中译翻译文库

李长栓 著

非文学翻译理论与实践

理解、表达、变通

上册

中国出版集团
中译出版社

图书在版编目(CIP)数据

非文学翻译理论与实践：理解、表达、变通：汉文、英文 / 李长栓著. -- 北京：中译出版社，2022.6
（中译翻译文库）
ISBN 978-7-5001-7005-1

Ⅰ.①非… Ⅱ.①李… Ⅲ.①英语-翻译-研究 Ⅳ.①H315.9

中国版本图书馆CIP数据核字（2022）第038648号

出版发行 / 中译出版社
地　　址 / 北京市西城区新街口外大街28号普天德胜大厦主楼4层
电　　话 / (010) 68359827, 68359813（发行部）；68359725（编辑部）
邮　　编 / 100044
传　　真 / (010) 68357870
电子邮箱 / book@ctph.com.cn
网　　址 / http://www.ctph.com.cn

出 版 人 / 乔卫兵
总 策 划 / 刘永淳
策划编辑 / 范祥镇　钱屹芝　王诗同
责任编辑 / 钱屹芝　杨佳特
营销编辑 / 吴雪峰　董思嫄

封面设计 / 黄　浩
排　　版 / 北京竹页文化传媒有限公司
印　　刷 / 北京顶佳世纪印刷有限公司
经　　销 / 新华书店

规　　格 / 710毫米×1000毫米　1/16
印　　张 / 38.75
字　　数 / 593千字
版　　次 / 2022年6月第一版
印　　次 / 2022年6月第一次

ISBN 978-7-5001-7005-1　定价：98.00元（全两册）

版权所有　侵权必究
中译出版社

编写说明

本书将刘重德先生提出的"信达切"三个字另作解释，作为翻译的标准，然后从理解、表达、变通三个方面，说明如何实现这三个标准，兼顾作者、读者和用户的利益。

所谓"信"（"忠实"），即译文准确表达原文意思，至少不违背原文。忠实的译文不见得与原文逐字对应。译者可以根据情况对原文作一定的变通取舍，只要在精神上与原文保持一致、在意图上与作者保持一致就达到了"忠实"的要求。这样说，不意味着降低了"忠实"的标准，可以只翻译大意；而是说，如果翻译目的要求我们逐字逐句翻译、与原文全面对等，我们就这样翻译；如果翻译目的和情景要求我们对原文作出变通取舍，也不要担心被指责不忠。"信"是译者对作者的义务。

所谓"达"（"通顺"），就是在忠实于原文意思或意图的基础上，按照译入语的写作规范进行翻译。具体来讲，就是在用词、搭配、句型、衔接、逻辑等方面，要符合译入语的要求，争取做到像母语创作那样通顺，避免"翻译腔"或中式英文、欧化中文。"达"是译者对读者的义务。

所谓"切"（"好用"），就是要符合翻译的用途，要根据翻译的目的，决定采取"全面对等"的翻译策略，还是采用"功能对等"的翻译策略，或者是超越对等的羁绊，通过省略或编译实现翻译目的。所谓"全面对等"，就是严格按照原文的意思和形式进行翻译，不增、不减、不作解释，制作一篇原文的孪生姐妹；所谓"功能对等"（或者叫"动态对等"），就是对原文的字面意思和表达形式作适当变通取舍，以更好实现语篇的功能；但有

i

时译文的功能和原文并不相同，这时则不必追求对等，而是可以通过省略、补充、改编等方式实现翻译目的，满足用户需求。"切"是译者对翻译委托人（用户）的义务。

实现"信达切"的方法，可以概括为"理解、表达、变通"三个方面。为了做到忠实，首先要理解原文。理解分为宏观理解和微观理解。宏观上，要理解 6W1H——Who is speaking to whom? About what? When, where and why, and how？即作者是谁？读者是谁？关注的问题是什么？什么时候、在哪里、为什么写这篇文章？以及语言风格如何（how）？任何作品都不是无病呻吟，都有其创作背景。对背景的了解，有助于理解文章细节。在微观层面，译者要理解原作的每个词语以及词语、句子、段落之间的关系和前后联系。理解是翻译的基础，只有透彻理解，才能准确传达。译者的理解要接近、达到甚至超过作者的水平。

为了做到语言通顺，就要在理解的基础上，以读者可以接受的方式来传达作者清楚表达、希望表达甚至应该表达的意思，包括用词要准确、搭配要正确、句子结构要牢靠、衔接方法要得当、信息流动要通畅等等。译者可要把自己视为一个作者，从作者的视角看自己的作品（译文）是否经得起推敲：意思是否清楚、逻辑是否连贯、表达是否欧化或中式英语。在通顺方面，本书重点介绍了如何运用简明英语，做好汉译英。

为了使译文符合用途，译者需要根据情况，决定是否以及在多大程度上对原文进行变通取舍。这要求译者在翻译之前，了解翻译活动发生的情境，同样回答 6W1H：Who is asking you to translate? For whom? When, where, why, and how is the translation to be used, by whom? 如果委托人没有提供以上信息，译者要主动询问，或者根据翻译的内容作出判断。只有了解了翻译情景，才能正确决定某个地方是否要翻译，如何翻译，是概括翻译还是逐字逐句翻译，是否要作解释，解释添加在译文中，还是作为译文的注释，或者是给用户看的一个批注。换言之，译者也要像作者那样，根据写作的具体背景，决定在文章中提供哪些信息，不提供哪些信息，以什么方式提供。译文的表达形式可以和原文相同、相近甚至完全不同。

贯穿全书的，是译者的思维方式：逻辑思维、宏观思维、批判性思维。译者通过逻辑思维，发现字词、句子之间的关系，通过宏观思维发现篇章前后以及篇章与大千世界之间的关系，通过批判性思维发现原文的逻辑和事实瑕疵。译者通过逻辑思维、宏观思维、批判性思维发现理解、表达、变通方面的问题，然后通过思考或调查研究解决这些问题。

笔者在《如何撰写翻译实践报告：CEA框架、范文及点评》一书中提出了"理解、表达、变通"的分析框架，本书可以视为对该框架的拓展和具体化；写作所需的分类，可以参照本书相应章节。为便于大家用英文写作，"信达切"可以译为Faithful, Natural and Fit for Purpose。

新版前言

2012年《非文学翻译理论与实践》第二版出版,迄今已印刷二十余次,共计六万册,原全国翻译专业学位研究生教育指导委员会主任委员仲伟合校长称本书"是翻译实践类教材中使用最为广泛的一种专业教材"。

为了使本书更加系统全面,笔者结合近些年对翻译的思考,并基于更多的翻译教学和实践经验,再次修订了本书,并更名为《非文学翻译理论与实践:理解、表达、变通》。新版主要涉及以下十二个方面:

(1) 重新整理了本书的结构。第二版已经作了结构调整,但仍没有理顺整体逻辑。新版以前两版提出的非文学翻译标准"方法得当、意思准确、语言朴实通顺"为基础,将翻译标准进一步概括为"信达切",进而把全书内容重新划分为理解、表达、变通三个版块。"理解"是为了实现"意思准确"或"信";"表达"是为了实现"语言朴实通顺"或"达";"变通"是为了实现"方法得当"或"切"。

(2) 明确提出翻译的三大理念,即翻译是沟通、翻译是写作、翻译是发现和解决问题的过程,以此作为实现"信达切"的思想基础。

(3) 提出译者的三大思维方式:逻辑思维、宏观思维、批判性思维。

(4) 提出理解和变通的抓手——两套6W1H。

(5) 新增关于理解的专门论述,提供实现"信"的思想方法和操作方法。

(6) 以英语写作方法(主要是简明英语)统领表达部分,提供实现"达"的抓手。

（7）把涉及原文内容和形式调整的章节，归为"变通"，作为实现"切"的手段。

（8）保留的部分重组或重新编辑，并增补大量权威著作汉译英实例和本人翻译实例，删除部分原有例子。

（9）新增大量英译汉的例子，使两个方向的内容较为均衡。

（10）将每章所用例句的原文提取出来，制成电子文档，供读者扫码获取，在阅读前预习，并可在群组讨论。

（11）在每章末尾增加课后练习。第二版所附练习作为综合训练，可扫码获得。

（12）增加了全书的思维导图，使全书结构一目了然。

为控制篇幅，本次修订还简化了理论阐述，删除了个别章节和原有附录，但新增了《欧洲委员会英语写作与翻译指南》作为附录，可扫码获取。

经过修订，本书与拙著《如何撰写翻译实践报告——框架、范文及点评》（中译出版社，2020）等著作在结构上趋于统一，为后者提供了更多例证，因此也希望本书对翻译实践的报告写作起到促进作用。

本书新增内容难度较大，汉译英基础薄弱的同学，可以先读第一章以及第八至十六章。

最后感谢北外高翻学院2020级全体同学（曹洋、单铮、董文洁、封鹏程、李媛、卢俊宇、吕光如、钱梦怡、王雅明、熊诗音、薛朝权、杨若彤、杨洋、朱思颖等）以及自由职业译员康利为本书提供的反馈、例证和建议。

2021年11月11日
李长栓
北京外国语大学高级翻译学院

第二版前言

本书自 2004 年 12 月问世以来，得到了广大读者的认可和喜爱，已经印刷五次，发行量达 15000 册。有同学告诉笔者，他们把这本书称为学习翻译的"黄宝书"。

这次借再版的机会，调整了书的结构，精简了理论概述，修订了笔误，完善了译例，更换了练习和参考译文，改进了注释体例。在修订过程中，新加坡自由译者周蕴仪（Chow Wan Ee）女士帮助修改了例证译文，并与我共同制作了练习的参考译文，我在此向她表示感谢。

本书所强调的理念和方法，经检验是行之有效的，所以没有做任何修改。对其中一些理念的深化探讨，见外语教学与研究出版社出版的《非文学翻译》（2009 年）和外文出版社出版的《理解与表达：汉英翻译案例讲评》（与施晓菁合著，2012 年）。

各章"参考资料"与书后"参考文献"中列出的英文写作指南，是笔者许多想法的来源，提醒读者按图索骥，延伸阅读。

李长栓

北京外国语大学高级翻译学院

2012 年 1 月 15 日

第一版前言

本书是根据笔者1999年至2001年在北京外国语大学高级翻译学院讲授汉英笔译课时使用的讲义编写的。翻译学院历来以培养实用型翻译人才为目标，所以教学中十分重视学生实践能力的培养。本书也重在探讨各类翻译问题的解决方法。

本书有以下特点：（1）**专门探讨非文学翻译**。一般翻译理论没有区分文学和非文学翻译。本书探讨了非文学翻译的特点，提出非文学翻译要做到"方法得当、意思准确、语言朴实通顺"。（2）**以写作指导翻译**。本书以功能翻译理论为基础，首次把英语写作原则引入汉英翻译实践。（3）**以翻译过程为导向**。重点探讨常见问题的解决方法，如怎样查找词语，翻译比喻、句子、段落和篇章，进行篇章调整等。（4）**操作性强**。即使英语能力不足，按照本书提供的方法和思路也可以大大提高翻译质量。本书还详细介绍了网络资源在翻译中的应用，相信对所有从事翻译的人都会有极大帮助。（5）**实用性强**。市场上绝大多数翻译活动是非文学翻译，本书从翻译实践者的角度，帮助广大翻译工作者解决工作中面临的实际问题。（6）**示例丰富**。在对相关理论作简要介绍后，举出大量的实例加以说明。

本书举例虽以汉译英为主，但所阐述翻译理论同样适于英译汉。在有些地方，笔者也同时举了英译汉的例子。笔译是口译的基础，本书中推荐的多数技巧可以直接运用到口译中，包括同声传译。

职业译员应当具备翻译各种专业文件的能力，条件是拥有充足的资源，允许我们在翻译前或翻译过程中进行充分的调查研究。专业不懂，可以把有关的专业知识学习一遍。这是一个职业译员应具备的工作态度。当然，开始时这样做会影响翻译速度，时间也往往不允许，但随着知识经验的积累，速度会逐渐加快。所以笔者劝告学习翻译的同学，不要急于求成，要踏踏实实地打好基础，养成良好的翻译习惯和工作态度。当然，为兼顾效率和质量，翻译的专业化分工是必要的。

学习翻译离不开练习。做练习不应当只做单词和单句的翻译，要把单词和句子放在篇章的角度加以考虑，所以一开始就要翻译文章。选取材料时要考虑文章的内容在国际交往或自己未来的工作中是否可能用到。如果选取的材料不常用，一是浪费时间，学了无用的东西，二是查找资料也不容易。

本书提供的练习材料不一定适合所有读者的需要，而且随着时间的推移会很快过时。所以，学习者可以选取其他练习材料。所提供参考译文属于一般意义上的翻译，没有大的篇章调整。大家可以为同一篇文章设定不同翻译目的（用途），从而尝试不同译法。参考译文多数是经过笔者修改的他人的译文，仅供参考。

在教学过程中，笔者的同事、加拿大汉英同声传译专家、国际口译协会（AIIC）会员杜蕴德（Andrew Dawrant）教授提供了有价值的资料和参考书，使笔者深受启发。本书初稿完成后，请笔者的师长，美国 Monterey Institute of International Studies 施晓菁教授修改了例句译文。施教授是为数不多的、精通汉英双语的同声传译专家。本书二稿完成后，联合国日内瓦办事处语文司中文科资深译员赵兴民先生通读了全书，指出不少疏漏之处，提出了宝贵的修改意见。因为他知道"翻译理论与实务丛书"主编罗进德老师正在物色作者组织撰写侧重应用研究的书稿，便不远万里热心推荐。罗老师在百忙中通读了全书，对本书内容给予充分肯定，同时也提出了中肯的修改意见。关于非文学翻译特点等方面的论述就是在罗老师建议下增加的。可以说，本书能够最终和大家见面，凝聚了许多人的心血，在此对他们的支持和帮助表示衷心感谢。

书中多数例子是笔者自己的翻译，有些例子取自经外国专家审校过的文件。但初稿完成后，又做了补充整理，增加的例句或段落没有经过英语母语人士把关，所以大家使用时要持批判态度，如有疏漏之处，都是笔者的责任。

第一版前言

  虽然本书从动笔到现在已经有四五年的时间，经多人批评、指正，仍然不敢保证没有错误。正如看自己过去翻译的东西一样，每次都能发现不足之处，这本书也一定存在不尽如人意的地方。发现问题，欢迎大家提出来，我们共同讨论。

李长栓

北京外国语大学高级翻译学院

2004 年 9 月 10 日

非文学翻译理论与实践——理解、表达、变通

第一部分：第一章指出，翻译的目的是沟通，主要面向三个利益主体：原文作者、译文读者和翻译客户。面向作者，译者负有确保译文忠实（"信"）的义务；面向读者，译者负有确保译文通顺（"达"）的义务；面向客户，译者负有确保译文好用（"切"）的义务，每次翻译任务，都需要平衡兼顾三者的利益，据此提出翻译的三个标准"信达切"。第二至四章把翻译类比为写作，进而提出如何通过"理解""表达""变通"分别实现翻译中的"信达切"。第五章举例说明如何以批判性思维为工具，解决理解、表达、变通中的难点问题。

第二部分：在第五章基础上，深入探讨理解的重点，第六章谈理解的广度和深度。理解的广度，归纳为6W1H，深度包括理解原文所有的概念和关系。第七章提出译者的三种思维方式：逻辑思维、宏观思维和批判性思维。通过逻辑思维，发现字词之间、句子之间、段落之间的联系；通过宏观思维，发现前后文的关系以及篇章与外部世界的联系；通过批判性思维，发现原文的逻辑瑕疵与不合常理之处。

第三部分：在第五章基础上，深入探讨表达的重点，首先介绍简明英语的基本要求，然后以字词句篇为线索，举例说明如何把简明英语和英文写作的各项要求，运用到翻译中。无论以人工还是机器翻译得到一稿，只要按写作原则来修改，即可得到通顺的译文。

第四部分：在第五章基础上，深入探讨变通的重点。比喻、俗语、口号等文化负载词的翻译，往往不能直译，需要通过各种办法变通处理，所以归入变通部分。还有些情况下需要根据英语的写作习惯，对原文结构或内容进行编辑调整，甚至把原文作为创作素材，这属于更高层次的变通。变通时同样需要考虑6W1H。

第五部分举例说明如何通过反复修改实现"信达切"。

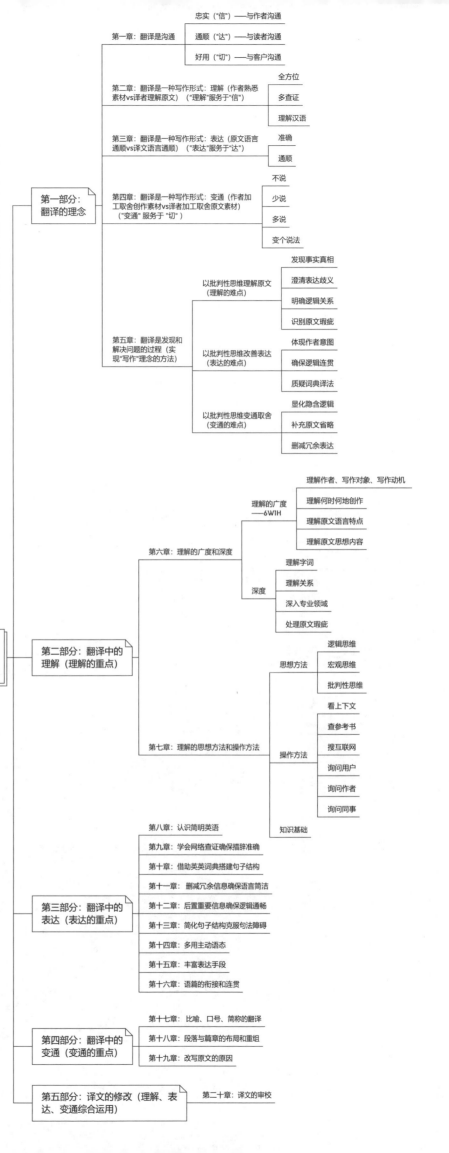

目 录

第一部分 翻译的理念

第一章 翻译是沟通 　　　　　　　　　　　　　　　2
　　1.1　翻译的历史 　　　　　　　　　　　　　　　2
　　1.2　翻译的历史作用 　　　　　　　　　　　　　3
　　1.3　职业翻译是一种沟通行为 　　　　　　　　　4
　　1.4　直译与意译之争 　　　　　　　　　　　　　5
　　1.5　翻译的目的论 　　　　　　　　　　　　　　8
　　1.6　翻译中的"信达切" 　　　　　　　　　　　10
　　1.7　"信达切"是文学和非文学翻译的共同标准 　14
　　1.8　如何做到"信达切" 　　　　　　　　　　　15
　　1.9　小结 　　　　　　　　　　　　　　　　　16

第二章 翻译是一种写作形式：理解 　　　　　　18
　　2.1　全方位 　　　　　　　　　　　　　　　　19
　　2.2　多查证 　　　　　　　　　　　　　　　　25
　　2.3　理解汉语 　　　　　　　　　　　　　　　27
　　2.4　小结 　　　　　　　　　　　　　　　　　33

第三章　翻译是一种写作形式：表达　　　　　34
　3.1　准确　　　　　　　　　　　　　　　34
　3.2　通顺　　　　　　　　　　　　　　　59
　3.3　小结　　　　　　　　　　　　　　　94

第四章　翻译是一种写作形式：变通　　　　　97
　4.1　不说　　　　　　　　　　　　　　　98
　4.2　少说　　　　　　　　　　　　　　　103
　4.3　多说　　　　　　　　　　　　　　　110
　4.4　变个说法　　　　　　　　　　　　　113
　4.5　小结　　　　　　　　　　　　　　　125

第五章　翻译是发现和解决问题的过程　　　　126
　5.1　批判性思维　　　　　　　　　　　　126
　5.2　以批判性思维理解原文　　　　　　　128
　5.3　以批判性思维改善表达　　　　　　　146
　5.4　以批判性思维变通取舍　　　　　　　154
　5.5　综合举例　　　　　　　　　　　　　159
　5.6　小结　　　　　　　　　　　　　　　162

第二部分　翻译中的理解

第六章　理解的广度和深度　　　　　　　　　164
　6.1　理解的广度（6W1H）　　　　　　　　164
　6.2　理解的深度　　　　　　　　　　　　170
　6.3　小结　　　　　　　　　　　　　　　213

第七章　理解的思想方法和操作方法　　　　　215
　7.1　逻辑思维　　　　　　　　　　　　　215
　7.2　宏观思维　　　　　　　　　　　　　218
　7.3　批判性思维　　　　　　　　　　　　225

7.4	调查研究	226
7.5	批判性思维需要知识基础	242
7.6	小结	243

第三部分　翻译中的表达

第八章　认识简明英语　　246

8.1	简明英语和简明英语运动	246
8.2	简明英语的基本原则	260
8.3	小结	279

第九章　学会网络查证确保措辞准确　　280

9.1	利用搜索引擎辅助翻译	280
9.2	当你找不到现成的译法时	302
9.3	小结	311

第十章　借助英英词典搭建句子结构　　312

10.1	外语表达难以自如的原因	313
10.2	成语优先原则	314
10.3	词典介绍	315
10.4	电子语料库 WebCorp 用法介绍	318
10.5	利用英语词典和电子语料库搭建句子结构	321
10.6	小结	333

第十一章　删减冗余信息确保语言简洁　　334

11.1	活用英语词形变化	334
11.2	调整篇章衔接手段	338
11.3	多用强势动词	344
11.4	化解一些动词	347
11.5	省略汉语范畴词	348
11.6	省略不必要修饰语	355

11.7	慎用加强词	357
11.8	慎用限定词	362
11.9	少用陈词滥调	364
11.10	减少同义词并列现象	365
11.11	减少更高层次的重复	372
11.12	使用简单句型	379
11.13	精简慢启动句子	380
11.14	小结	385

第十二章 后置重要信息确保逻辑通畅　387

12.1	介绍	387
12.2	不重要信息左移	392
12.3	重要信息右移	393
12.4	使用倒装句	396
12.5	删除多余的结尾	397
12.6	使用被动语态	398
12.7	重组句子主语和从句	400
12.8	减少插入成分	401
12.9	几种表示强调的句法手段	402
12.10	小结	405

第十三章 简化句子结构克服句法障碍　406

13.1	核心句概念	406
13.2	核心句种类	407
13.3	核心句分析	408
13.4	核心句分析在汉译英中的应用	411
13.5	小结	419

第十四章 多用主动语态　421

14.1	为什么用主动语态	421
14.2	如何把被动语态变为主动语态	422

14.3　什么时候用被动语态　　　　　　　　　423
　　14.4　使用被动语态应注意的问题　　　　　426
　　14.5　翻译中多用主动语态　　　　　　　　427
　　14.6　翻译中也可用被动语态　　　　　　　432
　　14.7　小结　　　　　　　　　　　　　　　438

第十五章　丰富表达手段　　　　　　　　　　　439
　　15.1　简明英语提倡长短句搭配使用　　　　439
　　15.2　英语句子总体变短的原因　　　　　　440
　　15.3　译者仍要学会理解长句　　　　　　　441
　　15.4　如何化繁为简　　　　　　　　　　　443
　　15.5　如何化简为繁　　　　　　　　　　　451
　　15.6　三种修饰方法　　　　　　　　　　　456
　　15.7　平行结构　　　　　　　　　　　　　462
　　15.8　小结　　　　　　　　　　　　　　　466

第十六章　语篇的衔接与连贯　　　　　　　　　467
　　16.1　语篇的衔接　　　　　　　　　　　　467
　　16.2　语篇的连贯　　　　　　　　　　　　477
　　16.3　小结　　　　　　　　　　　　　　　489

第四部分　翻译中的变通

第十七章　比喻、口号、简称的翻译　　　　　　492
　　17.1　比喻的概念　　　　　　　　　　　　492
　　17.2　比喻的翻译方法　　　　　　　　　　496
　　17.3　比喻翻译的双重标准　　　　　　　　499
　　17.4　特色表达翻译举例　　　　　　　　　502
　　17.5　政策口号的翻译方法　　　　　　　　511
　　17.6　数字简称的翻译方法　　　　　　　　517
　　17.7　小结　　　　　　　　　　　　　　　520

第十八章　段落与篇章的布局和重组　521
　18.1　是否调整原文结构取决于多种因素　521
　18.2　调整或增加段落主题　522
　18.3　各句主题相对一致　528
　18.4　重组逻辑不清的段落　531
　18.5　简化臃肿的段落　536
　18.6　大规模调整　541
　18.7　小结　546

第十九章　改写原文的原因　548
　19.1　文化差异　548
　19.2　意识形态差异　551
　19.3　外语能力不足　559
　19.4　小结　564

第五部分　译文的修改

第二十章　译文的审校　568
　20.1　关注事项　568
　20.2　审校他人译文　571
　20.3　接受他人审校　587
　20.4　小结　597

附录一　欧洲委员会英语写作与翻译指南　598
附录二　汉英翻译综合训练　598
附录三　汉英翻译综合训练参考译文　598
参考文献　598

第一部分　翻译的理念

第一至五章为本书的第一部分，提出译者应当具备的三个理念，即翻译是沟通、翻译是写作、翻译是发现和解决问题的过程。

翻译既然是沟通，译者就必须想尽一切办法理解原文，忠实传递原文的意思，确保译文通顺易懂，必要时还需要根据用户要求或读者需要，对原文做一些变通取舍。树立了沟通者的理念，就不会把自己当成文字转换的机器，而是想办法理解原文，并根据实际情况产出符合需求的译文。

翻译是写作，只不过传递的是原作者的思想。以写作的标准要求翻译，同样需要译者理解原文，以通顺易懂的语言表达出来，并在必要时对原文做一些编辑加工，就好比作者需要了解素材、通顺表达、选择使用创作素材一样。树立了译者即作者的理念，就会时刻关注译文是否可以被读者理解或接受。

翻译是发现和解决问题的过程。翻译中遇到的问题不外乎有三个：原文理解问题、译文表达问题、无法直译或直译不妥时如何变通的问题。译者要时刻以批判性思维发现问题，并通过调查研究或对翻译情景的思考解决问题。

第一章　翻译是沟通

1.1　翻译的历史

由于地域的分割，各民族在其历史发展过程中形成不同的语言。两个操着不同语言的民族，只要进行交往，就离不开翻译。所以，翻译的历史可能与人类语言的历史一样久远。中国最早记载翻译的书籍是《周礼》和《礼记》。两书记载了周王朝的翻译官职，其具体任务就是负责接待不同民族和国家的使节与来宾。秦始皇统一中国之后，改周代之"行人"为"典客"（意为"译者"），又另设典属国一职，掌管蛮夷降者。西汉因秦制。魏、晋、南北朝和隋代掌管四方民族和外国交往事务并配有译员的官方机构，大体上沿两汉之制，或有所损益，或有所省并。从东汉末年到宋代，官方组织了大规模的佛经翻译。辽宋时期，辽国占据了中国北方的广大地区，作为少数民族政权，统治着占人口多数的汉族和其他民族，因为沟通的需要，不得不聘用大量译员，在州以上官署置译史，从事文字翻译工作。同时，还首置通事，从事口译工作。金代和辽代一样，也有译史和通事职称，在政府机构内从事口笔译工作。元朝同样设有译史和通事。元朝译史有蒙古译史和回族译史之分。明朝永乐五年（1407），为适应外事翻译需要，设四夷馆，原为八馆，后又增添两馆，毕业生分发各部，充当译员，凡外国人与中国官员往还，谈话交际，都由他们翻译。明末清初，大量西方传教士来华，知名的总计七十名以上，他们与中国士大夫结合翻译编写书籍三百余种，除了经院哲学、神学和其他宗教文献外，科技书籍计一百二十来种，涉及天文学、数学、物理学、机械工程学、采矿冶金、军事技术、生理医学、生物学、舆地学、语言学、文学等。清朝更加重视翻译。清军入关前，就建立文馆，以"翻译汉字书籍""记注本朝政事"。清军入关后，设立"笔贴式"，以沟通满汉两族。清朝重视各族语言教学，培养通晓满、蒙、朝、汉文的各级官吏、笔贴式和口译人员。清朝的科举考试，还特设翻译一科。在中央一级设立多种翻译机构，负责满、汉、蒙、藏诸语之间的翻译。鸦片战争以后，有识之士和政府组织的西学翻译，其规模之大，范围之广，达到了前所未有的程度。（马祖毅，2001）

纵观中国翻译史，可以发现官方翻译机构发挥三个作用。一是进行国家的日常管理，这在多民族国家是必需的，尤其是少数民族统治时期。二是外交，在汉族统治时期外交似乎是翻译的主要功能。三是吸收其他民族的先进文化，如东汉末年至宋代的佛经翻译、伴随佛经翻译进行的印度药书和历法的翻译、清末对西学的大量翻译，都是汉民族吸收其他民族的先进文化；而辽、金、夏、元、清等少数民族统治时期，把汉籍翻译为少数民族语言，则是少数民族学习汉民族的先进文化。可以说，翻译的历史，就是世界各民族沟通交融的历史。

1.2 翻译的历史作用

翻译推动了世界文化交流和社会进步。各民族历史上的启蒙时期，无不以翻译为开端。纵观世界翻译历史，凡是一个民族认为自己需要向另一个民族学习的——无论是科学技术、政治制度，还是宗教文化——就必然产生大规模的翻译活动。所以，在知识的传播过程中——无论是从古希腊到波斯，从印度到阿拉伯国家，从伊斯兰世界到基督教世界，还是从欧洲到东方，从中国到日本，再从日本到中国——翻译都发挥着独一无二的作用。从翻译的角度考察世界思想文化史发现，各种思想文化正是通过翻译不断传播，同时也通过翻译吸收新鲜血液。所以，东西方文化在不断交融，并不存在严格的界线。

以中日文化交流为例。中日文化交流历史上可以说有两次高潮。第一次是 630 年至 894 年间的遣唐使时代。当时中国正处于封建经济与文化高度发达的盛唐时期，而日本则处于从奴隶制向封建社会过渡的时期，当权的新贵族富有进取心，在 260 年间先后向中国正式派遣使团 18 次，大批的留学生和学问僧随同使团前来中国，学习中国的思想文化和典章制度，回国后改革和构建日本的政治、经济、文化等制度，促进了日本封建制度的建立和巩固。第二次高潮是在近代。如果说第一次高潮主要是日本向中国学习，那么第二次高潮则主要是中国向日本学习。日本通过明治维新摆脱了民族危机，走上了资本主义道路，这对当时正处于半封建半殖民地状态的中国来说是一个莫大的震动和刺激。明治初期，日本全面学习西方近代科学技术，英美书籍的翻译介绍盛行。在中国，官方也设立了洋务机构，翻译出版西方书籍；中日甲午战争之后，为求速效，从日语转译了大量西方书籍，内容涉及哲学、法律、文学、教育、地理、历史、自然科学、军事、医学等各个领域。清末自然科学方面的教科书几乎全部转译自日文译本，如《物理译解》《分析化学》《动物学新论》《微分积分学纲要》等，甚至可以说近代中国人的新知识大部分是通过日本书籍得到的（王青，2002）。总而言之，翻译在民族沟通、知识传播、文明互鉴方面的作用，怎么强调都不过分。

1.3 职业翻译是一种沟通行为

从事翻译的人可以分为三类：学习外语的学生、翻译爱好者、职业译员。

学习外语的学生最熟悉的翻译活动可能是翻译练习。翻译练习的目的是检验学生对外语的掌握情况：从汉语翻译到外语，可以检测或提高学生的外语写作能力，至少是强化学生对两种语言语法差异的理解；从外语翻译到母语，可以检测或提高对外语词语和句子结构的理解情况。把翻译作为外语学习的手段，往往要求译者逐字逐句翻译，尽量贴近原文用词并进行结构转换，以检验对原文或译文词语和结构的理解情况。翻译练习的结果，往往只有自己或老师作为读者。译者不需要考虑译文的使用情景，因此基本不需要对原文进行编辑加工。

另一种翻译活动，是把翻译视为娱乐。例如，译者觉得翻译有趣，把他人或自己的作品翻译出来，供自己欣赏。这样的翻译不受外部约束，译者可以自定标准，包括对原文进行自己认为合适的任何改编，甚至意思完全错误，也不会产生任何后果。

职业翻译不是翻译练习，不是一种爱好，而是受到用户委托，为用户提供的专业沟通服务。翻译过程即译者与作者、读者和用户三个行为主体沟通的过程，翻译结果则在三者之间实现沟通。具体来说，**译者理解作者意图和语言表达细节的过程，是与作者建立沟通；译者重新表达原文意思的过程，是与读者建立沟通；译者对原文进行变通取舍的过程，是译者和委托人进行沟通的过程**。每次具体的翻译活动，译者都试图寻求三方利益的平衡，最终实现原文作者、翻译委托人和译文读者之间的沟通。

1.4 直译与意译之争

翻译是一种沟通行为，对此恐怕不会有人提出异议。但如何实现沟通，却有不同的观点。自汉代佛经翻译开始，我国就有"直译""意译"之争，一直持续至今。但笔者认为，直译和意译都是有效的沟通手段，要视具体情况决定采取哪种。所谓直译，就是既正确传达原文的意思，又尽量保留原文的表达形式，即原文和译文全面对等。鉴于语言之间的相通之处很多，很多情况下采用直译是行得通的。但是，由于各民族语言结构不同，定义世界的范畴不同，加上各种社会文化差异，有时采用原文的形式无法准确传递原文的意思，这时就要舍弃原文的表达形式，换一种形式表达原文的意思，这就是意译。注意，直译不是不求甚解的"硬译"或"死译"，意译不是无视原文意思的信口开河。

纽马克（1988）根据表达方式是接近源语习惯还是译语习惯，对翻译方法做了更加详细的分类。笼统来讲，接近源语习惯的翻译方法，可以算作我们所谓的"直译"；接近译语表达习惯的翻译方法，可以算作我们的"意译"。

接近源语习惯（程度由高到低）：

- Word-for-word translation（逐字对译）
- Literal translation（字面翻译）
- Faithful translation（忠实翻译）
- Semantic translation（语义翻译）

接近译语习惯（程度由低到高）：

- Communicative translation（交际性翻译）
- Idiomatic translation（地道的翻译）
- Free translation（自由翻译）
- Adaptation（改写）

从逐字对译到改写是一个连续体，逐字对译与原文的形式最为对应，改写最强调译文的交际功能。与此类似，周兆祥（1996）根据"翻译的自由度"，把翻译分为以下几类：

- 逐字对译（Word-for-word translation）
- 字面翻译（Literal translation）
- 语义翻译（Semantic translation）
- 传意翻译（Communicative translation）
- 编译（Free translation）
- 改写（Adaptation）

可以通过下面一句话的翻译[①]，体会几种翻译方法的区别：

原文：

　　Mr. Dewar slipped and fell outside his official Edinburgh residence on Tuesday morning. He picked himself up and went on to carry out two lunchtime engagements. (BBC news 11/10/2000)

逐字对译：

　　杜瓦先生滑了和跌倒在外面他的官方爱丁堡居所在星期二早晨。他拣自己起来和继续去实行两个午餐约定。

---

① 本例来自 http://teacher.cyivs.cy.edu.tw/~hchung/freedomontranslate.htm，2004年3月1日访问；译文有改动。

字面翻译：
　　星期二早晨杜瓦先生滑倒在他的爱丁堡官邸外面。他爬起来继续去参加两个午餐约会。

语义翻译：
　　星期二早晨，杜瓦先生在爱丁堡官邸外滑倒了，但他仍爬起来继续去参加两个午餐活动。

传意翻译：
　　杜瓦先生的官邸在爱丁堡。星期二早晨，他不小心在屋外摔一跤。不过他仍奋力爬起，去参加了两个午餐活动。

编译：
　　杜瓦先生在爱丁堡有一座官邸。星期二早晨，他刚出门就摔了一跤。不过，他觉得没事，就爬起来继续参加当天的活动，午餐时还与两个团体进行了正式会谈。

改写：
　　爱丁堡的早晨空气新鲜。杜瓦先生喜欢晨练。那天一大早，他穿着运动装出门，正要开始晨跑，不小心踩到一块香蕉皮上，跌倒在地。他奋力爬起，打消跑步的念头，出门上班，午餐时还坚持参加了两个见面会。

　　这个例子仅仅用来说明不同的翻译方法，而不是可以任意选用其中一种译法。现实中采取哪一种方法，取决于原文性质、读者背景以及委托人的要求。如果原文本身就是虚构的事实，甚至可以根据读者情况和委托人要求，在译文中添加原文没有的细节。但如果原文是对真实事件的报道，译者虽然可以用不同方式来表达，但不能脱离原文背后的事实。内容的增加，要有事实依据，例如，根据其他报道，了解到更多事实。也就是说，如何翻译，受到文本类型、翻译目的、社会环境等多方面因素的影响（见下一节"翻译的目的论"）。但无论如何翻译，其基本功能都是为了实现作者、读者、委托人之间的沟通。

再举几个生活中见到的例子，说明翻译的不同方法：

把"请勿践踏草地"翻译为"Please do not step on the grass."是照顾源语表达习惯的翻译；翻译为"Keep off the grass."是照顾译语表达习惯的翻译。"妥善保存，遗失不补"翻译为"Please safekeeping, lose no reissue."（某宾馆）是逐字翻译；翻译为"Please keep it safe. No replacement if lost."或者"Please keep it safe. Not replaceable if lost."大概属于字面翻译；翻译为"Please keep this voucher in a safe place. It will not be replaced if lost."大概属于交际性翻译。而某娱乐场所把"歌舞厅"翻译为"sinner room"（注意不是 singer）则是"乱译"（应为"song and dance room"）。

虽然在理论上可以把翻译方法分得很细，但实践中并无此必要。纽马克（1988）在其翻译举例中，就只区分了 semantic translation 和 communicative translation。翻译方法分为几类并不重要，重要的是要知道不同情况下需要采取不同的翻译方法：有时需要照顾源语，有时要照顾译语；可以是逐字翻译，可以较为自由，还可以对原文作较大幅度的调整。在实际生活中，各种翻译方法都可以看到实例。所以，每种方法都有其存在的必要性与合理性。

笔者认为，直译可以达意且满足委托人需要的，就直译；直译不能达意的，就意译；遇到特殊情况或委托人有明确要求，可以对原文进行必要的调整、增删，甚至改写。这就是翻译的"目的决定论"。前述关于"直译""意译"的讨论，以及纽马克的翻译分类，都没有关注也无法解释根据翻译目的对原文进行增删的情况。目的论的出现，恰当解释了翻译中的增删变通情况。

1.5 翻译的目的论

目的论[①]是功能派翻译理论中最重要的理论，20 世纪 80 年代由德国翻译理论家弗米尔（Hans J. Vermeer）和赖斯（Katharina Reiss）创立。当时

---

① 关于目的论，可参见维基百科词条：https://en.wikipedia.org/wiki/Skopos_theory，2021 年 3 月 8 日查阅。

正是等效论及语言学派盛行的时期。目的论摆脱等效论的束缚，以目的为总则，把翻译放在行为理论和跨文化交际的框架中进行考察，为世界翻译理论界包括中国译学界开辟了一条崭新的道路。

目的论将"行为理论"引入翻译理论中，认为翻译是一种行为，一种跨文化的交际行为。任何一种行为都有其自身的目的，翻译行为所要达到的目的决定了翻译所应采取的方法策略。这就是目的论的第一条原则——目的原则（Skopos rule）。目的原则认为，一项具体翻译任务的目的决定了翻译一个文本需要采用哪种方法。例如，把一般小说编译为儿童读物，语言就要适合儿童的特点；为电影翻译脚本，需要考虑音节多少，词的发音与原文口形是否一致，等等。这样就终结了关于各种翻译方法孰是孰非的争论。

目的论也可以用来解释"不译"的翻译策略。例如：有人请你把几个外国地址翻译为中文，你可以问他作何用。如果是给国外写信，就告诉他不用翻译——翻译了反而寄不到外国。这时的翻译策略就是不译。同样，参考书目是否翻译？如果该书没有外文或中文译本，可能还是不译为好，因为译出来反而不利于查找原书。

但按照目的决定手段的逻辑，译者是否可以无视原文，为达到目的任意操纵原文？回答是否定的。因为译者作为沟通者的本质，决定了译者要对作者和读者承担忠实的责任，不能夹带私货；对读者而言，还要确保译文便于理解。这就是目的论（后来补充）的第二和第三条原则：忠实原则（fidelity rule）和连贯原则（coherence rule）。

目的论中的忠实原则，是指译文不违背原文，译文和原文存在某种联系。该原则并不要求译文和原文在内容上一字不差；差异的程度和形式，由译文的目的和译者对原文的理解决定。连贯原则，则是指译文必须在目的语文化以及译文的使用环境中有意义，这就隐含了译文必须符合逻辑、符合译语的表达习惯。连贯原则也称为"语内连贯"（intratextual coherence），忠实原则也称为"语际连贯"（intertextual coherence）。上述三个原则的优先顺序是：目的原则＞连贯原则＞忠实原则（见图1.1）[①]。

[①] https://en.wikipedia.org/wiki/Skopos_theory，2021年3月8日查阅。

> **Rules** [edit]
> The three main rules of the Skopos Theory that encompass the six underlying directives are:[28]
>
> 1. The Skopos rule
> 2. The Coherence rule
> 3. The Fidelity rule
>
> The third rule, the Fidelity rule, is subordinate to the second rule, the Coherence rule, which in turn is subordinate to the Skopos rule.

图 1.1　目的论的三原则

笔者对此公式的理解是：翻译时如何做，要优先考虑翻译目的，其次考虑译文作为独立的语篇，是否通顺连贯，最后才考虑对原文的忠实程度。

1.6　翻译中的"信达切"

根据目的论和中国传统译论，笔者认为翻译应当做到"忠实""通顺""好用"；用三个字来表达，就是"信达切"。

所谓"忠实"（"信"），相当于目的论中所说"忠实"（fidelity），即译文不违背原文意思，但不见得与原文逐字对应。译者可以根据情况对原文作一定的变通取舍，只要在精神上与原文保持一致、在意图上与作者保持一致就达到了"忠实"的要求。这样说，不意味着降低了"忠实"的标准，可以只翻译大意；而是说，如果翻译目的要求我们逐字逐句翻译、与原文全面对等，我们就这样翻译；如果翻译目的和情景要求我们对原文作出变通取舍，我们也不要担心被指责不忠于原文。

所谓"通顺"（"达"），相当于目的论中的"（语内）连贯"（coherence），就是在忠实于原文意思或意图的基础上，按照译语的写作规范进行翻译。具体来讲，就是在用词、搭配、句型、衔接、逻辑等方面，要符合译语的要求，就像作者用译语直接写作那样，尽量避免"翻译腔"（中式英文或欧化中文）。

所谓"好用"("切"），相当于目的论中的"目的决定论"（Skopos rule），就是根据翻译的目的，决定采取"全面对等"的翻译策略，还是采用"功能对等"的翻译策略，或者是超越对等的羁绊，通过省略或编译实现翻译目的。所谓"全面对等"，就是严格按照原文的意思和形式进行翻译，不增、不减、不做解释，制作一篇原文的孪生姐妹文；联合国文件的翻译往往采取这种策略。所谓"功能对等"（或者叫"动态对等"），就是对原文的字面意思和表达形式作适当的变通取舍，以更好实现语篇的功能；广告、标识往往采用功能对等的翻译。但有时译文的功能和原文并不相同，这时则不必追求对等，而是可以通过省略、补充、改编等方式实现翻译目的，满足用户需求。

"信达切"作为翻译标准，与目的论内容相同，但排列的顺序相反，原因有三。一是因为"信达切"来源于"信达雅"，而"信达雅"已经被广泛接受，不便于改变表达顺序。二是因为忠实是翻译的本质特征，不忠实于原文，就算不上翻译。对原文的变通取舍，也要把握一定的度。三是在中国所有的译论中，也一贯把"忠实"放在首位，"通顺"放在第二。

古今中外，关于翻译标准的提法多种多样。清末翻译家严复在《天演论》"译例言"中提出的"译事三难，信、达、雅"，被后人奉为翻译原则或翻译标准，虽然几十年来引起不少争议，但至今仍有广泛影响。其中的"雅"，其本义是指"雅言"，即"汉以前的字法句法"，现在解释为"文雅"。但笔者认为可以从另一个角度理解严复提出的"雅"，即译文的读者对象，迫使严复把英语的白话，翻译为中国的古文。清末还没有推广白话文，如果把英文翻译为白话文，不符合当时的学术规范和阅读习惯。因此，严复的"雅"，是基于当时的翻译情景，对表达形式的变通，是为了做到切合读者需要，是"切"的一种表现形式。所以，"信达切"与"信达雅"没有矛盾，而是具有更广的内涵。

林语堂提出"忠实、通顺、美"的标准，但基本上没有超出"信达雅"的范畴——文雅就是一种美。傅雷提出了"形似神似"，属于"信"的范畴；钱锺书提出"化境"，可以认为包含"信达切"三个方面。王佐良认为，"一切照原作，雅俗如之，深浅如之，口气如之，文体如之"也是基于对等的翻译主张，归结起来就是一个字"信"。葛传椝认为，"翻译必须在把原文变成另一种文字时,做到不增,不减,不改",仍然是"信"。

朱文振在《翻译与语言环境》(1987)一书中提出"信达当"的说法,其中的"当",是指"翻译时在作品的品种格调方面,既应当对原文注意'恰当'的认知,又必须在译文上做到'恰当'的处理"。这里的"当",应该是指译文风格得当(与原文相同或相近),也属于"信"的范畴。

笔者所用"信达切"三个字,来自刘重德(1979)《试论翻译的原则》一文:

> 参考上述中外两家意见,取其精华,并结合个人翻译体会,拟把翻译原则定为既一目了然又比较全面的"信达切"三字:
> 一、信——保全原文意义
> 二、达——译文通顺易懂
> 三、切——切合原文风格

但刘重德提出的"切",是指切合原文风格,包含在笔者所说的"信"之中。笔者所说的"切"("好用"),是指切合翻译目的,包括根据委托人要求或翻译的实际情况,对原文作出译与不译、译多译少、如何翻译的决定,来自于目的论的"目的原则"。

古今中外,译者对翻译的感悟十分相似。苏格兰法学家、历史学家泰特勒(Sir Alexander Fraser Tytler)在1791年出版的 *Essay on the Principles of Translation* 中提出翻译的三原则就是朱文振的"信达当"或刘重德的"信达切":

- The translation should give a complete transcript of the ideas of the original work.
- The style and manner of writing should be of the same character with that of the original.
- The translation should have all the ease of the original composition.(转引自 Munday, 2008)

第一条相当于"信",第二条相当于"切"或"当",第三条相当于

"达"。

《圣经》翻译专家奈达在《翻译科学的探索》(1964)一书中提出了"动态对等"的概念(后改为"功能对等"),是指翻译不应拘泥于原文的语法结构和字面意义,而应着重译文读者的反应,使译文读者获得与原文读者在阅读、欣赏原文时相似的心理感受。这就要求译文在词汇意义、文体特色等诸层面上尽可能地与原文保持一致,要求译文是原文"最近似的自然对等语"。"对等"的概念,归根结底还是一个"信"字;"自然"的要求,还是一个"达"字。

综上所述,传统译论中更多地强调"忠实"("信",包括风格上的"信")和"通顺"("达"),但如果仅仅依赖这两个标准,一些翻译问题无法解决,一些翻译现象也无法解释。例如,在英语已成为世界语的今天,很多英语文件都是非母语人士起草的,文字上的问题很多。如果按照"信"的观点,译文也要文理不通。但是,如果我们这样做,是否对原文作者不公?再如,把中国古典作品翻译为外文时,如果按照"一切照原作,雅俗如之,深浅如之,口气如之,文体如之"的观点,则外文也必须用古文。接下来问题就是用哪个时代的英语? 2000年前是否有英语?用古英语是否可以为现代读者理解?

还有,在翻译法律文件时,译者是否有足够的权力完全抛开原文的形式,做到"神似"和"化境"?客户要求删减或编译时,是否还要坚持"不增、不减、不改"?作为职业翻译,是否可以说我的工作是忠实地翻译原文,改编不是我的职责?

这些问题在目的论下都可以解决,即根据翻译目的——包括跨文化沟通的总目的和具体翻译情景——来决定如何翻译。这样,原文如有瑕疵,译者就有责任纠正,因为翻译的目的不是为了让作者出丑,而是为了沟通——再现原文不足,难以达到沟通目的。当然,如果具体的翻译情景是,法庭要求你翻译一封恐吓信,译者就要尽量再现作者的文化水平和精神状态,恐怕还需要通过译注的形式向用户说明,译文中的语法错误和逻辑不通,是译者对原文的忠实反映,不是译者语言能力不足。但一般情况下,遇到原文词不达意,则必须查找有关资料、询问作者,理解作者要表达的客观事实,把意思表达得比原文更清楚。

同样，古汉语当然就要翻译为现代英文，因为翻译目的是让现代西方读者了解中国古代的智慧，而非语言形式；法律文件的翻译，不同于小说和诗歌的翻译，可能做不到出神入化，但原文的意思必须准确传递，重要的概念必须翻译出来。

　　总之，翻译目的和需求多种多样，译者不能盲目按照原文字面翻译，而必须考虑具体翻译情景，决定采用什么翻译策略。这就要求译者在翻译之前，向委托人了解译文的用途、对翻译有无特殊要求。当然，更多的情况则是译者根据文件内容，合理推定译文用途。如果译者认为根据译文用途，需要对原文进行较大调整甚至改写，可以向委托人提出建议或依据自己的判断作出决定，从而真正担当起文化使者的角色。简而言之，在"忠实""通顺"之外，还要考虑译文是否"好用"。"目的论"或者"信达切"可以为翻译实践提供更好的指导，两者在操作层面并无不同。

1.7 "信达切"是文学和非文学翻译的共同标准

　　"信"和"达"作为各类题材的翻译标准毋庸置疑；"切"（取"好用"之义）的概念虽然没有在传统译论中出现，但却贯穿各类翻译实践。在文学翻译历史上，对原文进行大幅删减或改编的事例数不胜数。例如，苏曼殊翻译《悲惨世界》(《惨社会》)，在十四回的小说里，除开头六回半和结尾一回半依托着雨果的小说，中间的六回皆是苏曼殊自己的创作，其目的是宣传革命纲领。① 近代文学家、翻译家林纾不懂外文，但与人合作翻译多国小说百余种，都是采用的编译方法。钱锺书在《林纾的翻译》一文中说："林纾不但喜欢删削原文，有时候还忍不住插嘴，将自己的意思或评语加进去②。"葛浩文在翻译莫言的作品时"连删带改"，翻译《天堂蒜薹之歌》时，甚至把原作的结尾改成了相反的结局，从而让莫言的外译本跨越了"中西方文化心理与叙述模式差异"的"隐形门槛"，成功地进入了西方的主流阅

---

① http://www.shubao90.com/read/23083/36，2021年3月8日查阅。
② https://www.xzbu.com/1/view-5624886.htm，2021年3月8日查阅。

读语境。①

非文学翻译同样如此。严复翻译《天演论》，就加入了很多发挥。他在《译例言》中解释《天演论》署"侯官严复达旨"之意道："题曰达旨，不云笔译，取便发挥，实非正法。"可见，严复并非忠实地逐字逐句"翻译"赫胥黎原著，只是传达大意而已，且指出此乃"取便发挥"的权宜之计，而非翻译之"正法"。（关爱和，2013）虽然严复自认为这种编译的方法不是"正法"，但作为一种翻译实践，是客观存在的，而且有其存在的迫切理由，否则他不会这么翻译。

中华人民共和国国家标准 GB/T 19682—2005《翻译服务译文质量要求》规定：

> 6.2 当采用原文的句型结构或修辞方式不能使译文通顺时，可以在不影响原文语义的前提下，在译文中改变句型结构或修辞或增删某些词句，以使译文更符合目标语言的表达习惯。
>
> 6.6 如果原文存在错误，译者可按原文字面含义直接译出，并在译文中注明，也可予以修正并注明。
>
> 如果原文存在含混、文字缺失现象而顾客又不能给出必要的说明，译者可采取合理的变通办法译出，并在译文中注明。

由此可见，必要时对原文进行加工处理，是所有翻译活动的常规操作，可以作为翻译标准之一。

1.8　如何做到"信达切"

要做到信达切，可以从三个方面入手：理解、表达、变通。

要忠实于原文的思想或作者意图，首先要理解原文。理解分为宏观理解和微观理解。宏观上，要理解 6W1H——Who is speaking to whom? About

---

① http://www.yeeworld.com/article/info/aid/12803.html，2021 年 3 月 8 日查阅。

what? When, where and why, and how? 即作者是谁？读者是谁？关注的问题是什么？什么时候、在哪里、为什么写这篇文章？语言风格如何（how）？任何作品都不是无病呻吟，都有其创作背景。对背景的了解，有助于理解文章细节。在微观层面，译者要理解原作的每个词语、每个词语之间的关系、句子之间的关系、段落之间的关系以及前后联系。理解是翻译的基础，只有透彻理解，才能准确传达。译者的理解要接近、达到甚至超过作者的水平。

要做到语言通顺，就要在理解的基础上，以读者可以接受的方式，来传达作者明确表达、希望表达甚至应该表达的意思，包括用词要准确、搭配要正确、句子结构要牢靠、衔接方法要得当、信息流动要通畅等等。译者要把自己看成一个普通作者，从普通作者的视角看自己的作品（译文）是否经得起推敲：意思是否清楚、逻辑是否连贯、表达是否有欧化倾向或中式英语。

为了使译文"好用"，译者需要根据情况，决定是否以及在多大程度上对原文进行变通取舍。这要求译者在翻译之前，了解翻译活动发生的情境，回答 6W1H: Who is asking you to translate? For whom? When, where, why, and how is the translation to be used, by whom? 如果委托人没有提供以上信息，译者要主动询问，或者根据翻译的内容作出知情判断。只有了解了翻译情景，才能正确决定某个地方是否要翻译，如何翻译，是概括翻译还是逐字逐句翻译，是否要做解释，解释添加在译文中，还是作为译文的注释，或者是给用户看的一个批注。换言之，译者也要像作者那样，根据写作的具体背景，决定在文章中提供哪些信息，不提供哪些信息，以什么方式提供。译文的表达形式可以和原文相同、相近甚至完全不同。

1.9 小结

本章简要回顾了翻译的历史及翻译的历史作用，指出翻译的本质是沟通，即在原文作者、委托人和译文读者之间架起沟通的桥梁。为了实现沟通目的，可以采取直译或意译的方法，但这两种方法无法涵盖翻译中对原文的变通取舍现象，于是出现了翻译的目的论，即根据翻译目的决定直译、意译还是对原文进行较大幅度的编辑，笔者将此概括为"变通"。最后，笔者指出，应当把"信达切"作为翻译的标准，通过透彻理解原文实现"信"，通过遵守写作规则实现"达"，通过变通取舍实现"切"。

〔课后练习〕

1. 请在网上搜索并阅读 Wikipedia 词条 Skopos theory。

2. 请在网上搜索并阅读刘重德《论翻译的原则》一文，说明刘重德提出的"信达切"与本书的解释有何不同。

3. 分析自己所知道的任何翻译理论，对比本书对"信达切"的定义，看其内容要素是否可以归入"信达切"或实现"信达切"的手段。

4. 本章提及了两套 6W1H，分别适应的场景是什么？两套 6W1H 分别指什么？

第二章　翻译是一种写作形式：理解

扫码预习

请扫码下载本章涉及的例句。先做练习，再看解答，学习效果更佳。

如果译者把自己视为普通的作者，各种翻译问题就会迎刃而解，因为译者和作者关注的问题基本相同。

首先是理解。作者在创作任何作品之前，都必须透彻理解所有写作素材。同样，译者在翻译之前，也必须透彻理解原文。译者对原文的理解要接近、达到甚至超过作者的水平。所谓达到作者水平，就是明白写作的目的、字词句段的含义和逻辑关系，以及作者希望达到的交际目的；所谓超过作者的水平，就是能够指出作者所犯的错误，包括笔误、引用错误、计算错误、事实错误、方位错误、逻辑瑕疵，等等。为此，译者必须以批判的眼光审视原作；如果对原文有疑问，则需要通过询问作者或调查研究加以解决。刚入行的译者，知识水平往往低于作者，但在对待原作时，仍要敢于质疑，要有"初生之犊不畏虎"的胆量，通过耐心细致的查证，确保真正理解原文，必要时向作者求教。译者不妨把自己当作编辑，时刻质疑作品的表达方式和内容。只有这样，才能透彻理解原文，甚至发现原文的不足之处。

其次是表达。作者无论创作什么体裁的作品，包括文学和非文学作品，都必须符合一般的写作规范，包括用词准确一致、搭配得当、句子结构严谨、信息流动通畅、前后逻辑连贯、篇章结构合理、意思清楚明了，等等。这些写作规范，同样也是译者需要关注的地方。译者无论采用什么方式（包括用机器翻译）生成初稿，都需要从中／英文写作的角度进行修改编辑，使译文符合一般的写作规范。我们常用的翻译技巧，例如增译／减译、词类／句型／语态转换、拆句／并句、正译／反译、结构调整／重组，等等，也都是为了达到这一目的。把自己当成作者，还意味着即使原文不太通顺连贯，译文也要保证通顺连贯（除非原文不连贯是作者故意为之）。因为译文是一部独立的作品，应当达到普通作品的基本要求。

最后是取舍变通。作者写作时选用什么材料、说什么话，需要根据写作背景和写作目的决定。同样，翻译活动也不是发生在真空中。译者一方面不能扭曲原文的意思；另一方面也要照顾到翻译情景和翻译目的。哪些内容必须译出，哪些可以或必须省略变通，需要视情况决定。例如，如果某些内容翻译出来对委托人有害或不利于实现翻译目的，译者可以自行决定或与委托人沟通后决定省略不译；如果某些内容需要解释才能更好实现沟通目的，译者可以添加注释或在正文中加以解释；如果具体情景不需要逐字逐句翻译，译者可以概括总结；如果读者喜欢文雅的语言，译者可以把白话翻译为古文。简而言之，写作和翻译都服务于特定目的，要根据目的决定写作和翻译的方法。

2.1　全方位

译者对原文的理解是全方位理解，可以用 6W1H 来概括：Who is speaking to whom? About what? When, where, why, and how? 即原文的作者是谁？读者是谁？内容是什么？原文是在什么时候、什么地点、在什么背景下创作的？原文的语言是否有特色？任何文章都不是无中生有，只有了解作者的知识结构、个人经历和创作背景，才能透彻理解文章的内容。即使待翻译的原文没有显示如上信息，也要通过询问或调查研究加以确定。对文章内容的理解不能只停留在字词的表面意思，而是要深入到字词的深

层含义、句子和段落之间的关系和逻辑,以及原文要表达的中心思想。请看这篇短文:

> I could not have known at the time but, when I was five years old, some 500 miles northeast of my rural Texas home, a young man named John Lewis <u>crossed a bridge for me</u>. That historic day, like many others in his extraordinary life, Congressman Lewis <u>endured the unconscionable</u> to challenge and change the <u>conscience</u> of the nation he loved—to make our union more perfect; to bring us closer to our founding ideals; so that little black children, like me, could pursue our American dreams.
>
> Late last night, Congressman Lewis, my hero, <u>crossed another bridge</u>, from <u>elder to ancestor</u>, with characteristic courage and grace. In <u>marking this passage</u>, we need not idealize Congressman Lewis beyond who he was: A founder of—a righteous force for—a <u>more American United States</u> and a fairer, better world.

虽然这篇短文看起来没有什么难度,但如果不知道作者和写作背景,恐怕很难理解,尤其是段落中下划线部分。在不理解的情况下,即使能够按字面翻译为通顺的汉语,也难免前言不搭后语:

> 当时我不知道,但是,当我五岁的时候,在我得克萨斯州乡下的家东北大约 500 英里的地方,一个叫约翰·刘易斯的年轻人帮我过桥。在这历史性的一天,和其他许多人一样,刘易斯国会议员忍受着不合理的挑战,改变他所热爱的国家的良知,使我们的联邦更加完美;使我们更接近我们的建国理想;让像我一样的黑人儿童能够追求我们的美国梦。
>
> 昨晚深夜,我心目中的英雄,国会议员刘易斯,以其特有的勇气和优雅跨过了另一座桥,从长者到祖先。在标记这一段时,我们不需要把刘易斯议员理想化,超越他是谁:一个正义的力量的创始人,一个更加美国化的美国和一个更公平、更美好的世界。

以上译文是机器翻译的结果。大家看到,虽然机器翻译已开口"说人话",即句子的用词、搭配、语法基本符合规范,但仍然有些句子不知所云,导致全文缺乏逻辑,让人感觉如雾里看花。

机器翻译之所以出现这种结果,是因为机器缺乏全方位的理解。机器翻译只是依据概率,推测每一个词的意思和句子结构,然后依据句子结构进行转换。如果推测正确,转换结果有可能正确;如果推测错误,转换结果一定错误。换言之,机器翻译还停留在文字和结构转换的基础上,目前还不能像人类一样理解语言背后的意思和前后逻辑。

人工翻译与机器翻译的差别,在于人首先要理解原文,包括 6 个 W 和 1 个 H,然后再进行转换。例如,人在翻译这段话时,首先要问:这段话的作者是谁?通过委托人或调查研究可知,作者为 Darren Walker,是美国某个基金会的会长,是个黑人。为什么写这篇文章?为了纪念美国黑人国会议员 John Robert Lewis,因为 Lewis 刚刚去世(这篇文章的题目是 "Remembering John Lewis and His Legacy of Good Troublemaking")。为什么要纪念 Lewis?因为他是个政治家和民权领袖[①],而该基金会也是一个民权机构。读者是谁?这篇文章放在该基金会的网站,读者应该是对该基金会及其社会贡献感兴趣的大众或合作机构,以及怀念 Lewis、想要了解 Lewis 的人。

有了这样的背景,我们就可以理解原文中的一些说法。例如:(crossed a bridge) for me,是因为 Lewis 和 Walker 同为黑人,前者曾为后者("me")争取权利;crossed another bridge, from elder to ancestor,是指 Lewis 从一个老者变成一个逝者("成为先贤");marking this passage 意思是"纪念他的过世"——passage 就是 crossing another bridge(指"去世");marking 是"纪念",不是"标记"。

但仅仅依靠以上背景情况,文中的其他细节还是难以理解。例如:crossed a bridge (for me),字面意思是穿过一座桥,但背后的意思是什么?通过调查可知,Lewis 年轻时为了替黑人争取权利,带领黑人群众游行示

---

① John Robert Lewis (February 21, 1940 – July 17, 2020) was an American politician and civil-rights leader who served in the United States House of Representatives for Georgia's 5th congressional district from 1987 until his death in 2020 from pancreatic cancer.

——https://en.wikipedia.org/wiki/John_Lewis_(civil_rights_leader), accessed August 20, 2020.

威，在穿过一座桥之后，遭到骑警镇压，头部遭重击，颅骨开裂。① 尽管翻译时不必补充这些知识，但做到了心中有数。

看似简单的 like many others，机器翻译为“和其他许多人一样”，也是理解错误。从全句来看（That historic day, like many others in his extraordinary life...），others 显然是指 other days。

再例如，endured the unconscionable 是指什么？通过查找英英词典，如 Merriam-Webster 可知 unconscionable 的含义（见图 2.1）②：

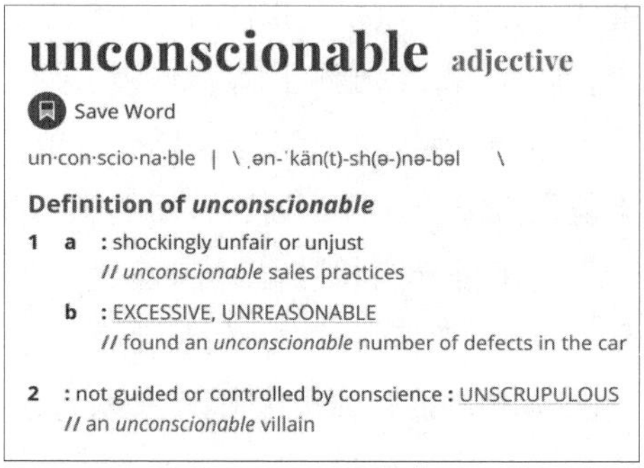
unconscionable adjective

Save Word

un·con·scio·na·ble | \ ˌən-ˈkän(t)-sh(ə-)nə-bəl \

Definition of *unconscionable*

1 a : shockingly unfair or unjust
// *unconscionable* sales practices

b : EXCESSIVE, UNREASONABLE
// found an *unconscionable* number of defects in the car

2 : not guided or controlled by conscience : UNSCRUPULOUS
// an *unconscionable* villain

图 2.1　unconscionable 定义

结合 Lewis 在游行示威时的遭遇，可以推断，此处的 unconscionable 是指没良心的武装镇压。Unconscionable 来自 conscience，后者的意思英文解释（见图 2.2）③：

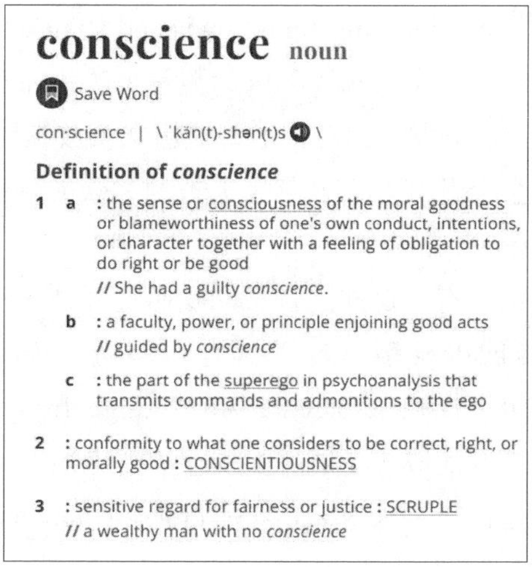
conscience noun

Save Word

con·science | \ ˈkän(t)-shən(t)s \

Definition of *conscience*

1 a : the sense or consciousness of the moral goodness or blameworthiness of one's own conduct, intentions, or character together with a feeling of obligation to do right or be good
// She had a guilty *conscience*.

b : a faculty, power, or principle enjoining good acts
// guided by *conscience*

c : the part of the superego in psychoanalysis that transmits commands and admonitions to the ego

2 : conformity to what one considers to be correct, right, or morally good : CONSCIENTIOUSNESS

3 : sensitive regard for fairness or justice : SCRUPLE
// a wealthy man with no *conscience*

图 2.2　conscience 定义

从英文解释可知，conscience 的意思是“良知”“道义”“是非观念”。endured the unconscionable to challenge and change the conscience of the nation 意思是“为

① Lewis became nationally known during his prominent role in the Selma to Montgomery marches when, on March 7, 1965—a day that would become known as “Bloody Sunday” — Lewis and fellow activist Hosea Williams led over 600 marchers across the Edmund Pettus Bridge in Selma, Alabama. At the end of the bridge, they were met by Alabama State Troopers who ordered them to disperse. When the marchers stopped to pray, the police discharged tear gas and mounted troopers charged the demonstrators, beating them with night sticks. Lewis's skull was fractured, but he escaped across the bridge to Brown Chapel, a church in Selma which also served as the movement's headquarters. Lewis bore scars on his head from the incident for the rest of his life. — ibid

② https://www.merriam-webster.com/dictionary/unconscionable, accessed August 20, 2020.

③ https://www.merriam-webster.com/dictionary/conscience, accessed August 20, 2020.

了挑战和改变国人的是非观念而忍受是非不分的行为"。

最后，a more American United States 如何理解？考虑到 make our union more perfect 来自美国《宪法》的建国理想（…in order to form a more perfect union, establish justice …①），接下来又说 to bring us closer to our founding ideals，同时 "little black children" 又指向美国民权运动领袖马丁·路德·金 1963 年 8 月 28 日在林肯纪念堂台阶上发表的著名演讲 *I Have a Dream*②，因此，a more American United States 应当理解为 "一个更加理想的美国"。

在扫除理解障碍之后，才可以下笔翻译。翻译过程中，可能还会发现更多的理解问题，都需要一一解决。笔者对机器翻译修改如下：

> 我在得克萨斯州的乡村长大。五岁那年，我并不知道家乡东北 500 英里开外的地方，有一位叫约翰·刘易斯的青年，为了争取黑人权利，跨过了一座桥。在那历史性的一天，国会议员刘易斯像其他许多日子那样，忍受着善恶不分的暴行，去挑战和改变他所爱国家的善恶标准，目的是让我们的联邦更加完美，让我们更加接近建国理想，让我这样的黑人儿童能够追求美国梦。
>
> 昨日深夜，我心目中的英雄，国会议员刘易斯，以特有的勇气和风度，跨过了另一座桥，从长者转变为先贤。在纪念这一转变时，我们不需要再去抬高他，只需要实事求是——他是正义的化身、美国理想的奠基人、公正美好世界的建设者。

我们进行了这么多调查研究和思考，才勉强改出两小段说得过去的译文，难以设想机器不经过任何思考，单凭结构转换就能得到理想的结果。以上两段，总共四句话，机器翻译就出现 5 处严重错误：

- crossed a bridge for me 按字面理解为 "帮我过桥"

---

① We the people of the United States, in order to form <u>a more perfect union</u>, establish justice, insure domestic tranquility, provide for the common defense, promote the general welfare, and secure the blessings of liberty to ourselves and our posterity, do ordain and establish this Constitution for the United States of America.

② "I have a dream that one day right there in Alabama little black boys and little black girls will be able to join hands with little white boys and white girls as sisters and brothers."

- like many others，望文生义为"和其他许多人一样"
- endured the unconscionable + 表示目的的 to challenge and change，被理解为 endured the unconscionable ~~to~~ challenge +~~and~~ change<u>d</u>
- In marking this passage，没有结合上下文，而是根据概率理解为"在标记这一段时"
- A founder of—a righteous force for— 本来为并列关系，机器理解为偏正关系 A founder of a righteous force

从以上例子可知，译者必须像作者一样，从宏观到微观，熟悉原文的每个细节，才能形成准确达意的译文。

全方位理解也需要考虑到译文读者和原文读者所在的文化环境差异。相同的词语在不同文化环境中代表的含义也许完全不同。此处引用人民网2015年关于破解养老难题的一段文字进行分析：

> 比起养老床位总量不足的问题，养老机构结构性紧缺的趋势更应引起重视——大多数中低收入的老人难以"挤进"为数不多的普通养老机构，而豪华养老机构的兴建只能满足少数富裕老人的需求；中心城区的公办养老机构一床难求，**地处郊区的民办养老机构**床位却大量空置。①

以下是最后一句话机器翻译的结果：

> It is hard to find a bed in public pension institutions in the central city, but there are a large number of vacant beds in private pension institutions in the suburbs.

机器翻译将"地处郊区"译为 in the suburbs，乍看来没有什么问题，但是 suburb 在西方语境中多为中产阶级居住的区域，请看英英词典的例句和搭配（见图2.3）②：

---

① 韩秉志，《人民日报纵横：以结构性思维破解养老难》，2015年8月3日，引自人民网：http://opinion.people.com.cn/n/2015/0803/c1003-27398905.html, accessed August 20, 2020.

② https://dictionary.cambridge.org/dictionary/english/suburb, accessed August 20, 2020.

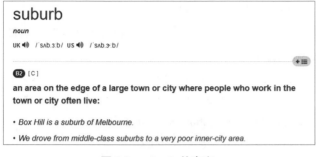

图 2.3 suburb 的定义

然而,"郊区"在中文的语境中多为"城市和农村过渡地带"的含义,如果直接把郊区处理为 in the suburbs,则会让英文读者产生困惑:"富裕的郊区养老院条件优厚,为什么反而会出现空置",也体现不出与前文的对比。因此,笔者认为,此处处理为 out of town 可能更为合适。从英英词典的解释看来,out of town 仅仅表示地理位置上的对比,而没有像 suburb 一样的隐含意思(见图 2.4):①

图 2.4 out-of-town 的定义

因此改译:

> It is hard to find a bed in public elderly care institutions in the central city, but there are a large number of vacant beds in private nursing homes out of town.

总体来看,译者在翻译时,要时时为译文的读者着想,站在译文读者的立场和文化环境中思考,进行翻译,才能更准确地传达原文的含义。

2.2 多查证

多数情况下,仅靠原文本身,无法确知作者的想法,必须通过一系列查证,才能接近甚至达到作者的认知水平。上例已经说明这个问题,这里再举一例:

---

① https://dictionary.cambridge.org/dictionary/english/out-of-town, accessed August 20, 2020.

Descriptive trademarks describe some feature of the product such as quality, type, efficacy, use, shape, etc. (<u>eg. SWEET for marketing chocolates as it would be considered unfair to give a single chocolate manufacturer the exclusivity over the word sweet for marketing its products</u>). They have little distinctiveness and are only eligible for protection if it can be shown that a secondary meaning has been acquired and a distinctive character has been established through extensive use in the marketplace.

原译：

描述性商标描述了产品的一些特征，如质量、类型、功效、用途、形状等（例如，<u>SWEET 代表巧克力，因为让一家巧克力制造商独占 SWEET 这个词来销售其产品是不公平的</u>）。这种商标的显著性很低，获得保护的前提是经过长期使用，商标逐渐获得了第二层含义并且确立了独特性。

译文划线部分显然逻辑不通。如果译者把自己视为普通作者，就绝不会允许这样的句子出现在自己的文章中。如果作者不理解描述性商标的含义，可以上网查资料：

我国商标分为四类：臆造型商标、任意型商标、暗示型商标和描述性商标。描述性商标是指由具有描述性的文字、图形或其组合构成的商标，描述性商标具有双重含义：第一含义是指对商品或服务用途、大小、颜色、成分、产地等的描述，即对描述性的文字、图形或其组合公共领域含义的使用；第二含义是指示商品或服务来源的使用。描述性商标禁止他人使用的权利范围仅限于"第二含义"，他人使用"第一含义"属于商标法上的合理使用。然而实践中对"第一含义"和"第二含义"的边界模糊不清，因此有必要对描述性商标相关法律概念进行梳理。①

由此可见，原文的意思是，生产巧克力的厂商，不能用"甜味"作为商标。因为一旦"甜味"成为一家企业的商标，别人就不能再用这个词营销产品；如果使用，就是侵犯他人的商标权，这对其他巧克力生产商显然是不公平的。在明白了意思之后，原文的用词、结构并无难译之处。修改如下：

---

① https://zhuanlan.zhihu.com/p/29535151, accessed August 20, 2020.

描述性商标描述产品的某种特征，如质量、类型、功效、用途、形状等（例如，以"甜味"作为巧克力的商标——但只允许一家厂商使用"甜味"商标，对其他厂商来说是不公平的）。这种商标的显著性很低，获得保护的前提是经过广泛使用，商标逐渐获得了第二含义并确立了显著性（"显著性"也可以译为"区分度""辨识度"）。

实际上，原文的表述也有问题。如果改为"SWEET for marketing chocolates, <u>but</u> it would be considered unfair to give a single chocolate manufacturer the exclusivity over the word sweet for marketing its products."，意思就清楚了。但在翻译实践中，原文表述不清的情况很多，有的是因为原文语言表述不当，有的是因为译者不懂相关专业，无论如何译者都必须根据上下文或文本之外的资料确定作者的真实想法，然后以更清楚的方式表达出来。

2.3 理解汉语

我们往往认为，英译汉时，鉴于我们的母语不是英语，也不熟悉国外的背景，因此需要查证的地方较多。实际上，汉译英时，也同样面临理解问题。甚至习以为常的说法，从翻译的角度看，也不容易理解。例如：

> 市政公用设施<u>大配套费</u>和土地出让金政府净收益，应当用于前述设施的建设与维护。

原译：

<u>The large utility fee</u> for municipal utilities and the net government revenue from land transfers should be used for construction and maintenance work on the facilities mentioned above.

"大配套费"是什么？不做翻译，我们不知道自己不理解。按字面翻译为 large utility fee 显然不正确。经查证：

> 第二条 本办法所称<u>大配套费</u>，是指为新建住宅和公建项目建设

27

的用地界线以外相关城市规划道路（含路灯、绿化、交通设施），给水，燃气，排水（含雨水、污水），再生水等工程费用。

由此可见，这个"大"是小区之外的一般性配套费。改译：

The general charges for municipal utilities and the net government revenue from land transfers should be used for construction and maintenance of the facilities mentioned above.

再如：防控和救治两个战场协同作战

这是一个小标题，来自2020年6月国务院新闻办发布的"抗击新冠肺炎疫情的中国行动"。从普通读者的角度看，不存在任何理解问题。但如果让机器翻译，就会凸显理解问题：

Coordinated Operations on the Two Battlefields of Prevention, Control and Rescue

中文是两个战场，但英文变成了三个：prevention、control和rescue。这就迫使我们问自己：prevention和control有什么区别？"对确诊病例、疑似病例、无症状感染者的早隔离，是控制传染源、防止疫情扩散的重要措施。"[①] 由此可见，"控制"是手段，"防止"是结果，两者属于同一行为，因此不必都翻译出来。"协同"是否"协调"？这涉及是否译为coordinated。该标题下有五个次级标题：

（一）建立统一高效的指挥体系

（二）构建全民参与严密防控体系

（三）全力救治患者、拯救生命

（四）依法及时公开透明发布疫情信息

（五）充分发挥科技支撑作用

其中并没有特别强调预防和救治的"协调"，所以中文的用词是"协同"，强调的是"并肩作战"。因此翻译时不一定是coordinate。另外，rescue的意思是"紧急救援"，此处的"救治"是指"治疗"，用treatment

---

① http://www.shanghai.gov.cn/nw2/nw2314/nw32419/nw48516/nw48536/u21aw1436322.html, accessed August 20, 2020.

才能达意；两个战场的隐喻可以保留。所以，可以改为：Two Battle Fields: Prevention and Treatment。其中的 prevention 也可以改为 control。还可以简化为：Prevention and Treatment。

再例如，北京市某年的政府工作报告中有这样一句话："切实发挥规划的<u>刚性管控</u>作用"，原译为 use it [the plan] as a powerful tool for <u>rigid control</u>。笔者后来改为 use it as a <u>binding instrument</u> for development control。原译者反思说，她"把'刚性管控'看作了一个短语，但不求甚解，字对字翻译，导致英文不知所云"。任何作品（包括报告）都不是无病呻吟，而是有感而发（6W 当中的 Why）。此处针对的问题，是过去政府制定了发展规划，但并没有严格遵守，没有做到"一张蓝图绘到底"。这句话的意思是，今后的规划，要发挥约束作用（"刚性管控"），不能朝令夕改，因此改用 binding。如果不敢确定是什么意思，可以上网查找相关解释（见图 2.5）：

图 2.5 "刚性管控"查证

另外，rigid 一词不要随便用。即便 rigid control 这一搭配存在，也暗示缺乏灵活性（见图 2.6）：

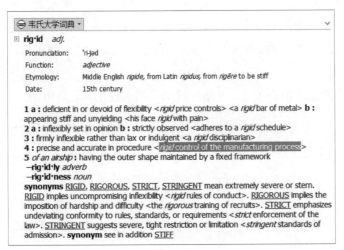

图 2.6 rigid 的定义

再举一例（出处为某年北京市政府工作报告）。原文为"北京经济技术开发区要优化提升，建立与三大科学城的<u>对接转化</u>机制。"原译为：

We will upgrade Beijing Economic-Technological Development Area as well as build a coordination and transformation mechanism connecting the Area with the three science parks.

原译是按照原文结构和字面意思转换的结果。句子基本通顺，但具体要表达什么，恐怕不容易理解。

透过文字，笔者的理解为：北京经济技术开发区要把三大科学城的科研成果接过来，投入商用。如果不敢确信，可以上网搜索。请看北京经济技术开发区网站提供的资料：

> 于长辉表示，"三城一区"科创中心主平台是落实北京城市新总规，实现首都高质量发展的重要基础。高新技术产业发展的关键在落地，<u>而北京经济技术开发区就是承载科技成果转化的最佳区域</u>。双方要建立合作沟通对接机制，密切开展科技创新及成果转化应用、干部人才等方面的交流合作，实现两区在主平台上的融合发展。①

因此改译为：Beijing Economic-Technological Development Area must improve itself and collaborate with the three science parks to build a mechanism for commercializing the latter's research results.

在了解情况的人看来，原文是可以理解的。但译者不是专业人士，对原文的理解可能达不到专业人士的水平。为了弥补这一不足，译者必须进行调查研究或得到内行的帮助。如果仅仅按照自己的一知半解来翻译，读者多半是看不懂的。

词语之间是并列还是偏正关系，也是理解中应当关注的问题。例如：

> 在向个人信息主体推送<u>新闻信息</u>服务的过程中使用个性化展示的，应为个人信息主体提供简单直观的退出或关闭个性化展示模式的选项。

原译：

Where personalized display is used in the process of pushing news

---

① http://kfqgw.beijing.gov.cn/zwgk/xwzx/yzxw/201909/t20190911_220347.html, accessed August 20, 2020.

<u>information</u> services to PI Subjects, the PI Controller shall provide a simple and intuitive option for the PI Subjects to exit from or turn off the personalized display mode.

"新闻信息服务"理解为"新闻和信息服务"才符合逻辑。若不是看到 news information 搭配不当，恐怕不会认真思考"新闻"和"信息"之间的关系。

译者往往需要翻译不熟悉的领域，这时必须通过调查研究，现学现卖。例如，2020年的政府工作报告中有一句话：

> 加强监管，防止资金"空转"套利，打击恶意逃废债。

机器翻译的结果如下：

> We will strengthen oversight to prevent "idle" arbitrage of funds and crack down on malicious evasion of junk bonds.

可以注意到原文中涉及两个专业名词，即"资金'空转'套利"和"逃废债"，要想翻译准确，首先要了解这两个名词的含义。

通过在网上查找资料，了解到"资金'空转'套利"是指：

> 银行业金融机构通过多种业务使资金在金融体系内流转而未流向实体经济或通过拉长融资链条后再流向实体经济来获取收益的套利方式。①

机器翻译将"空转"译成了"idle"。根据英英词典，idle 一词有形容词和动词两种词性，在此句中所用的应该是形容词。经过筛选，比较贴近"空转"这一意思的解释为（见图 2.7）：

ADJECTIVE [verb-link ADJECTIVE]
If machines or factories are idle, they are not working or being used.
Now the machine is lying idle.
...factories that had been idle for years.
Synonyms: unused, stationary, inactive, out of order   More Synonyms of idle

图 2.7 idle 的定义

---

① https://zhidao.baidu.com/question/561132531.html, accessed August 20, 2020.

但根据英文解释可知，这里说的"idle"是指不再运行或被使用。而原文中所说的"空转"是指资金在金融体系内流动却未流向或延迟流向实体经济。如果找不到对应的英文形容词，不妨直接根据中文背后的意思来解释，不追求字面对应。

而"逃废债"是指：

> 一种民事违约行为，不是所有的欠债不还都是逃废债，它强调债务人的主观故意：确切地说，有履行能力而不尽力履行债务的行为就是逃废债。所谓"有履行能力"是指有收入来源，或者虽无收入来源，但有可供履行债务的资产，能够部分或全部履行债务。从债务人主观上来看，逃废债有两种表现形式：一种是积极地逃避履行债务，另一种是消极的不作为。我们通常把前一种称之为"恶意逃废债"。①

这里我们还可以发现机器翻译的一个明显错误，即"逃废债"是指"逃（避）废（除）债务"，是简化的动宾短语，而机器却将"废"理解成了"债"的修饰语，将"废债"看作了偏正式短语，并且将"债"理解成了"债券"，所以才有了"junk bonds"的译法。实际上，这里讲的就是逃避债务，而且没有特别区分是积极的还是消极的，所以官方译文里也没有将"恶意"翻译出来（实际上，evasion 本身就隐含了主观故意）。

官方译文：

We should tighten regulation, prevent funds from simply circulating in the financial sector for the sake of arbitrage, and crack down on debt evasion.

还可以再改得更明确：

We should tighten regulation, make sure that funds go to the real sector, and crack down on debt evasion.

---

① https://zhidao.baidu.com/question/1895947823999007220.html?fr=iks&word=%B6%F1%D2%E2%CC%D3%B7%CF%D5%AE&ie=gbk, accessed August 20, 2020.

2.4　小结

　　作者如果对素材和写作目的不熟悉，是无法下笔写作的。同样，译者对翻译素材和译文使用的情景不熟悉，也无法下笔翻译。因此，翻译和写作在理解上的要求是一致的。译者必须熟悉原文的 6 个 W 和 1 个 H，在理解上接近、达到，甚至超过作者水平，才有可能作出准确的翻译。同时，译者还需要理解翻译的情景，才能产出符合需要的译文。

　　鉴于我们翻译的文件，往往是不熟悉的内容，因此，要想充分理解原文，必须进行大量的查证，确保译者的理解与作者的理解保持一致，而不是以自己个人理解为基础进行翻译。第四章还将专门讨论理解的广度和深度。

〔课后练习〕

1. 翻译和写作的共同点和区别是什么？
2. 理解的全方位，是指什么？
3. 为什么要进行查证？

第三章 翻译是一种写作形式：表达

 **扫码预习**

请扫码下载本章涉及的例句。先做练习，再看解答，学习效果更佳。

翻译就是写作，只是参照物不同。写作的参照物可以是直接经验，也可以是间接经验，而翻译的参照物永远是间接经验，直接经验起到帮助理解的作用。既然翻译是一种写作方式，就要符合中英文写作的要求，做到意思准确，语言通顺。

3.1 准确

写作要准确反映客观现实和作者的思想，译文则必须透过作者的文字，并结合文章之外的其他资料，还原作者描述的客观事实和主观思想，然后以另一种语言准确传达出来。

3.1.1 符合原意

如同写作要准确表达作者的意思，翻译也要准确传递作者的意思。例如，某遗址公园的门票价格内外有别，笔者相信不是翻译错误，而是公园的政策（见图 3.1）：

但如果确为公园政策，应当明确指出：Chinese visitors: 30 yuan/person; foreign visitors: 60 yuan/person. 否则，外国游客可能会有受骗的感觉。

图 3.1　某公园票价说明

3.1.2　用词得当

在理解的基础上，译者需要结合语境，找到专业、地道、能传达作者意图的词语来表达。例如，某化妆品的介绍中有这样一段：

> Love your skin and feel your best with smooth, vital, and elastic skin. To defy the signs of aging skin, our powerful and innovative products help preserve the skin's youthful beauty and <u>firmness</u>.

原译：

> 爱护您的肌肤，让肌肤变得光滑、有活力、有弹性，展现您的最美风采。为了抵挡岁月痕迹，我们强有力的创新产品帮助保护肌肤的年轻美丽和<u>硬度</u>。

原文为该品牌网站的营销用语，且不说第一句话翻译得是否传神，对消费者是否具有吸引力，看第二句"firmness"一词被翻译成"硬度"，让读者着实大吃一惊。查阅柯林斯字典可知，"firm"作为形容词，其释义为 If something is firm, it does not shake or move when you put weight or pressure on it, because it is strongly made or securely fastened。牛津字典释义为：having a solid, almost unyielding surface or structure。显然如果将"firmness"翻译成"坚硬""结实"，不仅缺乏美感，还无法起到宣传作用。参考美妆行业平行文本，可将其翻译成"紧致"，与衰老的"松弛"皮肤相对应。

再如：

本标准代替 GB/T35273—2017《信息安全技术 个人信息安全规范》，与 GB/T35273—2017 相比，除编辑性修改外主要<u>技术变化</u>如下：……

原译：

This standard replaces GB/T 35273-2017 Information security technology — Personal information security specification. In addition to a number of editorial changes, the following <u>technical deviations</u> have been made with respect to the GB/T 35273-2017 (the previous edition).

原译把"技术变化"译为 technical deviations。但这个短语的意思是"技术偏差"：

<u>Technical deviations</u> are deviations from drawings, specifications and other technical requirements. Possible deviations should be proposed and agreed before they are implemented. In case they impact on cost and/or schedule then the change procedure shall be followed first.[①]

根据资料（见图3.2）[②]，此处应当使用 technical changes 或 technical revisions：

```
Editorial review is intended to improve the clarity of the text or address obvious errors or omission of information.

Technical changes are those that have an effect such that change an outcome, procedure, equation, unit (load/force/temperature/time), etc. The intent and output of the standard is affected.

Examples of technical changes:
  - Referencing another standard should be considered a technical change, since the referenced standard itself has technical content.
  - Equations
  - Units (load/force/temperature/time/etc...)
  - Equipment
  - Technical changes to a footnote in a table or an annex

Examples of editorial changes:
  - Wording/rephrasing for clarity
  - Punctuation
  - Addition of a unit equivalence
  - Editorial or technical changes to non-mandatory language (notes and appendices)
```

图 3.2 "技术变化"英文查证

---

① https://www.klinkercmc.com/technical-deviation, accessed August 20, 2020.
② https://materials.transportation.org/wp-content/uploads/sites/24/2017/04/Editorial-vs-Technical-Revisions-in-Standards.pdf, accessed August 20, 2020.

改译：

This standard supersedes GB/T 35273-2017 Information security technology—Personal information security specification. In addition to a number of editorial changes, the following <u>technical revisions</u> have been made with respect to the previous edition.

注意："Information security technology—Personal information security specification"当中的字母大写，是制定标准文件时的要求，故没有修改。

鉴于英语不是母语，我们往往想不到确切的说法，只能翻译大概意思，例如：

个人信息保护政策应公开发布且易于访问，例如，在网站主页、移动互联网应用程序安装页、附录C中的交互界面或设计等<u>显著位置</u>设置链接。

原译：

The PI protection policy shall be publicly released and easily accessible, for example, <u>a link at an eye-catching place</u> on a website homepage, an installation page of a mobile-Internet application (APP), or an interface or interactive design included in Annex C.

原译"显著位置"译为"an eye-catching place"，怀疑不够正式，法律中应该有更严肃的说法。通过查找，原译确实没有用例，而且意思也有差异（见图3.3）[①]：

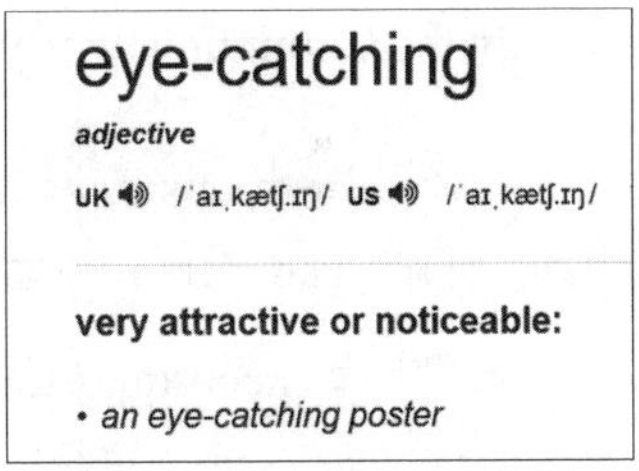

图 3.3 eye-catching 的定义

进一步查找，看到这样的表述：

The Privacy Policy should be **displayed in a prominent location**, such as a website footer or in the main menu of an app.

据此改译：

The PI protection policy shall be made publicly available, for example, <u>through its prominent display</u> on a homepage, an APP installation page, or an

---

① https://dictionary.cambridge.org/zhs/ 词典 / 英语 /eye-catching, accessed August 20, 2020.

interface or interactive design under Annex C.

再例如：

据不完全统计，从 1921 年到 1949 年，我们党领导的革命队伍中，<u>有名可查</u>的烈士就达 370 多万名。

原译：

According to incomplete statistics, there were more than 3.7 million martyrs <u>who had names in the revolutionary troops</u> of the CPC from 1921 to 1949.

其中的"有名可查"译为 who had names，与 in the revolutionary troops 连起来，容易产生歧义：这些烈士有名字，其他烈士没有名字？实际情况是，其他烈士也有名字，只不过查不出来。但因为译者表达能力有限，想不到更好的表达方法，只能权且这么说。如果把"有名可查"转化为"能够识别"，恐怕大家就可以翻译出来了：

According to incomplete statistics, from 1921 to 1949, there were more than 3.7 million <u>identifiable</u> martyrs in the revolutionary forces led by the Communist Party of China.

改译还把 troops 改为 forces（力量），因为这些烈士不一定都是在部队工作，他们可能是中央领导人、地下工作者、农会干部，等等。

如果怀疑 according to incomplete statistics 是否正宗，可以查语料库。查找发现，这个说法尽管在英语国家也会用到，但与中国相关的报道占绝大多数，说明中国媒体更喜欢用这个词。以下是语料库统计全球 20 个使用英语的国家和地区，来自中国香港的用例占绝大多数（见图 3.4）。

既然英语中有人用，改译决定不变。有些概念来自国外，翻译时回译为国外概念，不另起炉灶。例如：

确保安全——具备与所面临的安全风险相匹配的安全能力，并采取足够的管理措施和技术手段，保护个人信息的保密性、完整性、<u>可用性</u>。（取自《个人信息安全规范》）

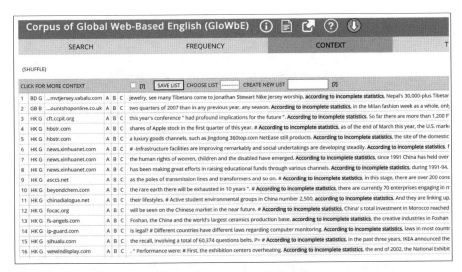

图 3.4 "据不完全统计"英文查证

原译：

Security assurance — have the security capabilities that match potential security risks and adopt sufficient administrative and technical measures to protect the confidentiality, integrity, and <u>availability</u> of PI.

根据同一语境下对"可用性"的解释，"可用性是根据授权实体的要求可访问和利用的特性"。据此，英文似乎应该使用 accessibility，因为 availability 是指数据是否存在，accessibility 是指能否访问（隐含"使用"），但国外相关资料用的是 availability（意思仍然是 accessibility）：

(1) The term "information security" means protecting information and information systems from unauthorized access, use, disclosure, disruption, modification, or destruction in order to provide:

 A. Integrity, which means guarding against improper information modification or destruction, and includes ensuring information nonrepudiation, accuracy, and authenticity;

 B. Confidentiality, which means preserving authorized restrictions on access and disclosure, including a means for protecting personal privacy and proprietary information; and

C. Availability, which means ensuring timely and <u>reliable access to, and use of</u>, information.[①]

因此，原译已经符合国际用法，不必修改，但需要增加主语：

Security. <u>PI Controllers</u> shall possess security capabilities that match potential security risks and adopt adequate administrative and technical measures to protect the confidentiality, integrity, and <u>availability</u> of PI.

由于译者并非具体领域的专家，一些专有名词往往不知道如何翻译，这时候就要通过查证来找到恰当的译法。例如：

国际临床评价指标同样认为，对于新冠肺炎轻症患者，真正反映疗效的关键指标是<u>转重率</u>。"中医药治疗发挥的核心作用正是有效降低<u>转重率</u>，特别是在早期介入，能显著降低<u>轻症病人发展为重症病人的机率</u>。"张伯礼说。

原译：

International clinical evaluation indicators also believe that for patients with new coronary pneumonia, the key indicator that truly reflects the efficacy is this <u>severeness conversion rate</u>. "The core role played by Chinese medicine treatment is to effectively reduce the <u>severeness conversion rate</u>, especially in early intervention, which can significantly reduce the incidences of <u>mild patients developing into severe patients</u>," said Zhang Boli.

"转重率"如何表达？笔者怀疑 severeness conversion rate 表述不够专业。通过使用关键词（如 mild moderate severity progression rate

Outcomes				
Time from illness onset to admission, days	7 (4.25–14)	8 (4–14)	7 (5–11)	0.135
Severe progression	—	—	155 (61.75%)	
Critical progression	—	—	50 (19.92%)	
Death progression	—	—	46 (18.33%)	

图 3.5 "转重率"英文查证

---

① https://www.tylercybersecurity.com/blog/fundamental-objectives-of-information-security-the-cia-triad, accessed August 20, 2020.

Covid-19）反复查找，笔者看到一些资料（见图 3.5）[①]：

其中的 severe/critical/death progression，就是指中症转为重症、危重症、死亡的情况（见图 3.6）：

> **Methods**
> All adults with COVID-19 of moderate severity diagnosed using quantitative RT-PCR and hospitalized at the Central Hospital of Wuhan, China, from 1 January to 20 March 2020 were enrolled in this retrospective study. The main outcomes were <u>progress</u>ion from moderate to severe or critical condition or death.

图 3.6 "转重率"英文资料

资料的来源是国际英文期刊，因此用法是可靠的，据此改译：

International clinical evaluation indicators also suggest that the key indicator on the effect of treatment for COVID-19 is <u>the severe progression rate</u>. "The core role of TCM treatment is precisely to reduce <u>this rate</u>. Through early intervention, TCM is able to significantly reduce the incidences of <u>mild cases developing into severe ones</u>," said Zhang Boli.

3.1.3 突出重点

每句话都有一个重点，翻译时要抓住这个重点，并突出呈现出来，通常是将其置于句末。例如：

These working groups, composed of senior colleagues from relevant Sectors and areas in WIPO, have met regularly since that time. While they are <u>progressing</u> in <u>their respective areas</u>, the issues with which they are dealing are often complex and interconnected and their deliberations are ongoing.

原译：

这些工作组由 WIPO 有关部门和地区的资深员工组成，自组建起定期会面。虽然各工作组<u>各有分工</u>，但处理的问题往往复杂且相互联

---

① https://www.sciencedirect.com/science/article/pii/S1198743X20303797, accessed August 20, 2020.

系，需要不断进行商议。

While 从句的重点是 progressing，不是 their respective areas，否则和主句的重点 ongoing 无法形成对照，因此原译是错误的，有望文生义之嫌。改译：

> 这些工作组由世界知识产权组织有关部门和领域的资深同事组成，自组建起定期会面。虽然各工作组<u>均取得进展</u>，但涉及的问题往往错综复杂，所以还在不断讨论中。

改译还纠正了 area 的译法——是"领域"，不是"地区"；以及 are ongoing 的译法——是"还在不断讨论"，不是"需要不断商议"。

3.1.4 表达到位

句子的意思要清晰传达出来，不能含混不清。比如：

原文：

> In the course of the examination, the authority may grow the variety or carry out other necessary tests, <u>cause the growing of the variety or the carrying out of other necessary tests</u>, or take into account the results of growing tests or other trials which have already been carried out.

原译：

> 审查过程中，可以种植该品种或进行其他必要试验，<u>或要求种植该品种或进行其他必要试验</u>，或对其他试验的结果予以考虑。

这是解释 UPOV 公约（植物新品种保护公约）的一段话。原文下划线部分 cause the growing or carrying out 是指政府机关在审查植物新品种申请时，如果自己没办法试种或测试申请中的品种，可以让别人去做。cause 的意思是"使……发生"，"使种植发生"意思就是让别人种植。原译"要求种植该品种"虽然可以理解为"要求他人种植该品种"，但意思表达不到位。改译：

审查中，受理主管机关可种植该品种或进行其他必要测试，<u>委托他人种植该品种或进行其他必要测试</u>，或考虑现有种植测试结果或其他试验结果。

3.1.5 当心歧义

翻译时，要时刻当心译文可能存在的歧义。比如：

原文：国内首家外资控股飞机维修企业落地运营。

原译：The first <u>foreign-holding</u> aircraft maintenance company in China has landed in Beijing and started operation.

控股公司叫作 holding company。但 holding company 是指控制其他公司的公司：

What Is a Holding Company?

A holding company is a form of corporate ownership structure or conglomerate. It involves a parent corporation, limited liability company (LLC), or limited partnership (LP) that owns enough equity and voting stock in another company that it can control that company's policies and oversee its management decisions. Although a holding company owns the assets of other companies, it often maintains only oversight capacities and therefore does not actively participate in running a business's day-to-day operations of these subsidiaries.[①]

此处的"外资控股企业"，不是由外国投资的控股企业（foreign (-invested) holding company），而是被外资控制的在华企业，应当译为 company held by foreign investors，简称 foreign-held companies。就像 state-owned enterprises 意思是 enterprises owned by the state，不能说 state-owning enterprises，后者的语法意义是 enterprises that own states，那是不可能的。

改译：

The first foreign-held（或 controlled）aircraft maintenance company

---

① https://www.investopedia.com/terms/h/holdingcompany.asp, accessed August 20, 2020.

in China has landed in Beijing and started operation.

再例如：

在验证个人信息主体身份后，应及时响应个人信息主体基于8.1~8.6 提出的请求。

原译：

After verifying the identity of a PI Subject, the PI Controller shall <u>make a timely response</u> to the request of the PI Subject <u>in accordance with</u> 8.1-8.6.

如果不看原文，可能以为 in accordance with... 修饰 make。把 in accordance with... 改为 under 并简化用词，就可以解决这个歧义：

After verifying the identity of a PI Subject, the PI Controller shall promptly respond to the PI Subject's request <u>under</u> 8.1-8.6.

3.1.6 当心假朋友

所谓"假朋友"（false friends），是指两种语言（或方言）之间看起来形态相同或相似，但实际上意思不同、不完全相同甚至相去甚远的一对词。例如，"手纸"二字，在日语中表示"信件"；"汽车"二字，在日语中表示"火车"。西方语言之间，假朋友也多，以下是英语和法语之间的几个例子（见图 3.7）[①]：

FRENCH	ENGLISH Incorrect	Correct
Achever	~~Achieve~~	Complete or finish
Actuellement	~~Actually~~	At the moment, currently
Affluence	~~Affluence~~	Crowds
Agenda	~~Agenda~~	Diary
Ancien	~~Ancient~~	Former
Assister a	~~Assist~~	Attend

图 3.7 英语和法语之间的"假朋友"

---

① https://www.learn-english-today.com/lessons/lesson_contents/grammar/faux_amis.html, accessed August 20, 2020.

维基百科中给出了更多例子。下表中的"other word"是指英文单词的假朋友;"other meaning"是"假朋友"的真正含义(见图3.8)①:

English word	English meaning	Other language	Other word	Other meaning
assist	to help	Spanish	asistir	to attend
		French	assister	
attend	to go to	Spanish	atender	to meet
		French	attendre	to wait
become	to develop into	German	bekommen	to receive
cafeteria	dining room	Spanish/Portuguese	cafetería	coffee house
confetti	small, colored paper pieces used for decoration	Italian	confetti	sugared almonds
		Russian	конфеты	candy
embarrassed	ashamed	Spanish	embarazada	pregnant
fabric	cloth	German	Fabrik	factory
gift	present	German	Gift	poison
		Swedish, Danish, Norwegian	gift	married
machine	device or equipment	Russian	машина	car
magazine	periodical	Italian	magazzino	store
		French	magasin	
		Russian	магазин	
ordinary	common	Portuguese	ordinário	vulgar
print	publication	Japanese	purinto プリント	advertising handout
smart	intelligent	Japanese	sumaato スマート	not fat
vulgar	crude	Portuguese	vulgar	ordinary

图3.8 欧洲语言及日语之间的"假朋友"

中日、中韩、中越之间也存在不少"假朋友"(同形异义词)。例如(见图3.9、3.10、3.11)②:

---

① https://www.elc.edu/english-grammar-lesson-false-friend-words/#, accessed August 20, 2020.
② https://zh.wikipedia.org/wiki/ 同形异义 oldformat=true, accessed August 20, 2020.

| 日文汉字与汉语的同形异议词列举 |||
日文汉字	平假名	意思
愛人	あいじん	情妇
悪心	あくしん	坏心眼[a]
暗算	あんざん	心算
安息	あんそく	安静地休息
石頭	いしあたま	如石般坚硬的头部、顽固不化的人
依頼	いらい	委托[b]
運転	うんてん	驾驶
得体	えたい	来历
遠慮	えんりょ	客气[c]
大家	おおや	房东
必死	ひっし	拼命

图 3.9　日语和汉语之间的"假朋友"

| 朝鲜汉字与汉语的同形异议词列举 |||
谚文	朝鲜汉字	意思
감독	監督	导演、主教练
감자	甘藷	马铃薯
거래	去來	交易、交涉
검토	檢討	研究、审查、探讨
결속	結束	团结
경리	經理	财务会计
공부	工夫	学习
공정	工程	工序、工艺
근신	謹愼	停职反省[d]
기차	汽車	蒸汽火车

图 3.10　朝鲜语和汉语之间的"假朋友"

越南语虽然已经不使用汉字，但如果写成汉字，就会出现同形异义词：

汉英的书写形态不同、发音不同，本无所谓"假朋友"，但存在一些看似对等但意思和用法却不一定相同的所谓"对等词"，我们姑且也称之为"假朋友"。例如，大家一看到"一批……"，就想翻译为"a batch of"，但是"a batch of"一般情况下只能形容一批机器货物；倘若指的是一群人，则是非正式用法（意思是"一帮"）（见图 3.12）：

国语字	越南汉字	意思
Bản đồ	版圖	地图
Biểu tình	表情	示威
Đông Dương	東洋	中南半岛
Giám đốc	監督	经理
Giáo sư	教師	教授
Phong lưu	風流	富有
Phương phi	芳菲	丰满
Phương tiện	方便	手段
Sách	冊	书本
Tai nạn	災難	事故
Thời sự	時事	新闻
Thời tiết	時節	天气
Văn phòng	文房	办公室

图 3.11　越南语和汉语之间的"假朋友"

```
New Oxford English-Chinese Dictionary

batch
noun
    a quantity or consignment of goods produced at one time
    一批生产量
    ■(informal)a number of things or people regarded as a group or set
    (非正式)一组、一批、一群（人）
    a batch of loyalists and sceptics.
    一批勤王者和怀疑者。
    ■(Computing)a group of records processed as a single unit, usually without input from a user
    (计算机)（通常不需要用户输入的）批量、成批（数据）
```

图 3.12　batch 的定义

David W. Ferguson 在《我可能学的是假英语》中也指出，“batch”一般只能在工业语境下形容一批货物，例如“The first batch of engines came off the new production line yesterday.”所以说，“a batch of”和“一批……”也是一对“假朋友”。

再例如“操场”和 playground 也是一对“假朋友”。A playground, play-park, or play area is a place specifically designed to enable children to play there.（https://en.wikipedia.org/wiki/Playground）朗文词典解释为（见图 3.13）：

play·ground / ˈpleˌgraund ; ˈpleɪgraʊnd /
noun [C]
1. an area for children to play, especially at a school or in a park, that often has special equipment for climbing on, riding on etc

图 3.13　playground 的定义（一）

韦氏词典的解释更直接（见图 3.14）：

playground noun
Save Word
play·ground | \ ˈplā-ˌgrau̇nd \
Definition of *playground*
1 : a piece of land used for and usually equipped with facilities for recreation especially by children

图 3.14　playground 的定义（二）

可知，playground 是具有一定娱乐设施的场地，供小孩子玩耍。而在谷歌上键入 playground，搜索图片，出来的都是类似的图片（见图 3.15）：

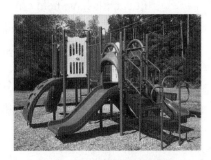

图 3.15　playground 的图片

而我们经常说的“操场”是“田径场”，应该是“field”“school field”“sports field”“pitch”。下图为搜索“school field”出现的图片（见图 3.16）：

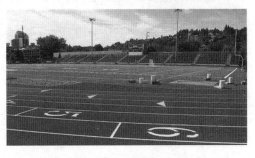

图 3.16　school field 的图片

连接词也可能是“假朋友”。例如，“一方面……另一方面”。一个似乎“完美”的对等词是“on one hand...on the other (hand)”。但实际上中文说的“一方面……另一方面”是递进或者并列的关系，而英文中的“on the other hand”是提出与“on one hand”相反的看法或事物（见图 3.17）。

> **WordNet English Dictionary**
>
> adv.
>
> - (contrastive) from another point of view; then again, but then
>
>   on the other hand, she is too ambitious for her own good
>
>   then again, she might not go

图 3.17　on the other hand 的定义

下面我们以“四风”的翻译为例，说明如何鉴别和翻译“假朋友”。“四风”——形式主义、官僚主义、享乐主义、奢靡之风，人们经常翻译为 Four Undesirable Working Styles — formalism, bureaucracy/bureaucratism, hedonism and extravagance。

例如，《中国日报》的报道：

> PLA units have held criticism and self-criticism meetings and submitted reports to echo a Communist Party of China drive to clean up undesirable work styles such as formalism, bureaucracy, hedonism and extravagance.①

但路透社在转述这个报道时，却把 formalism 变成了一个省略号：

> PLA units have held criticism and self-criticism meetings and submitted reports to echo a Communist Party of China drive to clean up undesirable work styles such as ... bureaucracy, hedonism and extravagance.

究其原因，可能是实在不明白为什么要反对 formalism（见图 3.18）②：

> ## Formalism (art)
>
> From Wikipedia, the free encyclopedia
>
> In art history, **formalism** is the study of art by analyzing and comparing form and style. Its discussion also includes the way objects are made and their purely visual or material aspects. In painting, formalism emphasizes compositional elements such as color, line, shape, texture, and other perceptual aspects rather than content, meaning, or the historical and social context. At its extreme, formalism in art history posits that everything necessary to comprehending a work of art is contained within the work of art. The context of the work, including the reason for its creation, the historical background, and the life of the artist, that is, its conceptual aspect is considered to be external to the artistic medium itself, and therefore of secondary importance.

图 3.18　formalism 的解释（一）

---

① http://cpcchina.chinadaily.com.cn/special/cleanparty/2013-11/05/content_17133019.htm, accessed August 20, 2020.

② https://en.wikipedia.org/wiki/Formalism_(art) , accessed August 20, 2020.

下面这个解释，虽然强调形式和内容的对立，但仍然限于文学、艺术、哲学领域（见图 3.19）[①]：

> The term *formalism* describes an emphasis on form over content or meaning in the arts, literature, or philosophy. A practitioner of formalism is called a *formalist*. A formalist, with respect to some discipline, holds that there is no transcendent meaning to that discipline other than the literal content created by a practitioner. For example, formalists within mathematics claim that mathematics is no more than the symbols written down by the mathematician, which is based on logic and a few elementary rules alone. This is as opposed to non-formalists, within that field, who hold that there are some things inherently true, and are not, necessarily, dependent on the symbols within mathematics so much as a greater truth. Formalists within a discipline are completely concerned with "the rules of the game," as there is no other external truth that can be achieved beyond those given rules. In this sense, formalism lends itself well to disciplines based upon axiomatic systems.

图 3.19　formalism 的解释（二）

我们来看看"四风"到底是什么意思：

> 四风问题表现，一是形式主义，群众反映最突出的是追求形式、不重实效，图虚名、务虚功、工作不抓落实。二是官僚主义，群众最不满意的是办事推诿扯皮多，效率低下，不作为、不负责任。三是享乐主义，基层和群众反映最多的是一些领导干部安于现状、贪图安逸，缺乏忧患意识和创新精神。四是奢靡之风，主要是条件好了，许多方面做过头，大手大脚、铺张浪费。（百度百科："四风"问题）

按照这个解释，可以把"形式主义"翻译为 form over substance（重形式不重实质）。近年来官方媒体翻译为 formalities for formalities' sake 或 pointless formalities，也是一种不错的表达，但不如 form over substance

图 3.20　formality 的定义

全面，因为 formalities 意思是"走过场""守礼节"（见图 3.20）：

form over substance 也是一句地道的表达，含义与"形式主义"相同：

[①] https://en.wikipedia.org/wiki/Formalism_(philosophy), accessed August 20, 2020.

What do I mean by the triumph of form over substance? Well, it typically means that content or the subject does not matter, what matters is how a thing looks. In other words, the subject itself does not have to have any depth or true meaning, it only has to look good and feel good.[①]

去掉 triumph 意思不变（见图 3.21）[②]：

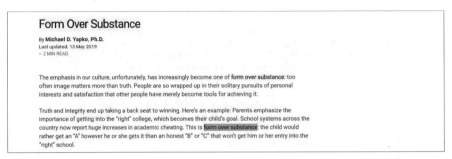

图 3.21　form over substance 的解释

因此，"形式主义"可以译为 form over substance，必要时加动词：emphasize form over substance。

"官僚主义"被《中国日报》译为 bureaucracy，更多的地方则使用 bureaucratism。bureaucracy 有两个意思，一是"官僚制度""科层制度""文官系统""公务员制度"，没有褒贬；二是"官僚主义"，相当于 red tape，有贬义（Oxford Languages）（见图 3.22）：

图 3.22　bureaucracy 的定义

使用 bureaucratism 可能是觉得 bureaucracy 会产生歧义。确实，bureaucratism 更多地包含贬义（见图 3.23）[③]：

---

① https://acalltotheremnant.com/2016/02/24/the-triumph-of-form-over-substance/, accessed August 20, 2020.
② https://blogs.psychcentral.com/blog/2018/12/form-over-substance/, accessed August 20, 2020.
③ https://www.lexico.com/definition/bureaucratism, accessed August 20, 2020.

bureaucratism

Pronunciation ⓘ /bjʊˈrɒkrətɪz(ə)m/ /bjɔːˈrɒkrətɪz(ə)m/

NOUN

derogatory

A system of government or administration characterized by bureaucracy; advocacy or practice of such a system.

图 3.23 bureaucratism 的定义（一）

但也有词典认为，这两个词没有什么区别（见图 3.24）[①]：

Definition of "bureaucratism" []

Nonelective government officials: same as bureaucracy. *(noun)*

Gnu Collaboartive International Dictionary of English: licensed under The Code Project Open License (CPOL)

图 3.24 bureaucratism 的定义（二）

况且，bureaucratism 这个词在 Word 中是标红的，说明不常见。既然两者区别不大，用简单的更好。为了避免误解，建议直接翻译为 red tape（见图 3.25）：

en.wikipedia.org › wiki › Red_tape ▾ 翻译此页

Red tape - Wikipedia

Red tape is an idiom referring to regulations or conformity to formal rules or standards which are claimed to be excessive, rigid or redundant, or to bureaucracy claimed to hinder or prevent action or decision-making. It is usually applied to governments, corporations, and other large organizations.

Origins · Red tape reduction

图 3.25 red tape 的定义

维基百科的解释正是我们要表达的意思。

“享乐主义”翻译为 hedonism 是否可以呢？我们看这个词的定义（见图 3.26）[②]：

可见，hedonism 是一种意识形态，就像 Marxism、capitalism、social-

① http://definition.org/define/bureaucratism/, accessed August 20, 2020.

② https://en.wikipedia.org/wiki/Hedonism, accessed August 20, 2020.

Hedonism

From Wikipedia, the free encyclopedia

For other uses, see Hedonism (disambiguation).

Hedonism is a school of thought that argues seeking pleasure and avoiding suffering are the only components of well-being.[1]

Ethical hedonism is the view that combines hedonism with welfarist ethics, which claims that what we should do depends exclusively on what affects the well-being of individuals. Ethical hedonists would defend either increasing pleasure and reducing suffering for all beings capable of experiencing them; or just reducing suffering, in the case of negative consequentialism and negative utilitarianism.[2][3][4][5] Ethical hedonism is said to have been started by Aristippus of Cyrene,[6] a student of Socrates. He held the idea that pleasure is the highest good.[7]

Part of a series on
Hedonism
Thinkers [show]
Schools of hedonism [show]
Key concepts [show]
Related articles [show]
V•T•E

图 3.26 hedonism 的定义

ism、liberalism、individualism 一样。我们反对的不过是“安于现状、贪图安逸，缺乏忧患意识和创新精神”的现象，译文不必上纲上线。通过反复查找同义词，发现可以用 shiftlessness 来表达这个意思（见图 3.27）：

shiftless 词汇频率
Collins COBUILD

(ʃɪftləs)
形容词

If you describe someone as shiftless, you mean that they are lazy and have no desire to achieve anything.

[*disapproval*]

...the lives of two shiftless, violent ex-convicts in 1950s America.

同义词：lazy, idle, indolent, irresponsible shiftless 的更多同义词

COBUILD Advanced English Dictionary. Copyright © HarperCollins Publishers

图 3.27 shiftless 的定义

该词也用于描述官僚作风（见图 3.28）：

www.heraldtribune.com › news › accountant-s... - 翻译此页
'Accountant' squanders its early potential - News - Sarasota ...
2016年10月13日 - Somewhere in here is a romance that gets dropped down a well, and a redemptive tale of a shiftless bureaucrat who found his calling late in life ...

mannyteodoro.com › wp-content › uploads ▾ PDF 翻译此页
A Labor Market Theory of Bureaucratic Politics - Manny Teodoro
politicians sometimes tolerate shiftless, incompetent, or rebellious bureaucrats? Why do politicians sometimes fire competent, hard-working bureaucrats?
作者：M Teodoro - 2017 - 相关文章

图 3.28 shiftlessness 的用例

另一个可以使用的词是 inertia（见图 3.29）[①]：

```
inertia
noun [U]
UK /ɪˈnɜː.ʃə/ US /ɪnˈɜː.ʃə/

inertia noun [U] (LACK OF ACTIVITY)

lack of activity or interest, or unwillingness to make an effort to do anything:
• The organization is stifled by bureaucratic inertia.
```

图 3.29　inertia 的定义

"奢靡之风"翻译为 extravagance 也不太准确。extravagance 的解释是"打肿脸充胖子"（见图 3.30）：

```
extravagance                                    词汇频率
Collins COBUILD

(ɪkˈstrævəɡəns )
词形 plural extravagances

1. 不可数名词
Extravagance is the spending of more money than is reasonable or than you can afford.
...gross mismanagement and financial extravagance.
When the company went under, tales of his extravagance surged through the industry.
同义词：overspending, squandering, profusion, profligacy   extravagance 的更多同义词

2. 可数名词
An extravagance is something that you spend money on but cannot really afford.
Her only extravagance was horses.
Why waste money on such extravagances?
同义词：luxury, treat, indulgence, extra   extravagance 的更多同义词
```

图 3.30　extravagance 的定义

但奢靡之风"主要是条件好了，许多方面做过头，大手大脚、铺张浪费"。外交部翻译室孙宁提出用 profligacy（见图 3.31）：

[①] https://dictionary.cambridge.org/zhs/ 词典 / 英语 /inertia, accessed August 20, 2020.

```
profligacy
noun [C or U]
UK 🔊 /ˈprɒf.lɪ.gə.si/  US 🔊 /ˈprɑː.flɪ.gə.si/

the act of spending money or using something in a way that wastes it and is not wise:
• The profligacy of the West shocked him.
• Years of **fiscal** profligacy have left the country deeply in debt.
• The party took 12 months to plan and featured the type of profligacies that only the super rich can afford.
```

图 3.31 profligacy 的定义

这个词的意思很准确,但可能不够通俗。笔者提出用这个词的解释即 wastes,孙宁认为前三项都是抽象含义,此处也用抽象的 wastefulness 更好,笔者赞同。

作为总结,"形式主义、官僚主义、享乐主义、奢靡之风"可以翻译为:form over substance, red tape, inertia, and wastefulness。作为概括这四种问题的"四风",是否是一种 work(ing) style 呢?这是人们对 working style 的理解(见图 3.32):

```
www.tonyrobbins.com › ... › Career & Business ▼ 翻译此页
What is Your Working Style? Find Out Now! - Tony Robbins
Work style types · 1. Independent · 2. Cooperative · 3. Proximity · 4. Supportive · 5. Big picture.
```

图 3.32 work style 的例证

可见,working style 是指办事风格,而"四风"是四种不良现象,所以可以译为 four undesirable phenomena。

假朋友的例子还有很多。例如,我们所说的"个人主义"和 individualism 也是"假朋友"。什么是个人主义?"个人主义者心中只装着自己的小九九,而党和人民利益却没有半点位置[1]",而英文的 individualism 是指"自力更生":

> Individualism is all about taking care of yourself; it is the belief and practice that every person is unique and self-reliant. A belief in individualism also implies that you believe that the government should bud out of

---

[1] http://theory.people.com.cn/n1/2017/0906/c40531-29517462.html, accessed August 20, 2020.

your individual affairs.①

"反对自由主义"当中的"自由主义"和西方的 liberalism 也是一对"假朋友"。我们反对的"自由主义"是指自由散漫：

> 坚决防止和反对自由主义，是我们党在 97 年的发展历程中一直着力强调的。早在 1937 年，毛泽东同志在《反对自由主义》一文中就分析了自由主义的种种表现及其危害。例如，"不负责任的背后批评，不是积极地向组织建议。当面不说，背后乱说；开会不说，会后乱说。心目中没有集体生活的原则，只有<u>自由放任</u>。""命令不服从，个人意见第一。只要组织照顾，<u>不要组织纪律</u>。"党的十八大以来，随着全面从严治党深入推进，党内政治生态显著改善，但像毛泽东同志剖析的那些自由主义表现，在个别党员、干部身上还不同程度地存在。例如，个别党员、干部<u>口无遮拦，对中央的大政方针说三道四</u>；在工作中"挑肥拣瘦"，中央的决策部署<u>对自己有利的就执行、对自己不利的就消极对待</u>。这些虽然只是个别现象，但如果不采取有效措施加以整治，就可能蔓延开来，影响党中央权威和集中统一领导。②

西方的 liberalism 是一种意识形态和哲学，强调人身自由、法律面前人人平等，其中的积极方面，我们是不反对的（见图 3.33）：

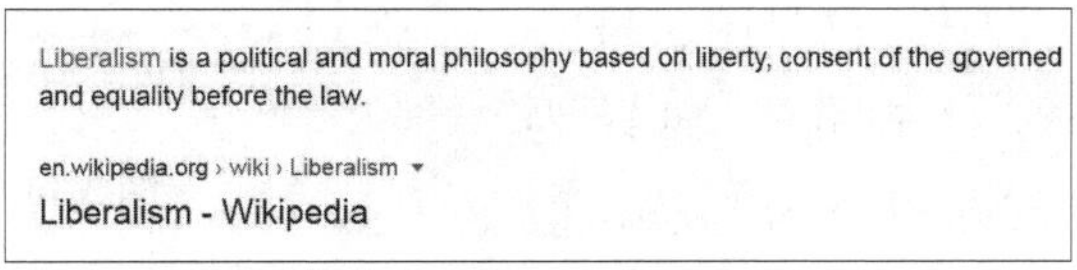

所以，陈明明大使在一次讲座中说：

图 3.33　liberalism 的定义

> 还有两个核心的概念，从过去一直就没有翻对过。一是"反对个人主义"，我们一直认为个人主义是"individualism"，好像这个词很坏，很糟糕，其实它是西方价值观念中最核心的理念，人是最重要的，它不是贬义的表述。马克思主义也主张人要全面发展，所以这个一定要改掉。

---

① https://www.vocabulary.com/dictionary/individualism, accessed August 20, 2020.
② http://theory.people.com.cn/n1/2018/0503/c40531-29961796.html, accessed August 20, 2020.

还有一个更糟糕的，“反对自由主义”。这个概念一开始从《毛选》翻译的时候，就用的“oppose liberalism”。很多人都知道 liberalism 是什么含义，它不是一个很高深的概念，而是西方文化的基础，我们不一定赞成，也没有必要在党的报告里去反对。而我们反对的“自由主义”是什么呢？是不听领导指挥，不守纪律。所以，十九大报告的翻译彻底解决了这个问题：“坚决防止和反对个人主义、分散主义、自由主义……”译成了 We must guard against and oppose self-centered behavior, decentralism, behavior in disregard of the rules...[①]

陈明明大使还指出：“基层”不是 grassroots，是指 community 或 primary level；“宣传”不是 propaganda，是 communication；即使翻译为 publicity 也不好。“科学”仅限于科研层面，与“科学发展”当中的“科学”意思不符；“文明”不一定总翻译为 civilized 或 civilization。

陈大使这番话是多年翻译审校经验的总结，也是实事求是的建议。大家不妨看看 propaganda 的意义，就知道为什么（见图 3.34）：

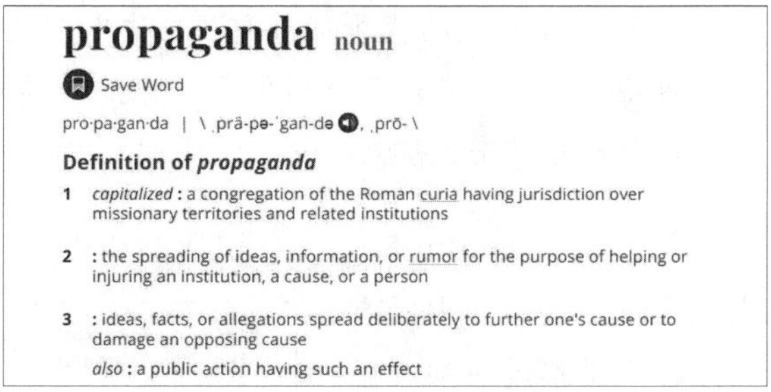
propaganda noun

Save Word

pro·pa·gan·da | \ ˌprä-pə-ˈgan-də, ˌprō- \

Definition of *propaganda*

1 *capitalized* : a congregation of the Roman curia having jurisdiction over missionary territories and related institutions

2 : the spreading of ideas, information, or rumor for the purpose of helping or injuring an institution, a cause, or a person

3 : ideas, facts, or allegations spread deliberately to further one's cause or to damage an opposing cause
also : a public action having such an effect

图 3.34　propaganda 的定义

“宣传”翻译为 publicity 不算错误，但它更像是“广告”的意思（见图 3.35）：

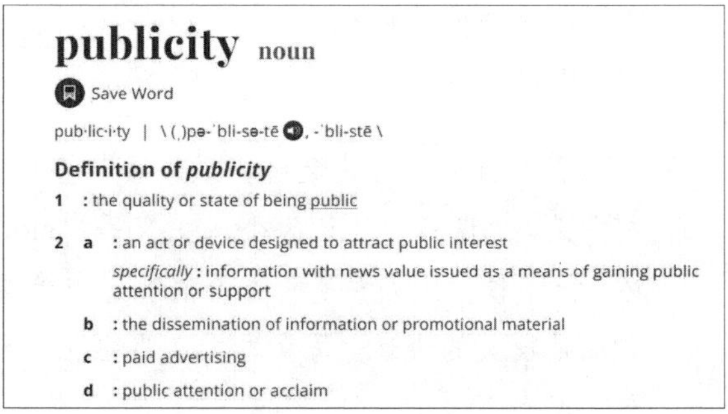
publicity noun

Save Word

pub·lic·i·ty | \ (ˌ)pə-ˈbli-sə-tē, -ˈbli-stē \

Definition of *publicity*

1 : the quality or state of being public

2 a : an act or device designed to attract public interest
specifically : information with news value issued as a means of gaining public attention or support

b : the dissemination of information or promotional material

c : paid advertising

d : public attention or acclaim

图 3.35　publicity 的定义

再看“分散主义”怎么翻译。十九大报告中有这样一句话：

> 坚决防止和反对个人主义、分散

---

① https://zhuanlan.zhihu.com/p/39904022, accessed August 20, 2020.

主义、自由主义、本位主义、好人主义，坚决防止和反对宗派主义、圈子文化、码头文化。

其中的"分散主义"能不能翻译成 separatism 呢？查一下分散主义的意思①：

> 指损害集中统一领导的错误倾向。主要表现是<u>违反民主集中制，特别是违反下级服从上级、全党服从中央的原则</u>，对于党和国家的方针、政策、指示和决定，采取各行其是、各自为政的态度，合意的执行，不合意的就不执行，甚至进行抵制。这是一种违反党的政治纪律的行为。

而 separatism 的意思是（见图 3.36）②：

separatism
noun [U] · POLITICS
UK /ˈsep.ər.ə.tɪ.zəm/ US /ˈsep.ɚ.ə.tɪ.zəm/

the belief held by people of a particular race, religion, or other group within a country that they should be independent and have their own government or in some way live apart from other people:

图 3.36　separatism 的定义

也就是分裂的意思，和 split 比较相近，分裂国家。因此这里违反民主集中制，翻译成 decentralism 更合理。

官方译文：

> guard against and oppose self-centered behavior, decentralism, behavior in disregard of the rules, a silo mentality, unprincipled nice-guyism, and sectarianism, factionalism, and patronage.

从以上众多的例子可以看出，很多看似对等的说法，意思却相距甚远，

---

① https://baike.sogou.com/v11027569.htm?fromTitle=%E5%88%86%E6%95%A3%E4%B8%BB%E4%B9%89, accessed August 20, 2020.

② https://dictionary.cambridge.org/zhs/%E8%AF%8D%E5%85%B8/%E8%8B%B1%E8%AF%AD/separatism, accessed August 20, 2020.

译者必须时刻警惕，对有疑问的译法，要反复查证，确信无疑后再用。

3.1.7 括号位置正确

翻译中经常忽视的一个问题，是括号的位置。译者要正确判断括号的修饰关系，确保经过翻译，括号仍然被置于适当的位置。即使原文括号位置不当，译文也应当纠正。例如：

> 个人信息控制者业务运营所使用的信息系统，具备自动决策机制且能对个人信息主体权益造成显著影响的（例如，自动决定个人征信及贷款额度，或用于面试人员的自动化筛选等）应……

原译：

> For the information systems used in business operations of a PI Controller, which has an automatic <u>decision-making mechanism</u> and can have a significant impact on the legitimate rights and interests of PI Subjects <u>(e.g. automatically determining personal credit and loan amount, or being used for automated screening of candidates)</u>, the PI Controller shall…

仔细阅读译文，发现 automatically determining… 并不能作为括号之前 have a significant impact… 的例子。仔细观察，发现括号中的内容是 automatic decision-making 的例子，因此，需要把括号提前至相应位置：

> Where the information system used in business operations of a PI Controller has an automatic <u>decision-making mechanism (e.g. automatically determining personal credits and loan amounts, or automatically screening interview candidates)</u> that may have a significant impact on the legitimate rights and interests of PI Subjects, the PI Controller shall…

再回头看原文，发现原文当中括号的位置也不恰当。翻译真是比绣花还要细的活儿啊！

3.2 通顺

3.2.1 写作视角

译者可以在融会贯通的基础上，不受原文形态的束缚，重新写作。下面这段话的三种译文，意思都准确，但第一种译法显然受到英文语法的影响，后两种则脱离了原文的影响（本段取自 2019 年联合国圣杰罗姆翻译竞赛，全文见本章附录）：

> We headed for the food hall. "I'm not feeding my children Kobe beef or Russian caviar," I muttered as I swerved us past heavy marble counters groaning under the weight of gleaming ice crystals and a meat counter offering a platter of "baby chicken, half duck, lamb cutlets and Merguez sausage" for £100.

译文 1：

> 我们朝美食馆走去。"我是不会给我的孩子吃神户牛肉或是俄罗斯鱼子酱的。"当我们急转弯经过因承受着闪烁的冰晶重量而呻吟作响的沉重的大理石柜台，和一个提供一种要价一百英镑的"雏鸡，半只鸭子，羊排和梅尔盖兹肉肠"套餐的肉类柜台时，我小声地咕哝道。

该译文虽然意思基本正确，但句子结构没有完全汉化，因此读起来不够流畅。下面这两种译文，就符合汉语行云流水般的叙事方式：

译文 2：

> 我们来到餐饮区。"我可不给孩子吃什么神户牛肉或者俄罗斯鱼子酱。"我一边嘟囔一边把一家子从沉沉的大理石柜台旁引开，那亮闪闪的冰晶把柜台压得喘不过气来。又经过一个肉食柜台，柜台上标着：装盘"童子鸡、半只鸭、小羊排和北非牛羊肉肠"，售价 100 英镑，于是我们转身离开。

译文 3：

我们朝着美食厅走去。"我才不会给孩子吃什么神户牛肉、俄罗斯鱼子酱"，我一边低声咕哝着，一边领着家人绕开那些沉甸甸的大理石柜台，下面堆砌的碎冰块儿闪闪发亮，压得柜台暗自呻吟。一个肉制品柜台上，摆了一盘"嫩鸡肉、半份鸭、羊排、北非风味香肠"，售价 100 英镑。

3.2.2 符合语法

符合语法是翻译的基本要求，包括单复数、动词形态、句型、搭配等。例如，某国家标准中文标题是这样（见图 3.37）：

最初提供的英文译文是这样（见图 3.38）：

图 3.37　某国家标准的标题　　　　图 3.38　某国家标准的标题（英文）

其中的 replace 的形态不对。按照逻辑关系，replace 应该是 -ing 形式（在用词上，superseding 更为正式）。这是国外标准的格式（见图 3.39）：

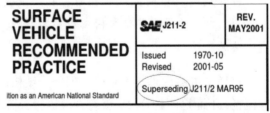

图 3.39　某国外标准的标题

再例如（凡涉及个人信息保护的例子，都来源于上述标准）：

显著区分的方式包括但不限于：标明"定推"等字样，或通过不同的栏目、版块、页面分别展示等。

原译：

Significant distinction <u>includes</u> but is <u>not limited to</u>: <u>mark</u> words such as "push", and <u>display</u> in different columns, sections, or on different pages.

include 和 limited to 后面应该跟名词，因此 mark/display 的语法形态是错误的（另外，mark words such as… 意思是为某些单词做标记，词不达意）。改译：

Methods for prominent distinction include but are not limited to: <u>indicating with words such as "push"</u>, and <u>displaying</u> in different columns, sections, or on different pages.

又如：

个人信息主体注销账户后，应及时删除其个人信息或匿名化处理。

原译：

After a PI Subject de-registers, his/her PI shall be deleted or anonymized <u>timely</u>.

timely 是形容词，无法修饰动词。改译：

After a PI Subject de-registers, his/her PI shall be deleted or anonymized <u>promptly</u>.

"及时"也可以说 in a timely manner，但不够简洁。还可以翻译为 without delay。

下面的例子不符合 require 要求的句型。原文：

确因工作需要，需授权特定人员超权限处理个人信息的，应经个人信息保护责任人或个人信息保护工作机构进行审批，并记录在册。

原译：

Where the job <u>requires to authorize</u> a particular person to process the PI beyond his/her access, it shall be approved by the person or the department responsible for PI protection, and it shall be documented.

61

require 的用法不包括 require to do（见图 3.40）：

```
柯林斯高级英语学习词典第5版

♦♦ re|quire /rɪkwaɪəʳ/ (requires requiring required)
1 [VERB] V n, V n to-inf, V-ed
If you require something or if something is required, you need it or it is necessary.
(FORMAL)
If you require further information, you should consult the registrar...
This isn't the kind of crisis that requires us to drop everything else...
Some of the materials required for this technique may be difficult to obtain.
2 [VERB] V n to-inf, V n, V that, be V-ed of n
If a law or rule requires you to do something, you have to do it. (FORMAL)
The rules also require employers to provide safety training...
At least 35 manufacturers have flouted a law requiring prompt reporting of such
malfunctions...
The law now requires that parents serve on the committees that plan and evaluate school
programs...
Then he'll know exactly what's required of him.
3 [PHRASE] v-link PHR, oft PHR for n
If you say that something is required reading for a particular group of people, you mean
that you think it is essential for them to read it because it will give them information which
they should have.
...an important research study that should be required reading for every member of the
cabinet.
```

图 3.40　require 的用法

因此，只能按照 require 的正确用法修改：

Where the job <u>requires</u> a particular person <u>to</u> process the PI beyond his/her access, authorization shall be made by the person or the department responsible for PI protection and shall be documented.

下面这个例子更为复杂，涉及平行结构的使用：

发布个人信息保护政策是个人信息控制者遵循公开透明原则的重要体现，是保证个人信息主体知情权的重要手段，还是约束自身行为和配合监督管理的重要机制。

原译：

A published PI protection policy is <u>an important manifestation of the PI Controller following</u> the principle of openness and transparency, <u>an important means to ensure</u> PI Subjects' right to know, and an <u>important mechanism that restricts</u> the PI Controller's behavior and <u>cooperates</u> with supervision and administration.

下划线的部分意思并列，但结构却不并列，尤其是 mechanism that cooperates with supervision and administration 在意思上也不搭配。改译使用并列的动词结构：

A published PI protection policy <u>demonstrates the PI Controller's intention to be open and transparent</u>, <u>guarantees the PI Subjects' right to know</u>, and <u>compels the PI Controller to cooperate with regulators</u>.

3.2.3　逻辑清晰

汉语属于意合语言，较少使用关联词，也没有动词的 -ing 形式，因此各小句都呈现并列结构。但仔细分析，会发现小句之间可能隐含条件、因果、目的等关系，翻译时可能需要以一定的语法手段，把这些关系明确表达出来。例如，《中国的北极政策》白皮书中有一句话：

近年来，<u>全球气候变暖</u>，北极冰雪融化加速。在经济全球化、区域一体化不断深入发展的背景下，北极在战略、经济、科研、环保、航道、资源等方面的<u>价值不断提升</u>，<u>受到国际社会的普遍关注</u>。

译文是：

<u>Global warming in recent years has accelerated the melting of ice and snow in the Arctic region</u>. <u>As</u> economic globalization and regional integration further develops and deepens, <u>the Arctic</u> is gaining global significance for its rising strategic, economic values and those relating to scientific research, environmental protection, sea passages, and natural resources.

本段中，"全球气候变暖"和"北极冰雪融化加速""价值不断提升"和"受到国际社会的普遍关注"是因果关系，但中文没有明显的词语提示；译文则通过不同手段明确了这种关系。

再如：

北极问题已超出北极国家间问题和区域问题的范畴，涉及北极域外国家的利益和国际社会的整体利益，攸关人类生存与发展的共同命运，具有全球意义和国际影响。

译文是：

The Arctic situation now goes beyond its original inter-Arctic States or regional nature, having a vital bearing on the interests of States outside the region and the interests of the international community as a whole, as well as on the survival, the development, and the shared future for mankind. It is an issue with global implications and international impacts.

原文由四小句组成，第二第三小句为北极问题的影响，是对第一小句的进一步说明，其意义又包含在最后一小句。译文将二三小句降级，用分词短语表示，第四小句另起一句翻译，显化了信息的重点和层次。

3.2.4　主语相对一致

译者必须时刻提醒自己：如果我不是在翻译，而是在写作，会不会这么说？这个问题不仅会帮助自己发现逻辑不通之处（如有，则可能是理解错误），还可以帮助自己发现语言表达的不当之处。例如：

In other words, if a patent has not been granted in a given country, the invention will not be protected in that country. That means that anyone can make, use, import or sell your invention in that country.

原译：

换言之，如果一个国家没有授予专利，发明就不会在该国受到保护。这意味着任何人都可以在那个国家制造、使用、进口或销售你的发明。

这段话讲的是专利的地域性。即，你的专利要想得到某个国家的保护，必须在这个国家提出申请。如果仅仅在中国申请了保护，其他国家就可以免费使用你的专利，因为在中国申请保护时，已经把专利技术的细节公之于众，全世界都可以看到。

原译的意思正确，语言也比较通顺，一般的审校可能会放过去。但如果严格遵守写作规范，还是有修改余地的，例如，第一句话的主句和从句主语不一致，可以统一，从而把已知信息置于句首：

> 换言之，如果<u>你的发明</u>没有在某个国家获得专利，就得不到该国的保护。这意味着该国任何人都可以制造、使用、进口或销售你发明的产品。

再举一例。原文：

> 5. Registration
> Once it has been determined that there are no grounds for refusal, the trademark is registered and a registration certificate issued. The certificate is generally valid for 10 years. Registrations can be renewed indefinitely upon payment of a renewal fee.

原译：

> 5. 注册
> <u>一旦</u>确定不存在驳回的理由<u>后</u>，商标就会给予注册并颁发注册证书。该证书有效期一般为10年，可在缴纳续展费后无限期延续。

这句话的翻译意思正确，但语言表述可以改进。除了"一旦……后"搭配不当外，动词"确定"隐含的逻辑主语"商标局"，与主句的主语"商标"不一致。用"商标局"作主语，这个问题迎刃而解：

> 5. 注册
> 一旦<u>商标局</u>确定不存在驳回的理由，<u>就会</u>注册商标并颁发注册证书。注册证书有效期一般为10年，可通过缴纳续展费无限次续延。

另请注意，最后一句原译有歧义（缴纳一次续展费永久延续），改译纠正了这个问题。

再举一例。原文：

> The Chicago school, built on the work of Aaron Director, an economist from the mid-20th century, reached its zenith in the writing of the legal scholars Robert Bork and Richard Posner.

原译：

> 芝加哥学派建立在亚伦·戴雷科特的研究的基础之上，他是一位20世纪中叶的经济学家。芝加哥学派达到顶峰是在罗伯特·伯克和理查德·波斯纳的著作中。

这句话的翻译意思正确，但中间变换主语破坏了句子的流畅性；再者，一个学派的思想在某著作中"达到顶峰"，在汉语中也较为生硬。可以修改如下：

> 芝加哥学派发轫于20世纪中叶经济学家亚伦·戴雷科特的研究，通过法学家罗伯特·伯克和理查德·波斯纳的著述达到顶峰。

3.2.5 少用不定式

有时可以用定语从句代替不定式，改进句子的逻辑关系。例如：

> 采用交互式页面（如网站、移动互联网应用程序、客户端软件等）提供产品或服务的，宜直接设置便捷的交互式页面提供功能或选项，便于个人信息主体在线行使其访问、更正、删除、撤回授权同意、注销账户等权利。

原译：

> If a product or service is provided through an interactive interface (e.g. website, mobile-Internet application (APP), and client software), the PI Controller should set up a convenient interactive page <u>to provide</u> functions or options, <u>so that</u> PI Subjects could exercise online their rights such as access to and rectification & deletion of PI, consent withdrawal and de-registration.

原译 to provide functions or options 似乎意思没有表述完整，但如果改

为定语从句，意思顿觉明朗：

> If a product or service is provided through an interactive interface (e.g. a website, a mobile-Internet application (APP), or a client software), the PI Controller should set up <u>a convenient interactive page that provides functions or options for PI Subjects to exercise online their rights</u> such as access to and rectification & deletion of PI, consent withdrawal and de-registration.

再如：

> 注销过程不应设置不合理的条件或提出额外要求增加个人信息主体义务，如注销单个账户视同注销多个产品或服务，要求个人信息主体填写精确的历史操作记录作为注销的必要条件等。

原译：

> The de-registration process shall not impose unreasonable conditions or <u>make additional requirements</u> <u>to increase</u> the obligation of the PI Subject, such as stipulating that the de-registration of a single account is deemed de-registration from multiple products or services, or requiring the PI Subject to provide accurate operating records as a necessary condition for the cancellation.

原译 to increase 意思正确，但有指责个人信息主体的隐含意思。如果改为 that 就比较客观：

> The de-registration process shall not impose unreasonable conditions or make additional requirements <u>that increase</u> the obligation of the PI Subject, such as stipulating that the de-registration of a single account is deemed de-registration from multiple products or services, or requiring the PI Subject to provide accurate operating records as a precondition for cancellation.

3.2.6　避免中式英文

由于受到汉语用词和结构的影响，译文往往不够地道。不敢确定英文表达方法时，应当多查找英文平行文本。例如，北京地铁站免费取用的《地铁服务指南》英文为 The service guide of metro（见图 3.41）：

图 3.41 某服务指南的英译

原译为字对字直译，故有 service guide 一说。这个说法符合语法，意思也正确，但西方国家可能会直接用 guide 一词来表达服务指南（见图 3.42 和图 3.43）：①

图 3.42 国外某服务指南的英文说法（一）

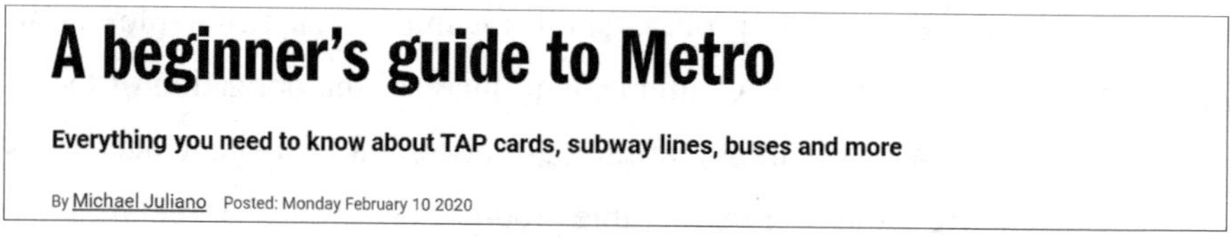

图 3.43 国外某服务指南的英文说法（二）

北京地铁手册中主要介绍地铁线路图以及购票方法，与西方国家的 guide 涵盖的内容相同，故可简化为 Guide to metro 或 Metro Guide。又鉴于北京地铁翻译为 Beijing Subway，所以最好说 Subway Guide 或者 Guide to Subway。将 of 改为 to，是由于 guide 搭配的介词为 to（见图 3.44）：

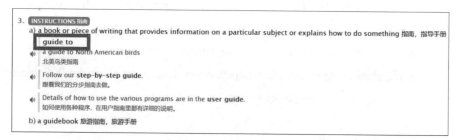

图 3.44 guide 的用法

---

① https://www.timeout.com/los-angeles/things-to-do/los-angeles-metro-guide, accessed August 20, 2020.

再如：

个人信息保护政策的内容应清晰易懂，<u>符合通用的语言习惯</u>，使用标准化的数字、图示等，避免使用有歧义的语言。

原译：

The content of PI protection policy shall be clear & understandable, <u>comply with common language habits</u>, use standardized figures and diagrams, and avoid ambiguous language.

"符合通用的语言习惯"本身就有问题：既然是大众的习惯，就一定是通用的，所以可以去掉原译中的 common，简化为 comply with language habits。但这个说法是否存在？上网搜索，发现只有两个用例，还是中国人写的英文（见图3.45）：

```
ieeexplore.ieee.org › document - 翻译此页
Integrating Part of Speech Guidance for Image Captioning ...
2020年3月2日 - ... generated by the proposed method contain more accurate visual information and comply with language habits and grammar rules better.
作者：J Zhang - 2020 - 相关文章

wenku.baidu.com › view
文艺复兴时期英国的翻译家及其理论_修订稿_图文_百度文库
The translating of Bible should comply with language habits. William Fulke suggested that religious words should be translated according to its concret meaning ...
```

图 3.45 "符合语言习惯"的中式英语

进一步查找，发现这样的用例（见图3.46）：

```
www.juiceanalytics.com › design-principles ▼ 翻译此页
Use common language — Juice Analytics - Build Data ...
2014年2月27日 - This principle is all about the words you use. It is important to use common language that is easily understandable. If someone using your website ...
```

图 3.46 "符合语言习惯"的英语查证

因此改译如下：

The PI protection policy shall <u>use common language that is easily understandable</u>, use standard figures & diagrams, and avoid ambiguous language.

除了用词和搭配容易造成中式英语外，中文的结构，也容易带入英文。例如，中文常用的主题 + 讨论（topic/discussion）式的表达（也叫主位 - 述位的表达方式），虽然英文中也有，但仅限于对比两种状况，平时用得较少。汉译英时，应当酌情避免。例如：

> 张伯礼对于这个结果挺满意。"事实证明对于新冠肺炎轻症患者，用中药完全可以达到治疗目的。"

原译：

> Zhang Boli was quite satisfied with these results. "It turns out that, <u>for patients with new coronary pneumonia</u>, Chinese medicine can completely meet the goal of medical treatment."

其中的 for patients with new coronary pneumonia 就是主题，英文应尽量避免。改译：

> Zhang Boli was quite satisfied with these results. "It turns out that patients with COVID-19 can be effectively treated with Chinese medicine," he noted.

改译还把比较虚的说法 can completely meet the goal of medical treatment 改为具体说法 can be effectively treated。

再例如：

> 他对比类似条件下的 108 例病例后发现，西医治疗转重率在 10% 左右，而中西医结合治疗转重率约为 4.1%。<u>对发热、咳嗽、乏力改善等症状，中药起效非常快，对肺部炎症的吸收和病毒转阴都有明显效果。</u>

原译：

> He compared 108 cases under similar conditions and found that the rate of severeness conversion in applying WM alone was about 10%, while the rate of severeness conversion with integrated TCM and WM regimens was about 4.1%. <u>For the symptoms of fever, cough and fatigue improve-</u>

ment, Chinese medicine works very quickly, it can absorb the inflammation of the lungs and shows obvious effects in turning the virus indicator negative.

原译用 for...the Chinese medicine...，就是主题+讨论的结构。改译为英文正常的叙述方式：

改译：

He compared 108 cases under similar conditions and found that the severe progression rate in applying WM alone was about 10%, while the rate with integrated TCM and WM regimens was about 4.1%. <u>TCM worked quickly to reduce symptoms of fever, cough and fatigue and was effective in mitigating lung inflammations and turning the virus indicator negative</u>.

改译还纠正了理解问题，如"发热、咳嗽、乏力<u>改善</u>等症状"应理解为"<u>改善</u>发热、咳嗽、乏力等症状"。

另外，虽然法律文本中为了准确起见，可以像中文那样在主语和谓语之间插入修饰成分，但尽量少用。例如：

原文：

个人信息控制者开展个人信息处理活动应遵循合法、正当、必要的原则。（取自《个人信息安全规范》）

原译：

PI Controllers, <u>in carrying out PI processing activities</u>, shall follow the principles of lawfulness, justification and necessity.

改译：

PI Controllers shall follow the principles of lawfulness, justification, and necessity <u>in PI processing activities</u>.

原译中主语和谓语之间的介词短语影响信息流动；改译把介词短语置于正常位置。

关于如何避免中式英语，请大家阅读 Joan Pinkham 的《中式英语之鉴》

（外语教学与研究出版社）和 David Ferguson 的《我可能学的是假英语》（石油工业出版社）。本书第九章也有详细论述。

3.2.7 避免欧化中文

汉语欧化有多种表现方式，例如，用代词过多、被动句过多、前置定语过长等等。例如：

As a general recommendation, if you intend to exploit your patent outside your country, make sure to file for protection in all the markets that interest you as early as possible.

原译：

作为总结，如果你打算在国外利用你的专利，你要尽早在你有意涉足的所有市场申请保护。

改译：

总的来说，如果你打算在国外利用专利，就要尽早在相关市场申请保护。

汉语不常使用代词，因此删除几个"你""你的"。如果译者自己用汉语创作，是不会出现这种欧化现象的。所以，译者只要有避免欧化的意识，就可以解决这个问题。

同理：

Where and how you practice will vary depending on the area of law you specialise in. You may be working on criminal cases, where you could be defending or prosecuting in a Magistrates or Crown Court. You may also work in civil courts and employment or residential property tribunals. (source: https://www.ucas.com/ucas/after-gcses/find-career-ideas/explore-jobs/job-profile/barrister)

原译：

根据您所擅长的法律领域，您在何处以及您如何进行执业会有所不同。**您**可能正在处理刑事案件，**您**可能在治安法庭或王室法庭进行辩护或起诉。**您**也可以在民事法院和劳资或住宅物业审裁处工作。

改译：

  您的法律专长决定了今后的执业地点和方式。**您**可以专职处理刑事案件，作为辩护律师或公诉人参与治安法庭或刑事法庭的工作；也可以在民事法院、劳资或住宅物业裁判所代理诉讼。

原译用了 6 个"您"，改译减少了 4 个。

汉语不常用被动语态。如果勉强使用，虽然可以理解，但不符合汉语习惯。译者往往需要找到施动者，改用主动形式表达。施动者有时候一目了然，有时则需要在语篇之外寻找线索。请看这段话：

  The building of wind turbines has virtually ground to a halt since **subsidies were cut back**. Meanwhile, compared with others in the European Union, Danes remain above-average emitters of the greenhouse gas carbon dioxide. For all its wind turbines, **a large proportion of the rest of Denmark's power is generated by plants** that burn imported coal.

机器翻译：

  自从补贴被削减以来，风力涡轮机的建设实际上已经停止了。同时，与欧盟其他国家相比，丹麦的温室气体二氧化碳排放量仍然高于平均水平。在丹麦所有的风力涡轮机中，**丹麦其余的电力很大一部分是由燃烧进口煤炭的工厂产生的。**

第一句的被动表达显得僵硬。根据上下文判断，削减补贴的人应为丹麦政府，可以补充出来，转为主动句。第二句虽然用被动语态（"由"字结构也是一种被动形式），不过问题不大，但转化为主动句更符合汉语习惯。改译：

  自从丹麦政府削减补贴以来，风机建设实际上已经停止。同时，与欧盟其他国家相比，丹麦的温室气体二氧化碳排放量仍然高于平均水平。尽管丹麦的风电占比颇高，**但其余电力仍大部分来自燃烧进口煤炭的火电厂**。

下面这个例子,找到施动者就不容易:

Indian scientists at TBGRI used tribal TK and know-how to develop the drugs and isolated 12 active compounds from the plant. <u>Patents were filed, and the technology was later licensed to the AVP</u>, an Indian manufacturer pursuing the commercialization of herbal formulations. <u>A trust fund was established</u> to share the benefits arising from the commercialization of the TK-based drug.

其中的两个被动句,原译分别为:

- 专利得到申请,技术后来转让给了 AVP
- 信托基金被建立起来

此处可以推测是 TBGRI 申请的专利,但也不敢绝对肯定,所以需要证据支撑。经查:

1996 年,TBGRI 就这种药物申请了 2 项相关专利,并将专利技术许可给了印度从事草药商业化生产的私营医药公司。

因此,可以确认专利申请人是 TBGRI。信托基金是谁建立的呢?也需要核实:

1997 年 11 月,TBGRI 协助 Kani 部族注册了一个信托基金(The Kani Samudaya Trust),以分享 Jeevani 商业化后所带来的利益。

在明白了施动者之后,就可以灵活翻译被动语态:

为研制这种药物,印度热带植物园研究所的科学家利用部族的传统知识和技艺,从植物中分离出 12 种活性化合物。<u>研究所申请了专利,后将技术许可转让给 AVP</u>,一家从事草药配方商业化的印度制药公司;<u>研究所还协助部族建立了一家信托公司</u>,来分享传统草药知识商业化所得到的利益。

再如,《每日电讯报》2019 年 6 月 9 日的一篇文章,以英国足球队母狮队(Lioness)为例,讲述了英国女子足球的发展,这篇文章的题目为:

As a girl, I was told football was for men. Today, the Lionesses could launch a thousand careers

题目当中的被动句,原译为:

当我还是小女孩时,被告知足球是男人的运动;如今,母狮队麾下拥有上千女队员

"被告知"虽然可以理解,但我们会问"被谁告知?为什么不交代清楚?"所以,这有必要弄清楚动作的发出者。在本篇文章中,有这样两段描述:

Take, for instance my first career goal. I wanted, in 1999, to be a "farmer's wife". Thankfully, after quick correction by <u>my progressive parents</u>, that morphed into "farmer"…

I remember the exact moment I told my dad I was interested in doing what my big sister did. I was watching the game with him in the living room as a pre-teen and it just came out: "It makes me sad I can't be a footballer." He asked why not, and I answered: "Because I'm not a boy." <u>He immediately responded by telling me that women's football was "great" and that I could play if I wanted to.</u>

显然,作者对"足球为男人运动"的刻板印象不来自于家庭。因而,我们可以排除是"父母告诉我"或者"我的爸爸告诉我"的译法。既然在文章中没有找出动作的发出者,是将"I was told"翻译成"有人告诉我",还是"人们都说"更好呢?回顾原文第一段:

Retrospect is a wonderful thing. It allows you to — with a slightly more critical eye — see what led you here, how you turned into who you are and, hopefully, <u>how society has changed and improved.</u>

原文作者在本段最后一句提出了社会的变迁和进步,表明是从整个社会的角度提出对女子之与足球运动的看法,因而施动者偏向为大多数人或社会。了解施动者之后,就可以灵活翻译被动语态。该标题试译为:

20年前,足球是男人的运动;如今,母狮队麾下拥有上千女队员

英语句子结构是开放的,可以通过后置定语或状语任意延长。汉语句子是封闭的,前置定语或状语不能太长。遇到英语定语或状语从句,往往需要把句子断开。例如:

> The SCT has examined in depth member states' legislation and trademark office practice in relation to the registration of three-dimensional marks, color marks, sound marks and other types of marks, such as motion marks, position marks, hologram marks, slogans, and smell, feel and taste marks.

原译:

> 委员会[1]深入审议了成员国有关立体商标、颜色商标、声音商标以及动作商标、位置商标、全息图商标、广告语、气味、触觉和味觉商标等其他各类商标的注册方面的立法和商标主管机关的做法。

动词和宾语之间的距离太远。改译:

> SCT 深入研究了成员国有关各类商标注册的立法和商标主管机关的做法,包括立体商标、颜色商标、声音商标,以及动作商标、位置商标、全息图商标、广告语、气味、触觉和味觉商标等。

改译先用"各类商标"作为概括,随后列举各类商标。

关于欧化中文,建议阅读余光中的《翻译乃大道》(商务印书馆和外语教学与研究出版社)[旧版书名《余光中谈翻译》(中译出版社)],其中列举了很多我们不曾意识到的欧化现象。例如,频繁使用"进行""的的不休""西而不化",等等,这本书对我们提高语言敏感性、克服欧化中文很有帮助。

3.2.8 表述尽量一致

表达中的另一个问题是一致性问题。这个问题在写作和翻译中都需要注意,特别是多人共同完成一篇报告或一个翻译项目时。例如,一本教程

---

[1] 指 The Standing Committee on Trademarks, Industrial Designs and Geographical Indications (SCT) 商标、工业品外观设计和地理标志常设委员会,承前用简称。

中有练习，有答案，如果这两部分的译者互不通气，用词就难以统一，甚至答非所问。一份文件需要统一的地方很多。赵兴民在《联合国文件翻译案例讲评》（2011）中把一致性作为一个重要的翻译标准，包括：

- 术语、专有名词、固定用语
  - 前后一致
  - 与主要参考文件一致
  - 无权威译法时，与多数同类文件一致
- 目录与正文一致
- 正文与脚注一致
- 正文与附件一致
- 阿拉伯数字和汉字数字使用规则一致
- 相同的句子／概念译文相同
- 引自其他文件的句子／短语与出处译法相同

这些都是我们在统稿时应当注意的问题。一位同学总结得很到位：

> 同一文件的翻译中，不同译者没有提前协商或是采用权威的译法，反而各自为政进行翻译，这种情况十分常见，也经常导致同一专有名词出现五花八门的中文译法。
>
> 在翻译外国政要或是其他重要人物姓名时，首先要考虑是否存在官方译法或权威译法。如果已经有了广为流传的版本，就不要再另起炉灶。这也符合译者在翻译之前应先查证的要求。比较官方的来源有中国政府网站，例如外交部、商务部等。如果还没有官方译法，则要参照新华社、人民日报等权威媒体的译法。如果实在找不到可靠的版本，就要考虑根据专有名词的发音和内涵进行翻译。翻译人名时，可以参照人名辞典上的译法进行翻译。
>
> 例如，我在 2019 年初为中东欧研究院翻译斯洛伐克的国别报告时，需要翻译现任总统 Zuzana Čaputová（苏珊娜）这个名字。由于她当时还未当选总统，网上还找不到权威的译法，这就需要自己进行翻译。Zuzana 虽然是斯洛伐克语，但是和英文名字的翻译规则是类似的。我了解了斯洛伐克语的发音规则后，将这一人名翻译为苏珊娜·恰普托娃，结果和之后的官方译法是一致的。但是在网上搜索时就会发现，翻

译的版本五花八门，有祖扎纳·卡普托娃、祖桑娜·查普托娃等等。不同的版本虽然读音大同小异，但容易给不熟悉的读者带来误解。

以上仅仅是一个很小的例子，但是反映出许多译者在翻译时求快不求精，没有读者意识，或认为细节正确与否无关紧要，忽视译文的严谨性。这也提醒我们，在着手翻译之前，一定要先做好准备工作，同一个翻译任务中的译员一定要统稿，这不仅是给读者行方便、给审校者减轻负担，也是为了避免不知其然的翻译。

另一位同学提供了另一种常见情况：

> 大企业的稿件通常情况下量大且留给翻译的时间较短，仅凭一名译员完成整个稿件的翻译显然不现实，这时便需要多名译员共同协作，完成客户的稿件，并按时交付。笔者曾经参与国内某互联网企业的某重大合同翻译的校对，笔者就发现了本章所述"表述不一致"的问题。例如：
>
> 原文：Appendix/ Schedule
> 译文1：附表 / 附录
> 译文2：附录 / 附表
>
> 由于在译前准备阶段，项目经理（PM）没有统一好这些看似不起眼的词语的翻译，导致在翻译过程中，不同译员将相同的英文词翻译成不同的英文词。如果只看单个词，而忽略合同的语境，本质上译文1和译文2的译文是没有问题的，合同也确实提供的是列表型的附录。但是，如果考虑到整个合同，译法不统一就会造成很大的麻烦。试想一下，在不同的地方，条款本应该与Appendix（附录）有关，而因为不同译员把Appendix翻译成"附表"，而导致不懂英语的甲方去关注附表（Schedule）的内容，并产生纠纷，影响谈判过程，造成巨大损失。这是任何一方都不愿意看到的结果，严重时译员还需要承担造成的损失。所以，翻译时要确保表述一致，这一点至关重要。

* * *

翻译中所犯的错误，往往是综合性的，无法归到以上单个类别。下面一例，就包含多个问题：

Suggestive trademarks hint at the nature, quality or attributes of the product, without describing those attributes (e.g. SUNNY for marketing lamps which would hint that the product will bring light to homes). In some countries, a suggestive trademark may be considered too descriptive and as such may be rejected.

原译：

暗示性商标暗示产品的性质、质量或属性，但<u>不对属性进行描述</u>（例如，<u>代表</u>灯具的 SUNNY 暗示产品为家庭带来光明）。在<u>一些国家</u>，<u>暗示性商标可能被</u>认为过于描述性，因此有<u>被驳回</u>的可能。

改译：

暗示性商标仅仅暗示产品的性质、质量或属性，但不直接描述（例如，销售灯具时用 SUNNY 商标，暗示产品为家庭带来光明）。一些国家可能会认为暗示性商标描述性太强，因此可能驳回申请。

改译关注的问题如下：

- "对……进行描述"，改为强势动词"描述……"；汉语写作和英汉翻译中，有滥用"进行"的倾向，应予以纠正
- "代表灯具的 SUNNY"为错译，改为"销售灯具时用 SUNNY 商标"
- 汉语少用被动语态，第二句改为用人物（"一些国家"）作主语，全句变为主动语态

再看看下面一段话（摘自 2011 年的政府工作报告），这里面涉及很多英文表达问题：

——我们要大力发展社会事业。坚持优先发展教育，稳步提升全民受教育程度。坚持自主创新、重点跨越、支撑发展、引领未来的方针，完善科技创新体系和支持政策，着力推进重大科学技术突破。研究与试验发展经费支出占国内生产总值比重达到 2.2%，促进科技成果更好地转化为生产力。适应现代化建设需要，加强人才培养，努力造就规模宏大的高素质人才队伍。大力加强文化建设，推动文化改革发展实现新跨越，满足人民群众不断增长的精神文化需求。大力发展体育事

业。进一步深化医药卫生体制改革，健全基本医疗卫生制度，加快实现人人享有基本医疗卫生服务的目标。创新社会管理体制机制，加强社会管理法律、体制、能力建设，确保社会既充满活力又和谐稳定。

我们以机器翻译为例，通过逐句修改，强调译者关注的表达问题。

第一句：我们要大力发展社会事业。

MT (Machine Translation): We must vigorously develop social undertakings.

外交部资深翻译专家程镇球（2002）指出：

> 在汉语里，说话和写文章习惯于用四字词组，因而"贯彻"前加上"全面"，"推行"前加上"认真"，好像无可非议。其他如"广泛开展""深入批判""切实采取""严肃处理""大力整顿""努力做到""紧密联系""热烈拥护""胜利完成"等等，也觉得说来顺口，写来顺手。

程先生说"要把汉语文章里所用的修饰词全都翻译过来，有时会产生很大的困难"。怎么办呢？"凡是英语里的动词或名词，已经把汉语里修饰名词或动词的形容词或副词的含义包括进去了，就可以在英语里把这些形容词、副词删去不译"。

鉴于此处以及后续的"大力""进一步"等修饰语已经隐含在所修饰的动词中，翻译出来除了削弱动词的意思外，还导致句子冗长拗口，弊大于利，因此需要省略。

根据百度百科，社会事业：

> 是指中央和各级地方政府领导的社会建设和社会服务事业，是与行政部门和企业（包括金融机构）行为相并列的活动。具体而言，社会事业是指国家为了社会公益目的，由国家机关或其他组织举办的从事教育、科技、文化、卫生等活动的社会服务。

"社会事业"传统上翻译为 social undertakings。通过互联网查证，发现该词只有中国的英文媒体在广泛使用。进一步调查发现，social services 可能是一个更好的选择：

<u>Social services</u> are a range of public services provided by the government, private, profit and non-profit organizations. These public services aim to create more effective organizations, build stronger communities, and promote equality and opportunity.

Social services include the benefits and facilities like education, food subsidies, health care, police, fire service, job training and subsidized housing, adoption, community management, policy research, and lobbying.

"要大力发展"当中的"要"如何翻译，并不容易决定。有人翻译为must，有人翻译为should，有人翻译为will。哪一个更合适？要从宏观上考虑（Who is speaking to whom?）。根据百度百科，政府工作报告的主要内容有：

一年内工作回顾

回顾并总结前一年的政府工作情况。汇报政府取得的成绩和基本经济指标完成情况，然后再将政府工作分为几个大类（如经济、社会事业、劳动等），分别详细阐述工作举措和成绩。

当年工作任务

归纳当年政府各项工作，汇报这一年政府的工作计划和目标。首先提出一段纲要性的文字，说明当年政府工作的基本思路和主要任务。然后再将政府工作分为几个大类（如经济、社会事业、劳动等），分别详细阐述将要施行的工作举措和工作计划。

政府自身建设

详细阐述对当年政府内部的政府职能、民主化建设、依法行政、政风建设等方面将要施行的工作举措和工作计划。

其他

国务院总理所作的政府工作报告一般还包括外交和国际形势方面的内容。每个"五年规划"开始之年，报告中还需包含过去五年的总结和今后五年的基本规划。部分政府工作报告后，对报告中出现的一些新名词或专有名词还附有"名词解释"。

可见，政府工作报告即国务院总理向人大代表汇报前一年的工作情况，报告未来一年的工作计划和目标，以供代表审议，代表有建议可以提出来。"我们要大力发展社会事业"这段话，就出现在来年工作计划部分。既然是工作计划，最恰当的用词是 will（见图 3.47）①：

2. MODAL VERB
You use **will** in order to make statements about official arrangements in the future.
The show will be open to the public at 2pm; admission will be 50p.
When will I be released, sir?

图 3.47　will 的用法

should 和 must 都表示"建议"，should 语气弱一些，must 语气更强；must 还表示个人意见（见图 3.48）②：

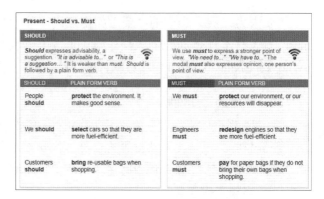

图 3.48　should 和 must 用法比较

总理面对人大代表作政府工作报告时，显然不是建议别人怎么做，或者个人认为应当怎么做，而是本届政府打算怎么做，因为总理本人就是政府首脑，只能是别人给他提建议；经他说出后就变为政府的意志（will）。

改译：We will expand social services.

"发展"译为 develop 没有问题。但 develop 也不是唯一的选项。

第二句：坚持优先发展教育，稳步提升全民受教育程度。

MT1: <u>Insist on</u> giving priority to the development of education, and steadily improve the education level of all people.

MT2: We <u>will</u> give priority to ~~the development of~~ education and ~~steadily~~ improve the education level of all people.

---

① https://www.collinsdictionary.com/dictionary/english/will, accessed March 21, 2021.
② https://www.grammar-quizzes.com/modal3.html, accessed March 21, 2021.

MT1 和 MT2 是两台机器翻译的不同结果。MT1（包括后面几句）没有主语，是显而易见的语法错误，不在我们讨论之列。机器和很多人把"坚持"翻译为 insist on，属于严重用词不当。insist on 的意思是尽管别人反对，还固执己见，非要做一件事（见图 3.49）[①]：

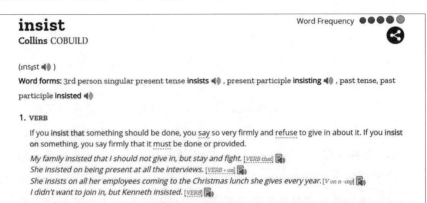

图 3.49　insist 的用法

因此，除了英英词典列举的这些情况，其他时候不要使用 insist 一词。可以视情况省略或改用其他说法，例如 be committed to、continue to 等。

MT2 语法上没有问题，语言也通顺，但情态动词用错，并且还可以更简洁。改译：We will give priority to education and improve the education level of our nation. 还可以把 give priority to 改为动词 prioritize。

第三句：坚持自主创新、重点跨越、支撑发展、引领未来的方针，完善科技创新体系和支持政策，着力推进重大科学技术突破。

MT1: Adhere to the policy of independent innovation, key leapfrogging, supporting development, and leading the future, improve the scientific and technological innovation system and supporting policies, and strive to promote major scientific and technological breakthroughs.

MT2: We should adhere to the principles of independent innovation, key leapfrogging, supporting development and leading the future, improve the system of scientific and technological innovation and support policies,

---

[①] https://www.collinsdictionary.com/dictionary/english/insist, accessed March 21, 2021.

and ~~strive to~~ promote major ~~scientific and technological~~ breakthroughs.

"坚持自主创新、重点跨越、支撑发展、引领未来"如何理解？译者要找到依据，不能根据个人的理解翻译。《国家中长期科学和技术发展规划纲要》①对此的解释是：

> 自主创新，就是从增强国家创新能力出发，加强原始创新、集成创新和引进消化吸收再创新。重点跨越，就是坚持有所为、有所不为，选择具有一定基础和优势、关系国计民生和国家安全的关键领域，集中力量、重点突破，实现跨越式发展。支撑发展，就是从现实的紧迫需求出发，着力突破重大关键、共性技术，支撑经济社会的持续协调发展。引领未来，就是着眼长远，超前部署前沿技术和基础研究，创造新的市场需求，培育新兴产业，引领未来经济社会的发展。这一方针是我国半个多世纪科技发展实践经验的概括总结，是面向未来、实现中华民族伟大复兴的重要抉择。

《纲要》的英译如下：

> The guiding principles for our S&T undertakings over the next 15 years are: "indigenous innovation, leapfrogging in priority fields, enabling development, and leading the future". Indigenous innovation refers to enhancing original innovation, integrated innovation, and re-innovation based on assimilation and absorption of imported technology, in order to improve our national innovation capability. Leapfrogging in priority fields is to select and concentrate efforts in those key areas of relative strength and advantage linked to the national economy and people's livelihood as well as national security, to strive for breakthroughs and realize leaping developments. Enabling development is an attempt to strive for breakthroughs in key areas, enabling technologies that are urgently needed for the sustainable and coordinated economic and social development. Leading the future reflects a vision in deploying for frontier

---

① http://www.nsfc.gov.cn/nsfc/cen/ghgy/02/01.htm, accessed March 21, 2021.

technologies and basic research, which will, in turn, create new market demands and new industries expected to lead the future economic growth and social development. The guideline is a summary of China's practice and experience in S&T development for more than a half century, and an important choice for realizing the great renaissance of the Chinese nation.

"自主创新"最初翻译为 independent innovation，结果在国外企业中引起轩然大波，以为中国关闭了对外合作的大门，要搞独立研发。为此政府专门澄清，我们的自主创新，是指拥有知识产权的创新，并非关闭对外合作的大门，后来就把"自主创新"改译为 indigenous innovation[①]：

'Indigenous Innovation' is a national strategy put forward by the Chinese government for the purpose of promoting the development of technological innovation in domestic firms, eventually leading to the ownership of their own core IP rights.

《纲要》中就翻译为 indigenous innovation。也可以翻译为 proprietary innovation。proprietary 的意思就是专有的，拥有产权的（见图 3.50）[②]：

proprietary
in British English
(prəˈpraɪətərɪ, -trɪ)
ADJECTIVE
1. of, relating to, or belonging to property or proprietors
2. privately owned and controlled
3. medicine
   of or denoting a drug or agent manufactured and distributed under a trade name
   Compare ethical (sense 3)

图 3.50　proprietary 的定义

proprietary innovation 这一搭配也确实存在（见图 3.51）[③]：

---

① https://www.chinalawinsight.com/2010/09/articles/intellectual-property/chinas-indigenous-innovation-policy-and-its-effect-on-foreign-intellectual-property-rights-holders/, accessed March 21, 2021.
② https://www.collinsdictionary.com/dictionary/english/proprietary, accessed March 21, 2021.
③ https://www.english-corpora.org/iweb/, accessed March 21, 2021.

CLICK FOR MORE CONTEXT					[?] SAVE LIST CHOOSE LIST --------- CREATE NEW LIST [?] SHOW DUPLICATES
1	skullcandy.com	A	B	C	athletic audiophiles looking for best in class fit, construction and materialization. Featuring a **proprietary innovation** called Stickybuds, which allows for maximum su
2	nike.com	A	B	C	bladder. # The ball's NIKE AEROW TRAC grooves, Nike Football's newest **proprietary innovation** are engineered to grip and channel air to produce the truest trajector
3	capsugel.com	A	B	C	28119941 1819941/ # DBcaps capsules are a **proprietary innovation** developed by Capsugel for use in pharmaceutical clinical studies. The capsules are specially
4	merlotmommy.com	A	B	C	gets you clean enough to " go Commando. " Cottonelle CleanRipple Texture is a **proprietary innovation** that removes more than the leading value brand. Cottonelle C
5	supplementsource.ca	A	B	C	of a set. Agent-M is transported using Bullet Caplet Technology, which is a **proprietary innovation** exclusive to Fusion Bodybuilding. This allows immediate and accura
6	freshconsulting.com	A	B	C	to commencing work on Phase 2. Clearly defined processes for each service **Proprietary Innovation** App July 18, 2017 # Thanks to everyone who made it out
7	soccerreviewsforyou.com	A	B	C	Nike Ordem 2 is debossed with NIKE AEROW TRAC grooves. Nike Football's newest **proprietary innovation**, these grooves are engineered to grip and channel the air t
8	wholesalesolar.com	A	B	C	to withstand the most rigorous operating conditions while still offering high power output. Their **proprietary innovation** in surface texturing of panels increases their
10	johnaugust.com (1)	A	B	C	for an inventor to get paid per unit for the right to use some **proprietary innovation**. So it may help to think of screenplays as " literary inventions,
11	podcastgarden.com	A	B	C	the founder of LaunchStreet, the online innovation program and community and creator of the **proprietary innovation** Quotient Edge, the only assessment able to he
12	kyocera.com	A	B	C	bending the media in order to print on rigid materials such as plastic. A **proprietary innovation**, Kyoceras printheads place the heater element (head which prints ima
13	footballfashion.org	A	B	C	bladder. # The ball's NIKE AEROW TRAC grooves, Nike Football's newest **proprietary innovation** are engineered to grip and channel air to produce the truest trajector
14	footy-boots.com	A	B	C	running, but also downwards. # Assisting this is the Adaplite upper; a **proprietary innovation** from PUMA, this unique material will only stretch in one direction down
15	samedaysupplements.com	A	B	C	SUB-Qs powerful formula is transported with Bullet Caplet Technology. Bullet Caplet Technology is a **proprietary innovation** exclusive to FUSION BODYBUILDING. Wh
16	chaordix.com	A	B	C	served to community participants. It's here where we showcase the power of our **proprietary Innovation** Challenge Engine. 2 QUICK QUESTIONS # Wildly popular am
17	spectrum.ieee.org	A	B	C	Open Source Hardware innovation model of the DIY Drones dev teams is designed to beat **proprietary innovation** models in the speed and cost dimensions, but not
18	www.innovationexcellence.com	A	B	C	e.g. innovation clusters, strategic innovation alliance, lead user integration, university co-operations or **proprietary innovation** networks) should be used that other fi
19	radar.oreilly.com	A	B	C	. There's often good reason to do this, particularly those systems that use **proprietary innovation** and are essential for market differentiation. Outside of this categor
20	business.financialpost.com	A	B	C	to market, " Forbes said. # The trio of banks will share their **proprietary innovation** strategies and exchange key technology talent, with an eye to co-developing digita

图 3.51　核实 proprietary innovation

“重点跨越”机器译为 key leapfrogging 意思不明确。可以改为 leapfrogging 或 breakthroughs in key areas。《纲要》翻译为 leapfrogging in priority fields 也很好。“支撑发展”译为 support development 没问题。《纲要》译为 enabling development 技高一筹。“引领未来”本身意思含糊，但《纲要》的解释是清楚的，因此翻译为 leading the future 未尝不可。

改译：

Under the principles of indigenous innovation, leapfrogging in priority fields, enabling development, and leading the future, we will improve the system and policy for innovation and facilitate major breakthroughs.

如果不敢确定 facilitate breakthrough 的搭配是否存在，也可以上网核实：

Home Virtual Humans: Helping Facilitate Breakthroughs in Medicine Friday, 14 February 2014: 1:30

together the most progressive leaders to facilitate breakthroughs in thinking and action in combatting human

we've mastered the essential skills needed to facilitate breakthroughs smoothly. In this webinar series, Adam Hailstone

Ure will walk you through the skills you need to facilitate breakthroughs for your kids. You'll know how to better support

“坚持”翻译为 adhere to 也可以不改；改译用介词短语，不再需要翻译"坚持"。the system of 改为 the system for，介词 for 表示"服务于"。两处 scientific and technological 已经隐含在 innovation 和 breakthrough 当中，故省略。如果有必要保留，可以把"科技创新"翻译为 scientific and technological innovation，但更符合英语逻辑的说法是 scientific <u>discovery</u> and technological innovation，因为 science 的本义是知识①：

> Science (from the Latin word scientia, meaning "knowledge") is a systematic enterprise that builds and organizes knowledge in the form of testable explanations and predictions about the universe.

而人们认为知识（knowledge）或真理是先天存在的，只是等待我们去发现、去揭示，因此只能说 scientific discovery，不能说 scientific innovation。谷歌搜索也发现，scientific discovery 有 381 万条检索结果，scientific innovation 有 126 万条检索结果，说明前一搭配更常用。实际上，汉语中也经常说"科学发现""技术创新"；"科技创新"很可能仅仅指"技术创新"。

第四句：<u>研究与试验发展</u>经费支出占国内生产总值比重达到 2.2%，促进科技成果更好地转化为生产力。

MT1: Expenditures for <u>research and experimental development</u> accounte<u>d</u> for 2.2% of GDP, which promote<u>d</u> the conversion of scientific and technological achievements into productivity.

MT2: Expenditure on <u>research and experimental development</u> account<u>s</u> for 2.2% of GDP, which promote<u>s</u> the better transformation of scientific and technological achievements into productivity.

这句话两个机器翻译时态不同，但都不正确，说明机器翻译缺乏宏观思维。单独看这句话，无法判断作者是在讲过去、现在还是未来。但这句话出现在未来一年工作计划部分，毫无疑问，应当使用将来时。

这句话中的"研究与试验发展"是否就是我们平时所说的 R&D（Research and Development）？如果是，直接翻译为 R&D；如果不是，则需要按中文概念翻译（"试验""发展"应为并列关系，机器翻译译为偏正，显

---

① https://en.wikipedia.org/wiki/Science, accessed March 21, 2021.

然错误）。查证可知，“研究与试验发展”就是 R&D（见图 3.52）：

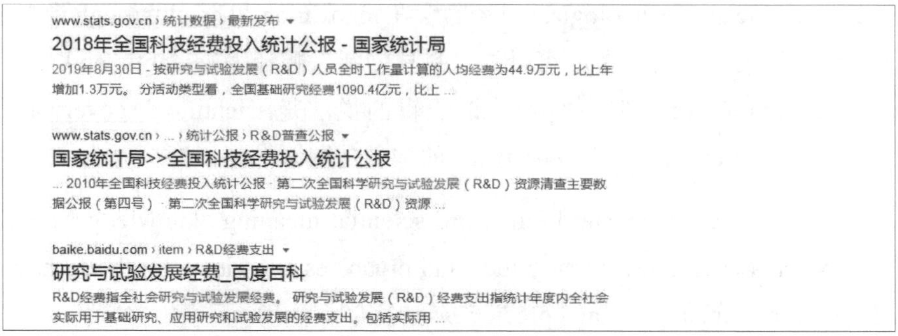

www.stats.gov.cn › 统计数据 › 最新发布 ▾
2018年全国科技经费投入统计公报 - 国家统计局
2019年8月30日 - 按研究与试验发展（R&D）人员全时工作量计算的人均经费为44.9万元，比上年增加1.3万元。分活动类型看，全国基础研究经费1090.4亿元，比上 ...

www.stats.gov.cn › ... › 统计公报 › R&D普查公报 ▾
国家统计局>>全国科技经费投入统计公报
... 2010年全国科技经费投入统计公报 · 第二次全国科学研究与试验发展（R&D）资源清查主要数据公报（第四号）· 第二次全国科学研究与试验发展（R&D）资源 ...

baike.baidu.com › item › R&D经费支出 ▾
研究与试验发展经费_百度百科
R&D经费指全社会研究与试验发展经费。研究与试验发展（R&D）经费支出指统计年度内全社会实际用于基础研究、应用研究和试验发展的经费支出。包括实际用 ...

图 3.52　核实“研究与试验发展”与 R&D 的关系

这句话逗号前后是并列关系还是偏正关系？从 R&D 的定义来看，其中的 development 就是开发新产品，也就是科技成果转化（见图 3.53）：

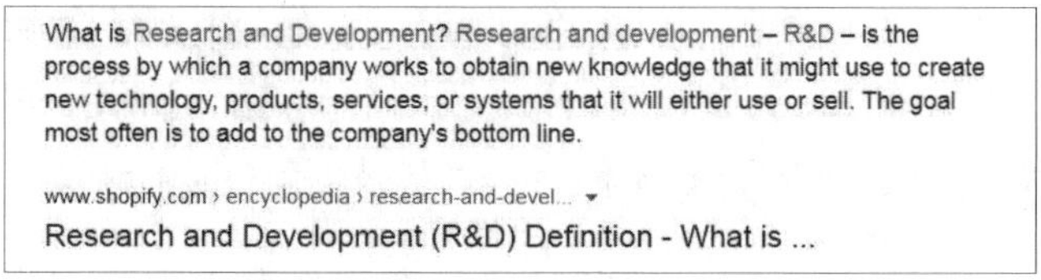

What is Research and Development? Research and development – R&D – is the process by which a company works to obtain new knowledge that it might use to create new technology, products, services, or systems that it will either use or sell. The goal most often is to add to the company's bottom line.

www.shopify.com › encyclopedia › research-and-devel... ▾
Research and Development (R&D) Definition - What is ...

图 3.53　R&D 的定义

因此前后两部分是偏正关系。机器翻译不算错，但语言比较啰嗦，可以改为直接使用动词：

改译：

R&D expenditure will be increased to 2.2% of our GDP to better transform scientific and technological achievements into productivity.

其中的“科技成果转化”翻译为 transform scientific and technological achievements into productivity 是传统的译法。在英文中则经常用 research/technology commercialization（见图 3.54）：

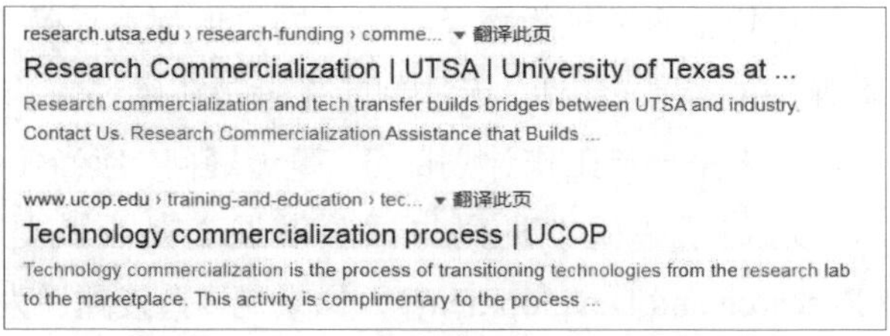

research.utsa.edu › research-funding › comme... ▾ 翻译此页
Research Commercialization | UTSA | University of Texas at ...
Research commercialization and tech transfer builds bridges between UTSA and industry. Contact Us. Research Commercialization Assistance that Builds ...

www.ucop.edu › training-and-education › tec... ▾ 翻译此页
Technology commercialization process | UCOP
Technology commercialization is the process of transitioning technologies from the research lab to the marketplace. This activity is complimentary to the process ...

图 3.54　“科技成果转化”英译查证

因此，这句话也可以译为：R&D Expenditure will be increased to 2.2%

of the GDP to facilitate research/technology commercialization。

第五句：适应现代化建设需要，加强人才培养，努力造就规模宏大的高素质人才队伍。

MT1: To meet the needs of modernization, strengthen personnel training, and strive to create a large-scale high-quality personnel team.

MT2: Adapt to the needs of modernization, strengthen personnel training, and strive to create a large-scale high-quality talent team.

MT3: In order to meet the needs of modernization, we should strengthen personnel training and strive to create a large-scale and high-quality talent team.

汉语中的无主句很多，给机器翻译带来很大困难，因为机器不考虑上下文，无法根据上下文添加主语，因此，就会出现把无主句翻译为祈使句的情况（MT1/2）。MT3 添加了主语 we，是碰对了（其他场合不一定是 we），但情态动词不应该用 should，而应该用 will。strive to 也可以省略，因为 create 隐含了努力。a large-scale team 搭配不当。人才的素质用 high-quality 不如 high-caliber①，因为 high caliber 专门用于指人（见图 3.55）：

"人才"不容易找到英文对应词。talent 是指有天赋的人、天资聪颖的人（"天才"），不是培养出来的（见图 3.56、3.57、3.58）②：

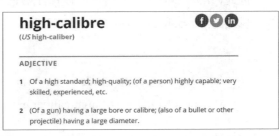

图 3.55　high-calibre 的定义

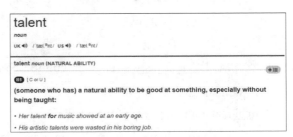

图 3.56　talent 的定义（一）

---

① https://www.lexico.com/en/definition/high-calibre, accessed March 21, 2021.

② https://dictionary.cambridge.org/dictionary/english/talent, accessed March 21, 2021.

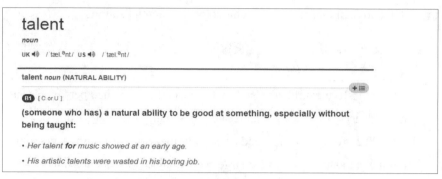

图 3.57　talent 的定义（二）

```
a person or people with a natural skill or ability:
• The company has shown that it can attract and retain top talent.
• Other industries facing a talent shortage can easily outsource jobs overseas.
• He's considered one of the greatest talents in the programming world.
```

图 3.58　talent 的定义（三）

因此，汉译英时，并非所有时候都能够把"人才"翻译为 talent，有时候可以译为 personnel 或 people。机器翻译部分正确。

改译：

In order to meet the needs of modernization, we <u>will</u> strengthen training <u>to</u> create a large pool of high-caliber experts.

改译还删除了 personnel，以避免重复。

第六句：<u>大力</u>加强文化建设，推动<u>文化改革发</u>展实现新跨越，满足人民群众不断增长的<u>精神文化</u>需求。

MT1: <u>Vigorously</u> strengthen cultural <u>construction</u>, promote <u>cultural reform and development</u> to achieve a new leap, and meet the growing <u>spiritual</u> and cultural <u>needs</u> of the people.

MT2: We should <u>vigorously</u> strengthen cultural <u>construction</u>, promote <u>cultural reform and development</u>, achieve new leaps, and meet the growing <u>spiritual</u> and cultural <u>needs</u> of the people.

cultural construction 在英文里意思是“文化建构”，与中文的“文化建设”是两码事。此处可以用 cultural development。“大力”基本上是为了和“加强”配够四个音节，并无实质意义，不译。“推动……实现新跨越”可以理解为“实现突破”。“文化改革”翻译为 cultural reform，意思变为“改革我们的文化”，可能并非此处的意思。查“文化改革”，出现的都是“文化体制改革”（见图 3.59）：

解读文化体制改革-中国政府网
www.gov.cn/zhuanti/jieduwenhuatizhigaige.htm
2022-5-4 · **文化**部部长蔡武：全面推进**文化**系统体制**改革**工作. 2013年以来，**文化**系统在以往**改革**工作取得显著进展的基础上，坚持稳中求进，锐意**改革**创新，对重点领域和关键环节的**改革**进行了新的实践探索，取得明显成效。. 深化**文化**体 ...

文化体制改革-文明百科-中国文明网
www.wenming.cn/special/bk_whtzgg
2013-11-11 · 文化领域体制改革工作在探索中不断推进。. 1996年十四届六中全会通过的《中共中央关于加强社会主义精神文明建设若干重要问题的决议》提出了文化体制改革的任务和一系列方...

图 3.59 “文化改革”含义查证

因此，此处的“文化改革”应当理解为“文化体制改革”，可以译为 reform of cultural institutions。

“精神”翻译为 spiritual[①] 增添了一层宗教含义（见图 3.60）：

2. ADJECTIVE

Spiritual means relating to people's religious beliefs.

...the spiritual leader of Ireland's 3.7 million Catholics.
A man in priestly clothes offered spiritual guidance.

Synonyms: sacred, religious, holy, divine More Synonyms of **spiritual**

图 3.60 spiritual 的定义

这一含义与执政党的无神论世界观不相符。可以认为，加上“精神”二字，也是为了凑够四个字，“精神文化需求”就是“文化需求”。改译省略 spiritual。

① https://dictionary.cambridge.org/zhs/ 词典 / 英语 /spiritual, accessed March 21, 2021.

改译：

We will strengthen <u>cultural</u> development and promote breakthroughs in <u>relevant institutions</u> to meet the growing ~~cultural~~ <u>demands</u> of the people.

改译还避免重复三个 cultural。needs 和 demands 有区别①：

In short, needs are things that satisfy the basic requirement. Wants are requests directed to specific types of items. Demands are requests for specific products that the buyer is willing to and able to pay for.

此处显然是指大众对文化产品的需求，因此用 demands。

第七句：<u>大力发展体育事业</u>。<u>进一步深化医药卫生体制改革，健全基本医疗卫生制度</u>，<u>加快实现</u>人人享有基本医疗卫生服务的目标。

MT1: Vigorously develop sports. <u>Further deepen the reform</u> of the <u>medical and health</u> system, improve the basic <u>medical and health</u> system, and <u>accelerate the realization of the goal of</u> everyone enjoying basic <u>medical and health</u> services.

MT2: Vigorously develop sports <u>undertakings</u>. <u>Further deepen the reform</u> of the <u>medical and health</u> system, improve the basic <u>medical and health</u> system, and <u>accelerate the realization of the goal of</u> everyone enjoying basic medical and health services.

"大力"翻译为英文多余，故需要省略；"体育事业"当中的"事业"是范畴词，需要省略；further deepen the reform 就是 further reform；medical and health 重复三次，需要简化；accelerate the realization of the goal of 属于"慢启动"或者 unnecessary introductory phrases，需要简化。

改译：

We will develop <u>sports</u>. We will <u>further reform</u> the <u>medical and health institutions</u>, improve basic services, and <u>make such services accessible to all</u>.

改译减少了 medical and health 的重复，省略了范畴词"加快实现……

---

① https://www.baillie.com/hardwood-lumber-blog/item/420-understanding-needs-wants-and-demands-of-customers, accessed March 21, 2021.

目标";"人人享有……"简化为 accessible to all。

修改过程中考虑过是否把"基本医疗卫生服务"译为 primary healthcare（初级保健），但调查发现两者含义不同：

> Primary healthcare is a term used to describe the first contact a person has with the health system when they have a health problem or issue that is not an emergency. It is the part of the health system that people use most and may be provided, for example, by a general practitioner (GP), physiotherapist or pharmacist.①

基本医疗卫生服务含义更广：

> 第十五条 基本医疗卫生服务，是指维护人体健康所必需、与经济社会发展水平相适应、公民可公平获得的，采用适宜药物、适宜技术、适宜设备提供的疾病预防、诊断、治疗、护理和康复等服务。
>
> 基本医疗卫生服务包括基本公共卫生服务和基本医疗服务。基本公共卫生服务由国家免费提供。②

第八句：创新社会管理体制机制，加强社会管理法律、体制、能力建设，确保社会既充满活力又和谐稳定。

MT1: Innovate social management systems and mechanisms, strengthen social management laws, systems, and capacity building to ensure that the society is full of vitality, harmony and stability.

MT2: We should innovate the system and mechanism of social management, strengthen the construction of law, system and capacity of social management, and ensure that the society is full of vitality, harmony and stability.

机器翻译 social management laws 等等，前置定语过长；construction of law, system and capacity 搭配不当；full of…harmony and stability 搭配不当；"既……又……"包含相对立的两个意思，需要体现出来，不是简单的并列（and）。

---

① https://www.betterhealth.vic.gov.au/health/ServicesAndSupport/primary-healthcare-explained, accessed March 21, 2021.

② http://www.xinhuanet.com/politics/2019-12/28/c_1125399629.htm, accessed March 21, 2021.

改译：

We will innovate social management systems, including <u>building stronger laws, institutions and management capacity</u> to create a vibrant, harmonious and stable society.

改译还省略了"稳定"，因为"和谐"隐含了"稳定"。中文的"和谐稳定"，是为了凑足四个音节，"和谐"和"稳定"意思相近。另外，表达形式也从抽象名词改为更简短的形容词。

innovate 常用作不及物动词，例如：

Some expressed the view that fewer and fewer employers are willing to take risks with ideas or to <u>innovate</u>.

也可以用作及物动词，例如：

Sometimes it's hard to imagine that there's still room to <u>innovate your product or service</u>.

也见到过 innovate new ideas/products 一类的说法:We continue to innovate new products。但这种说法不符合逻辑:innovate 的本义就是 make new（nov- 的意思是 new），"make new"与 new products 意思重复。与 new idea 搭配的应该是 generate、create、unlock、embrace、capture、inspire、adopt、spread、explore 等等；与 new product 搭配的是 develop、launch、build、introduce 等等。

3.3 小结

翻译是写作的一种形式。翻译像写作一样，必须做到意思准确、用词得当、重点突出、表达到位，必须关注"假朋友"可能带来的用词不当、译文可能产生的歧义，以及包括括号位置在内的修饰关系。译文还必须做到语言通顺。要从写作的视角看待翻译，必要时抛开原文用词重新表达。要避免语法错误，做到前后逻辑清晰；每段话主语相对一致；尽量避免多个不定式连用。要尽量避免源语结构对译语的影响，减少中式英文和欧化中文。同一概念的译法尽量做到前后一致、与历史文件一致。

〔课后练习〕

1. 翻译和写作在表达方面有哪些相似之处？
2. 你平时翻译是以写作的原则指导自己，还是依靠结构转换？
3. 请检查自己最近一篇译文，看是否有本章所述的表达问题。
4. 请在网上搜索"从十九大报告英译看政府公文翻译最新趋势"，阅读陈明明大使的演讲实录。
5. 请在网上搜索"欧化中文"，阅读维基百科或百度百科文章。

附：2019年联合国翻译竞赛原文

Out of My Comfort Zone, Wandering Around Harrods in the Wrong Trousers[①]

1. I've rarely felt as adrift from my comfort zone as I did last week when I found myself wandering slack-jawed through the gilded halls of Harrods in the wrong trousers.

2. As soon as I walked through the heavy metal doors I knew it wasn't the place for me. Beautiful men with perma-tans, artfully sculpted facial hair and teeth as white as their crotch-hugging jeans strutted the halls like they owned them. Some were so dazzled by their amazingness that they had to wear sunglasses indoors. Armies of perfectly made-up women looking like—I imagine—Kardashians struggled with bags from designers so exclusive I'd never even heard of them.

3. We headed for the food hall. "I'm not feeding my children Kobe beef or Russian caviar," I muttered as I swerved us past heavy marble counters groaning under the weight of gleaming ice crystals and a meat counter offering a

---

① 可在此查看电子版：https://languagecareers.un.org/dgacm/Langs.nsf/files/14th_St_Jerome_English_text_final/$FILE/St%20Jerome%2014%20-%20English%20original.pdf, accessed March 21, 2021

platter of "baby chicken, half duck, lamb cutlets and Merguez sausage" for £100. Harrods is a most confusingly laid out shop with lifts that go to random floors and stairs more suited to an Escher print. After several wrong turns, which took us repeatedly through a diamond hall maze where staff looked through us, I had to do a thing I hate doing. I had to ask someone for directions to somewhere other than the food hall where food might be found.

4. We were directed to the tea rooms and after more wrong turns, found a brassy lift which agreed to take us there. As we waited for a table, I'd cause to regret my wardrobe choice. The skanky shorts and t-shirt combo was wrong for a place where stooped men of advancing years gently vacuumed red velvet sofas as beautiful people in sharply cut waistcoats delivered morsels of sharply cut sandwiches to bored diners.

5. I hid my shorts of shame using my family as a shield and we were shown to a table under a flowering tree. I felt more comfortable when another family arrived and I noticed the solitary man in their party also wearing shorts. My comfort turned to more shame when I realized they were Irish. "What will all these men in tight white jeans, Armani loafers and ankles untroubled by socks make of us Paddies who can't even afford trouser legs," I thought.

6. After lunch we explored the children's clothes section, walking floors covered with carpets richer and thicker than minor royals. The stock prices horrified, amused, depressed and outraged me to varying degrees. I looked at my gorgeous little baby in her Penney's leggings and M&S t-shirt covered in drool and lunch and wondered if I'd failed at life because I couldn't afford a handwash-only cashmere onesie to cover her perfect skin.

7. Then I felt indignation. Much to the mortification of my family, I marched up to a shop assistant and asked who in their right mind would pay 300 quid for a romper suit? The question clearly caught her off guard but rather than calling security she smiled. "Oh you'd be amazed. There really is a market for this stuff. And it is really good quality and... No, you're right," she said. "They're just paying for brand names because they can."

Adapted from: Conor Pope, "Out of My Comfort Zone, Wandering Around Harrods in the Wrong Trousers", *The Irish Times*, 29 August 2018.

第四章　翻译是一种写作形式：变通

 扫码预习

请扫码下载本章涉及的例句。先做练习，再看解答，学习效果更佳。

作者需要根据写作要求、目的、读者等因素选择加工写作材料，确定表达方式；翻译作为二次创作，原文即是写作素材，也需要视情况对原文进行变通取舍。变通取舍是指翻译时删减原文信息、添加原文隐含但没有明确表达的信息、采用不同方式传递原文信息或体现作者意图。

影响变通取舍的因素多种多样，其中意识形态的影响可能是最根本的，因为不符合意识形态的内容，会被排除在翻译选材的范围之外。意识形态整体符合要求的作品，也会对局部不适当的内容作编辑处理。

文本类型也会影响变通取舍。有些文本，例如公约、法律、决议，译者变通取舍的余地很小；有些文本，例如广告宣传材料，译者有较大的灵活余地。有些情况下则必须变通，才能达到应有的效果，例如笑话或双关语的翻译。

变通取舍也受到具体翻译情景的影响。例如，如果译文呈现的空间受限，则必须简洁或简化；如果翻译出来对委托人有害，可以建议委托人不译。还有些情况下没有必要逐字逐句翻译，因为逐字翻译可能给读者带来理解负担，耽误读者的时间。

还有些情况下，原文表述有瑕疵，译者既然发现了，不妨顺手纠正，这不仅帮了原文作者，也可免去译文读者的困惑。

如前文所述，为了作出正确的变通取舍决定，译者需要回答以下问题：Who is asking you to translate? For whom? When, where, why, and how is the translation to be used, by whom? 在此基础上，作出不说、少说、多说还是换个说法的决定。

4.1 不说

4.1.1 完全省略

有时候忠实翻译，可能会给客户惹麻烦。例如，下面这则旅行提示：

> London is generally a safe place to travel. However, precautions are needed when entering areas mainly populated by Indians, Pakistanis and black people. We advise tourists not to go out alone at night, and females always to be accompanied by another person when traveling.

这段话的原文是：

> 到伦敦旅行很安全，但有些印巴聚集区和黑人聚集区相对较乱。夜晚最好不要单独出行，女士应该尽量结伴而行。

对照原文和译文，发现译文既忠实又通顺，完全达到了基本的翻译要求。但一些外媒记者却借题发挥，在国外媒体大肆渲染，指责旅行提示涉嫌歧视黑人，造成恶劣影响。为什么达到基本翻译要求的译文却引起轩然大波呢？因为译者没有文化敏感性，把不该翻译的内容翻译出来了。这段话是针对中国游客讲的，完全没有必要翻译为英文。西方国家种族矛盾、宗教矛盾、男女平等问题突出，任何相关言论都可能被曲解，因此遇到相关问题，应当十分谨慎。如果译者当初意识到这个问题，就可以建议委托人，不要翻译这一段。

4.1.2 音译代替意译

根据功能主义的翻译观，有些信息翻译出来反而不如保留原文更容易实现翻译的目的，比如，下例中的中药名称：

国家中医药管理局此前已发布消息，初步证实清肺排毒汤、化湿败毒方、宣肺败毒颗粒、金花清感颗粒、连花清瘟胶囊、血必净注射液等3个中药方剂和3个中成药对新冠肺炎有明显疗效。

原译：

The State Administration of Traditional Chinese Medicine has previously released news that initially confirmed [*Qingfei*^{1} *Detox*] Decoction, [*Huashi*^{2} *Baidu*^{3}] Recipe, [*Xuanfei*^{4} *Baidu*] Granule, and [*Jinhua*^{5}*Qinggan*^{6}] granule, [*Lianhua*^{7} *Qingwen*^{8}] capsule, [*Xuebijing*] injection, etc. The aforementioned 3 TCM prescriptions and 3 manufactured products have obvious curative effect on new coronary pneumonia.

[1] "Clear the lung."
[2] "Reduce the dampness."
[3] "Detox."
[4] "Reduce stuffing."
[5] A popular over the counter Chinese medicine for cold and flu relief. Main ingredients include Honeysuckle, *Fritillaria thunbergii*, *Baical* skullcap root, achene of creat burdock and Sweet wormwood.
[6] Get rid of cold.
[7] Lotus flower.
[8] "Clear pandemic diseases."

这是一份新闻报道，翻译为英文的目的是让国外普通读者了解中医的疗效，从而在世界范围内宣传中医。至于这些药的具体成分和含义，对读者来说意义不大。即使他们真的去尝试中药，恐怕也要到中医诊所。这时，拿着翻译出来的药方，恐怕还不如拼音药方管用。因此，从翻译的功能出发，药名不翻译的作用更大，原译煞费苦心，甚至添加了注释，但沟通效果不一定好。改译如下：

Earlier, the State Administration of Traditional Chinese Medicine released information preliminarily confirming that three TCM prescriptions and three manufactured products exert clear curative effects on COVID-19. They are Qingfei Paidu Tang, Huashi Baidu Fang, Xuanfei Baidu Granule, Jinhua Qinggan Granule, Lianhua Qingwen Capsule, and Xuebijing Injection.

4.1.3　保留原文

有时需要保留原文，才能达到翻译目的。下面的例句来自 WIPO 的一份专利检索教程，内容是如何找到自己想要的专利文件：

Looking at the documents you will see that many of them are not relevant to what you are looking for; the word *farming* is far too general. What is another term that would describe better your invention? Is it best to use the word *plough* itself?

原译：

查看文件时，您会看到其中许多文件与您正在寻找的内容无关；"农业"一词过于宽泛。那么哪个术语能更好地描述您的发明呢？是否最好直接使用"犁"字本身？

原译意思正确，符合一般的翻译要求，但不"好用"（切合用途）。因为该文件是教授读者如何在具体数据库中查找专利文件，而这个数据库只有英文。因此，把 farming 和 plough 都翻译出来，读者反而无法搜索。改译：

查看文件时，你会看到其中许多文件与你正在寻找的内容无关；farming（农业）一词过于宽泛。那么哪个术语能更好地描述你要检索的发明呢？使用 plough（犁）本身是否更好呢？

改译在英文后面括注了中文，便于读者理解。

4.1.4 删减

译者在翻译或编译过程中，还会对中国人不熟悉的背景做一些补充说明，对中国人熟悉的背景，则删去不译。例如，以下德新社关于新冠肺炎的报道，《参考消息》编译的中文版，就删除了关于中国公共卫生制度的一句说明（粗体下划线部分）：

原文：
WHO Admits Wuhan May not be the Origin of Covid-19

<u>While Chinese researchers have conducted studies around initial cases and around the Wuhan seafood market, there are gaps in the epidemiological landscape.</u>

The Chinese city of Wuhan may not be the origin of the novel coronavirus, senior UN health official Mike Ryan said on **Monday**, announcing extensive studies to track down the animal species that transmitted the virus to humans.

"The fact that that fire alarm was triggered doesn't necessarily mean that that is where the disease crossed from animals into humans," WHO emergency operations chief Ryan said during a press conference in Geneva.

The World Health Organization (WHO) and China are to put together an international team that is to go to Wuhan to trace back the chain of infections from the first Covid-19 cases that appeared there late last year, **after the outbreak was detected by the city's pneumonia surveillance system.**

While Chinese researchers have conducted studies around initial cases and around the Wuhan seafood market to find the source animal, "there are gaps in the epidemiological landscape," Ryan said.

"What is required is going to be a much more extensive retrospective epidemiological study" to look at the links between the first human cases, he added.

A Team to China

WHO chief Tedros Adhanom Ghebreyesus had announced **in late June** that a small WHO advance team would go to China to prepare this work.

It took a month until the WHO experts and their Chinese counterparts drafted the outlines of a work plan.

On **Friday**, an international expert group that advises the WHO on the Covid-19 pandemic said the UN health agency should speed up research to find the animal source of the novel coronavirus.

编译：

据德新社日内瓦 8 月 3 日报道，联合国高级卫生官员迈克尔·瑞安当地时间 3 日说，中国城市武汉未必是新冠病毒的源头。他宣布将开展广泛研究，追踪将这种病毒传给人类的动物种类。

世界卫生组织突发卫生事件规划执行主任瑞安在日内瓦举行的记者会上说："警报响起这一事实并不一定意味着病毒是在这个地方由动物传给人类的。"

报道称，世卫组织专家将与中国专家组成国际专家组前往武汉，追踪去年年底该地出现的最早一批新冠病例的传染链。

瑞安说，虽然中国研究人员围绕最初病例及武汉那家海鲜市场进行了研究，寻找源头动物，但"流行病学调查仍存缺口"。

他还说"需要进行更加广泛的流行病学回溯研究"，探究最早一批感染病例之间的关联。

报道介绍，世卫组织总干事谭德塞**数周前**曾宣布将派先遣队前往中国从事筹备工作。世卫组织专家及其中国同行用了一个月时间起草工作计划纲要。

为世卫组织提供新冠疫情建议的国际专家团队 **7 月 31 日**说，该组织应加快研究速度，寻找新冠病毒的动物源头。

《参考消息》的上述编译还作了其他变通处理，例如：

- 省略了原报道中导语部分，因为这句话与正文内容重复（非粗体下划线部分）
- 改用转述德新社报道的叙述方式（"报道称""报道介绍"）

- 改变日期的表达方式（把星期几改为更加具体的几月几日）
- 把 late June 改为"数周前"，免得读者再去计算过了多久
- 删去了原文的一个小标题（A team to China）

至于《参考消息》这些改动是否具有普遍指导意义，恐怕也不一定；只能说这是该报的做法。今后翻译新闻报道，是否需要对时间、货币、重量、长度进行转化，还需要服从用户的规定。

4.2 少说

4.2.1 简洁

译文应尽量简洁。可以删除重复累赘的表达，采用更为直接的表达方式。例如：

当产品或服务提供多项需收集个人信息的业务功能时，个人信息控制者不应违背个人信息主体的自主意愿，强迫个人信息主体接受产品或服务所提供的业务功能及相应的个人信息收集请求。

原译：

When a product or service provides a number of business functions that require the collection of PI, the PI Controller shall not <u>force</u> PI Subjects to accept the business functions provided by the product or service and the corresponding requests for PI collection <u>against their independent will</u>.

原文"违背意愿"和"强迫"意思重复，"自主意愿"和"意愿"意思相同。译文要避免重复，因此改译删除了"违背自主意愿"：

When a product or service provides a number of business functions that require the collection of PI, the PI Controller shall not force PI Subjects to accept the business functions provided by the product or service and the corresponding requests for PI collection.

再如：

收集年满 14 周岁未成年人的个人信息前，应征得未成年人或其监护人的明示同意；不满 14 周岁的，应征得其监护人的明示同意。

原译：

Before the collection of PI of minors at 14 years old and above, the PI Controllers shall obtain explicit consent from the minors or their guardians; <u>for minors under 14 years old, ~~the PI Controllers~~ shall obtain explicit consent from their guardians.</u>

改译：

Before the collection of PI of minors at 14 years old and above, the PI Controllers shall obtain explicit consent from the minors or their guardians; <u>for minors under 14 years old, explicit consent from their guardians is required</u>.

改译用被动语态，避免重复主语，使译文简洁。

英译汉同样需要简洁。例如：

The greatest improvement in the productive powers of labour, and the greater part of the skill, dexterity, and judgement with which it is anywhere directed, or applied, seem to have been the effects of the division of labour.[①]

原译：

分工出现之后，劳动生产力得到了最大的增进，运用劳动时的熟练程度、技巧和判断力也得以加强。

改译：

分工最大限度提高了劳动生产力，大幅提升了劳动技巧、熟练度和判断力。

---

① *The Wealth of Nations*. Adam Smith. New York: Random House, Inc., 2003.

4.2.2 简化

有时直译甚至解释虽然并不困难，但可能没有必要。例如：

1685 年，按照人出生就算一岁，过了年就两岁的习惯，45 岁的蒲松龄已经结结实实地算是年近半百了。

这段直译加解释也不难：

In 1685, in accordance with the traditional way of calculation—by which a person is one year old after birth and two years after the first Chinese New Year — Pu Songling was already 46, approaching "half-hundred", as the saying goes.

但作者这样写，也许仅仅是为了通过"年近半百"这个成语，传达蒲松龄年纪不小了的含义。如果介绍中国文化不是作者的主要目的（这本书的主题是物联网），就可以简化为：In 1685, Pu Songling was 45, or 46 by the Chinese tradition. 或者：In 1685, Pu Songling was already 45, more than half-way through his life. 或者更简单些：In 1685, Pu Songling was already 45（经查，蒲松龄生于 1640 年，卒于 1715 年）。

有时都翻译出来还可能引起误解。例如：

据张伯礼介绍，现在的中医医生以高校培养为主，除了学好中医理论外，西医课程占 40%，真正的中医学生没有完全不懂西医的。

原译：

According to Zhang Boli, TCM doctors are mainly trained in colleges and universities, now. In addition to learning TCM theories, Western medicine courses account for 40% of the trainings. <u>Real TCM students</u> cannot be without knowledge on western medicine.

"<u>Real TCM students</u> cannot be without knowledge on western medicine"给人的印象是"不懂西医的中医是假中医"，恐怕有失偏颇。张院长的意思

是所有中医学生都懂一些西医。改译如下:

> According to Zhang Boli, TCM doctors today are mainly university-trained. In addition to TCM theories, TCM students must also take Western medicine courses, which account for 40% of their training. <u>All TCM students have some knowledge of Western medicine.</u>

本句还修改了"learning"的逻辑主语与句子主语 Western medicine courses 不一致的问题。

有时翻译出来显得多余或者低估读者智力(patronizing/condescending),也需要删除。例如:

> 应要求第三方产品或服务建立响应个人信息主体请求和投诉等的机制,以供个人信息主体查询、使用。

原译:

> The PI Controller shall require the third-party product or service provider to establish mechanisms to respond to the PI Subjects' requests, complaints, etc., <u>so that the PI Subjects can access and use</u>;

初读原译,还以为 access and use 后面少了宾语。再读原文,发现两个词的宾语就是 mechanism。但句子前半部分已经把意思表达清楚了——提供这样的机制就是为了使用,下面再把明摆的意思说出来,就是画蛇添足。改译:

> The PI Controller shall require the third-party product or service provider to establish mechanisms that respond to the PI Subjects' requests, complaints, etc.

改译还通过使用从句,把两个连续的不定式变为一个。

4.2.3 不该省的不省

变通原则还要求不该变通的时候不要变通,尤其是不要漏掉本应翻译的内容,也不要增加错误的内容。这里略举几例。

原文：

The term "traditional" <u>qualifies</u> a form of knowledge or an expression which has a traditional link with a community, meaning that it is developed, sustained and passed on within a community, sometimes through specific customary systems of transmission. It is the relationship with the community that makes knowledge or expressions "traditional".

原译：

"传统"表明知识或表现形式与某一社群有着传统联系，它在一个社群中发展、延续、代代相传，有时通过特定的习惯传递体制。所以是它与社群的这种关系使知识或表现形式变得"传统"。

原译的意思总体上并无大错，只是没有把 qualify 这个具有实质意义的词翻译出来。在重要的文件中，除非有充分理由，否则，所有具有实质意义的词都需要翻译出来。这里 qualify 的意思是 to limit the strength or meaning of a statement①，即"限制""限定"，翻译出来并不困难，所以改译为：

"传统"一词用于限定知识或表达的形式，表明该知识或表达形式与某一社群存在传统联系，是在该社群中形成、维系、传承的，有时还需要通过具体的传承制度加以传承。知识或文化表达形式与社群的这种关系，使之成为"传统"。

注意：原文表述有一定瑕疵。The term "traditional" qualifies a form of knowledge or an expression <u>which has a</u> traditional link with a community. 其中的 which has a… 需要改为 to indicate its… 才能清楚表达句子的逻辑关系。

下一个例子来自关于个人信息安全的国家标准。原文：

去标识化建立在个体基础之上，<u>保留了个体颗粒度</u>，采用假名、加密、哈希函数等技术手段替代对个人信息的标识。

原译：

De-identification is a concept based on individual personal informa-

---
① https://dictionary.cambridge.org, accessed March 21, 2021.

tion. It uses pseudonyms, encryption, hash functions and other technical means to replace the identifying element of personal information.

对照原文和原译，发现漏掉了下划线部分。可能是有意的，也可能是无意的。前者的可能性更大。实际上，个人信息保护的资料网上很多，下面是笔者查到的几段文字，可以从中借鉴译法：

De-identification is the process used to prevent someone's personal identity from being revealed. For example, data produced during human subject research might be de-identified to preserve the privacy of research participants.

When applied to metadata or general data about identification, the process is also known as data anonymization. Common strategies include deleting or masking personal identifiers, such as personal name, and suppressing or generalizing quasi-identifiers, such as date of birth. The reverse process of using de-identified data to identify individuals is known as data re-identification. Successful re-identifications cast doubt on de-identification's effectiveness.

其中可以借鉴"个人信息标识"的译法 personal identifiers。下面一段可以找到"颗粒度"的译法：

Granular data is detailed data, or the lowest level that data can be in a target set. It refers to the size that data fields are divided into, in short how detail-oriented a single field is. A good example of data granularity is how a name field is subdivided, if it is contained in a single field or subdivided into its constituents such as first name, middle name and last name. As the data becomes more subdivided and specific, it is also considered more granular.[①]

根据这些资料，原文的"个体颗粒度"应当是指"个体数据的颗粒度"。改译如下：

---

① https://www.techopedia.com/definition/31722/granular-data, accessed March 21, 2021.

De-identification is individually based and maintains data granularity. It uses pseudonyms, encryption, hash functions and other technical means to replace personal identifiers.

译者不能随意省略原文内容，也不能添加违背原文意思的内容，例如：

如果产品或服务的提供者提供工具供个人信息主体使用，提供者不对个人信息进行访问的，则不属于本标准所称的收集。例如，离线导航软件在终端获取个人信息主体位置信息后，如果不回传至软件提供者，则不属于个人信息主体位置信息的收集。

原译：

Where a product or service provider provides a tool for the personal information subject to use, but the provider does not access the personal information, ~~such act of obtaining the personal information by the provider~~ is not deemed an act of collecting for the purpose of this standard. For example, if an offline navigation software on the terminal obtains the personal information subject's location information, and if it does not transmit the information back to the software provider, then ~~such act of obtaining location information of the personal information subject~~ is not deemed an act of collecting for the purpose of this standard.

原文明明指出产品或服务的提供者并不收集信息，但初译者却增加了提供者收集信息的内容（删除部分），简直是画蛇添足。改译如下：

Where a product or service provider provides a tool for PI Subjects, but the provider does not access the PI collected by the tool, the situation is not deemed an act of collection for the purpose of this document. For example, if an offline navigation software on a terminal obtains a PI Subject's location information, the situation is not deemed an act of collection if the software does not transmit the information back to the software provider.

4.3 多说

4.3.1 译者现身

即使在非常严肃的文本中,译者有时也不得不通过译注让读者更清楚原文的意思。

下面一句话来自联合国国际法委员会的一份文件(A/CN.4/SR.3357):

> Draft guideline 9 was entitled "guiding principles on interrelationship", which suggested the existence of at least two principles. The text of the guideline, however, only identified one: a so-called "principle of interrelationship".

其中涉及英文复数形式如果有意义,应该如何翻译的问题。例如,如果英文原文是"person(s)",表明单复数是个重要问题,译文可以说"一人或多人";但此处的"guiding principles on interrelationship"翻译为"相互关系的多个指导原则"并不符合汉语习惯,因为"原则"在汉语中本来就可以理解为复数,而不用"多个"又不能表明"原则"是复数形式,从而与下一句话的逻辑脱节。在两难之中,译者不得不增加一个注释:

> 准则草案9的标题是"相互关系的指导原则"("原则"在英文中用复数形式),这表明存在至少两个原则。但是准则的案文只明确了一个原则,就是所谓的"相互关系原则"。

4.3.2 补充信息

有些文件十分严肃,译者会尽最大努力把全部信息都翻译出来,包括在行文中作适当解释或补充隐含的信息,例如(来自北京市政府工作报告):

> 完善整治类专项任务"动态清零"认定标准和长效机制,巩固"散乱污"企业治理、"开墙打洞"、违法群租房整治等治理成效,严

防新生反弹。

其中的"动态清零""长效机制""散乱污""开墙打洞",都通过调查研究,用最简单的语言作了解释:

We will improve the criteria for "<u>continuous clearance</u>" under special remediation operations and establish a <u>long-term mechanism to prevent relapse</u>. We will consolidate achievements in <u>shutting down small, unlicensed and polluting companies</u>, in cleaning up <u>shop fronts illegally modified from residential buildings</u>, and in rectifying illegal group lease.

如果中文简称包含的意思过于丰富,在正文作解释过于冗长,可以通过脚注加以说明。例如:

积极支持国防和军队改革,深化国防动员和<u>双拥共建</u>,人民防空工作得到加强,军民融合发展成效明显。

其中的"双拥共建"内涵十分丰富,正文先做简化处理(enhanced civil-military relations),再通过注释解释含义:

We have supported the military and national defense reforms, improved the capacity for national defense mobilization, and enhanced <u>civil- military relations</u>* and the civil air defense; civil-military integrated development has produced fruitful results.

注释:

*Known as *Shuangyong Gongjian*. *Shuangyong* refers to the tradition by which the government honors those in military service and their families, and the military honors the government and cares for the people; *Gongjian* means the military and the people working together to promote cultural progress. — Translator

如此处理的依据是:

Civil-military relations (Civ-Mil or CMR) describes the relationship between civil society as a whole (and its <u>civil authority</u>) and the military organization or organizations established to protect it.①

再举一例：

> 深入落实反恐"六住"措施，反恐防恐能力不断提升。

根据资料，"六住"措施是指：

> 盯住人、把住口、管住房、看住物、守住点、<u>控住面</u>。具体来说，就是盯住涉恐可疑人员，把住出入境口岸、环京外围检查站等通道，管住出租房屋、行业场所等易藏污纳垢部位，看住枪支弹药以及易制爆、易燃易爆等危险物品，守住重点要害部位以及公交、地铁、火车站、大型活动、人员密集场所等重点目标，<u>做好社会面安全防控工作</u>，坚决守住绝不发生暴恐活动的底线。

据此，决定把"六住措施"翻译为 six measures，再加注释：

> We have improved our counter-terrorism capability through "six measures"**.

脚注：
**These include suspect tracking, city border control, accommodation control, explosives control, critical venues control, and patrol service. — Translator

其中的"控住面"比较抽象，进一步查询，了解到主要是指"武装巡逻"：

> 中秋、国庆双节即将到来之际，全市公安机关严格按照市委、市政府和省公安厅的部署要求，紧密结合近期治安特点，进一步强化推进社会面治安防控，持续开展武装巡逻、应急处突等工作，全力维护全市社会治安持续稳定的良好局面。

英文讲求具体，因此，注释中直接翻译为 patrol service。

---

① https://en.wikipedia.org/wiki/Civil%E2%80%93military_relations, accessed March 21, 2021.

4.4 变换说法

4.4.1 超越字面

如果按字面翻译词不达意，可以换一种说法。例如：

这是世界知识产权组织（WIPO）文件中的一幅插图（见图4.1），所在部分介绍如何通过知识产权制度保护传统知识（Traditional Knowledge），包括中草药。需要翻译的是这幅插图的说明，即：

Caterpillars with emerging *Cordyceps sinesis*

图 4.1 某文件的插图及图片说明

Caterpillars with emerging *Cordyceps sinesis*。做一稿的同学译为"萌发出冬虫夏草的毛虫"。确实，如果去查 *Cordyceps sinesis*，所有资料给出的译文都是"冬虫夏草"，而 caterpillars 的对应词是"毛虫"，emerging 译为"萌发"，三者加起来可不就是"萌发出冬虫夏草的毛虫"？

但"萌发出冬虫夏草的毛虫"这个说法不合逻辑："冬'虫'夏草"里面已经有个虫子，难道是这个虫子长在另一个虫子身上？

为了弄清这个问题，就需要了解冬虫夏草到底是怎么回事。说实话，笔者在此次翻译之前，还真是不清楚，总是觉得这个东西冬天是虫子，夏天变成草，实在是太神奇。通过调查了解到：

> 通俗地讲，就是蝙蝠蛾为繁衍后代，产卵于土壤中，卵之后转变为幼虫；在此前后，冬虫夏草菌侵入幼虫体内，吸收幼虫体内的物质作为生存的营养条件，并在幼虫体内不断繁殖，致使幼虫体内充满菌丝，在来年的 5—7 月天气转暖时，自幼虫头部长出黄或浅褐色的菌座。菌座生长后冒出地面呈草梗状，就形成我们平时见到的冬虫夏草。因此，虽然兼有虫和草的外形，却非虫非草，属于菌藻类生物。[1]

---

[1] http://wap.zhongguotuijie.com/assets/health/zybk/zyck/12034.html, accessed March 21, 2021.

图 4.2　生长中的冬虫夏草

原来并不是虫子变成草,而是虫子身上长出"草"(真菌)!怪不得图片上有一半像虫子,它本来就是虫子!请看长在地里的虫草(见图 4.2):

现在明白了 WIPO 图片就是晒干的冬虫夏草。那么,能否直接看图说话,把图片说明译为"冬虫夏草"——无论英文怎么说?

译者心里想这么做,但担心审校问:你为什么只翻译了 Cordyceps sinesis(冬虫夏草),而没有翻译 caterpillars 和 emerging?

通过调查,发现 sinesis (sinensis) 的意思是 from China,Cordyceps 的意思是 club(棒)+ head(头部):

> Traditionally, *Ophiocordyceps sinensis* was classified under the genus *Cordyceps*. The etymology of the scientific name is from Latin: cord "club", ceps "head", and sinensis "from China".[①]

仔细观察地面的草,确实是一根短棒加上一个较粗的头部。这个样子的物件,中文里不是有一个现成的名字——叫"棒槌"吗?*Cordyceps sinesis* 的字面意思,不就是"中国棒槌"吗?Caterpillars with emerging *Cordyceps sinesis* 的字面意思不就是"长出中国棒槌的毛毛虫"吗?"长出中国棒槌的毛毛虫"又是什么呢?那不就是"冬虫夏草"吗?所以,这幅图片的说明完全可以翻译为"冬虫夏草"。如果有人不服气,你可以把以上论据拿出来。但如果没有做这些调查,你可能会被人家问住。

另外,既然"毛虫"是指"冬虫","中国棒槌"是指"夏草",Caterpillars with emerging *Cordyceps sinesis* 也可以译为"长出夏草的冬虫"。但"长出夏草的冬虫",仍然是冬虫夏草。是否需要翻译为"冬虫夏草——死去的毛虫身上长出了草"? 笔者认为,既然译文读者是中国人,而中国人通常都听说过冬虫夏草,这个解释没有必要。而且在联合国文件翻译中,一般会尽量避免增加译者注。

---

① https://microbewiki.kenyon.edu/index.php/Ophiocordyceps_sinensis, accessed March 21, 2021.

最后，英文说明 Caterpillars with emerging *Cordyceps sinesis* 也有些逻辑问题。emerging 用 -ing 形式，表示正在长出，但实际上图片展示的是已经采收并炮制好的冬虫夏草。如果要笔者修改，可以把 emerging 去掉。

4.4.2 编辑原文

原文表达不当之处，译者有义务作适当编辑。例如：

> 包括通过积极的行为作出授权（即明示同意），或者通过消极的不作为而作出授权（如信息采集区域内的个人信息主体在被告知信息收集行为后没有离开该区域）。

原译：

> Including authorization through active action (i.e. explicit consent) or through passive inaction (e.g. the personal information subject in the information collection area has not left the area after being informed that their information was going to be collected).

原文"消极的不作为"措辞不当，正确的措辞应该是"消极的行为"或简单说"不作为"，相对于"积极的行为"或"作为"。原译 passive inaction 犯了同样的错误。如果不确定如何表达，可以上网查资料（可查谷歌图书）（见图 4.3）：

> **3.3.1.2 Omissions count as practice**
> As summarized by one writer, what matters for the creation of customary norms is what 'States have done, or abstained from doing'.[195] Thus, both *positive* acts (actions) and *passive* acts (inaction, omission, abstention) are components of State practice.[196] Scholars generally recognize that in *certain circumstances* States' abstentions to take action can give rise to customary rules.[197] What matters is that the abstention is not ambiguous

图 4.3 "作为"和"不作为"英译查证

据此，可以改译：

> Including authorization through a positive act (i.e., explicit consent)

or through a <u>passive act</u> (e.g., PI Subjects in the information collection area have not left the area after being informed that their information was to be collected).

原文重复啰嗦之处，可以精简。例如：

> <u>我们已使用</u>符合业界标准的<u>安全防护措施保护您提供的个人信息</u>，防止数据遭到未经授权访问、公开披露、使用、修改、损坏或丢失。<u>我们会采取一切合理可行的措施，保护您的个人信息</u>。例如，……

原译：

> <u>We have employed security protection measures</u> according to industry standards <u>to protect your personal information</u>, prevent unauthorized access to, disclosure, use, modification, damage or loss of data. <u>We will take every practical measure to protect your personal information</u>. For instance…

原译下划线部分显得意思很重复，这是因为原文意思重复。译文可以进行适当合并编辑：

> We have employed reasonable and practical security measures in conformity with industry standards to protect your PI against unauthorized access, public disclosure, use, modification, damage or losses. The measures include…

下面这个例子选自北外招生宣传短片的字幕，为笔者的恩师——98岁高龄的陈琳教授谈北外英语教材的编写。大家注意下划线部分的时态。陈教授在描述自己一辈子教学生涯时，最初的时态有些不确定（"能够"和"干了"意思上有冲突），接下来的用词也给译者选择时态带来困扰。原译选择使用现在时和将来时，笔者的改译选择使用过去时和完成时，因为陈教授早已退休，是在回顾过去。

原文	原译	改译
在50年代中期的时候	As early as in the mid-1950s,	We began to compile our own textbooks
我们就自己开始编写教材了	we began to compile our own textbooks.	as early as in the mid-1950s.
那个是我们自己国家新编的	It was the first English textbook collection	These were the first English textbooks
新中国的第一套英语的教材	ever compiled by ourselves ever since the founding of the PRC.	published since the founding of the PRC.
我们的国家的人民需要外语	Our people need to learn foreign languages.	Our people needed to know foreign languages.
我们的国家的工作需要外语	Our country needs people who know foreign languages well.	Our country needed them to communicate with the world.
我这一辈子能够干了英语教学的工作	Since I <u>am devoted to</u> English teaching,	I <u>have taught</u> English my entire life.
那就要把我全身的力量	I <u>shall</u> devote myself	I <u>put</u> all my energy into this cause.
能够投入到这个	to this mission,	I am happy
能够为国家做一点有益的工作	<u>to do</u> something for my country.	<u>to have done</u> something useful for my country.
为什么	Why?	Why?
还是这五个字	Simply three words	The same answer
为人民服务	Serve the people.	We are serving the people.

  这个例子要说明的问题是，即使原文有些逻辑上的瑕疵，译文也应该加以改进，除非作者故意为之。特别是在翻译采访记录时，用词不当、逻辑不顺、语言啰嗦甚至表达失误的地方很常见，译者要借用翻译的机会，尽量让英语观众得到更加准确的信息。字幕的时间和空间限制，也要求译文尽量简洁。

4.4.3 纠正瑕疵

从笔者的经验来看，汉译英时需要变通的地方更多一些。一是因为笔者翻译的英文文件种类比较单一，基本上都是正式文件，译者的能动性较小，而汉语文件则五花八门，既有正式文件，也有广告宣传、解说字幕、摘要目录，有的文件翻译需要较大灵活性。二是因为很多汉语文件质量比较差，前言不搭后语的地方较多，译者不得不做较多编辑工作。请看这个广告牌（见图4.4）：

不清楚原译是怎么做出来的，显然不是正确的英文。如果按字面意思翻译，可以说：If you build fitness in a scientific way, the world will be more wonderful. 可是，大家仔细想一下：你身体好了，与世

图 4.4 某广告牌的英译

界精彩有关系吗？世界会因为你身体好坏而有改变吗？显然，原文本身也是逻辑不通。但作为译者，不能因为原文差而拒绝翻译。我们可以变通处理，让译文更有逻辑，例如翻译为：Keep fit to see wonders of the world. 这样翻译虽然不忠实于原文字面，但并不违背作者意图，甚至能更好地体现作者意图。这就是所谓的"目的论"（The Skopos Theory），即根据翻译的目的，决定是否对原文进行变通取舍、加工改造。

4.4.4 功能对等

在翻译广告、标牌的时候，我们经常寻找译入语中功能相近的说法，而不是按字面翻译。例如，右面的标识并没有逐字翻译，而是借鉴英语国家的类似说法（见图4.5）：

汉语中告诫行人不要践踏草地的说法数不胜数，每种说法都充满诗情画意，但所配译

图 4.5 较好的公共标识译例

图 4.6　有关爱护花草的各式错误翻译

文基本都是"神翻译"（见图 4.6）：

而在英语国家，同样的情况下并不用诗词去感化，而是直截了当地警告，表达方式不过三四种（见图 4.7）。

我们在翻译中文标牌时，以不变应万变，直接借用英语说法即可。

翻译具有文化特色的内容或跟语言特点相关的内容，也往

图 4.7　英语国家关于爱护花草的各式标识

往不得不作文化层面的转换。例如，新冠肺炎流行期间，美国政府抗疫不力，却拼命"甩锅"中国，外交部发言人华春莹在回答记者提问时说：

这些人试图制造出一只世界上最大的"锅"甩给中国，让中国成为最大的替罪羊。但这"锅"太大了，对不起，甩不出去的。

如果按照字面翻译为：

These people are trying to create the world's largest "pot" and throw it to China, making China the biggest scapegoat. But the pot is too big. I'm sorry. You can't throw it out.

英语中不存在 throw the pot 的说法，所以读者可能无法透彻理解。官网译文达意，但也没有译出幽默的效果：

They are trying to shift the biggest blame of the century to China and make it the biggest scapegoat. However, such an attempt is just impossible as the blame is too heavy to be shifted. Sorry, it won't work.

如何翻译才能既达意又有幽默效果，作为英语非母语的我们，并没有好的办法。笔者请教了北外高翻学院外教冯爱苏（Ursula Friedman）老师，她给出的译文如下：

These people are dumping all their manure on China, in an attempt to blame China for the world's problems. But China won't stand for this. The pile of dung is overflowing, and can't simply be tossed out quietly.

如果笔者来翻译，最多也就是翻译成这个样子：

These people are putting all the blame on China. But the blame is groundless and we simply cannot accept that.

如上例所示，语言中的隐喻，如果按照字面翻译无法理解，往往需要抛弃原文的表达方式，有时还会因此丧失表达的生动性。党政文献翻译中也有类似的例子。如：

有了学习的浓厚兴趣，就可以变"要我学"为"我要学"，变"学一阵"为"学一生"。（某时政文献）

出版的译文为：

With a keen interest in study we will be enthusiastic volunteers rather than reluctant conscripts, and study will be a lifelong habit instead of a temporary pastime.

四对引号中的内容都做了阐释性翻译，失去了原文的生动性。

再如：

"其实翻译成中医理论，炎症就是毒，凝血就是淤。"刘清泉接过了话茬儿。

原译：

"In fact, translated into the theory of Chinese medicine, inflammation is poison, and coagulation is stasis." Liu Qingquan <u>took over the stubble of the conversation</u>.

"接过话茬儿"是个隐喻。但把"茬"直接翻译为 stubble（麦茬、胡茬），在英语中没有意义。

Portrait of joyful adult stylish man with *stubble* is having pleasant *conversation* on modern smartphone. He is looking aside with wide smile wearing eyeglasses.

改译只翻译直白的意思：

"In fact, when translated into TCM terms, inflammation is called *du*, or poison, and coagulation is called *yu*, or stasis," Liu Qingquan joined the conversation and explained.

再例如：

"中国有<u>两套医学保驾护航</u>。真正把两种医学吃透了，优势互补，中西医结合不仅能实现，还能起到非常好的效果。"

原译：

"China has <u>two sets of medical escorts</u>. Only when the two medicines' disciplines can be thoroughly digested, with their complementary advantages, not only we could fuse the two systems, we could also obtain very good results."

"保驾护航"是个隐喻，但已经失去新意，没有必要按字面翻译。翻译背后的意思就足以起到沟通作用：

"China is protected by two medical systems. When you know the two systems well enough, you can take advantage of both. A combination of the two systems is possible and will produce excellent results."

另外,"中西医结合"本身不是目的,增强疗效才是目的。因此,"不仅……还能……"的说法比较勉强。这种不太严谨的表述在采访中经常出现,译文可以淡化不合逻辑之处。因此改译为"A combination of the two systems is possible and will produce excellent results."

陈明明大使在关于抗击疫情涉外翻译的一场讲座中提到,翻译表述要考虑外国人的理解习惯,必要时可适当灵活。例如,北京市健康宝的使用说明中有这样一句话:

红色状态:表明您符合集中隔离医学观察条件。

机器翻译:

Red status: indicates that you meet the conditions of centralized isolation medical observation.

改译:

The red code on the Health Kit indicates that you need to be quarantined in a designated facility.

大使提醒,此处"符合……条件"是委婉语,其意思是该隔离了,不宜机械地译为 you meet the condition of…。"meet the condition"有积极含义,指为了达到某项要求而应具备的条件。这就是功能对等的翻译观。

另外,笔者认为,原文此处的委婉语如果换成"表明您需要集中隔离,进行医学观察"也无不妥之处。这样的表述方式有助于提高翻译效率。但是,我们不能指望所有原文都以最便于翻译的形式呈现。译者必须具备变通能力,站在读者的角度传达作者的意思。

上述例子强调译文发挥的功能与原文对等,不强调文字层面的死板对应,这就是美国语言学家尤金・A. 奈达(Eugene Nida)提出的功能对等理论。

4.4.5 改变形式

变通还包括在信息的呈现形式上做些改进,例如把一长段拆分为几段,或者把一段之中的信息用图表和清单方式列举出来。例如,十九大报告的译文中就有这样的处理:

第二个阶段,从二〇三五年到本世纪中叶,在基本实现现代化的基础上,再奋斗十五年,把我国建成富强民主文明和谐美丽的社会主义现代化强国。到那时,我国物质文明、政治文明、精神文明、社会文明、生态文明将全面提升,实现国家治理体系和治理能力现代化,成为综合国力和国际影响力领先的国家,全体人民共同富裕基本实现,我国人民将享有更加幸福安康的生活,中华民族将以更加昂扬的姿态屹立于世界民族之林。	In the second stage from 2035 to the middle of the 21st century, we will, building on having basically achieved modernization, work hard for a further 15 years and develop China into a great modern socialist country that is prosperous, strong, democratic, culturally advanced, harmonious, and beautiful. By the end of this stage, the following goals will have been met: • New heights are reached in every dimension of material, political, cultural and ethical, social, and ecological advancement. • Modernization of China's system and capacity for governance is achieved. • China has become a global leader in terms of composite national strength and international influence. • Common prosperity for everyone is basically achieved. • The Chinese people enjoy happier, safer, and healthier lives. • The Chinese nation will become a proud and active member of the community of nations.

在《中国人权法治化保障的新进展》白皮书中,就出现了将长段切分为小段呈现信息的方法,请看:

> 依法保障公民在行政决策中的参与权。优化决策程序,把公众参与、专家论证、风险评估、合法性审查、集体讨论决定确定为重大行政决策法定程序。推行政府法律顾问制度和公职律师制度,推动

县级以上各级党政机关普遍设立法律顾问、公职律师，为重大决策、重大行政行为提供法律意见。探索建立行政决策咨询论证专家库，对专业性、技术性较强的决策事项组织专家、专业机构进行论证，提高依法行政的能力水平。有关部门在规范网约车、快递行业等民生领域事项决策过程中广泛征求各方意见，统筹兼顾不同群体的利益诉求。

Safeguarding in accordance with the law the citizens' right to participate in administrative decision making. The government has improved decision-making procedures, which define public participation, expert evaluation, risk assessment, legality review, and discussion and decision as the legal procedures for making major administrative decisions.

The central government has encouraged local governments at or above the county level to employ legal advisers and lawyers to provide legal opinions for major administrative decisions and actions.

China has also explored to set up a consulting expert database for administrative decisions. The governments invite experts and specialized institutes to discuss on those decision matters of strong professional or technological nature, so as to increase their capabilities in law-based administration.

When making decisions on people's livelihood like E-hailing and express delivery services, the related departments of the Chinese government solicited opinions from a wide range of circles to balance the interests and requests of different groups.

在处理信息集中的长段时，这种方法不仅能给读者一个清楚明了的视觉体验，省去阅读的烦恼，还能够凸显信息要点和重点。

4.5 小结

写作需要根据写作目的，对掌握的素材进行选择加工；翻译也同样需要根据翻译目的，决定是否对原文提供的素材进行加工取舍。有时需要严格按照原文翻译，有时则有一定的变通取舍余地。译者需要根据文本类型、作者的权威性、原文的质量、用户的翻译目的等客观情况，作出适当决定。

作为整个第二、三、四章的总结，翻译和创作都需要对相关素材有深刻的理解，都需要以通顺自然的语言表达出来，都需要根据需要对相关素材进行变通取舍，因此，翻译和写作极其相似，唯一的区别在于：翻译是表达别人的思想，创作是表达自己的思想。翻译和创作都是一种写作形式，都需要遵守写作的一般规律。

〔课后练习〕

1. 为什么需要对原文进行变通取舍？是否所有情况下都需要变通？
2. 有哪些变通取舍的办法？
3. 你在翻译实践中是否经常对原文进行编辑加工？

第五章　翻译是发现和解决问题的过程

扫码预习

请扫码下载本章涉及的例句。先做练习，再看解答，学习效果更佳。

　　翻译中遇到的问题不外乎三类：理解、表达、变通。翻译的过程是发现和解决这些问题的过程。

　　发现问题依靠逻辑思维、宏观思维、批判性思维。通过逻辑思维，可以发现字词之间、句子之间、段落之间的联系；通过宏观思维，可以发现前后文的关系以及篇章与外部世界的联系；通过批判性思维，可以发现原文的逻辑瑕疵与不合常理之处。宏观思维和批判性思维的基础是逻辑思维，批判性思维是逻辑思维的最高级形式。关于逻辑思维和宏观思维的更多论述和举例，见第七章"理解的思想方法和操作方法"。本章举例说明什么是批判性思维，以及如何通过批判性思维，发现翻译中的理解、表达、变通问题，并通过调查研究解决这些问题。

5.1　批判性思维

　　什么是批判性思维（critical thinking）？*Critical Thinking*（Bassham 等，

2012）一书这样解释：

> Often when we use the word *critical* we mean "negative and fault-finding." This is the sense we have in mind, for example, when we complain about a parent or a friend who we think is unfairly critical of what we do or say. But *critical* also means "involving or exercising skilled judgment or observation." In this sense critical thinking means thinking clearly and intelligently. More precisely, critical thinking is the general term given to a wide range of cognitive skills and intellectual dispositions needed to effectively identify, analyze, and evaluate arguments and truth claims; to discover and overcome personal preconceptions and biases; to formulate and present convincing reasons in support of conclusions; and to make reasonable, intelligent decisions about what to believe and what to do.[①]

笔者译文：

通常，"批评"或"批判"一词（critical）表达消极、挑剔的态度，比如，抱怨父母或朋友的"批评"不公，用的就是这个意思。但批评或批判还有"评判"或"评价"的意思。在这个意义上，"批判性思维"就是指清晰、理性的思考。更准确地说，批判性思维是个统称，指一系列的认知技能和智力倾向，只有具备这种认知技能和智力倾向，才能够有效认识、分析和评价一个论点或主张，发现并克服个人的先入之见和偏见，构思并提出支持论断的可信理由，并就该信什么、该做什么作出合理明智的决定。

我们在理解原文时，运用的正是批判性思维。我们总是假定待译文本前后一致、意思连贯，否则该文本就不值得翻译。在阅读原文时，我们力图发现原文的逻辑。如果发现某个地方逻辑不通，或与我们的知识或常识不符，就要通过查阅资料等手段，判断是我们的理解错误，还是原文本身不通。

---

① *Critical Thinking: A Student's Introduction*, Fifth Edition, Gregory Bassham, William Irwin, Henry Nardone, James M. Wallace, King's College, McGraw Hill, 2012.

在修改自己或别人的译文时，我们同样运用批判精神。两者的区别是，在阅读原文时，我们努力寻找原文符合逻辑的证据；在审校译文时，我们努力寻找译文不符合逻辑的证据，然后予以纠正。

笔者在网上看到这样一个关于误译的故事，反映了翻译中的批判性思维，翻译出来供大家参考：

> 有一部描写二战期间德军占领波兰的电影。在华沙，一群波兰艺术家决定加入波兰抵抗运动，但他们不敢肯定波兰抵抗运动是否仍在活动。一天晚上，他们到外边寻找抵抗运动的成员，突然，听到火车站传来一声剧烈的爆炸声。他们走近车站，其中一个人叫道："火车站被炸了！地下组织（Underground）还在活动！"葡萄牙语字幕是："火车站被炸了，但地铁（Subway）还在运营！"
>
> 这一误译说明了两点：第一，译者时刻不能忘记上下文。显然，译者在这里忘记了这群艺术家的目的是找到抵抗运动（即地下组织Underground，与地铁没有关系）。否则，错误本可以避免。第二，译者对任何事情都应该刨根问底，怀疑一切，包括自己翻译的初稿。这里，译者如果问一下自己："1940年华沙有地铁吗？"问题也许可以得到解决。事实上，华沙的地铁是几年前才建造的，大概是1996年！

在根据翻译活动的情景和用户要求灵活处理译文时，运用的仍然是批判性思维。下面分别从理解、表达、变通三个方面，举例说明批判性思维在翻译中的运用。

5.2 以批判性思维理解原文

5.2.1 发现事实真相

翻译不仅是翻译文字，而要透过文字了解作者希望表述的客观事实。如果原文的表达方法直译过去，无法向译文读者传达这一客观事实，译者有权使用他认为更好的表达方法。

例1.

当时，农业人口和非农业人口的收入水平，被估计为相差 3—6 倍。而从农业人口中选举出的全国人大代表所代表的人口数则 8 倍于从非农业人口中选举出的代表所代表的人口数。

这句话看来没有什么难处，可以按结构轻易转换为英语。原译：

At that time, income differences between the agricultural and non-agricultural population were estimated at 3-6 times, *whereas* deputies to the National People's Congress elected from the agricultural population represented a population 8 times the population represented by deputies elected from the non-agricultural population.

如果进一步思考："从农业人口中选举出的全国人大代表所代表的人口数则 8 倍于从非农业人口中选举出的代表所代表的人口数"这句话是什么意思？"从农业人口中选举出的全国人大代表"所代表的人数多，是因为中国的农民多，有什么不正常？为什么还用"而"表示转折？再者，从农业人口中选出的代表当然代表农民，但中国的农民虽多，也没有达到非农业人口的 8 倍，这句话到底是什么意思？作为一份学术研究报告，作者不可能突然冒出一句谁也不懂的话，这时就要深入研究，看上下文有没有线索；或者查人大的相关资料；或者询问作者。经过调查，译者发现这句话的意思是："如果一个非农业人口人大代表所代表的人数为 1000 人，那么一个农业人口代表所代表的人数为 8000 人！"这显然是不公平的，也是作者要指出的问题。原文使用的"而"字，应当理解为"而且"。原文的"全国人大代表"前如果加上"一个"，意思就明确多了。翻译为英语时，可以把意思进一步明确，而且"deputy"不能用复数形式：

改译：

At that time, their income differences were estimated at 3–6 times; *moreover*, the agricultural and non-agricultural population were not represented in the same proportion at the National People's Congress: the constituency represented by one deputy elected from the agricultural population is eight times the size of a constituency represented by one deputy elected from the non-agricultural population.

在这里，constituency 的意思是 "the whole body of voters, or a district or population, represented by a member of parliament, etc"。① 后来觉得以上翻译比较啰唆，于是又改为：

… moreover, the agricultural and non-agricultural population were not equally represented at the National People's Congress: a rural constituency is eight times the size of an urban constituency.

例 2.

The 1986 Childhood Vaccine Act requires *patient information on vaccines*, gives FDA authority to recall biologics, and *authorizes civil penalties.*

什么是"关于疫苗的病人信息"？什么是"授权民事处罚"？经过在网上查询该法有关内容，理解后翻译如下：

1986 年颁布的《儿童期疫苗法》要求向患者提供疫苗信息，赋予食品与药物管理局召回生物制剂的权力，并确定了民事罚款制度。

下面这个例子，选自程镇球（2002）先生的《翻译论文集》，也是运用批判性思维，发现问题、解决问题的很好例证：

例 3.

我们对于苏共中央先后两次提出的宣言草案，提出了自己的意见，并且在作了相当多的原则性的重大修改后，提出自己的修改草案。

We expressed our views on the two successive drafts put forward by the CC of the CPSU and *made* a considerable number of major changes of principle, which we presented as our own revised draft.

程先生指出，汉语原文意思有些含糊。可能会有人问：既然对苏联的

---

① *The Chambers Dictionary.* Copyright © 1994 by Chambers Harrap Publishers, Ltd. All rights reserved.

草案提出许多重大修改，为什么还要提出自己的草案？事实情况是，我们的草案就是经我们修改后的原苏联草案。所以，如果按字面翻译为"after many major changes of principle had been made, we provided our own draft"就不符合客观情况。

例 4.

（一位同学在一家媒体实习时，翻译过一个宣传片的字幕。视频中，一位自行车厂员工介绍该厂产能）"我们厂 3 条生产线，……，一分钟就能装好 8—9 台出口的自行车。"

这句话看似不难理解，最后一个分句机器翻译为：8–9 export bicycles can be installed in one minute。

该译法看似没什么问题。但按照机器翻译的译法理解，该厂一分钟就能安装 9 台自行车，即使是三条生产线，那每台生产线也仅需要 20 秒就能安装一台自行车。

该同学查看了视频中对应的画面（见图 5.1），还通过其他网上视频①和网页了解工厂里自行车的组装流程。该同学发现，每台自行车有几十个零部

图 5.1　自行车生产线

件，且每一步都需要工人站在生产线两侧手动安装，每一步安装都要很细致，节奏并不快。一台自行车从光秃秃的车架到全部零部件安装完毕、离开装配线，至少要几十分钟，绝非 20 秒就能完成。原文中"一分钟就能装好 8—9 台出口的自行车"产生歧义，实际意义应为"一分钟就有 8—9 台出口的自行车完成装配，从装配线上下来"。因此改译为：Every minute, eight bicycles for export come off the assembly lines.

---

① https://www.bilibili.com/s/video/BV1xJ41157kJ, accessed March 21, 2021.

5.2.2 澄清表达歧义

歧义（ambiguity）是指意思可以有多种解释。歧义分为两种：词汇歧义（lexical ambiguity）和句法歧义（syntactical ambiguity）。如"The school had many poor students on scholarships."其中的 poor 既可以理解为"贫穷的"，也可以理解为"成绩差的"，属于词汇歧义。"He did not marry her because he loved her."可以作两种解释："他因为爱她，所以没有与她结婚"或者"他不是因为爱她才与她结婚的"，属于句法歧义。

歧义可能是作者故意创造的，例如作者使用双关语、隐喻等模糊语言托物言志、借景抒情；歧义也可能是作者无意间造成的，如在讲话或写作的特定时间、地点、场合等背景下，本来没有歧义，只是读者不了解当时的背景情况，才导致歧义产生。

从使用情况来看，文学作品（如诗歌、幽默），经文等有意使用歧义的情况比较多，但即使在经文里面，"原文中的大多数歧义也是由于我们不了解文本的文化和历史背景产生的。"（Nida, 1986）[①] 就是说，这些作品里面的歧义也不是作者故意制造的。相反，信息性文本中的歧义多属于作者无意间造成的，但不排除也故意含糊的情况，如法律规定、政治决议等本来要求明白无误，但有时为了照顾不同的利益，不得不含糊其词，使各方均能按照自己的意思解释；在执行遇到问题时再想办法。

从歧义的处理方法来看，对于作者故意创造的歧义，翻译起来十分困难，因为译语很可能找不到一个与原文词语产生同样歧义的对等词或结构。译者往往需要想很多办法，包括通过注释或解释的方式进行翻译。很多时候译者可能根本没有注意到原文有歧义，而只是翻译了其中的一个意思。关于如何翻译作者刻意制造的歧义，这里不详细讨论。

对于作者无意造成的歧义，在翻译时应当运用批判性思维，通过上下文、背景知识、常识和逻辑，推断作者的真实意思，然后予以准确传递。如通过常识判断，上文中的 The school had many poor students on scholarships.

[①] "Most ambiguities in the original text are due to our own ignorance of the cultural and historical backgrounds of the text."

恐怕只能是指贫困学生。从逻辑上判断，He did not marry her because he loved her.恐怕只能解释为"他不是因为爱她才与她结婚的。"以下再举几例。

例 5.

  血源性疾病是一个长期存在的严重问题，艾滋病同梅毒、乙型肝炎、丙型肝炎一样可以通过血液传播。据1992年组织进行的第二次全国肝炎流行病学调查结果表明：中国人群中乙肝病毒平均感染率在60%左右，表面抗原阳性携带近10%。中国发现的供血（浆）员艾滋病病毒感染者大部分合并有乙型肝炎、丙型肝炎感染。这就提示艾滋病病毒也能和乙肝、丙肝一样以相同的方式广泛传播。而艾滋病病毒血源性传播的后果是将远远超过其他血液源性传播疾病的。

10%是否是60%当中的10%，还是与60%并列？这是句法结构引起的歧义，从语言本身难以找到答案，如果直译，可以翻译为：

  Findings of the 1992 national epidemiological investigation for hepatitis showed that hepatitis B virus infections among the Chinese population groups averaged about 60%, nearly 10% had a positive surface antigen.

但意思不明确。用 Google 搜索文本外的资料，发现 10% 是指中国人群的 10%，所以翻译为：

  The national epidemiological investigation for hepatitis conducted in 1992 found that *among different Chinese population groups*, an average of about 60% were infected with HBV (hepatitis B virus), and nearly 10% were HbsAg (hepatitis B surface antigen) carriers.

例 6.

  土地资源是三大地质资源（矿产资源、水资源、土地资源）之一，是人类生产活动最基本的资源和劳动对象。人类对土地的利用程度反映了人类文明的发展，但同时也造成对土地资源的直接破坏，这主要表现为不合理垦殖引起的水土流失、土地沙漠化、土地次生盐碱化及土壤污染等，而其中水土流失尤为严重，乃当今世界面临的又一个严重危机。据估计，世界耕地的表土流失量约为 230 亿吨/年。

这也是一个句法有歧义的句子。"不合理垦殖引起的"修饰一个短语还是几个短语？从上下文看，"不合理垦殖引起的水土流失、土地沙漠化、土地次生盐碱化及土壤污染等"是"人类对土地的利用……造成对土地资源的直接破坏"的具体化，如果"人类对土地的利用＝不合理垦殖"，那么，"土地资源的直接破坏＝水土流失、土地沙漠化、土地次生盐碱化及土壤污染等"。所以，"不合理垦殖引起的"修饰一串短语。所以译为：

> Land is one of the three major geological resources (mineral, water and land). It is a resource that provides the basis for Man's production and labor activities. Although *exploitation of land resources* reflects the degree of development of a civilization, it destroys the land. Such destruction is often the result of *unsound cultivation practices that cause soil erosion, desertification, secondary salinization, or soil pollution.* Soil erosion is the most serious problem and is one crisis that the world is facing today. According to estimation, topsoil loss from the world's arable land is about 23 billion tonnes a year.

例 7.

某双语词典对 hayride 一词的英语释义是：

> Hayride: A ride taken for amusement, usually by a group of people in the evening in a wagon or other vehicle piled with hay or straw.

翻译是：

> 乘装有干草无蓬卡车夜游，常指一群人在夜间乘坐马车或其他装着干草或麦秸的车辆进行的娱乐性旅行。

暂不评论其他部分译文是否准确，只看"in a wagon or other vehicle piled with hay or straw"一个短语的翻译。是译为"马车或其他装着干草或麦秸的车辆"还是"装着干草或麦秸的马车或其他车辆"？从逻辑上不难判断应当是后者。一句话在没有上下文时，可以有多种解释；一旦确定上下文，解释只有一种，除非作者是在玩文字游戏。

5.2.3 明确逻辑关系

有时原文会缺少一个逻辑环节，或逻辑关系不甚明确，译文往往需要补充出来或予以明确意思才完整。

例 8.

在文本中，国务院、法院、检察院同由人民代表大会产生，在实际中，法院和检察院比国务院低半个级别。这种制度安排到了地方上，就会使行政机关有可能影响司法。

In the legal texts, the State Council, the Supreme People's Court, and the Supreme People's Prosecution Office are all created by the National People's Congress, *and therefore are equal*; in reality, the court and the prosecution office are half a rank lower than the State Council. Such institutional arrangements make it possible for local executives to interfere with the judiciary.

原文省略了逻辑中的一环：国务院、法院、检察院同由人民代表大会产生，所以级别相当。译文中补充了这个意思，以更好与下文的"低半级"相衔接。

例 9.

社会保障的支出是随着市场经济的增长或下降的运行变化情况而增减的。在经济发展强劲、失业率下降时，社会保障的支出会进行相应的缩减，社会保障基金的存储规模必然会因此增大，从而减少社会需求的急剧膨胀；而当经济衰退、失业增加时，社会保障的支出会相应地增多，给失去职业和生活困难的人们提供相应的购买能力，唤起社会的有效需求，并在一定程度上促进社会的经济复苏。

In a market economy, social security spending levels fluctuate in inverse proportion to economic growth. When the economy is booming and unemployment is low, spending falls, resulting in increase in the net balance of funds in the social security account. This will help curb the expansion of demands. In times of recession and high unemployment, spending increases, as benefits are paid out to individuals who have been laid off and who require temporary assistance. This results in increased purchasing power and effective demand, and helps, in a certain extent, in economic recovery.

单看加点部分，还以为社会保障支出随着经济的增长而增加；看完这一段，才知道两者是反比关系。译文用 fluctuate，避免原文措辞可能引起的误导。

例 10.

通过对几种权威的电子出版物和出版物的检索及网络上的查找，选出法律及其他文献 300 余种，分为两类……

Drawing on several authoritative *electronic publications*, *paper publications*, and the Internet, I have selected more than 300 legal and other texts. They fall into two types …

"出版物"包括"电子出版物"，不能并列。所以，译文明确"出版物"实际是指 paper publications。

例 11.

血站和单采血浆站是由卫生行政部门设置的卫生事业单位。

Whole blood stations and blood plasma-only stations are non-profit health institutions set up by health administrative authorities.

此例问题同上。再举一个较为复杂的例子：

例 12.

Please outline the measures, both legislative and practical, preventing entities and individuals from recruiting, collecting of funds or soliciting other forms of support for terrorist activities to be carried out inside or outside Norway, including in particular:

— *the carrying out, within or from Norway, of recruiting, collecting of funds and soliciting of other forms of support from other countries; and*

— deceptive activities such as recruitment based on a representation to the recruit that the purpose of the recruitment is one (e.g. teaching) different from the true purpose and collecting of funds through front organisations.

译文 1：

请概述挪威已制定哪些立法和实际措施，防止实体和个人为在挪威境内或境外开展恐怖活动而招募成员、筹集资金或争取其他形式的支持，尤其是

——在挪威境内或从挪威境内招募人员、筹集资金和向其他国家争取其他形式的支持；以及

——欺骗活动，例如在招募时向应招者隐瞒招募的真实目的（如谎称招聘教师）以及通过掩护组织筹集资金。

译文 2：

……在挪威境内或从挪威开展从其他国家招募人员、筹集资金和争取其他形式支持的活动……

译文 3：

……在挪威境内或以挪威为基地招募人员、筹集资金和从其他国家争取其他形式的支持……

译文 4：

……在挪威境内招募人员、筹集资金和争取其他形式支持，或以挪威为基地，从其他国家招募人员、筹集资金和争取其他形式的支持……

显然，第四种译法更符合逻辑。第一种译法有歧义，可以理解为禁止：

- 在挪威境内招募人员、筹集资金和向其他国家争取其他形式的支持
- 从挪威境内招募人员、筹集资金和向其他国家争取其他形式的支持

这时，我们的疑问是："在挪威境内"和"从挪威境内"有什么区别？也可以理解为（禁止）：

- 在挪威境内招募人员、筹集资金
- 从挪威境内招募人员、筹集资金
- 向其他国家争取其他形式的支持

这时,我们的疑问除了第一个外,还有:"在挪威争取其他形式的支持"是否包括在内?显然,这一译法无法自圆其说。

第二种译法可以理解为禁止:

- 在挪威境内开展从其他国家招募人员、筹集资金和争取其他形式支持的活动
- 从挪威开展从其他国家招募人员、筹集资金和争取其他形式支持的活动

我们的疑问是:

- "在"和"从"有什么区别?
- "在挪威境内招募人员、筹集资金和争取其他形式的支持"是否包括在内?

第三种译法可以理解为禁止:

- 在挪威境内招募人员、筹集资金
- 以挪威为基地(从其他国家)招募人员、筹集资金
- 从其他国家争取其他支持

这一译法,把 from 的意思表达清楚了,但我们还有一个疑问:是否禁止在挪威境内"争取其他形式支持"。从逻辑来看,是要禁止的,但文字上有漏洞。

第四种译法可以理解为禁止:

- 在挪威境内招募人员、筹集资金和争取其他形式支持
- 以挪威为基地,从其他国家招募人员、筹集资金和争取其他形式的支持

虽然麻烦一点儿,但逻辑上填补了以上漏洞。

本例造成翻译错误的原因，是原文企图把太多的东西糅在一起，导致句子结构的多种解释。所以，对于斩不断、理还乱的句子，要批判性地阅读和思考，根据上下文逻辑关系、背景资料和常识，重新组织，不能硬译。要力图使译文清晰易懂，真正起到沟通的作用。

下面是同一句话的西班牙语和法语翻译，学习过这两种语言的读者可看意思是否清楚：

西班牙语：

Sírvanse explicar las normas y prácticas vigentes para impedir que las en-tidades y los particulares recluten a personas, recauden fondos o recaben otro tipo de apoyo para realizar actividades terroristas dentro y fuera de Noruega, incluidas en particular:

La realización dentro de Noruega o desde Noruega de actividades encami-nadas a reclutar, recaudar fondos y recabar apoyo de otra índole de otros países; y

Las actividades engañosas, como el reclutamiento de una persona a la que se manifiesta que va a ser contratada con un objetivo (impartir enseñan-za), pero el verdadero objetivo es recaudar fondos mediante organizacio-nes que sirven de fachada.

法语：

Veuillez décrire les mesures législatives et les mesures pratiques destinées à empêcher des entités et des particuliers de recruter des personnes, de collecter des fonds ou de solliciter toute autre forme d'appui en vue d'activités terroristes à exécuter sur le territoire national ou à l'étranger, en particulier les activités ci-après:

Le fait de recruter des personnes, de collecter des fonds, de solliciter toute autre forme de soutien provenant d'autres pays, et ce, sur le territoire national ou à l'étranger;

Les activités reposant sur une tromperie, comme le fait de recruter des personnes en justifiant ce recrutement par un but différent (par exemple, l'enseignement) du but véritable et de collecter des fonds par l'entremise d'organisations de la ligne de front.

附带说明，即使在英语作为世界性语言的今天，许多英语文件都不是英语是母语的人写的，文字上的问题很多，造成意思含糊不清，甚至理解困难。

从翻译的最终目的来看，翻译是为了交流，不是文字转换。所以，原文的含糊不清之处，除非是作者故意为之，译文均应当做到清楚、通顺，就好比原文作者用母语写的。遇到词不达意的地方，应当通过批判性思考，发现问题，并通过常识、上下文或有关资料，吃透原文含义，把意思表达得比原文更清楚。笔者不同意译文无须高于原文的观点。

另外，"原文表达不清，译文也应该不清"的想法对原文作者是不公平的。作者之所以写出蹩脚的英文，不是故意的，而是英语能力不足，如果让他用自己的母语起草，肯定不会如此。原文作者如果知道你故意把他的东西翻译得文理不通，一定会非常生气。

5.2.4 识别原文瑕疵

翻译时只要努力理解原文，核对自己没有把握的事实，很容易发现原文的错误。译者对于是否指出和改正原文错误有不同看法。实践中原文错误的处理方法有四种：在译文中改正，不加说明；在译文中改正，加以说明；照原样译出，不加说明；照原样译出，加以说明。从各方面看，改正或指出原文错误更为可取。

发现原文错误

译者是最细心的读者。专业译员不是翻译文字，而是翻译意思。他十分注意文章的内在联系，注意文章的连贯性，对于自己不敢确定的事实，都要一一核实，决不想当然。所以，除了显而易见的打印错误外，译者时常发现原文的笔误和事实性错误。

发现原文错误并不是一件困难的事情，我们不需要去主动寻找。翻译时，只要把自己作为一个真正需要了解原文提供信息的读者，而不是一个

"翻译"，从而真正去理解上下文逻辑关系，按照常识及各种背景知识做出判断，对原文事实进行核实，会很容易发现原文的不当或错误之处（如果有）。这里略举几例。南斯拉夫提交联合国的报告中有这样一段话：

> At the beginning of 1997 macroeconomic indicators showed a decline in industrial output, retail trade and exports. All this led to the drop in GDP in that year by one-fifth of its value in 1998 (-19.3%). Thus, the FRY entered the last year of the 20th century as one of the poorest countries in Europe.

> 1997年初，南斯拉夫联盟共和国宏观经济指数表明，工业产出、零售和出口呈下降趋势，导致1999年国内总产值比1998年下降五分之一（负19.3%），因此，进入20世纪最后一年时，南斯拉夫联盟共和国成为欧洲最贫困的国家。

原文说1997年GDP比1998年下降五分之一，又说1997年是20世纪最后一年，这显然不符合逻辑。最合理的猜测（也是唯一的可能）是作者笔误，把1999误为1997。经与审校协商，译文直接改正，没有报请有关部门更正原文。审校认为，这样改正没有疑问。再者，报告来自南斯拉夫国内，即使问联合国文件控制部门，那里的人也无法做出决定，让他们再联系南斯拉夫国内十分麻烦，说不定是南斯拉夫翻译的错。

另有一篇英文提到7 bore 62mm AK rifles。我们不懂枪械。查字典发现，bore与枪械有关的意思有"枪膛""口径"。那么，"7枪膛/口径62毫米步枪"是什么意思？好像说不通。怀疑原文有问题。用关键词查Google发现这样的信息："AK-47式7.62mm突击步枪是苏联著名枪械设计师卡拉什尼科夫设计的，俗称冲锋枪……"数字、型号太巧合，7.62mm也是指口径，所以，一定是原文笔误，不管原文如何改，该短语的意思应该是"口径为7.62mm的AK式步枪"。

一篇文章谈到中国的法制历史时说："……1860—1949年，被现代化时期。其中，1990年以前属于中华法系时期，1990年以后，属于学习、模仿西方现代法制时期，1924年以后，属于党治时期……"显然，"1990年"是错误的。查资料无法确定正确的年代，只能与作者核实。作者更正为

"1900 年"。

还有的错误是在核对有关事实时偶然发现的。如有这样一段话：

> 中国在 1995 年签字加入的《巴黎宣言》宣称："不管其性别、种族、宗教、民族背景、社会地位或健康状况（包括 HIV 感染）如何，每个人均有被别人宽容的权利和宽容他人的责任。"

如果引用国外资料，最好能够找到原文。实在找不到时，变为间接引语翻译意思。在查找这段引文的原文时，发现《巴黎宣言》中并没有这段话。这段话来自联合国艾滋病规划署主任皮奥特博士在某一场合的讲话。通知作者后，作者改为：

> 中国政府的卫生部早在 1995 年发布的《世界预防和控制艾滋病日主题：共享权利，同担责任》中即引用联合国艾滋病规划署主任皮奥特博士的话，宣称……

译文：

> In its World AIDS Day 1995: "Shared Rights, Shared Responsibilities", the Ministry of Health quoted Dr. Peter Piot, Director of the United Nations Program on HIV/AIDS, as saying . . .

处理原文错误

在翻译中如何处理原文的错误，是每个译员都会遇到的问题。就笔者个人而言，如果属于打印错误或笔误，且自己可以肯定正确内容的，翻译时不请示作者或委托人，自行改正，在提交译文时说明原文有哪些问题，请作者修改原文；如果发现事实错误，则告诉委托人或作者，请修改后再译。无法与作者取得联系的，将错误之处译出，向委托人说明。

据了解，各翻译公司和机构的翻译部门对于如何处理原文错误，有不同的做法。有的公司在服务合同中规定，译者有义务指出原文的错误或疏漏[1]；有的公司在服务合同中规定，译者无义务指出原文错误、疏漏

---

[1] "The Company shall be under an obligation to indicate or correct errors or omissions in original material supplied by the Client." http://www.astls.co.uk, accessed September 2, 2004.

或不准确之处，但可以提醒客户注意这些问题可能存在[①]；有的翻译公司在其标准服务合同中明确表示，译者没有义务指出或纠正原文出现的错误[②]；也有的翻译公司把发现和纠正原文错误作为一项增值服务推销给客户。[③]

国际公务员制度委员会（ICSC）[④]人事政策司在其《工作分类手册和用户指南》第一卷中，对联合国系统笔译和审校的工作描述包括："发现原文明显或可能的错误，并酌情告知编辑或作者。"[⑤] 据了解，在纽约联合国中文处，作为一般译员，发现原文有误或怀疑原文有误时，按以下处理方法处理：

> 对于明显的印刷错误或笔误，译者能够改正的，在译文中改正，并在译稿上注明，由审校定夺是否报告有关部门修改原文；译者无法改正的，与资深译员协商，必要时报请有关部门，要求作者澄清。对于实质性错误（推理错误、事实错误等），译者要译出，并在翻译稿上注明，请审校定夺是否报告有关部门修改原文，译者无权自行改动原文。

国外的翻译工作者采取的方法也不外乎以上几种，这里引述一位日本专利文件翻译工作者 William Lise 的几段话：

---

① Teknos will not be under any obligation to correct or indicate any errors, omissions or inaccuracies found in the text of a document submitted for translation, but may draw these to the Client's attention, particularly if they impact the accuracy of the translation." http://www.teknos-translations.co.uk/terms.htm, accessed September 2, 2004.

② "SBC shall be under no obligation to correct or indicate errors in the original language." www.sbcco.com, accessed September 2, 2004.

③ "A professional translator has good knowledge of his/her fields of expertise, to such an extent that errors in the original text (not so infrequent as one might expect) can be detected and corrected, thus offering their clients a value-added service." http://www.languagesrus.com/interviews.htm, accessed September 2, 2004.

④ The International Civil Service Commission (ICSC) is an independent expert body established by the United Nations General Assembly. Its mandate is to regulate and coordinate the conditions of service of staff in the United Nations common system, while promoting and maintaining high standards in the international civil service.

⑤ "spot manifest or possible errors in the original text and inform the editor and the author when appropriate." http://icsc.un.org/ppd/index.htm, accessed September 2, 2004.

原文错误：在翻译过程中，我经常发现作者的错误，例如引用标记错误，对照附图错误，从属权利要求中引用的独立权利要求错误等。在翻译专利文件时，如果译者努力去理解专利内容（并非所有译者都这样做），上述错误是很容易发现的。原文出现错误时，有几种处理方法：一是自行改正，加批注说明。如果可以肯定原文有误，并知道如何修改，就直接把正确内容纳入译文，并用 Word 的批注功能，标出修改的地方。大多数客户对这种做法表示满意，而不希望把错误留在译文中。

二是把错误译出，加批注说明。如果发现错误，但不敢肯定如何修改，就采用这一方法。例如，有时我发现文中使用“上述”二字，但上文却没有相应的内容。

三是把错误译出，不加说明。应该说，这种方法是不能采用的，但我听到有些同事支持这种做法。他们认为，识别原文错误根本就不是译者的分内的事。

由于客户是日本人，批注以日语做出（这一点恐怕是不言自喻的）①

从以上论述可以看出，对于是否指出和修改原文错误，译者有不同的意见和做法。下例中，译者直接纠正了原文笔误：

The great pre-Socratic systems that we have been considering were confronted, in the latter half of the fifth century, by a skeptical movement, in which the most important figure was Protagoras, chief of the Sophists.

这是《西方哲学史》第十章首句。原文中的时间为五世纪下半叶，而实际上前智者时期是在公元前。查证 Protagoras 的生卒年份，是前五世纪下半叶，而不是五世纪下半叶（见图 5.2）：

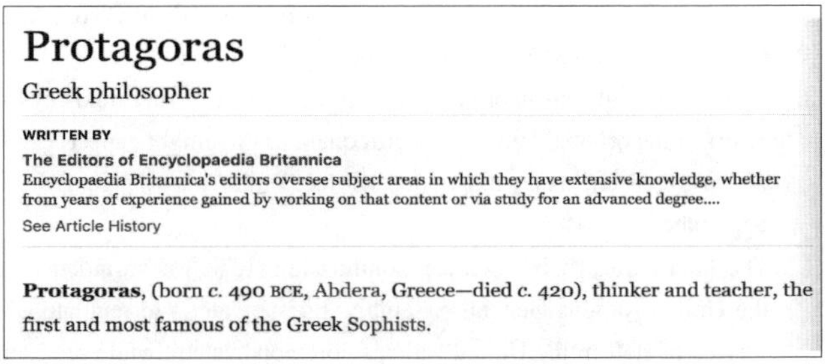
Protagoras
Greek philosopher

WRITTEN BY
The Editors of Encyclopaedia Britannica
Encyclopaedia Britannica's editors oversee subject areas in which they have extensive knowledge, whether from years of experience gained by working on that content or via study for an advanced degree....
See Article History

Protagoras, (born *c.* 490 BCE, Abdera, Greece—died *c.* 420), thinker and teacher, the first and most famous of the Greek Sophists.

图 5.2　Protagoras 的介绍

① http://www.lise.jp/approach.html, accessed September 2, 2004.

何其武的中译本直接改正错误,译为:

> 我们所考察过的前苏格拉底时期的那些伟大的体系,在公元前五世纪后半叶就遭到了怀疑运动的反对。怀疑运动中最重要的人物就是智者派领袖普罗泰哥拉。

提供增值服务

从客户来看,肯定欢迎译者指出原文错误。① 在翻译作为商业性服务的今天,如果客户能够为这一增值服务提供相应的酬谢,必定可以鼓励译者指出原文的错误。原文错误带来的消极影响,毕竟要比支付一点翻译费用大得多。况且,如果客户专门雇用审校人员,也是要付费的。确实有用户因译者指出错误而给译者奖励的。纽马克举了一个例子:一位荷兰译者因指出一篇财经文章里的错误得到了三倍于平时翻译的报酬(Newmark, 2001)。

从商业交易的角度看,译员或翻译公司把自己工作的"副产品"——发现的原文错误——拿来交换应该无可厚非。工业生产中的副产品也不是白白扔掉的。关于"副产品"的交易可以在"买卖合同"中加以规定。在纯粹的商业翻译中,可以做到这一点。即使客户不愿付费,与其将副产品白白扔掉,也不如送人落个人情,同时也提高了自己的声誉。

从译者对自己角色的定位来看,如果你认为自己的任务是翻译文字,当然没有必要指出(当然也不容易发现)原文的错误,即使客户要求,你也可以说我没有发现;如果你认为自己的任务是帮助别人沟通,则肯定会主动指出(当然也会更容易发现)原文错误,即使客户没有要求。笔者认为,后者应当是翻译工作者的态度。对于机构内部翻译人员来说,更应当强调团队精神,与文件起草部门合作,提高各种语言文本的质量。

当然,有时译者受客观条件限制,无法与作者取得联系,或许作者早已离开人世,这时,本着对读者负责的态度,要把原文错误之处改正过来,必要时加注说明;或者将错误译出,以注释方式说明原文有误,并提供调查结果。

---

① 这里是一封委托人的感谢信: "... First of all thank you for the file where you indicated errors in the English original. I am sure the client will appreciate it as much as I do. Not many translators will spend their valuable (let alone, unpaid) time for correcting errors in the original text! As far as my many thanks is concerned, you deserved it!" http://users.otenet.gr/~alsims/docs/comments.htm, accessed September 2, 2004.

特殊情况下，原文出现的错误不能更改。如为维护毛利人使用本民族语言的权利，新西兰 Waikato 大学制定了使用毛利语进行学术评价的政策，允许毛利人用本族语撰写论文，并用本族语评阅；但在找不到毛利语评阅人时，则指定译员负责将毛利语论文翻译为英语，再予以评阅。对译者的要求是："不纠正原文出现的错误，不进行润色，但可以向评阅人指出含混不清之处。必要时，评阅人可以要求论文译者澄清译文，但禁止学生和译者之间的接触，当然也禁止学生与评阅人的接触。"①

5.3 以批判性思维改善表达

5.3.1 体现作者意图

译者不仅要知道作者说什么，还要努力搞清楚作者为什么这么说。清楚作者的意图后，我们就可以更好地选择翻译策略，否则，译文只能亦步亦趋：

例 13.

"儿童公园是什么？我从来没听说过。"七岁的小姑娘晶晶怯生生地问老师。她是父母到杭州打工后出生的，父母一天到晚忙着卖大饼油条的生意。节假日城里的孩子能与大人外出旅游，她想都不敢想，因为那时候父母总是最忙碌的。（来自北外高翻学院入学试题）

"What's the Children's Park? I have never heard of it," a 7-year-old girl asked her teacher shyly. She was born after her parents migrated to Hangzhou in search of work. Now they are busy selling *fast food* from morning to night. She cannot imagine spending holidays away from home with her parents, as the urban children do, because her parents are most busy during that period.

"大饼和油条"难倒了不少人。出现很多种译法，如：pie and deep-fried twisted dough sticks, a kind of large flatbread and *youtiao*。文化词语的翻译，不同场合有不同的处理方法。如果出现在菜谱中，恐怕不仅要给出详细的英

---

① http://www.waikato.ac.nz, accessed September 2, 2004.

语解释，还要给出汉语拼音，再给出用料和制作方法。出现在这样一篇报道中，就没有必要那么复杂，分散读者的注意力。如果翻译为拼音，读者只知道是一种东西（从搭配 selling 可以推测出），也许是高档的、特殊的东西。如果翻译为 a kind of large flatbread and deep-fried twisted dough sticks，读者知道是一种食品，可能极力想象这种东西是什么样子，但无法知道它的档次。如果我们问一下自己，作者写大饼油条的意图是什么，也许可以帮我们找到翻译策略。笔者想，作者想要表达的，不过是说她的父母在忙于料理一个小本生意，更具体一些，在卖一种普通快餐。这时，简单翻译为 fast food 或 snacks 就足以传达作者的意图，也不会分散读者的注意力，甚至可以翻译得更笼统：busy running their small business。当然，也可以翻译为美国或英国人经常吃的快餐，但细心的读者会问：中国人也吃这个吗？

例 14.

目前，伊利产品已经广销全国 30 个省市自治区的 500 多个大中城市。

Now Yili products are sold in more than 500 medium and large cities in *nearly every province.*

作者说"30 个省市自治区"的意图是什么？仅仅是想告诉读者这个事实，还是说产品几乎销售到全国所有地方？中国读者读到"30"，想到的是全国各地；外国人知道中国有几个省吗？会产生同样的联想吗？所以，如果翻译为 ... in 30 provinces, municipalities and autonomous regions of China 不一定能更好传递作者的信息。

例 15.

乙方在代理该产品期间，必须严格遵守诚实可信的商业道德，不得更换产品的包装或经销假冒伪劣产品欺骗消费者，若有违反，甲方有权取消乙方代理资格，并保留诉讼的权利。（某合作意向书）

Party B, as a sales agent for Party A, must act in good faith and may not change the packaging of the products or *sell counterfeits.* If Party B fails to comply, Party A has the right to terminate the agency and retains the right to take legal action.

原文是不严谨的。"假、冒、伪"可以认为是同义词，都可以翻译为 counterfeit / fake / phony (products)；"劣质"产品是 inferior products，不一定是假冒的。"假冒伪劣"产品就是"counterfeit and inferior products"。乙方不得销售"假冒甲方的产品"可以理解，但乙方销售其他品牌的劣质产品与甲方有何关系？中方（甲方）的意思更有可能是把"假冒伪劣"作为同一概念理解的，即伪劣产品也是指假冒甲方的产品。所以这里的"伪劣"已经包含在"假冒"当中，不用译出。这样翻译应不违反合同双方的意图。

5.3.2 确保逻辑连贯

有些句子直译出来看似没有问题，但仔细进行逻辑分析就会发现，译文逻辑上出现脱节。这是由于原文不够严谨，导致关系密切的两部分被其他句子隔开，这时需要对句子进行局部调整：

例 16.

为鼓励乙方组织更多学生来华学习，甲方决定给乙方以如下优惠政策：即每班每期不少于 10 人，每超 5 人，学费可减免 10%（食宿及生活费不在此列）。为确保学习质量，每班限报 30 人。

如果翻译为：

In order to encourage Party B to bring more students to China, Party A offers the following favorable policy to Party B: each class may not have less than 10 students; for every additional 5 persons, the tuition may be reduced by 10% (not including boarding and living expenses). In order to guarantee quality of study, each class may not exceed 30 students.

就显得语气不连贯，因为所谓的优惠政策是指学费减免，"即每班每期不少于 10 人"并非优惠政策，而是苛刻的条件。译文中"favorable policy"距离所说明的"be reduced"太远，所以可以改为：

As an incentive for Party B to bring more students to China, *Party A offers to reduce the tuition* (excluding board & lodging and living expenses) *by* 10% for every additional 5 persons above 10 in each class. Each class may not have less than 10 students and to ensure quality, may not exceed 30.

5.3.3 纠正原译问题

翻译是一个永远没有结束的过程，无论是自己的译文，还是别人的译文，什么时候拿起来，只要以批判的眼光去看待，总是可以发现问题。笔者并不是要求译文完美。译文永远做不到完美。笔者只是强调，有时翻译时会想当然，结果译文不符合常识，在校订译文时一定把好最后一关。

例 17.

先看原译文：

图腾作为重要的文化被用来防止一个部族的灭亡、识别构成朝代古代文明的不同部族。

因为逻辑不通（图腾如何防止部族灭亡？构成古代文明的不同部族又是什么意思？），怀疑是翻译错误。查看英文原文，是这样的：

Totems are critical cultural aspects used towards prevention of extinction of fauna. Totems are used to identify different clans that make up ancient civilization of dynasties.

fauna 的意思是"动物"。但"图腾"如何防止动物灭绝呢？查资料可知，当地部族认为，图腾中的动物不可猎杀，有些部族甚至有多种动物作为图腾，因此，图腾客观上起到了保护动物的作用。译者没有作背景调查，明知 fauna 是"动物"的意思，但因为不知道这个道理，想当然引申为"部族"（人类，也属于动物），结果犯了常识性错误。

"构成古代文明的不同部族"也是不求甚解的字面翻译。这段话来自津巴布韦概况介绍，译者可能不敢相信非洲也有古代文明，因此不敢灵活翻译。实际上，稍作调查，就会发现津巴布韦各民族也有悠久的历史和引以为傲的文化。因此，可以译为：

图腾作为文化的重要组成部分，有助于防止相关动物的灭绝，还用以识别不同部落，这些部落曾在历史上建立王朝，创造了古代文明。

例 18.

　　此后，由于人民公社制度的设立，以及粮食（包括粮食制品）和副食（包括肉、蛋、菜、奶等）供应的票证制度、乘车购票和住宿的介绍信制度，及临时户口的申报制度等一系列制度的设立，使得数量较大的农村人进城已不大可能。但数量较少的，被称为"盲流"的边缘人小群体始终是存在的。

加点部分原来翻译为：... *when a ticket had to be bought to take the train and a letter of introduction had to be shown to stay in a hotel*。

但读了这个译文马上产生了疑问：哪个国家乘车不购票呢？人民公社之前我们乘车不用购票吗？再仔细查看原文，发现句子结构可以产生歧义，加点部分既可以理解为"乘车购票制度"和"住宿的介绍信制度"，也可以理解为"乘车购票的介绍信制度"和"住宿的介绍信制度"。根据常识判断，显然后一种理解更符合逻辑。这样的常识性错误是谁都可能犯的。

因此改译为：

　　Later, when coupons were needed to buy foodstuff, *when a letter of introduction was needed to buy a train ticket and to stay in a hotel*, and when a person had to apply for a permit for temporary residence in the city, it became practically impossible for large numbers of rural people to come to the city. But there has always been a small group of marginalized "aimless drifters".

例 19.

　　1997 年，中国全国人大常委会通过了《献血法》。在此之前 1996 年国务院行政法规《血液制品管理条例》和在此之后 1998 年卫生部规章《血站管理办法（暂行）》将原料血浆的采集和临床用血的采集区分开来。这三个法律文件的制定已经考虑到临床用血的安全和保证血液制品的质量，预防和控制经血液途径传播疾病的问题。这三个法律文件的主要内容是：一、国家实行无偿献血制度和单采血浆统一规划、设置制度。二、卫生行政部门监督管理献血工作。三、血站是不以营利为目的的公益性组织；血站实行执业许可证制度，血站技术工作人员实行考试合格证书制度，<u>血源、采供血和检测原始记录实行 10 年保存制度</u>。四，血站对献血者必须进行健康检查；医疗机构对临床用血必须进行核查……

加点部分有人翻译为：

As non-profit organizations, blood-stations *have* to be licensed and their employees *have* to be certified. The original records of blood sources, blood collection and distribution and blood tests *are kept* for 10 years.

这段文字表面看起来是陈述性的，但实际上是对血站的强制性要求，所以 As non-profit organizations, blood-stations *have* to be licensed and their employees *have* to be certified. 是可以传达原文意思的，但"血源、采供血和检测原始记录实行 10 年保存制度"翻译为陈述性的"The original records of blood sources, blood collection and distribution and blood tests *are kept* for 10 years."就无法表达原文意思，与上文意思不连贯，所以可以改为：

A blood station is a non-profit, public service institution; it *must* have a license; its technical personnel *must* be examined and certified; its original records relating to blood source, blood collection and distribution and blood test *must be kept* for ten years.

例 20.

There are concerns that in the absence of adequate legal <u>protection</u>, documentation could mean that the originating community unwittingly loses control over its TK, or that documentation may lead to <u>misappropriation</u> of TK, and use in ways that were not anticipated and were not intended by the TK holders.

原译：

人们担心，对<u>记录缺乏适当法律保护</u>这一问题可能意味着提供传统知识的社区不知不觉失去了对传统知识的控制，或传统知识记录可能导致对传统知识的<u>滥用</u>和通过以难以预料的和违背传统知识持有人意愿的方式进行使用。

本段讲的是传统知识保护可能带来的后果。例如：为了保护即将失传的工艺，有人以录像方式加以记录（document），但记录之后，广为流传，别人开始仿造，当地人失去了对这门手艺的控制。

其中的 protection，从上下文来看，是指对传统知识的法律保护措施，原译理解为对记录的保护，是错误的。这个例子提醒我们，遇到动词变来的抽象名词（如 protection），必须在思想上把它变为动词，问自己 Who does (protects) what？如果这个问题能回答出来，翻译就不易出错，也方便添加逻辑主语或宾语。

改译：

有人担心，如果对传统知识缺乏适当法律保护，记录工作可能会导致提供传统知识的社区无意中丧失对知识的控制，也可能导致他人<u>盗用</u>或以知识持有人没有料到或不希望看到的方式使用传统知识。

改译还纠正了 misappropriation 的翻译。该词的意思不是"滥用"，是"盗用"（见图 5.3）：

```
misappropriate [,misə'prəuprieit]
vt. 侵占, 霸占, 盗用
[法] 侵占, 私吞, 贪污

朗文当代英语词典

misappropriate
mis·ap·pro·pri·ate /,misə'prəuprieit US -'prou-/ v [T]
formal to dishonestly take something that someone has trusted you with, especially
money or goods that belong to your employer
= embezzle
  ▪ He claimed the finance manager had misappropriated company funds.
> misappropriation /,misəprəupri'eiʃən US -prou-/ n [U]
  ▪ the misappropriation of public funds
```

图 5.3　misappropriate 的定义

关于补充抽象名词的逻辑主语，这里再举一例：

Joint Submission 4 (JS4) noted the <u>adoption</u> of the Law on the Elimination of All Forms of Discrimination in 2014 and that the Public Defender had been charged with monitoring its implementation. It was concerned that the Government had not considered NGO demands to strengthen the mechanism and that the law did not provide for sanctions in cases of discrimination.

其中的 adoption 是 adopt 变来的抽象名词。如果不找到这个词的逻辑主语，就不容易翻译——“某某注意到什么的通过”并不通顺。从常识判断，通过法律的一定是立法机关，因此可以在译文中 补充出来：

> 联合提交材料 4（JS4）注意到 2014 年<u>立法机关</u>通过了《消除一切形式歧视法》并授权公设辩护人监督其实施。JS4 关切地认为，政府没有考虑非政府组织增强该机制的要求，并指出法律并未就歧视案件规定处罚。

5.3.4 质疑词典译法

受字典翻译的影响，我们经常认为中英文之间有一一对应的译法，但很多情况下，这些对应是所谓的“假朋友”（false friends），即并非真正对应，而是有些情况下对应。例如，在词典上，“内涵”的对等词是 connotation，因此，很多人（包括机器翻译）把“内涵式发展”翻译为 connotative development。但是，connotation 的意思仅仅指一个词的隐含意义，除此之外没有别的意思（见图 5.4）：

柯林斯高级英语学习词典第5版

con|no|ta|tion /k'ɒnət'eɪʃᵊn/ **(connotations)**
[N-COUNT] usu with supp, oft N of n
The **connotations** of a particular word or name are the ideas or qualities which it makes you think of.
It's just one of those words that's got so many negative connotations...
'Urchin', with its connotation of mischievousness, may not be a particularly apt word.
= association

维科英汉词典

connotation [con·no·ta·tion || ˌkɒnəʊ'teɪʃn]
n. 含蓄; 内涵; 储蓄的东西

图 5.4　connotation 的定义

而“内涵式发展”是指重视质量的发展，相对于“外延式发展”（强调数量扩张的发展）。

根据学术界的观点，“外延式发展”就是 growth，“内涵式发展”就是 development：

> “Growth is the expansion of some object, institution or population which is measurable and is always quantitative whereas development is

related to qualitative improvement," said the Reader of the department of Economics, Mangalore University Prof Shripathi Kalluraya.[①]

也可以把"外延式发展"称为"quantitative growth",把"内涵式发展"称为"qualitative development"(见图 5.5)[②]:

**Quantitative Growth and Qualitative Development:
An Overview from Pakistan (2002-2009)**

Saira Batool, Saif–ur-Rehman Saif Abbasi , Adeela Rehman*

International Islamic University Islamabad, Pakistan
*Corresponding Author: dradeelarehman@yahoo.com

图 5.5 "内涵式发展"和"外延式发展"英译查证(一)

中国也有学者分别称之为"quantitative growth"和 qualitative enhancement(见图 5.6)[③]:

— HIGHER — EDUCATION — POLICY —
© 2005 International Association of Universities 0952-8733/05 $30.00
Higher Education Policy, 2005, 18, (117–130)
www.palgrave-journals.com/hep

Qualitative Enhancement and Quantitative Growth: Changes and Trends of China's Higher Education

Futao Huang
Research Institute for Higher Education, Hiroshima University, Kagamiyama 1-2-3, Higashi Hiroshima 739-8523, Japan.
E-mail: futao@hiroshima-u.ac.jp

图 5.6 "内涵式发展"和"外延式发展"英译查证(二)

5.4 以批判性思维变通取舍

5.4.1 显化隐含逻辑

汉语表达有一定模糊性,需要运用批判性思维,澄清句子含义并在英

---

① https://www.deccanherald.com/content/54922/growth-quantitative-development-qualitative.html, accessed March 21, 2021.

② http://www.hrpub.org/download/20141001/SA1-19602538.pdf, accessed March 21, 2021.

③ http://bcct.unam.mx/adriana/bibliografia%20parte%202/HUANG,%20F..pdf, accessed March 21, 2021.

语中明确表达出来。

例21.

　　但事实上，在法律保护妇女、社会尊重妇女、男女平等的今天，男女不平等的现象依然或多或少地存在着。这是"男尊女卑"、女性依附男性的历史留下的"后遗症"。（来自北外高翻学院入学试题）

考试中，绝大多数同学没有处理好加点部分，一般都是直译，导致译文逻辑矛盾。例如：

But in fact, today when women are protected by law, respected in society, and enjoy equal rights with men, the phenomena of gender inequality still exist to some extent. This is a legacy of our history where women were considered inferior or subordinate to men.

试想，既然"男女平等"，怎么还会有不平等的现象存在？这是明显的矛盾。但汉语听起来似乎还说得过去，那是因为我们在理解时自动补充了原文缺少的内容：尽管倡导社会尊重妇女，尽管法律规定男女平等，尽管理论上男女平等……，但实际上，男女还是不平等。基于这样的理解，我们可以翻译为：

译文1：

Although *in principle* women should be equally protected by law, respected in society, and enjoy equal rights with men, instances of inequality do exist. This is a legacy of our history where women were considered inferior or subordinate to men.

译文2：

But in fact, instances of gender inequality do exist although *it is believed that* women are protected by law, enjoy equal rights under the law, and are respected in the society. This is a legacy of our history where women were considered inferior or subordinate to men.

译文3：

But although *it seems* that women are protected by law, respected in society, and enjoy equal rights with men, instances of gender inequality do exist. This is a legacy in our culture, where women are considered inferior or subordinate to men.

5.4.2　补充原文省略

现在我们所翻译的大多数文章都不是什么"经典"之作，作者的汉语或英语水平并不太高；再就是很多文章是匆忙之中写出来的，毫无文采可言，甚至文理不通的情况也不少，所以，译文能达到比原文通顺、达意，也是理所应当的。这时，译者要抛弃对等的观念。

例 22.
　　剥离国有商业银行不良资产，并组建相应的资产管理公司收购、管理、处置国有商业银行和国家开发银行的不良资产，是我国借鉴亚洲金融危机教训，深化国有企业和金融体制改革，着眼于在 21 世纪初建立一个良性发展环境的大政策。

　　Learning from the Asian financial crisis, China has decided to deepen reforms of state-owned enterprises and the banking sector and build an enabling environment for them in the new century. A major component of the reform is to remove troubled assets from state-owned commercial banks (*and the state development bank*) and establish assets management companies (AMCs) to acquire, manage, and dispose of such assets.

从这段文章可以看出，资产管理公司管理的资产包括两部分：商业银行的和开发银行的。但为什么开头谈剥离资产时只谈商业银行不谈开发银行呢？这不是矛盾吗？如果尊重客观事实，翻译时应当把丢失的信息补充出来；但考虑到发言人来自商业银行，不想强调开发银行，所以，我们可以把补充出来的"开发银行"放在括号里面。

例 23.
　　对国有商业银行来说，这个大政策的目标含义至少有三个方面：其一，国家把国有商业银行长期以来由政策的、历史的、客观的、主观的原因而形成的不良贷款包袱予以解脱、还了多年积欠银行的"旧债"。

This policy will have at least three implications: Firstly, the government will pay back the old "debts" it owes the banks by removing the NPLs *caused by its decisions.*

政府欠银行"债",理应是政府的决策(所谓"政策的、历史的、客观的"原因)为银行造成的不良贷款,严格地讲,不包括"主观的"原因(银行自己经营不善)造成的不良贷款。如果译文把"主观原因"也翻译出来,会显得逻辑不通。

5.4.3 删减表达冗余

批判性思维在对原文的变通取舍中也发挥重要作用。以下例子是笔者翻译过的一篇文章(开头一段),后来节选刊登在《中国日报》(02/06/2003)。笔者本想删除一部分,但觉得没有权力,最后中国日报还是删了。

例 24.

【题目】中国:加入 WTO 与改革的新阶段

中国加入 WTO,为什么会引起国内国际相当广泛的影响?入世一周年,国际上各个方面的评价是正面的、积极的、肯定的。我想这个原因应该概括为两个方面:第一,中国是一个发展中的大国,是有着庞大国内市场需求且又保持经济持续增长的一个大国;第二,中国又是一个从传统计划经济向市场经济转轨的大国。中国作为经济体制转轨的大国能够在不长的时间内,纳入到世界市场经济的主流,这本身就是一个奇迹。因此,中国加入 WTO,最深刻、最有实质性或者最有长远意义的,我把它叫做中国的第二次改革、第二次开放。中国加入 WTO,开放进入新阶段,改革也进入新阶段。

原译:

Why has China's accession into WTO aroused so much attention both at home and abroad? The comment in the international arena on China's accession into WTO has been positive. There are several reasons attributed to this: China is a large developing country with great potentials in the domestic market demand and sustainable economic growth; it is also a country in transformation from a planned economy to a market economy. It is itself a miracle for China, as a large country in economic transition, to have joined WTO in such a short period of time. Therefore, the greatest significance of China's accession into WTO is that it brings about another period of reform and opening up in China.

改译：

China's accession to the World Trade Organization (WTO) has attracted much attention both at home and abroad. Responses of the international community in the past year have been positive. This is because firstly, China is a large developing country with great market potential and sustainable growth; and secondly, China has created an economic miracle through its successful economic transition and quick integration into the world economy despite the size of the country. But to China, the most important thing is that with accession, China has entered into a new period of reform and opening-up.

原文逻辑关系不清，需要在翻译时理顺。例如，原文所说的两个理由，按照逻辑应当理解为是对"为什么会引起国内国际相当广泛的影响"的回答，而不是对"入世一周年，国际上各个方面的评价是正面的、积极的、肯定的"的回答，尽管在形式上好像是对后者的回答。"入世一周年……"一句话的意思是"一年来，中国履行了入世承诺，得到了国际社会肯定，"把它夹在问题和回答之间妨碍了逻辑的通畅。这时，可以把这句话调到别的地方或省略不译。但这个问题以后没有展开讨论，所以没有其他地方可调。如果选择省略，又怕超越了译者权限（不是最后决策者）。最后采用折中的方法，在翻译时把两句合并，尽量弱化第二句的意思，把疑问留给了译文使用者。尽管译文下一句中 This 的指代还是比较模糊，但似乎没有更好的办法。

再例如，文章给出的第二个原因，也不是到第一个句号为止。相反，第二个原因的重要信息包含在下一句中,即"中国作为经济体制转轨的大国能够在不长的时间内,纳入世界市场经济的主流,这本身就是一个奇迹"(所以,中国入世举世瞩目)。故而有"改译"的处理方法。

第三,如果上述分析成立,原文中的"因此"是不妥当的,因为"因此"前后并没有明显的因果关系,而是一种话题的转变,表示闲话不再多说,进入正题了(别忘了文章的题目是《中国:加入 WTO 与改革的新阶段》),所以,顶多翻译为 but,或者不译。

实际上,"因此"之前的部分对于全文来说,并不起什么作用,因为全文的主题包含在"因此"之后的两句话:"中国加入 WTO,最深刻、最有实质性或者最有长远意义的,我把它叫做中国的第二次改革、第二次开放。中国加入 WTO,开放进入新阶段,改革也进入新阶段。"所以,把"因此"之前的部分去掉,并不影响文章的意思。

那么,如何解释"因此"之前那部分内容存在的意义呢?只能理解为属于汉语作文"起承转合"中的"起",其作用是引出话题而已,而英语却没有这种叙事方式,而是讲求开门见山。如果笔者有权,就直接把前半部分省掉了。果然,最后在《中国日报》刊登出来的译文是:

[Title] Cut Gov't Red Tape to Reform Economy

China's accession to the World Trade Organization (WTO) has aroused much attention both at home and abroad.

What is of the greatest significance to China is that its accession to the World Trade Organization (WTO) brings about a new period of reform and opening-up.

5.5 综合举例

下面这个例子①,说明通过调查研究解决的各种理解和表达问题。原文:

A year ago, I joined a sailing trip to Islay, an island in western

---
① 此案例由苏玥玥提供。

Scotland and famous for peaty malt whisky that can singe the hair off your nostrils. The mooring was in front of a distillery called Ardbeg, its name painted in huge black letters on a whitewashed wall facing the sea. Its breakfast included haggis — and a dram of scotch. Then came the distillery tour, and more samplings. Even at midnight, the air reeked with the smoky vapours coming from the mash tun. Night workers cooed over the spirit as it flowed through pipes and jars. They said demand was so strong that production was running round the clock.(选自 *The Economist*)

原译（机器翻译）：

　　一年前，我参加了一次前往伊莱岛（Islay）的航海之旅，这是苏格兰西部的一个岛屿，以泥煤麦芽威士忌（peaty malt whisky）闻名，这种威士忌可将鼻孔上的发丝烧成灰烬。停泊处位于一家名叫阿德贝的酒厂前，酒厂的名字用巨大的黑色字母写在一面面对大海的白色墙壁上。早餐包括羊杂碎和一杯苏格兰威士忌。接着是酒厂之旅和更多的取样。即使在午夜，空气中也弥漫着从酒桶里冒出来的烟雾。当烈酒从管道和罐子中流过时，夜班工人们对它咕咕哝哝。他们说，需求如此强劲，以致于生产昼夜不停。

可以看到，虽然机器翻译已经有很大进步，但还是只能翻译大概意思，许多细节模糊不清，甚至让人哭笑不得，究其原因就是因为缺少调查研究的环节。

首先是地名和酒厂名的翻译，Islay 国内暂无统一译名，频率较高的译名有艾拉岛、艾雷岛两种；Ardbeg 比较高频率的译名为雅柏，作为商品名称出现在某购物网站上。

查找时发现 Ardbeg 这家酒厂是奢饰品集团 LVMH 旗下的子品牌，所以可以通过 LVMH 的官网看一下是否有官方译名。官网上将 Islay 译为艾雷岛，而 Ardbeg 始终以英文出现，所以暂且可以选择译为雅柏，括号中注明英文。

综上，这两个名词可以译为艾雷岛（Islay）和雅柏（Ardbeg）。同时，在官网还看到了艾雷岛更确切的位置，是苏格兰西海岸，比译为苏格兰西部更佳。

原译最好笑的一句翻译恐怕就是"这种威士忌可将鼻孔上的发丝烧成灰烬"。何为鼻孔上的发丝？不就是鼻腔内的绒毛嘛！这句英文的背景含义可以通过了解泥煤威士忌来求证。某美食网对泥煤威士忌是这样介绍的："这种泥煤麦芽威士忌不仅有麦芽的香甜气息，还有浓浓的泥煤味，熏辣呛口，让人欲罢不能""在烘烤的过程中，燃烧泥煤的热气直接与大麦接触，就像熏鱼或熏肉一样，泥煤的烟熏味直接进入烘干的大麦中，让最后制成的威士忌更有泥煤的风味"。所以可以判断，这句话用了夸张修辞，说明这种威士忌的泥煤味浓烈，仿佛可以将鼻毛熏焦。

下一处，"早餐包括羊杂碎和一杯苏格兰威士忌"。哪里的早餐？是停泊处提供的早餐？还是参观酿酒场时酒厂提供的早餐？单从语法结构分析，its 指代的应当是 Ardbeg，但是不能大意。去 Ardbeg 官网一看，刚好有一张图片符合作者描述的停泊时的画面："The mooring was in front of a distillery called Ardbeg, its name painted in huge black letters on a whitewashed wall facing the sea."（见图 5.7）

图 5.7 某酒厂厂房及标识

这样一看，停泊处只是一个小码头，无任何设施，肯定是不能提供早餐了。接着又在官网看到，Ardbeg 提供食宿，可以网上预订住宿，OLD KLIN CAFÉ 甚至提供了菜谱。一看，确实有 haggis 这道菜，这下可以确定，早餐是酿酒厂提供的了。

下一处，"接着是酒厂之旅和更多的取样"。"取样"代表的是什么？经查，酒厂提供的 TOURS 服务，就是让参观者参观酒厂并且品尝一些酒品，那么这里的 samplings 指的就是每去一处参观，酒厂提供的酒了。

经过上述查证，将译文修改如下：

一年前，我参加了一次前往艾雷岛（Islay）的航海之旅，这座小岛位于苏格兰西海岸，以泥煤麦芽威士忌（peaty malt whisky）而闻名。这种威士忌熏辣呛口，泥煤味恨不得将鼻腔内的绒毛熏焦。船停在一座酒厂前，酒厂的白色外墙面朝大海，上面用巨大的黑色字母写着酒厂的名字——雅柏（Ardbeg）。酒厂提供的早餐包括哈吉斯和一杯苏格兰威士忌，早餐后参观酒厂并品尝各种样酒。即使在午夜，空气中也弥漫着一桶桶麦芽浆散发出来的泥煤味。烈酒不断流过管道，进入酒坛，夜班工人在一旁轻声聊天。他们说，由于市场需求巨大，生产昼夜不停。

5.6 小结

综上所述，批判性思维是透彻理解、通顺表达、恰当变通的思想武器，而调查研究是解决翻译问题的操作方法。两者在翻译中的作用，再强调都不过分。

〔课后练习〕

1. 什么是批判性思维？在翻译中批判性思维可以解决哪些问题？
2. 批判性思维在理解中有哪些应用？
3. 批判性思维在表达中有哪些应用？
4. 批判性思维在变通中有哪些应用？
5. 请总结学习每个例句后的感悟。
6. 请阅读《翻译论文集》（程镇球著，外语教学与研究出版社，2002.）

第二部分　翻译中的理解

　　第六至第七章为本书的第二部分，探讨翻译中的理解问题，包括理解的广度和深度（第六章）以及理解的方法（第七章），目的是实现"信达切"当中的"信"（"忠实"）。

　　译者的理解是广泛的。仅仅依靠原文本身，译者可能无法完成翻译任务，因为原文展现出来的信息，仅仅是冰山之一角，译者必须挖掘原文背后的信息，深入水下部分，才能真正理解原文的思想内容。这就要求译者去认识作者、作者的写作动机、写作的时间地点、写作方式、原文预设读者群体等各方面的信息。第六章举例说明理解的广度。

　　同时，作为二次创作者，还要了解自己的创作/翻译情景：委托人是谁、为何翻译、预设读者是谁、译文使用场景、发布媒介等各种信息。这些信息有助于作出变通取舍决定，因此相关内容放在本书的第四部分。

　　译者的理解是深入的。首先，译者的理解超过一般的读者。一般读者可能只需要了解大意，看不懂的地方可以跳过去，译者却需要理解每个词、每个短语、上下文所有的逻辑关系。其次，译者的理解甚至可以超过作者，尤其是作者引用他人的话，作者不必全懂，但译者必须完全理解。有时译者为了准确表达，需要核实作者引用的事实，在此过程中可能发现原文引用或事实错误。这些情况都可以说译者的理解超越了作者。第六章还举例说明理解的深度。

第六章　理解的广度和深度

扫码预习

请扫码下载本章涉及的例句。先做练习,再看解答,学习效果更佳。

翻译中的理解不同于平时阅读的理解。平时阅读时,理解大意即可,不懂的地方可以跳过去,或者仅仅关注自己感兴趣的信息。但翻译时则需要理解每一个词、每一个短语、每一个句子、句子之间的关系、段落之间的关系以及全篇的中心思想。有些地方作者不见得完全理解,但译者必须理解。例如,作者引用他人文献时,不一定懂得其中的每个字,但译者必须弄懂。

为了理解文本,译者还需要了解作者背景和写作背景;为了更好地满足客户需求、向读者传递信息,译者还需要了解客户的需求和读者的需求。可以说,译者的理解是广泛、深入和全方位的。

6.1　理解的广度(6W1H)

任何著作、报告、文章、标语、口号都是特定的作者在特定情景下创作的。译者必须了解作者和创作背景(6W1H),才能真正理解文字背后的含义,真正传达作者的意图。在不理解背景的情况下,单凭语言翻译,可能带来理解的偏差。同时，译者也必须了解（或假定）翻译情景，才便于作出变通取舍的决定。

在第二章，我已经举例说明了解作品本身6W1H的重要性，这里我再次借用2019年联合国举办的圣•杰罗姆翻译竞赛，强调6W1H的重要性，以及了解或假定翻译情景的重要性。以下是笔者作为联合国译员组评委，在比赛结束时写的一个总结（节选，至6.1.4结束）[1]：

The Ws and H in Translation

译者完成任何一项翻译任务，都需要回答一系列问题，这些问题可以归结为Who is speaking to whom? About what? When, where, why and how? 即：作者是谁？对谁说话？说了什么？说话的时间、地点、原因和方式是什么？通常情况下，翻译客户不会提供这些问题的答案，也不会告知你翻译活动情景。联合国的竞赛也一样，除了在末尾提供了作者和文章出处，并没有其他说明。关于作者和写作背景，译者可以通过调查获知；关于译文的用途，鉴于这是翻译竞赛，区别于通常的翻译情景，译者只能假定用户要求做到最大限度的对等。但即便如此，译者也需要假定一个读者群，以便于作出具体变通取舍。

6.1.1　作者、读者、动机（Who, to Whom and Why）

关于作者、原文读者和写作动机，这里借用一位参赛同学的调查[2]：

> 本文作者Conor Pope是《爱尔兰时报》消费者事务记者（Consumer Affairs Correspondent）兼价格观察编辑（Pricewatch Editor），同时他还是爱尔兰有名的消费者权益倡导者。消费者电台节目（Consumer 999）

---

[1] 全文见：http://blog.sina.com.cn/s/blog_67d1e1980102yvq0.html, accessed March 21, 2021.
[2] 这是参赛选手张旭同学进行的调查，参考了以下网站：
https://www.irishtimes.com/profile/conor-pope-7.1008780, accessed March 21, 2021.
https://en.wikipedia.org/wiki/Conor_Pope, accessed March 21, 2021.
https://www.irishtimes.com/news/consumer, accessed March 21, 2021.
http://youandyourmoney.ie/consumer-999/, accessed March 21, 2021.
https://www.amazon.co.uk/Stop-Wasting-Money-Holiday-Instead/dp/1905483341.

主持人，拥有英文和哲学学士学位。在《爱尔兰时报》Pricewatch 栏目中，Conor Pope 通过回答消费者提出的问题教给人们如何经济地消费，维护自己的合法权益，辛辣地指出商家的营销陷阱。综合自己多年来在消费领域的见闻和思考，Conor Pope 于 2007 年出版消费者建议书籍 *Stop Wasting Your Money*，旨在帮助消费者避免盲目消费，节省金钱。

本文还涉及另一个 why：作者作为消费者权益保护领域的记者，此次哈罗德之行是有意安排的，还是误打误撞？从调查中可知，作者逛哈罗德并非专门安排，而是带家人闲逛，无意中闯入。实际上，如果是故意安排的，作者也许就不会感到窘迫了。因此，译文使用的字眼如果暗示这是一场故意安排的活动，就不准确了。例如：We headed for the food hall. 译为"我们向美食厅走去"没有问题，但译为"第二站，我们准备前往食品大厅"，就暗示这是一场安排好的活动。实际上，如果看看这篇文章的全文，原文是 The Popes had to eat so we headed for the food hall，完全没有这种暗示，也从一个侧面说明这不是安排好的活动。这句话还提醒我们，今后参加翻译竞赛，一定要设法找到全文，才方便全面透彻理解。

翻译时需要关注的另一个 whom，是译文的读者。由于译文和原文读者来自不同语言、社会、文化背景，原文读者熟知的事物，译文读者不一定清楚。译者要根据译文读者对原文背景的了解，决定采用归化或异化的翻译策略以及简化、补充、解释的翻译方法。例如，如何翻译本文出现的 Harrods、perma-tans、Escher print、Irish、Penney's leggings、M&S t- shirt 等说法。

6.1.2 何时、何地（When and Where）

关于文章创作的时间和地点（或发表平台），这里再次借用上述同学的调查[①]：

[①] 张旭的调查，参考了以下网站：
https://www.irishtimes.com, accessed March 21, 2021.
https://www.irishtimes.com/life-and-style, accessed March 21, 2021.
https://en.wikipedia.org/wiki/The_Irish_Times, accessed March 21, 2021.
https://www.irishtimes.com/life-and-style/people/conor-pope-out-of-my-comfort-zone-wandering-around-harrods-in-the-wrong-trousers-1.3605609, accessed March 21, 2021.

本文摘自《爱尔兰时报》(*The Irish Times*)的"生活时尚"版块，刊登日期为 2018 年 8 月 29 日。《爱尔兰时报》是爱尔兰的主流大报，创建于 1859 年，总部位于首都都柏林。该报每日出版，主要报道内容覆盖：时事政治、体育、经济、社会、生活、文化、汽车、求职等。"生活时尚"版块提供关于饮食、家居、健康、家庭、旅游、汽车、时尚等话题讨论，观点贴近生活，语言轻松幽默。本篇文章刊登在人物专栏，介绍了作者在英国伦敦的豪华百货商场中的轶事。

翻译中需要考虑的另一个 when 和 where 就是原文和译文存在的时空差异。如果这篇文章翻译为法文，可能就不需要对 Harrods、perma-tans、Escher print 等中国读者（可能）不熟悉、但法国读者（可能）熟悉的事物作任何解释。如果中国还处在 20 世纪 70 年代的发展状况，可能还需要解释 Kobe beef（这里的牛肉有什么特别）、Russian caviar（鱼子酱有什么好吃的）、tea rooms（茶室怎么会卖吃的）、gleaming ice crystals（当时可能还很少见到冷藏食品柜台）。

即使在今天的中国翻译这篇文章，如果假定的读者不同[①]，对某些概念的处理方式就会不同。例如，如果假定读者是对西方文化相当了解、紧跟时代潮流的时尚青年，则 Harrods、perma-tans、Armani loafers、Penney's leggings、M&S t-shirt 等可能不需要任何解释；如果假定读者是普通的中国大众，包括教育程度不高的中老年人，他们甚至可能不知道什么叫 comfort zone，100 英镑值多少钱，更不用说 Irish 代表了什么，因此就需要更多解释。

6.1.3 写作方式（How）

How 是指作者的写作风格：是正式，还是随意；是严谨厚重，还是轻松活泼；是独白，还是对话。上述同学调查发现[②]：

[①] 翻译竞赛情景特殊，实际读者只有评委，但笔者建议无论组织何种翻译竞赛，主办方都为译者设定具体翻译情景，包括翻译的委托人、译文的用途、读者是谁等等。

[②] 张旭同学调查：https://www.irishtimes.com/life-and-style/people/conor-pope-most-people-are-good-and-kind-and-other-truths-i-hold-dear-1.3747767, accessed March 21, 2021.

Conor Pope 整体写作风格非常风趣幽默，他所写的话题非常贴近生活，语言也平易近人，敏锐的观察力和精妙的用词能够抓住读者的注意力，因此是非常受欢迎而且很高产的撰稿人。Pope 在回顾 6 个月的专栏写作体验时[1]，点出了他写作的源泉，即从小事中发现生活的闪光点，其中还专门提到竞赛使用的这篇文章：

The Little Things

But most of all I've learned that it's worth dwelling on the little things, those passing conversations with strangers on a plane, the melodramas at the doorstep, the baby steps towards a tottering Christmas tree, <u>the random visit to Penney's with excited family members or to Harrod's in the wrong trousers</u> and the rainy walks to school with children under inappropriate umbrellas.

从这一段中可以体会出，Pope 擅长从生活的琐碎中提炼有益的感受，并用灵动的文字传递给读者，以小见大，这也是读者喜爱他的原因。

了解了作者的语言风格，就需要在译文中尽量再现这一风格。例如：

We were directed to the tea rooms and after more wrong turns, found a brassy lift which *agreed to* take us there.

其中的 agree to，就是拟人的表达方式：电梯无法 agree。如果译文平铺直叙，意思虽然不错，但失去了一点趣味：

我们被指向咖啡茶点零食部，又转错了几个弯，然后发现了一个古铜色升降机，终于把我们带到那里。

按照原文的拟人方式翻译，则更为有趣：

虽然问到了去茶室怎么走，我们还是走了些冤枉路，才找到一部黄铜色电梯愿意载我们过去。

---

[1] 发表于 2019 年 1 月 9 日，见 https://www.irishtimes.com/life-and-style/people/conor-pope-most-people-are-good-and-kind-and-other-truths-i-hold-dear-1.3747767, accessed March 21, 2021.

6.1.4 思想内容（About What）

本文描写作者作为普通工薪阶层，带领全家逛商场，误打误撞进入面向富有阶层的哈罗德商场后的经历和心理感受，尤其是作者当天还穿了一条与高雅的购物环境格格不入的短裤。

译者除了从宏观上把握写作内容外，还需要理解原文的每个细节，例如中国读者可能不了解的概念（Harrods、perma-tans 等）。另外，由于译者的英语并非母语，普通的语言表达也可能需要调查。例如，

> After several wrong turns, which took us repeatedly through a diamond hall maze where staff *looked through* us, I had to do a thing I hate doing.

其中的 look through，参赛者有两种理解，一是对我们视而不见，二是注视着我们，可谓截然相反。但如果查英语词典，可以看到明确的解释：

> If you say that someone looks through another person, you mean that they look at that person without seeming to see them or recognize them, for example because they are angry with them or are thinking deeply about something else.[1]

再例如：

> "I'm not feeding my children Kobe beef or Russian caviar," I muttered as I *swerved* us past heavy marble counters groaning under the weight of gleaming ice crystals and a meat counter offering a platter of "baby chicken, half duck, lamb cutlets and Merguez sausage" for £100.

其中的 swerve 是指 to turn aside or be turned aside from a straight course[2]，言外之意是看到这么贵的食物，不敢在旁边停留，生怕哪个孩子哭着闹着要吃，所以带领家人火速绕过，而不是简单的"经过"，更不是"突然转向"

---

[1] https://www.collinsdictionary.com/dictionary/english/look-through, accessed March 21, 2021.
[2] http://definition.org/define/swerve/?xsmr=1, accessed March 21, 2021.

这个柜台。

参赛者对 minor royals（After lunch we explored the children's clothes section, walking floors covered with carpets richer and thicker than *minor royals*.）的理解也是五花八门，例如"皇室""小皇室""皇室小贵族""皇室小成员""少数皇家贵族""皇室成员小孩们""皇室幼童"；准确的译法包括："王室远亲""皇室七大姑八大姨""皇亲国戚""王室旁系成员"等。

6.2 理解的深度

译者对原文的理解包括字词和短语的含义、句子结构和意思重点、前后逻辑关系、局部与整体的关系等，甚至包括发现并在必要时纠正原文的语言、事实和逻辑瑕疵。译者对原文的理解要接近、达到甚至超过作者水平。

6.2.1 理解字词

6.2.1.1 理解概念

译者要理解每一个概念。不清楚时，要勤于调查研究。例如，联合国关于老年人权利的一篇报告中有这样一段话：

> Social exclusion is a relative concept, which refers to the fact that it is assessed against a population base, for example the general population. It further involves agency: older persons are being excluded against their will or lack the agency to achieve integration for themselves, or choose to exclude themselves from mainstream society.

原译是：

> 社会排斥是一个相对概念，是相对于一个人口基数（如总人口）而言。社会排斥还涉及机构：或者是社会违背老人意愿，将其排除在外，或者是老人缺乏融入社会的能动性，或者是老人不愿意融入主流社会。

这里面涉及两个词的理解：against 和 agency。前者根据逻辑就可以理解：既然社会排斥是个相对概念，那一定是一部分相对于另一部分受到排斥。因此，assessed against a population base 不是什么"根据一般人口来评估"，而是相对于一个人口基数来评估。agency 翻译为"机构"，结合上下文看没有意义，需要调查 agency 的具体意义。通过使用 social exclusion、agency 等关键词检索，看到这样的资料：

资料1：

The issue of agency is key to the social exclusion debate. This focuses on the role of various agents, as well as more impersonal forces and processes, in causing exclusion. These agents and forces can potentially include globalisation, international organisations, nation states, elites, and excluded groups and individuals themselves.①

资料2：

Although schools are usually regarded as important agents for social inclusion, research has shown that they may also function as agents of exclusion itself.②

通过直找词源，发现这样的信息：

Middle English, from Medieval Latin *agent-, agens,* from Latin, present participle of *agere* to drive, lead, act, do; akin to Old Norse *aka* to travel in a vehicle, Greek *agein* to drive, lead③

由此可见，agency 的本义是驱动、领导、行动、作为；与此相应的行动者 agent，就是驱动者、领导者、行动者、行为主体。实际上，在本段中，老人被排斥在主流社会之外，是因为老人缺乏行动能力，无法抵抗被排斥，也无法主动融入。因此，本段中可以译为"行动能力"或"能动性"：

社会排斥是一个相对概念，是相对于一个人口基数（如总人口）

---

① https://gsdrc.org/topic-guides/social-exclusion/dynamics/social-exclusion-as-a-process/, accessed March 21, 2021.
② https://www.tandfonline.com/doi/abs/10.1080/13603116.2012.742145, accessed March 21, 2021.
③ https://iklearn.com/en/?r=dictionary/collegiate/agent, accessed March 21, 2021.

而言。社会排斥还涉及<u>能动性</u>：老年人受到排斥或者是违背了老年人的意愿，或者是因为老年人缺乏主动融入社会的能动性，或者是老年人自外于主流社会。

再例如：<u>健全层级监督工作机制</u>，加强常态化监督，完善纠错问责机制。原译为：

We will improve <u>oversight mechanism at different levels</u> and on a regular basis; improve the system for redressing wrongs and holding the culprit accountable.

"层级监督工作机制"原译理解为"不同级别的监督机制"，但实际上是指上级对下级的监督：

层级监督是指行政机关监督纵向划分为若干层级，各层级的业务性质和职能基本相同，不同层级的监督范围自上而下逐层缩小，各层级分别对上一层级负责而形成的层级节制的监督体制。①

因此可以改为：

We will improve the <u>hierarchical oversight mechanism,</u> strengthen regular supervision, and improve the accountability system.

一位审读本书初稿的同学②怀疑 hierarchical 是否有必要，作了如下查证，值得肯定：

"上级对下级的监督"，和上级对下级的管理似乎区别不大，查找后发现在政治话语中，区别主要在于监督可以是平级监督、上级对下级的监督、群众对官员的监督等不同方向上的，而管理则是上级对下级的。而层级监督既然已经说明了是上级对下级的，是不是一个 oversight/supervision/control 就已经能够说明了？不需要再强调 hierarchical？根据简明英语和国际英语的原则，加上一个形容词可能

---

① https://baike.baidu.com/item/ 层级监督 /1312904, accessed March 21, 2021.
② 刘桐杉同学。

会另 E2（以英语为第二语言）的读者不解。因此我对监督的几个英文表达进行了查询（见图 6.1）[①]：

> **oversight**
> *noun*
> UK /ˈəʊvəsaɪt/ US
>
> [U] · LAW, GOVERNMENT, MANAGEMENT
>
> systems or actions to control an activity and make sure that it is done correctly and legally:
>
> - *In commodity trading, key goods such as oil or uranium are traded with almost no oversight.*
> - **government/regulatory oversight** *Lawmakers are questioning whether the industry needs more government oversight.*
> - **oversight of sth** *The report criticized weak oversight of the contractors.*

图 6.1　oversight 的定义

再看一些例句（见图 6.2、6.3）：

> **oversight mechanism**
> - *It provides a clear independent oversight mechanism which never existed previously.*
>
> From the Hansard archive
>
> **proper oversight**
> - *Proper oversight appeared to be assured by the demand that the serum's production be supervised by a trained pharmacist.*
>
> From the Cambridge English Corpus
>
> **regulatory oversight**
> - *Proposed improvements in bank regulatory oversight, stalled before the crisis, were now rammed through.*
>
> From the Cambridge English Corpus

图 6.2　oversight 的用例（一）

发现 oversight 虽然从构词上有自上而下的意思，但这个词因为有多种搭配，单独出现时，并不一定表示自上而下的监督，因此我认为需要保留 hierarchical。

[①] https://dictionary.cambridge.org/dictionary/english/oversight, accessed March 21, 2021.

```
These are words often used in combination with oversight.
Click on a collocation to see more examples of it.

civilian oversight
• Article 330 led to a secret budget, completely shielded from civilian oversight.
From the Cambridge English Corpus

congressional oversight
• This story came to be viewed as credible, as media coverage and congressional oversight shifted to revealing significant gaps in the food inspection system.
From the Cambridge English Corpus

judicial oversight
• The resulting zoning litigation illustrates the ways in which administrative indiscretion helped retain a role for judicial oversight of newly empowered municipal bureaucrats.
From the Cambridge English Corpus
```

图 6.3　oversight 的用例（二）

那么 supervision 可不可以本就表示自上而下的监督呢？查找如下（见图 6.4）[①]：

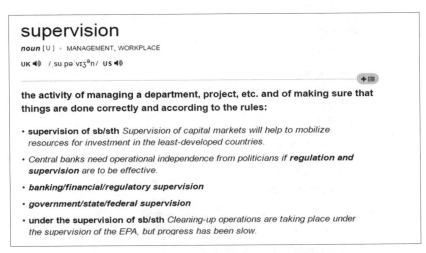

图 6.4　supervision 的用例

又观察了一些例子：

---

① https://dictionary.cambridge.org/dictionary/english/supervision, accessed March 21, 2021.

Thus, where *supervision* is lax, district leaders, including local bureaucrats, may use their budgetary discretion and the force at their disposal for personal gain.

It gives way to another form of production preferring flexibility, moderating the contrast between *supervision* and execution, and combining the domains of competition and cooperation.

Pressures to tighten the net of prudential *supervision* emerged after several failures of large central banks, particularly after the second oil crisis in 1979.

Growing official interference in private spaces was a logical consequence of stronger government *supervision* over public places.

发现这个词确实用在自上而下的监督比较多，或者说"监管"更合适。谷歌中对 oversee 和 supervise 的区别这样定义：

As verbs the difference between supervise and oversee is that supervise is to <u>direct, manage, or oversee</u>; <u>to be in charge</u> while oversee is (literally) to survey, look at something in a wide angle.

加上 supervise 的构词方式，所以本人认为 supervise 更多的表示自上而下的监管，即不仅有监督，还有在监督的基础上采取行动进行管理；而 oversee 也有这种意思，但它侧重于监督、调查、检查，全面地去看了之后并不一定有下一步的管理，因为它的方向可以是平级监督、下对上的监督等，而这种监督之后并不一定能够有权力采取措施进行管理。

了解之后发现老师改译的 hierarchical oversight 是合理的，但过程中更深入的了解了 oversight 和 supervision 两个词，所以这种查找是有意义的吧。

6.2.1.2 理解用词不当

在 3.1.6 "当心假朋友"中，已经从产出（译文）的角度，举了很多例子，这里再举几个例子，说明"假朋友"给输入（理解）带来的问题。

由于欧洲语言之间的"假朋友"较多，而大多数欧洲国家母语都不是英语，因此，这些国家提供的英文文件中可能存在"假朋友"。译者如果觉得难以理解，还需要把这些“假朋友”还原为源语，再通过源语词典确认这个单词的意思。例如，佛得角（曾为葡萄牙殖民地）提交给联合国的文件中有这样一段话：

> Among the infra-constitutional legislative measures, stands out the approval in 2000 of Law no. 122/V/2000, on the general bases of prevention, rehabilitation and integration of people with disabilities, which was regulated in 2010.

其中的 infra-constitutional 在英语中并不存在，想必是直接从葡语翻译过来的。但意思可以理解：上文讲了宪法对残疾人的保护，而 infra- 作为一个前缀，意思是 below、under，所以，infra-constitutional 一定是位阶低于宪法的法律规定——这个不算难点。难点是 regulated——regulate 的意思是“规范”“监管”“调整”（见图 6.5）：

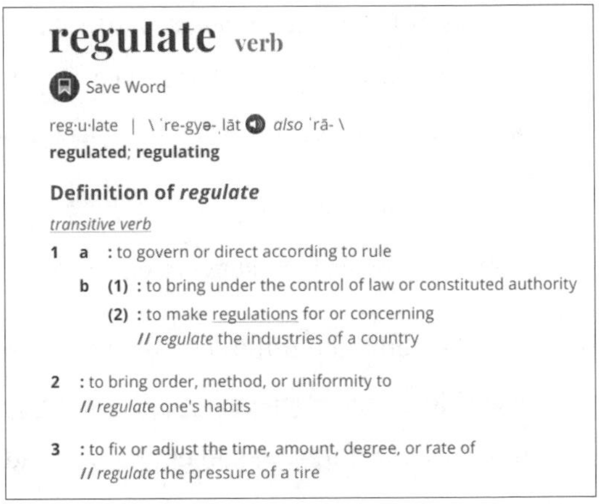
regulate verb

Save Word

reg·u·late | \ ˈre-gyə-ˌlāt also ˈrā- \

regulated; regulating

Definition of *regulate*

transitive verb

1 a : to govern or direct according to rule

b (1) : to bring under the control of law or constituted authority

(2) : to make regulations for or concerning

// *regulate* the industries of a country

2 : to bring order, method, or uniformity to

// *regulate* one's habits

3 : to fix or adjust the time, amount, degree, or rate of

// *regulate* the pressure of a tire

图 6.5　regulate 的定义

但原文的搭配是 regulate Law no. 122/V/2000。一部法律，怎么能够被 regulate? 笔者想到在中国，一部法律出台后需要通过实施条例（regulation）来具体实施。说不定是 2010 年通过了这部法律的实施条例。经查，regulation 的葡语是 regulamento，后者的意思之一是（葡英机器翻译）①：

> Set of governmental provisions that contain rules for the enforcement of a law, decree etc.: regulation of water consumption.

该国宪法当中也有相关条款：

> Article 205

① https://www.dicio.com.br/regulamento/, accessed March 21, 2021.

(Administrative powers)

The Government, in the exercise of its administrative functions, shall have the power:

a) …;

b) To make the regulations necessary for the proper execution of the laws;

…

因此，可以断定，原文的 regulate，意思是 make a regulation for，不同于英语 regulate 的本义，可能是葡萄牙语直译的结果。

据此，例句翻译为：

宪法以下的法律措施中，突出的有 2000 年批准的第 122/V/2000 号法，该法为残疾预防、残疾人康复和社会融入设立了基本框架。2010 年，该法出台了实施条例。

更常见的"假朋友"是因为理解不到位（输入错误）而造成的误译。例如，一些文件中常把 sexual abuse 翻译为"性虐待"，但这两个概念并不对等。

维基百科中对 child sexual abuse 的定义是：Child sexual abuse, also called child molestation, is a form of child abuse in which an adult or older adolescent uses a child for sexual stimulation. 也就是把这里的 abuse 等同于 molestation，而 molest 是什么意思呢①？（见图 6.6）

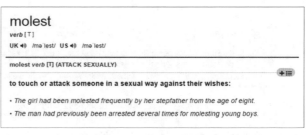

图 6.6　molest 的定义

再看 mayo clnic. org 对 sexual abuse 的定义：Sexual child abuse is any sexual activity with a child, such as fondling, oral-genital contact, intercourse, exploitation or exposure to child pornography.

还有世界卫生组织给 child sexual abuse 的定义（见图 6.7）②：

---

① https://dictionary.cambridge.org/zhs/%E8%AF%8D%E5%85%B8/%E8%8B%B1%E8%AF%AD/molest

② https://www.who.int/violence_injury_prevention/.../guidelines_chap7.pdf, accessed March 21, 2021.

```
7.1  Definition of child sexual abuse
These guidelines adopt the definition of child sexual abuse formulated by the
1999 WHO Consultation on Child Abuse Prevention (62) which stated that:
    "Child sexual abuse is the involvement of a child in sexual activity that he or
she does not fully comprehend, is unable to give informed consent to, or for
which the child is not developmentally prepared and cannot give consent, or
that violates the laws or social taboos of society. Child sexual abuse is evidenced
by this activity between a child and an adult or another child who by age or
development is in a relationship of responsibility, trust or power, the activity
being intended to gratify or satisfy the needs of the other person. This may
include but is not limited to:
    — the inducement or coercion of a child to engage in any unlawful sexual
      activity;
    — the exploitative use of a child in prostitution or other unlawful sexual
      practices;
    — the exploitative use of children in pornographic performance and
      materials".
```

图 6.7 child sexual abuse 的定义

可见，sexual abuse 不只是"暴力侵害"，还有性剥削等多种形式。而"性虐待"的意思是（见图 6.8）①：

```
性虐待症  ✎ 编辑
[同义词] 性虐待一般指性虐待症
⚠ 本词条缺少概述图，补充相关内容使词条更完整，还能快速升级，赶紧来编辑吧！

   虐待狂，现在我们将它称之为"虐待症"是一种非常难以界定的病症。在临床上，性虐待症包括主动的和被动的两种表现。以
前法国一个侯爵叫做撒德，他在生活中喜欢对女性施加虐待，在他的著作里也描写了许多这类性的变态现象，所以，Kraft-
Ebing 把主动的虐待症，也就是喜欢虐待别人，命名为撒德现象（Sadism），中文译为施虐症。
```

图 6.8 "性虐待狂"的定义

英文一般叫作 sadism，是一种心理上的疾病。

还有的"假朋友"源于外来说法，直译为中文后，意思发生了变化，再译为外文时，不能恢复为外文原来的说法。例如，"底线思维"源于英文的 bottom line thinking。但"底线思维"进入中文后，意思却发生了变化。请大家查证下文中的"底线思维"是什么意思、如何翻译（选自习近平总书记 2020 年初视察云南时的讲话）：

---

① https://baike.baidu.com/item/%E6%80%A7%E8%99%90%E5%BE%85%E7%97%87/1052147?-fromtitle=%E6%80%A7%E8%99%90%E5%BE%85&fromid=4738020, accessed March 21, 2021.

要树立正确政绩观，处理好稳和进、立和破、虚和实、标和本、近和远的关系，坚持底线思维，强化风险意识，自觉把新发展理念贯穿到经济社会发展全过程。①

机器翻译：

We should set up a correct view of achievement, handle the relationships between stability and progress, between stability and failure, between emptiness and reality, between standards and foundation, between the near and the far, stick to the bottom line thinking, strengthen risk awareness, and consciously apply new development concepts throughout the whole process of economic and social development.

机器翻译把"底线思维"翻译为 bottom line thinking，大多数译者也可能这样翻译。毕竟机器翻译的数据库，就来自人工翻译。

要确定两个说法是否对应，需要分别查证中英文说法的含义。bottom line 的意思有三个（见图 6.9）②：

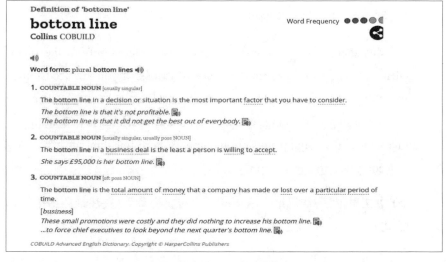

图 6.9　bottom line 的定义

分别是：1）"最重要的（考虑）是"；2）"底限""最起码的条件"；3）

---

① https://m.yunnan.cn/system/2020/02/24/030597882.shtml, accessed March 21, 2021.
② https://www.collinsdictionary.com/zh/dictionary/english/bottom-line, accessed March 21, 2021.

“盈利”。其中前两个意思来源于第三个意思。请看图 6.10：

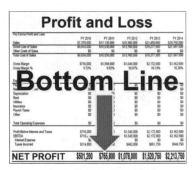

图 6.10　bottom line 图示

大家看到，利润表的最后一行（bottom line），就是盈利情况，所以有“盈利”的意思。对企业来说，盈利最重要，因此引申为“最重要的考虑”；做生意要盈利，因此引申为“最起码的条件”“底限”。bottom line thinking 就是对标（关注）是否盈利的思维（见图 6.11）：

> In business, most decisions that need thought need that extra consideration because there are multiple matters to consider, often in conflict with each other. ... **Bottom-line thinking** is placing the greatest weight or priority on the impact upon the final profits or net earnings of the company. Aug 3, 2019
>
> www.quora.com › What-is-the-meaning-of-bottom-line-t...
>
> What is the meaning of bottom-line thinking? - Quora

图 6.11　bottom line thinking 的含义

是对标（关注）最终结果的思维：

> Most people see bottom-line thinking as related only to the financial world. They see it as financial profit or loss. If you are accustomed to thinking of the bottom line as it relates to financial matters, then you may be missing some things crucial to you and your ministry. Bottom-line thinking is really about results or outcome. Bottom-line thinking asks, “Are we accomplishing our mission?”

而在中文里，“底线思维”演变成了“居安思危”“关注最坏结果的思维”的意思：

> 底线思维就是从忧患意识出发分析社会存在的问题，从最坏处着眼谋划工作，把风险、困难估计得更多一点，做到有备无患、遇事不慌，在此基础上稳中求进。[①]

① http://www.71.cn/2019/0408/1039869.shtml, accessed March 21, 2021.

总书记讲话中正是这个意思："坚持底线思维，强化风险意识"。党的十八大以来，总书记多次表达过这个意思。在十八届中央政治局第四十次集体学习时，他强调维护金融安全，要坚持底线思维，坚持问题导向；在主持召开国家安全工作座谈会时，他强调要坚持底线思维，把维护国家安全的战略主动权牢牢掌握在自己手中；在庆祝中国人民解放军建军90周年大会上，他强调必须强化忧患意识，坚持底线思维，全部心思向打仗聚焦，各项工作向打仗用劲；在中央外事工作会议上，他强调对外工作要坚持底线思维和风险意识。

由此可知，尽管英语的"底线思维"一词通过翻译进入了中文，但意思发生了变化。因此，在把"底线思维"翻译为英文时，不能直译为 bottom line thinking。试译如下：

> We must correctly understand what constitutes an official's achievements. In governing our country, we must manage the relationship between <u>stability and progress</u>, <u>creation and abolition</u>, and <u>tangible and intangible results</u>; we must also balance the treatment of <u>symptoms and their causes</u> and <u>short-term and long-term interests</u>. <u>We must raise our awareness of risks, prepare for the worst-case scenario,</u> and apply the new development concepts in our economic and social decisions.

综上，坚持"底线思维"，可以用 brace ourselves（或 prepare）for a worst-case scenario（见图6.12）：

```
2) https://uk.reuters.com/article/uk-mauritius-environment/mauritius-must-brace-for-worst-case-scenario-after-oil-spill-says-pm-idUKKCN25616Q
Text, Wordlist, text/html, UTF8 (Content-type), 2020-08-11 (Meta tag)

3:   11:07 AM / 19 days ago Mauritius must brace for 'worst case scenario' after oil spill, says PM Katharine Houreld,
4:   but the island nation must still prepare for "a worst case scenario", Prime Minister Pravind Jugnauth said late on
5:   Reuters by his office. "We should prepare for a worst case scenario. It is clear that at some point the ship will
```

图 6.12 "底线思维"英译查证

最后，译文对"稳和进、立和破、虚和实、标和本、近和远"的解释都围绕起首"要树立正确政绩观"展开。稳和进，解释为维护稳定和锐意进取；立和破，解释为创立新制度、打破旧制度；虚和实，解释为有形的成绩和无形的成绩；标和本，解释为表面问题和背后的原因；近和远，解释为近

181

期和远期利益。这些都是衡量一个官员政绩的指标。

6.2.2 理解关系

译者必须理解篇章各部分之间的关系,包括词语之间、短句之间、段落之间的关系。原文有时还会出现结构歧义,译者应该根据上下文和相关资料作出符合逻辑的判断。

6.2.2.1 词语之间

词语之间可能是并列关系,也可能是偏正关系(主谓、动宾、因果、手段等)。例如,"科技抗疫"当中的"科技",就表示手段,翻译时要体现出来:combat COVID-19 with science and technology。再如:

> 原文:开放发展动力不足
> 原译:open development lacks momentum
> 改译:opening up (as a driver for development) is losing momentum

原译把"开放发展"直译为 open development,但这个英文表述意思是"公开的发展""透明的发展",没有意义。经调查,"开放发展"是十八届五中全会提出的五大发展理念之一——五大发展理念即创新、协调、绿色、开放、共享的发展理念。因此,这里的"开放发展"意思是通过开放求得发展,开放作为发展的动力。因此可以译为:opening up as a driver for development is losing momentum。但因为 as a driver for development 已经隐含在上下文,所以可以省略。而"创新发展"则是 innovation-driven development。

> 原文:强化企业投资主体地位
> 原译:strengthen the dominant position of enterprise investment
> 改译:strengthen the role of enterprises as principal investors

原译断句为"企业投资 // 主体地位",但实际含义是"企业投资主体 // 地位"。根据上下文可知,政府要简政放权,不再包揽投资,要提升企业这个主体的地位。

另外,"主体"用 principal (=most important) 更恰当;dominant 的意思是"处于支配地位的":Someone or something that is dominant is more powerful, successful, influential, or noticeable than other people or things.[①]

再如:"人口资源环境承载能力"原译为 bearing capacity of the population, resources and environment,显然是把"人口资源环境"理解为"人口""资源""环境"三个并列项目,但:

> <u>资源环境承载能力</u>指在某一时期、某种状态或条件下,某地区的<u>环境资源</u>所能承受的人口规模和经济规模的大小,即<u>生态系统</u>所能承受的人类经济与社会的限度。

因此,"人口资源环境承载能力"应当理解为"资源和环境承载人口的能力"。而这样的说法在英文中的表述为 the carrying capacity of an environment,不用说"资源":

> The **carrying capacity** of an environment is the maximum population size of a biological species that can be sustained in that specific environment, given the food, habitat, water, and other resources available. In population ecology, carrying capacity is defined as the environment's maximal load, which is different from the concept of population equilibrium, which may be far below an environment's carrying capacity.[1] The effect of carrying capacity on population dynamics may be modelled with a logistic function.

因此改译为:the carrying capacity of the environment。

再如,"证据裁判"能否翻译为 judging evidence(对证据的判断)?根据资料:

> 证据裁判原则,又称证据裁判主义,是指司法人员对案件事实的认定,必须依据有关的证据作出。没有证据而认定案件事实,或者仅凭司法人员的内心推测而认定案件事实,都是违背证据裁判原则的。

因此,"证据裁判"意思是依据证据作出的裁判,应当译为 **judging by**

---

① https://www.collinsdictionary.com/dictionary/english/dominant, accessed March 21, 2021.

evidence 或者 evidence-based decision(-making)。

再如:"案件事实清楚,证据确实充分",机器翻译为"the facts of the case are clear and the evidence is <u>indeed sufficient</u>"是否正确?"确实充分"既可以理解为"真的充分",也可以理解为"确实、充分",这里显然是后者。因此应当改为:"the facts of the case are clear and the evidence is reliable and sufficient."

英语也有结构歧义。例如,WIPO 的一份文件的名称为:

> Promoting Access to Medical Technologies and Innovation — Intersections between Public Health, Intellectual Property and Trade

应当理解为 A: Promoting Access to [Medical Technologies and Innovation],还是 B: [Promoting Access to Medical Technologies] and [Innovation],还是 C: Promoting [(Access to Medical Technologies) and (Innovation)]? 三种理解都说得通。但报告的正文颠倒了 innovation 和 access to medical technologies 的位置,意思一下清晰起来: Insights into the intersections between public health, the IP system, trade and competition rules, and <u>measures to promote innovation and access to medical technologies</u>。由此可见,C 的理解正确。报告前言部分也证实了这个理解: focusing on access to and <u>innovation of medicines</u>。因此译为:促进医疗技术获取和创新——公共卫生、知识产权和贸易的交集。当然,这个翻译也有歧义,但根据后文可以理解。

译者必须理解所有指代关系。上下文不能明确的,可以通过文本外资料确认。例如:

> Article 76 of the Constitution recognizes the right of persons with disabilities to the special protection of <u>the family, society and public authorities</u>, giving **them** full responsibility for the prevention, treatment, rehabilitation and full social inclusion of persons with disabilities. (HRI/CORE/CPV/2017)

这是佛得角提交联合国的一份报告,介绍国内人权保护立法。本段的问题是: them 是指谁? 从语法上来看,应该是指 the family, society and public authorities，但从常理上讲，把责任交给家庭不太正常。既然原文给出了出处，不妨查一下佛得角的宪法。没查到英文版，这是葡语版的英译文（机器翻译）（见图 6.13）：

> Artigo 76º
> (Direitos dos portadores de deficiência)
>
> 1. Os portadores de deficiência têm direito a especial protecção da família, da sociedade e dos poderes públicos.
> 2. Para efeitos do número anterior, incumbe aos poderes públicos, designadamente:
>   a) Promover a prevenção da deficiência, o tratamento, a reabilitação e a reintegração dos portadores de deficiência, bem como as condições económicas, sociais e culturais que facilitem a sua participação na vida activa;

图 6.13　某文件的葡语版

Article 76 (Rights of the disabled)

1. People with disabilities have the right to special protection for the family, society and public authorities.

2. For the purposes of the preceding paragraph, it is incumbent upon public authorities, namely:

Promote disability prevention, treatment, rehabilitation and reintegration of people with disabilities, as well as the economic, social and cultural conditions that facilitate their participation in active life;

虽然机器翻译不太好，但用来协助我们做出判断没问题。从宪法规定看，这个 them 应该仅仅指 public authorities。因此翻译为：

《宪法》第 76 条确认残疾人有权获得家庭、社会和公共机关的特别保护，规定公共机关对残疾预防和治疗、残疾人康复和充分融入社会承担全部责任。

6.2.2.2　短句之间

汉语经常省略关联词，形式上并列的短语、句子之间的关系，可能是并列关系，也可能是偏正关系，要注意分辨。例如，在新冠疫情的背景下，有这样一个新闻标题："中国驻法大使：美国无权在中国开展调查，指责中国应该拿出证据"。

作为一个了解疫情动态的读者，我们完全可以判断"指责中国应该拿出证据"的意思是"如果要指责中国，必须拿出证据"，但机器翻译就会犯错：

> China's Ambassador to France: The United States has no right to investigate in China, <u>accusing China of producing evidence</u>.

正确的翻译是：China's Ambassador to France: US has no right to investigate in China, must produce evidence to support its accusation

若不是看了机器翻译，我们可能还不知道这个结构存在歧义。因此，译者应时刻关注结构歧义，特别是在修改机器翻译时。再如：

> 证据确实、充分<u>，</u>应当符合以下条件：……（三）综合全案证据<u>，</u>对所认定事实已排除合理怀疑。

原文的两个逗号，是表示并列还是偏正？从前后逻辑来看，是表示偏正。但机器翻译不懂逻辑，就会翻译为并列：

> The evidence is true and sufficient, and shall meet the following conditions: ... (3) Synthesizing the evidence of the whole case and removing reasonable doubts about the facts identified.

应当修改为：

> Reliable and sufficient evidence shall meet the following conditions: ... (3) all evidence taken together, there are no reasonable doubts about the facts to be determined.

以上的例子人工翻译通常不会犯错，但并非所有情况下都一目了然，有时需要深入思考才能作出判断。例如，北京市政府工作报告中有这样一段话（在计划部分）：

> 健全行政决策机制<u>，</u>推进重大行政决策程序地方立法<u>，</u>明确事项范围、程序和责任<u>，</u>把公众参与、专家论证、风险评估、合法性审查、集体讨论决定作为重大行政决策法定程序。

原文几个短句用逗号隔开,所以最初都翻译为并列结构:

We will improve the mechanism for administrative decision-making, advance local legislation on major administrative decision-making procedures, clarify the scope, procedures and responsibility of decision-making, and codify public participation, expert argumentation, risk assessment, validity review, collective discussion and decision-making as legal procedures.

但实际上,"健全行政决策机制"是概述,"推进重大行政决策程序地方立法"是具体做法。"明确事项范围、程序和责任"和"把公众参与、专家论证、风险评估、合法性审查、集体讨论决定作为重大行政决策法定程序"是地方立法的重点内容。

根据以上逻辑关系,可以让译文更有层次:

We will improve the administrative decision-making process through local legislation on major decisions, which will define the coverage, procedure and makers of decisions and make public participation, expert evaluation, risk assessment, legality review and deliberation statutory procedures.

再如:

采取鼓励居民消费的综合政策,提高居民消费能力,扩大商品和服务消费,降低流通成本,更好发挥消费对经济发展的支撑作用。

原译各短句处理为列结构:

We will take a comprehensive set of policies to boost consumer spending, raise people's spending power, increase consumption of goods and services and reduce distribution costs so that consumption can provide greater support for economic development

但实际上,"采取……综合政策"是概述,"提高……能力""扩大……消费""降低……成本"是具体采取的措施,"更好发挥……"是预期目的。

因此可以修改为:

We will take a comprehensive set of policies to boost consumer spending, such as raising people's spending power, increasing consumption of goods and services and reducing distribution costs so that consumption can provide greater support for economic development.

英译汉时，同样需要判断短句之间的逻辑关系。例如，联合国大会第七十四届会议主席在一次发言中指出：

While swift action is also needed in the areas of debt relief and concessional finance to enable vulnerable countries scale up health responses and provide social protection, we must remember that effective public revenue generation will be key to financing resilient systems, now and in the future.①

原译为：

同时，在债务免除和优惠融资领域也需要迅速采取行动。为了使脆弱国家能够扩大卫生应对措施和提供社会保护，我们必须记住，在现在和将来，有效地创造公共收入将是为有弹性的系统提供资金的关键。

其中 while 从句和主句要表达的逻辑关系是：虽然 A 很重要，但 B 更重要（见图 6.14）。②

B2
(also formal **whilst**)
despite the fact that; although:
- While I accept that he's not perfect in many respects, I do actually like the man.
- While I fully understand your point of view, I also have some sympathy with Michael's.

图 6.14　while 的用法

但原译没有体现出这一逻辑关系。改译：

虽然我们在免除债务和优惠融资领域也需要迅速采取行动，使脆弱国家能够扩大卫生应对措施、提供社会保护，但我们必须牢记，有效创造公共收入，是当前和未来为卫生系统提供资金、提高系统韧性的关键。

---

① https://www.un.org/pga/74/2020/05/04/high-level-contact-group-meeting-of-the-heads-of-state-and-government-of-the-non-aligned-movement/, accessed March 21, 2021.

② https://dictionary.cambridge.org/dictionary/english/while, accessed March 21, 2021.

6.2.2.3　句段之间

译者不仅必须了解句子内部各成分的相互关系，还必须了解句子之间、段落之间的相互关系。请看这段话：

> 必须深刻认识又好又快发展是全面落实科学发展观的本质要求。
>
> 我国正面临着重要战略机遇期，又处于经济快速增长阶段，坚持又好又快发展，是落实科学发展观、实现全面建设小康社会目标的必然要求，是调动各方面积极性、发挥各类生产要素潜力的有效途径，是紧紧抓住发展机遇、实现综合国力整体跃升的必由之路。又好又快发展是有机统一的整体，既要求保持经济平稳较快增长，防止大起大落，更要求坚持好中求快，注重优化结构，努力提高质量和效益。
>
> 我国已具备支撑经济又好又快发展的诸多条件，关键要在转变增长方式上狠下功夫，当前特别是要在增强自主创新能力和节能降耗、保护生态环境方面迈出实质性步伐。①

作为普通读者，我们读完之后没有特别感觉。可能是因为我们作为普通百姓，并不关注讲话的逻辑和内涵。但作为译者，我们却发现了问题，即开头两个短句（删除部分）和该段其他内容逻辑联系不够紧密：

> 必须深刻认识又好又快发展是全面落实科学发展观的本质要求。
>
> ~~我国正面临着重要战略机遇期，又处于经济快速增长阶段，~~坚持又好又快发展，是落实科学发展观、实现全面建设小康社会目标的必然要求，是调动各方面积极性、发挥各类生产要素潜力的有效途径，是紧紧抓住发展机遇、实现综合国力整体跃升的必由之路。又好又快发展是有机统一的整体，既要求保持经济平稳较快增长，防止大起大落，更要求坚持好中求快，注重优化结构，努力提高质量和效益。
>
> <u>我国正面临着重要战略机遇期，又处于经济快速增长阶段，</u>~~我国~~已具备支撑经济又好又快发展的诸多条件，关键要在转变增长方式上狠下功夫，当前特别是要在增强自主创新能力和节能降耗、保护生态环境方面迈出实质性步伐。

---

① 胡锦涛，"转变经济发展方式，实现又好又快发展"，2006 年 12 月 5 日。

"我国正面临着重要战略机遇期，又处于经济快速增长阶段"在逻辑上的自然延伸是"所以具备又好又快发展的条件"，跟第二段的内容正好衔接。因此，翻译时可以把这两句移至第二段。这样，第一段讲又好又快发展的必要性，第二段讲可能性，逻辑更加清晰。

大家可能会问：译者有这么大的权利吗？这可是胡锦涛同志的讲话啊！是否对原文进行优化，由委托人或定稿人决定。译者发现问题，可以与他们协商，或交由他们决定。如果他们认为优化原文有利于对外传播，通常会作出优化的决定。当然，如果自己有最终决定权，就可以采用自己认为合适的翻译方法。

另外，这两段话中还有一处需要注意，即"好中求快"的重点在"好"（需重读"好"字），不在"求快"，因为"求快（+求稳）"是"既要……"的重点：

又好又快发展是有机统一的整体，既要求保持经济<u>平稳较快</u>增长，<u>防止大起大落</u>，更要求坚持好中<u>求快</u>，注重优化结构，努力提高质量和效益。

试译如下：

We must understand that sound and speedy development is essential for fully implementing the Scientifically-based Approach to Development (SAD)[①].

Sound and speedy development is an essential part in implementing the SAD and building a moderately prosperous society in all respects. It is also a means to motivate all stakeholders and tap the potential of all factors of production, as well as the necessary path for seizing development opportunities and elevating our composite national strength. Sound and speedy development is a coherent whole in that it <u>demands speedy but steady growth by avoiding major fluctuations; and more importantly, it demands the soundness of growth</u>, which emphasizes structural optimization, development quality and outcomes.

---

① 此处没有使用官方译法 Scientific Outlook on Development，具体原因见《非文学翻译》（李长栓，外语教学与研究出版社，2009）第122页。

<u>Our country is in an important period of strategic opportunity and fast growth.</u> It already possesses many conditions for sound and speedy development, but the key is to transform the growth mode. Particularly, we need substantive progress in indigenous innovation, energy conservation, and environmental protection.

6.2.2.4 版块之间

译者必须根据上下文来理解句子的含义和重点，包括理解文本的不同部分之间的联系。以下例子选自关于植物新品种保护的介绍，是一道测试题的答案：

<u>Q6 Answer</u>:

(a) All varieties of common knowledge must be considered in accordance with Article 7 of the UPOV Convention.

原译：

问题 6 回答：

所有已知品种认定应遵照《UPOV 公约》第 7 条。

这样的翻译，显然没有回头看看问题是什么。哪怕前面的问题部分不是自己翻译的，在翻译答案部分时，也必须了解问题是什么，否则根本无法理解答案的意思，更无法抓住答案的重点。我们看看问题：

Q6. When examining distinctness of a candidate variety, it <u>is not necessary</u> to consider all varieties whose existence is a matter of common knowledge (varieties of common knowledge). Please indicate true or false.

  a. true

  b. false

正确的译文：

问题 6　在审查申请品种的特异性时，<u>没有必要</u>考虑所有人所共知的品种。请判断对错。

  a．对

  b．错

我们看到了问题，就知道答案中的 (a) 并不是一个序列号，而是"选择 (a)"的意思。consider 也不是"认定"的意思，而是"考虑"；句子的意思重点是 must be considered，翻译时应置于句子末尾。改译：

问题 6 答案：

选择 (a)。根据《UPOV 公约》第七条，所有人所共知的品种都必须加以考虑。

句子的修饰关系，也必须通过上下文来判断。例如（来自某国机构的《工作人员条例》）：

Regulation 9.8 (a) (1) Termination Indemnity
Months of separation remuneration <u>as defined in Regulation 9.13</u>

下划线部分是修饰 months 还是 remuneration？从语法上来看，应遵循就近修饰原则，但为了做到确信无疑，我们要回头查看 9.13 的规定。但 9.13 并无相关规定（见图 6.15）：

> **Regulation 9.13**
> 条例 9.13
> **Last Day for Pay Purposes**
> 计酬最后日期
> (a) On separation from service, the date on which entitlement to salary, allowances and other benefits shall cease shall be determined according to the following provisions:
> (a) 离职后，薪酬、津贴和其他福利待遇的终止日期依照以下规定确定：

图 6.15 某条例规定（一）

相关规定在 9.15（见图 6.16）：

> **Regulation 9.15**
> 条例 9.15
> **Separation Remuneration**
> 离职补贴
> (a) "Separation remuneration" – the basis for the calculation of any payments due upon separation from service pursuant to Regulations 9.8, 9.9 and 9.12 – shall be the amount determined in accordance with the following provisions:
> (a) "离职补贴"为依照条例 9.8、9.9 和 9.12 计算离职后任何应付款项的基础，其数额根据以下规定确定：

图 6.16 某条例规定（二）

据此，我们不仅明白了修饰关系，还发现了原文的错误。鉴于这是一份国际文书，内容相当重要，译者不能擅自修改。因此，暂时按照原文翻译,并提醒用户注意。

译文:
　　条例 9.8 (a) (1)　终止任用赔偿金
　　条例 9.13　所述离职补贴的月数

6.2.3　深入专业领域

译者往往没有其他学科背景,但又不得不翻译专业性很强的内容。因此,译员必须学会现学现卖,在短时间内了解一个专业的语言习惯、把握所需的专业知识,努力做到"以假乱真"。

6.2.3.1　理解专业语言

任何专业都有自己的一套行话,外人看起来高深莫测,译者望而生畏。但实际上只要做充分调查研究,行话背后的道理可能十分浅显。例如,WIPO 一本培训专利检索的教材需要翻译为中文,内容涉及一件专利。该专利是制作封闭型无硬边三明治(a sealed crustless sandwich,类似我们的馅饼)的方法,权利要求包括:

> We claim:
> A sealed crustless sandwich, comprising:
> a first bread layer having a first perimeter surface coplanar to a contact surface;
> at least one filling of an edible food juxtaposed to said contact surface;
> a second bread layer juxtaposed to said at least one filling opposite of said first bread layer, wherein said second bread layer includes a second perimeter surface similar to said first perimeter surface;
> a crimped edge directly between said first perimeter surface and said second perimeter surface for sealing said at least one filling between said first bread layer and said second bread layer; wherein a crust portion of said first bread layer and said second bread layer has been removed.

我们看完之后可能觉得不知所云。描述具体空间布局的文字，必须配以图画才能够理解。但培训手册中只提供了一幅附图（见图 6.17）：

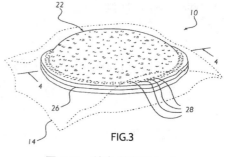

图 6.17　某专利附图（一）

我们可以通过截取权利要求中任意一句话，在搜索引擎中检索专利文件全文。全文提供了更多解释和附图，例如（见图 6.18）：

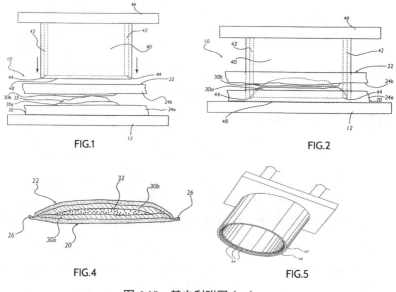

图 6.18　某专利附图（二）

对照文字和附图看专利，需要特别细心。为了便于理解，可以在谷歌图片中查找实物图。结果发现确实有生产：

> A sealed crustless sandwich is a type of sandwich which has a filling sealed between one big layer of bread. The big layer of bread is crimped together to seal in the filling and the crust is removed.

A number of patents have been issued for various versions of the sealed crustless sandwiches.

通过这些调查研究，我们发现制作密封型无硬边三明治没有那么复杂：在两个面包片之间放上填料，用个筒状刀片（FIG.5）切一下，切掉面包的硬边；筒状装置有一圈牙齿，把两片面包咬合到一起，把馅儿密封在里面。再回头看权利要求：

A sealed crustless sandwich, comprising:

a first bread layer having a first <u>perimeter surface</u> <u>coplanar to</u> <u>a contact surface</u>;

at least one filling of an edible food <u>juxtaposed</u> to said contact surface;

a second bread layer juxtaposed to said at least one filling opposite of said first bread layer, wherein said second bread layer includes a second perimeter surface similar to said first perimeter surface;

a <u>crimped</u> edge directly between said first perimeter surface and said second perimeter surface for sealing said at least one filling between said first bread layer and said second bread layer; wherein a crust portion of said first bread layer and said second bread layer has been removed.

这里面有几个说法不熟悉，需要查证。首先是 perimeter surface，调查发现，这两个词并不是一个短语（见图 6.19）：

> Perimeter is the distance around a shape while surface area is the area contained within it. 2019年3月1日
>
> www.thoughtco.com › Chemistry › Basics ▼
> **Perimeter & Surface Area Formulas: 2 Dimensional Shapes**

图 6.19　perimeter 的定义

perimeter 是周长，surface 是表面。为了万无一失，加引号查 "perimeter surface"，发现这两个词确实不是一个短语；即使出现在一起，中间也有逗号隔开（见图 6.20）：

www.amazon.com › Broccis-Perimeter-Surfac... ▾ 翻译此页
Bossy Brocci's Area, Perimeter, Surface Area ... - Amazon.com
Amazon.com: Bossy Brocci's Area, Perimeter, Surface Area & Volume Student Workbook: Calculating and Solving for the Area, Perimeter, Surface Area ...

www.teacherspayteachers.com › Browse ▾ 翻译此页
Perimeter Area Surface Area Worksheets & Teaching ...
Results 1 - 24 of 714 - This is the perfect game to review problems involving area, perimeter, surface area, and volume. This is a working Jeopardy® (Power Point) ...

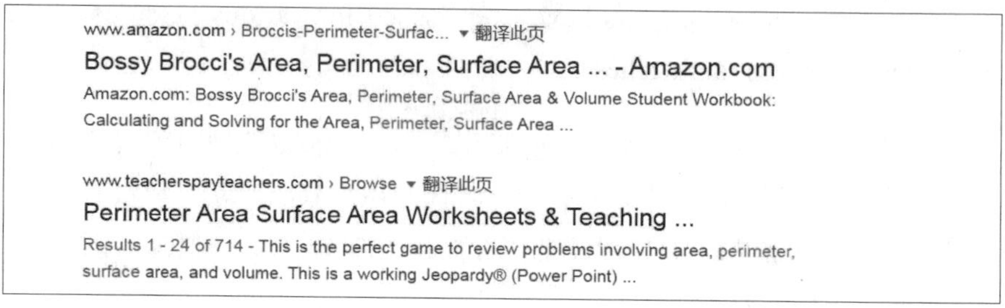

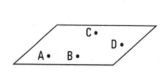

图 6.20　查证英文说法是否存在

由此推断，所谓 perimeter surface，作者希望表达的可能是“由周长包围的一个面积”，但哪块面积没有周长呢？

coplanar 的意思是“位于一个平面的”（见图 6.21）：

coplanar adjective
Save Word
co·pla·nar | \ (ˌ)kō-ˈplā-nər, -ˌnär \
Definition of *coplanar*
: lying or acting in the same plane

图 6.21　coplanar 的定义

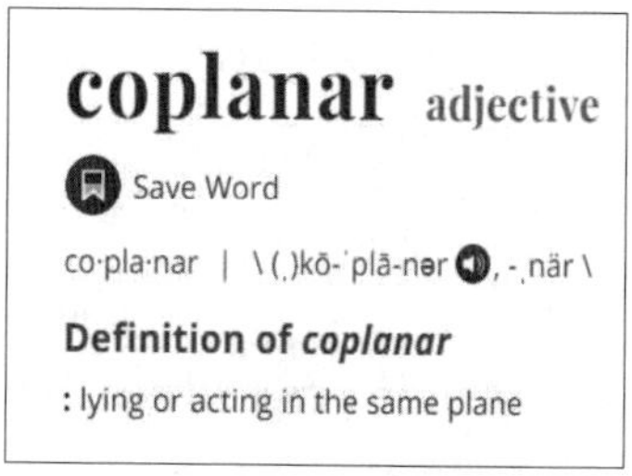

下图（图 6.22）中，A、B、C、D 位于同一平面，右侧立方体任何一面的四个点都位于同一平面。

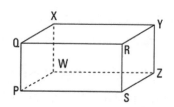

图 6.22　coplanar 图示

什么是 contact surface（接触面）？就是和三明治填料接触的面。所谓 a surface coplanar to a contact surface，字面意思是“与接触面位于同一平面的表面”，给人的印象是一个平面的两个位置。但从专利文件（其实就是常识）可知，填料直接放在第一个面包片的一个表面，接触面就是这个表面。所以“coplanar to”用法不当，改为 serving as 才贴切。综上，第一句话这样修改意思才清楚：

> a first bread layer having a first ~~perimeter~~ surface ~~coplanar~~ serving as a contact surface

第一片面包,其第一面为接触面

第二句的原文是:

at least one filling of an edible food <u>juxtaposed</u> to said contact surface;

Juxtapose 的意思是(图 6.23):

```
juxtapose  [ juhk-stuh-pohz, juhk-stuh-pohz ]  SHOW IPA
SEE SYNONYMS FOR juxtapose ON THESAURUS.COM

verb (used with object), jux·ta·posed, jux·ta·pos·ing.
1  to place close together or side by side, especially for comparison or contrast.
```

图 6.23 **juxtapose** 的定义

根据常识,填料是放在面包片之上的,并非与面包片并排放置以便于比较。由此可见,juxtapose 也是词不达意。不过,也不妨碍理解。因此,第二句可以翻译为:

至少一种可食用填充物,覆盖在第一片面包的接触面;

said 在专利文件中很常见,意思是"上述"。第三句:

a second bread layer <u>juxtaposed to said</u> at least one <u>filling</u> opposite of ~~said~~ first bread layer, wherein said second bread layer includes a second ~~perimeter~~ surface similar to said first ~~perimeter~~ surface;

这句话的结构是: a second layer juxtaposed to said one filling,即第二层面包压在馅儿上。opposite of first bread layer 是说第二片面包和第一片面包面对面(扣在一起)。其实不说也罢——都扣在馅儿上了,难道还不是面对面?试译:

第二片面包,相对于上述第一片面包,置于上述至少一种填充物之上;第二片面包包括与上述第一个接触面类似的第二接触面;

第四句(删除多余部分便于理解):

197

a <u>crimped</u> edge ~~directly~~ between ~~said~~ first ~~perimeter~~ surface and ~~said~~ second ~~perimeter~~ surface for sealing ~~said at least one~~ filling between ~~said~~ first bread layer and ~~said~~ second bread layer; wherein a crust portion of ~~said~~ first bread layer and ~~said~~ second bread layer has been removed.

其中的 crimp 意思是（图 6.24）：

> 牛津高阶英汉双解词典
>
> **crimp**
> / krɪmp; krɪmp/ v [Tn] **(a)** press (cloth, paper, etc) into small folds or ridges 把（布、纸等）压出小的摺痕或皱纹. **(b)** make (hair) wavy by pressing with a hot iron 把（毛发）烫成拳曲状；烫发.

图 6.24　crimp 的定义

试译：

　　上述第一接触面和第二接触面压成褶子的边缘，用于密封两片面包之间上述至少一种填充物；上述第一片面包和第二片面包的硬边已经切除。

由于专利要求的第一句是 A sealed crustless sandwich, comprising——（一种封闭型无硬边三明治，包括——），因此，接下来的清单都用名词短语，不用句子。

看似不可能的事情，经过我们不懈努力，还是能够圆满完成。我相信译文的质量比原文要高。所有这一切，有赖于对原文的准确和批判性理解。没有理解，翻译结果会是这样（学生初稿）：

　　一种密封的无硬边三明治，包括：
　　第一面包层，具有与接触表面共面的第一周边表面；
　　至少一个与所述接触表面并置的可食用食品的填充物；
　　与第一面包层相对的至少一个填充物并列的第二面包层，其中第二面包层包括类似于第一面包层的第二周边表面；
　　在第一周面和第二周面之间直接卷曲的边缘，用于密封第一面包层和第二面包层之间的至少一个填充物；其中第一面包层和第二面包层的硬边部分已被移除。

其中难以理解的地方没有经过任何加工消化，读者很难理解。可能有同学会问：这样翻译是否不忠实于原文？回答是：任何翻译活动都有发起人，都有既定的翻译目的。就上述专利而言，如果发明人有意在中国申请专利，就必须提交中文版的申请书，申请书必须符合中国法律要求。如果采用直接翻译的方法，专利审查员看不懂，就会打回来修改。所以，忠实于原文文字并非主要目的，主要目的是能够通过专利审查。做到意思清楚、语言通顺是必然的要求。当然，如果你是一个专利翻译，遇到原文有很多瑕疵，要向审校或用户提出来，由他们决定如何处理。实际上，上述专利要求的翻译，并非出于申请专利的目的，而是作为专利教程中的一个例子，告诉大家如何进行专利检索。因此，为便于阅读而进行优化处理，不需要专利权人同意。

还可能有同学会问：为什么外国专利写得这么差？回答是：这也许是个特例。但不排除专利撰写人故弄玄虚，让委托人觉得专利撰写高不可攀，花钱请人物有所值。但作为翻译，我们的价值取向是明确的，即让读者明白我们在说什么。

最后，译者工作中会涉及很多领域的知识，这些领域看似难以理解，但只要勤于查证，勤于请教，没有解决不了的问题。

6.2.3.2　理解行业背景

除了语言问题，专业和行业背景对于理解原文也至关重要。例如，在下例中，如果了解一点知识产权知识，就不会产生理解错误：

3. Substantive examination

In a number of countries, no search is made and no examination as to substance is carried out prior to registration of the industrial design. In some countries a substantive examination is conducted[,] where the design is checked against designs on the register for novelty and/or originality.

原译：

3. 实质审查

在一些国家，在工业品外观设计获得注册之前<u>不进行任何检索，也不进行任何实质审查</u>。在有些国家，实质审查是<u>相对于在册外观设</u>

计的新颖性和/或原创性进行的。

申请专利、商标、工业品外观设计保护的时候，受理机关通常会在数据库中查找一下，判断你的申请是否符合专利、商标、外观设计的条件；如果不符合，就会驳回。这就是实质性审查。但在授予工业品外观设计权的时候，有些国家（包括中国）不进行检索和审查，只要申请符合形式要求就批准，等将来有人告你侵权，那时候可以撤销。了解到这个背景后，就会知道，原文 no search is made and no examination as to substance is carried out 并非两个动作——search 只是 examination 的手段；因此翻译为"不……也不……"意思错误。同样，原文第二句 conducted 后面应该有个逗号，即 where 从句是非限定性的，说明审查的方式。原译"在有些国家，实质审查是相对于在册外观设计的新颖性和/或原创性进行的"，言外之意是，在其他国家不是这样，这不符合事实。在所有国家，实质审查都是针对新颖性进行的。改译：

在一些国家，在工业品外观设计的注册<u>不需要进行检索和实质审查</u>。在有些国家则需要进行实质审查，<u>即对照已注册外观设计进行新颖性和/或原创性检查</u>。

下面这个例子[①]，则说明理解行业背景的重要性：

Unlike owners of Apple phones, Android users can buy software, including "Fortnite", from various vendors, <u>limiting Google's power</u>; in 2018 Epic launched its own web-based store for PC games, where it takes a 12% cut from developers.

试译：

和苹果手机用户不同，安卓用户可以从各种应用商店上购买软件，包括"堡垒之夜"，这就限制了谷歌的权力；在 2018 年，艺铂游戏（Epic Games）推出了自己的网上电游商城，在这个平台上艺铂向游戏开发者抽取 12% 的分成。

---

① 本例由封鹏程提供。

这一段选自《经济学人》一篇讨论苹果公司和游戏开发者争端的文章，想要完全理解这句话需要具备背景知识。例如，其中 limiting Google's power 表达很简单，但到底是怎么回事？联系上下文并搜集背景知识后我们发现，原来因为苹果公司的产品使用的都是其自行开发的 IOS 系统，所有用户想要下载应用只能通过苹果公司的软件平台；而安卓系统是谷歌公司开发的，其源代码公开，所以安卓用户可以便利地从任意来源下载安装应用，但这也限制了谷歌公司，使其无法垄断，所以限制了谷歌的权力。

本例同样涉及表达的问题。此处我们合理推测《经济学人》的读者长期关注科技行业，具有相应的知识，所以不必在此处添加注释；但如果面向的读者发生变化，译者可能会需要向读者解释这背后的关系。

在翻译组织或者机构名称时也要查证。首先看该组织是否有已经决定的官方译名，这是最优先的选择；如果没有，则看是否已经有约定俗成的称呼；最后如果找不到可以采信的译名，则自己动手拟定。文中提到的"Fortnite"明显是一款应用，经过简单搜索我们发现其为一款近年来流行于各个国家的射击类游戏，在中文社区中已经有了广泛接受的译名"堡垒之夜"，故采用此译名。Epic 是一家美国游戏开发商，没有官方的中文译名，因为哪怕是中文用户也是直接称呼 Epic 这一英文名称的。但是在搜集资料的过程中我们发现，在一些用户的讨论中其被译为了"艺铂游戏"，所以我们暂且把其译为"艺铂游戏（Epic Games）"。

6.2.4 处理原文瑕疵

任何人都会犯错，所以，原文中出现错误也不足为奇。前面已经有很多原文出现瑕疵的例证。遇到原文笔误，如果原文来得及修改，可以和作者或委托人沟通，建议其修改原文。如果原文已经发表，无法修改，可以和用户沟通译文如何处理。通常情况下，很小的笔误，译者直接纠正即可，也可以在译文中批注说明。

6.2.4.1 笔误

原文的错误多种多样，有些属于笔误，稍微有一点逻辑思维就能够发现。例如：

> However, the work on the substantive issue on GRs [genetic resources] had not yet received attention, <u>and time allocated for its discussion during the eighteenth session</u>. The substantive issues were reflected as options as contained in WIPO/GRTKF/17/6.

下划线部分是半句话。这样的句子只能提请委托人修改。如果修改原文不现实，译者可以保留错误，加注说明"原文句子未完"，或者根据上下文猜测意思。此处很可能是说讨论的时间不够；如果足够的话，就不用专门提出来。

再如，下面的例子中，原文漏掉了 meeting，译者根据逻辑添加：

> The representative of FAIRA thanked Member States for their comments. At Tuesday night's drafting group <u>meeting</u>, there had been a number of pieces of text proposed by Indigenous representative that were indiscriminately eliminated with no attempt to rationalize the text and look to see if it should be supported.

有些错误可能来自语音识别错误。例如，下文中的 diversification 意思显然不符合逻辑；经查，应该为 desertification：

> They may also refer to relevant national communications to the Convention on Biological <u>Diversity</u>, the United Nations Convention to Combat ~~Diversification~~ <u>Desertification</u> and the United Nations Framework Convention on Climate Change.

出错的原因，可能是刚刚出现一个 diversity，因此，语音识别软件把 desertification 听成了 diversification。

6.2.4.2　表述不当

原文表述不当的情况很多，尤其是英语不是作者母语时。如果译者觉得逻辑上不通，或者违反常识的时候，就要去核实信息。例如，爱沙尼亚向联合国提交的一份报告中有这样一段话：

The Gender Equality Act <u>applies to</u> all areas of social life except professing and practising faith or working as a minister of a religion in a registered religious association; <u>and to</u> relations in family or private life.

学生译文：

《性别平等法》适用于社会生活的所有领域，但不包括传教或注册宗教团体的牧师；但适用于家庭或私人生活关系。

《性别平等法》到底是否适用于家庭？在家里推行性别平等是否可行？从句式结构看，适用于家庭。但如果已经说了适用于所有领域，自然包括家庭在内，无须再次专门提及；如果不适用于家庭，表述方式则应该调整如下：

The Gender Equality Act <u>applies to</u> all areas of social life except **to** professing and practising faith or working as a minister of a religion in a registered religious association; <u>and to</u> relations in family or private life.

为了弄清这个问题，笔者找到了该法的英文本：

1) This Act applies to all areas of social life.
2) The requirements of this Act do not apply to:
   i. professing and practising faith or working as a minister of a religion in a registered religious association;
   ii. relations in family or private life.

看来第二种理解是正确的，是原文表述不清。爱沙尼亚文是这样：

1) Seadust kohaldatakse kõigis ühiskonnaelu valdkondades.
2) Seaduse nõudeid ei kohaldata:
   i. registrisse kantud usuühendustes usu tunnistamisele ja viljelemisele või vaimulikuna töötamisele;
   ii. perekonna- või eraelu suhetes.

不需要懂爱沙尼亚语，单从排版就可以知道与英文版意思相同。但为了慎重起见，再用机器翻译做一下：

1) The law applies to all sectors of society.
2) Legal requirements shall not apply to:
   i. recognition and cultivation of religion or clergy in registered religious associations;
   ii. family or private relationships.

结果还是一样。改译如下：

《性别平等法》适用于社会生活的所有领域，但不适用于加入教会、参加宗教活动或担任注册宗教团体的神职人员，也不适用于家庭生活或私人关系。

6.2.4.3 指向错误

这类错误不容易发现。译者必须充分发挥逻辑思维、宏观思维、批判性思维的作用，才会发现线索，并通过进一步调查研究，确定问题所在。如属原文问题，应采取适当的方式处理。

大家请看这幅图及其说明（来自 WIPO 的一份文件，主题是传统知识的保护）（见图 6.25）：

图片说明初稿译为：卡尼部落成员发现了锡兰毛柄花中的有效成分。identify 确实可以译为"发现"（尽管更确切的意思是"识别出"），但难道这张图的意义就在于让我们看看卡尼部落的人长什么样？那个有效成分是什么？在哪里？怀着这种疑问，我们搜索了谷歌图片，发现这张图片配错了，应当配上另外一幅图片（见图 6.26）：

Kani tribal members identify components of the *arogyapaacha* plant

图 6.25 某文件的插图及错误的图片说明

图 6.26 本应当使用的图片

相应的，图片说明应该翻译为：卡尼部落成员展示锡兰毛柄花的有效部分。配错的那幅图，其实是卡尼部落的一位医生，资料来源如下（见图6.27）：

图 6.27　核实应使用的图片

此处原文错误，译者无法修改，只能告诉委托人更换图片。

6.2.4.4　数字错误

数字也是容易出错的地方。作者引用的时候会抄错，涉及计算的会出错，有时仅仅是笔误。译者只要勤于核实，或注意从数字中读出意义，便会可能发现数字错误。例如，下面这段文字：

> 例如，2007年1月30日《苹果日报》报道屯门泥围的邓兆伙诉陶枝盛等人，原因是在屯门围（村）的"'陶福德公'祖堂的三个氏族村民起纷争，""祖堂共有113个户口，其中4户姓陶及2户姓邓"，大姓"陶氏一族认为姓邓及姓衷的少数村民并非祖堂成员，03年开始停止向他们分发祖堂赔偿金。"

这是一篇介绍中国古代调解制度的论文，这段话因为涉及香港，所以需要查证香港地名如何拼写。在香港地图上没有查到"屯门围"的村名，也没有怀疑"屯门围"就是"屯门泥围"。倒是查到几个类似地名：屯门新村（Tuen Mun San Tsuen）；屯子围（Tuen Tsz Wai）；屯门新墟（Tuen Mun San Hui）；屯门旧墟（Tuen Mun Kau Hui）。后来居然发现本案的英文判决，其中不仅找到了所有专有名词，还发现《苹果日报》（或论文作者）的三处错误，包括数字错误：

- "屯门围（村）"应为"屯门泥围"
- "113 个户口"应为"131 个户口"
- "4 户姓陶"应为"4 户姓袁"

鉴于这是一篇学术论文，英译文将来要发表，经与作者沟通，译文改正了原文的上述（及其他一系列）错误：

> To cite an example: *Apple Daily* (Hong Kong) reported on 30 January 2007 of a case of Tang Siu For v. Tao Chi Shing & Others, where "the disputing parties were villagers of three clans" in Nai Wai, a village situated in Tuen Mun, Hong Kong, where villagers are surnamed To, Tang and Yuen. The ancestral temple ("Tong") To Fuk Tak Kung includes 131 households, of which, only 4 were Yuen households and 2 were Tang households. The majority households, To, argued that minority villagers with surnames Tang and Yuen cannot be members or acquire the household status of the Tong, and have stopped distributing compensation money from the Government for resumption of land since the end of 2003.

以下例子（见图 6.28）来自 WIPO 文件，其中规定了雇员搬家的时候，带多少东西可以报销费用。其中的 46 显然少个 0，因为如果 150 千克折算为 0.93 立方米的话，75 千克应该是 0.46 立方米。

> (h) In cases where the shipment by air is not more economical than by surface the maximum authorized shall be:
>
> (1) 225 kg (445 lb) or 1.40 m3 (49.5 cubic feet) for the staff member;
>
> (2) 150 kg (330 lb) or 0.93 m3 (33 cubic feet) for the first dependant;
>
> (3) 75 kg (165 lb) or 0.46 m3 (16 cubic feet) for every other dependant authorized to travel at the expense of the International Bureau.

图 6.28　某文件中的数字错误

笔者向委托人提出后，没想到引发更多修改。最后的文件是这样（见图 6.29）：

> (h) In cases where the shipment by air is not more economical than by surface the maximum authorized by air shall be:
> (1) 225 kg (495 lb) or 2.25 m³ (80 cubic feet) for the staff member;
> (2) 150 kg (330 lb) or 1.50 m³ (53 cubic feet) for the first dependant;
> (3) 75 kg (165 lb) or 0.75 m³ (26 cubic feet) for every other dependant

图 6.29　订正后的文件

在 UNOG（联合国日内瓦办事处）翻译文件时，遇到中国汽车标准化技术委员会的结构图，需要从英文翻译为中文（见图 6.30）：

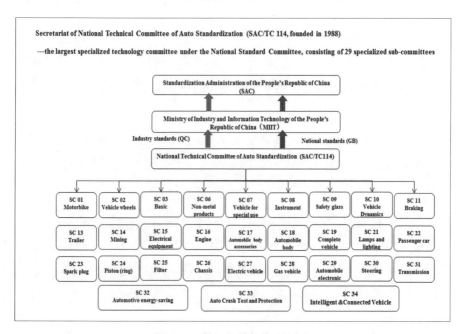

图 6.30　某组织的架构（英文）

这种情况下需要还原，而不是翻译。找到中文版之后，发现中文版中是 30 个专业分委员会，而英文版是 29 个。笔者建议用户采用更新的版本（见图 6.31）：

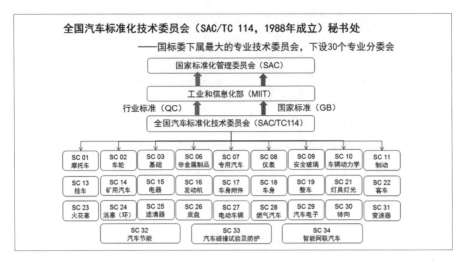

图 6.31　某组织的架构（中文）

6.2.4.5　方位错误

翻译方位描述时，一定要找到相应的地图。单凭文字描述，容易造成理解或表达错误。例如，这是杭州九里云松酒店的一段介绍：

> 作为一家新开张的奢华度假酒店，隐匿于山环水抱之间。坐落于杭州灵隐路18-8号，可谓是风水灵秀之地，<u>向西面对西湖美景、西溪湿地</u>，<u>北面即是千年古刹灵隐寺和天下第一财神庙</u>，仅有几步之遥，酒店后门即是古往今来香客祈福的必经之路——白乐桥村。

如果不看地图，文字描述看不出什么问题来：西面是西湖和西溪湿地；北面是灵隐寺，很近，仅有几步之遥；酒店后门是白乐桥村。但如果看看地图，发现描述并不准确（不是地图错误，其他地图也一样）（见图 6.32）：

西湖不在酒店西面，而是在东面！西溪不在

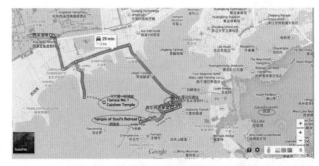

图 6.32　在地图中核实某酒店的方位

西面，而是在西北！这是否是作者表述错误呢？如果我们向作者求证，作者可能会辩解说，我要表达的是"向西面对作为西湖美景一部分的西溪湿地"，西溪湿地属于西湖地区的美景，"西湖美景、西溪湿地"中间的顿号，表示同位关系。我们作为读者，也可能无话可说。谁让我们不仔细呢！至于"西"和"西北"，也不算大错。

"北面即是千年古刹灵隐寺和天下第一财神庙，仅有几步之遥"，是否正确呢？地图上显示，这两处古迹分别在西南面和西面，作者恐怕无法辩解。"仅有几步之遥"是否正确呢？看起来不止几步。经查询，步行需要20多分钟，打车5分钟。但这句话作者可以辩解："仅有几步之遥"是跟在下一句："仅有几步之遥，酒店后门即是古往今来香客祈福的必经之路——白乐桥村"。好吧！我们又无话可说了——除了说：您能不能把那个逗号改为分号或句号？

我们作为译者，在做一件十分被动的事情，人家给什么，我们都要逆来顺受。据了解，华为的译者可以把不合格的原文退回去，他们真是有福气。一般的译者虽然不能退稿，也要尽力去理解原文，发现问题，还是可以提出来。对方听不听，另当别论。

上面这个例子是给学生布置的翻译作业，因此没有责任向任何人反馈。但假如是实际的翻译情景，可以改正并反馈给用户，请用户修改原文。试译如下：

> Nestled among lush hills and amid crystal waters, this newcomer to luxury boutique resorts is situated in the picturesque West Lake area. To its northwest is the Xixi National Wetland Park; to the west and southwest are the Temple of Fortune Gods and Lingyin Temple, both built 16 centuries ago. Behind and within hailing distance is the Baileqiao Village, through which visitors to the Lingyin Temple must pass.

6.2.4.6　引用错误

作者引用其他数据来源或报告，偶尔也会出错。例如一位同学在参与翻译《2019新常态下的区域经济大变局》时，发现其专栏1-23中存在引用

错误[1]。专栏原文如下:

> 据统计,1978—2008 年,中央财政向民族地区的财政转移支付累计达 20889.40 亿元,年均增长 15.6%。其中,2008 年为 4253 亿元,占全国转移支付总额的 23.8%。<u>从西藏自治区成立的 1955 年到 2008 年,中央给予新疆的财政补助累计达 3752.02 亿元</u>,年均增长 11%,其中 2008 年达 685.6 亿元。

细心的译者一定会发现,最后一句话前后不一致,先说的是"西藏自治区成立",为什么又变成"中央给予新疆财政补助"呢?而且资料显示,西藏自治区的成立时间为 1965 年,新疆维吾尔自治区才是成立于 1955 年。因此我们可以合理怀疑,此处引用存在错误。根据专栏最后提供的资料来源,可以搜索到中华人民共和国国务院新闻办公室在 2009 年发布的《中国的民族政策与各民族共同繁荣发展》[2]白皮书,相关内容如下(见图 6.33):

> 不断加大财政支持力度,积极组织对口支援
>
> 60年来,中央和地方各级政府逐步加大对民族地区的财政转移支付力度。从20世纪50年代开始,国家对民族地区实行"统收统支、不足补助"、提高预备费的设置比例(比一般地区高2个百分点)等优惠财政政策。1980年至1988年,中央财政对5个自治区和少数民族较为集中的贵州、云南、青海等省实行年递增10%的定额补助制度。1994年,国家进行分税制改革,对民族地区实行政策性转移支付。2000年起,除按照相关规定拨付一般性转移支付和专项转移支付外,还设立民族地区转移支付。据统计,1978年至2008年,中央财政向民族地区的财政转移支付累计达20889.40亿元,年均增长15.6%。其中,2008年为4253亿元,占全国转移支付总额的23.8%。
>
> 据不完全统计,从实行民主改革的1959年到2008年,中央给予西藏的财政补助累计达2019亿元,年均增长近12%;从自治区成立的1955年到2008年,中央给予新疆的财政补助累计达3752.02亿元,年均增长11%,其中2008年达685.6亿元。

图 6.33 核实原文信息

阅读白皮书原文,我们不难发现,专栏想表述的是新疆接收到的财政补助,确实是专栏作者引用笔误。遇到这种情况,译者需要及时向委托方反映,及时降低基础性错误带来的影响。

此外,若是引用的资料有官方译文,译者在翻译时还需要参考官方译文进行翻译,确保术语、信息的准确(参照官方译文时也需要保持批判性思维和逻辑)。通过互联网,译者找到了该白皮书的官方译文[3],并在此基础

---

[1] 本例由董文洁提供。
[2] http://www.gov.cn/zhengce/2009-09/27/content_2615773.htm, accessed March 21, 2021.
[3] http://english.cctv.com/20090927/104030.shtml。

上产出以下译文：

From 1978 to 2008 the total transfer payments by the central financial authorities to the minority areas totaled 2,088.94 billion yuan, with an annual increase of 15.6 percent. In 2008 alone, the amount was 425.3 billion yuan, making up 23.8 percent of the nation's total transfer payments. From 1955, when the Xinjiang Uyghur Autonomous Region was established, to 2008, the fiscal assistance from the central budget to Xinjiang reached 375.202 billion yuan, with an annual growth of 11 percent; the sum in 2008 was 68.56 billion yuan.

由此可见，译者在翻译时需要替原文内容把关，担当起"校对"的职责，确保每处引用都正确无误，不能对双引号内的内容完全迷信。

6.2.4.7　日期错误

在以下例子中，笔者要了解 National Strategic Roll-out Plan 的内容，以便准确翻译这个文件的名字，结果发现该文件的发布日期不是 10 月，而是 11 月，于是在提交译文时，向委托人提出（译文没有改）。后来发现原文改了，译文也相应修改。

这份文件的背景是：联合国消除对妇女歧视委员会审查了某国的履约报告，之后向该国提出一些问题，要求澄清情况。

原文：

Please provide updated information on the implementation of the National Strategic Roll-out Plan for the implementation of the three gender acts launched on 25 ~~October~~ November 2008 (para.13), including the challenges faced, and indicate whether any monitoring mechanisms have been established to determine the main achievements. (CEDAW/C/SLE/Q/6)

译文：

请提供 2008 年 11 月 25 日为落实三部性别法启动的《国家战略展开计划》的最新信息，包括面临的挑战，并说明是否建立了用以认定主要成果的监测机制。

译者并不是为了挑错而挑错,而是为了理解原文,在调查研究的过程中偶然发现原文错误。

6.2.4.8 标点错误

有的标点错误不影响理解,有的却会造成重大错误。这里举一个例子。前文提到的专利查询教程中,还有一份权利要求书需要翻译,其内容是:

> A spider ladder comprising a thin flexible latex rubber strip, means for attaching the latex to <u>a bath, a basin or sink inner and outer steps</u> and a wide base.

这是一个人发明的蜘蛛梯,申请了专利。梯子的用途是帮助不慎落入浴缸或盥洗池的蜘蛛爬出来。因为陶瓷表面十分光滑,蜘蛛在上面行走困难。原译是这样的:

> 蜘蛛梯包括一条有弹性的薄乳胶橡胶条,用于将乳胶与<u>浴缸、水盆或水槽的内外阶梯</u>和一个宽的基座相连。

下划线部分难以理解。浴缸、水槽哪来的阶梯?通过搜索下载并研读专利说明书的详细内容,发现原文少了一个逗号。请看查到的资料(见图6.34):

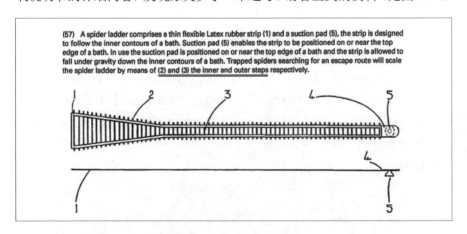

图 6.34　核实发现标点错误

从文字解释和附图可以了解到：蜘蛛梯一端有个吸盘（5），把吸盘粘在浴缸外边，顺着浴缸内壁的走势，把梯子铺开。蜘蛛可以顺着梯子"扶手"外侧的踏板（2）（outer steps）或者内侧的踏板（3）（inner steps）爬出去。请看内（3）外（2）踏板的放大图（见图6.35）：

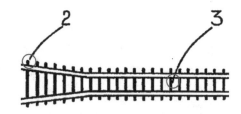

图 6.35　某专利附图（局部放大）

所谓"扶手"（蜘蛛当然不需要扶），就是一个橡皮条。明白了蜘蛛梯的基本原理后，再去看文字，就可以看懂了，原来在 sink 和 inner 之间，漏掉了一个逗号：

> A spider ladder comprising a thin flexible latex rubber strip, means for attaching the latex to a bath, a basin or sink, inner and outer steps and a wide base.

其中的 a thin flexible latex rubber strip，就是扶手；means for attaching the latex to a bath, a basin or sink 就是指吸盘；a wide base 就是左侧加宽的部分。全段改译如下：

> 一种蜘蛛梯，包括一条柔软纤细的乳胶条、一个将胶条附着在浴缸、水盆或水槽上的装置、多个内外侧踏板以及一个加宽的基部。

注意：其中的 means 意思是名词"手段"，不是动词 mean 的第三人称单数。

6.3　小结

译者的理解需要广泛而深入，既包括原文产生的背景，如 who is speaking to whom, about what, when, where and why，又包括原文的细节，如字词的含义、逻辑关系、专业知识；译者甚至需要发现原文的瑕疵。只有在准确理解的基础上，才能产出准确的译文。

〔课后练习〕

    1. 你最近做的一次翻译练习，6个W分别是什么？是否有人告知？如果没有，自己是否询问或做了调查？

    2. 你的理解是否深入？是否在理解句子结构的基础上，就开始翻译？这样做与机器翻译有何区别？

    3. 你的调查研究是否仅限于查询不会翻译的单词？还需要调查或考虑哪些方面？

    4. 是否需要纠正原文瑕疵？是直接纠正还是与作者沟通？

    5. 每个例子对自己有何启发？

第七章　理解的思想方法和操作方法

 **扫码预习**

请扫码下载本章涉及的例句。先做练习，再看解答，学习效果更佳。

理解原文的思想方法是逻辑思维、宏观思维和批判性思维，操作方法是调查研究。在前几章的举例中，已经举过很多例子，本章再举若干例证，以示强调。

7.1　逻辑思维

逻辑思维就是能够根据常识和专业知识，发现句子之内、句子之间和上下文的逻辑关系。以下例子来自 WIPO 文件，内容是告诉读者如何在专利库中检索专利文件：

The searcher will find it interesting to search the patent documents by using names of the parties involved in patenting.

原译：

通过使用专利申请中相关者的姓名，检索人会发现专利文件检索的乐趣。

原译意思不清。原文的意思其实很简单：看到一份专利文件，搜一下发明人还有什么发明，不是很有趣吗？这是凭借常识就可以得出的判断，把这个意思交代清楚即可。

改译：

通过专利文件列出的人员姓名检索，查询这些人的其他发明，也是一件有趣的事情。

以下段落仍然来自WIPO的一份文件，内容是传统知识的保护：

Indigenous people, local communities and their governments – mainly in developing countries — are seeking IP protection for traditional forms of creativity and innovation, which are not adequately protected under the conventional IP system. For instance, a traditional remedy could be developed by a pharmaceutical company and patented; an indigenous folk song could be adapted and protected by copyright; an invention derived from a genetic extract from a plant could be protected by patents or plant breeders' rights — all with no benefit going to the local community.

原译：

土著人民、地方社区及其政府，主要是发展中国家政府，正在为传统形式的创造力和创新寻求知识产权保护，而传统的知识产权制度并没有充分保护这些传统形式的创造力和创新。例如，制药公司可以开发一种传统的治疗方法并获得专利；土著民歌可在改编后受版权保护；源自植物遗传提取物的发明可以受到专利或植物育种者权利的保护——而这些专利并不能给当地社区带来利益。

原译最主要的问题是没有理解all。全段的意思是：外人可以以某种方式对传统知识加以包装改造，获得不同形式的知识产权的保护，从中获利，但这些传统知识的最初创造者，却一无所获。All前面的破折号，指分号隔开的三个句子，而不是仅仅最后一个。改译如下：

土著民族、地方社区及其政府（主要在发展中国家），正在为传统形式的创造和创新寻求知识产权保护，因为常规知识产权制度无法有效发挥作用。例如，制药公司可以通过开发传统疗法获得专利；改编后的土著民歌可以得到版权保护；源自植物基因提取物的发明可以受到专利或植物育种者权利的保护——而<u>所有这些保护</u>都不能给地方社区带来任何利益。

以下例子仍然来自 WIPO 文件，内容是介绍一种创意耳机：

> A listener who is using <u>earphones</u> to listen to streamed <u>music</u> provided by an online service may occasionally need to <u>remove them</u>. Unless the user manually stops playing the music, he or she will miss some; and there will also be wastage of the electronic device's battery life and of cellular data usage, of which the user may only be allotted a certain amount per month. In order to solve this problem, an inventor called Alessandro produced a pair of earphones having ear presence sensors. In response to determining that the earphones have been removed from the ears, a control circuit pauses the music.

原译：

> <u>耳机用户收听在线服务商提供的流媒体音乐后有时可能需要将音乐删除</u>。如不手动停止播放，用户会错过一些音乐；还会浪费电子设备的电池寿命和蜂窝数据流量，而用户每月的流量是有限的。为解决这一问题，一位名叫 Alessandro 的发明家生产出带入耳感应器的耳机。从耳中取出耳机后，控制电路便会暂停播放音乐。

原译有个显而易见的错误，就是把 them 错误理解为 music，实际上是指的耳机。出错的原因，是没有结合生活常识和下面几句来理解。改译：

> <u>耳机用户收听在线服务商提供的流媒体音乐时可能偶尔需要取下耳机</u>。如不手动停止播放，用户会错过一些音乐；还会浪费电子设备的电池电量和手机数据流量，而用户每月的流量是有限的。为解决这

217

一问题，一位名叫 Alessandro 的发明家制造出带人耳感应器的耳机。从耳中取出耳机后，控制电路便会暂停播放音乐。

7.2 宏观思维

宏观思维能力是指译者能够通过作者背景、写作背景、上下文等宏观背景，解决微观层面的理解或表达问题的能力。笔者称之为 Act local, think global。宏观思维是逻辑思维在更大背景下发挥作用。还以前文提到的联合国圣杰罗姆翻译竞赛为例，译者关于作者和写作背景的调查，都是为了从宏观上把握一篇文章。宏观思维使译者在遇到微观问题时，能够根据宏观背景作出正确判断。例如：

> Armies of perfectly made-up women looking like — I imagine — Kardashians *struggled with bags* from designers so exclusive I'd never even heard of them.

其中的 struggle with 到底是买包太多，招架不住，还是面对不同牌子的包包，心中纠结，不知道买哪一个？参赛者两种理解都有。

从宏观背景考虑，这些俊男靓女都是出手阔绰的土豪，不在乎花钱多少。调查卡戴珊的家庭背景，观看一些她的日常生活视频，就可以理解她平时花钱如流水。据此判断，他们只要看到满意的手袋，都会统统买下，因此，struggled with 解释为买包太多拎不动可能更有道理，而不是纠结于到底要哪个。

另外，文章后文（竞赛节选之外）还提到了包（bag），作者借此讽刺那些来哈罗德购物就是为了拎着购物袋到处炫耀的人：

> Despite my outrage, I resolved not to leave without buying at least one thing for at least one of my little girls. I settled on a teether for a tenner. After chatting amicably with the woman at the till I collected my receipt, put the teether in my skanky shorts pocket and left.

"Where's the bag," my better half asked as we headed towards the Knightsbridge Tube Station.

"Oh, I didn't bother with one," I said.

"You didn't get the bag? Everyone gets the bag. What is the point of shopping in Harrods if you don't get to walk around with the bag afterwards?"

此处的包，一定是购物袋。由此可以推测，女士们购买的手袋，也一定是装在购物袋里，她们拎着的大包小包，也一定是购物袋，里面装着名牌手袋。

再举一例，说明即使一个简单的词，也需要通过宏观背景界定词义。

原文：

This second function – the publication of patent information – has resulted in the accumulation of millions of technological solutions to the many challenges that people face. In this course, we will discuss this rich accumulation of scientific knowledge and technological information that is disclosed in patent documents.

原译：

专利制度的第二项功能即专利信息的公布。专利制度目前已积累数百万技术解决方案，应对人们面临的各种挑战。在本课程中，我们将讨论专利文件中公布的大量科学知识和技术信息。

原译把 millions 理解为"数百万"，不一定准确。因为汉语的"数"通常限于个位数，而英文中"millions"可以达到几百个百万。如果原文和网上查不到更具体信息，可以翻译为"数以百万计的"，但在这份文件中，后文有一段给出了具体数字：

It is estimated that over 70 million patent documents have been published to date. It is important to note that about two-thirds of the technical information revealed in patents is never published elsewhere.

据此，millions 可以大胆翻译为"数千万"。

下面一例来自 WIPO 一份专利检索教程：

Also, since functionality and screen layout also change regularly, what you see on your screen may differ from what is shown in the Module. The Academy does not take responsibility for the visual changes that patent databases make and we appreciate your sending a note to your tutor or the course administration where you find functional changes to a patent database during the offering of the course <u>so we may adapt the screens in the course content</u>.

原译：

此外，由于功能和页面布局也定期变化，您在页面上所见的内容可能与模块中显示的内容不同。本学院不对专利数据库进行的视效变更负责，在听课过程中，如您发现专利数据库出现功能变化，我们谨请您向导师或课程管理部门发送说明，<u>以便我们根据课程内容调整页面</u>。

下划线部分的意思是：以便我们调整教材中的页面截图。这是一份教程，教授人们在具体网站检索专利文献，所以用到了多页面截图。网站不断变化，教材不一定跟上变化。所以，老师告诉学生：如果谁发现变化，随时告诉我，我们更新截图。如果译者把握这个大背景，就不会出现相反的理解和翻译。改译：

此外，由于数据库功能和页面布局也定期变化，你在页面上所见的内容可能与模块中显示的内容不同。本学院不对专利数据库的视效变更负责；在听课过程中，如发现专利数据库出现功能变化，请向导师或课程管理部门发送说明，<u>以便我们调整教材中的页面截图</u>。

请大家阅读以下短文，通过查证和宏观思维，说明家暴为什么被称为 "a perfect storm"：

Domestic Violence: A Perfect Storm

America is facing a "spiraling crisis" of domestic violence, said Julie Bosman in *The New York Times*. With women and children "cooped up at home for months" with abusive husbands and fathers during government-imposed lockdowns, evidence is mounting of a surge in domestic violence. A new study from Brigham Young University found a 10.2 percent increase in domestic violence calls across 15 large U. S. cities. Houston saw five domestic violence deaths over the Memorial Day weekend alone. The National Domestic Violence Hotline said at least 5,000 people have called since mid-March and cited the pandemic as a trigger. In Los Angeles and New York City, authorities say calls to hotlines are actually down, probably because women can't call while confined "in such close quarters with their abusers." Unfortunately, women's shelters no longer are accepting new residents, to prevent the spread of Covid-19. Sara Hirsch, who staffs a victim hotline in New York, said of her clients, "It feels like there's no escape."

"It's hard to imagine a set of circumstances that would facilitate abuse so much as the ones we've been living under," said Ashley Fetters and Olga Khazan in *TheAtlantic.com*. Beyond being simply isolated, "people are stressed," with job losses causing financial worries and their kids home 24/7. Soaring unemployment rates make it more difficult for victims to flee a family bread winner. A 2017 study by Oxford University linked a 1 percent rise in U.S. unemployment with a 25 percent increase in child neglect and a 12 percent increase in physical abuse. The news from the front lines is not good, said Adiel Kaplan and Wilson Wong in *NBCNews.com*. A survey of 35 domestic violence support groups in 19 states found that most reported "major disruptions" in their ability to help victims. "Hotline calls became shorter and callers more frantic." In some cases, the calls suddenly grew "eerily silent as trapped victims" had to hang up.

As a child, I got a taste of "the brutal reality" people are surely experiencing, said Wendy Knight in *USAToday.com*. For years, I was trapped in the house "with a man who slapped, shoved, cursed, threatened, and belittled" my mom. "What I didn't see, I heard from my bed or the closet where I hid." It left me with lasting trauma that haunted me for years, as it does for so many kids. "Decades after the bruises fade," the pain of this terrible time will endure. (*THE WEEK* June 5, 2020)

本文的主要意思是新冠疫情导致美国的家庭暴力增加。主要原因包括：妇女儿童被迫待在家里，长期与丈夫/父亲"圈"在一起；家暴受害者庇护所无法接收家暴受害者，受害者无处可逃；失业率升高，经济压力增大，受害者不敢逃；孩子无法上学，给孩子带来精神压力。

而英文的 perfect storm 意思是：

… an event in which a rare combination of circumstances drastically aggravates the event. The term is used by analogy to an unusually severe storm that results from a rare combination of meteorological phenomena.①

这一解释，正好符合文章的内容。因此，把 a perfect storm 翻译为"家暴：一场强（大、总）风暴""家暴：一场完美（巨大、无声、十足、极端、绝对、完全、彻底、可怕、真正、汹涌、肆虐、嚣张）的风暴""家暴：一场无法逃脱（席卷而来、不折不扣、已成定局、席卷全美、势头之上）的风暴"难以和正文建立联系，或者以偏概全。

自拟类的标题，如"家暴风波""家庭暴力之殇""疫情期间的狂风暴""风暴已经来临""特殊时期的危机""席卷而来的家暴事件""家庭暴力高发""席卷全美的家暴风波""家庭暴力来袭社会风暴激增""家暴：风暴来袭""家暴：一次大爆发""家暴：一场风暴危机""家暴：家庭中的狂风暴雨""家庭暴力：嚣张中席卷而来""风暴袭来：家暴日益严重"，同样没有准确理解 perfect storm 的含义及其和正文的联系。

比较好的翻译有："家暴：祸不单行""家暴：雪上加霜""家暴：一场扣准时机的风暴""家暴：疫情带来的'完美'契机""家暴偏逢连月封城""家庭暴力：一场适逢新冠疫情的风暴""家庭暴力：一场'完美'的

---

① https://en.wikipedia.org/wiki/Perfect_storm, accessed March 21, 2021.

风暴""家暴：一场'适时'的风暴""家庭暴力，趁疫猖獗""一场天地人完美结合的风暴"。

有的同学把标题译为"国内暴乱：一场难以击退的困难风暴"，显然是把 domestic 理解为"国内"，与正文完全失去了联系，这是缺乏宏观思维的典型表现。

如果笔者来做，可能译为："家暴：天时地利人不和""家庭暴力：天地人的完美组合""新冠疫情导致家暴激增""新冠疫情成为家暴温床"。大家可以再想想有无更好译法。

本段还有多处需要宏观视角才能理解。例如，domestic violence calls 当中的 call——从上下文来判断，此处的 call 也是指热线电话。再例如，第二段的 front lines 是指下面所说的 domestic violence support groups（他们运营 shelters 和 hotlines 等）。

宏观思维还包括利用自己的常识作出判断，例如：

<u>The news from the front lines is not good</u>, said Adiel Kaplan and Wilson Wong in NBCNews.com. A <u>survey</u> of 35 domestic violence support <u>groups</u> <u>in 19 states</u> found that most reported "major disruptions" in their ability to help victims.

一个同学的译文是：

NBCNews.com 的 Adiel Kaplan 和 Wilson Wong 则表示，<u>实地调查看到的景象也不容乐观。有一项调查在美国 19 个州进行</u>，覆盖了 35 个为家暴受害者提供帮助的组织，结果表明，大多数组织帮助受害者的能力正经受"严重干扰"。

译者的表述方式（下划线部分），给人的印象是调查人员亲自到 19 个州区调查。但根据常识，获取反家暴团体的数据，并不需要亲自过去；in 19 states 从语法上来看，也更接近 groups，修饰 survey 的可能性较小。

改译：

Adiel Kaplan 和 Wilson Wong 在 NBC 新闻网（NBCNews.com）撰

223

文指出，来自反家暴前线的消息也不容乐观。一项对 19 个州 35 个家暴受害者支持组织的调查显示，大多数组织称，他们提供帮助的能力受到"严重影响"。

最后举个例子，说明在发挥宏观思维的时候，避免先入为主。CNN 在关于巴西重开一处旅游胜地的报道中写道：

"To land on the archipelago, the tourist will need to present the result of a positive PCR test that is <u>at least 20 days old</u>, or the result of the serological test showing the presence of antibodies against Covid," its administrator, Guilherme Rocha, told a news conference on Thursday. During the news conference, Rocha didn't explicitly explain why Brazil would accept only tourists to the islands that had already had the disease.①

新华社编译了这条新闻，这段的翻译是：

伯南布哥州政府官员吉列尔梅·罗沙 27 日在新闻发布会上宣布，游客若想登上该州辖内的费尔南多—迪诺罗尼亚群岛，"需要出示<u>至少 20 天内</u>接受的新冠病毒核酸检测结果呈阳性的证明，或者证明体内已产生新冠病毒抗体的血清学检测结果"。罗沙没有说明提出这一要求的原因。②

原译中将"at least 20 days old"理解为"至少 20 天内"意思是不清楚的，甚至是错误的。在这里，原文指的是在"至少 20 天前"核酸检测呈阳性的人群。因为这一句话的整体意思是，患过新冠肺炎、已经产生抗体的人群，才可以到这里旅游。虽然发言人没有解释为什么，但也容易理解：患过之后，就不容易再患了，免得为当地增加负担。产生这个错误的原因，是国内通常要求游客出示若干天之内新冠肺炎检测阴性的报告，于是译者不假思索地套用了这个表达方法。实际上，这段话的前面一句就是：And now

---

① https://edition.cnn.com/travel/article/fernando-de-noronha-brazil-reopens-covid-19/index.html, accessed March 21, 2021.

② https://xhpfmapi.zhongguowangshi.com/vh512/share/9363397?channel=weixin, accessed March 21, 2021.

it's open to travelers again—but with an unexpected catch. You can go only if you show you have had Covid-19. 沿着这句话的逻辑，就不会被国内的情况带偏。

改译：
  伯南布哥州政府官员吉列尔梅•罗沙 27 日在新闻发布会上宣布，游客若想登上该州辖内的费尔南多－迪诺罗尼亚群岛，"需要出示<u>至少 20 天前</u>接受的新冠病毒核酸检测结果呈阳性的证明，或者证明体内已产生新冠病毒抗体的血清学检测结果"。罗沙没有说明提出这一要求的原因。

7.3　批判性思维

  批判性思维就是能够根据上下文逻辑、常识和专业知识，发现原文的语言瑕疵、逻辑问题和事实性错误，并在必要时予以纠正。批判性思维是逻辑思维的高级形式。在前文"家暴"一例中，如果去核实文章引用的资料，会发现所谓 "1 percent rise in U. S. unemployment with a 25 percent increase in child neglect and a 12 percent increase in physical abuse"，表述并不准确，其中的 1 percent，实指一个百分点，而不是百分之一。同样，所谓 most reported "major disruptions" in their ability to help victims，表述也不准确；原始出处说的是受害者求救的能力遭受巨大打击，而不是援助机构的接待能力。现实中遇到这种情况，可以询问委托人如何处理。下面再看一个例子：

  Policy makers have been guided by economists' findings that a country's economic growth rate is influenced by government Intellectual Property policies (see Module 2). This recognition of the importance inherent in the "<u>endogenous growth theory</u>" (a theory that economic policy and <u>external factors</u> can drive economic growth) suggests that governments should give a higher priority to policies that promote research and engineering activities to create a solid base for indigenous technologies.

原译：

　　经济学家发现，一个国家的经济增长率受政府知识产权政策的影响，这一发现成为政策制定者的决策指导（见模块2）。这种对"内生增长理论"（经济政策和外部因素可以推动经济增长的理论）内在重要性的认识表明，政府应该更加重视能够促进研究和工程活动的政策，为本土技术创造坚实基础。

"endogenous growth theory"译为"内生增长理论"没问题。但"内生增长"怎么会来自外部因素呢？调查可知：

> Endogenous growth theory holds that economic growth is primarily the result of endogenous and not external forces. Endogenous growth theory holds that investment in human capital, innovation, and knowledge are significant contributors to economic growth.

因此，可以断定，原文的 external 纯属笔误，译者直接改正即可。也可以告诉委托人原文有问题，请委托人注意。关于批判性思维在翻译中的运用，请见第五章"翻译是发现和解决问题的过程"。

7.4　调查研究

翻译中通过逻辑思维、宏观思维、批判性思维发现的问题，有的通过思考可以解决，大多数则需要通过调查研究才能解决。前面很多例子已经说明了这个问题，这里再举几例，说明调查研究的手段，包括：看上下文、查参考书、搜互联网、询问作者。

7.4.1　看上下文

译者必须通过上下文判断词义、修饰关系、逻辑关系、意思重心等。可以说，没有上下文，就没有确定的意思。比如，在前文"家暴"案例中，"In

Los Angeles and New York City, authorities say calls to hotlines are actually down"当中的 authorities 并非指市政当局,而是家暴热线负责人,因为上文讲到调查了 15 个城市的家暴热线,这里一定仍然是家暴热线反馈的情况。再比如:下例中的 when filing... 是修饰 provided 还是 found?

Q5. If it is <u>found</u> that the information <u>provided</u> by the breeder to assess uniformity and stability <u>when filing the application</u> was not accurate and the variety was wrongly determined to be uniform and stable, this would lead to:

a. Cancellation

b. Nullity

虽然从语法判断修饰哪个都可以,但如果看了前文内容,就一定知道是修饰 provided,也只有修饰后者,句子才有意义。以下译文,就是没有看上文的结果(上文是另一个同学做的):

题 5. <u>在提出申请之际</u>,倘若发现育种提供的评估一致性和稳定性信息不准确,于是/并且错误地确定本品种是一致和稳定的,这将导致:

a. 取消

b. 无效

改译:

问题 5. 如发现育种者<u>在申请时</u>提供的用于评估一致性和稳定性的信息不准确,导致品种被错误认定为具有一致性和稳定性,这将导致育种者权利——

a. 被取消

b. 被宣告无效

7.4.2 查参考书

字词典等参考书是翻译不可或缺的工具,尤其是英英词典(关于词典等查询工具的详细介绍,见第九章"学会网络查证确保措辞准确")。对于拿不准的词,必须通过英英词典加以核实,不能凭空猜测或望文生义。例如，上文家暴案例中有一句话：

> Sara Hirsch, who <u>staffs</u> a victim hotline in New York, said of her clients, "It feels like there's no escape."

有同学翻译为：

> Sara Hirsch 是<u>负责纽约一个家暴热线机构的职员</u>，她感觉求助者"无处可逃"。

给人的印象是此人是个负责人，但她其实是一位接听电话的雇员（见图 7.1）：

因此要改为：Sara Hirsch 是纽约一个家暴热线的职员，她感觉求助者"无处可逃"。

图 7.1　staff 的定义

```
staff verb
staffed; staffing; staffs
Definition of staff (Entry 2 of 2)
transitive verb
1 : to supply with a staff or with workers
2 : to serve as a staff member of
// an organization staffed by volunteers
```

再如，2020 年耶鲁大学校长在毕业典礼上有这样一段话[①]：

> These are no ordinary times. The world needs each of you prepared to tackle whatever challenges come your way. I am confident, with eyes open and hearts full of compassion, you will take Yale's mission of light and truth to neighbors near and far.

原译：

> 今时不同以往。世界需要你们每一个人都做好迎接前方挑战的准备。诸位视野广阔、满怀热忱，我相信你们把耶鲁"光明与真理"的使命带到远近邻舍面前。

原译把 with eyes open 译为"视野广阔"令人生疑。一查英英词典，原来 with eyes open 另有其他意思[②]：

[①] https://law.yale.edu/yls-today/news/yale-law-commencement-2020-coming-together-while-apart, accessed March 21, 2021.

[②] https://idioms.thefreedictionary.com/with+eyes+open, accessed March 21, 2021.

with (one's) eyes (wide) open

<u>With keen or complete knowledge, awareness, or expectations</u>.

I know they're offering you a lot of money, but make sure you go into this situation with your eyes open—it could be a scam.

Considering John's history of infidelity, Claudia knew she could only take him back with her eyes wide open.

with (one's) eyes (wide) open

Fig. <u>totally aware of what is going on</u>.

I went into this with my eyes open.

We all started with eyes open but didn't realize what could happen to us.

with (one's) eyes open

<u>Aware of the risks involved</u>.

从三处解释来看，with eyes open 确实是个比喻用法，字面意思是睁大眼睛，引申为"加倍小心"，此处从积极的角度看，翻译为"审时度势"也许更为合适：

改译：

　　今年不同寻常。世界需要你们作好准备，迎接前进道路上的任何挑战。我相信只要大家审时度势、满怀热忱，就一定不负耶鲁大学的使命，把光明与真理带到四邻八方。

另外，原译"把使命带到面前"搭配不当，但可以把"光明和真理"带到某个地方。原译"远近邻舍"搭配不当：距离远的，就不是"邻舍"。可以改为"近邻远舍"，但"舍"是个去声字，不够响亮，因此改为"四邻八方"。These are no ordinary times. 是指 2020 年新冠疫情爆发，不同寻常，尽管不影响翻译，但译者心里要清楚。

7.4.3 搜互联网

很多疑难问题通过原文难以解决，必须通过互联网查询。例如，上文关于家暴的短文中，有这样一句话：

The National Domestic Violence Hotline <u>said</u> at least 5,000 people have <u>called</u> since mid-March and <u>cited</u> the pandemic as a trigger.

下划线的三个单词，是 said 和 called 并列，还是 called 和 cited 并列？仅通过语法分析，是无法做出判断的，因为两种结构都说得通。第一种结构意思是：家暴热线称，有 5000 人打电话，还称疫情是（有些案例的）诱因。第二种结构意思是：家暴热线称，有 5000 人打电话并告诉他们疫情是家暴诱因之一。要想做出确信无疑的判断，必须通过网络获得更多信息。通过关键词搜索，2020 年 4 月 6 日的报道是：

In the U.S., since March 16, 2020, the National Domestic Violence Hotline has received <u>2,345 calls in which COVID-19 was cited as a condition of abuse</u>, Crystal Justice, chief marketing and development officer, told *Forbes* on Monday.

其措辞显然是第二种理解，即"受害者打电话并声称……"，而我们要翻译的报道是 6 月 5 日的报道（见图 7.2）：

www.pressreader.com › usa › the-week-us - 翻译此页
The Week (US): 2020-06-05 - Domestic ... - PressReader
2020年6月5日 - The National Domestic Violence Hotline said at least 5,000 people have called since mid-March and cited the pandemic as a trigger. In Los ...

图 7.2　某新闻报道截图

两个报道的数据来源相同，数字差距合理，显然是在讲同一件事情。因此，可以断定第二种结构正确。

再例如（来自 WIPO 文件，主题是药品贸易、知识产权和公共健康的关系）：

This represents an annual average growth of almost 10 percent. Growth in trade in health-related products is dominated by <u>formulations</u> (i.e. <u>active pharmaceutical ingredients **packaged** together with non-drug substances in form of pills, capsules, liquids, etc.</u>) followed by hospital inputs and medical equipment (Figure 6).

第七章 · 理解的思想方法和操作方法

原译：

> 医疗产品贸易的增长主要来自配方（即片剂、胶囊、液体等形式的<u>非药品物质中的活性药物成分</u>），其次是医院投入和医疗设备（图表 6）。

原译下划线部分的意思简化一下，就是"配方＝活性成分"，显然不对。通过互联网调查发现：

> Pharmaceutical formulation, in pharmaceutics, is the process in which different chemical substances, including the active drug, are <u>combined</u> to produce a final medicinal product. <u>The word formulation is often used in a way that includes dosage form</u>.[1]

所以，formulation 不是抽象的配方，而是制剂的制作过程，其结果还叫作 formulation（制剂）。制剂的制作过程，并非把活性成分和辅料包装在一起，而是混合在一起。所以原文用 package 并不恰当。以下中文资料也说明了这个道理：

> 药物制剂是由活性成分的原料和辅料所组成，因此辅料是制剂生产中必不可少的重要组成部分，也可以说"没有辅料就没有制剂"。[2]

改译：

> 保健产品贸易的增长主要来自制剂（即<u>活性药物成分与辅料一起制成的片剂、胶囊、液体等</u>），其次是医院投入和医疗设备（图表 6）。

再举一个例子[3]，美国企业家芭芭拉·柯克兰曾经为 Big Think 网站录制了一系列演讲视频，讲述了她的创业经历与秘诀。译者需要将柯克兰的演讲翻译成简单、易懂的中文，投放到中文电台上。以下是演讲内容的节选：

> I discovered the power of the press by publishing **a statistical survey in the 1970s on the value of New York City apartments. I was a real estate broker at the time. We had 11 sales to base my statistic on as the**

---

[1] https://en.wikipedia.org/wiki/Pharmaceutical_formulation, accessed March 21, 2021.
[2] http://blog.sciencenet.cn/blog-47391-239287.html, accessed March 21, 2021.
[3] 此案理由江依梵提供。

average apartment sale.** It was preposterous but, of course, thanks to the fact that I was so young and too stupid to know any better I published the report and **it was written up on the front page of** *The New York Times* **real estate section**, which was the bible of the industry. **I realized immediately it put me on the map. I had power in my brand immediately.** People started giving us **listings**. My salespeople even started respecting me more. Go figure. All it really was was a third party endorsement. And a third party endorsement you can't pay for but when they give it to you your name starts to have meaning.

在翻译这段内容之前，译者已经对柯克兰的创业经历有了大致的了解，知道她在创立自己的房地产中介公司之前，曾经在另一家房地产公司担任过接待员，但同时也在偷偷兼职做中介工作：

After graduation, she taught school for a year, but soon moved on working various jobs including a side job renting apartments in New York City. **While she was a waitress, her boyfriend convinced her to work for a real estate company. She wanted to be her own boss, and in 1973, while working as a receptionist for the Giffuni Brothers' real estate company in New York City**, co-founded The Corcoran-Simonè with her boyfriend, who loaned $1,000. She split from her boyfriend 7 years later after he told her he was going to marry her secretary and she then formed her own firm, The Corcoran Group.①

"I landed a job as a receptionist at a builder's office. I moonlighted renting apartments." Corcoran saw that there was money to be made and she especially like being her own boss.②

根据演讲段落的上下文，译者推测她在发表房地产行业观察报告时，应该已经建立了自己的公司，而她用到的 11 个销售案例应该也是来源于自己的中介公司。为了查证，译者随即在互联网上进行搜索，得知柯克兰提到的报告即行业内大名鼎鼎的"The Corcoran Report"。该资料也与柯克

---

① https://en.wikipedia.org/wiki/Barbara_Corcoran.

② https://cooperator.com/article/the-corcoran-group/full#cut.

兰演讲中的自述相印证：

> By the mid-70's Corcoran created her first marketing masterpiece: "The Corcoran Report." The report, an insider's data-driven analysis of the real estate market, **put her company on the map, giving it the authoritative voice it needed to grab the attention of the press and the industry.**[①]

由此得知，柯克兰正是通过这篇报告打响了"柯克兰"这个品牌。因此，在翻译"I was a real estate broker at the time"一句时，为避免听众误以为柯克兰仍是一名中介职员，可以译为"我那时还在经营自己的房地产中介公司"（这也正是原文时态表达的含义）。再准确一点，柯克兰应该是公司的合伙人。

另外还有一个问题，译者是否需要在翻译稿里点明报告的内容呢？经过思考与权衡，译者认为没有必要将"柯克兰报告"进行补充说明。一方面是因为普通的中国听众对柯克兰以及这份行业报告并不熟悉；另一方面，柯克兰在演讲里做了很多铺垫，说以现在的眼光来看，当年的这篇报告实在是不够严谨（当然也很有可能是自谦），以此来鼓励创业者大胆创造、努力抓住宣传的机遇。因此，只要模仿柯克兰叙述的语气将演讲翻译出来即可。

同时，该段中还有一句"People started giving us listings"，那么这个 listing 指的是什么呢？译者在词典中查找到的释义如下（见图 7.3）：

词典释义只能给出一个模糊的范围，译者只能推测柯克兰

listing

listing¹ | listing² | listing³
[TOP]**listing**
list·ing / ˈlɪstɪŋ /
noun
1.[C] a list, especially an official or published list of people or things, often arranged in alphabetical order
(尤指按字母顺序排列的)表册, 目录, 列表：
a comprehensive listing of all airlines
所有航线的综合目录
2. listings [pl.] information in a newspaper or magazine about what films / movies, plays, etc. are being shown in a particular town or city
(报章或杂志有关某城市电影、戏剧等的)上映信息, 演出信息：
a listings magazine
演出信息杂志
3.[C] a position or an item on a list
(表册上的)位置, 项目：**(business 商)**
The company is seeking a stock exchange listing (= for trading shares).
这家公司正在争取上市。

■出处：牛津高阶英汉双解词典

图 7.3　listing 的定义

---
① https://cooperator.com/article/the-corcoran-group/full#cut.

所说的"listings"是类似名录一样的东西，且和房地产有关。为了查证，译者利用互联网，输入"real estate""listings"进行检索，随后出现了许多房地产中介公司网站，打开任意一个网站，便出现了以下示例（见图7.4）：

图7.4　通过图片查证listing的含义

由此可知，"listings"指的是房地产的出租或销售信息。为了便于听众理解，译者将"People started giving us **listings**"译为"越来越多的业主把房子挂到我们这里来了"。

译者对整段演讲试译如下：

在一九七几年的时候，我曾经就纽约市的公寓价格发表了一篇调查统计报告，也因此见识到媒体的巨大影响力。那时候我还是"柯克兰-西蒙"房地产中介公司的合伙人。在报告里，我用到了公司的11个销售案例。我用这些销售数据计算出了纽约公寓的平均销售价格。这听上去很扯，不过，幸亏那时的我太过年轻，虽然无知但足够自负，就这么把报告投了出去，最后它登上了行业圣经——《纽约时报》房地产栏目的头版。我随即意识到自己的公司出名了。我的品牌"柯克兰"突然之间就有了影响力。越来越多的业主把房子挂到我们这里来了。甚至我的销售员工对我的态度都愈加恭敬。因此，多多去争取类似的机会吧。你需要第三方媒介的支持。虽然这种机会花钱也买不到，但是，一旦你抓住了这个机会，你的品牌就能在市场占有一席之地。

再举两个汉译英的例子。北京市政府工作报告中有句话"推动职住平衡"，如何翻译？首先要理解意思：

职住平衡是指在某一给定的地域范围内，居民中劳动者的数量和就业岗位的数量大致相等，大部分居民可以就近工作；通勤交通可采用步行、自行车或者其他的非机动车方式；即使是使用机动车，出行距离和时间也比较短，限定在一个合理的范围内，这样就有利于减少机动车尤其是小汽车的使用，从而减少交通拥堵和空气污染。

经查，这个理念叫作 jobs-housing balance：

One of the issues in land use planning today in Santa Barbara County is that of "jobs-housing balance." The purpose of the job-housing balance concept is to match the number of workers who reside in an area with the number of jobs provided in that same area (one resident worker for each job).①

因此译为：try to achieve jobs-housing balance

再如：统筹老城内房屋腾退和征收政策（北京市政府工作报告计划部分），原译为：We will coordinate the house relocation and expropriation policies in the old town. 其中的"腾退"是否表示"把房屋迁移到新的地方"（楼房整体迁移）？根据新闻报道，房屋腾退是指把占用文物单位的住户清理出去：

在北京市十五届人大一次会上，代市长陈吉宁作政府工作报告时指出，要贯彻习近平总书记"老城不能再拆了"的重要指示精神，研究制定推进老城整体保护实施方案。此外，要统筹老城内房屋腾退和征收政策，配套建设定向安置房，做到在保护中改善民生，在改善民生中实现更好的保护。

这为老城保护指明了政策方向。昨天新闻发布会上，东城区常务副区长陈之常介绍，东城区组建了一个由书记、区长挂帅的领导机构，编制了十三五文物腾退修缮利用的规划，到2020年时计划腾出47处文物。

---

① https://www.cityofgoleta.org/home/showdocument?id=619.

"去年腾退了 11 处，修了 9 处，今年计划有太庙、天坛、社稷坛三处文物开始修缮。"陈之常介绍，从市级层面，老城保护受到高度重视，作出了很好的举措，市里面主管领导挂帅，在市文物局，列出了未来几年市、区两级政府包括东、西城共同完成的文物腾退的清单。

今年东城区要完成对天坛公园内的住户腾退，推进前门地区所有会馆的腾退。"文物的腾退有很多难题需要破解，腾退的政策、产权的不统一，腾退之后的利用和平衡的问题。"陈之常说。

所以，房屋腾退并非文物的整体搬迁，而是让住户离开占用的房屋，这个意思英语用 vacate（见图 7.5）：

因此改为：We will coordinate policies for the vacation and expropriation of buildings in the old town.

图 7.5　vacate 的定义

再如：开展社区服务社会化改革，原译为：We will carry out social reform of community services。根据资料①：

> "社区服务社会化"即政府部门采取向专业社工机构购买专业化服务的方法，引入社会力量共同参与社区治理，满足居民群众多元化、个性化、专业化服务需求，其实质是对社区公共服务的供给侧改革。

因此，"社会化改革"不是"社会改革"，而是让私人主体参与社会服务。因此改译为：We will introduce non-government players in the provision of community services.

在翻译过程中，除了通过网页了解具体词语含义外，维基百科、百度百科等网上百科词典，是我们快速熟悉不同领域的重要资源。

---

① http://minzhengju.suzhou.gov.cn/mzj/sqdt/201704/52f1a39861bc4a2bb4d29d4fd2adf038.shtml.

7.4.4 询问用户

对原文存疑或发现瑕疵时,译者可以询问委托人;委托人如认为有必要,可以与原文作者联系。前面讲到某 WIPO 文件中的笔误,这里再举一例,说明通过与委托人沟通,可以参与到文件的制定工作中,意义重大。原文:

(2) tax rates used in conjunction with gross salaries for staff members <u>without dependants</u>:

(i) <u>assessable amounts</u> for staff members <u>with neither a dependent spouse nor a dependent child</u> shall be equal to <u>the difference between the gross salaries at different grades and the corresponding net salaries at the single rate</u>;

这一段讲的是联合国专门机构的工作人员如何缴税。在联合国系统,会员国缴费、个人纳税,都用 assess(税额评估)这个词(图 7.6)①:

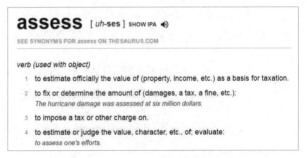

图 7.6　assess 的定义

本例中的"assessable amount"意思是"应纳税所得额"(字面意思是"可用作纳税评估的数额"),是纳税的基础("计税依据")。与之对应的是"应纳税额"(assessments)(图 7.7):

图 7.7　assessment 的定义

例如,你每月税前收入 10,000 元,税率 10%,假定免税额为零,应纳

---
① https://www.dictionary.com/browse/assess.

税所得额（assessable amount）就是税前收入的 10,000 元，应纳税额（assessments）就是 1,000 元，净收入就 9,000 元。换言之，应纳税所得额 – 应纳税额 = 净收入。

据此，原文所说"assessable amounts … shall be equal to the difference between the gross salaries and the corresponding net salaries…"的表述是错的，因为毛收入（应纳税所得额）– 净收入 = 应纳税额（assessments）。因此，原文的 assessable amounts 应该改为 assessments。

笔者向委托人提出原文修改意见：

> Should "assessable amounts" be "assessment"? Because "the difference between the gross salaries at different grades and the corresponding net salaries at the single rate" is exactly the assessment. The assessable amount is the gross salary.

委托人表示，自己是秘书处工作人员，无权修改缔约国作出的决定，答应写个提案，交给下次缔约国大会讨论通过。后来果然看到修改：

STAFF REGULATIONS AND RULES
OF THE INTERNATIONAL BUREAU OF WIPO

> (2) tax rates used in conjunction with gross salaries for staff members without dependants:
>> (i) staff assessable amounts for staff members with neither a dependent spouse nor a dependent child shall be equal to the difference between the gross salaries at different grades and the corresponding net salaries at the single rate;

译文：
> (2) 与无受养人的工作人员薪金毛额相关的税率：
>> (i) 既无受养配偶，亦无受养子女的工作人员，<u>其薪金税额</u>等于各职等薪酬毛额与相应的单身薪酬净额之差。

这是笔者看到的提案（见图 7.8）：

Staff Regulation	Current text	Proposed/new text	Purpose/Description of amendment
Regulation 3.19(a)(2)(i) Internal Taxation	assessable amounts for staff members with neither a dependent spouse nor a dependent child shall be equal to the difference between the gross salaries at different grades and the corresponding net salaries at the single rate;	<u>staff assessment</u> ~~assessable~~ amounts for staff members with neither a dependent spouse nor a dependent child shall be equal to the difference between the gross salaries at different grades and the corresponding net salaries at the single rate;	To correct the terminology (the "difference between the gross salaries at different grades and the corresponding net salaries at the single rate" is the staff assessment, whereas the *assessable* amount is the gross salary).

WO/CC/70/3
Annex II, page 4

图 7.8　某国际机构的提案

作为背景知识，grade 是指"职等"（职务的高低），联合国专业类（Professionals）人员共分五级，从低到高为 P1—P5，每个"职等"之下，又分为若干"职级"（steps）。另外，single rate（单身税率）是指适用于单身员工的税率，相对的是 dependency rate（家庭税率）。请关注双划线词语之间的联系：without dependants=with neither a dependent spouse nor a dependent child = single。最后，笔者译文中采用了联合国系统约定的译法，与我们平时的说法不尽相同。

7.4.5　询问作者

原文难以理解的地方，绝大多数可以通过查资料解决，万不得已时，可以询问作者。笔者在翻译联合国文件时，就求助过作者。例如，原文：

> Even though civil society groups were usually well informed about the issues faced by communities, they were not always consulted in the development of counter-narratives. By contrast, technology-based solutions, such as the use of machine learning to identify online extremist texts, were particularly susceptible to bias. Further thought should be given to whether the approaches adopted by a State or a private company were positive, in the sense that they contributed to fresh thinking about an issue, or negative, in the sense that they moderated content or curtailed liberties. It should also be recalled that some approaches used by States, civil society and private companies, such as the <u>trolling</u> of right-wing extremists, were

beneficial but defied simple categorization. (S/AC.40/SR.332/Add.1)

这是根据联合国安理会某项决议设立的一个反恐委员会的会议记录，讨论如何针对极端主义、恐怖主义在网络宣传（narrative）这一现象做好反宣传（counter-narrative）。其中的 categorization 难以理解。该词只有一个意思，即"分类"（见图 7.9）①：

```
categorize
verb [T] (UK usually categorise)
UK 🔊 /ˈkæt.ə.gəʳ.raɪz/ US 🔊 /ˈkæt̬.ə.gə.raɪz/

to put people or things into groups with the same features:
• The books are categorized into beginner and advanced.
• I would categorize this as a very early example of Tudor art.
```

图 7.9　categorize 的定义

我们遇到一个抽象名词，通常都会把它还原为动词，然后为这个动词添加主语和宾语。在这里，我们要问：Who categorize what into what? 我们能回答前两个 W，但无法回答 into what：We categorize the approaches used by States, civil society and private companies into [?]。会议记录中也没有其他线索。不得已，只能根据此人所在机构，找到该机构的网页，通过网页提供的公共邮箱，联系到作者。没想到作者详尽热情地回答了这个（及其他）问题。作者说：

> This 'defies simple categorisation' in the sense that it is difficult to look at their responses or estimate the effect that this kind of counter-narrative activity might have. I should have used a more precise term about the effects of such kinds of activity — we cannot simply categorise the effects of counter-narratives (including the use of more informal methods such as trolling) as good or bad, effective or not, because we don't have clear information on what effect this might have had on the person to whom the counter-narrative was targeted.

---

① https://dictionary.cambridge.org/dictionary/english/categorize.

据此，可以把译文说得清楚一些：

> 尽管民间社会团体通常非常了解各个社区所面临的问题，但他们不一定被邀请参与开发反宣传内容。相比之下，基于技术的解决方案，如通过机器学习来识别在线极端主义宣传，特别容易产生偏见。还应当进一步思考国家或私营公司采取的方法是积极的（即这些方法有助于就某个问题创新思维）还是消极的（即这些方法用于审查内容或限制自由）。还应指出，一些国家、民间社会团体和私营公司采用的方法（如<u>讥讽右翼极端主义分子</u>）是有益的，但<u>无法简单地评价效果</u>。

在翻译这段话的时候，trolling 一词也是个难点。因为笔者不熟悉网络用语（包括汉语的），所以要调查 trolling 的含义。据网络资料，troll 在中文语境下，可以指"钓鱼""引战""卧底""洗版""刷屏""小白""菜鸟"等，但在此处都不符合逻辑。经查英英词典，找到比较符合的意思（见图 7.10）[①]：

> **c** : to harass, criticize, or antagonize (someone) especially by provocatively disparaging or mocking public statements, postings, or acts
> // The switch came after the Chargers became the butt of jokes, memes and derision on social media. The NFL tweeted the initial logo Thursday, but later deleted it as the Chargers even got *trolled* by other pro and college sports teams over the logo that looked like a cross between baseball's Dodgers and hockey's Lightning.
> — Arnie Stapleton

图 7.10 trolling 的定义

这个意思也得到作者的确认：

> Trolling refers to a particular kind of activity of antagonizing and bullying users of a social media platform (a good place to get some context on this is a book *This is why we can't have nice things* by Whitney Phillips (2015), MIT Press). <u>In this case, trolling was using a kind of social media style that is antagonistic as a way of trying to counter right wing extremists.</u>

遗憾的是，笔者没有找到一个合适的中文网络用语，来传达这个意思。想到用"吊打"，但又担心意思偏差，最终采用了保守无趣的用词"讥讽"。

---

① https://www.merriam-webster.com/dictionary/troll.

编写本书时，熟悉网络语言的同学指出：trolling 可以理解为"带节奏""口嗨"，是指在网上发表一些明显具有争议性的，可能挑起两方甚至多方网络骂战的言论。Troll 这个词应该是同时涵盖了"钓鱼""引战""带节奏""口嗨""网暴"等等。此处更偏向"网暴"和"口嗨"。还有同学说："嘲讽"现在也可以算网络用语，因为在王者荣耀等游戏中有嘲讽技能，被称为"开嘲讽"；打游戏的人很多，这个词语也被广泛应用。

7.4.6　询问同事

笔者曾经听到一个知名翻译机构的老领导说：现在的年轻人不会沟通。专家就坐在你的身边，你不懂可以随时间，可是这些孩子从来不问。眼看你交上来的稿子乱七八糟，事前请教一下专家，不是事半功倍吗？

另一位在国家机关工作的校友也跟笔者说：现在的孩子不太懂事，不知道请教领导。什么地方不会翻，你问我一下，我就可以告诉你——我好歹也做了十几年了，还是有些经验啊！

看来，领导喜欢会沟通的部下，领导不觉得麻烦。你去请教他，正好可以体现领导的价值，他们心里会很高兴。当然，在去请教别人之前，自己要做好功课，把该查的都查遍，到时候也可以跟领导分享。

最后提醒大家，在接受翻译任务的时候，记住向客户索要背景资料，这些资料可能更有针对性，也可能包含网上查不到的资料。等到查不到的时候再去索要，可能已经浪费了大量时间。

7.5　批判性思维需要知识基础

批判地看待原文，需要一定的知识基础。对某个专业领域一无所知，便会轻易相信专家所言。因此，翻译专业性较强的内容，需要先了解该专业的基础知识。例如，下文中的计量单位问题，如果对美军装备不了解，就不可能发现。[1]

---

[1] 此案例来自微博"军武菌"：https://weibo.com/AdmiralJunwu?is_all=1. 杨洋同学提供。

译者在翻译文件时需要注意文件中所使用的单位,特别是要注意由美国人起草的文件。虽然目前全球绝大多数国家都采用了国际标准单位制,但美国(还有利比里亚以及缅甸)是为数不多的官方仍在使用英制单位制的国家。这也就表明在某些时候可能会导致误判。右面是一张关于美国M88A3 式坦克救援车的介绍(见图 7.11):

图片介绍,该救护车可回收最大重量为 80 "ton(英吨)"(也就是 81.28 公吨重)的坦克。但是如果对美军坦克稍微有点了解就会意识到美军并没有这么大吨位的坦克。仔细观察右下角详细数据(见图 7.12)发现,该救援车的牵引能力为 16 万磅(lb)。

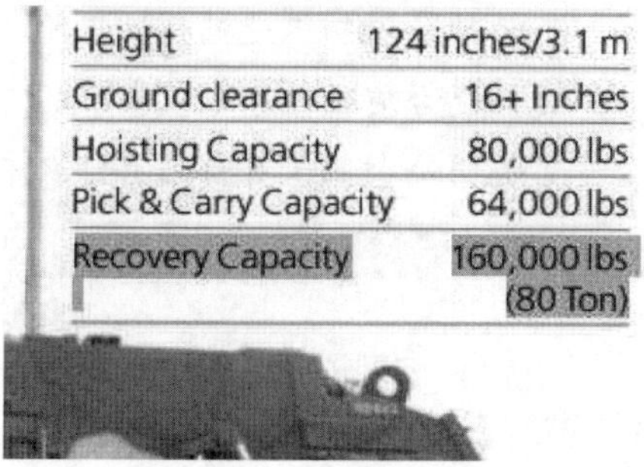

图 7.11 某款军用车辆的图片

图 7.12 某军用车辆数据

一磅是 0.45 公斤,查证后可以发现,美国人使用的是 1ton= 2000lbs 的美式英制单位制(即 short ton),而非英式单位制里的 1ton=2240lbs(即 long ton)。实际上该牵引车最多只能拖动 72 吨重的坦克(这也符合美军目前坦克的最大吨位数)。美军在制作册子时有意或无意地删去了 "short",译者如果不注意,就很可能导致读者对美军能力的误判。(注:公吨的英文是 tonne。)

7.6 小结

本章举例说明如何运用逻辑思维、宏观思维、批判性思维三种思想武器发现翻译中的问题,然后通过调查研究解决这些问题,最后指出批判性思维需要知识支撑。学习翻译的过程,就是培养思维能力和查证能力的过程,而这些能力的获得,不仅有助于做好翻译,也有助于做好任何一项工作。从这个意义上讲,翻译是一种通识教育。翻译学习者要不断积累知识,提高分辨能力,并通过调查研究解决翻译中的难题。

〔课后练习〕

1. 逻辑思维、宏观思维、批判性思维有什么联系和区别?
2. 调查研究有哪些方式?你经常使用哪几种方法?
3. 为什么说知识是批判性思维的基础?
4. 你是否质疑过原文或书上的资料?如有,请举例说明。
5. 说明每个例子对自己有什么启发。

第三部分　翻译中的表达

　　第八至十六章为本书的第三部分，关注翻译中的表达问题，重点介绍简明英语运动以及如何以简明英语的原则指导汉译英。本部分首先介绍简明英语的基本要求，然后以字、词、句篇为线索，举例说明如何把简明英语和英文写作的各项要求，运用到翻译中。无论以人工还是机器翻译得到一稿，只要按写作原则来修改，即可得到通顺的译文。第三部分的目的是实现"信达切"中的"达"（通顺）。

第八章　认识简明英语

扫码预习

请扫码下载本章涉及的例句。先做练习，再看解答，学习效果更佳。

8.1　简明英语和简明英语运动

信达切当中的"达"，就是要求译文符合语言习惯。汉语作为我们的母语，只要时刻提醒自己：我会这样说吗？就可能避免原文带来的干扰。但什么是好的英语？我们凭直觉可能还难以判断。因此，我们应当首先树立好英文的标准，才能在翻译中自觉遵守。在这一章，笔者向大家介绍最近几十年风靡英语世界的简明英语运动，让大家认识到母语人士眼中的"好英语"，以便为汉译英树立标杆。

首先，我们做一道测试题，看你的判断是否正确。请问如果是政府公文，下面两种说法，哪种更好？

　　A: Our lack of knowledge about local conditions precluded determination of committee action effectiveness in fund allocation to those areas in greatest need of assistance.

　　B: Because we knew nothing about local conditions, we could not determine how effectively the committee had allocated funds to areas that most needed assistance. (Williams, 1990)

在受试学生中，几乎所有的学生都认为 A 更好，理由是政府公文属于正式文体，所以越抽象越好。但写作手册上给的答案是 B。这句话是 Joseph M. Williams（1990）在 *Style: Toward Clarity and Grace* 一书中举的例子。*Style* 是一本很有影响的英语写作指南，已经发行十多版，可见其流行程度。所以，作者的见解，应当是代表性的，应成为我们追求的目标。Williams 指出，a 句之所以不好，是由于抽象名词太多。

很多学习外语的人认为，一个句子中抽象名词用得越多，文字越优雅，外语水平显得越高。尤其是政府公文，属于正式文体，更应当多用抽象名词。我们在学校可能受到这个观点的影响很大，所以倾向于用大词、抽象名词，认为像 A 这样的句子才是标准的英文，是我们模仿的典范。

但事实并非如此。美国前总统克林顿执政时，与副总统戈尔共同发布了一项总统备忘录，要求所有面向公众的政府文件均使用简明英语（plain English），国会随后于 2010 年通过《简明写作法》（Plain Writing Act of 2010）。简明英语与我们传统的观点正好相反。它要求篇章布局、句子结构、用词等要简单明了，因为我们写出来的东西毕竟是让人读的，人们读起来越容易，越能达到交流的目的。所以，根据总统（以及各种英语写作手册）的要求，答案就应当是 B，越简单越好。

克林顿的备忘录也不是空穴来风，而是简明英语运动的结果。数十年来，简明英语运动在很多国家蓬勃发展。简明英语作为与公众有效沟通的手段，已深入人心。所有的英语写作指南，无论是否使用简明英语这一说法，所提倡的基本原则与简明英语都是一致的。看来，在这个问题上，我们应当转变观念，跟上时代步伐。况且，简明英语对于以英语作为外语的我们来说，相对容易掌握，所以没有必要舍简就繁。就翻译而言，至少在翻译非文学作品时，我们应当遵循简明英语的原则。

8.1.1 关于简明英语的总统备忘录

我们来看看美国总统关于使用简明英语的备忘录:

Presidential Memorandum on Plain Language
The White House
June 1, 1998
Memorandum for the Heads of Executive
Departments and Agencies

The Vice President and I have made reinventing the Federal Government a top priority of my Administration. We are determined to make the Government more responsive, accessible, and understandable in its communications with the public.

The Federal Government's writing must be in plain language. By using plain language, we send a clear message about what the Government is doing, what it requires, and what services it offers. Plain language saves the Government and the private sector time, effort, and money.

Plain language requirements vary from one document to another, depending on the intended audience. Plain language documents have logical organization, easy-to-read design features, and use:

- common, everyday words, except for necessary technical terms;
- "you" and other pronouns;
- the active voice; and
- short sentences.

To ensure the use of plain language, I direct you to do the following:

- By October 1, 1998, use plain language in all new documents, other than regulations, that explain how to obtain a benefit or service or how to comply with a requirement you administer or enforce. For example, these documents may include letters, forms, notices, and instructions. By January 1, 2002, all such documents created prior to October 1, 1998, must also be in plain language.

- By January 1, 1999, use plain language in all proposed and final rule-making documents published in the Federal Register, unless you proposed the rule before that date. You should consider rewriting existing regulations in plain language when you have the opportunity and resources to do so.

The National Partnership for Reinventing Government will issue guidance to help you comply with these directives and to explain more fully the elements of plain language. You should also use customer feedback and common sense to guide your plain language efforts.

I ask the independent agencies to comply with these directives.

This memorandum does not confer any right or benefit enforceable by law against the United States or its representatives. The Director of the Office of Management and Budget will publish this memorandum in the Federal Register.

(Presidential Sig.) William Clinton

我们看到，为了建立"亲民"形象，美国政府明确要求，美国联邦政府的所有文件，一律使用简明英语；以前没有使用简明英语的，限期"整改"，把推广简明英语提高到了"讲政治"的高度。

简明英语作为一个国际运动，甚至可以追溯到 William Strunk 早在 1918 年出版的 *The Elements of Style*。该书尽管没有使用 Plain English 的概念，其基本内容与今天倡导的简明英语是相同的（这本书今天仍然是一本不可多得的写作参考书）。近年来，随着公众知情权概念的提出、消费者权利意识的提高、政府服务意识的增强、商家竞争的加剧，简明英语运动进一步发展壮大。倡导使用简明英语的范围，已经远远超过克林顿所提出的政府文件，而是涵盖社会生活的各个方面，包括法律、金融、商业、技术、医疗，乃至一切实用性文本。前文提到的 Style 就是针对各种类型的写作的。如果你上网搜索 Plain English，可以看到数不胜数的介绍和写作指南(本章和下一章提供了一些网址)。我们作为英语学习者和翻译工作者，不能不注意到这一发展趋势，并把简明英语的原则应用到我们的写作和翻译中。

8.1.2 简明英语

什么是简明英语

"We define plain English as something that the intended audience can read, understand and act upon the first time they read it. Plain English takes into account design and layout as well as language."("我们把简明英语定义为：预期受众只需读一遍即可以理解并据此采取行动的语言。简明英语不仅强调语言，也强调外观设计和排版。")[①]

——Plain English Campaign, U.K.

"Plain English is good, clear writing which communicates as simply and effectively as possible. But it is not a childish or simplistic form of English."("简明英语是一种适当、清楚的写作方法，它以尽可能简单的方式，达到有效沟通的结果。但简明英语不是幼稚或过分简单化的英语形式。")[②]

——Plain English at Work, Australia

"Plain language writing is a technique of organizing information in ways that make sense to the reader. It uses straightforward, concrete, familiar words."

("简明语言是以读者感到清楚的方式组织信息的技巧。简明语言使用直白、具体和常见的词汇。")[③]

——Minister of Multiculturalism and Citizenship of Canada, in *Plain Language: Clear and Simple*

"Plain language matches the needs of the reader with your needs as a writer, leading to effective, efficient communication. It is **effective** because

---

[①] http://www.plainenglish.co.uk/introduction.html, accessed September 2, 2004.
[②] http://www.detya.gov.au/archive/publications/plain_en/contents.htm, accessed September 2, 2004.
[③] http://www.gopdg.com/plainlanguage/whatisplain.html, accessed September 2, 2004.

readers can understand your message. It is **efficient** because readers can understand your message the first time they read it."("简明语言把读者的需求和作者的需求统一起来，可以增强交流效果、提高交流效率。可以增强交流效果是因为读者可以理解作者传递的信息；可以提高交流效率是因为读者理解作者传递的信息，只需阅读一遍。")①

— Garbl's Plain Language Resources

维基百科甚至出现了"简明英语"词条：

简明英语（Plain English）是一种英语的沟通风格，这种沟通风格讲求的是简单易懂，也就是一种强调简洁、明晰且避免使用过于复杂的单词的简明语文。这种风格常见于政府官方与商业交流中。简明英语的目标是要写出和讲出让听众容易了解的内容，因此清晰、直白、不落俗套、避免行话、切合听众的程度（包括听众的发展程度、教育水平和对谈论主题的熟悉度等）成了这种风格的特色。

—https://zh.wikipedia.org/wiki/ 简明英语

为什么使用简明英语

美国卫生知识普及专家、简明语言专家和跨文化交流专家协会 Clear Language Group (CLG) 是这样概括的：

- 简明的语言比复杂的语言更容易阅读，读者更可能耐心地把文件读完。
- 即使阅读能力很强的读者也喜欢看简明的语言。大家都很忙，如果材料不容易理解，即使看得懂，也可能没有足够的动力去看。
- 简明语言节省时间和金钱。如果读者在印刷材料里面找到了答案，就不会再打电话询问。如果机构内部使用简明语言，雇员阅读业务往来函件时，一遍就可以看懂，从而节约了时间。
- 简明的医学材料使读者了解如何治疗慢性病、如何为手术做准备、为什么要及早检查诊断，从而挽救患者生命。

---

① http://members.home.net.garbl/writing/plaineng.htm, accessed September 2, 2004.

简明英语的基本原则

以下概括了简明英语的基本原则,详细内容将在本章 8.2 阐述。

- 使用读者熟悉的词汇
- 用人称代词拉近与读者距离
- 避免性别歧视语言
- 使用强势动词
- 以"人物加动作"搭建句子
- 避免含糊不清
- 使用短句
- 多用主动语态
- 信息流动通畅
- 少用否定表达,尤其是双重否定
- 语言简洁明了
- 外观设计醒目

消除对简明英语的误解

简明英语不同于传统观念上的文学、艺术语言——虽然很多伟大的作家强调,清楚、易懂的语言很重要。简明英语是以读者为中心传递信息的方式,即在了解读者需求和知识水平的基础上,使用日常语言和熟悉的词汇,有效传递信息的方式。简明英语不使用不必要的专业术语,但绝不是过分简单化的语言。简明英语不是儿童语言,也不是对儿童说话时用的语言。

简明英语不是流行音乐使用的语言,不是小学生作文,不是被降低等级的语言,不是缺乏美感和词汇贫乏的语言,不是缺乏表现力的语言。它是按照公认的语法规则,在结构得当的句子中正确使用所有词汇,是针对特定受众的,简单、清楚、有效的交际方式。

使用简明英语语言,并不意味着削减要传达的信息,即使在撰写法律文件或高度技术性的文件时,也仍然可以使用简明英语。

简明英语不仅使用简单的语言,还使用其他工具,保证清楚有效的交流,如小标题、清晰的排版设计、图表等;起草法律时,可以使用目的条款、序言段、定义条款等,清楚揭示立法意图。

8.1.3 简明英语运动

简明语言不仅是一种方法,也是一项运动,其目的是向使用者提供他们可以理解的信息。数十年来,简明英语运动在很多国家蓬勃发展。英国、澳大利亚、新西兰、加拿大、南非、瑞典等国一直是这一运动的积极推动者。后来,美国也活跃起来。爱尔兰、印度、加纳、巴西、丹麦、芬兰等地也纷纷加入进来。简明英语的使用已经扩展到许多领域,如法律、金融、商业、技术、医疗等领域。

简明英语的倡导者包括世界各地的企业、组织、机构和个人,并得到政府的大力支持,很多国家的政府制定了简明英语政策,直接参与简明英语的推广应用。笔者所看到的所有的英语写作指南,无论是否使用"简明英语"这一说法,其所提倡的基本原则与简明英语是一致的。

英国

英国的"简明英语运动"(Plain English Campaign)提出,语言要做到"水晶般透彻"(crystal clear)。它反对使用别人不懂的行话、官样文章和其他含糊不清的语言。

简明英语运动主张,所有公共信息均应使用简明英语,如表格、传单、协议、合同等。简单地说,就是普通百姓赖以做决定的任何信息,都应当使用简明英语。

英国的"简明英语运动"是一个基层非政府组织,成立于 1979 年,总部设在英格兰 New Mills, Derbyshire,创始人是 Chrissie Maher 女士。

1979 年,当 Maher 女士看到两位年长女士因不会填写住房补贴申请表,无法获得取暖补贴而不幸身故时,愤怒地从利物浦驱车赶到伦敦,在议会广场当众撕碎数百张申请表以示抗议,标志着英国简明英语运动的开始。

英国政府对此作出反应。1981 年,该运动作为政府表格审查委员会的成员,帮助政府对 58,000 种表格进行审查和改写,从而为政府节约开支 1500 万英镑。

1980 年,该组织开始颁发"简明英语奖"。

1983 年，运动出版了题为 *Small Print*（小字条款）的一份报告，批判了合同中冗长难解的语言，并包括一些如何用简明英语改写合同的实例。

1982 年，英国政府开始正式实行简明英语政策。政府资助公务员大学开设有关简明英语课程，传授信息的编排设计以及如何把复杂的信息以简单易懂的格式陈列出来。

1990 年，英国简明英语运动开始为经过其技术测试和公众测试的文件颁发文件清晰性标志（Crystal Mark）。消费者在购买金融、保险等服务时，可以据此判断有关文件是否明白易懂。到 2002 年 3 月，简明英语运动已经认证了 7000 份文件，并授予其清晰性标志。

1994 年，简明英语运动资助一个国际专家组，赴南非为新政府提供有关简明英语的建议。专家组帮助南非政府把《人权委员会法案》改写为简明英语，证明不使用法言法语照样行得通。

1996 年，简明英语运动出版了《审判语言》(*Language on Trial*) 一书，用清晰易懂的语言，旗帜鲜明地反对使用法言法语。该书出版后受到了读者的热烈欢迎，简明英语运动于是开始向律师提供专门的简明英语培训课程。

1999 年，英国上议院首席大法官、上议院议长改革了英国的法律制度，在英格兰的民事法院禁止使用拉丁语和法言法语。这也许是简明英语运动最辉煌的时刻。

在简明英语运动的帮助下，英国航空航天公司（British Aerospace）把一份长达 150 页的国际租赁协议简化为 50 页。因为协议使用简明英语，价值 1.2 亿英镑的交易仅用了不到一个月的时间就顺利完成。而在过去，平均需要 6 个月的时间。

由于简明英语运动在欧洲的游说活动，目前在欧洲，消费合同如果不使用简明易懂的语言，根本无法执行。

Chrissie Maher 的简明英语运动感召了世界各地的简明语言倡导者，她的精神和培训材料传遍了全世界。

英国简明英语运动的另一起源——Clarity

1983 年，英国一个地方政府法律部事务律师（solicitor，也译"初级律师""沙律师"）约翰·沃尔顿（John Walton）在事务律师协会会刊上看到一封房屋鉴定人的来信，信中称，由于房屋租赁合同晦涩难懂，其工作十分辛苦。

沃尔顿在会刊上公开复信称，如果有人愿意与他共同发起一项运动，促进简明语言在法律中的应用，请写信给他并寄去 5 英镑。有 200 名律师作出响应，最远的来自澳大利亚。沃尔顿第二年召开了第一次会议，创办了通讯，并主持新协会的工作，直到 1987 年。从此以后，沃尔顿的通讯就成为一本严肃的法律杂志，得到知名的上诉法院法官的赞助。沃尔顿所创办的组织 Clarity 已经成长为一个世界性的团体，会员超过 1000 多人，遍及全球近 30 个国家，其中包括执业律师、法官、议员、政府部门法律工作者、教育工作者、图书管理员、法律翻译工作者、语言学家和简明英语顾问。

澳大利亚

在澳大利亚，简明英语运动开始于 1976 年。1976 年 8 月，澳大利亚国家道路和驾驶员协会颁布了澳大利亚第一份简明英语文件。这是一份保险合同，它一改过去晦涩难懂的法律语言，使用清晰易懂的语言。第二年，新南威尔士不动产学会颁布了一份用简明英语起草的住房租赁协议。

1983 年，澳大利亚政府发起了"简明英语和简化表格项目"，给日渐壮大的简明英语运动以全面支持。在 1990 年国际扫盲年，澳大利亚政府发起了数项活动，推动各行各业使用简明英语。

1990 年，悉尼大学成立了"简明英语法律语言中心"。该中心是世界上少数几个专门从事简明英语应用研究的机构之一。它的任务是推动在所有法律和行政文件中使用简明英语。

1993 年，政府启动修改公司法项目，改进公司法的语言、编排和结构；同时还开展了另外两个法律项目——重新设计立法项目以及税法改进项目。

1996 年，澳大利亚就业、教育和培训委员会颁布了指导公共和私有部门使用简明英语的政策。

现在，大多数澳大利亚联邦和州政府部门，以及许多工商企业，都制定了简明英语政策。例如，澳大利亚律师事务所 Phillips-Fox 放弃了原来的程式化语言，用简明语言对它们进行改写，让现有客户大为高兴，还给它带来了新客户。

加拿大

从 1970 年开始，政府、企业和律师开始从保护消费者利益的角度出发，改进针对普通消费者或普通公民的商业和法律文件的语言、设计和排版。

从 1971 年开始，加拿大法律改革委员会开始审查所有联邦法律，并对法律的改进提出建议。委员会提倡在立法中使用简明语言。

1988 年，加拿大律师协会和加拿大银行家协会成立了简明语言文献联合委员会。

1992 年，加拿大政府在 14 个联邦政府部门工作的基础上，编辑出版了一本关于简明英语写作的手册 *Plain Language: Clear and Simple*。这本仅有 55 页的简明英语写作指南本来是为联邦政府公务员编写的，出版后却一举成为加拿大畅销的写作指南。与此同时，萨斯喀彻温省开始在所有政府部门实施一项"清晰语言项目"，出版了写作手册 *Clear Language for the Saskatchewan Government*.

许多杰出的个人和机构，如加拿大简明语言协会、加拿大法律信息中心、多伦多大都市识字运动等，为推动简明英语作出了不懈努力。成立于加拿大的国际简明语言协会（The Plain Language Association International, or PLAIN）是简明英语倡导者和专业人员的领导机构，它的成员来自加拿大、美国、澳大利亚、英国、瑞典、南非和新西兰。

美国

1971 年，美国英语教师全国委员会成立了一个关于使用简明英语的委员会，引起公众注意。

1975 年，美国出现了第一份简明英语文件。

1978 年，卡特总统签发第 12044 号行政命令，要求联邦政府的行政规章使用简明英语，从而使简明英语运动获得了更广泛的支持。但 1981 年，里根总统废止了这一命令。

虽然政府不再推动简明英语的应用，但民间的推动却时刻没有停止。密歇根州律师协会成立了简明英语委员会；国家教育研究院成立了美国文件设计中心，该中心从 1979 年开始，经过 20 年的研究，把人类学、认知心理学、写作、绘图、表格设计、立法起草、语言学、组织心理学、修辞学和社会学等多个学科运用到文件设计中，极大地推动了文件设计的发展。

1989 年，律师、语言学家 William Lutz 出版 *Doublespeak: From "Revenue Enhancement" to "Terminal Living," How Government, Business, Advertisers, and Others Use Language to Deceive You*，发扬美国光荣传统，向官样文章开战。

1998 年，克林顿总统发布一份总统备忘录，要求所有政府机构在编写书面材料时，使用简明英语，至今仍未被废止。所以，所有联邦机构在编写或更新其面向公众的印刷材料时，都应当使用简明英语。

很多联邦机构，如内政部土地管理局、财政部、联邦航空管理局、美国国立卫生研究院、联邦公报办公室、小企业管理局等都积极响应简明英语的号召，在其编写的文件中应用简明英语，力求改善政府与人民的沟通。

美国证券与交易委员会专门制定了一套简明英语标准，要求招股说明书中的某些内容，必须使用简明英语。

美国有 36 个州立法要求使用清楚的语言。很多州的规定对字号提出具体要求，尤其是要消除法律文件中的"小字条款"。有些州规定，保险合同必须使用简明英语，以照顾人们的阅读水平。美国很多州都编写了法律起草手册，鼓励使用简明的法律语言。有些州甚至要求法官的判决书使用简明英语。

过去几年中，卫生保健行业越来越强烈地认识到，他们大多数的印刷材料太难，绝大多数病人看不懂。越来越多的卫生保健机构正在学习如何更好地与病人沟通，如何编写简明易懂的材料，并研究健康和识字水平之间的关系。

南非

南非有 11 种官方语言，很多南非人以英语作为第二语言，所以英语的清晰性至关重要。南非宪法规定，公民有获得信息的权利，所以政府十分重视在立法和行政中使用简明的英语，有效向公民传递信息，保护公民权利。

瑞典

瑞典政府专门雇用简明英语专家,帮助政府制定便于理解的立法。

欧盟

欧洲委员会的翻译部门发起了一场名为"Fight the FOG"的运动,指导撰稿人和译员使用百姓的语言,更清楚地写作,消除欧盟各机构与公众之间的距离。该运动编写了指导写作和翻译的手册 *How to Write Clearly*,其基本原则与简明英语是一致的。

8.1.4 简明英语流行的原因

印刷术的产生和发展,教育的普及,使文字不再成为统治阶级的工具,不再由少数僧侣、贵族垄断,普通大众具备了初步的阅读能力,为简明英语的流行创造了条件。

公众权利意识提高,法律赋予公众知情权,要求政府提供便于公众理解的信息。同时,消费者权益保护运动的兴起,要求商家以简单明了的语言确定与消费者之间的权利义务关系,避免商业合同中的"小字条款"。

政府服务意识的提高,要求政府更加接近群众。克林顿总统简明英语备忘录中的"We are determined to make the Government more responsive, accessible, and understandable in its communications with the public."("我们决心使政府在与群众的交流中反应更快、更易接近、更易理解。")更是把简明英语的使用提到"讲政治"的高度。南非政府推行简明英语更是直接服务于保护人权。

商业竞争的需要。商家为了塑造平易近人的形象,需要使用简单明了的语言与客户沟通,向客户介绍自己的企业,推销自己的产品和服务。

英语的全球化。英语在全球处于主导地位。许多英语文件的读者已经不限于英语本族语者,有些文件就是专门为英语作为外语的人写的,所以,必须考虑这些人的语言能力。这些国际读者的基本特点是,对英语的掌握并非十全十美,缺乏共同的文化背景,但对所谈的题目有兴趣或有一定了解。在为国际读者写作时,要考虑他们的特点,达到在国际上有效交流的目的。①

当然，并不是所有的人都拥护和使用简明英语。如果不是消费者的压力，商家宁愿在标准合同中把自己的义务和消费者的权利写得不明不白；一些大企业为了掩盖自己不可告人的目的，继续使用世代相传的程式化语言，欺骗投资者。《华盛顿邮报》2003 年 3 月 2 日的报道就揭露了很多大公司不使用简明语言，避免让投资者了解可能影响公司未来业绩的真实趋势和不确定因素：

English, Not Legalese

Continuing its campaign to force corporations to come clean with shareholders, the Securities and Exchange Commission ordered 350 of the Fortune 500 companies to rewrite their last annual reports or make better disclosures next time. The special review of the country's biggest firms was instituted in the wake of the Enron scandal. The SEC said companies continued to rely on boilerplate rather than using plain English to give investors a true sense of trends and uncertainties that are likely to affect future results.

用不用简明英语，看作者的立场、写作目的。如果是为了真正与读者沟通，必然选择简明英语；如果甘当资本家的雇用文人，愚弄百姓，当然要使用群众看不懂的语言。

8.1.5 掌握简明英语不容易？

简明英语的倡导者认为，简明英语并不容易掌握。作者要时刻提醒自己遵循简明英语的原则，而不是盲目采用世代相传的写作格式和陈词滥调。作者要问问自己到底想说什么，然后明白地表达出来。

倡导者认为，写作离不开修改，只有反复修改和润色，才能使文章简洁有力。当然，修改润色需要时间。丘吉尔一次给朋友写了一封长达五页的信，最后解释说："本来可以写短一些，但是没有时间。"

---

① 请查找并阅读 "The Elements of International English Style: A Guide to Writing Correspondence, Reports, Technical Documents, and Internet Pages for a Global Audience" by Edmond H. Weiss.

美国证券和交易委员会也在其写作指南中称:"完成向简明英语的转变,需要新的思维方式和写作风格……过去的法言法语和外人难以理解的行话必须让位于日常用词,从而清楚地传递复杂的信息……很多公司已转向使用简明英语,因为这是一项好的商业决策。"

我们认为,对于英语作为外语的中国人,简明英语相对传统英语还是比较容易掌握的,因为我们没有历史包袱,比如千年不变的程式化法律语言;简明英语竭力避免的,正是我们英语学习中的弱项,如结构冗长复杂的句子、法言法语和行话等。但是,在其他很多方面,我们也同样需要付出努力,才能达到简明英语的要求。

8.1.6 简明英语的启示

简明英语发展到今天,已经超出英语的范围,其基本原则也被其他欧洲语言所采用,如法语、德语,所以出现了简明语言的概念。我们可以研究,这些原则是否也同样适用于汉语。也许我们当年的白话文运动,就是中国的简明语言运动,不过,简明英语的某些特点,仍然值得我们借鉴。

简明英语的原则,不但对我们的英语写作有直接和重大的借鉴意义,对汉英(甚至英汉)翻译也有重要意义,因为翻译和写作在本质上是一致的,只不过参照物有所不同。实际上,欧盟出版的写作手册就是由欧盟的专职译员编写,同时用于指导写作和翻译的。简明英语也是以读者为中心的翻译取向对译者提出的要求。我们应当对简明英语进行深入的研究,在英语写作和翻译中加以运用。

8.2 简明英语的基本原则

简明英语首先要求确定写作的目的和读者群,根据读者的需求和知识水平,确定写作的内容和风格。从简明英语运动的发展来看,简明英语一直是面向大众的英语。由于大众的受教育程度不一定很高,所以,简明英语从内容、句式到用词，都力图做到清晰易懂、言简意赅；形式上做到一目了然。简明英语不仅受到一般公众的欢迎，也受到专业人士喜爱，所以，即使撰写学术论文，也提倡使用简明英语。

8.2.1 使用读者熟悉的词汇

避免使用大词、抽象词、行话、拉丁语、流行词、外来语、古语

例如：

不用	可用
accede to	agree to
determine	set
domicile	house / address
eliminate	cut out
emphasize	highlight
employment opportunities	jobs

避免使用：

afore-mentioned, aforesaid, hereby, herein, hereinafter, hereinbefore, hereunto, pursuant, thenceforth, thereunto, wheresoever, whereas, whereof, whosoever

一个词可以说清楚的，不用短语

例如：

不用	可用
in view of the fact that	as
with respect to	on
a certain number of	some
the majority of	most
pursuant to	under
within the framework of	under

下面多个说法意思相同：

| the reason for |
| for the reason that |
| due to the fact that |
| owing to the fact that | } because, since, why
| in light of the fact that |
| considering the fact that |
| on the grounds that |
| this is why |

| despite the fact that |
| regardless of the fact that | } although, even though
| notwithstanding the fact that |

8.2.2 用人称代词拉近与读者距离

使用人称代词，如 you、I、we 等，拉近与读者的距离。把自己的机构称为 we，把读者称为 you：

以前：An information helpline is also operated by ABC Hospital Trust for the convenience of patients.

现在：We also operate an information helpline for your convenience.

以前：This Summary does not purport to be complete and is qualified in its entirety by the more detailed information contained in the Proxy Statement and the Appendices hereto, all of which should be carefully reviewed.

现在：Because this is a summary, it does not contain all the information that may be important to you. You should read the entire proxy statement and its appendices carefully before you decide how to vote.

8.2.3 避免性别歧视语言

表示职业的词，使用中性词：

Fireman — fireperson is awkward, but firefighter is not

Policeman — policeperson sounds silly, but police officer sounds natural

Mailman — mailperson seems awkward, postal worker does not

Cleaning woman — house cleaner, office cleaner, custodian are all preferable

用好代词。英语中有些句子不好处理，如 Everyone must do his work. 语法上正确，但属于性别歧视语言。此类问题有三种处理方法：

- 使用 their

如 Every officer must do their best. 这个说法语法上虽然不正确，但语感上过得去。

- 使用"his or her"

这种用法很安全，但不能总用，因为比较拗口。

- 用复数代替单数

如 All officers must do their best. 这种解决方法最好，但不是每个地方都适用。有时为了精确，必须使用单数。所以，也许三种办法应结合使用。

8.2.4 使用强势动词

避免使用动词变来的名词；把动词变来的名词转为动词：

A: I will make adjustments to the procedure

B: I will adjust the procedure

A: Upon the approval of your request

B: When (If) your request is approved

A: Before consideration can be given to X

B: Before we can consider X

A: Indication was made in your letter that

B: Your letter indicated that

使用强势动词也使句子更简洁。

8.2.5 以"人物加动作"搭建句子

人物加动作原则是指把句子的主语留给动作的执行者,把谓语留给关键动作。① 例如:

> A: Our lack of knowledge about local conditions precluded determination of committee action effectiveness in fund allocation to those areas in greatest need of assistance.

如果要在剧中把这句话演出来,需要哪些人物或角色?需要"we"(从句子中的"our"可以推断出);需要"the committee"(可能就是"we");需要"area"。可是,在本句中,这些人物出现在什么地方呢? our 不是主语,而是 lack 的定语:our lack;committee 不是主语,而是定语:committee action effectiveness;area 不是主语,而是介词的宾语:to areas。这句话的主语是谁呢?是一个抽象名词:our lack of knowledge,后面跟着一个模糊的动词 precluded。

我们看一看 B 句:

> B: Because we knew nothing about local conditions, we could not determine how effectively the committee had allocated funds to areas that most needed assistance.

We 是 knew 和 could not determine 的共同主语:Because we knew nothing..., we could not determine...。The committee 是动词 had allocated 的主语:...the committee had allocated...。虽然 area 仍然是介词宾语(to areas),它同时也是 needed 的主语:areas that most needed assistance

再看两句中人物所执行的动作是如何表达的。在第一个句子中,动作不是由动词表示的,而是用抽象名词表示的:lack, knowledge, determination, action, allocation, assistance, need。在第二个句子中,动作都是由动词

---

① "人物加动作"(character/action)的说法出自 Joseph M. Williams. *Style: Toward Clarity and Grace*, University of Chicago Press, 1995。

表示的：we knew nothing, we could not determine, the committee allocated, areas needed。只有一个动作仍由名词表示：assistance。

综上所述，A 句没有把人物放在主语的位置，没有用动词表示关键的动作，从而违反了"人物加动作"的原则，而 B 句则把人物放在了主语的位置，用动词表示关键动作，因而符合"人物加动作"的原则。

需要指出的是，"人物"的种类很多。最重要的是动作的发出者（包括比喻性质的）：

- *Faculties of national eminence* do not always teach well.
- *Mayor Daley* built Chicago into a giant among cities.
- *The White House* announced today the President's schedule.
- *The business sector* is cooperating.
- *Many instances of malignant tumors* fail to seek attention.

有时，我们用动作执行者的"工具"，而不是动作执行者作句子的主语：

- Studies of coal production reveal these figures.
- These new data establish the need for more detailed analysis.
- This evidence proves my theory.

如果用真正的动作执行者，就是：

- When we study coal production, we find these figures.
- I have established through these new data that we must analyze the problem in more detail.
- With this evidence I prove my theory.

但没有必要把"人物加动作"的原则绝对化。

符合"人物加动作"原则的句子，可以满足简明英语的数项要求，例如，信息流动更加通畅；被迫使用连接词，明确句子逻辑关系；使用了强势动词；句子必然变短；避免了被动语态；避免了介词短语的连用。分别举例如下：

信息流动更加通畅

A: The closure of the branch and the transfer of its business and non-unionized employees constituted an unfair labor practice because the purpose of obtaining an economic benefit by means of discouraging unionization motivated the closure and transfer.

B: The partners committed an unfair labor practice when they closed the branch and transferred its business and non-unionized employees in order to discourage unionization and thereby obtain an economic benefit.

在 A 句中，所有动作都由抽象名词表示，通过介词把名词串联起来，从而打乱了动作的先后顺序；而 B 句遵守了人物加动作的原则，更符合事物发展的逻辑顺序。

被迫使用连接词

在下例 B 中，由于人物加动作原则的使用，迫使我们通过连接词表示句子的逻辑关系，从而使意思更加清楚：

A: The more effective representation of needs by other agencies resulted in our failure in acquiring federal funds, despite intensive lobbying efforts on our part.

B: *Although* we lobbied Congress intensively, we could not acquire federal funds *because* other interests presented their needs more effectively.

使用了强势动词

A: There has been affirmative decision for program termination.

B: The director decided to terminate the program.

避免了介词短语连用

A: An evaluation *of the program* by us will allow greater efficiency *in service to clients*.

B: We will evaluate the program so that we can serve clients better.

句子必然变短

实际上，句子长关系不大，关键是要符合人物加动作的原则。但遵守这一原则的必然结果是句子变短。请比较以下例句：

A: After Czar Alexander II's emancipation of the Russian serfs in 1861, many now-free peasants chose to live on a commune for purposes of cooperation in agricultural production as well as for social stability. Despite some communes' attempts at economic and social equalization through the strategy of imposing a low economic status on the peasants, which resulted in their reduction to near-poverty, a centuries-long history of important social distinctions even among serfs prevented social equalization.

B: In 1861, Czar Alexander II emancipated the Russian serfs. Many of them chose to live on agricultural communes. There they thought they could cooperate with one another in agricultural production. They could also create a stable social structure. The leaders of some of these communes tried to equalize the peasants economically and socially. As one strategy, they tried to impose on all a low economic status that reduced them to near-poverty. However, the communes failed to equalize them socially because even serfs had made important social distinctions among themselves for centuries.

C: After the Russian serfs were emancipated by Czar Alexander II in 1861, many chose to live on agricultural communes, hoping they could cooperate in working the land and establish a stable social structure. At first, those who led some of the communes tried to equalize the new peasants socially and economically by imposing on them all a low economic status, a strategy that reduced them to near-poverty. But the communes failed to equalize them socially because for centuries the serfs had observed among themselves important social distinctions.

应该澄清一点，清晰易懂并不要求把文章写成儿童读物（如B），而是让读者更容易读懂。我们可以使用某些技巧，如并列、从属等，把一连串过短、过于简单的句子变为更复杂、更成熟，但仍然易于读懂的句子（如C）。

8.2.6 避免含混不清

避免结构歧义

句子结构不当可能产生歧义。例如：

A: The Deputy Minister cancelled *her appointment to tour the drought stricken area.*

此句可能把斜体部分理解为一个整体，但其实意思可能是：

B: The Deputy Minister cancelled her appointment so she could tour the drought-stricken area.

避免连续使用两个以上的介词短语

介词短语连用，会导致修饰关系不清：

A: He discussed the question of stocking the proposed hog operations *with his associates.*

此句中 with 短语不知道修饰那个中心词。修改：

B: He and his associates discussed the question of stocking the proposed hog operation.

使用单数名词，不使用复数

在法律起草中，用单数名词会更准确。不说：

The guard shall issue security badges to employees who work in Building D and Building E.

要改为：

The guard shall issue a security badge to each employee who works in Building D and each employee who works in Building E.

除非表示：

The guard shall issue a security badge to each employee who works in both Building D and Building E.（还可能有其他意思）

避免一连串的名词修饰名词

名词修饰名词造成名词之间逻辑关系不清,要使用介词澄清各词之间的关系:

A: Underground mine worker safety protection procedures development

B: Developing procedures to protect the safety of workers in underground mines

8.2.7 多用短句

用简单的句型

如有简单句型可用,不用复杂句型。例如:

A: There are three common types of splices that are used in electrical connections.

B: Three types of splices are used in electrical connections.

A: It is important that all employees read the safety handbook.

B: All employees must read the safety handbook.

A: There are three other considerations that outweigh …

B: Three other considerations outweigh …

A: The state court had proposed that there be a bellwether trial …

B: The state court had proposed a bellwether trial …

A: Petitioner would seek to have this Court …

B: Smith seeks to have this Court …

C: Smith asks this Court …

A: An example would be …

B: An example is …

限制句子长度

根据美国证券和交易委员会编写的写作手册,句子平均长度应为15—20个单词,句子要长短结合,长句不超过三项信息。

以前:

If you could let me have the latest typed version of the form in the next seven days, whereupon I suggest we meet here on 19 December to finalize the text so that you could then give me an estimate of the cost of producing a typeset proof.

现在：

Please let me have the latest typed version of the form in the next seven days. I suggest we meet here on 19 December to finalize the text. You could then give me an estimate of the cost of producing a typeset proof.

以前：

The following description encompasses all the material terms and provisions of the Notes offered hereby and supplements, and to the extent inconsistent therewith replaces, the description of the general terms and provisions of the Debt Securities (as defined in the accompanying Prospectus) set forth under the heading "Description of Debt Securities" in the Prospectus, to which description reference is hereby made. The following description will apply to each Note unless otherwise specified in the applicable Pricing Supplement.

这段话的问题，不仅在于句子长，包含复杂的信息，还在于没有向读者提供必要的背景情况。以下是两种改写方法，一种没有采用列表方式，一种采用了列表方式。

现在1：

We provide information to you about our notes in three separate documents that progressively provide more detail: 1) the prospectus, 2) the prospectus supplement, and 3) the pricing supplement. Since the terms of specific notes may differ from the general information we have provided, in all cases rely on information in the pricing supplement over different information in the prospectus and the prospectus supplement; and rely on this prospectus supplement over different information in the prospectus.

现在 2：

We provide information to you about our notes in three separate documents that progressively provide more detail:

The Prospectus

General information that may or may not apply to each note.

The Prospectus Supplement

More specific than the prospectus, and to the extent information differs from the prospectus, rely on the different information in this document.

The Pricing Supplement

Provides that details about a specific note including its price. To the extent information differs from the prospectus or the prospectus supplement, rely on the different information in this document.

8.2.8　多用主动语态

主动语态简短、清楚；被动语态较长，有时意思不清。主动语态应占 90%。在 10% 的情况下，使用被动语态更合适。

试比较：

A. New guidelines have been laid down by the President in the hope that the length of documents submitted by DGs will be restricted to 20 pages.

B. The President has laid down new guidelines in the hope that DGs will restrict the length of documents to 20 pages.

下面是把被动语态变为主动语态的例子。

不好：

A recommendation was made by the European Parliament that consideration be given by the Member States to a simplification of the award procedure.

稍好：

The European Parliament made a recommendation that the Member States give consideration to a simplification of the award procedure.

较好：

The European Parliament recommended that the Member States consider simplifying the award procedure.

被动语态在某些情况下可以使用。施动者显而易见，没有必要说明：

All Commission staff are encouraged to write clearly.

但提请读者注意动作的接受者时，可以加上施动者：

One of the most controversial members of the European Parliament has been interviewed by the press about the proposal.

需要把新奇或重要的信息放在句末：

After the Summit the President was interviewed by a ten-year-old pupil from the European School.

当然，如果你想逃避责任，可以用被动语态：

"In my department the advice on clear English has been disregarded."

8.2.9 信息流动通畅

按照人的认识规律，人们对新事物的认识是在已有知识基础上进行的。所以，在介绍新知识时，应当以旧知识作铺垫，引出新知识。同样，在写作时，也要把先发生的事情或已知的内容（旧信息）放在前面，把新信息放在后面。排列顺序不当，违反人的认识规律，可能会造成理解困难，有时需要读几遍才能掌握句子强调的重点，有时更可能无法读懂（口头交流时可以不遵守这一规律，因为可以通过较重的语调表示强调）。写作和翻译时可以采用以下方法排列信息：

指出每个施动者，按逻辑顺序叙述各项动作

以前：

Its decision on allocation of ESF assistance will be taken subsequent to receipt of all project applications at the Committee's meeting.

现在：

When all applicants have submitted their project applications, the Committee will meet to decide how much ESF aid it will grant to each one.

必须指出，这条规则不可绝对化。英语把时间、条件、原因状语放在后面的例子同样常见。谁先谁后，取决于上下文的衔接（见下一条规则）。脱离上下文，无论怎样排列都可以。这是一条处理句子信息结构的规则；至于段落的信息结构，则是首先提出问题，然后回答问题。

保证段落各句层层推进

把旧信息或已知信息放在句首，新信息或复杂信息放在句末，可以使论述层层推进，帮助读者抓住论证的线索。比如：

The court of auditors' report criticizes agricultural spending and *proposes* some new measures to prevent fraud.

Their proposals include setting up a special task force with *powers* to search farms.

Such powers are not normally granted to Commission officials, but fraud prevention is now one of the EU's main priorities.

句子的结尾要有力

如有必要，把不重要的信息移向句子左侧，避免有气无力的结尾。比如：

A. Complete institutional reform is advocated by the report in most cases.

B. What the report advocates, in most cases, is complete institutional reform.

通过其他手段把句子重心后移：

A. For EU enlargement several alternative scenarios could be considered.

B. There are several scenarios that we could consider for EU enlargement.

A. The accession of new Member States in several stages now seems likely.

B. It now seems likely that new Member States will join in several stages.

读者或听众印象最深的，是最后看到的或听到的。

8.2.10 少用否定表达，尤其是双重否定

在阅读否定句时，读者需要把它变为肯定句才容易理解，不如肯定句直截了当。有不少否定的意思可以用肯定的方式来表达。例如：

not many = few
not the same = different
not different = alike/similar
did not = failed to
does not have = lacks
did not stay = left

再比如：

A: It is not uncommon for applications to be rejected, so do not complain unless you are sure you have not completed yours incorrectly.

B: It is quite common for applications to be rejected, so complain only if you are sure you have completed yours correctly.

8.2.11 语言简洁明了

简明英语要有清楚的条理。如果要传达的信息很多，一定要把信息拆分成符合逻辑的信息单元。每个单元使用标题和小标题。标题和小标题要有内容，不仅仅是为了打破文件形式的单调。对于每一个信息单元，应当首先陈述要点，然后予以解释和论证。遇到复杂的信息，要使用列表（bullet points），或举例、画图加以解释。

言简意赅

"Vigorous writing is concise. A sentence should contain no unnecessary words, a paragraph no unnecessary sentences, for the same reason that a drawing should have no unnecessary lines and a machine no unnecessary parts."

—William Strunk, Jr., *The Elements of Style*

简明英语的一个重要特点是言简意赅，要言不烦。这一特征显然继承了 William Strunk, Jr. 自 1918 年出版 *The Elements of Style* 以来所提倡的文风。文件是否受到重视，不在于它的长短。很多国际机构和政府部门就明确规定不接受过长的文件。要缩短文件，做到言简意赅，可以从很多小的地方着手。

避免重复

已经说过的，不再说；读者知道的，不再说；读者可以推知的，不再说。试比较：

原文：

In my personal opinion, we must listen to and think over in a punctilious manner each and every suggestion that is offered to us.

分析：

personal：任何意见都是个人的；

opinion：所说的任何话都是一种意见；

listen to and think over：两个词的意思相同，可以概括为 consider；

in a punctilious manner：较短的说法是 punctiliously，更简单的说法是 carefully；

each and every：同义词并列；

suggestion that is offered to us：suggestion 一定是提给别人的，已经隐含在 offer 中。

改写：

We must consider each suggestion carefully.

消除意思重复，可以使用以下手段：

一、两个词意思相同的，只留一个

英语中有一些同义词对（redundant pairs），其中一个来自法语或拉丁语，意思几乎相同，使用时只需保留一个简单的。如：

- full and complete
- true and accurate

- hopes and desires
- each and every
- first and foremost
- any and all
- various and sundry
- basic and fundamental
- so on and so forth

二、修饰语的意思已经被隐含的，不用修饰语

有些修饰语的意思已经包含在中心词里（redundant modifiers），应当去掉该修饰语，如以下各例斜体的词：

- The *end* result of this merger will be higher unemployment.
- The *underlying* principle of this document.
- This policy will *completely* eliminate computer crime.
- The problem of dishonesty *still* remains.

其他例子有：
- each individual
- consensus of opinion
- important essentials
- future plans
- final outcome
- initial preparation
- free gift

三、词本身已经隐含其范畴的，不用范畴词

通常，一个词本身就可表明其范畴（类别），所以不必再用表示范畴的词。如 time 的范畴是 period，所以不用说 time period；同样，不用说 pink in color, shiny in appearance。英语叫 redundant categories。

有时，可以把形容词变为副词，以消除范畴词（A 是不符合要求的句

子，B 是修改后的句子。下同）：

A: The holes must be aligned in an accurate manner.

B: The holes must be accurately aligned.

有时，可以把形容词变为名词，把多余的名词去掉：

A: The educational process and athletic activities are the responsibility of county governmental systems.

B: Education and athletics are the responsibility of county governments.

四、避免冗长的表达方式和"慢启动"句子

有些表达方式，没有太大实际意义，却推迟了主要意思的到来，应当尽量不用或少用：

试比较：

A: For all intents and purposes, American industrial productivity generally depends on certain factors that are really more psychological in kind than of any given technological aspect.

B: American industrial productivity depends more on psychological than on technological factors.

A: The point I am trying to make is that the NAFTA policy will not benefit the country.

B: The NAFTA policy will not benefit the country.

类似的词还有：

usually, often, sometimes, almost, virtually, possibly, perhaps, apparently, seemingly, in some ways, to a certain extent, sort of, somewhat, more or less, for the most part, to all intents and purposes, in some respects, in my opinion, at least, may, might, can, could, seem, tend, try, attempt, seek, hope.

以及：

as everyone knows, it is generally agreed that, it is quite true that, as we can plainly see, literally, clearly, obviously, undoubtedly, certainly, of course, indeed, inevitably, very, invariably, always, key, central, crucial, basic, fundamental, major, cardinal, primary, principal, essential.

直截了当

有些文章故弄玄虚,把简单的问题复杂化、抽象化,这是简明英语所应避免的。

试比较:

A. Pursuant to the recent memorandum issued August 9, 1996, because of financial exigencies, it is incumbent upon us all to endeavor to make maximal utilization of telephonic communication in lieu of personal visitation.

B. As reported in our August 9 memo, use the telephone as much as possible, instead of making personal visits, to save the company money.

以下摘自对两个雇员的评估报告:

The attitude of each, that he was not required to inform himself of, and his lack of interest in, the measures taken by the other to carry out the responsibility assigned to such other under the provision of plans then in effect, demonstrated on the part of each lack of appreciation of the responsibilities vested in them, and inherent in their positions.

改写为简明英语是:

Neither took any interest in the other's plans, or even found out what they were. This shows that they did not appreciate the responsibilities of their positions.

8.2.12　外观设计醒目

良好的文件设计包括:

- 留有足够的空白。较宽的行距和较大的字体便于阅读。每行字符数量以 50—70 个为宜。
- 避免全部使用大写字母和下划线。使用小写字母黑体或变换字体表示强调,不要使用全大写。全大写和下划线不利于阅读。全大写仅限于题目和标题。

- 使用 Times New Roman、Century Schoolbook，甚至 Courier 等字体。这些字体的字母带有小尾巴，易于辨认。
- 最后，使用左对齐，不要使用两端对齐。缺乏变化使眼睛容易疲劳。

8.3 小结

本章介绍了简明英语运动及其基本原则，并指出实施某些原则的手段。笔者尽量把有关联的一些原则归纳在一起，但各原则之间的交叉和重叠是无法避免的。如希望了解更详细的要求，请大家阅读本书提供的参考文献，大部分均可在网上检索获得。

第九至十六章，将介绍英语的写作规则（包括简明英语规则）在翻译中的运用。第九、十章关注基本的遣词造句方法，第十一章关注如何删减冗余信息，做到简洁明了；第十二章介绍如何做到信息流动通畅，关注重点信息的位置；第十三章关注如何通过核心句分析，把长句变为"人物＋动作"的简单表述方式；第十四章关注主动语态和强势动词；第十五章关注长短句搭配使用；第十六章关注语篇的衔接和连贯。其中最基本的规则是简洁规则、强势动词规则、"人物＋动作"规则和信息流动规则。

〔课后练习〕

1. 为什么会流行简明英语？简明英语是否儿童英语？
2. 简明英语的基本原则是什么？
3. 请搜索 Claire's Clear Writing Tips，下载并阅读欧盟的《简明英语写作指南》。
4. 请阅读维基百科的"简明英语"条目（https://zh.wikipedia.org/wiki/简明英语）。
5. 请阅读 Wikipedia 的 Plain English 条目（https://en.wikipedia.org/wiki/Plain_English）

第九章　学会网络查证确保措辞准确

扫码预习

请扫码下载本章涉及的例句。先做练习，再看解答，学习效果更佳。

网络资源在翻译中发挥重要作用，既可以帮助我们查找背景资料，理解原文，又可以帮助我们找到合适的表达方法，包括单词用法、专业术语、原始说法等，本章聚焦英汉互译中如何通过网络查证，确保措辞准确无误。

9.1　利用搜索引擎辅助翻译

国内最常用的搜索引擎是百度，但百度搜索英文资料的能力捉襟见肘，因此，要查找高质量的英文文本，还必须借助国外常用的搜索引擎，比如谷歌、必应、Ecosia.org 等等，其中最好用的是谷歌。谷歌可以查询数万亿网页，提供网站、新闻、图片、视频、图书等多种资源的查询，内容无所不包，查询结果准确、相关性高、速度快。

9.1.1　利用谷歌查术语和平行文本

翻译中常见的专业问题、热点问题，基本上都可以在网上找到相关文章，不仅有中文的，还有其他语言的，有些网站还提供了相关问题的单语或双语词汇，为翻译带来很大方便。译者有任何地方不懂，或者希望检验某个译法是否存在，可以直接用谷歌搜索。

有些词可以逐字翻译出来，但不知道是否地道，可以用谷歌检验。比如，要翻译"水蚀面积""风蚀面积"，可以先猜一个译法，再进行检验。因为字典上"水蚀"和"风蚀"的翻译分别是 water erosion 和 wind erosion，所以，这两个词可能译为 water erosion area 和 wind erosion area（可以看到，双语词典是我们研究的开端）。

在谷歌中输入"water erosion area"或"wind erosion area"。注意加引号。加引号后，引号内的词作为一个整体搜索，搜索出来的几个词是连续的。否则 water、erosion 和 area 可能被别的词隔开。搜索结果发现，两种说法在英语文本中都存在，但仔细观察，发现都是中国或日本的网站内容，所以不完全可信。去掉双引号作更大范围的搜索，查看平行文本。在众多的平行文本中，发现这两个词应该这样说：water eroded area 和 wind eroded area。从词的形态上看（过去分词，"被水侵蚀"），这两种说法也显然更符合逻辑。

有些词不知道如何翻译，但知道上一级概念，不妨查找上一级概念。比如，需要翻译"旱厕"，但你不敢确定，可以上网查 toilet，维基百科提供了以下信息：

> A flush toilet (also known as a flushing toilet, water closet (WC) — see also toilet names) is a toilet that disposes of human waste (urine and feces) by using water to flush it through a drainpipe to another location for disposal, thus maintaining a separation between humans and their waste. Flush toilets can be designed for sitting (in which case they are also called "Western" toilets) or for squatting, in the case of squat toilets. Most modern toilets are designed to dispose of toilet paper also. The opposite of a

flush toilet is a dry toilet, which uses no water for flushing.①

从这些解释中不仅知道"旱厕"是 dry toilet（与汉语何其相似！），还可以学习关于厕所的一系列表达方式。

有些时候完全不知道汉语是什么意思，更不用说如何翻译。比如，要把一篇关于保险和再保险的文章从中文翻译为英文，专业不太懂，有些词（分出公司、分入公司）甚至没有听说过，那么如何利用谷歌来帮助我们呢？有很多种方法：

同时输入英文和中文关键词，点击搜索所有网页，可能找到英汉对照的词语或相关解释。

比如，在搜索框里输入"再保险 分出公司 insurance"，便会出现众多的搜索结果，进入其中一条：

Ceded Company 分进公司

分进公司系指接受原保险人（Original Insurer）所分出之业务之保险人，即再保险人（Reinsurer）。

Ceding Company 分出公司

分出公司系指依再保险契约之规定，将其所承保之业务分予再保险人（Reinsurer）以获取再保险保障之保险公司，又称原保险人（Original Insurer）、原签单公司（Original Writer）或被再保险人（Reinsured）。

我们不仅查到了词语，还学习到了专业知识，知道许多说法原来是同义词。也可以使用以下查找方法：

在搜索框里输入"insurance ＋其他英文关键词"（各个关键词以空格隔开），点击搜索所有网页，可以找到无数有关的文章（平行文本），你可能从中找到所需词语；或者输入"insurance glossary（或 terminology、terms、dictionary 等）"，你可以找到英英保险词语表或词典，可以据此确定某个英文术语的含义与中文是否完全一致；或者输入"保险词语（或术语、词典）英汉对照"，可能找到英汉对照保险词语表。

再比如，要翻译"理财"，你可以输入"理财 management"（如果仅

---

① https://en.wikipedia.org/wiki/Flush_toilet#Etymology, accessed August 31, 2021.

输入"理财",搜索结果中含有英语的很少。你可能会猜到用 management 一词,所以输入该词),发现很多网页中有相关内容,你发现"理财"有很多种说法,如 financial management, assets management, wealth management, personal wealth management,这时,你可以把这些说法逐一输入谷歌,加双引号,检验其出现的上下文是否符合中文的意思。你可能会发现 wealth management 和 personal wealth management 比较符合中文的意思。

又比如,要翻译"专升本",可以输入"专升本 college",得到线索,即美国的两年制大学叫 junior college 或者 community college,相当于中国的大专,毕业后发放 associate degree。据此,你可以推测是否可以译为"associate-to-bachelor" degree,输入谷歌检验,发现果然有类似说法:

- Associate's to Bachelor's Degree Programs
- Associate to Bachelor Programs
- Associate to Bachelor
- Associate to Bachelor Degree
- associate-to-bachelor degree program
- to launch an accelerated transition program that would enable nurses to move from associate to bachelor's degree status
- Students can now enjoy a smooth transition from their associate's to bachelor's degrees through …
- To change from Associate to Bachelor degree

你也许以为这是一个具有中国特色的词语,没想到外国也有类似机制!请你自己查找一下"硕博连读"怎么说。另外,词典上查不到的俚语、俗语,可以用谷歌搜索,即使查不出解释,也可以找到无数上下文供你猜测其含义。

谷歌的特点是,输入的关键词越多,查出来的结果越少,但越有针对性。有时,关于某个专业的文章或资料较少,输入一组关键词没有查到任何结果,你可以减少关键词的数量,或者换一组,重新查找。关键词不仅限于文本中出现的词,也可以是文本之外大背景中的词。例如,文章中虽未提及"中国"一词,但因讲的是中国的事情,"中国"也是关键词。把英语译为汉语时也一样。即使找不到一个英语词的汉语翻译，至少可以通过平行文本或英英词典了解它的意思。当然，如果网上查不出来，还可以用其他方式查找，包括请求原文作者或翻译委托人协助。

9.1.2 使用谷歌查人名、地名等专有名词

9.1.2.1 英语到汉语

翻译外国专有名词，需要先查阅《世界人名翻译大辞典》《世界地名译名词典》及《GB/T 17693〈外语地名汉字译写导则〉国家标准应用手册》，其中没有收录的，则按照译音表翻译。各种语言的"译音表"，可在网上获得。请查找"外语译音表"。

如果查找上述资料不方便，可以在网上搜搜是否有人翻译过。如有，则可借用。可以在谷歌中输入英语名称，再加上一个限定语境的汉语词（如"科学家"）检索，会发现在中文网页中，会有译者在汉语名称后，括注原文名称。括注名称之前，就是你找的译文。如果查出的译法不止一种，选择权威的一种（如外交部网站），或中国大陆使用的说法；如果无法判断哪个常用，就把不同的汉语名称分别输入谷歌查找，哪个结果多，哪个就更常用。但最常用的也可能不是最好的，所以还要依据自己的判断。此方法也可以用来查找刚进入汉语、译名尚待确立的专业术语，因为一般的译者会在自己拿不准的译法后加注原文。他们的译法至少可以作为你的参考。汉英双向皆可使用。

例如，要查找缅甸领导人 Aung San Suu Kyi 的中文译名，可以在谷歌搜索框里输入 Aung San Suu Kyi，加上"缅甸"，可以看到基本上有三种译法：昂山淑姬、翁山苏姬、昂山素季。如果只有一种，自然没有选择余地；现在出现了三种，就要决定使用哪一个。你可以把三种译名分别输入搜索框，点击搜索，看哪个结果多。最终发现：昂山淑姬有 610 项，翁山苏姬有 186 项，昂山素季有 5620 项。从数量上来看，应当使用"昂山素季"。如果你要进一步确保该译法与我国外交部的译法一致，则要看有关文章是否包含中国官方媒体的文章。检查结果是肯定的。

9.1.2.2　汉语到英语

要把翻译为汉语的英语人名（以及日本、港澳台和海外华人名字）翻回到英语，可以使用以下方法：

在谷歌中输入该汉语名称，查找汉语网站，希望在找到的结果中，有用心的译者把英语放在括号中

如，要查"史迪威"将军的英文拼写，在谷歌搜索框里输入"史迪威"，其中一个搜索结果就显示："史迪威在中国，约瑟夫·沃伦·史迪威（Joseph Warren Stilwell）是一位与中国有着不解之缘的美国人……"

如果你知道专有名词中的一部分用英语怎么说，同时把这一部分输入搜索框，可以加快搜索速度

如，要查找"诺尔曼·白求恩"，你已经知道 Norman，可以把"诺尔曼 白求恩 Norman"同时输入（注意关键词之间加空格），一下就可以找到（当然，这个名字不用输入英语也很容易找到）。

如果单独输入汉语，搜索出来的结果很多，一下子没找到哪个附有英语说法，可以在关键词中加一个英语单词，缩小搜索范围（限于搜索既有汉语也有英语的网站）

如，要查找"利马窦"的英语说法，输入"利马窦"后，发现搜索结果不计其数，你可以同时输入"利马窦 Italy"，一下子就找到了：

……地图信息咨询 Dear sir, Thank you very much for your web and it is very well organized. Congratulations! We are from Matteo Ricci (Li Madou in Chinese) Institute in Italy… Best wishes. Filippo Mignini. 这位先生想了解有关利马窦的有关信息……

查日语汉字也一样。例如，英翻中时谈到美日贸易关系，有一个词 kei-retsu，要查日语原文（汉字），在谷歌搜索框里输入该词，搜索中文网站，即可看到不少文章介绍这一制度。日语汉字是：系列。如果以上方法查不到，可以用以下方法：

查找关联的英文词

如要查日本前首相"小泉纯一郎"和"靖国神社"的英语说法，你可以在谷歌搜索框里输入 Japanese prime minister visit war criminal China Korea protest。

要查前澳门特首贺一诚的英语拼法,可以查 Macao special administrative region chief。

顺藤摸瓜

可以查这个人所在机构名称(大学、研究所、公司、国际组织等),希望其中有该人的介绍或其他线索(如果不知道该机构的确切说法,可以试查几个关键词)。如要查下句中的人名:

> 但是,正如奈娜·卡比尔所说:"没有任何一组方法本身对男女之间的差异和不平等具有敏感性;一个方法的社会性别敏感度完全取决于其使用者"。(卡比尔,1995)

用中文搜索"奈娜·卡比尔",仅得到这样的信息:"本文的分析框架选择的是英国萨赛克斯大学发展学研究所奈娜·卡比尔创立的社会关系分析法……"笔者又用相关关键词法查了多次,均未查到。后来在搜索框里输入"Sussex university development institute",找到研究所网站,在网站的 bookshop 下,发现 "Gender Mainstreaming in Poverty Eradication and the Millennium Developing Goals: A Handbook for policy-makers and other stakeholders, Published by the Commonwealth Secretariat, By Naila Kabeer"。

问题迎刃而解。顺便说一句,这个名字的译者一定是个南方人,n 和 l 分不清楚,否则应该是"奈拉"。

查这个人的著作名称(及其他有关信息)

如要查找下文中的人名及著作名:

> 针对女性(或者说是妇女)这一有特色的区别性范畴进行分析研究,应该归功于丹麦经济学家 E. 鲍塞罗普,他 1970 年的著作《经济发展中妇女的作用》,可以说是"妇女"作为一个有特色的区别性范畴在发展思想中的标志……

汉语网站查不到,可以输入 "Danish economist women role economic

development", 一下子便可以找到: "… In 1970, Ester Boserup, a Danish economist, wrote a book (Women's Role in Economic Development) showing that women's work had been ignored or underestimated by…"

查这个人的合作者名称

如, 要翻译"《中国居民收入分配再研究》——赵人伟、李实、卡尔·李思勤著——中国财政经济出版"中的人名"卡尔·李思勤", 用其他方法搜索不出来, 可以输入"zhao renwei li shi", 一下子便找到了: "…S Björn Gustafsson & Li Shi 'Is China Becoming More Unequal?' pages 212-252 in Zhao, Renwei, Li Shi & Carl Riskin (Eds) Re-study on Income Distribution of . . ."

查与这个人有关的任何其他关键词

如果要查下一句话中的人名: "1993 年, <u>卡罗琳·摩塞</u>从妇女参与发展的角度出发, 第一次对社会发展过程中的性别平等问题的理论和政策实践进行了分类……", 在中文网站没有查到, 但你比较肯定"卡罗琳"是 Caroline, 你可以在搜索框里输入"Caroline gender", 搜索所有网站, 便可以很快找到: "Caroline Moser…and social capital, social protection, human rights and sustainable livelihoods and mainstreaming gender into development practice. Caroline recently moved to…"

如果还查不到, 可以猜测几个可能的拼法, 在所有网站中查询, 如"卡比尔"可能是 Kabil, Carbil, Carbir 等。还不行, 查别的辞书, 或者问作者, 找委托人协助。

要把翻译为汉语的地名翻回到英语, 可以使用以下方法:

- 在汉语网站查找, 希望有用心的译者把原文放在括号中
- 在英语网站中查找与此地名有关的事件
- 查找所在国家或地区的地图(输入国家或地区的英语名称＋map)

但对于一些小地名, 查找起来确实不易, 比如, 有一次笔者翻译"越南义安省义禄县义莲社", 是这样查的: 上网搜索"义安省", 找到维基百科该省词条, 该词条下有"宜禄县(Huyện Nghi Lộc)", 应该是"义禄县"的正确译法; 点开"宜禄县"链接, 可看到该县下辖 1 市镇 28 社, 其中没

有"义莲社",与之相近的,是"宜延社(Xã Nghi Diên)"和"宜林社(Xã Nghi Lâm)"。考虑到与 Diên 拼写相似的 điện 读音听起来像"莲"(其实 đ 读作高度浊化的[d],介于汉语 d 和 l 之间),因此可以断定,Xã Nghi Diên(宜延社)就是所谓的"义莲社"。顺带指出,越南过去使用汉字,改为拼音后,这个拼音对应于哪个汉字,并不容易确定,因此,中国作者用不同汉字转写越南语名字也不奇怪。另外,遇到一些小语种的人名地名,可以用谷歌翻译的朗读功能确定当地语言读音,然后转写为最接近的汉字,而不用按照英语中可能的发音来转写。

9.1.3 利用谷歌查机构名称、翻译法律条文等

9.1.3.1 组织机构

包括政府机构、国际组织、非政府组织、公司等名称。可以使用以下方法:

输入中文,可能把你带到该机构的中文网站,进而可进入英文网站

如,输入"劳动和社会保障部",便可以看到"简介: Ministry of Labour and Social Security, PRC"

输入可能的英文关键词,会帮你找到准确的说法

如,查找"英国萨赛克斯大学发展学研究所",可以输入"Sussex university development institute",一下子便可以找到"Welcome to the Institute of Development Studies"。不敢肯定的关键词不要输入。

9.1.3.2 条约

如果要把翻译为汉语的某公约、国际法等条文翻回英语,在搜索框输入被引用部分可能的英语关键词,就可能直接把你带到这段原文。如要翻译:

> 但在 2009 年 1 月 1 日以前,中国的出口还要受到数量约束,"<u>控制在不超过提出磋商请求的当月前的最近 14 个月中,前 12 个月进入该成员数量的 7.5%(羊毛产品类别为 6%)的水平</u>。"

可以输入"'14 months' request consultations 7.5 6",因为这几个词可以肯定英语如此(注意不输入百分号是因为你不知道原文用百分号还是文字

percent)。搜索结果中,"沈阳与 WTO"项下有:

(c) Upon receipt of the request for consultations, China agreed to hold its shipments to the requesting Member of textile or textile products in the category or categories subject to these consultations to *a level no greater than 7.5 percent (6 percent for wool product categories) above the amount entered during the first 12 months of the most recent 14 months preceding the month in which the request for consultations was made.*

如果把引用的国际公约条文译为汉语,可以用汉语输入公约名称,在汉语网站查找,看是否有现成的译文。

查中国的官方文件、法律文书的英语译本,可以输入英语可能的关键词查找。如果想知道某段文字是否来自网上,只需把这段文字中任意几个连续的字词输入,加双引号,搜索,即可找到。

9.1.3.3 回译

有时需要把已经翻译为汉语的概念,重新翻译到英文,这就是"回译"。网络可以帮助我们准确回译。比如,要查找下文中加点部分的原文说法:

首先,中国在短期内将扩大纺织服装的出口。加入 WTO 之后,一方面可以按照 ATC 协议,获得"一体化比例"和"额外增长率",争取到自由化带来的贸易利益……

可以先猜几个译法,如,integration proportion/ratio/rate, incremental/additional growth rate,然后在谷歌中分别查找,加以证实,可以发现,正确说法是:integration rate 和 additional growth rate。

再如,要翻译"优先采用世界卫生组织推荐的自愿、匿名、无关联方法"。显然,其中的关键词来源于卫生组织。"自愿""匿名"的翻译可以比较肯定使用 voluntary, anonymous,那"无关联"卫生组织用的是哪一个词?是 unconnected? 还是 unlinked? unassociated? 可以用谷歌输入 WHO voluntary anonymous 以及上下文提供的其他关键词,查找有关英文资料;或者,把你猜到的词分别进行验证。最后你会发现应该这么翻译:"Priority shall be given to adopt the WHO recommended *voluntary, anonymous, and unlinked protocol*"。卫生组织用了 protocol，可能是我们无法想到的。

再比如，要翻译：

1995 年，中国举办了第四届世界妇女大会。在此前为准备世界妇女大会召开而进行的一系列工作中，中国党政领导机关接受了"非政府组织"这一概念。此后，在扩大开放和增加与外部的交往中，又接受了"第三部门"和"非营利组织"的概念。

其中的"第三部门"是 the third sector 还是 the third department？用谷歌分别检验就知道了。该段翻译为：

In 1995, China hosted the Fourth World Conference on Women. In preparing for the conference, leading organizations of the Chinese Communist Party and the government accepted the concept of "NGO". Later, as a result of further opening and numerous exchanges with other countries, the concepts of "the third sector" and "non-profit organizations" were also adopted.

再如：

中国政府认为：是 70 年代末境外贩毒向云南渗透，开辟"中国通道"，使中国成为毒品贩运过境国。此后，中国政府很不情愿地看到中国成了毒品生产国和消费国。

其中的"中国通道"显然是外来词，翻译为 China path, China corridor, China road, 还是 China way？分别验证即可找到答案。本段翻译为：

The Chinese government believed that China first became a transit country for the drug trade via the *China Route* in the late 1970s when overseas drug traffickers penetrated into Yunnan. Later, the government reluctantly conceded that China has become a producer and consumer of drugs.

9.1.4　利用谷歌查中国特有概念

中国搞市场经济只有几十年的历史，西方有几百年的历史。我们发展中出现的很多现象和问题，都是西方经历过的。而且，对于中国的一举一动，国外都有人关注和研究。所以，即便是所谓中国"特有"的事物，西方人也可能经历过或研究过，我们只需找到即可借用。假如你翻译中国刑法中的拘役、劳改等概念，查 China criminal justice system 就可能发现这样的内容：

> There are mainly 5 types of incarcerating institutions: 1) prisons; 2) *reform-through-labor* institutions, in which criminals are sentenced to a minimum of 1 year fixed-term imprisonment; 3) reform house for juvenile delinquents; 4) Juyi house (criminal detention house), which houses offenders sentenced to criminal detention; and the 5) *Kanshou* house (detention house), which houses offenders awaiting trial.

不仅找到了要找的词，还学习了相关的说法。

中国的历史，国外研究更多，我们翻译的时候不必闭门造车。如要查下文中"废分封、立郡县"的译法：

> 从历史传统来看，中国是一个有几千年封建历史的国家，从秦始皇"废分封、立郡县"开始，每一个行政区划几乎就是一个政治经济实体，封建割据条件下长期形成的"诸侯经济"及其影响，成为滋生地方保护主义的历史根源。

在谷歌中搜索 qin shi huang，即可看到维基百科的相应词条，其中有这么一段：

Administrative reforms

Further information: History of the administrative divisions of China before 1912

Map of the Qin dynasty and its administrative divisions

In an attempt to avoid a recurrence of the political chaos of the Warring States period, <u>Qin Shi Huang and his prime minister Li Si completely abolished feudalism. The empire was then divided into 36 commanderies</u> (郡 , *Jùn*), <u>later more than 40 commanderies.</u> The whole of China was thus divided into administrative units: first commanderies, then counties (縣 , *Xiàn*), townships (鄉, *Xiāng*) and hundred-family units (里, *Li*, which roughly corresponds to the modern-day subdistricts and communities). This system was different from the previous dynasties, which had loose alliances and federations. People could no longer be identified by their native region or former feudal state, as when a person from Chu was called "Chu person" (楚人, *Chu rén*). Appointments were subsequently based on merit instead of hereditary rights.

下划线部分的说法，我们可以借鉴。经常用到的百科网站还有 Wikipedia 中文版、百度百科、MBA 智库百科、Investopedia 等。

9.1.5 利用谷歌检验普通词语的意思和用法

互联网不仅可以帮助我们方便、高效地解决专业词汇问题，还可以帮助我们确定普通词语的翻译方法，弥补我们英语的不足。具体程序是：使用汉英词典找到大致对等的词，使用英英词典、百科全书检验该词是否可用，根据英文解释或英语同义词词典找到更确切的词，使用英语搭配词典查找词的搭配。

例 1.
以往主流社会的意识形态以及一些不恰当的宣传，加大了艾滋病恐慌及人们对艾滋病病人和艾滋病病毒感染者的厌恶，而无助于预防和控制艾滋病。

"宣传"在汉英词典上给出的译法不外乎 propaganda, publicity, promotion, advertisement 等。查英英词典，promotion 是促销，advertisement 是广告，显然不符合上下文。

某百科全书给 propaganda 下的定义是：

noun the organized spreading of doctrine, true or false information, opinions, etc., especially to bring about change or reform; an association or scheme for doing this; the information, etc. spread; (with *capital* Propaganda) a Roman Catholic committee, founded in 1622, responsible for foreign missions and the training of missionaries.

从中可以看出 propaganda 用在这里也不合适。但这个解释给了我们提示：是否可以用 false information 或 misinformation。

misinform: *verb* transitive to inform or tell incorrectly or misleadingly

misinformation 的同义词还有 disinformation，但它的意思是 deliberate leakage of misleading information，显然不对。

publicity 的英语解释是 the process of making something known to the general public; advertising。

综合以上解释，这里的"不恰当宣传"可以用 misinformation, false information, misleading information, incorrect information, 甚至 inappropriate publicity。

同样，在逐个检验了"厌恶"的同义词后，你可能选用 aversion 或 prejudice against：

> Past mainstream thinking and *misleading information* about AIDS increased public fear of the disease and *an aversion for (or prejudice against)* its victims, all of which obstructed its prevention and control.

例 2.

> 最初的立法动议往往由国务院部、委提出，报国务院，由国务院法制机构列入立法计划，涉及多部门的，由国务院法制机构进行综合平衡，然后，由该事项的主管（或主要主管）部门的业务机构和法制机构合作起草，并征求地方政府的分管部门和相关单位（如国有大企业）意见，草案完成后，经过部、委办公会议，然后以部长或委员会主任名义报国务院……

"征求意见"如何译？"意见"常见的译法为 opinion。与它搭配的动词是哪一个？是否只有我们常听说的 solicit 一个词？可以查搭配词典，表示"征求"含义的搭配有：ask (consult, gather, hear, invite, obtain) the opinion of。"意见"还可以翻译为 comments，与它搭配的词是 invite (comments from)。可以在这里查询《牛津英语搭配词典》：www.ozdic.com。关于遣词造句的方法，下一章会专门介绍。

再比如，要翻译下文加点部分：

> 要"坚决打击卖淫、嫖娼、吸毒等社会丑恶现象"，"把预防和控制艾滋病的工作作为社会主义精神文明建设的一项内容切实抓好"，"只有坚持禁止吸毒、卖淫、嫖娼等丑恶行为，才能防止艾滋病蔓延流行"。

如果说这里的"卖淫、嫖娼"可以用一个词 prostitution 来概括的话，下面的"卖淫嫖娼人员"就不能用一个 prostitutes 来概括了，因为那显然是两类人：

> 公安、司法部门抓获的卖淫嫖娼人员和吸毒人员

查普通词典，"嫖客"的译法是 whorehouse visitor，"嫖妓"是 wench，"嫖"是 go whoring, visit prostitutes。反查英语词典，发现 wencher 的意思是：(*old*) a man who associates with prostitutes."属于旧用法，可以排除。剩下的可能是 whorehouse visitor 和 prostitute visitor。通过互联网验证"whorehouse visitor"和"prostitute visitor"（各种单复数组合），发现 whorehouse visitor 不存在；prostitute visitor 只有两个结果，说明不常用。

这时，我们只能想别的办法，扩大搜索范围。比如，根据上下文，输入 China prostitutes detention drug users 等关键词，耐心查阅平行文本，你会发现英语更多地使用 (prostitutes and) their clients。

一个词在不同的上下文可能有不同的译法。因为双语词典没有提供上下文，所以双语词典提供的译法不一定符合你的需要。双语词典的作用在于为你提供词语翻译的线索和进一步研究的基础。对于双语词典中查到的译法，要通过平行文本逐一检验，以确定是否适用于当前的上下文。

9.1.6　利用谷歌辨析词义

如果不清楚两个说法哪个正确，可以通过网络检索加以确定。比如，"公共卫生安全治理体系"有人翻译为 public health safety governance system，你怀疑应该把 safety 改为 security，可以分别检索 public health safety 和 public health security。查前者，发现这三个词并不连用（见图 9.1）：

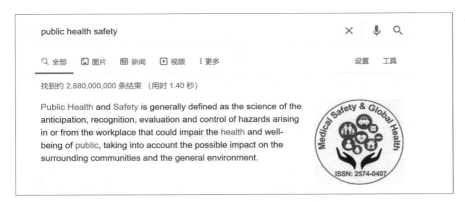

图 9.1　public health and safety 释义

查后者,发现是统一说法(见图 9.2):

图 9.2　public health security 查询结果

所以改译为 the governance system for public health security。虽然 safety 和 security 都翻译为"安全",但含义有所不同。根据《牛津英语词典》,safety means the condition of being safe and protected from danger or harm,强调的是一个系统、组织或个人按照自己的机制正常运转的"稳定状态"。Security 其中一个意思是 Procedures followed or measures taken to ensure the security of a state or organization,security 强调的是免受来自外部或内部"蓄意或恶意"的伤害,采取必要的措施防止这样的伤害发生,确保国家、组织或个人正常运转。

基于这一本质区别,food safety 是指"食品安全",即食品中是否含有有害物质，如苏丹红、三聚氰胺（见图 9.3）：

> Food safety refers to routines in the preparation, handling and storage of food meant to prevent foodborne illness and injury. From farm to factory to fork, food products may encounter any number of health hazards during their journey through the supply chain.
> 2020年1月29日
>
> www.sesotec.com › apac › resources › blog › what-is-foo...
> **What is Food Safety? - The Importance of Food Safety in ...**

图 9.3　food safety 释义

food security 是指"粮食安全"（见图 9.4）[①]，即人类是否会遭受粮食短缺的威胁（是外在威胁，不是来自 food 本身的威胁）：

> What is Food Security? Food security means having, at all times, both physical and economic access to sufficient food to meet dietary needs for a productive and healthy life. A family is food secure when its members do not live in hunger or fear of hunger. 2020年9月22日
>
> www.usaid.gov › what-we-do › agriculture-and-food-sec...
> **Agriculture and Food Security | U.S. Agency for International ...**

图 9.4　food security 释义

nuclear safety（核安全）是指核设施本身的设计是否安全，是否会出故障；nuclear security（核保安）是指核设施是否会受到恐怖袭击、核材料是否会被扩散等（见图 9.5）：

> **Nuclear safety and security**
> From Wikipedia, the free encyclopedia
>
> **Nuclear safety** is defined by the International Atomic Energy Agency (IAEA) as "The achievement of proper operating conditions, prevention of accidents or mitigation of accident consequences, resulting in protection of workers, the public and the environment from undue radiation hazards". The IAEA defines **nuclear security** as "The prevention and detection of and response to, theft, sabotage, unauthorized access, illegal transfer or other malicious acts involving nuclear material, other radioactive substances or their associated facilities".[1]

图 9.5　nuclear safety and security 释义

aviation safety 是指飞机是否可以安全起飞（见图 9.6）：

---

① food security 翻译为"粮食保障"更恰当，但鉴于"粮食安全"已经在官方文件中使用，再改比较困难。

en.wikipedia.org › wiki › Aviation_safety ▼ 翻译此页
Aviation safety - Wikipedia
Aviation safety means the state of an aviation system or organization in which risks associated with aviation activities, related to, or in direct support of the operation of aircraft, are reduced and controlled to an acceptable level.
Statistics · Aviation safety hazards · Human factors · Runway safety

图 9.6　aviation safety 释义

aviation security 是指是否有人到飞机上搞破坏（见图 9.7）：

Aviation security is a combination of measures and human and material resources in order to safeguard civil aviation against acts of unlawful interference. Unlawful interference could be acts of terrorism, sabotage, threat to life and property, communication of false threat, bombing, etc.

en.wikipedia.org › wiki › Airport_security
Airport security - Wikipedia

图 9.7　aviation security 释义

因此，机场的安全检查是 security check，而不是 safety check。

如果不清楚两个概念或单词之间的区别，还可以直接在谷歌上输入 what's the difference between A and B，比如（见图 9.8）：

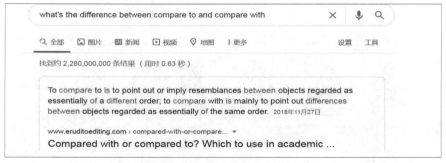

图 9.8　查找词义区别的方法

也可以使用 https://wikidiff.com/ 网站，搜索两个近义词区别和相似点。

9.1.7　用谷歌查找图片

如果我们翻译的内容可能存在于图片中，可以利用谷歌的图片搜索功能。比如，有人要你翻译毕业证，你想知道英语毕业证的格式，可以输入

certificate of graduation，然后仿照实例翻译，确保万无一失（见图 9.9）：

图 9.9 "毕业证"英译查证

在使用谷歌图片搜索公共标识时，可以用关键词加上 signs。比如，要翻译"小心地滑"，可以搜索 slip signs，然后直接借鉴英文说法，而不必另起炉灶来翻译（见图 9.10）：

图 9.10 "小心地滑"英译查证

有时遇到难以想象的事物，如动植物、机器设备、操作流程，也可以借助谷歌的图片搜索功能找到有关事物的图片。例如，有人翻译下面一段话时，由于无法想象斜体部分的意思而不敢翻译（乌龟壳怎么会是黄色的？）：

He loved green turtles and hawk-bills with their elegance and speed and their great value and he had a friendly contempt for the huge, stupid loggerheads, *yellow in their armour-plating*, strange in their lovemaking, and happily eating the Portuguese men-of-war with their eyes shut.（Hemingway. *The Old Man and the Sea*）

如果用谷歌查 loggerhead，搜索图片，你会看到许多漂亮的乌龟图片，这种乌龟果然是鲜艳的黄色。

9.1.8　其他常用网站

汉译英时还可以借助以下网站查找用词是否准确或常用：

- 维基百科

前文已经提及维基百科，这里再次推荐。维基百科人人可以编辑，这意味着其中的文章经过无数次审核，质量相当可靠，内容也十分丰富，对于我们系统了解某个学科的知识和表达方法，非常有帮助，是英文参考资料的首选。维基百科可通过谷歌或维基百科界面查询，包括中英文版，其中甚至收录中国最新的政治缩略语（见图 9.11）：

Four Comprehensives

From Wikipedia, the free encyclopedia

The **Four Comprehensives**, or the **Four-pronged Comprehensive Strategy**[1] (Chinese: 四个全面战略布局) is a list of political goals for China, put forward by Xi Jinping, General Secretary of the Communist Party of China in 2014. They are:

1. Comprehensively build a moderately prosperous society
2. Comprehensively deepen reform
3. Comprehensively govern the nation according to law
4. Comprehensively strictly govern the Party.[2]

Some scholars argue that there are the same or very similar statements of the "four comprehensives" in Deng Xiaoping Theory.[3]

图 9.11　"四个全面"英译查证

- 语料库

语料库的使用可以让译者清楚直观了解到一些词语／搭配在各种学术

文章中是如何使用的。english-corpora.org 网罗了大多数英文语料库，我们可以从中选择使用。界面如下（仅展示了其中的一半语料库）（见图 9.12）：

Corpus (online access)	Download	# words	Dialect	Time period	Genre(s)
iWeb: The Intelligent Web-based Corpus		14 billion	6 countries	2017	Web
News on the Web (NOW)		11.0 billion+	20 countries	2010-yesterday	Web: News
Global Web-Based English (GloWbE)		1.9 billion	20 countries	2012-13	Web (incl blogs)
Wikipedia Corpus		1.9 billion	(Various)	2014	Wikipedia
Corpus of Contemporary American English (COCA)		1.0 billion	American	1990-2019	Balanced
Coronavirus Corpus		591 million+	20 countries	Jan 2020-yesterday	Web: News
Corpus of Historical American English (COHA)		400 million	American	1810-2009	Balanced
The TV Corpus		325 million	6 countries	1950-2018	TV shows
The Movie Corpus		200 million	6 countries	1930-2018	Movies
Corpus of American Soap Operas		100 million	American	2001-2012	TV shows

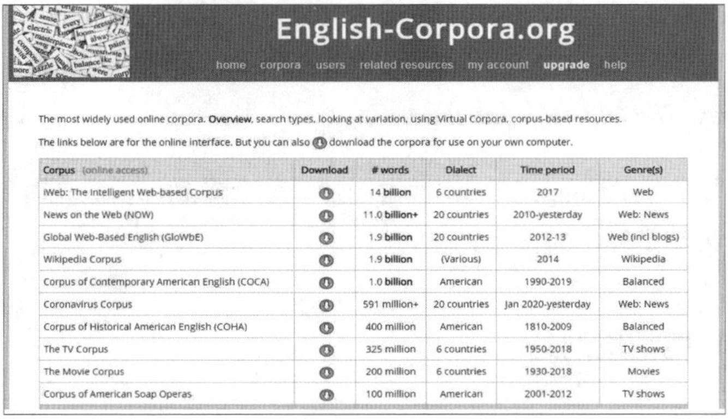

图 9.12　English-Corpora.org 网站截图

- Google Books Ngram View

网站：https://books.google.com/ngrams。可以查一个词从什么时候开始流行以及使用情况。以下是查 brainwash 的图片，说明该词从 20 世纪 50 年代开始使用（见图 9.13）：

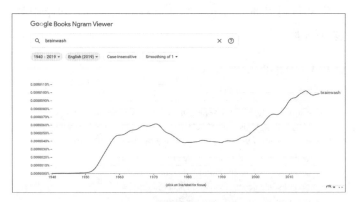

图 9.13　单词使用历史查询

- 中国重要政治词汇对外翻译标准化专题库

该专题库由中国外文局中国翻译研究院主持建设，是国内首个国家级政治词汇对外翻译标准化专题库，旨在规范重要政治术语译法，为对外传播翻译工作提供数据资源，确立国家主导的政治词汇外译标准。可通过标题搜索网址。

- 中国核心语汇

网站：https://www.cnkeywords.net/index。界面（查"四个意识"）如下（见图 9.14）：

图 9.14 "四个意识"英译查证

- 术语在线

网站：http://www.termonline.cn/index.htm。界面（查"海市蜃楼"）（见图 9.15）：

图 9.15 "海市蜃楼"英译查证

注意：以上术语库提供的译法，也不能照单全收。必须根据上下文，重新检验这个译法是否合适。

301

9.2 当你找不到现成的译法时

以上介绍了如何使用电子手段查找单词的译法。如果使用任何手段都无法查到，我们就需要自己翻译，也许会成为这个词的第一个译者。在翻译词语时，通常可以采取以下几种方法：

9.2.1 使用近义词

相近的词这里指上义词、下义词、中性词。具有种属关系的一组词称为上下义词，其中表示属概念的词是上义词，表示种概念的词是下义词。如"笔"是"钢笔"的上义词，"钢笔"是"笔"下义词。例如："嫂子"译为 sister-in-law（sister-in-law 不仅指嫂子），"叔叔"译为 uncle（uncle 的词义更广），lap 译为"腿"（lap 指的是 the front part of the lower trunk and thighs of a seated person），"楼堂馆所"可以用 hotels 或 buildings 一言以蔽之。grandfather 根据情况翻译为"爷爷"或"姥爷"，uncle 译为"叔叔""伯父""舅舅"等。如果无法翻译一个生动、具体的词，可以改用一个中性词或表达力不够强的词。比如，在特定情况下，argue、claim、assert、believe、think 等词都可以翻译为"认为"；"大吃大喝"可以译为 wining and dining。

9.2.2 文化替代

翻译时放弃原文的文化内涵，用译入语的文化取而代之。例如，raining cats and dogs 倾盆大雨；a piece of cake 易如反掌；milky way 银河；The child lays his head upon his mother's lap. 孩子把头依偎在妈妈的怀里；饺子 dumpling；鄙人 I；贵公司 your company；maternal aunt 姨妈等。

9.2.3 使用原文

汉语倾向于把外语一律转变为汉字，但在特定情况下，某些词语经常可以不翻译，尤其是这个词成为讨论的对象时。如：

例 3.

Abandon and surrender both imply no expectation of recovering what is given up; surrender also implies the operation of compulsion or force: abandoned all hope for a resolution; surrendered control of the company.

abandon 和 surrender 都暗含已经 give up 的事物没有指望重新获得；surrender 还暗含使用了强迫手段或者武力。如：abandoned all hope for a resolution; surrendered control of the company。

例 4.

……位于西洋楼景区最东部。在方河东岸修筑七道"八"字形左右对称的断墙，墙面挂西洋风景油画，从西岸眺望，形成透视深远的西方街市风光。此景亦称线法墙。

This attraction is situated at the far east end of the European Palaces. Originally, there had been seven continuous pairs of symmetric walls resembling the Chinese character "eight（八）", on which were hung Western oil landscapes. Viewed from the western side of the Square Lake, the oil paintings appeared like actual Western landscapes in natural perspective.

9.2.4　音译

可以利用音译、解释或两种方式的组合，来处理一些难译的词，这样做目的不是为了向另一种语言输入新词，而是为了准确表达或交流方便，英文文献中很常见。单是一个"民办"和"私立"，要表达出来就需要各显神通：

- *Minban* Teachers vs. Gongban (public) teachers: How to achieve equal pay for equal work?
- At the bottom of the teaching profession are the low-paid and academically less qualified *minban, or "community sponsored"* peasant teachers like Bai, who make up 40 percent of China's primary school instructors

- Private institutions (*Sili or Minban*) are in control over budget and spending Market Study of Chinese Private (*Minban*) Higher Education;
- Community-run schools as well as community-paid (*Minban*) teachers have played a crucial role in the overall expansion of basic education.

再比如，有人把"拘役"先翻译为 criminal detention，再给出拼音：

Criminal detention *or Juyi* range from one month to six months in a place near one's residence, overseen by the local police department and the convicted is allowed return home one or two days per month. They may need to work while detained and will receive some pay.

音译和解释相结合的方法有一个好处，即可以避免同一概念因不同人的译法相异而造成的误解，因为读者至少可以从汉语拼音看到这是同一概念。

9.2.5 字面翻译

就是按照音素或单词直接译出。这是一种常见的翻译方法。现代汉语中很多词和术语都是从外语直接翻译过来的。例如：

superman 超人；postmodernism 后现代主义；United Nations 联合国；armed to the teeth 武装到牙齿；全国人大 National People's Congress 等。再如，下文的"体制内""体制外"：

所谓"支持系统"分两部分：体制内——由官方提供的支持；体制外——民间社会提供的支持。

The support system has two parts: intra-institutional — support provided by the governments, and extra-institutional — support provided by the civil society.

在字面翻译的基础上，还可以解释，如下文中对"政务院"的解释：

1951年2月，政务院发布了《中华人民共和国劳动保险条例》，这是新中国成立后的第一部社会保险法规，奠定了我国社会保障的基础。

The Labor Insurance Regulations of the People's Republic of China were promulgated as early as February 1951 by the then Administrative Council [*the precursor of the State Council*]. This was the first labor regulation of the People's Republic of China and served as the foundation of China's social security system.

也可以在字面翻译后夹注原文或其缩写。例如：

- 入世后，我国应全面履行 WTO 法律体系中《服务贸易总协定》(GATS)、《GATS 的金融服务附录》
- 由经济合作与发展组织（简称 OECD）着手起草并组织谈判的《多边投资协定》(Multilateral Agreement on Investment，以下简称 MAI)……
- 融资激励（financial incentives）包括政府资助（government grants）、补贴贷款（subsidized loans）和贷款担保（loan guarantees）……
- China's reforms have made it impossible to deliver social services to the majority of urban residents through the former work unit (*danwei*)(单位) system.

9.2.6 概括和解释

一些汉语的说法可以用简单的英语单词加以概括。如：

所有访谈录音均整理成文字。
All interview audio recordings were *transcribed*.
我们也认为在当前背景下，全球化与劳工标准是非常重要的现象，有必要作为重点题目研究。
We agree that under the current situation, globalization and labor standards are extremely important and *merit* a major study.
在市场经济条件下，竞争机制所形成的优胜劣汰，必然会造成部分劳动者退出劳动岗位，从而使本人和家庭因失去收入而陷于生存危机。

In a market economy, competition engenders natural selection, resulting in *unemployment* for some members of the workforce. Loss of income can put these individuals and their families in financial crisis.

与概括相反的，是解释性翻译。例如：

准备设立"农民工的需要和支持系统"项目，研究二者的契合及错位。

"契合"是指"支持系统满足了需要"；"错位"是指"支持系统没有满足需要"。据此，翻译为：

We plan to set up a project named Migrant Worker Needs and Support Systems to study what needs have been met and what have not.

再如：

In U.S. v. 95 Barrels Alleged Apple Cider Vinegar, the Supreme Court rules that the Food and Drugs Act *condemns* every statement, design, or device on a product's label that may mislead or deceive, even if technically true.

在美国诉 95 桶所谓苹果酒醋一案中，最高法院认定，产品标签中的任何声明、设计或图案如果可能造成误导或欺骗，即使在技术上符合事实，也违反《食品与药物法》。

"法案"谴责某一行为，即意味着某一行为"违反"了法律。

9.2.7 词类转换

如果原文的词类无法移植到译文，可以转换词类：

In 1976 residents staged large-scale protests *against* the South African government's policy of apartheid.

1976 年，居民发动了大规模的抗议示威，反对南非政府的种族隔离政策。

再如：

In 1966, Fair Packaging and Labeling Act requires all consumer products in interstate commerce to be *honestly and informatively labeled*, with FDA enforcing provisions on foods, drugs, cosmetics, and medical devices.

1966年，《公平包装和标签法》要求州际贸易中所有消费品粘贴内容翔实的标签，FDA负责实施有关食品、药物、化妆品和医疗器械的条款。

又如：

因此，美国转变立场的可能性还是存在的。
It may *be possible*, then, that the US changes its position.

但是否转换，还是要凭借语感，并无固定规则。

9.2.8 视角变换

从不同的角度描述同一事物，例如：自学 self-teach；远程教育 distance learning。再如：

In his 1776 work *The Wealth of Nations*, Scottish economist Adam Smith proposed that *specialization in production leads to increased output.*

苏格兰经济学家亚当·斯密在其1776年所著《国富论》中认为，专业化生产会引起产出增加。

这里，把"生产的专业化"转变为"专业化生产"，"增加的产出"转变为"产出增加"。

FDA publishes Guidance to Industry for the first time. This guidance, "Procedures for the Appraisal of the Toxicity of Chemicals in Food," came *to be known* as the "black book."

FDA首次发布《产业指导》。该指导题目为"食品中化学制剂毒性的评估程序"，人们习惯称之为"黑皮书"。

这里把被动转变为主动。

"正话反说,反话正说"也属于视角变换:

In 1954, Miller Pesticide Amendment spells out procedures for setting safety limits for pesticide residues on *raw* agricultural commodities.

1954年,《米勒杀虫剂修正案》详细规定了制定未加工农产品杀虫剂残留标准的程序。

再如:

The bill *was defeated*, but during the next 25 years more than 100 food and drug bills were introduced in Congress.

虽然议案未获通过,但在随后的25年中,有100多个食品与药物法案被提交到国会。

又如:

Food Quality Protection Act amends the Food, Drug, and Cosmetic Act, *eliminating application* of the Delaney provision to pesticides.

《食品质量保护法》修订了《食品药物与化妆品法》,戴勒内限制性条款不再适用于杀虫剂。

抽象的事物可以具体化,具体的事物也可以抽象化:

Shocking disclosures of unsanitary conditions in meatpacking plants, the use of poisonous preservatives and dyes in foods, and cure-all claims for *worthless and dangerous* patent medicines were the major problems leading to the enactment of these laws.

之所以通过以上法律,主要是因为肉类包装厂卫生条件恶劣,被披露后引起了人们的震惊;商人在食品中使用有毒的防腐剂和染料;药厂声称包治百病的专利药品却没有任何药效甚至危害身体健康。

原文是"无价值的"和"危险的",译文变为具体的"没有任何药效甚至危害身体健康"。

9.2.9 完形填空

如果一个词不容易翻译出来,可以把原文中这个词去掉,看能否根据上下文,换成一个容易翻译的词。或者在翻译时先把这个词的翻译空出来,然后根据译文上下文填出一个词,而不管原文用什么词。例如:

In 1937, Elixir of Sulfanilamide, containing the poisonous solvent diethylene glycol, kills 107 persons, many of whom are children, *dramatizing* the need to establish drug safety before marketing and to enact the pending food and drug law.

1937年,含有毒性溶剂二甘醇的磺胺酏剂致使107人丧生,包括多名儿童。这一事件强烈地提醒人们,需要在营销前确定药物安全性,需要讨论中的食品与药物法。

dramatizing 不易翻译,可以先不译,而是把其他部分译出后,根据上下文意思,补充一个可以承前启后的说法。

9.2.10 省略不译

有些情况下,省略不译并不妨碍意思的表达:

调查以问卷和访谈方式进行。
Questionnaires and interviews were used in our investigation.

"方式"属于范畴词,可以省略。关于这类省略见第十一章"删减冗余信息确保语言简洁"。再如:

伊利奉行"人才为本"战略,将之列为企业发展的第一战略。他们早就废除了"三铁"(铁饭碗、铁交椅、铁工资),实行全员合同制,公开招聘人才,总公司的14名部长有10名是从社会公开招聘的。伊利也注重对在职干部的培养。

Yili pursues a policy of meritocracy that gives top priority to human resource development. It has long abolished the practice of "*no dismissal, no demotion,* and *no wage reduction*". Instead, staff is employed on contract and recruited through an open competitive process; this was how it recruited ten of its fourteen department heads. Yili also emphasizes on-job training of managers.

"三铁"的具体内容已经按意思翻译，再直译"三铁"失去意义。再如：

Chain 坦言，董事局现在面临的许多挑战，均来自大家对公司治理（corporate governance 或称企业治理）的新关注。

Chain admitted that many of the board's challenges arose from new concerns in corporate governance.

括号中是关于译法的解释，翻译出来没有意义。

9.2.11　翻译的遗憾

以上是翻译词语遇到困难时使用的一些变通方法。这样归纳不一定全面、准确，仅仅希望起到启迪思考的作用。我们经常遇到这样的情况：想尽了一切办法，到了交稿时，对某个词或句子的译法还是不满意，使我们感到终身遗憾。不过，只要你作了足够努力，即便是没有找到满意的答案，这个词或句子本身也会长时间留在脑子中，说不定哪一天你就能碰到满意的译法。

比如，下面几段话中的"规制"：

本报告将尽力阐释处于动态之中的中国的规制与结构的变化，及其在具体的与艾滋病相关的法律中的表现、实际作用和意义……

因此，如何设立规制，创造一种有利于修复传统，促使社会平稳转型的环境，促进主流社会和多数人认同的法律理念的形成，就成了至关重要的问题。

我们注意到社会的结构与规制——主要是法律之间的一种对应关系……

笔者在哪里都查不到"规制"的译法，问作者，作者只是说这是个日语词，不知道英语怎么说。查日英词典，给出的翻译是 regulation，但本文中 regulation 已经用来翻译"规章"，如果用同一个词表示两个不同的意思，显然读者无法区分是哪个意思；况且这里的意思似乎与 regulation 不同。最后不得已，还是用了 regulation。

交稿后不久，发现了它的译法应当是 institution（多译为"制度"）：

> Third, the less-than-fully-developed state of domestic institutions, especially the legal system, increases the prospect that China will fall short of full compliance with its WTO commitments.

尽管这个错误已经无法补救，但是今后再遇到这个词的时候，是不会出错了。需要注意，"规制"也可能翻译为 regulation，视情况而定。

9.3　小结

本章详细介绍了网络查证的方法，以及查不到时该如何处理。根据本人的经验，几乎所有的翻译问题，都可以通过网络查询解决，需要请教他人的情况极少。对译者来说，最重要的是责任心和耐心。只要坚持不懈查下去，一定会查出结果。

〔课后练习〕

1. 按照本章提供的方法，请把本章所用例子再查询一遍，看结果有何不同？如果查不出来，请换一种方法，反复尝试，直到查清。
2. 请在今后的翻译中，坚持使用谷歌搜索。
3. 翻译公共标识、证书等可能有图片的资料，可以尝试搜索谷歌图片。
4. 如需了解事物原理，可查询百度、谷歌等网站提供的视频。

中译翻译文库

李长栓 著

非文学翻译理论与实践
理解、表达、变通 下册

中国出版集团
中译出版社

第十章　借助英英词典搭建句子结构

扫码预习

请扫码下载本章涉及的例句。先做练习，再看解答，学习效果更佳。

一般认为，理想的翻译模式是把外语翻译为母语，这是因为，"一个人即使学习和使用外语多年，也不一定能够完全达到自如的程度"（Sofer, 1998）。①

但实际情况是，如果一个国家的政治、经济、文化等处于劣势，学习该国语言的外国人就会很少，其中愿意从事该语言翻译的人更少。而这些弱势国家出于政治、经贸和文化交流的需要，往往要把大量的文献译为外语，依赖外国人翻译是不现实的，所以，大多数情况下需要由本国人把文献资料从母语翻译为外语。

与英语相比，汉语处于劣势，虽然随着中国国力的增强，学习汉语的外国人越来越多，但短期内由中国人自己做中翻外的局面不会有根本性改变。鉴于以上情况，我们对汉译英的语言质量应有合理的预期。

本章针对母语译为外语的薄弱环节，提出可操作的解决方案，用具体

---

① 转引自 Chi-Chiang Shei. Combining Translation into the Second Language and Second Language Learning: An Integrated Computational Approach. Ph. D. Thesis. Division of Informatics, University of Edinburgh, 2002.

案例说明如何利用英英词典、英语搭配/用法词典、英语同义词词典、英语语料库及其他网上资源解决汉译英时的语法搭配、词汇搭配和句子框架问题。

10.1 外语表达难以自如的原因

研究表明，外语水平难以达到自如，除其他原因外，主要是因为没有掌握足够的英语习语、搭配和句套子（idioms, collocations and sentence stems）。

英语习语经常是比喻性的，其组成部分不能随意替换，如 bark up the wrong tree、have sticky fingers 等，因此，拿不准的话必须核实。

搭配分为有标记搭配和无标记搭配。无标记搭配是指人们日常使用的普通搭配。有标记搭配是指作者为了制造某种语言效果而创造出来的搭配。例如，虽然 damage 的直接宾语一般是无生命的事物，而在 The driver of the car was badly damaged. 这句话中作者却用有生命的 driver 作 damage 的逻辑宾语，作者在这里的意图是要拿车祸本身开玩笑，制造幽默的效果。本章介绍的方法针对无标记搭配。

搭配还可以分为语法搭配（grammatical collocations）和词汇搭配（lexical collocations）。语法搭配是一个短语，由一个主导词（dominant word），即名词、形容词和动词，加一个介词或不定式、从句等语法结构组成，如 account for、apathy towards、offer to help、a pleasure to do something、and afraid that it would rain。

词汇搭配不包括介词、不定式或从句等，而是由名词、形容词、动词和副词构成，如 strong tea、rough estimates、readily available、sorely needed、deeply absorbed。词汇搭配比成语更为灵活（如 sorely needed 也可以说 badly needed），但比单词的自由组合更为固定。所谓自由组合，是指只要符合语法规则，就可以几乎不受限制地进行组合。如与 put 搭配的宾语可以是任何物体；run 表示"管理"的意思时，其宾语的选择范围虽受到一定限制，但仍可以在意思上归纳为任何可以管理的机构，如 business、 institution 等。

句套子是指一个句子的骨架（也叫 sentence builders、lexicalized sentence stems），如 at the heart of ... is ...、demand for ... is high、with all the ...、it should be no surprise that ...、to be sorry to have kept you waiting、there's no doubt that X or my point here is X。

另外，还有一些固定的短语和句子，似乎无法归入以上各类，如 by the way、can I help you 等。

10.2 成语优先原则

研究认为，人们在表达思想时，常常遵守"成语优先原则"（idiom principle），即首先选用语言中业已存在的表达方式，当找不到现有的表达方式时，再使用自由选择原则（open-choice principle），即根据语法规则创造新的表达方式。业已存在的表达方式就是指成语、搭配、句套子等。我们在学习外语时，传统上强调语法规则，按照语法规则造句，没有遵循成语优先的原则，从而导致语言不符合习惯。但现在的问题是，尽管我们知道应当遵循成语优先的原则，我们却没有足够的"成语"（包括习语、搭配和句套子）可供使用，无论在口头表达、写作或翻译时都是如此。正所谓"巧妇难为无米之炊"。

口头表达和写作当然要符合英语习惯。翻译是否一定要符合英语习惯呢？回答是显而易见的。古今中外，许多翻译家提出的翻译标准中，都强调了译文要符合语言习惯，如"信达雅"中的"达"，"忠实""通顺"中的"通顺"；纽马克（1988）也说过，在进行交际性翻译（communicative translation，相对于 literal translation）时，无论翻译的是信息性文本、通知或广告，"自然"（naturalness）都是至关重要的。

纽马克的结论是："所以，如果目的语不是译者惯用的语言，就没有办法翻译好。"然而，我们面临的工作恰恰是无法做好的工作。

从以上论述可以看出，外语学习者所缺乏的不是语法知识，而是惯用表达方法。语法知识是有限的，容易在短时间内掌握，而惯用表达方法的数量要大得多，短时间内充分掌握有很大困难。为此，一方面我们在英语教学中应充分重视惯用表达方法，另一方面，对于翻译专业的学生以及广大从事中英翻译实践的人士来说，由于他们很少有时间再专门学习外语，因此必须学会通过翻译实践提高英语表达能力，使译文尽量符合英语习惯。一个临时抱佛脚的做法，就是拿不准时充分查证。

10.3　词典介绍

传统上，我们查词的工具书包括双语词典，如《新世纪汉英大词典》（第二版，杜瑞清，外语教学与研究出版社），《新世纪英汉大词典》（胡壮麟，外语教学与研究出版社）；单语词典，如《现代汉语词典》（商务印书馆）；英英词典，如 Collins COBUILD Essential English Dictionary；英语搭配词典，如《牛津英语搭配词典》（Oxford Collocations Dictionary for Students of English）（外语教学与研究出版社）；英语同义词词典；英语用法词典等。

双语词典用来查找一个单词在另一种语言中的对应说法。没有学过翻译的人认为，只要把每个单词查出来，按照英语的语法排列出来，就是翻译。这是很大的误解。暂且不把句子放在篇章中考虑，仅仅翻译句子本身，也要保证用词、搭配、句型符合英语习惯（不仅是语法）。这就要求我们对于没有把握的单词，需要通过查找英语同义词词典、英英词典和英语平行文本，确定其意义确实是我们要表达的意思；查找英语用法词典和搭配词典，确定该词的搭配和句型。

随着网络和手机的普及，这些传统词典纷纷推出网络版和手机版，为用户带来很大方便。笔者常用的网络英语释义和用法词典包括 Oxford Languages、Merriam-Webster、Cambridge、Collins、Longman、The Free Dictionary 等等[①]。如果要查一个单词，在谷歌搜索框输入该词（可以再加上 define 或 definition），排在搜索结果前面的就是这些词典的释义。当然也可

---

① 这里是几个常用词典网站：www.zdic.net（汉语词典）；www.dictionary.com（英语词典）；www.ozdic.com（英语搭配词典）；www.thesaurus.com（同义词典）。

以直接使用这些词典的界面查询。

笔者常用的搭配词典是 *Oxford Collocation Dictionary*（www.ozdic.com）。比如，查找 recovery 的搭配，结果如下（局部）（见图 10.1）：

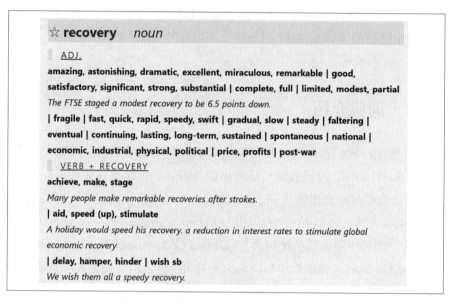

图 10.1　搭配词典查询截图

最近发现的一个网站（https://linggle.com/），可以查到各种搭配关系。比如，不确定是用"in such context"还是"in such a context"，可以查"in such? a context"（图 10.2）：

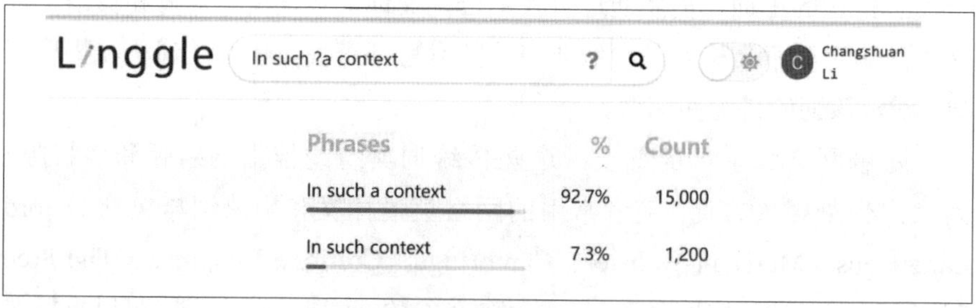

图 10.2　Linggle 搭配查询示例（一）

结果显示大多数人用冠词。不敢确定是 spread wide 还是 widely，可以查"spread widely/wide"，结果是（见图 10.3）：

spread widely/wide		
Phrases	%	Count
spread wide	76.4%	94,000
spread widely	23.6%	29,000

图 10.3　Linggle 搭配查询示例（二）

大部分人使用 wide。"促进……发展"不想用 promote the development of（上句刚用过 promote），想换一个动词，可以查"v. the development of"，结果是（见图 10.4）：

v. the development of		
Phrases	%	Count
support the development of	12.2%	330,000
is the development of	9.4%	250,000
promote the development of	6.2%	170,000
encourage the development of	5.6%	150,000
facilitate the development of	4.8%	130,000
including the development of	4%	110,000
include the development of	3.4%	91,000

图 10.4　Linggle 搭配查询示例（三）

具体使用方法，可以点击查询框后的问号。

手机 APP 方面，笔者有时使用《新世纪英汉汉英大词典》（外语教学与研究出版社），该词典双向打通，比如，查"大局"的英文，不仅可以看到"大局"词条下的英文，还可以看到其他汉英或英汉词条下含有"大局"的例句；以及《朗文当代高级英语辞典》（外语教学与研究出版社），这本词典不仅包括单词的解释，还包括丰富的用法信息和词语搭配，对于翻译工作者特别有用；该词典也可以作为汉英词典使用；还有网易有道词典。另外有一个 APP，叫作 pleco，是外国人学习中文/翻译时使用的，例句语言地道，不妨尝试一下。

还有可以安装在电脑桌面的词典软件，如灵格斯词霸（见图 10.5）：

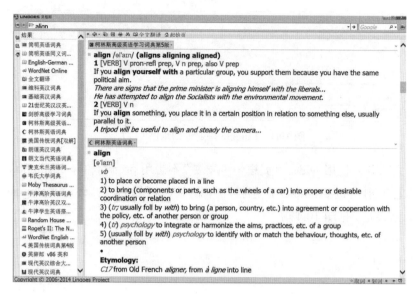

图 10.5 灵格斯词霸查询示例

以及 GoldenDict（见图 10.6）：

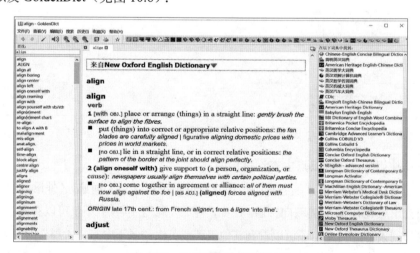

图 10.6 GoldenDict 查询示例

10.4 电子语料库 WebCorp 用法介绍

除了可以利用网络词典外，语料库也是语言学习和翻译的强大工具。

这里以 WebCorp（http://www.webcorp.org.uk/）为例加以介绍（界面见图 10.7）。更多语料库请见 https://www.english-corpora.org/。

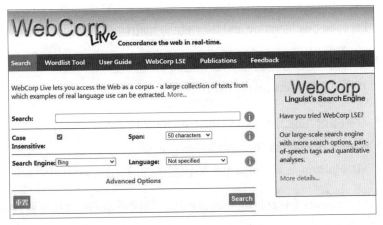

图 10.7　WebCorp 查询界面

WebCorp 语料库以 Google 等搜索引擎的搜索结果为基础，搜索功能极为强大。我们举例说明其用法。例如，《婚姻法》英译本把"子女应当尊重父母的婚姻权利"翻译为"Children shall have respect for their parents matrimonial rights"。是否存在 matrimonial right 这一搭配？用 WebCorp 搜索 matrimonial right*（"*"是通配符，见下文解释），发现下列例句：

- that neither spouse has a <u>matrimonial right</u> to the property of the
- that a spouse has no <u>matrimonial right</u> to certain property belonging to
- and Raija, neither has a <u>matrimonial right</u> to the property of the
- and wife may use their <u>matrimonial right</u> even during the days of
- the intention of limiting the <u>matrimonial right</u> itself to the periods of

这些例句说明：1）right 用复数是不正确的；2）matrimonial right 的意思是"因婚姻而获得的权利"，不是"结婚的权利"。所以，这里使用 matrimonial right 是错误的。那么，能否使用 the right to marriage 呢？我们用 Webcorp 可以查到如下结果：

- that is fighting for our <u>right to marriage</u>), agrees. He believes the work

319

- Literature and the <u>Right to Marriage</u> (9/20/02; ACLA, 4
- the complex question of the <u>right to marriage</u> in response to at least
- the claim upon a universal <u>right to marriage</u> would at once contest the
- between this literature and the <u>right to marriage</u>? Does the literary

我们可以断定 right to marriage 是正确的。那么，用 respect for their right 是否可以呢？查 respect for the right，得到如下结果：

- The <u>respect for the right</u> of the individual to privacy
- namely <u>respect for the right</u> to freedom of
- Mr. Mahamade Houmed and <u>respect for their right</u> to be assisted

所以，respect for their right to marriage 是说得通的。全句可以译为：
Children must have respect for the right to marriage of their parents.
或者用动词：
Children must respect the right to marriage of their parents.

如果用 WebCorp 查找中国特有的概念，要注意查找的结果是出现在中国人写的文章里，还是西方的媒体报道里，如果是前者，则结果不一定可靠。可以用 Advanced Search Options 限定搜索的范围。

另外，Webcorp 可以通过特殊符号，查找符合某一条件的单词、短语或句型。

通配符（*）

通配符可以用在单词词尾（如用 run* 匹配 *running*、*runners* 等），也可以用来代替短语中的一个单词（如用 the* sank 匹配 *the boat sank*、*the ship sank*、*the ferry sank* 等）。

同一短语中可以使用多个通配符，通配符也可以连续使用（如用 the** sank 匹配 the *'unsinkable' ship sank*、*the ship that never sank* 等）。注意，短语开头和结尾不必使用通配符。

字符组

the* sank 表示任何以 the 开头，以 sank 结尾的由三个单词组成的短

语，而 the [ship|boat] sank 仅仅表示 the ship sank 或者 the boat sank。

该短语最后一个单词中可以加括号，变为 the [ship|boat] s [a|u] nk，匹配 the ship sank、the ship sunk、the boat sank or the boat sunk。

更复杂的用法还有，用 r [u|a] n [ning|s|] 匹配 running、runs、run、ranning、rans、ran。

10.5 利用英语词典和电子语料库搭建句子结构

为解决英语表达习惯问题，尤其是句子框架和词语搭配问题，笔者根据自己的实践和教学，提出以下几个操作步骤：

- 确定句子的关键词；
- 根据汉英词典查找关键词的英语译法；
- 根据英英词典或平行文本检验关键词的英语译法是否符合特定上下文的意思；如果不符合，则……
- 根据英语同义词词典（thesaurus）寻找更为贴切的译法；
- 根据英语搭配（用法）词典、语料库等电子手段等确定该关键词的语法搭配（句型）、词汇搭配，从而确定译入语句子框架；
- 把原文各个组成部分按照语法要求逐项纳入句子框架，注意各成分内部的搭配。

当然，并非翻译每个句子都要遵守以上步骤。如果对各种句子结构、搭配都很熟悉、有把握，当然不需要每个地方都查。这些步骤是遇到问题时的解决方法。下面举例说明。

10.5.1　welcome 用法考证

请大家翻译下面一句话：

中国政府欢迎外国私人资本参与中国的基础设施和基础工业建设。

本句话中关键的动词是"欢迎"，根据我们已有的英语知识，找到这个词的英语对应词 welcome 应该不会有问题。下一步是确定该词的句型。如果不敢肯定，我们可以用搭配（用法）词典查 welcome 的用法。下面是 *The Collins Cobuild Student's Dictionary Online* 对 welcome 一词用法的解释：

1. If you **welcome** someone, you greet them in a friendly way when they arrive.

He moved eagerly towards the door to welcome his visitor.
welcome n.
I was given a warm welcome by the President.

2. You can say '**Welcome**' to someone who has just arrived.

Welcome to Peking.
Welcome back.

3. If someone is **welcome** in a place, people are pleased when they come there.

All members of the public are welcome.

4. If you tell someone that they are **welcome** to do something, you are encouraging them to do it.

You will always be welcome to come back.

5. If you **welcome** something new, you approve of it and support it.

I warmly welcomed his proposal.

6. If something that happens or occurs is **welcome**, you are pleased about it or approve of it.

This is a welcome development.

可以看出，动词 welcome 有 6 种用法，我们使用 welcome 一词时，应符合这 6 种用法之一。根据本句所需表达的意思，我们可以选择第 4 项、第 5 项或第 6 项用法作为句子框架：

根据第 4 项用法 someone is welcome to do something 翻译：

Private foreign investors are welcome to invest in China's infrastructure and basic industries.

第十章 · 借助英英词典搭建句子结构

为符合该句型的要求，我们把"物"（资本）改为"人"（投资者）。原文的主语"中国政府"没地方加入，但这可以从上下文推断出来，所以不译也可以。基础产业是否是 basic industries? 上网查一查发现有这一搭配。

根据第 5 项用法 someone welcomes something 翻译：

The Chinese government welcomes private foreign investments in China's infrastructure and basic industries.

根据第 6 项用法 something is welcome 翻译：

Private foreign investments are welcome in the development of China's infrastructure and basic industries.

是否可以用 A welcomes B to do something? 这似乎是我们期待的句型，但字典中却没有说明（字典中是 B is welcome to do something）。如果存在这一句型，则本句也可以翻译为：

The Chinese government welcomes private foreign investors to invest in China's infrastructure and basic industries.

我们可以用 Google 搜索 "welcomes*** to"（一个 * 号代表任意一个单词，以此控制 welcome 与 to 之间的单词数目），发现大多数场合是 to welcome someone to some place, 以及 to welcome something, 如：

- President Bush **Welcomes** Prime Minister Sharon to White House. Dr. Dreary **welcomes** you to Creep Street!
- UNFPA **Welcomes** Anglo-Dutch Action to Avert Condom Crisis
- Vladimir Putin **Welcomes** U.S. Decision to Recognize Russia as Market Economy

也有个别例子用句型 to welcome someone to do something：

- The Chinese government **welcomes** students studying abroad to return and develop their careers at home, Vice Minister of Personnel Shu Huiguo said Sunday.

- Sidhu **welcomes** visitors who are interested to come and watch the performance of this talented martial artist.

鉴于我们无法断定这样的用法是否来自英语国家的媒体，我们可以用英语国家的语料库，如 Collins Cobuild Concordance Sampler 进一步搜索 welcome 的用法。检索结果与 Google 搜索结果类似。笔者作了这样的检索：

输入 welcome@/VERB 检索 welcome 作为动词的例句，在所显示的 40 个索引行中发现只有一句可以归入 to welcome someone to do something 的句型：Judge Sporkin today said, "I welcome you back to sue Exxon. For …" 输入 welcome@/VERB+PPO+to+VERB 搜索 welcome+人称代词＋动词不定式的例句，结果为：

1. She knows that no one will **welcome** her to share the festivities and
2. Here, everybody else had **welcomed** me to take photographs of their
3. Act as an historic village and we **welcome** you to join us on a special tour

用 welcome@/VERB+NOUN+to+VERB 检索动词 welcome＋一个名词＋不定式的用法，其中符合 welcome someone to do something 的例句有：

1. We are an open society. We **welcome** people to come and work with us.
2. the Conservation Tent but they would **welcome** volunteers to help design the
3. Christmas Fair. The Committee will **welcome** volunteers to help before, during

输入 welcome@/VERB+NOUN+NOUN+to+VERB 查动词 welcome＋两个名词＋不定式的用法，其中符合 welcome someone to do something 的例句有：

1. and Governor Clinton have said they **welcome** Mr. Perot to join their debates,

2. David O'Brien. The priest **welcomed** wage earners to join a larger mass

从以上调查可以发现，welcome someone to do something 的用法是存在的，但不常用。所以，该句翻译为 The Chinese government welcomes private foreign investors to invest in China's infrastructure and basic industries 应该是没有问题的。

以上关于 welcome 用法的检验，如果使用 https://linggle.com/，会更简便。下图阴影部分的用例说明，welcome sb. to do 尽管不常用，也可以使用（见图 10.8）：

Phrases	%	Count
welcome email to log	23.6%	6,300
welcome return to form	11.8%	3,200
welcome donations to help	8.5%	2,300
welcome calls to calls	5.4%	1,500
welcome parents to come	5.4%	1,500
welcome decision to resist	3%	810
welcome calls to solving	2.7%	730
welcome sight to see	2.2%	600
welcome volunteers to help	2%	540
welcome buyer to send	1.9%	520
welcome readers to share	1.7%	460
welcome others to join	1.7%	450

图 10.8　welcome 用法查询

最后提醒读者，孤立地翻译一个句子与在上下文中翻译是不同的。有了上下文，就需要考虑其他因素对句子结构、信息排列的影响。如果段落的主题是投资者，可能需要以投资者作主语；如果段落的主题是中国政府，可能需要以中国政府作主语。因此，尽管一个句子可以有多种译法，但在一定的上下文，可能只有少数译法是合适的。

10.5.2　request 用法考证

请大家判断这句话的原译是否正确：

个人信息主体发现个人信息控制者所持有的该主体的个人信息有错误或不完整的，个人信息控制者应为其提供请求更正或补充信息的方法。

原译：

Where a PI Subject finds his/her PI held by a PI Controller erroneous or incomplete, the PI Controller shall provide a channel for the PI Subject to <u>request to rectify the error or provide supplemental information</u>.

此例中的 request 用法不正确。请看 request 的解释（见图 10.9）[①]：

```
1. VERB
   If you request something, you ask for it politely or formally.
   [formal]
   Mr Dennis said he had requested access to a telephone. [VERB noun]
   She had requested that the door to her room be left open. [VERB that]

2. VERB
   If you request someone to do something, you politely or formally ask them to do it.
   [formal]
   They requested him to leave. [VERB noun to-infinitive]
   Students are requested to park at the rear of the Department. [be VERB-ed to-infinitive]
   [Also VERB with quote]

   Synonyms: invite, call for, beg, petition    More Synonyms of request
```

图 10.9　request 用法查询

由此见，request 只有两个用法：或者后跟名词，或者后跟 sb.+to do sth.。没有 request to do sth. 的用法。造句时，应符合用法要求：

Where a PI Subject finds his/her PI held by a PI Controller erroneous or incomplete, the PI Controller shall provide a channel for the PI Subject <u>request rectification or supplementation</u>.

---

① https://www.collinsdictionary.com/dictionary/english/request.

10.5.3　句法综合考证举例

我们再举一例,综合呈现翻译句子时的各种考虑。请大家先翻译这句话:

一种观点认为,既然我国刑法没有把丈夫和妻子排除在外,如果丈夫违背妻子意愿,强行与妻子发生性行为,就应定为强奸罪……

原译:

First opinion, now that Criminal Law in China does not exclude husband and wife, if a husband forces his wife to participate in unwanted sexual activity, he has committed rape.

查汉英词典和同义词词典①,"观点"可能译为 view、viewpoint、point of view、opinion;"一种观点"可能翻译为 one view、one opinion、one point of view。

接下来看这些说法如何与句子其他部分搭配。在 Simple Search of BNC-World 上搜索 one view,共检索到 76 个包含 one view 的例句,显示了其中的 50 个(免费用户最多可以看到 50 个),比如:

1. One view of the art market is that it is like a staircase with several landings.

2. One view is that the Corporation can now afford to do this.

3. One view has it that they are the trusted preservers of law and order …

4. One view sees the development of fairness as a correlative of the expansion of procedural rights post Ridge v. Baldwin.

5. One view saw Suharto's motive in encouraging greater activism on the part of Golkar as an attempt to acquire a reforming image to help counteract pressure on him to stand down before the 1993 election.

6. On one view, this was a bilateral dispute between Israel and Egypt

---

① 在谷歌上搜索一个单词,会发现很多英英词典的解释,包括同义词词典。

regarding the right of transit for Israeli shipping through the Canal.

7. On one view, expert determination is not a form of dispute resolution at all.

据此，我们可以总结出 one view 所使用的句套子：One view is that …, one view has it that …, one view sees something as something else, on one view+ 句子。根据本句的特点，我们可以选用简单的 one view is that … 我们可以再搜索一下 one opinion 的用法。同一语料库，one opinion 仅有 6 个例句，可以用作本句翻译"模板"的只有一个：

> Taking a more global view, one opinion is that the manufacturing industries should indeed move to developing countries whilst the advanced industries orientate their labour forces toward information and other service industries.

可以看出，虽然 one view is that … 与 one opinion is that … 都可以使用，但前者更为常用。

从另一个角度看，也可以从"认为"入手进行翻译。"认为"的英语可以是 think、believe、consider。在同义词词典上查 think，不仅得到 think 的同义词，还可以得到各词的例句，可以据此决定各词在句子中的用法，比如，think 的第一义项是：

> think, believe, consider, conceive — (judge or regard; look upon; judge; "I think he is very smart" "I believe her to be very smart""I think that he is her boyfriend" "The racist conceives such people to be inferior")
> EX: They think that there was a traffic accident

因为 think 或 believe 的主语必须是人（从例句可以看到），所以，"一种观点认为"，就应变为"有人认为"：some believe …, some think …

下面看"既然"一词的意义和用法。"既然"在字典上有两个译法，一是 now that，二是 since。原译选择了 now that。Cobuild 对 now that 的解释是：

You also use **now** or **now that** when you are talking about the effect of an event or change.

Now that she's found him, she'll never let him go.

可见，now that 表示"既然结果是……"，BNC-World 众多例句也说明了这一意思。例如：

1. Sir: Now that the dust kicked up by the mass raid on the Broadwater Farm estate last week has begun to settle, it is time to embark upon an assessment of its effects.

2. Now that Caen had fallen, some of the villagers were beginning to drift back to their homes.

3. Now that Czechoslovakia is stepping out of the Stalinist ice-box, nationalist voices in Slovakia are beginning to be heard again.

Cobuild 对 since 的解释如下：

You use **since** to introduce a reason.
Aircraft noise is a problem here since we're close to Heathrow Airport.
Since it was Saturday, he stayed in bed an extra hour.

所以，since 表示原因，更符合本句的意思。

我们看下一个关键词"排除"。"排除"可以翻译为 exclude。Cobuild 对该词的解释和用法举例如下：

1. If you **exclude** something from an activity or discussion, you deliberately do not include that thing in it.
The retail prices index, excluding housing costs, rose by 646.6 percent.

2. If you **exclude** a possibility, you reject it.
A fake call from some local phone box was not excluded.

3. If you **exclude** someone from a place or activity, you prevent them from entering the place or taking part in the activity.
… jobs from which the majority of workers are excluded.

我们由此知道，exclude 的句型是 exclude something 或 exclude someone or something from …，但笔者怀疑这个词是否可以表示法律上的"不适用于"，查到钱伯斯电子词典中有一条解释：to exempt (from a law, regulation, etc.)。所以，笔者的怀疑是没有根据的，这里可以用 exclude。字典也提醒我们，还可以用 exempt。

所以，前半句可以翻译为：One view is that since the criminal law of China does not exclude husband and wife… 或者用被动语态：One view is that since husband and wife are not excluded from the criminal law of China…（考虑到后半句主语是"丈夫"，为保持话题的一致，用被动更好一些）。也可以用 exempt 翻译：One view is that since husband and wife are not exempted from the criminal law of China… 这半句还有一个小问题：是 criminal law in China 还是 criminal law of China？在 BNC-World 上查 criminal law of，结果有：

1. The criminal law of England (it might well be argued) is shot through with inconsistencies and irrationalities

2. … suggested that Imelda Marcos would be charged under the criminal law of the Philippines at some point in the future.

3. There are plenty of examples in English criminal law of crimes which appear to include …

所以，我们不仅可以说 the criminal law of China，还可以说 the Chinese criminal law。至于 the criminal law in China，查询结果共有 12 项，其中 3 项与我们的要求在形式上相似，它们是：

1. The Dutch courts applied Roman-Dutch criminal law in the Low Country, though it is unlikely that it was adhered to by headmen or officials trying minor offences.

2. His lecture took as its starting point the distinction drawn by the Wolfenden Committee between public and private behaviour, and what it thus considered to be the proper role of the criminal law in these areas.

3. There is growing interest in the possibility of introducing a formal

system of plea bargaining and discounts into the systems of criminal law in the UK.

但仔细分析，发现介词 in 组成的短语并不修饰 law：第一句应当理解为 to apply ... in some place；第二句应理解为 the proper role ... in these areas；第三句应理解为 the systems ... in the UK。所以不能用介词 in。接下来看下半句：

如果丈夫违背妻子意愿，强行与妻子发生性行为，就应定为强奸罪……

学生的原译：

... if a husband forces his wife to participate in unwanted sexual activity, he has committed rape.

原译选用的关键词是 force。我们查 Cobuild 看动词 force 的意思和搭配：

1. If you **force** someone to do something, you cause them to do it, although they are unwilling.
They forced him to resign.
She forced herself to kiss her mother's cheek.
... the campaign to force the closure of the factory.
Weekend gales forced him to change his plans.

2. If you **force** something into a particular position, you use a lot of strength to make it move there.
I forced his head back.

3. If you **force** a lock, door, or safe, you break the lock in order to open it.

学生的用法符合第一个句型 to force someone to do something。从第 1 项解释还可以看到，force 本身有违背某人意愿的意思，所以，"违背妻子意愿"不译出来是对的。

我们看 to participate in unwanted sexual activity 这个词汇搭配是否说得通。

查 Google: "participate in unwanted sexual activity"，结果有：

Date/Acquaintance rape occurs when an individual is forced by someone he or she knows to *participate in unwanted sexual activity.*

这样看来，学生的这部分译文是站得住脚的。我们看最后一部分：

……就应定为强奸罪……

原译：… he has committed rape.

这部分译文显然与原文意思不太相符。原文是表达一种观点，译文是陈述事实，因为译文没有把"应定为"翻译出来。对此，我们从"强奸罪"的译法入手，看能否找到解决方案。"强奸罪"的译法在字典上可能无法直接查出来，但"强奸"是可以找到的：rape。那么，"强奸罪"是否可以说crime of rape？我们可以用 Google 或其他电子手段查一下这个搭配是否成立。答案是肯定的。 那么，下一步就是决定与 crime of rape 搭配的动词是什么。用 Cobuild Concordance Sampler 查 VBN+5crime of rape（表示要搜索一个过去分词＋ crime of rape，两者之间的单词数不超过 5 个），结果有两个符合我们需要的意思：

1. be adjudged guilty of the crime of rape …
2. person convicted of the crime of rape shall be imprisoned in a …

我们可以从中抽出两个搭配：someone is adjudged guilty of a crime 以及 someone is convicted of a crime。

基于这个结果，我们可以把原译文修改如下：… he should be convicted of the crime of rape. 由于 rape 本身就是犯罪，可以不用 crime 加以限制。所以，整个句子翻译为：

One view is that since husband and wife are not excluded from the criminal law of China, if a husband forces his wife to participate in unwanted sexual activity, he should be convicted of the crime of rape.

或者：

One view is that the husband should be convicted of the crime of rape if he forces his wife to participate in unwanted sexual activity, since husband and wife are not excluded from the criminal law of China.

当然，一句话的译法可以多种多样，只要意思正确，符合英语习惯就可以，不必拘泥于原文的字词。比如，下面的译文虽然脱离了原文字面，但与原文意思相同，同样可以接受：

Coercive sex within marriage should be a criminal offense since husband and wife are not exempted from the Chinese criminal law.

10.6 小结

综上所述，笔者认为只要充分利用现有资源，尤其是电子资源和网络资源，我们在汉译英方面是可以避免死译、硬译，做到达意、通顺的。我们应当针对外语学习的薄弱环节（各种搭配及句子结构），勤查英英词典、英语搭配词典、用法词典、同义词词典、英语语料库和有关英语文献，不要轻易相信汉英词典。虽然每个人的英语水平不同，但只要掌握了方法，多查资料，都可以保证翻译质量，只不过英语差的人多用些时间罢了。另外，建议大家在学习外语、阅读和翻译外语材料时，注意抽取其中的成语、短语、搭配和句子骨架，以备汉译英时使用。

〔课后练习〕

1. 如何提高英语表达能力？
2. 汉译英时确保语法正确是否已经足够？
3. 请逐个尝试本章提到的英语语料库。
4. 请用本章介绍的方法检验自己最近做的一段汉译英。

第十一章
删减冗余信息确保语言简洁

扫码预习

请扫码下载本章涉及的例句。先做练习,再看解答,学习效果更佳。

译文臃肿是汉译英的一个严重问题。琼·平卡姆(Joan Pinkham)在《中式英语之鉴》一书中,从英语写作的角度,对这个问题进行了深刻的剖析,列举了众多鲜活的用例,对汉英翻译工作者有极大的帮助。本章结合简明英语的要求,总结了平卡姆提出的"减肥"方法,并加入了自己的一些思考。所选译例有的来自《中式英语之鉴》(标记为 Pinkham),有的来自权威著作的出版译文,包括《毛泽东选集》第四卷(Mao-IV),《邓小平文选》中英文版第三卷(Deng-III),《习近平谈治国理政》第一、二卷(Xi-I/II)中英文版,有的则是笔者的翻译实践(未标记)。由于《中式英语之鉴》为纯英文著作,没有提供译例原文,本书所用原文或者是从其他地方找到的原文,或者是回译(不一定准确)。

11.1 活用英语词形变化

现代英语的曲折变化,主要有性、数、格、时态、体、语态、语气、人称、词类和比较级等变化。英语的曲折变化翻译为汉语时有的消失，有的转换为词的形式。反过来，汉译英时，有些词语的意思可以利用英语的曲折变化传达，没有必要翻译出来。这样可以避免英语表达中的意思重复，使译文更为简洁。这方面尤其值得注意的是时态和数的表达方法。

11.1.1　时态表达方法

汉语中表示时态的词，如"现在""过去""已经"，如果已经通过英语时态清楚传达，在英语中可以省略。

例1.

现在，同过去相比，中国改革的广度和深度都大大拓展了。(Xi-I)
China's reform has been greatly furthered in both breadth and depth.

例2.

为什么我们现在有这样的底气？(Xi-I)
Why are we so confident?

例3.

又比如上海，目前完全有条件搞得更快一点。(Deng-III)
Shanghai is another example. It has all the necessary conditions for faster progress.

例4.

当前，全世界都在关注着我国的改革。(Deng-III)
The whole world is watching the reforms in our country.

例5.

现在，同过去相比，中国改革的广度和深度都大大拓展了。(Xi-I)
China's reform has been greatly furthered in both breadth and depth.

如果有强调意味，则需要译出。如：

例6.

现在，大家都在讨论中国梦。(Xi-I)

We are *now* all talking about the Chinese Dream.

例 7.

我们要精兵简政，真正下放权力，扩大社会主义民主，把人民群众和基层组织的积极性调动起来。现在机构不是减少了，而是增加了。设立许多公司，实际是官办机构，用公司的形式把放给下面的权又收了上来。(Deng-III)

We must streamline the administration, delegate real powers to lower levels and broaden the scope of socialist democracy, so as to bring into play the initiative of the masses and the grass-roots organizations. *At present*, the number of organizations, instead of being reduced, has actually increased. Many companies have been established that are actually government organs. Through these companies people at higher levels have taken back the powers already delegated to lower levels.

例 8.

现在，我们这一代共产党人的任务，就是继续把这篇大文章写下去。(Xi-I)

Now, the job of the Communists of our generation is to continue with this mission.

11.1.2 数的表达方法

汉语中许多复数概念可以转化为英语的复数形式，不必再译出汉语表示复数的词。

例 9.

围绕这些重大课题，我们强调，要有强烈的问题意识，以重大问题为导向，抓住关键问题进一步研究思考，着力推动解决我国发展面临的一系列突出矛盾和问题。(Xi-I)

To carry out these resolutions, it must be stressed that we should be fully aware of our problems, focus on the key issues for further study and research, and strive to solve the *major dilemmas and problems* challenging our development.

dilemmas and problems 作为复数形式已经包含一系列的意思，不用再说 a series of。

例 10.

今天，坚持和发展中国特色社会主义，全面深化改革，有效应对前进道路上可以预见和难以预见的各种困难与风险。（Xi-I）

Today, new problems will arise while we adhere to and develop socialism with Chinese characteristics, drive reform to a deeper level, and deal effectively with foreseeable and unpredictable *difficulties and risks* on our way ahead.

例 11.

第二个内容是权力要下放，解决中央和地方的关系，同时地方各级也都有一个权力下放问题。（Deng-III）

Second, we should transfer some of the powers of the central authorities to local authorities in order to straighten out relations between the two. At the same time, *local authorities* should likewise transfer some of their powers to lower levels.

例 12.

科技成果只有同国家需要、人民要求、市场需求相结合，完成从科学研究、实验开发、推广应用的三级跳，才能真正实现创新价值、实现创新驱动发展。（Xi-I）

Scientific and technological achievements can generate real value and pay off only if they meet the needs of the country, the people and the market, and only after they have gone through the *stages* of research, development and application.

stages 用复数形式，隐含了多级的意思。到底是几级，读者可以数一数。但如有强调意味，这些数量词还是需要译出。

例 13.

前两年我们曾指出各级领导上存在着软弱涣散的状况，对严重刑事犯罪分子下不了手也是一种表现。（Deng-III）

Two years ago I pointed out that many leaders *at various levels* were weak and lax, as was shown by their tender-heartedness in dealing with persons guilty of grave criminal offences.

例 14.

全会决定提出了一系列相互关联的新举措。（Xi-I）
The Decision proposes *a series of* targeted reform measures.

例 15.

全会决定提出一系列有针对性的改革举措。（Xi-I）
The Decision proposes *a series of* targeted reform measures.

例 16.

要利用各种时机和场合，形成有利于培育和弘扬社会主义核心价值观的生活情景和社会氛围，使核心价值观的影响像空气一样无所不在、无时不有。（Xi-I）

We should make use of *every* opportunity to make this happen, anytime and anywhere.

11.2　调整篇章衔接手段

语篇（discourse）是交流过程中的一系列连续的语段或句子所构成的语言整体，由一个以上的语段或句子组成，其中各成分之间，在形式上是衔接（cohesion）的，在语义上是连贯（coherence）的。

英语和汉语的语篇衔接手段均包括照应、替代、省略、连接、重复、同义词、反义词、上下义关系、搭配等。但不同手段在两种语言中使用的频率是不同的。所以，把一种语言转换为另一种语言时，衔接手段应当作相应调整。

与本章内容关系密切的是重复、照应、替代和省略。汉语大量使用重复，翻译为英语后应考虑是否要转换为照应、替代和省略等。

所谓重复，是指单词、短语、句子在同一语篇多次出现。所谓照应，是语篇中的指代成分与所指对象之间的相互解释关系，通过人称代词、指示代词、定冠词、指示性副词等实现。所谓替代，是指用替代形式取代上文中的某一成分。替代分为：1）名词性替代，如英语的 one, ones, the same, so；汉语的"的""者""同样的""一样的"。2）动词性替代，如英语的 do, do so；汉语："干""来""弄""搞"。3）小句性替代，如英语的 so, not；汉语的"（不）这样""（不）这么""（不）是""不然""要不"。所谓省略，指的是把语言结构中的某个成分省去不提。省略分为：1）名词性省略，如：— I received no message. — I didn't send any (message). 2）动词性省略，如：By birth he was an Englishman; by profession, (he was) a sailor; by instinct and training, (he was) a rebel. 3）小句性省略，如：— I thought you said there was a sapphire on the head, dear? — No, Lady Markby — (I said there was) a ruby.（朱永生，2001）。遇到汉语重复性衔接可以采取以下处理方法：

11.2.1 动词性重复

如果是动词性重复，可以变为动词性替代或省略。

例 17.

问题是：从医学上讲，哪些工作是有传染扩散艾滋病危险的工作，这些工作为什么有传染扩散艾滋病危险，这些工作通过什么途径或方式传染扩散艾滋病，在这些出自政府卫生行政部门的法律文件中，均未予以说明。

The problem is, from a medical point of view, what are the jobs that could spread AIDS? *Why and how?* These questions are not answered in the legal documents of the health administrative authorities.

例 18.

1986年，国家教育委员会、卫生部文件：外国留学生和研究学者，须做艾滋病检查，对坚持不接受检查，且劝说无效的，不得安排学习。

The 1986 document of the State Education Commission and MOH states: foreign students, researchers, and scholars must *undergo an AIDS test*; persons who refuse and cannot be persuaded *to do so* may not be accepted for studies.

例 19.

"文化大革命"十年浩劫，中国吃了苦头。中国吃苦头不只这十年，这以前，从一九五七年下半年开始，我们就犯了"左"的错误。

China suffered greatly from the *ten-year* disaster, the cultural revolution. In fact, not just from that: as early as the second half of 1957 we began to make "Left" mistakes.（Deng-III）

例 20.

中国有13亿多人，只要道路正确，整体的财富水平和幸福指数可以迅速上升，但每个个体的财富水平和幸福指数的提高就不那么容易了。（Xi-I）

We will accelerate China's *overall prosperity* and raise *the happiness index* for our 1.3 billion Chinese people as long as we are on the right path. Yet, it will not be easy to *make this happen* for every individual.

财富水平和幸福指数上升，第二次出现就没有重复翻译，而是简化为 make this happen。

11.2.2　名词性重复

如果是名词性重复，可以采取以下方法：

11.2.2.1 用代词照应

用代词与上文照应，而非重复名词。

例 21.

以往主流社会的意识形态以及一些不恰当的宣传，加大了艾滋病恐慌及人们对艾滋病病人和艾滋病病毒感染者的厌恶，而无助于预防和控制艾滋病。

In the past, mainstream mindsets and misleading information about *AIDS* increased the public's fear of *the disease* and prejudice against *its* victims, all of which impeded *its* prevention and control.

its 是与 AIDS 有关的代词；the disease 是 AIDS 的上义词。

例 22.

最后，20 年来，中国发生了很大的变化，包括中国的权力系统和中国的法律制度，但是，发生在中国的权力系统和法律制度方面的变化却并没有像有些人说得那么大，甚至可以说，在这方面没有发生本质性的变化，这就是中国官方说的"政治体制改革滞后"的问题。

Lastly, many changes have taken place in China in the past 20 years, including *those in the power structure and legal system*. However, *such* changes are not as great as some people have claimed. I would even argue that *they* are not fundamental. In the official language, "political system reform is lagging."

没有重复"权力系统和法律制度"，而是译为 such、they。

11.2.2.2 省略修饰语

即，省略中心词的修饰语，只剩下中心词。

例 23.

顾问委员会怎样做工作，总的说就是要按照新的党章办事。党章规

定，中央顾问委员会是中央委员会的政治上的助手和参谋。(Deng-III)

原译：

As far as the work of *the Central Advisory Commission* is concerned, its general functions are set forth in the new *Constitution of the Communist Party of China.* According to the *Party Constitution*, the members of the *Central Advisory Commission* are to act as political assistants and consultants to the Central Committee. (Pinkham)

改译：

As far as the work of *the Central Advisory Commission* is concerned, its general functions are set forth in the new Constitution of the Communist Party of China. According to the Party Constitution, the members of *the Commission* are to act as political assistants and consultants to the Central Committee. (Pinkham)

第二次出现"中顾委"时，省略了 the Central Advisory。

在《邓选》第三卷英文版中，本段译文另一个版本，名词重复的处理方式相似：

How is the *Central Advisory Commission* to go about its work? Generally speaking, *it* should act in accordance with the provisions of the new Party Constitution. According to the Constitution, the members of *the Commission* are to act as political assistants and consultants to the Central Committee.

例 24.

世界各国的社会保障制度，都不是凭空建立起来的，立法所确定的社会保障对象、社会保障项目、社会保障待遇水平，无一不受到本国社会经济发展阶段和经济发展水平的制约与影响。

No country builds its social security institutions in a vacuum. *Programs, eligibility, and benefits* as defined by legislation are defined and influenced by the social and economic *realities* of each country.

本例中的发展阶段和发展水平也做了概括处理。

11.2.2.3 用其他名词总结

除了可以用代词概括名词，也可以用名词概括名词。

例 25.

坚持"经济建设必须依靠科学技术，科学技术工作必须面向经济建设"的原则，促进科技与经济的有机结合。

原译：

We must ensure that *economic development is driven by science and technology,* and that development of *science and technology* is geared to the needs of *economic development*, and enable science *and technology* to serve the *economy*.

改译：

We must ensure that development of the economy is based on science and technology and that development of science and technology be based on the needs of the economy. *The two aspects* must be well-harmonised.

例 26.

中华人民共和国诞生以后，我国的社会保障工作就在党和国家的领导下开展起来了，50年代的政府工作文件中用过"社会保障"这一称谓。

In China, social security programs have been developed since the founding of the People's Republic of China in 1949 under the leadership of the Party and the government. *The term "social security"* appeared in government documents as early as the 1950s…

本例中，中英文均用名词短语"这一称谓/the term"概括"社会保障/social security"。

11.2.2.4 用首字母缩写

第一次提到时用全称，以后用缩写。如国有企业，第一次用 State Owned Enterprises (SOE)，以后用 SOEs。

11.3　多用强势动词

在英语中，一个动词往往可以变为"弱势动词＋名词化动词"的形式表示，如：

apply for	submit an application for
evaluate	carry out an evaluation of
investigate	implement an investigation of
review	conduct a review of
assess	perform an assessment of
renew	effect a renewal of

一个介词的宾语既可以使用名词化（nominalization）形式，也可以使用动名词（-ing）形式，如：

by the introduction of	by introducing
for the allocation of	for allocating
of the provision of	of providing

简明英语认为，应当优先使用强势动词，尽量避免名词化动词。按照这一原则，下例中的 A 应当变为 B：

A: The committee *came to an agreement* to the effect that *a study should be carried out* by the consultants into the feasibility of *the provision of* national funding.

B: The committee *agreed* that the consultants *should study* the feasibility of *providing* national funding. (Directorate-General for Translation European Commission: *How to Write Clearly*)

汉译英时，也尽量遵循这一规则。

例 27.

  解决这些问题，关键在于深化改革。（Xi-I）

  To solve these problems, the key lies in continuing the reform.

"解决这些问题"不必译为 to find solutions for…

例 28.

  第四，关于健全城乡发展一体化体制。（Xi-I）

  Fourth, *improving* mechanisms and institutions for the integrated development of urban and rural areas.

不必译为 making improvement in…

例 29.

  我们将积极参与国际航空运输市场的竞争，扩大国际市场的份额。

  We will *compete* in the international air transport market and expand international services.

不必译为 participate in the competition in…

例 30.

  自那时以来，为了实现中华民族伟大复兴，无数仁人志士奋起抗争，但一次又一次地失败了。（Xi-I）

  Countless people with lofty ideals rose up for *the rejuvenation* of the Chinese nation, but each time they failed.

"实现复兴"不必翻译为 realization of rejuvenation。rejuvenation 已经包含实现的意思。

例 31.

  推进局部的阶段性改革开放要在加强顶层设计的前提下进行。（Xi-I）

  Reform and opening up in a region at a certain stage should be *subject to top-level design*.

不译"加强"意思没有任何损失。

汉语中也有与英语类似的动词名词化情形,翻译时不必亦步亦趋。下面是一些常见的动词名词化说法和建议译法(基于《中式英语之鉴》编写):

序号	汉语	不建议	建议
1	发动进攻	launch an attack against	attack
2	加以改变	bring about a change in	change
3	加以改善	make an improvement in	improve
4	加以强调	place stress on	stress
5	进行调查	make an investigation of	investigate
6	进行斗争	carry out the struggle against	struggle against
7	进行分析	make an analysis of	analyze
8	进行改革	implement the reform of	reform
9	进行控制	exercise control over	control
10	进行评估	make an evaluation of	evaluate
11	进行审查	conduct an examination of	examine
12	进行讨论	engage in the discussion of	discuss
13	进行研究	make a study of	study
14	进行指导	give guidance to	guide
15	取得成功	achieve success in	succeed in
16	取得增长	experienced a growth	grow
17	实现现代化	accomplish the modernization of	modernize
18	实现转变	realize the transformation of	transform
19	实行配给	implement rationing	be rationed
20	提出建议	make a proposal	propose
21	提出申请	make an application for	apply for
22	提供援助	provide assistance to	assist
23	予以批准	give approval to	approve
24	作出决定	make a decision	decide

11.4 化解一些动词

汉语中的一些动词或动词短语,可以化解到英文句子中,尤其是在把汉语短句压缩为英语短语时。

例 32.

中国外交面临着诸多挑战,实行大国外交战略势在必行。

A great-power strategy is required to respond to China's foreign policy challenges.

省略了加点的词。

例 33.

适应经济全球化的发展趋势,对社会保障制度进行必要的调整。

Globalization is driving new social security reforms.

省略了加点的词。

例 34.

以大国姿态对待美国,确定既反对美国的强权政治又在世界事务中与美国进行合作的双向战略。

A great-power foreign policy strategy calls for opposition to US power politics *and* cooperation with the US in global affairs.

省略了加点的词。

例 35.

维护中美两国的正常关系,不光对维护中国进行现代化建设的外部环境具有重要意义,而且对整个国际局势的和平与稳定具有重要意义。

Normal relations between China and the United States are important not only for maintaining a sound external environment necessary for China's modernization, but also for global peace and stability.

省略了加点的词。

11.5　省略汉语范畴词

通常，一个词本身就可表明其范畴，不必再用表示范畴的词。如 time 本身就表示一个期间，所以不用说 time period; pink 本身就表示一种颜色，所以不用说 pink in color; shiny 本身就表示一种外表，所以不用说 shiny in appearance.

汉语中范畴词的使用要比英语广泛得多，已经成为我们的语言习惯，但直接翻译到英语中不增加任何实质内容，只能使句子变得冗长，翻译时应当注意删除。汉语范畴词可以分为名词性的和动词性的。

11.5.1　名词性范畴词

名词性范畴词相对于动词性范畴词。前者如"计划工作"当中的"工作"，后者如"坚持……原则"。

例 36.

我们要坚持不懈抓好宪法实施工作，把全面贯彻实施宪法提高到一个新水平。(Xi-I)

We must persistently ensure *the implementation* of the Constitution, and raise the comprehensive implementation of the Constitution to a new level.

"实施"本身就是一项工作，不必再翻译"工作"。

例 37.

为中华民族发展壮大、促进祖国和平统一大业、增进中国人民同各国人民的友好合作作出了重要贡献。(Xi-I)

They have made a major contribution to the growth of the Chinese nation, to *the peaceful reunification of the motherland*, and to the friendly people-to-people cooperation between China and other countries.

"和平统一"本身就是一项"大业"，不必再翻译为"the great cause of peaceful reunification"。

例 38.

当前，制约科学发展的体制机制障碍不少集中在经济领域。(Xi-I)

Currently, most structural and institutional barriers hindering China's proper development are found *in the economy*.

"经济领域"不必翻译为 economic sphere 或 field/area；经济本身就是一个领域。

例 39.

中国高度重视发展同中亚各国的友好合作关系，将其视为外交优先方向。(Xi-I)

China values its *friendship and cooperation* with these countries, and takes improving these relations as a foreign policy priority.

"合作"即是一种关系。

例 40.

对一切违反党纪国法的行为，都必须严惩不贷，决不能手软。(Xi-I)

All violations of Party discipline and state laws must be punished without exception, and we shall not be soft in dealing with them.

"违反党纪国法"本身就是一种行为，不必再说"acts"。

例 41.

各种可以预见和难以预见的风险因素明显增多。(Xi-I)

All kinds of foreseeable and unforeseeable *risks* are increasing significantly.

"风险"本身就是一个因素。

例 42.

大熊猫的数量很少。(Pinkham)

There are few pandas.

不用说 Pandas are few *in number*. "很少"本身就表示数量。

例 43.

中国民航决定开展提前订票业务。

The Civil Aviation Administration of China has decided to start advance booking and ticketing for connecting and return flights.

"订票业务"不必说：*the business of* advance booking and ticketing。因为"提前订票"本身就是一项业务。

例 44.

同时，与国内外形势发展变化相比，与党所承担的历史任务相比，党的领导水平和执政水平、党组织建设状况和党员干部素质、能力、作风都还有不小差距。(Xi-I)

However, in view of the need to manage changes in domestic and international conditions, and to accomplish its historic mission, there is still considerable room for our Party to *improve* its art of leadership, governing capacity and *organization*, and the quality, competence, and practices of its members and officials.

"建设状况"没有译出，因为 improve the organization 意思已经很清楚。

11.5.2 动词性范畴词

汉语中用范畴词概括具体词，并不限于名词；对一个动词短语，也可以进行类似的概括。如果这一概括没有实质意义，一般不用翻译出来，只需翻译该动词短语，如：

坚持（本着）……的原则

例 45.

坚持效率优先、兼顾公平的原则。

The first priority should be efficiency, with due consideration given to equity.

例 46.

不管建立和完善什么制度，都要本着于法周延、于事简便的原则。（Xi-I）

Any newly-developed or improved system must be easy to implement, *be coherent with the established laws, and function within the existing legal framework.*

例 47.

要本着互惠互利的原则同周边国家开展合作，编织更加紧密的共同利益网络，把双方利益融合提升到更高水平，让周边国家得益于我国发展，使我国也从周边国家共同发展中获得裨益和助力。（Xi-I）

We should cooperate with our neighbors *on the basis of reciprocity*, create a closer network of common interests, and better integrate China's interests with theirs, so that they can benefit from China's development and China can benefit and gain support from theirs.

例 48.

要铸牢听党指挥这个强军之魂，坚持党对军队绝对领导的根本原则和人民军队的根本宗旨不动摇。（Xi-I）

We must *ensure the absolute leadership of the Party over the military* that follows the commands of the Party and serves the people.

如果坚持的是真正的"原则"，则要把"原则"翻译出来，例如：

例 49.

而坚持社会主义，实行按劳分配的原则，就不会产生贫富过大的差距。

But if we stick to socialism and *apply the principle of* work-based distribution of income, wealth disparity will not be too great.

例 50.

中央国家安全委员会要遵循集中统一、科学谋划、统分结合、协调行动、精干高效的原则。（Xi-I）

The NSC should *abide by the principles of* centralized leadership, scientific planning, exercising power in both centralized and separated ways, coordinated actions, and high performance and efficiency.

采取（用）……办法

例 51.

近年来，许多国家如德国、法国、美国、意大利、瑞士等，已经采取了互相签订双边协议的办法，解决两国劳动者在对方国家从事工作遇到的社会保障问题。

In recent years, many countries, including Germany, France, the U.S., Italy and Switzerland, *have concluded bilateral agreements* to address the social security needs of their people employed in counterpart countries.

"互相签订双边协议"就是一种"办法"，不用重复表达。

例 52.

35 年来，我们用改革的办法解决了党和国家事业发展中的一系列问题。（Xi-I）

In the past 35 years we have overcome many problems hindering the development of the Party and the state *through reform.*

"用改革的办法"，就是"通过改革"。

处于……状态

例 53.

目前在社会保障方面发生争议进行仲裁或提起诉讼时，由于立法滞后，仲裁机构和人民法院无法根据有效的法律规定对社会保障争议、纠纷进行仲裁或判决，处于无法可依的状态。

Because legislation has fallen far behind, when claimants resort to arbitration or litigation to resolve a social security dispute, arbitration institutions and the people's courts *will be handicapped in making awards or decisions.*

省略了"处于……状态"。

发挥……功能（精神），起到……作用

例 54.

完整的法律规范应当由假定、处理和制裁构成，无法律责任、无制裁措施的法律规范，是一个有严重缺陷的系统，无法发挥法律规范的强制功能。（Xi-I）

A complete body of law should comprise presumptions, procedures, and sanctions. Existing legislation is seriously deficient in that it provides for no legal liability or sanctions. Since the law has no teeth, *enforcement is impossible.*

省略了"发挥……功能"。

例 55.

第一，必须充分发挥工人阶级的主力军作用。（Xi-I）
First, we must make sure that the working class is our main force.

省略了"发挥……作用"。

例 56.

全国各族人民都要向劳模学习，以劳模为榜样，发挥只争朝夕的奋斗精神，共同投身实现中华民族伟大复兴的宏伟事业。（Xi-I）

The people of all ethnic groups in the country should learn from model workers, follow their examples and, *with a sense of urgency*, strive to realize the rejuvenation of the Chinese nation.

省略了"发挥……精神"。

实施……战略

例 57.

中国将坚定实施科教兴国战略，始终把教育摆在优先发展的战略位置。（Xi-I）

China will reinvigorate the country through science and education and will always give priority to education.

省略了"实施……战略"。

采取……态度

例 58.

对恐怖主义、分裂主义、极端主义这"三股势力",必须采取零容忍态度,加强国际和地区合作,加大打击力度,使本地区人民都能够在安宁祥和的土地上幸福生活。(Xi-I)

We should *have zero tolerance* for terrorism, separatism and extremism, strengthen international and regional cooperation, and step up the fight against these three forces, so as to bring peace and happiness to the people of this region.

译文省略了"采取……态度"。

呈现……局面

例 59.

我们坚定不移全面深化改革,推动改革呈现全面发力、多点突破、纵深推进的崭新局面。(Xi-II)

We have carried all-round reform to a deeper level, making breakthroughs in key fields.

译文省略了"呈现……局面"。

出现……现象

例 60.

现在,一些地方出现干部作用发挥有余、群众作用发挥不足现象,"干部干,群众看""干部着急,群众不急"。(Xi-II)

Now, in certain places, village officials are really busy whereas farmers remain indifferent.

译文省略了"出现……现象"。

以上列举并非穷尽，只是提醒大家注意，汉语中常见的搭配或连用的词语，直译为英语不一定合适，需要根据情况，决定是否译出。一个判断标准是，如果不译出不妨碍意思传达，就可以省略。

11.6 省略不必要修饰语

官方文件中使用很多形容词和副词。这些词在汉语中司空见惯，但直译为英语后则显得多余，因为这些修饰语的意思已经包含在被修饰语或其他地方。翻译出来只会造成重复，削弱中心词本身的力度。以下分为"意思明显重复"和"意思不言而喻"分别介绍。

11.6.1 意思明显重复

这类修饰语的意思已经完全包含在中心词中，汉语中不觉得多余，但英文显得多余。

例 61.

  珍贵的思想财富。（Pinkham）

译为 a valuable ideology 即可，不必说 a *valuable* ideological treasure；treasure 必然是珍贵的。

例 62.

  经济发达国家（Pinkham）

译为 the developed countries 即可，不必说 economically developed countries."发达国家"就是指经济发达国家。

例 63.

  但我们自豪而不自满，决不会躺在过去的功劳簿上。（Xi-I）
  Nevertheless, we should never be complacent and rest on *our laurels*.

"过去的"不用译出,因为 laurels 一定是过去的。

例 64.

　　此外,随着市场经济的发展,日益增多的社会保障项目,必然给社会成员提供更多的社会保障服务,而社会保障的服务性工作的增多,也会增加劳动者的就业机会。

　　Moreover, continued development of the market economy spurs creation of more social security programs. More programs mean more services to beneficiaries, and more services means *more job opportunities*.

"就业机会"肯定是给劳动者的。因此,"劳动者"不用译出。再比如:提前预报,不必译为 advance forecasts,因为预报必定是提前的;女企业家,不必译为 female businesswoman,因为 businesswoman 一定是女性;严重的自然灾害,不必译为 a serious natural disaster,因为 disaster 就意味着是严重的;互相合作,不必译为 mutual cooperation,因为合作必然是相互的;不幸的悲剧,不必译为 an unfortunate tragedy,因为悲剧都是不幸的;民用住宅,不必译为 residential housing,因为 housing,必定是民用的;财政收支,不必译为 financial revenue and expenditure,因为 revenue and expenditure 一定指财务。

11.6.2　意思不言而喻

　　修饰语的意思严格地讲虽不重复,但仍然多余,因为它所表示的意思是不言而喻的。

例 65.

　　这九年是国家经济实力持续增长的九年。(Pinkham)

不必译为 These nine years constitute a period in which the *national economic strength* has increased. 可以译为 In these nine years *the economy* has grown stronger. 因为除非另有说明,"经济"就是指"国民经济"。

例 66.

　　要完善财政政策,适当加大财政性资金对保障性住房建设投入力

度。(Xi-I)

We should improve our fiscal policy and *use more public funds* to build such housing.

"加大投入"隐含着"适当"。政府的决策任何时候都应当"适当"。

例 67.

加快经济改革步伐 (Pinkham)

不必译为 to accelerate *the pace of* economic reform，可以译为 to accelerate economic reform，因为"to accelerate"="to increase the pace of"。

例 68.

农业获得大丰收 (Pinkham)

不必译为 there have been good harvests *in agriculture*，可以译为 there have been good harvests，因为汉语"丰收"与英语"harvest"均指农业，但汉语"丰收"获得了更多的比喻意义，英语却没有。

例 69.

城乡人民生活水平继续提高 (Pinkham)

不必译为 Living standards *for the people* in both urban and rural areas continued to rise. 可以译为 *Living standards* in both urban and rural areas continued to rise. 因为只有人类才有"生活水平"的概念。

11.7 慎用加强词

加强词用来加重中心词的意思，如"认真""努力""大力""坚决""充分"等。这些词在汉语中泛滥成灾，一般情况下不要移植到英语中。翻译时遇到这类汉语表达方式，有两种处理方法：合并和省略。

11.7.1　合并

如果被修饰语较弱，可以把加强词和被修饰语合并译为一个意思较重的英语词，如："极为重要"不译为 extremely important，而译为 essential、imperative、vital、indispensable、crucial 等；"坚信"不译为 firmly believe，而译为 be convinced。

例 70.

干部群众对这些问题深恶痛绝，必须下决心加以整治，使用人之风真正纯洁起来。（Xi-I）

Officials and the public *abhor* this practice very much, so we should make resolute efforts to change it and make it a clean process.

"深恶痛绝"没有翻译为 strong aversion 或 hate very much，而是改用更强的词 abhor。

例 71.

第一，必须充分发挥工人阶级的主力军作用。（Xi-I）
First, we must *make sure that* the working class is our main force.

"充分发挥作用"用一个 make sure 足以传达。

11.7.2　省略

如果被修饰语本身已经足以表达作者的意思，就不必翻译修饰语。如"伟大的历史意义"，不用翻译为 great, historic significance，因为英语中 historic 的意思本身已经十分强烈。"历史经验已经雄辩地证明"不用说 "historical experience has *convincingly* proved that ..."因为必须"雄辩"才能"prove"。再如：

例 72.

实践充分证明，中国特色社会主义是中国共产党和中国人民团结

的旗帜、奋进的旗帜、胜利的旗帜。(Xi-I)

Facts *prove* that Chinese socialism is a banner of unity, endeavor and victory for the CPC and the Chinese people as a whole.

一个 prove 就没有商量余地。

例 73.

规范收入分配秩序，有效保护合法收入，坚决取缔非法收入。

We will regulate income distribution, protect lawful income, and ban illegal income.

保护无效，算不上保护，所以省略 effectively；英语中 ban 已经是一种坚决的行为。

例 74.

积极回应广大人民群众对深化改革开放的强烈呼声和殷切期待，凝聚社会共识，协调推进各领域各环节改革，努力把改革开放推向前进。(Xi-I)

In response to *the call* of the people and *their expectations* for further reform and opening up, we should build a social consensus, and promote reforms in all sectors in a coordinated way.

中文的"强烈"和"殷切"多半是为了凑够四个音节，不必反映到译文中。

例 75.

要始终坚持这条道路，不断拓展这条道路，努力使这条道路越走越宽广。(Xi-I)

We should *keep to* this path and steadily widen it.

"始终"没有译为 persistently，因为已经包含在 keep to 之中。另请注意两个小句合并简化。

例 76.

社会各界对办教育表现出极大的热情。(Pinkham)

不必译为 All social circles are *tremendously* enthusiastic about providing education. 可以译为 Every social sector is enthusiastic about providing education. 因为 enthusiastic 本身已经表达强烈的意思（这个词的本义是 possessed by God/ 如鬼神附体般，因此意思强烈），再加副词是画蛇添足。但汉语中如果不加"极大的""很大的"，似乎强调不够。

例 77.

未来几年，我们将不遗余力地做好以下几件工作：切实确保航空运输安全、不断提高航空运输能力、继续加强基础设施建设。

Our tasks for the next few years are as follows: improve safety, increase capacity, and increase infrastructure.

如果修饰语都翻译出来，显得歇斯底里。

11.7.3 经常需要省略的加强词

汉语中有些加强词出现十分频繁，这里逐个列举，以便引起足够注意，如：

积极 active/actively

例 78.

希望大家继续弘扬中华文化，不仅自己要从中汲取精神力量，而且要积极推动中外文明交流互鉴。（Xi-I）

I hope all Chinese will continue to carry forward Chinese culture and draw strength from it, while *promoting* exchanges between Chinese civilization and other civilizations.

"积极"省略。因为不积极无法 promote。

例 79.

积极推动我国能源生产和消费革命（标题）（Xi-I）
Revolutionize Energy Production and Consumption

revolutionize 已经很积极了。如果确实需要强调，可以用别的方法，如:"we should vigorously promote," "make every effort to promote," "use all means to promote," "do everything possible to promote" 等等。

例 80.

未来几年，我们将根据我国经济和社会发展的需要，积极拓展航空运输市场。

In the next few years, we will *expand* the civil aviation transport market to respond to the needs of economic and social development.

expand 也需要积极行动。

例 81.

积极推进法制化、科学化的管理。
We will set up a law- and science-based management system.

有效 effective/effectively

例 82.

要对非法占有保障性住房行为进行有效治理，同时要从制度上堵塞漏洞、加以防范。(Xi-I)

We must *stop* illegal acquisition of basic-need housing, and block institutional loopholes in this regard.

在没有比 stop 更有效的措施了。

例 83.

要把发展直接融资放在重要位置，形成融资功能完备、基础制度扎实、市场监管有效、投资者合法权益得到有效保护的多层次资本市场体系。(Xi-II)

We should prioritize direct financing, and develop a functional and solidly-based multi-layer capital market which is effectively supervised and where the legitimate rights and interests of investors *are duly protected*.

"有效"换了个词 duly。

圆满、成功 successful/successfully

例 84.

全年主要目标任务顺利完成，"十二五"规划圆满收官。(Xi-II)

The year's major targets *were accomplished*, and the 12th Five-year Plan *was completed*.

顺利完成、圆满收官：to successfully accomplish = to succeed in accomplishing = to accomplish。

例 85.

经过改革开放37年来的努力，我们成功走出了一条中国特色扶贫开发道路，使7亿多农村贫困人口成功脱贫，为全面建成小康社会打下了坚实基础。(Xi-II)

Through 37 years of effort since we adopted reform and opening up in 1978, we *have followed* a poverty relief path with Chinese characteristics, and *lifted* more than 700 million rural people *out of poverty*, laying the foundation for moderate prosperity throughout the country.

两个"成功"都没有译出。因为动词意思中已经隐含成功。

11.8 慎用限定词

限定词是弱化被修饰成分的词，如"相当""比较""基本""有些"，英语有 kind of、really、basically、practically、actually、virtually、generally、certain 等。为了避免过于绝对，可以适当使用，但不能用得太多。

例 86.

我们有几十万留学生在国外学习，为他们归国后创造适当的工作条件相当重要。(Pinkham)

不要译为：We have dozens of thousands of students studying abroad, and it is *quite* important to create suitable conditions for their work after they come back.

可以译为：We have tens of thousands of students studying abroad, and it is important to create suitable conditions for their work after they return. 这里的"相当"应理解为"十分",是强化,用 quite 等于弱化"重要"的意思。

例 87.

非法集资、信息泄露、网络诈骗等案件相当猖獗。(Xi-II)
Illegal fundraising, information leakage, and cyber fraud are *widespread.*

道理同上。

例 88.

今年政府工作的任务相当繁重,我们肩负的责任重大而光荣。

原译:

This year, the work of the government will be quite arduous, and the responsibilities we shoulder are important and glorious.

改译:

This year, the government must accomplish many demanding tasks, but we are honoured to undertake these important responsibilities.

原译加上 quite,反而削弱了任务的强度。

例 89.

集团的领导班子应该说是比较强的。
The group has a strong team of leaders.

不用修饰语,语气更加肯定。如果说 It may well be said the group's leadership is quite strong. 给人的印象是一点儿不强,作为集团自己的宣传材料,就等于自我否定。

例 90.

你知道,承担我这样的工作,基本上没有自己的时间。(Xi-I)
As you know, I *almost* have no private time in the position I am in.

"基本上"不一定总翻译为 basically。

例 91.

中国正在实施"宽带中国"战略,预计到 2020 年,中国宽带网络将基本覆盖所有行政村,打通网络基础设施"最后一公里",让更多人用上互联网。

China is now implementing the Broadband China strategy. It is estimated that by 2020, the broadband network in China will, *by and large*, cover every village. The "last kilometer" of internet infrastructure will be linked up thanks to this strategy, and more people will have access to the internet.

"基本上"还可以说 by and large。

11.9 少用陈词滥调

政府文件中有许多陈词滥调,翻译时要有适当的变化,不要机械对译。遇到以下搭配需要引起注意:

编号	中文	直译
1	充分调动积极性	fully mobilize
2	大胆实验	bold experiments
3	大力促进	vigorously promote
4	大力发展	energetically develop
5	基本完成	basically accomplished
6	坚定不移地贯彻落实	carry out unswervingly
7	坚决和有效措施	firm and effective measures
8	坚决执行	resolutely enforce
9	艰巨任务	arduous tasks
10	艰苦卓绝的奋斗	painstaking efforts
11	绝大多数	overwhelming majority
12	科学分析	scientific analysis
13	认真学习	study conscientiously

（续表）

编号	中文	直译
14	深化改革	deepen reform
15	适当调整	appropriate readjustment
16	适当结合	properly combine
17	严格禁止	firmly forbid
18	正确理解	correct understanding
19	逐步改善	gradually improve

对于这些习惯性搭配，最简单的办法是在英语中省略修饰语；原文确实表示强调时，可以换一种说法，如把 arduous task 换成 demanding task，vigorous development 说成 intensive development 等，避免通篇都是重复的表达。

11.10 减少同义词并列现象

汉语的音韵美和节奏美，部分来自它的工整和对仗。用词方面，经常把两个意思相近的词（名词、动词、形容词、副词）并列使用。例如：

编号	汉语	中式英语
1	帮助和协助	help and assistance
2	挑起和煽动	stir up and incite
3	观点和意见	views and opinions
4	小心谨慎	prudent and cautious
5	情感和感情	sentiments and feelings

虽然英语中也存在与汉语类似的同义词连用现象，如 rules and regulations、bits and pieces、trials and tribulations、by leaps and bounds、betwixt and between、lo and behold、by hook or by crook，但数量很少，即

使这少数的一些用法，也受到了英语教师、作家和编辑的同声谴责，认为这是毫无意义的重复。所以，汉语的同义重复直译为英语并不符合英语习惯，也不能产生美感。

遇到汉语对仗性重复有三种处理方法。多数情况下删除一个并不妨碍意思的传达；有时需要用一个新词概括两个词的意思；偶尔需要补充解释，明确两个词隐含的区别。

有人也许会问，多数时候汉语的两个词是有区别的。回答是，没有两个词的意思完全相同。我们应当这样考虑：在这一特定场合，两个词的区别是否重要，第二个词是否增加了重要的意思，如果回答是否定的，那么，其中一个就是多余的。

例92.
　　创新是民族进步的灵魂，是一个国家兴旺发达的不竭源泉。(Xi-I)
　　Innovation is the soul driving a nation's progress and an inexhaustible source of a country's *prosperity*.

汉语中"兴旺"和"发达"没有太大区别，只需要翻译一个；不必说flourishing and prosperity，因为这两个词是同义词。

例93.
　　要树立正确的世界观、人生观、价值观，掌握了这把总钥匙，再来看看社会万象、人生历程，一切是非、正误、主次，一切真假、善恶、美丑，自然就洞若观火、清澈明了，自然就能作出正确判断、作出正确选择。(Xi-I)
　　You must form a correct world outlook, view of life and values, then you will *see – crystal-clear –*the true nature of society and have a better understanding of your life's experience, and be able to tell *what is right and what is wrong*, what is primary and what is secondary, what is true and what is false, what is good and what is evil, and what is beautiful and what is ugly before making judgments and decisions.

"是非、正误"意思重复，只翻译一次；"洞若观火、清澈明了"两者意思相同，只翻译一遍。

例 94.

保证党对军队的绝对领导，关系我军性质和宗旨、关系社会主义前途命运、关系党和国家长治久安，是我军的立军之本和建军之魂。(Xi-I)

This is central to the nature and mission of the armed forces, *the future* of socialism, the enduring stability of the Party, and the lasting peace of our country. It is *fundamental* to the existence and development of the armed forces.

"前途"和"命运"、"之本"和"之魂"都是同义反复，译文只翻译一次。"长治"和"久安"本是同义反复，但译文把"长治"分配给"党"，"久安"分配给"国家"，分别翻译，也是减轻重复的好办法。但把"长治"翻译为 long-term governance 可能比 enduring stability 更恰当。

例 95.

了解越多，理解越深，交流合作的基础就越牢固、越广泛。(Xi-I)

Mutual understanding is the foundation of state-to-state relations. Deeper mutual understanding will cement and broaden the foundation of our exchanges and cooperation.

"了解越多"和"理解越深"区别不大，译文合并为 mutual understanding。

例 96.

按照稳中求进的工作总基调，及时加强和改善宏观调控，把稳增长放在更加重要的位置。(Xi-I)

Following the general guideline of making steady progress, we have acted promptly to *improve* macro control and placed more emphasis on sustainable development.

"加强"和"改善"区别不大，只翻译为 improve。

例 97.

　　第六，现有外交战略是建立在两极分裂的世界的现状基础上，而现有的世界正进入全球化时代，各国相互依存、相互依赖的程度加深，独立自主战略与这一大趋势有摩擦和冲突之处。

　　The sixth pillar is based on a bipolar world. But the world today is entering into an age of globalization, where countries are increasingly *interdependent*; thus, in some ways, a strategy of independent diplomacy *contradicts* the general trend.

"相互依存"和"相互依赖"意思重复，只翻译一次；"摩擦"和"冲突"在此处无明显区别，只翻译一个。

例 98.

　　在贯彻落实上，要防止徒陈空文、等待观望、急功近利。（Xi-I）

　　While implementing the document we should avoid *empty talk, hesitation* or *seeking quick success and instant benefits*.

"徒陈"和"空文"、"等待"和"观望"、"急功"和"近利"是三组同义反复，前两组译文做了简化，第三组都翻译出来似无必要，可以删除 and instant benefits。

例 99.

　　城乡发展不平衡不协调，是我国经济社会发展存在的突出矛盾。（Xi-I）

　　The unbalanced development between urban and rural areas is a serious problem hindering the development of our economy and society.

"不协调、不平衡"意思相同，合并翻译。有时可以把两个词语概括为一个新的说法，例如：

　　各级领导干部要经常到学生们中去、同他们交朋友，听取他们的意见和建议。（Xi-I）

　　Leading officials at all levels should keep in communication with the students, make friends with them and listen to *what they have to say.*

此处的"意见和建议"合并处理为 what they have to say。

同义反复是汉语特色,数量庞大,随处可见,应当引起我们的高度重视。下面再给出一些例子,大家在翻译时注意进行必要简化。

编号	汉语	中式英语
1	诚实正直	upright and honest
2	挫折和失败	setbacks and defeats
3	措施和步骤	steps and measures
4	风俗习惯	practices and customs
5	腐化堕落	corruption and degeneration
6	高瞻远瞩	forward-looking and far-sighted
7	公平公正	fair and equitable
8	鼓励和促进	encourage and promote
9	技能和能力	skills and abilities
10	加强和改善	enhance and improve
11	坚决果断	firmly and resolutely
12	考虑和研究	consider and study
13	困难和问题	troubles and problems
14	情况和条件	the conditions and situation
15	缺点错误	errors and mistakes
16	缺点和弱点	shortcomings and weaknesses
17	认识和觉悟	consciousness and awareness
18	逃跑和撤退	flee and retreat
19	讨论和辩论	discuss and debate

（续表）

编号	汉语	中式英语
20	途径和方法	paths and routes
21	吸收合并	absorbing and incorporating
22	形象生动	vividly and dramatically
23	阴谋诡计	plots and intrigues
24	优柔寡断	irresolute and hesitant
25	预测预报	forecasts and predictions
26	赞成和支持	endorse and support
27	真心诚意	earnestly and sincerely
28	争议和纠纷	disputes and dissension
29	职能和责任	functions and responsibilities

最后需要指出，在审校译文时如果发现意思重复，不可轻易删除，需要仔细核实原文是否真的重复。如果两个概念有区别，则需要在英文中体现出来。

例 100.

团结统一的中华民族是海内外中华儿女共同的根，博大精深的中华文化是海内外中华儿女共同的魂，实现中华民族伟大复兴是海内外中华儿女共同的梦。（Xi-I）

出版译文：For Chinese people both at home and abroad, *a united Chinese nation* is our shared root, the profound Chinese culture is our shared soul, and the rejuvenation of the Chinese nation is our shared dream.

此处的"团结统一"包括两个意思：民族团结和国家统一。出版译文仅仅译出一个，可以改进：

For Chinese people both at home and abroad, *a unified and united*

Chinese nation is our shared root, the profound Chinese culture is our shared soul, and the rejuvenation of the Chinese nation is our shared dream.

例 101.
　　这表明，由于所有先进的交通和通讯手段都由人民掌管，过去遇到的困难不复存在。

本例来自《中式英语之鉴》。初稿译为 This shows that since all advanced *means of communication* and *communications equipment* are controlled by the people, so the difficulties of the past no longer exist. 在英语中，communications equipment 就是 means of communication，因此等于意思重复。但仔细对照原文发现，原文是"交通"和"通讯"两个概念，因此改为 This shows that since all advanced *means of transportation* and *communication* are controlled by the people, past difficulties no longer exist. 因此，这里的意思重复属于原译不准确，并非真的重复。

例 102.
　　各族人民为维护祖国统一、促进社会稳定、民族团结和经济繁荣作出了巨大贡献。

本例也来自《中式英语之鉴》。书中提供的初译为 People of all the different nationalities have made enormous contributions to *safeguarding the unity* of the motherland and to *promoting* stability and *unity* and prosperity. 作者认为：原译中"safeguarding…unity"和"promoting…unity"难以区分，但因为文章属于重要文本，不敢轻易修改，所以采取变换措辞的方法，把第二个 unity 改为 solidarity（尽管这不解决根本问题）。但回译为中文可以发现，safeguarding the unity of the motherland 很可能是"祖国统一"，promoting stability and unity and prosperity 很可能是"社会稳定、民族团结和经济繁荣"。"祖国统一"和"民族团结"所指不同。前者涉及国家领土完整；后者涉及各民族和睦相处。所以，可以把这两个意思明确表达出来。建议改为：People of all the ethnic groups have contributed enormously to maintaining the territorial integrity of the motherland, solidarity among ethnic groups, social stability and eonomic prosperity.

11.11　减少更高层次的重复

汉语中的意思冗余不仅表现在词语层面的重复，有时甚至整个短句都是冗余信息，必要时应当予以简化。短句层面的重复表现为三种形式：简单重复、不言自喻、正反表达。

简单重复即意思相同，措辞不同，如"厉行节约，减少不必要开支"，两部分意思完全相同；不言自喻，即一个意思已经隐含在另一个意思中，如"控制环境污染，努力保护环境""加强国防建设，增强国防实力"，前半句隐含后半句的意思；正反表达，即先用肯定形式说一遍，再用否定形式说一遍，如"要保持警惕，决不掉以轻心"。

意思表达重复的问题，往往在审校译文时才会发现。遇到意思重复时，可以这样问自己：（1）原文是有意重复还是无意？如果是无意中重复，可以删减。如果为了强调，可以保留。（2）同一说法在这篇文章中已经重复了多少次？如果是多次重复，更有理由删减。（3）这篇文章的作者是否权威？如果权威，尽量少删减，但可以通过改变措辞，使译文看起来不太重复；如果是普通文章，则灵活度更大。下面举例说明减少重复、维持重复、改变措辞三种情况。

11.11.1　减少重复

当重复没有正当理由时，要删除重复。

例 103.
国家安全和社会稳定是改革发展的前提。只有国家安全和社会稳定，改革发展才能不断推进。（Xi-I）

National security and social stability form the basis for further reform and progress.

句号前后意思重复，只需要翻译一半。

第十一章 · 删减冗余信息确保语言简洁

例 104.

我们自己要保持警惕，放松不得。(Deng-III)
We ourselves should *maintain vigilance*.

"保持警惕"和"不得放松"意思相同，只翻译一处。

例 105.

可以说，容易的、皆大欢喜的改革已经完成了，好吃的肉都吃掉了。(Xi-I)
It can be said that the easy part of the job has been done to the satisfaction of all.

"容易的"和"好吃的肉都吃掉了"表达的意思相同，官方译文没有重复翻译，而是合译，语言更简练。

例 106.

他强调，国务院各部门在反腐败斗争中责任重大，所处的地位非常重要。(李鹏在国务院全体会议上的讲话，1993年9月17日)

原译：

He stressed that all State Council departments *have an important responsibility* in the struggle against corruption and said they *are in a very important position.* (Pinkham)

改译：

He stressed that all State Council departments *have an important responsibility* in the struggle. (Pinkham)

"责任重大"，隐含了地位重要，故删除后者。

例 107.

在适合生产粮食的地区，要做好粮食生产工作，努力提高粮食单产，增加粮食品种，提高粮食质量。(Pinkham)

原译：

In areas that are suitable for grain growing, *a good job must be done in grain production and efforts be made to raise per-unit yield, increase variety, and improve quality.*

改译：

In areas suitable for producing grain, *we must try to raise per-unit yield, increase crop variety,* and *improve quality.*

"做好粮食生产工作"的具体内容就是"努力提高粮食单产，增加粮食品种，提高粮食质量"，因此省略概括部分。

例 108.

要对外汇外债实行集中管理，把外汇外债的管理权统一划归中央有关部门。(Pinkham)

原译：

We should *exercise centralized control* over the management of foreign exchange and foreign debts and *centralize such power in the hands of central authorities.*

改译：

We should *give the power to manage* foreign exchange and foreign debt *to the central authorities.*

同一意思重复三次：centralized control、centralize、in the hands of central authorities，修改后删除意思重复。

例 109.

"决定性作用"和"基础性作用"这两个定位是前后衔接、继承发展的。使市场在资源配置中起决定性作用和更好发挥政府作用，二者是有机统一的，不是相互否定的，不能把二者割裂开来、对立起来，既不能用市场在资源配置中的决定性作用取代甚至否定政府作用，也不能用更好发挥政府作用取代甚至否定使市场在资源配置中起决定性作用。(Xi-I)

"Decisive role" is a continuation and extension of "basic role." Letting the market play the decisive role in allocating resources and letting the government better perform its functions are not contradictory. It does not mean that the market can replace the government's functions, nor vice versa.

本段原文有多处正反表达，译文则十分简洁。

例 110.

  一、切实确保航空运输安全。加强对安全工作的组织领导，认真落实安全责任制。积极推进法制化、科学化管理，提高安全管理水平。实施对航空公司运行持续监督和对航空公司、机场、空管系统的安全评估，提高全运行质量。加强空防安全工作，重点反劫机、炸机和利用飞机进行恐怖活动，把隐患消除在地面。加大安全投入，大力采用先进的科学技术，增强安全工作的科技含量，全面提高确保安全的能力。

  First, safety of air transport. We will strengthen leadership and implementation of a safety responsibility system. A sound, rational management system based on law will be set up. Airline operations will be subject to continuous monitoring and airlines, airports, ATC systems will be assessed for safety. Air security will be stepped up, and the emphasis is on preventing hijacking, explosions and using aircraft as a weapon of terrorism, so that dangers can be eliminated on the ground. Resources for security will be increased by increasing investments in advanced technologies and facilities.

加点部分已经包含在小标题中，译文省略。

11.11.2 维持重复

有时为了强调，可以保留重复，尤其是正反表达的情况：

例 111.

  毫无疑问，我们必将胜利，敌人必将失败。（Pinkham）
  There is no question that *we will win and the enemy will be defeated.*

例 112.

正处在革命高潮中的中国人民需要有自己的朋友，应当记住自己的朋友，而不要忘记他们。（Mao-IV）

The Chinese people, now at the height of revolution, need friends and they should *remember their friends and not forget them*.

例 113.

在克服困难的斗争中，必须反对浪费，厉行节约。（Mao-IV）

In the struggle to do so, we must fight waste and practice economy.

有时保留重复是由于删除重复后，剩下的内容太少。

例如：

要加强农村地区的公共卫生，改善人民健康状况。

We must *improve public health services* in rural areas to *improve our people's health*.

11.11.3 改变措辞

从理论上讲，是否删除重复完全是一个技术问题，即看英语译文能否有效传递汉语的信息。但实践中却要考虑文本的性质和读者：是一般大众阅读的文章，还是将受到外国政府或公司仔细研究的法律文件或官方声明？是即席发言，还是精心准备的稿子？如果稿子很重要，你可能觉得没有修改的权力，这时你可以改变措词方式，使重复不太显眼。

例 114.

为保持经济的稳步增长，必须实行长期、稳定的经济发展政策。（Pinkham）

原译：

To *maintain steady growth of the economy*, we must implement a long-term *policy of steady economic growth*.

改译：

To *keep the economy growing,* we must implement a long-term *policy favorable to steady economic growth.*

《中式英语之鉴》的作者从英译初稿出发，认为修改后的译文归根结底还是"to maintain steady growth, we must have a policy of steady growth"，意思显然重复。如果我的回译正确，这句话似乎可以翻译为：To maintain steady growth, we must implement a long-term and stable policy. 把强调重点放在政策的稳定性上。

11.11.4　产生重复的原因

若不是平卡姆指出这些问题，我们也许不知道这些习以为常的说法翻译为英语是重复的。这一点再次提醒我们，我们对汉语中的一切表达方法都要持批判态度，不要想当然地认为，汉语说得通的，直译为英语一定没有问题。分析产生这一问题的根源，有助于我们识别哪种情况下可能引起英语译文的重复，从而在翻译时加以注意。

11.11.4.1　由总到分的思维习惯

分析以上例句，我们发现某些例句有一个共同特点：先抽象后具体。所谓先抽象后具体，是指先用一个成语（或"原则"）概括总的意思，再用白话解释这一具体场合该成语（或原则）的含义。例如，"我们要厉行节约，减少不必要开支""厉行节约"是概括，落到实处就是"减少不必要开支"。"工业生产中我们应当坚持'安全第一、预防为主'的方针"，"安全第一"是原则，"预防"是具体办法。英语讲求直截了当，不容忍重复。用英国作家 Robert Graves 和 Alan Hodge 的话说："Unless for rhetorical emphasis, or necessary recapitulation, no idea should be presented more than once in the same prose passage … Repetitiveness is nowadays considered a sign of pauperdom in oratory, and of feeble-mindedness in narrative." 所以，遇到这种情况，自然要对原文进行简化。

11.11.4.2　工整对仗的审美习惯

请看下面这些句子：

- 要进一步继续加强国防建设，增强国防实力
- 要控制环境污染，努力保护环境
- 要努力钻研业务，提高工作技能
- 要加强农村地区的公共卫生，改善人民健康状况
- 要减轻企业税负，增加企业留利，提高企业的财务能力

其他例子还有：发展体育运动，增强人民体质；提高警惕，保卫祖国；植树造林，绿化祖国等。

这些句子从汉语的角度，看不出任何问题。意思符合逻辑（前后有因果关系），句子结构工整，读起来朗朗上口，充分体现了汉语的特点。但这些句子翻译为英语后，平卡姆女士认为，属于 self-evident statement，因为后半部分的意思已经显然隐含在前半部分。我们只能认为这是两种语言审美观的不同。

汉语在写作时，非常注意长短句搭配和整散句的运用，甚至沉溺于词句的工整对仗而不重逻辑和事实。古代有一个文人写了两句诗："舍弟江南死，家兄塞北亡"，皇帝一看立刻安慰他。这个文人大言不惭地说：其实只有弟弟死在江南，不过为了对仗只好让哥哥死在塞北。这是一个极端的例子，但在汉语写作时我们确实十分注意音韵效果，不能排除为了达到音韵效果而凑字、凑句的可能。如"国务院各部门在反腐败斗争中责任重大，所处的地位非常重要"这句话，如果把后半部分去掉，意思没什么变化，但似乎句子不够平衡。以上其他例子也是如此。

英语也强调长短句搭配、平行结构的使用。但经过翻译的程序，长句可能变为短句，平行结构可能不再平行，原文的音韵效果丧失殆尽，原文的平衡被打破。这时，就需要建立新的平衡，而建立新的平衡只能以译入语为出发点，进行词句的调整取舍。

11.11.4.3　正反对比的修辞习惯

正反对比是汉语论证中的一种正当修辞手段，如"有毅力者成，反是

者败""得道者多助，失道者寡助""毫不利己，专门利人""扭亏为盈""脱贫致富""阴盛阳衰""男尊女卑""重男轻女""有害无益""男主外、女主内"等，这种格式的前后两部分意思完全相同，只是从相反的角度进行论述。对比和对偶不同。对偶主要是从结构形式上说的，它要求结构相称，字数相等；对比是从意义上说的，它要求意义相反或相近，而不管结构形式如何。一句话可能同时达到形式上对偶，意义上对比。比如：

- 目前，社会主义法制已基本确立，无法可依的局面已经改变。
- 我们要十分关心年度计划的编制工作，不能对此不闻不问。
- 要保持警惕，决不掉以轻心。
- 财政开支应按轻重缓急进行安排，不应当主次不分。
- 毫无疑问，我们必将胜利，敌人必将失败。

从上面对英译文的修改来看，英语不主张这种显而易见的意思重复。

11.11.4.4　汉语本身经不住推敲

像英语一样，汉语如果不经推敲，也可能出现重复啰嗦的情况，翻译时应注意甄别。比如：

> 回族人口数量大，是由于其同化了其他民族，这促进了其人口的增加。

这句话等于说：我今天早上起晚了，所以迟到，因为我起晚了。这种情况必须编辑原文。

11.12　使用简单句型

简明英语要求我们尽量使用简单的句型。比如：

例 115.
　　这九年是国家经济实力显著增强的九年。
　　In these nine years the economy has grown stronger.（Pinkham）

不必说：

These nine years *constitute a period in which* the national economic strength has increased.

例 116.

要积极探索建立非营利机构参与保障性住房建设和运营管理的体制机制，形成各方面共同参与的局面。(Xi-I)

We should also actively explore systems and mechanisms for non-profit organizations to build and manage basic-need housing, *so that all sides involved can join forces in this endeavor.*

不必说：

We should also actively explore systems and mechanisms for non-profit organizations to build and manage basic-need housing, to *form a situation in which* all sides involved can join forces in this endeavor.

例 117.

解决问题的关键是控制开支

可以译为：The solution is to cut spending。不必说：*The key to* the solution *lies* in the curtailment of expenditure。

11.13　精简慢启动句子

11.13.1　元话语

元话语（metadiscourse）是关于讨论本身的讨论。维基百科的解释很清楚：

Metadiscourse is a term that is used in philosophy to denote a discussion about a discussion, as opposed to a simple discussion about a given topic.

The term metadiscourse is also used in writing to describe a word or phrase that comments on what is in the sentence, usually as an introductory adverbial clause. It is any phrase that is included within a clause or sentence that goes beyond the subject itself, often to examine the purpose of the sentence or a response from the author. Metadiscourse includes phrases such as "frankly," "after all," "on the other hand," "to our surprise," and so on.

Below are some examples of metadiscourse in writing, denoting:

- the writer's intentions: *"to sum up," "candidly," "I believe"*
- the writer's confidence: *"may," "perhaps," "certainly," "must"*
- directions to the reader: *"note that," "finally," "therefore," "however"*
- the structure of the text: *"first," "second," "finally," "therefore," "however"*

Most writing needs metadiscourse, but too much buries ideas. Technical, academic, and other non-fiction writers should use metadiscourse sparingly.[①]

例 118.

The last point I would like to make here is that in regard to men-women relationships, it is important to keep in mind that the greatest changes have probably occurred in the way men and women seem to be working next to one another.

本句划线部分都是元话语，实质内容只有以下部分：

可改为：Greatest changes have ... occurred in the way men and women ... working next to one another.

翻译时，应注意少用或不用元话语：

众所周知，从 20 世纪 70 年代末开始，中国开始进行经济体制的深刻改革和全面对外开放，极大地促进了生产力的发展和社会的繁荣。

Starting in the late 1970s, China initiated a series of radical economic reforms and policies of overall opening-up to the world, leading to increased productivity and social prosperity.

---

① https://en.wikipedia.org/wiki/Metadiscourse, accessed 2021-09-02.

11.13.2 多余的引导性动词

汉语中有些词语和短语，如果直接翻译为英语，只能推迟主要动词的出现，不如省略不译。这和英语的慢启动句子（slow-starting sentences）是相同的。例如：

努力（大力、尽力）等
通常翻译为 make great efforts to、make every effort to、try our best to、do our utmost to、do everything possible to、strive to, endeavor to、work hard to、consciously、make conscious efforts to，建议尽量少用。

例 119.
　　第四，必须大力弘扬劳模精神、发挥劳模作用。（Xi-I）
　　Fourth, we must emulate model workers.

"大力"并没有译为"make great efforts to"，而是直接省略。

　　为建设一支听党指挥、能打胜仗、作风优良的人民军队而奋斗。（Xi-I）
　　build revolutionary, modernized and standardized people's armed forces that faithfully follow the Party's commands, are able to win battles and have fine conduct.

"为……而奋斗"没有翻译为 work hard for the building of…，而是省略不译，因为 build 本身就需要"奋斗"。

例 120.
　　我们要着重从以下几个方面作出努力。（Xi-I）
　　We should take the following steps.

没有翻译为 we should focus our efforts on the following aspects。take steps 就隐含了努力。

例 121.

要大力改革粮食购销价格形成机制,进一步采取措施,建立粮棉及其他主要产品储备的调控机制。

原译:

It is essential to *make vigorous efforts to* reform the system for determining the purchasing and selling prices of grain and take further steps to establish the institution of regulating the reserves of grain, cotton, and other such major products.

改译:

It is essential to reform the pricing mechanism of grains, and to further regulate the stockpiling of grain, cotton, and other basic products.

重视(注意、强调)

经常被翻译为 pay attention to、pay heed to、lay stress on、attach importance to、stress、emphasize,视情况决定是否翻译、如何翻译。

例 122.

对这些问题,我们必须高度重视,切实加以解决。(Xi-I)
We must *pay close attention to* and earnestly solve these problems.

有实际意义,译出。

例 123.

中央对扶贫开发工作高度重视。(Xi-I)
The Party and government have always *attached great importance to* the housing issue.

有意义,译出。

例 124.

中国重视联合国,将坚定地支持联合国。(Xi-I)
China *values* the UN and will support it.

有意义,译出,但选用更恰当的词。

例 125.

我们党历来重视抓全党特别是领导干部的学习。(Xi-I)

Our Party has always *worked to ensure* that all its members, especially leading officials, acquire further knowledge.

根据意思,译为"努力确保"(worked to ensure)。

搞好、做好(……工作)

经常被翻译为 do a good job in、make a success of、achieve success in、do successful work in、be good at,建议尽量少用。

例 126.

深入做好组织群众、宣传群众、教育群众、服务群众工作,虚心向群众学习,诚心接受群众监督。(Xi-I)

We must organize our people, communicate with them, educate them, serve them, learn from them, and subject ourselves to their oversight.

省略"深入做好……工作"。

例 127.

搞好上述领域合作,必须得到各国人民支持。(Xi-I)

To pursue productive cooperation in the above-mentioned areas, we need the support of our peoples.

省略"搞好"。

例 128.

我们要牢牢抓好党执政兴国的第一要务(Xi-I)

The most important thing for our Party is to govern the country well and rejuvenate the nation.

"抓好"没有译为 do a good job in。

例 129.

同时要搞好城市居民的医疗保健工作。(Pinkham)

原译：

A good job must be done in medical care *work* for the urban residents too.

改译：

Good medical care must be provided for city dwellers too.

换了一种说法，避免 do a good job。

11.14 小结

平卡姆从母语的角度，按照英语写作的原则，对汉译英出现的问题进行了精辟的分析，对很多司空见惯的译法提出了挑战，值得我们认真研究和借鉴。作为从事汉英翻译的中国人，我们的英语很难达到母语水平，但通过对这些问题的研究，至少可以增强我们对这些问题的敏感度，从而主动避免出现这些问题。

我们要树立"不是每个词、每句话都需要翻译出来"观念。译者要时刻问自己：这个词不译，意思有无损失。如果没有损失，就可以考虑省略。具体来讲，要注意汉语中有无多余的名词性和动词性范畴词，有无单词和句子层面的同义反复，有无可被中心词吸收的修饰限定成分，有无陈词滥调。如有，则进一步考虑如何精简。同时，也要利用英语的词形变化、衔接手段差异、强势动词、简单的句子结构，进一步简化英语的表达，做到清晰易懂。

对于无法确定取舍的成分，可以先翻译出来，最后批判性地通读译稿，把英语作为一篇独立的文章，按照英语写作原则进行审视。可以用各种网络资源检验可疑的并列或偏正词组是否存在。如果存在，看它的出处是否可靠，以及是否常见。

简洁不仅是英语作文的要求，在口译尤其是同声传译中也有重大意义，因为口译的时间是非常宝贵的。

〔课后练习〕

1. 你是否关注到翻译中的简洁问题？
2. 汉语中的冗余表现在哪些方面？
3. 请阅读附录一"欧洲委员会英语写作与翻译指南"。
4. 请阅读《中式英语之鉴》第一部分 Unnecessary Words。
5. 请以简洁为视角，修改自己最近一次翻译。

第十二章
后置重要信息确保逻辑通畅

扫码预习

请扫码下载本章涉及的例句。先做练习,再看解答,学习效果更佳。

12.1 介绍

在语篇分析中,可把句子切分为主位(theme/topic)和述位(rheme/discussion)两部分。主位在前,一般包含已知信息,是交际的背景;述位在后,通常包含新信息,是交际的重心。在组句成篇的过程中,主位和述位层层推进。例如:

> *The Court of Auditors' report* criticizes agricultural spending and proposes some new measures to prevent fraud. *Their proposals* include setting up a special task force with powers to search farms. *Such powers* are not normally granted to Commission officials, but fraud prevention is now one of the EU's main priorities. (Williams, 1995)

在上例中,the Court of Auditors' report 是已知信息或者作者假定读者已知的信息,是下面论述的出发点,所以放在句子开头;their proposals 属于已知信息，放在句首，因为上一句中提到 proposes some measures; such powers 是已知信息，放在句首，因为上一句提到 with powers to search farms。

再看下面的例子：

Now that China has joined the World Trade Organization, attention in the west has shifted to the prospects of China's compliance with the substantive commitments it has made.

There are some grounds for optimism that are frequently overlooked.

Most important, China has already gone a long way towards dismantling the pervasive protectionism that characterized its trading system two decades ago. (1a) *As shown in diagram 1, by the time China entered the WTO last year* the average nominal tariff had already fallen by three-quarters, from 56 percent in the early 1980s to an average of only 15 percent in 2001. That is roughly the average tariff level in Brazil and Mexico and about half the level of India. Equally important, China provides exemptions from import duties on parts and components used in export processing and on the machinery and equipment imported for installation in joint-venture and wholly foreign-owned factories. (1b) *Because of these exemptions in recent years*, about 60 percent of all goods imported into China have been entirely tariff free. (1c) *Thus for much of the 1990s*, tariff revenues collected were less than 5 percent of the value of imports. China, in effect, is already on a glide path that should allow it to meet relatively easily its commitment to reduce its average nominal tariff rate to only 9 percent by 2005.①

中国既已成为世贸组织成员，西方国家的注意力也随之转移。现在西方国家关注的焦点，是中国能否履行其实质性入世承诺。

关于中国履行入世承诺的前景，存在一些令人乐观的理由，但经常被人们忽视。

---

① Nicholas R. Lardy. Adjustment of Foreign Trade Policies and Foreign Direct Investment—Comment presented at the China Development Forum, 2002.

二十多年以前，在中国的外贸体制中，贸易保护主义措施无处不在；而今天，中国在消除贸易保护主义措施方面，已经取得了长足的进展。如表1所示，中国去年入世之前，平均名义关税税率已经下降了四分之三，从20世纪80年代初期的56%降至2001年平均只有15%的水平。这一关税水平大致相当于巴西和墨西哥现有平均关税水平，相当于印度关税水平的一半。这是令人乐观的最重要理由。同时，中国对于出口加工型企业的零部件进口，以及合资企业和外商独资企业的机器设备进口，免征关税。由于最近几年的免税措施，进口到中国的全部货物当中，大约有60%根本没有缴纳关税，因此，在20世纪90年代的多数年份，关税收入在进口总额中所占比重不到5%。中国承诺在2005年之前，将平均名义关税税率降至只有9%的水平。我想，中国实现这一目标，应当是没有困难的，因为如上所述，中国实际上已经以较快的步伐降低了关税。这也是令人乐观的重要理由之一。

我们重点分析斜体部分三个句子：

1a. *As shown in diagram 1, by the time China entered the WTO last year* the average nominal tariff had already fallen by three-quarters, from 56 percent in the early 1980s to an average of only 15 percent in 2001.

2a. *Because of these exemptions in recent years,* about 60 percent of all goods imported into China have been entirely tariff free.

3a. Thus *for much of the 1990s,* tariff revenues collected were less than 5 percent of the value of imports.

第一句（1a）下划线部分 As shown in diagram 1, by the time China entered the WTO last year，不是作者要强调的，所以放在句首；作者要告诉读者的是下面的数字，所以放在句末。紧接着一句"That is roughly the average tariff level in Brazil and Mexico and about half the level of India"（见原段落）当中的 that 承上启下，概括上一句的新信息，作为本句的旧信息，放在句首。

第二句（2a）下划线部分 because of these exemptions in recent years 当

中，these exemptions 也是对上一句内容的概括，所以放在句首。

第三句（3a）下划线部分 for much of the 1990s 也是在上文所提到的，所以放在句首。

我们在翻译时，要识别出原文每句话的信息重点（有时并不出现在句末），在译文中尽量将该信息置于句子末尾，以加强句子之间的联系，帮助读者抓住论证的线索。

这里要强调，学英文的人经常有一种误解，认为英文的语序是把句子的主干部分放在前面，修饰成分放在后面，这个观点有失偏颇。孤立的句子，其主句、从句、状语等信息单元的排列位置比较灵活，但一旦这个句子成为段落的组成部分，其中的信息排列顺序就受到认识规律的限制，即应当把旧信息前置，新信息后置；次要信息前置，重要信息后置。上述三个句子如果改为如下结构，虽然符合语法、意思也正确，但不符合认识规律：

1b. *The average nominal tariff had already fallen by three-quarters by the time China entered the WTO last year, from 56 percent in the early 1980s to an average of only 15 percent in 2001, as shown in diagram 1.*

2b. *About 60 percent of all goods imported into China have been entirely tariff free because of these exemptions in recent years.*

3b. *Thus tariff revenues collected were less than 5 percent of the value of imports for much of the 1990s.*

汉语行文也同样符合人们的认识规律，除非汉语语法不允许，通常也是把旧信息放在前面，新信息放在后面，翻译时不需要进行大幅调整。例如：

对比 2002 年与 2000 年的调查结果，虽然在答案的选择上，两年的调查是有些差异的，// 但如果将排在前五位的回答比较一下，// 就会发现，前五位的内容是完全一致的。排在前五位的因素，属于农村推的因素有三条（农村收入水平太低、农村缺乏发展机会、农村太穷），属于城市拉的因素有两条（城市收入高、外出见世面）。2002 年将"城市收入高"列为外出驱动的第一位因素，2000 年将"农村收入水平太低"列为第一位驱动因素。其实，农村的推的力量与城市的拉的力量是农民工外出流动这样一种行为的两个方面，所以这里的驱动因素实际上是一回事。笔者试将表1和表2列在第一位的因素总结为是"经济收入的驱动力"。

Although the two results differ in certain points, // the first five answers remain unchanged. Among the first five, // three are the rural pushing force (low-income, lack of career development opportunities and poor living standard) and two are the city pulling force (high-income and eye-opening access). In 2002 // *high-income in cities* // ranks first, while in 2000 // *low-income in rural areas* // tops the list. Actually, the rural pushing force and city pulling force // have same effects on the emigration of farmer workers. So *low-income in rural areas* and *high-income in cities* are, // in fact, one factor and I name it the economic driving force.

对比英汉各句"//"前后两（三）部分发现，翻译为英语后信息结构并没有发生变化，原来先说的，译文仍然先说；原来后说的，译文仍然后说。相反，如果按照一般的认识，把所有主句放在前面，从句或附属成分放在后面，上面一段话就可能翻译为：

The first five answers remain unchanged although the two results differ in certain points. Three are the rural pushing force (low-income, lack of career development opportunities and poor living standard) and two are the city pulling force (high-income and eye-opening access) among the first five. *High-income in cities* ranks first in 2002, while *low-income in rural areas* tops the list in 2000. Actually, the rural pushing force and city pulling force have same effects on the emigration of farmer workers. So *low-income in rural areas* and *high-income in cities* are, in fact, one factor and I name it the economic driving force.

读这段话是否觉得抓不住重点？

当然，由于受到语言结构的限制，有时不得不把新信息或重要信息放在句首，这时只能通过阅读时的语调和重音表示出来。

了解信息结构的特点，对于翻译有重要的意义。英汉的信息结构是相似的，翻译时不应破坏。为了促进信息的流动，翻译（和写作）时可以从下面几个方面入手。

12.2　不重要信息左移

这样可以避免结尾有气无力（A 是修改前的句子，B 是修改后的句子）：

例1.

　　A: Complete institutional reform is advocated by the report in most cases.

　　B: What the report advocates, in most cases, is complete institutional reform. (EC, 7)

例2.

　　A: The data that are offered to establish the existence of ESP do not make believers of us for the most part.

　　B: For the most part, the data that are offered to establish the existence of ESP do not make us believers. (Williams, 1995)

翻译中可以使用类似方法：

例3.

　　据1992年组织进行的第二次全国肝炎流行病学调查结果表明：中国人群中乙肝病毒平均感染率在60%左右，表面抗原阳性携带近10%。

如果翻译为：

　　The second national epidemiological survey for hepatitis conducted in 1992 found that an average of 60% were infected with HBV (hepatitis B virus) and nearly 10% were HbsAg (hepatitis B surface antigen) carriers *among different Chinese population groups*.

则结尾处的 among different Chinese population groups 使句子显得乏力，

因为它不是作者强调的重点。作者强调的重点是两个百分比。可以把这个短语移到前面：

> The second national epidemiological survey for hepatitis conducted in 1992 found that *among different Chinese population groups*, an average of 60% were infected with HBV (hepatitis B virus), and nearly 10% were HbsAg (hepatitis B surface antigen) carriers.

12.3 重要信息右移

无论中文还是英文，如果有意识把重要信息、新信息置于句子末尾，会更便于读者理解。

例 4.

A: Some complex issues run through these questions.

B: Through these questions run some complex issues. (Williams:55)

翻译中可以使用类似方法：

例 5.

　　市场经济是人类社会历史进步过程中不可逾越的经济发展阶段，而社会保障法律制度是市场经济建立和发展的必要条件之一。

原译：

> Market economy is a necessary stage of development in the progress of human society, and *the social security system* is a prerequisite for the establishment and development of market economy.

改译：

> Market economy is a necessary stage of development in the progress of human society, and its establishment and development *requires the support of a social security system*.

原译按照汉语中信息出现的顺序，把斜体部分放在第二句开头。但因为这部分是重要信息，必须重读才能突出其地位。改译把这一内容移到了英语句子末尾，阅读时重音自然落在了句尾。

例 6.

找到医治艾滋病的方法，要靠生物学家和医学家的努力，但解决今天肆虐全球的、作为一种社会病症的艾滋病问题，却不是仅靠生物学家和医学家所能做到的。

原译：

We need biologists and medical experts to find a cure for AIDS; but <u>biologists and medical experts alone are not enough</u> to cure AIDS as a social problem, a problem that has run wild globally.

改译：

To find a cure for AIDS, we need biologists and medical experts; but to cure AIDS as a social problem, a problem that has taken the world by storm, <u>biologists and medical experts alone are not enough</u>.

原译调整了原文信息出现的顺序，显得平铺直叙，改译把应该强调的内容放在句子的自然重心——结尾。

例 7.

Amendments to UN Regulations shall be <u>established by the Administrative Committee as described in Article 1, paragraph 2 and in accordance with the procedure indicated in the Appendix.</u>

原译：

<u>应由第一条第 2 款所述行政委员会按附录 1 列出的程序</u>，确定对规章的修订。

这句话（下面**突出显示**部分）在全段中的位置是这样的：

Article 12

<u>The UN Regulations</u> annexed to this Agreement may be amended in

accordance with the following procedure:

1. Amendments to <u>UN Regulations</u> shall be established by the Administrative Committee as described in Article 1, paragraph 2 and in accordance with the procedure indicated in the Appendix.

可见，UN Regulations 在上一段已经提过，属于旧信息，Amendments to UN Regulations 是和旧信息相关的信息，置于句首，便于和上文衔接，译文应当维持这一结构：

联合国条例的修订，<u>应由第 1 条第 2 款所述行政委员会按附录所列程序进行。</u>

注意：amendment 虽然也是重要信息，但相对于修订的机关和程序，较为次要，况且其附着在旧信息之上，所以置于句首。句首通常用来放置较重要信息，句尾放置最重要信息。

另外，本句中的 as described 是修饰 Administrative Committee，不是修饰 established，因为回头查看第 2 款，只有这一句相关：

The Administrative Committee shall be composed of all the Contracting Parties in accordance with the rules of procedure set out in the Appendix.

原译在这个问题上，没有犯错。

再举一个英译汉的例子：

原文：

Mengniu can tap high-quality Aussie milk. And it is one in the eye for Yili, its bigger cross-town dairy rival in Hohhot, the regional capital of Inner Mongolia.（选自 *Economist*）

原译：

蒙牛可以利用优质的澳洲牛奶。这让规模更大的竞争对手伊利很恼火，伊利总部同在内蒙古省会呼和浩特。

原译和原文的信息顺序保持一致，同位语位置保持不变。但按照信息流动的规律，新信息和重要的信息置于句末，这个同位语从句显然不是作者想要强调的内容，故可提前。

改译：

  蒙牛可以利用优质的澳洲牛奶。这让总部同在内蒙古首府呼和浩特、规模还更大的竞争对手伊利很恼火。

当然，维持原文顺序，以破折号补充说明伊利的情况也可以接受：

  蒙牛可以利用优质的澳洲牛奶。这让伊利很恼火——伊利是蒙牛的竞争对手，规模更大，总部同在内蒙古首府呼和浩特。

12.4　使用倒装句

这种做法与上一种做法类似。请大家观察句子修改前后的区别。A 为原文，B 为修改：

例 8.

  A: Those questions relating to the ideal system for providing instruction in home computers *are just as confused.*

  B: *Just as confused are* those questions relating to the ideal system for providing instruction in home computers. (Williams:69)

例 9.

  A: The source of the American attitude toward rural dialects is *more interesting [than something already mentioned].*

  B: *More interesting [than something already mentioned]* is the source of the American attitude toward rural dialects. (Williams:55)

例 10.

  A: The failure of the administration to halt the rising costs of hospital care *lies at the heart of the problem.*

  B: *At the heart of the problem lies* the failure of the administration to halt the rising costs of hospital care. (Williams:55)

翻译中可以使用类似的方法：

例 11.

　　查中国在 1994 年制定的《广告法》中可能与此相关的只有第七条第六项规定广告不得有"含有淫秽、迷信、恐怖、暴力、丑恶的内容"，但将有关安全套的公益性广告，解释为"含有淫秽内容"，是不恰当的。

　　Possibly related to this in the 1995 Advertisement Law is only Article 7.6, which states that advertisements shall not "contain obscenity, superstition, terror, violence, and evil." But it is inappropriate to interpret public service adverts on condoms as "contain[ing] . . . obscenity."

如果把斜体部分翻译为 Only Article 7.6 of the 1995 Advertisement Law is possibly related to this. . . 就需要重读 Only Article 7.6。

例 12.

　　法律是一种最结构化和外显化的社会制度。其表层有着大量的技术化的构成（这决定了在现代社会它必须要由专业化程度极强的职业群体来掌握），而在其深层则有着与文化传统和价值取向密切关联的理念。

　　Law is a highly structured and externalized social system. *On the surface are many technical components (requiring professionals to master), while beneath lies a belief system grounded in cultural traditions and value orientations.*

如果翻译为 A large number of technical components (requiring professionals to master) are on the surface, while a belief system grounded in cultural traditions and value orientations lies beneath. 就显得头重脚轻。

12.5　删除多余的结尾

下例中斜体部分就是对 behavior 的解释，可以删除：

改前：Sociobiologists are making the provocative claim that our genes largely determine our social behavior *in the way we act in situations we find around us every day.*

改后：Sociobiologists are making the provocative claim that our genes largely determine our social behavior. (Williams:68)

运用到翻译中：

集团的领导班子应该说是比较强的。

原译：The group's leadership is strong, we should say.
改1：The group has a strong leadership.
改2：The group has strong leaders.

12.6 使用被动语态

尽管在写作和翻译中提倡使用主动语态，但可以通过使用被动语态，把重要信息放在后面，避免头重脚轻，从而遵循英语的"尾重"原则，达到信息流动的通畅。试比较下面两组例句。A 组显得头重脚轻，B 组则更加平衡：

例 13.

A: During the first years of our nation, *a series of brilliant and virtuous presidents committed to a democratic republic yet confident in their own superior worth* conducted its administration.

B: During the first years of our nation, its administration was conducted by *a series of brilliant and virtuous presidents committed to a democratic republic yet confident in their own superior worth.* (Williams:54)

例 14.

A: *Astronomers, physicists, and a host of other researchers entirely familiar with the problems raised by quasars* have confirmed these observations.

B: These observations have been confirmed *by astronomers, physicists, and a host of other researchers entirely familiar with the problems raised by quasars.* (Williams:55)

翻译中可以直接使用这种方法。

例 15.

从 2001 年 3 月份开始，原油定价将进一步放开，国家计委不再公布国内原油基准价，改由本公司和中国石油按照国家计委的上述原则和办法自行计算和确认原油价格。

Since March 2001, the price of crude oil will be further liberalized. The SDPC will stop publishing domestic base price. *Instead, the price will be calculated and determined independently by our company and PetroChina according to the principles and methods mentioned above.*

原文加点部分形式上是主动语态，但用"由……"表示强调。译文斜体部分用的是被动语态，正好把旧信息 the price 作为主语，把要强调的部分（由……）放在句末。如果把这一句改为主动语态，语气是不通顺的：Instead, our company and PetroChina will calculate and determine the price independently according to the principles and methods mentioned above. 主动语态要表达原文意思，只能通过有意重读 our company and PetroChina 来实现，因为按照人们的阅读习惯，一般是把重音放在句末。

例 16.

汽、柴油零售价仍实行政府指导价，由国家计委制定并公布零售中准价；中国石化具体零售价可在规定浮动幅度内确定，浮动幅度由上下 [ ]％扩大为上下 [ ]％。

Retail prices of gasoline and diesel still follow the government benchmark price, which will *be fixed* and published by SDPC. The flexibility enjoyed by Sinopec in deciding its retail prices will expand from [ ]％ to [ ]％.

12.7 重组句子主语和从句

如果主语包含的信息过多（A），可以把它转换为独立的从句（B）：

律师在证据发现程序结束之后又发现了新的书证的，即使该书证与发现程序所涉事项关系极小，也必须立即通知法庭和对方律师。

A: *An attorney who uncovers after the close of a discovery proceeding documents that might be even peripherally relevant to a matter involved in the discovery proceeding* must notify both the court and the opposing attorney immediately.

B: *If a discovery proceeding closes and an attorney then uncovers documents that might be even peripherally relevant to the matter of the proceeding,* he/she must notify both the court and the opposing attorney immediately. (Williams:55)

我们按照以上方法修改下面一句法律条文的翻译：

第二十一条 经营者假冒他人的注册商标，擅自使用他人的企业名称或者姓名，伪造或者冒用认证标志、名优标志等质量标志，伪造产地，对商品质量作引人误解的虚假表示的，依照《中华人民共和国商标法》《中华人民共和国产品质量法》的规定处罚。(《反不正当竞争法》)

原译：

Article 21 *A business operator who counterfeits another's registered trademark, uses without authorization the name of another enterprise or person, forges or counterfeits authentication marks, famous-and-excellent product marks or other product quality marks, forges the origin of the products or makes false and misleading indications regarding the product quality,* shall be punished in accordance with the provisions of the Trademark Law of the People's Republic of China and the Law of the People's Republic of China on Product Quality. （中国法制出版社）

这句话的主语很长，原因是里面包含一个很长的定语从句。修改非常简单，只需把 who 去掉，开头加一个 if 或 where 就可以了：

修改 1：

Article 21　Where a business operator counterfeits a registered trademark of another person, or uses without authorization the name of another enterprise or person, or forges or unjustifiably uses a quality mark such as a certification mark or a famous-and-excellent-product mark, or forges the origin of a product, or makes false or misleading presentation of a product's quality, such operator will be punished under the Trademark Law of the People's Republic of China and the Product Quality Law of the People's Republic of China.

也可以在格式上做些调整，使句子结构一目了然：

修改 2：

Article 21　A business operator will be punished under the Trademark Law of the People's Republic of China and the Product Quality Law of the People's Republic of China if such operator —

- counterfeits a registered trademark of another person;
- uses without authorization the name of another enterprise or person;
- forges or unjustifiably uses a quality mark such as a certification mark or a famous / excellent product mark;
- forges the origin of a product; or
- makes false or misleading presentation of product quality.

12.8　减少插入成分

即使在法律文本中，也尽量减少在主谓之间或句子任何地方插入。法律中经常使用插入，是因为放在正常位置修饰关系不清楚。

改前：Industrial spying, *because of the growing use of computers to store and process corporate information, is* increasing rapidly.

改1：Industrial spying is increasing rapidly *because of the growing use of computers to store and process corporate information.*（消除了插入）

改2：*Because of the growing use of computers to store and process corporate information,* industrial spying is increasing rapidly. (Perdue, 2021)（重要信息后置）

在翻译中的应用：

原文：

行政复议机关应当自受理申请之日起六十日内作出行政复议决定。

原译：

An administrative reconsideration organ shall, *within 60 days from the date it accepts an application*, make a decision after administrative reconsideration.

改译：

An administrative reconsideration organ shall make a decision after administrative reconsideration within 60 days from the date it accepts an application.

12.9　几种表示强调的句法手段

12.9.1　There Be

下列B组例句中，通过使用there be突出了强调的重点（A组斜体部分）：

A: *A few grammatical patterns* add weight to the end of a sentence.

B: *There are* a few grammatical patterns that add weight to the end of a sentence. (Williams: 71)

A: For EU enlargement *several alternative scenarios* could be considered.

B: *There are* several scenarios that we could consider for EU enlargement. (DGT:7)

需要指出的是，there be 很多时候可以省略，比如：

例 17.

还有 18.5% 的女性尚有更加充足的时间可以从事另外一份工作。

原译：

There are still 18.5% having sufficient time to do a second job.

改译：

18.5% still have sufficient time to do a second job.（注意：这个句子就是把重点信息放在句首，需要重读。改为放在句末句子结构会比较麻烦）

例 18.

女性在初始就业或转换工作的时候，主要通过三种途径：一是亲戚、朋友介绍，二是劳务市场，三是其他。如：报纸广告、企业招聘广告、毕业分配、招工、接班等。

原译：

There are three main ways through which a woman finds her first job or changes job: recommendation by friends or relatives, the labor market, and other avenues, such as classified advertisements, company recruitment advertisements, government assignment upon graduation, worker recruitment, or replacement of retired relatives.

可以更简洁：

改译：

A female finds her first job or change her job in three ways ...

12.9.2　What

What 句型强调系动词之后的部分：

例 19.

国家立法滞后，地方立法分散，统一的社会保障制度被分割。

译文：

National legislation has fallen behind current realities, and local legislation varies so drastically that *what* China has currently is not an integrated social security system, but a large set of fragmented systems.

12.9.3　It

It 作为形式主语，可以把较长的主语后置：

A: The accession of new Member States in several stages now seems likely.

B: *It* now seems likely that new Member States will join in several stages. (DGT:7)

It is . . . that . . . 强调 that 之后的成分：

It was that image of calm, control and discipline *that* appealed to millions of voters.

12.9.4　倒装

倒装也是一种强调手段：

例 20.

在自然经济社会里，社会成员的生活保障是以自给自足的小农经济为基础的，体现为家庭自我保障，并未形成规范化、法制化的社会保障制度。市场经济开创了现代社会保障的先河。

译文：

In the natural economy, members of society secured their livelihood through small-scale farming, achieving self-sufficiency and economic security at the family level. *Only with the transition to a market economy did the first modern, law-based social security system emerge.*

例 21.

在你们身上，寄托着中国和人类的希望。

On you is placed the hope of China and mankind.

例 22.

这个人，他 20 年前就认识了。

This guy he has known twenty years.

正常的顺序是 He has known this guy for twenty years. 把一个成分放到不正常的位置，就是强调。与中文表达方式一致。

12.10　小结

以上总结了促进句子之间信息流动的几种手段，概括起来，其实只有一条：把重要信息或者新信息放在句子末尾。这不是一条绝对的规则，无须不惜一切代价做到，但关注到这一点，会使句子之间的逻辑通顺很多。

〔课后练习〕

1. 请任意找一篇英文文章，看每句话是否符合本章所述的信息流动规律。
2. 请从信息流动的角度总结重新审视自己最近的一篇翻译。
3. 请用 Improving Sentence Clarity 在网上搜索并阅读相关材料。

第十三章
简化句子结构克服句法障碍

 扫码预习

请扫码下载本章涉及的例句。先做练习，再看解答，学习效果更佳。

13.1 核心句概念

句子结构复杂是翻译的难点之一。尽管汉语也有长句、复杂句，但因为汉语无法添加后置从句和状语，大大限制了中文的长度和复杂性，因此，汉译英时句子结构造成的困难，远远少于英译汉的情况。但无论是哪种语言，句子结构有多么复杂，都可以通过核心句分析的方法，把复杂的表层结构转换为简单的语法结构，在此基础上翻译，句子结构造成的困难便迎刃而解。奈达和泰伯（Nida & Taber）在《翻译理论与实践》（*The Theory and Practice of Translation*）（1982:39）一书中指出：

> In fact, one of the most important insights coming from "transformational grammar" is the fact that in all languages there are half a dozen to a dozen basic structures out of which all the more elaborate formations are constructed by means of so-called "transformations." In contrast,

back-transformation, then, is the analytic process of reducing the surface structure to its underlying kernels. From the standpoint of the translator, however, what is even more important than the existence of kernels in all languages is the fact that languages agree far more on the level of the kernels than on the level of the more elaborate structures. This means that if one can reduce grammatical structures to the kernel level, they can be transferred more readily and with a minimum of distortion.

笔者译文：

　　事实上，"转换语法"的重要的观点之一是，在所有语言中都有六至十多个基本句子结构（核心句），其他更复杂的结构都是通过所谓的"转换"构建的。相比之下，"逆向转换"则是将复杂的表层结构简化为底层核心句的分析过程。然而，从译者的角度来看，所有语言中都存在核心句固然重要，但更重要的是各种语言在核心句层面比在复杂结构层面上更加一致。这意味着，如果能把复杂结构简化为核心句，复杂结构就更容易翻译，翻译时扭曲也最小。

13.2　核心句种类

奈达等（Nida &Taber, 1982:40）认为，英语中有七种核心句，更复杂的句子都是在这七种核心句的基础上转换生成的：

- John ran quickly.
- John hit Bill.
- John gave Bill a ball.
- John is in the house.
- John is sick.
- John is a boy.
- John is my father.

再复杂的句子，都可以分解为这七种结构。

13.3 核心句分析

核心句分析的实质是找到"谁做了什么"(即"人物+动作")。进行核心句分析时,我们通常需要先找到"动作"。在英语中,动作可能由一个动词表示,也可能由名词化动词(nominalization)表示。找到动作后,再根据逻辑关系、百科知识或常识,找到这个动作的发出者。比如:

> The current *estimate* is of a 50% *reduction* in the *introduction* of new chemical products in the event that *compliance* with the Preliminary Manufacturing Notice becomes a *requirement* under proposed Federal legislation. (Williams, 1995:20)

其中斜体单词是含有动词意味的词,我们需要根据逻辑找到其主语和宾语(如有):

- Who estimates? We.
- Who reduces what? The chemical industry reduces new products by 50%.
- Who introduces what? The chemical industry introduces new products.
- Who complies with what? The chemical industry complies with Preliminary Manufacturing Notice.
- Who requires what? The Congress requires that the chemical industry comply with . . .

根据核心句分析,考虑句子之间的关系,可以把结构复杂的句子重组为结构简单的句子(增加必要的关联词):

> If Congress requires that the chemical industry comply with Preliminary Manufacturing Notice, we estimate the chemical industry will reduce introduction of new products by 50%.

经过核心句分析和句子重组,不但意思更加清楚,翻译起来也会简单得多：

如果国会要求化学工业遵守《生产预告》，估计化学工业推出的新产品会减少 50%。

再举一例：

Our lack of *knowledge* about local conditions precluded *determination* of committee action effectiveness in fund *allocation* to those areas in greatest need of assistance. (Williams, 1995:17)

按表层结构可翻译为：

由于对当地情况缺乏了解，无法确定在向最需要援助地区提供资金时，委员会行动的有效性。

核心句分析：

- We did not know local conditions.
- We could not determine sth.
- (Committee) allocated fund to areas effectively.
- Some areas needed assistance most.

根据各句之间存在的关系，"翻译"为简明易懂的英语：

Because we knew nothing about local conditions, we could not determine how effectively the committee had allocated funds to areas that most needed assistance.

再翻译就比较容易：

由于我们不了解当地情况，无法确定委员会是否有效地向最需援助的地区提供了资金。

通过核心句分析，我们可以通过各种手段找到动词的逻辑主语和宾语。因此，对于我们真正理解原文也很有帮助。在下例中，如果不进行核心句分析，可能不会去深究每个动词的主语宾语是谁：

The *closure* of the branch and the *transfer* of its business and non-unionized employees constituted an unfair labor practice because the purpose of *obtaining* an economic benefit by means of *discouraging* unionization motivated the closure and transfer. (Williams, 1995:24)

核心句分析：

- (The partners) closed the branch.
- (The partners) transferred its businesses and non-unionized workers.
- (The partners) discourage unionization.
- (The partners) obtain economic benefits.
- (This) constitutes an unfair labor practice.

根据分析结果重组句子：

In order to discourage unionization and thereby obtain an economic benefit, the partners closed the branch and transferred its business and non-unionized employees. This constitutes an unfair labor practice.

再来翻译就较为容易：

为阻挠工人加入工会，牟取经济利益，合伙人关闭了这家分公司，并将分公司业务和非工会会员转移出去，从而构成不当劳动行为。

实际上，在进行核心句分析的基础上，对原文理解更加透彻，按表层结构翻译也成为可能：

关闭分支机构、转移业务和非工会员工构成不公平的劳动行为，因为其目的是通过上述关闭和转移行为打压工会，进而获取经济利益。

再看联合国文件中的一句话：

The *call* by Iraq for immediate *repatriation* of prisoners of war when *viewed* against its actions since the *establishment* of cease-fire clearly *manifests* Iraq's *intention* of *deceit* and public relation campaign in order to *divert* the international attention from *pinpointing* Iraq as the culprit for the *continued captivity* of tens of thousands of Iranian and Iraqi POWs whose *hope* of freedom immediately after cease-fire was *shattered* by Iraq's policy of intransigence.（李长栓等，2014:70）

粗略的核心句分析：
- Iraq called that [Iran] should immediately repatriate prisoners of war.
- When this call is viewed against Iraq's actions since cease fire,
- The call manifests that Iraq intends to deceit and hold public relations campaigns.
- Iraq intends to divert international attention from pinpointing Iraq as the culprit for the continued captivity of tens of thousands of Iranian and Iraqi POWs.
- POWs hope they will be freed immediately after cease-fire.
- Iraq's policy of intransigence shattered the hope.

翻译为：
　　伊拉克要求立即遣返战俘，但如果对照两国停火以来伊拉克所采取的行动，就会清楚发现伊拉克企图通过欺骗和公关活动，转移国际视线，避免国际社会将其指责为导致成千上万战俘继续遭受关押的罪魁祸首。这些战俘本希望两国停火后被立即释放，但伊拉克顽固不化的政策使他们的希望破灭。

13.4　核心句分析在汉译英中的应用

英语提倡简明易懂。作为译者，我们不能苛求作者使用简单的语言，但可以以身作则，运用核心句分析，让译文更加清晰易懂。核心句分析的关键是通过逻辑关系、百科知识或常识，找到各个动作的逻辑主语。在此基础上重组原文结构，然后再进行翻译。通过核心句分析可以摆脱原文句法对译文的影响，特别适用于翻译复杂句、长句、主题句。

13.4.1 翻译复杂句

结构复杂的句子，不容易一下子翻译出来，如果对其进行分解，可以变得较为容易。

例1．
　　保险人应保障被保险人由于货物遭受机器设备运输保险内所承保的风险造成工程中断或延误所引起的还本付息及固定成本的赔偿。

这句话结构非常复杂，难以一下子翻译出来。我们可以先对它进行核心句分析：

- （如果）货物遭受机器设备运输保险内所承保的风险

If its goods are exposed to risks covered by machinery and equipment transportation insurance

- （如果）机器设备运输保险内所承保的风险造成工程中断或延误

If risks covered by machinery and equipment transportation insurance cause disruption or delay of the project

- （如果）工程中断或延误引起（被保险人）还本付息及固定成本（损失） If the disruption or delay of the project cause losses related to debt service and fixed costs

- （保险人）应赔偿被保险人还本付息及固定成本损失

The insurer must compensate the insured for its losses related to debt service and fixed costs

通过分析发现原文少了"损失"，翻译时应当补上。在此基础上进行翻译：

译文1：
　　The insurer must compensate the insured for its losses related to debt service and fixed costs if:

a) its goods are exposed to risks covered by machinery and equipment transportation insurance;

b) the risks result in disruption or delay of the project; and

c) the disruption or delay result in losses related to debt service and fixed costs.

译文虽然仍然是一个长句,但结构简化了许多,每一个分句都不长,而且在外观上显得清楚明了。如果你愿意,可以把以上翻译变为结构复杂的句子,像原文一样,但这样做不一定可取:

译文2:

The insurer must compensate the insured for losses related to debt service and fixed costs incurred by the insured when the Project is disrupted or delayed as a result of its goods being exposed to risks covered by the machinery and equipment transportation insurance.

例2.

经人民法院调解结案或判决结案的案件,根据案情责任应由受援方承担的受理费和其他诉讼费用,受援人交纳确有困难的,人民法院应当酌情减、免。

我们可以翻译为"法言法语",但句子较长,不便于理解:

Court fees and other costs of action chargeable as against an assisted person pursuant to the assignation of responsibility in a case settled through mediation or concluded through adjudication by the people's court shall be waived in part or in whole, as appropriate, where payment would clearly create difficulty for the assisted person.

这句话的汉语并不难懂,因为汉语由很多小句组成;而英语只有一个长句,所以不易理解。为简化句子,可以先进行深层结构分析:

- 人民法院通过调解或判决结束了案件;(条件1,大前提)
The people's court closes a case through mediation or judgment.

- 根据案情受援方应当承担受理费用和其他诉讼费用;(条件2)

The assisted person has to pay court fees and other costs of action by the merits of the case.

- 受援人交纳受理费用和其他诉讼费用确实有困难;(条件3)

The assisted person has clear difficulty paying such fees and costs.

- 法院应当酌情减免受理费用和其他诉讼费用。(结果)

The court must exempt or reduce, as appropriate, such fees and costs.

可以依据分析结果进行多种组合:

译文1:

Where the people's court closes a case through mediation or judgment, if the assisted person has to pay court fees and other costs of action by the merits of the case, but has clear difficulty paying such fees and costs, the court must exempt or reduce, as appropriate, such fees and costs.

译文2:

In a case closed through mediation or judgment by the people's court, if the assisted person clearly has difficulty paying court fees and other costs of action chargeable against him or her by the merits of the case, the court must waive such fees and costs in part or in whole, as appropriate.

译文3:

Where the people's court closes a case through mediation or judgment, and if, based on the merits of the case the assisted person has to pay court fees and other costs of action but clearly has difficulty paying such fees and costs, the court must reduce or exempt them as appropriate.

说明:"酌情"也可以省略不译。因为"减"或"免"本身即是酌定行为。

13.4.2 翻译长句

长句翻译时经常需要断句。断句实际就是一种粗略的核心句分析。

例 3.

　　第二，中国现有的外交战略是建立在国际社会基本承认各国的独立自主权为基础的，但以美国为首的西方国家在人权问题尤其是科索沃问题上采取新干涉主义的立场，这不仅是对中国主张和坚持的以不干涉内政为核心的建立国际政治新秩序构成了威胁，而且也对中国按自己主张解决国内问题的原则形成了潜在的威胁。

首先把长句拆分为短句，并按照事务发展的顺序排列：

• 第二，中国现有的外交战略是建立在独立自主权基础上的 China's current strategy is based on the principle of independence of all nations.

• 国际社会基本承认各国的独立自主权 The principle has been generally recognized in the international community.（使用被动语态是为了与上文衔接）

• 中国主张和坚持建立以不干涉内政为核心的国际政治新秩序 China calls for the establishment of a new international political order based on non-intervention in the internal affairs of any country.

• 中国坚持按自己的主张解决国内问题的原则 China asserts that each country should handle its own domestic affairs as it sees fit.

• 但以美国为首的西方国家在人权问题尤其是科索沃问题上采取新干涉主义的立场对中国的主张／原则构成了威胁。But these principles are being challenged by the neo-interventionist approach to human rights issues that has been adopted by Western nations following the lead of the United States, as exemplified in the Kosovo case.（使用被动语态是为了与上文衔接）

适当调整后变为：

　　The second pillar of China's current strategy is the principle of independence of all nations, which has been generally recognized in the international community. China proposes that a new international political order be established based on non-intervention in the internal affairs of any country, and asserts that each country should handle its own domestic affairs as it sees fit. These principles are challenged, however, by the neo-interventionist approach to human rights issues, led by the United States and adopted by Western nations, as exemplified in the Kosovo case.

例 4.

1978 年，卫生部针对当时全国地、市以上输血站只有 30 多个，不少地区没有输血机构，自 1949 年前一直延续下来的卖血现象没有得到根本改造的情况，提出建立公民义务献血制度。

先进行核心句分析（略），然后再翻译：

In 1978, there were only some 30 blood donation centers at the prefecture or higher level. Many places did not have blood donation centers. Selling one's own blood, which existed before 1949, was still common. To deal with the problem, MOH proposed creating a voluntary system of blood donation.

13.4.3 翻译主题句

汉语往往先用介词短语（关于、对于、至于等）提出问题，然后再加以阐述，英语称为话题加讨论（topic-discussion）或主位-述位（rheme-theme）结构。虽然英语中也有类似结构，但用得不如汉语频繁。因此翻译时，多数情况下需要把汉语的主题句变为英语普通的主谓结构。可以通过简单的核心句分析，摆脱汉语结构的束缚。

例 5.

对于已经出现临床症状的感染者，经当地卫生行政部门指定的医学专家确诊为艾滋病病人，而关押场所内又无条件隔离治疗的，可保外就医。

粗略的核心句分析：
- 感染者已出现临床症状 If an infected individual demonstrates clinical symptoms

- 感染者被当地卫生行政部门医学专家确诊为艾滋病病人 the infected individual is confirmed to have AIDS by medical experts designated by local health administrative departments
- 关押场所不能提供隔离治疗 if no treatment in quarantine can be provided within the place of detention
- 感染者可以在交纳保证金的条件下寻求治疗 the infected individual may seek treatment outside the detention center on bail

重组后可以翻译为：

译文1：

An infected individual may seek treatment outside the detention center on bail if he or she demonstrates clinical symptoms and is confirmed to have AIDS by medical experts designated by local health administrative departments, and if no treatment in quarantine can be provided within the place of detention.

译文2：

Treatment may be sought outside the detention center on bail if an individual demonstrates clinical symptoms and is confirmed to have AIDS by medical experts designated by local health administrative departments, and if no treatment in quarantine can be provided within the place of detention.（避免了 he or she）

译文3：

If someone demonstrates clinical symptoms and if medical experts designated by local health administrative departments confirm that such person suffers from AIDS, the person may seek treatment outside the detention center on bail if no treatment in quarantine can be provided at the place of detention.

而不用翻译为：

For an infected individual that demonstrates clinical symptoms, if he or she is confirmed to have AIDS by medical experts designated by local health administrative departments and if no treatment in quarantine can be provided within the place of detention, he or she may seek treatment outside the detention center on bail.

例 6.

对于中国来说，问题更为复杂。

核心句分析：问题对于中国更复杂。译为：

The problem is more complex for China.

例 7.

此外，对于艾滋病病人和艾滋病病毒感染者家属的强制检查问题，也应予以关注。

核心句分析：也应关注对艾滋病病人和艾滋病病毒感染者家属的强制检查问题。译为：

In addition, we should highlight the issue of mandatory testing of family members of AIDS/HIV victims.

例 8.

1987 年，认为：对于艾滋病，开放是传入的重要途径；暗娼和同性恋存在，是传播蔓延的条件；此外，血液制品传播和医源性传播的可能也存在。

In 1987, it was noted that opening-up was a major reason for AIDS entering China; covert prostitution and homosexuality were reasons for the spread of AIDS; and infection through blood products and medical treatment are other possible reasons.

例 9.

对献血者，发给营养补助费和副食品票证，职工献血当日算公休，照发工资；农村社员照记工分。

Blood donors were given nutrition allowances and coupons to obtain meat, poultry and eggs. Donors did not have to work on donation day:

workers were paid as usual and farmers received credits for a day's work.

例 10.

至于世界经济暂时的不景气，中国民航业有着充足的信心去克服。

Our civil aviation industry is confident that we can overcome the global economic slowdown.

不过，少数情况下汉语的主题句仍须译为英语主题句，主要是为了确保重要信息后置。例如：

此后，一些有影响的学者和学术机构的量化研究反映：被调查人自认有婚外（含婚前）性交行为的，在上海刘达临教授 1988 年全国非随机抽样调查中占 6% 左右（20000 多个样本）；在中国社会科学院李银河教授 1991 年北京夫妻抽样调查中占 3.7%（500 个样本）……

Later, quantitative studies by some authoritative scholars and academic institutions showed that *to the question of "whether you had engaged in extra-marital (including pre-marital) sexual relations,"* about 6% of the respondents (more than 20,000 surveyed) answered "yes" in the 1988 national non-random sampling survey conducted by Professor Liu Dalin of Shanghai; 3.7% (500 couples surveyed) answered "yes" in the 1991 sample survey of Beijing's married couples conducted by Professor Li Yinhe of China Academy of Social Sciences (CASS)…

13.5 小结

本章介绍了什么是核心句以及如何进行核心句分析，并在此基础上举例说明如何通过核心句分析克服句法障碍。核心句分析不仅是克服句法障碍的工具，还可以加深译者对原文的理解。建议大家在翻译过程中，时刻关注中英文句子中有动词意味的词，主动思考或查找其逻辑主语或宾语，这样，即使不进行核心句分析的实际操作，也方便理解和翻译。

〔课后练习〕

1. 如何进行核心句分析？任意阅读一篇英文，并对其中的几个长句、复杂句进行核心句分析。

2. 汉译英时，核心句分析主要用于哪些情形？检查自己最近的一篇翻译练习，看是否可以通过核心句分析解决句子结构带来的困难。

3. 阅读李长栓、陈达遵《联合国文件翻译教程》第 3.4 节"表达篇"，学习如何翻译英语的长句和复杂句。

第十四章　多用主动语态

扫码预习

请扫码下载本章涉及的例句。先做练习，再看解答，学习效果更佳。

主动语态直接有力，在写作和翻译中应多用主动语态；被动语态的使用应限于特定情形，比如，无须提及主语或为了将新信息置于句子末尾。本章论述汉译英时主动语态和被动语态的使用情形，指出译文语态的选择不取决于原文，而是要服从译文需要。

14.1　为什么用主动语态

William Strunk 和 E. B. White 在 *The Elements of Style*（2000）中指出：The active voice is usually more direct and vigorous than the passive（主动语态比被动语态更直接、有力）。并举例说明：

I shall always remember my first visit to Boston.

要远远优于

My first visit to Boston will always be remembered by me.

因为后一句不够直接、有力,也不够简洁。如果省略 by me,句子会简洁一些:

My first visit to Boston will always be remembered.

但意思就不确定了:是谁来 remember 呢?作者、作者心里的某个人,还是全世界?

不仅在以动作为主的叙述性文章中如此,科技文献也不宜用太多被动语态。普渡(Purdue)大学在线写作指南指出:

> Active voice is used for most non-scientific writing. Using active voice for the majority of your sentences makes your meaning clear for readers, and keeps the sentences from becoming too complicated or wordy. Even in scientific writing, too much use of passive voice can cloud the meaning of your sentences.[①]

14.2　如何把被动语态变为主动语态

把被动语态变为主动语态时,有些情况下进行简单转换即可,有些情况下还要做更多加工。如把 A 改为 B 就是简单转换:

A: New guidelines *have been laid down by the President* in the hope that the length of documents submitted by DGs will be restricted to 20 pages.

B: *The President has laid down* new guidelines in the hope that DGs will restrict the length of documents to 20 pages.

但下面这句话,就做了更多改动:

A: The foregoing Fee Table *is intended* to assist investors in understanding the costs and expenses that a shareholder in the Fund will bear directly or indirectly.

---

① https://owl.purdue.edu/owl/general_writing/academic_writing/active_and_passive_voice/active_versus_passive_voice.html, accessed 2022-04-29.

B: *This table describes* the fees and expenses you may pay in connection with an investment in our fund.

再如：

A: *An error has occurred* with your account, but *every attempt was made* to remedy it.

B: *We made an error* with your account, but we *have made every attempt* to remedy it.

经过修改，义务主体更加明确，显示合作伙伴敢于承担责任，值得信赖。改为主动也使权利主体更加明确：

A: If there are any questions, I can be reached at the number below.

B: If *you* have any questions, call me at the number below.

14.3 什么时候用被动语态

14.3.1 信息流动的需要

即，使用被动语态是为了后置重要信息。

例1.

After the Summit *the President* was interviewed by a ten-year-old pupil from the European School.

"the President"属于已知信息，前置，自然使用被动。

例2.

After long debate, *the proposal* was endorsed by the long-range planning committee.

"the proposal"属于已知信息，前置。

例 3.

Some astonishing questions about the nature of the universe *have been raised* by scientists exploring the nature of black holes in space. A black hole *is created* by the collapse of a dead star into a point perhaps no larger than a marble. So much matter compressed into so little volume changes the fabric of space around it in profoundly puzzling ways.

两个被动语态都是为了把新信息放在句末。

14.3.2 段落主题要求

使用被动语态，是为了在主语位置放置段落的主题，以表示突出。例如，这两句话：

- The dramatists of the Restoration are little esteemed today.
- Modern readers have little esteem for the dramatists of the Restoration.

如果段落的主题是英国王朝复辟时期的戏曲家，应当用第一句；如果段落的主题是现代读者的口味，应当用第二句。从这两个例子可以看出，选用哪个词作句子的主语，往往决定了用什么语态。

再举一例：

A: By March of 1945, the Allies had essentially defeated the Axis nations; all that remained was a final, but bloody, climax. American, French, and British forces had breached the borders of Germany and were bombing both Germany and Japan around the clock. But they had not so thoroughly devastated either country as to destroy its ability to resist.

B: By March of 1945, the Axis nations had been essentially defeated; all that remained was a final, but bloody, climax. The borders of Germany had been breached, and both Germany and Japan were being bombed around the clock. Neither country, though, had been so devastated that it could not resist.

如果从同盟国的角度写，就用 A；如果从轴心国的角度写，就用 B，尽管里面用了很多被动语态。再比如，如果话题是 insulin，就以 insulin 作为主语，无论用什么语态：

> Insulin was first discovered in 1921 by researchers at the University of Toronto. It is still the only treatment available for diabetes.

14.3.3　动作发出者显而易见、不重要或不知道

使用被动句是因为没有必要提及动作发出者。例如：
- Rules are made to be broken.
- Every year, thousands of people are diagnosed as having cancer.
- All Commission staff are encouraged to write clearly.
- Visitors are not allowed after 9:00 p.m.
- An experimental solar power plant will be built in the Australian desert.

14.3.4　提请读者注意动作的接受者

使用被动句是为了提请读者注意动作的接受者。例如：
- One of the most controversial members of the European Parliament has been interviewed by the press about the proposal.
- Three hundred people are employed by the construction company in Station Road.

这两个例子把重要信息置于句首，需辅之以重读才能理解。

14.3.5　表示委婉

使用被动句是为了避免提及动作发出者，以示尊重。例如：
- This bill has not been paid.
- The procedures were somehow misinterpreted.

英语中不能连续使用两个被动结构。试比较：
- You have not paid this bill.
- You have somehow misinterpreted the procedures.

14.3.6 避免责任

如果说"we made a mistake"，显然责任在自己；如果说"a mistake was made"，则是有意推脱责任。再如：

　　Because the final safety inspection was neither performed nor monitored, the brake plate assembly mechanism was left incorrectly aligned, a fact that was known several months before it was decided to publicly reveal that information.

这个例子使用被动语态，是为了掩盖汽车缺陷的责任，不仅是写作风格问题。

14.4 使用被动语态应注意的问题

14.4.1 避免两个被动语态连用

英语中不能连续使用两个被动结构。试比较：
A: Gold was not allowed to be exported.
B: It was forbidden to export gold (The export of gold was prohibited).
再比较：
A: He has been proved to have been seen entering the building.
B: It has been proved that he was seen to enter the building.

14.4.2 避免使用弱势动词的被动语态

　　尽量减少使用弱势动词（make、carry out 等）的被动语态；改为强势动词的被动语态。试比较：

A: A survey of this region was made in 1900.

B: This region was surveyed in 1900.

再比较：

A: Mobilization of the army was rapidly carried out.

B: The army was rapidly mobilized.

A: Confirmation of these reports cannot be obtained.

B: These reports cannot be confirmed.

14.5　翻译中多用主动语态

汉译英时使用什么语态，取决于英语的需要，与汉语的语态没有直接关系。一般情况下，使用主动；只有在出现上文列举的需要使用被动语态的几种情况时，才使用被动语态。所以，整体上主动语态要比被动语态用得多。

从理论上讲，只要英语需要，汉语的主动语态可以译为英语被动语态，汉语的被动语态（包括隐性的被动句）也可以译为英语的主动语态。实际上，据笔者观察，汉语的主动句可能翻译为英语被动句，而汉语的被动句却极少翻译为英语的主动句。笔者认为，这与汉语中被动句本来就少有关。

14.5.1　汉语无主句不一定译为英语被动句

汉语中的主语经常省略，英语的主语不能省略，因此，遇到汉语的无主句，就需要找到主语。有时主语不明确，只能翻译为被动句。

例 4.
　　依法加强采供血机构建设，健全采供血机构网络；节约血液资源，做到合理、科学用血。建立健全省级血液中心。到 2002 年底前，要对不符合建设标准的地（市）中心血站进行必要的改造。

可以翻译为被动句：

A complete and up-to-standard network of blood collection and distribution will be created in accordance with law to strengthen institutional capacity. Blood resources will be conserved by using blood rationally and scientifically. Provincial blood centers will be established and improved. By the end of 2002, necessary changes will be made to prefectural and city blood centers that do not meet standards.

也可以用主动句，使用主动句使责任人更加明确：

We will strengthen the institutional capacity in accordance with law by creating a comprehensive blood collection and distribution network that meets the required standards. We will conserve blood resources by ensuring that blood is rationally and scientifically used. We will establish and improve provincial blood centers. By end 2002, we will upgrade substandard prefectural and city blood centers.

例 5.

要更加注重满足人民群众需要，更加注重市场和消费心理分析，更加注重引导社会预期，更加注重加强产权和知识产权保护，更加注重发挥企业家才能，更加注重加强教育和提升人力资本素质，更加注重建设生态文明，更加注重科技进步和全面创新。(Xi-II)

We must satisfy the people's demands, improve our analysis of market and consumer psychology, and upgrade our guidance of social expectations. *We* must strengthen the protection of property rights and intellectual property rights, explore the talent of entrepreneurs, and improve education and the quality of our human capital. *We* must promote ecological progress, advances in science and technology and all-round innovation.

这里就增加了主语 we，显示讲话者的责任和担当。

例 6.

加强西部地区商品和要素市场的培育和建设。

译文 1：Efforts will be made to develop markets of consumer goods and factors of production in the western region.

译文 2：We will develop markets of consumer goods and factors of production in the western region.

译文 1 中的 efforts will be made to 不增加实质意义，只是增加了句子的长度，不符合简洁的原则。所以，改为主动句好一些。

14.5.2　汉语被动句很少译为英语主动句

因为汉语的被动句与英语被动句功能相似，因此往往保持被动语态不变。

例 7.

这一点，不仅已经在理论上被证明是正确的，而且在实践上也被证明是正确的。

The truth of these statements has been proven not only in theory, but also by practice. (Xi-II)

因为话语的主题是"这一点"，用它作主语，就必须用被动。

例 8.

第二，世界上最不怕孤立、最不怕封锁、最不怕制裁的就是中国。建国以后，我们处于被孤立、被封锁、被制裁的地位有几十年之久。但归根结底，没有损害我们多少。(Deng-III)

Second, the last country in the world to be afraid of isolation, blockade or sanctions is China. For several decades after the founding of the People's Republic, we *were isolated and subjected to blockades and sanctions*. But in the final analysis, that did not do us much damage.

这段话没有提及谁"孤立、封锁和制裁我们"，可能是为了给某些国家颜面，所以翻译时也不必改变。

例 9.

公费医疗制度建立于 20 世纪 50 年代初，其法律的依据有 1952 年的《国家工作人员公费医疗预防实施办法》及 1965 年卫生部、财政部《关于改进公费医疗管理问题的通知》和 1989 年卫生部、财政部《公费医疗管理办法》。

The free medical care system *was established* in early 1950s, *based on* the 1952 Methods for Implementing Free Medical Care and Prevention for State Employees, Notice on Improving Management of Free Medical Care of MOH and Ministry of Finance in 1965, and Methods for Management of Free Medical Care issued by MOH and Ministry of Finance in 1989.

加点部分也是隐性被动句，译为英语不变，因为这段话的主题就是公费医疗，被谁建立不是重点。

例 10.

我们对解决香港问题所采取的政策，是国务院总理在第六届全国人民代表大会第二次会议的政府工作报告中宣布的，是经大会通过的，是很严肃的事。(Deng-III)

Our policy on the settlement of the Hong Kong problem *was made known* by the Premier of the State Council in his report on the work of the government to the Second Session of the Sixth National People's Congress [held in May 1984], and it *was approved* by the congress. That shows how serious we are about it.

加点部分也是隐性的被动句。汉语使用这一结构，是为了把重要的信息后移，起到强调的作用，与英语一样。如果翻译为主动句，反而打乱了这一信息安排，因此维持被动结构。

例 11.

改革以来中国所有制的结构变化十分明显，其突出特征是：公有制经济总量发展、比重下降但依然保持主体地位，国有经济增幅及比重下降但主导地位依旧，非公有制经济迅速发展，但是个体经济、私营经济、外商投资经济及混合所有制经济各具特色。

原译：

Since the adoption of the reform policy, marked changes have taken place in China's ownership structure. The most noticeable change is that the dominant position of the public sector *has been maintained* while continuous growth *has been achieved* in absolute amount despite its proportional decline in the total of the national economy. The growth rate and proportion of the state-owned sector have gone down but its leading position has remained. The non-public sector has witnessed a rapid growth. But, the development of the individual sector, the private sector, the foreign-funded sector and the sector operating under various forms of mixed ownership has shown different features. (*China's Economic Transformation Over 20 Years*)

改译：

China's ownership structure has changed considerably since the country introduced the reform policy. *The public sector has maintained* its "leading position", growing in size but declining in as a share of the economy. Within the public sector, the state-owned economy remains in a "dominant position", despite slower growth and a declining share. The non-public sector as a whole has grown rapidly, with self-employment, the private sector, the foreign-funded sector and the sector of mixed ownerships all displaying distinct features of development.

改译把原译中的被动语态（斜体部分）变为主动语态，消除了弱势动词的被动语态（continuous *growth has been achieved*），同时，还解决了以下问题：

• 理清了各种所有制的关系（公有和国有的关系，非公有和个体、私营的关系）

• 主题（topic）趋于一致。英语主张一个段落中各个句子的主题一致，原译没有做到。其实，原文的主题非常明确：所有制、公有制经济（包括国有经济)、非公有制经济(包括个体、私营、外商投资、混合经济等),英语中可以用同样的主题作为叙述的线索。

- 减少了抽象名词(adoption, growth, development)
- 消除了表达臃肿之处:"in the total of the national economy"是不言自喻的;"operating under various forms of"是文中隐含的。
- 纠正了自相矛盾之处:"the most noticeable *change*"怎么可能是the dominant position of the public sector *has been maintained* 呢?

14.6 翻译中也可用被动语态

无论原文是否为被动语态,只要英语表达需要,都可以用被动语态。

14.6.1 信息流动需要

如果有必要将信息后置,可以用被动语态。

例 12.

"一个国家,两种制度",我们已经讲了很多次了,全国人民代表大会已经通过了这个政策。有人担心这个政策会不会变,我说不会变。(Deng-III)

We have discussed the policy of "one country, two systems" more than once. *It has been adopted by the National People's Congress.* Some people are worried that it might change. I say it will not.

上句中如果把斜体部分变为 The National People's Congress has adopted it. 句子重心就不对了,因为 it 是已知信息,"全国人民代表大会"是新信息;也可以说用 it 作主语符合这一段的主题。

例 13.

针对以下两种情况:第一,中国 20 年大量立法而无立法程序(中国大量立法开始于 1979 年,而《立法法》制定于 1999 年);第二,党领导下的立法机关的办事机构立法和政府行政机关立法而缺少公众参与，本项目的目的在于：展示听证制度和探寻建立适于中国社会的听证制度以推进立法的公众参与。

Considering the following two situations: first, since 1979, and for 20 years, China enacted many laws without a proper procedure (the Law on Legislation was enacted only in 1999); second, *laws in China are made by clerk's office of the Party-led legislative body and administrative bodies of the government without public participation* — the project tried to demonstrate what the public hearing system was and how to set up a hearing system suitable for China, so as to promote public participation in the legislative process.

如果把斜体部分改为：The clerk's offices of the Party-led legislative body and administrative bodies of the government make laws without public participation. 读主语时无论如何声嘶力竭，都很难把重点读出来。用被动语态，句子中心自然落在句末。

例 14.
　　甲方与乙方的项目规定，乙方所有与政府合作的项目，均应由甲方提供其研究所需的文献资料。

这句话强调的是由甲方（而不是任何第三方）提供文献资料，所以不能译为：

The parties agree that that in all projects between Party B and the government *Party A must provide documentations* that Party B needs for research.

因为这样翻译，意思是"甲方应提供乙方研究所需的文献资料"，句子重心转移到"文献资料"上。阅读时无论如何重读主语 Party A，都很难传达原文意思。

翻译为被动句，问题就迎刃而解：

The parties agree that that in all projects between Party B and the government *documentations that Party B needs for research must be provided by Party A.*

翻译为被动句，句子的重音自然落在 Party A 所在位置——句子末尾。

14.6.2 段落主题要求

如果一段话围绕一个主题进行，则通常用这个主题做主语，无论这是否意味着使用被动句。

例 15.

新发展理念的提出，是对辩证法的运用；新发展理念的实施，离不开辩证法的指导。(Xi-II)

New development concepts have been proposed based on dialectical thinking, which is essential to their implementation.

新发展理念是句子的话题，不得不用被动。

例 16.

人民只有投票的权利而没有广泛参与的权利，人民只有在投票时被唤醒、投票后就进入休眠期，这样的民主是形式主义的。(Xi-II)

If the people merely have the right to vote but no right of extensive participation, in other words, if they *are awakened* only at election time but go into hibernation afterwards, this is token democracy.

段落的主题是"人民"，所以英语一直维持 people 作主语，哪怕这意味着用被动语态。

例 17.

"不要惊慌失措，不要认为马克思主义就消失了，没用了，失败了。哪有这回事！"(Xi-II)

"So don't panic, don't think that Marxism has disappeared, that it's not useful any more and that *it has been defeated*. Nothing of the sort!"

这句话的主题就是 Marxism，坚持用到底，哪怕是用被动语态。

例 18.

  存疑不起诉和批准逮捕是两个独立的诉讼决定，存疑不起诉和批准逮捕尽管都是由检察机关在刑事诉讼过程中作出的决定，但两者无论在适用阶段、适用条件还是目的、功能上都是截然不同的。

  "Dismissal due to weak evidence" and "approval of remand" are two independent decisions. *Although both are made by the prosecuting authority in the litigation process,* they apply in different stages and conditions and serve different functions.

如果把斜体部分变为主动：Although the prosecuting authority makes both decisions in the litigation process…，则句子的主语与段落主题（"存疑不起诉和批准逮捕"）不一致，导致强调重点错位。这实际上也是一个信息流动的问题。

14.6.3　动作发出者显而易见、不重要或不知道

无必要提及动作发出者时，用被动语态。

例 19.

  有人说，如果这一次还是出现反弹、出现回潮，那人民就失望了。(Xi-II)

  It has been said that if corruption makes a return this time the people will lose heart.

谁说的，不重要，也没有必要说出来。

例 20.

  中国特色社会主义是改革开放新时期开创的，也是建立在我们党长期奋斗基础上的。(Xi-I)

  China's socialist system *was pioneered* in the new era of reform and opening up, and it is an outcome of the Party's painstaking efforts.

谁开创的，不言自喻，不用提及，所以用被动。也可以说是因为段落的话题是中国特色社会主义，不得不用被动。

例 21.

过去学的本领只有一点点，今天用一些，明天用一些，渐渐告罄了。

The limited bank of abilities accumulated over the years had been depleted with each passing day, and the coffers were empty.

被谁用完不言自喻，译文用被动。

例 22.

我多次强调，要把权力关进制度的笼子里，一个重要手段就是发挥舆论监督包括互联网监督作用。(Xi-II)

I have repeatedly emphasized that power needs to *be confined* in the cage of regulations. An important means of doing this will be to exert the role of public scrutiny, including scrutiny on the internet.

谁来管，这里不需要强调。

14.6.4　提请读者注意动作的接受者

如要提请注意动作发出者，可将其置于句首，用被动语态。这时需要重读主语。

例 23.

政府每年还拨专款用于维修重点寺院教堂，仅 1999 年中央政府就拨款 760 万元人民币用于重修乌鲁木齐的洋行大寺、伊宁拜图拉清真寺、和田加麦大寺。

Every year, the government allocates specialized funds for the maintenance and repair of the key mosques, monasteries and churches. In 1999 alone, *7.6 million yuan was allocated* by the central government for the reconstruction of the Yanghang Mosque in Urumqi, the Baytulla Mosque in Yining and the Jamae Mosque in Hotan.(《新疆的历史与发展》白皮书)

这个例子中，原文用主动语态，译文用了语态被动，可以认为是为了提请人们注意动作的对象，即 "760 万元人民币"，强调数量之大。

例 24.

截至 2001 年底，福建共减少行政审批事项 606 项，占审批事项的 40.4%。

By the end of 2001, *606 items* had been eliminated — more than 40% of the total.

原文用主动，译文用被动，强调数量之大。

14.6.5　表示委婉

作者不说明动作发出者可能有其他考虑，属于故意含糊，译者只能用被动或其他含糊的方式进行翻译。

例 25.

一段时间以来，一些材料反映，一些地方为了做到精准识贫、精准扶贫，搞了一大堆表格要下面填写。(Xi-II)

For some time now, it has been reported that in order to identify the poor and implement targeted measures for poverty alleviation, some areas have issued reams of forms.

"一些材料反映"本来就是为了避免提及具体的人，正好用英语被动句。

要深化生态文明体制改革，尽快把生态文明制度的"四梁八柱"建立起来，把生态文明建设纳入制度化、法治化轨道。(Xi-II)

Reform for ecological progress *should be driven* to a new level, and a pertinent institutional framework should *be set up* as soon as possible, providing functional mechanisms buttressed by the rule of law.

原文是无主句，译文用被动语态。可以理解为领导核心对下级的的委婉要求。改为主动句，用 we 作主语，也未尝不可。

14.6.6　避免责任

如果翻译的文件涉及责任认定，原文如果含糊其辞，译文应当与原文保持一致。

14.7　小结

主动语态直接有力，在写作和翻译中应当多用，而被动语态的使用应限于特定情形。实际上，一个句子单独存在时，用什么结构没有大的妨碍，但把一个句子放在段落中时，它的结构就不自由了。应当根据信息流动的规律及前文提到的各种考虑，选择适当的语态或句式，正确传达作者的信息。

大多数情况下，主动和被动语态的选择不构成严重的翻译问题，因为汉语习惯使用主动语态，被动语态较少，如果按照汉语的语态翻译为英语，译文的主动语态即占大多数。

〔课后练习〕

1. 哪些情况下使用被动语态？
2. 不同的文体，主动语态和被动语态的使用频率是否一样？请观察科技论文和一般新闻报道是否有区别。
3. 请从语态的角度，审查自己最近的一篇译文，看是否有可修改之处。
4. 请在网上搜索 *The Elements of Style*，阅读有关主动语态的相关章节。

第十五章 丰富表达手段

 扫码预习

请扫码下载本章涉及的例句。先做练习，再看解答，学习效果更佳。

简明英语要求我们使用简洁明了的英语，但并不是要求我们全部使用简单句。简明英语要求我们长短句搭配使用，也要求我们使用丰富的表达手段。本章介绍如何把长句变短、把短句变长，以及如何使用平行结构。

15.1 简明英语提倡长短句搭配使用

简明语言提倡长短句搭配使用，尤其是信息型文本。以下建议就是长短句结合的典范：

> Informative writing should have an average sentence length of 15 to 20 words. This is short enough to be clear and long enough to make the text flow well. (The average sentence length of the main body of this guide is 15 words.)
>
> Be punchy. Mix short sentences (like the last one) with longer ones (like this), aiming for one main point, plus perhaps one other related point,

in each sentence.

We tend not to use short sentences enough. We need to vary the length in order to make our writing livelier.

For example, you have the short sentence "This is an important document and you should read it carefully" in the middle of longer sentences. This is fine. But how much sharper it would be as two sentences:

"This is an important document. You should read it carefully."

Remember: if you have two different things to say that are fairly short, don't be frightened to use two sentences.

— *How to Write Well*

Several sentences of the same length can make for bland writing. To enliven paragraphs, write sentences of different lengths. This will also allow for effective emphasis.

— *Strategies for Variation*

15.2　英语句子总体变短的原因

如果我们看十八、十九世纪的作品,动辄遇到一句话几十个甚至上百个词,插入语、从句叠床架屋,层层套叠,要想理清头绪非常困难,即使母语读者,也不是一目了然。比如,这是 19 世纪英国作家 John Ruskin 在 *The Stones of Venice* 中的一句话:

It is as if the soul of man, itself severed from the root of its health, and about to fall into corruption, lost the perception of life in all things around it; and could no more distinguish the wave of the strong branches, full of muscular strength and sanguine circulation, from the lax bending of a broken cord, nor the sinuousness of the edge of the leaf, crushed into deep folds by the expansion of its living growth, from the wrinkled contraction of its decay. (85 words)

如果今天的编辑看到这样一句话，可能会这样修改[①]：

> It is as if the soul of man, itself severed from the root of its health and about to fall into corruption, lost the perception of life in all things around it. Thus, while the wave of strong branches is full of muscular strength and sanguine circulation, the soul could not distinguish it from the lax bending of a broken cord. It would be equally clueless about the difference between the sinuousness of the edge of the leaf when crushed into deep folds by the expansion of its living growth from when it is wrinkled by the contraction of its decay.

即使在断为三句话之后，每句仍有三四十个单词，仍然属于今天的长句范畴。

英语句子之所以越来越短，是因为随着现代生活节奏加快，人们希望用更短的时间获得信息，而短句理解起来显然更省时间。即使以长句著称的法律领域，也非常注重使用简明英语。我们作为译者，应当顺应这一潮流。当然，英语作为我们的外语，即使希望搭建复杂的结构，也不一定做得到。况且越复杂越容易出错，还不如老老实实用简单的英语把意思表达清楚。

15.3　译者仍要学会理解长句

然而，我们无法要求其他作者使用简明英语，因此，在阅读和翻译实践中仍然会遇到非常复杂的句子，尤其是非英语国家的英文文件，特别是学术和法律文本。下面这段话来自欧洲法院的一份判决：

> Accordingly... Article 82 EC is to be interpreted as meaning that a copyright management organisation with a dominant position on a

---

[①] https://proofreadingpal.com/proofreading-pulse/writing-guides/run-on-sentence-or-long-sentence/, accessed September 4, 2021.

substantial part of the common market does not abuse that position where, with respect to remuneration paid for the television broadcast of musical works protected by copyright, it applies to commercial television channels a remuneration model according to which the amount of the royalties corresponds partly to the revenue of those channels, provided that that part is proportionate overall to the quantity of musical works protected by copyright actually broadcast or likely to be broadcast, unless another method enables the use of those works and the audience to be identified more precisely without however resulting in a disproportionate increase in the costs incurred for the management of contracts and the supervision of the use of those works.

这是笔者的译文：

  因此……《欧共体条约》第 82 条应被解释为：在共同市场的较大区域具有支配地位的版权管理组织如满足以下条件，则不构成滥用支配地位——在针对电视广播使用受版权保护的音乐作品取酬时，版权管理组织对商业电视频道采用的收费模式确保版税数额与商业频道的收入部分地对应，同时该部分又与实际播出或可能播出的受版权保护音乐作品的数量大体成正比，除非另一种方法能够更准确地确定作品的使用情况和观众，但又不会导致管理合同和监督作品使用所产生的费用过多增加。

这样的句子若不断开，完全没有办法翻译。本书第十三章介绍了如何通过核心句分析，把长句变为短句。这里就请大家通过核心句通过分析，将该句变为若干便于翻译的短句。需要强调，核心句分析建立在理解原文的基础上。如果不理解原文，即使能够断为若干短句，也无法重组为有逻辑联系的系列短句。因此，断句之前，必须进行语法分析，找到句子主干和各种修饰关系。而做到这一点，主要还得依靠专业知识。真可谓学无止境！

把长句翻译为若干短句，在中国翻译界是一种常识。无论翻译什么文本，如果不允许断句，翻译就无法进行。然而，欧盟要求在翻译法律条文时不能断句。如果必须断句，则在本应该用句号的地方使用分号，这样，从形式上来看，译文仍然是一句话。以下截图是欧盟委员会为译员编写的 Clear English Tips for Translators 当中的相关建议和例证（见图 15.1）：

> **But don't change sentence boundaries in legislation.**
> As a work-around, split with references and semicolons.
>
> All documents must be sent, once evidence has been taken, to the prosecutor, *who,* within a period of one month, shall submit them to the court, *which,* within a period of one month, shall either reject the case or issue a court order, *even for* related offences, regardless of how serious they are, *when it* considers that there is no indication of one of the crimes in Article 1.
>
> Once evidence has been taken, all documents must be sent to the prosecutor; *the prosecutor* has one month to submit the documents to the court; *the court* then has one month either to reject the case or to issue a court order; *this also applies to* related offences, regardless of how serious they are; *this provision does not apply if the court* considers that the case involves one of the crimes in Article 1.

图 15.1　欧盟翻译指南截图

15.4　如何化繁为简

汉语中句子的概念比较模糊，句号和逗号的使用有较大的随意性。如果以句号作为区分的标志，汉语句子可能很长；如果以逗号作为区分的标志，则有些逗号之间具备句子的完整成分，而有些逗号之间只是一个短语。为了方便，我们以句号作为划分句子的标准；以此为标准，则汉语的长句很多。其中有两类值得注意，一是流水句，二是结构复杂的句子，翻译时要避免翻译为英语的流水句（一逗到底），并视情况决定维持中文复杂句结构，还是进行简化。

15.4.1　流水句

汉语流水句的特点是一个分句接一个分句，很多地方可断可连，能省略的成分就省略。翻译流水句要注意断句和分清层次。

15.4.1.1　断句

一些句子必须断开才能够翻译。下例中的编号，即为断开后的英文句子单位。

例1.

　　(1) 在市场经济体制下，收入分配机制与竞争机制相联系，必然造成社会成员之间在收入分配方面的不均等，(2) 甚至收入相差十分悬殊，强者成为富翁，弱者陷于困境。(3) 为了解决这一社会问题，就需要运用政府的力量对社会经济生活进行干预，(4) 通过提供社会保障措施，通过对社会成员的收入进行必要的再分配调节方式，将高收入者的一部分收入适当转移给另一部分缺少收入的人，(5) 从而在一定程度上缩小社会成员之间的贫富差距，弥补市场经济的缺陷，缓和社会矛盾，以促进社会公平目标的实现。

以句号为界，这段话算作两句，但英文分为五句：

In a market economy, where income distribution is a function of competition, wealth is inevitably distributed unequally. Sometimes the income gap widens because the strong gets richer and the weak poorer. This is a problem that can be addressed only with government intervention. Social security is a form of intervention that increases social equity by redistributing wealth, for part of the income of the rich is rechannelled to the lower income groups. By narrowing the income gap and mitigating the flaws of the market economy in some extent, social security enhances social cohesion and equity.

我们以英语句子为单位，来分析一下翻译方法和思路。

(1) "在市场经济体制下，收入分配机制与竞争机制相联系，必然造成社会成员之间在收入分配方面的不均等"：翻译时将中间部分作为从句处理，这样英语就有了意思层次之分——次要的意思用从句表达，主要意思用主句表达。

(2) "甚至收入相差十分悬殊，强者成为富翁，弱者陷于困境"：从意思上判断，后两个分句是第一个分句的原因，在译文中以 because 显化，这样译文又分出了层次。

(3) "为了解决这一社会问题，就需要运用政府的力量对社会经济生活进行干预"：在此断开就可以形成一个意思完整的句子，因此断开。

（4）"通过提供社会保障措施，通过对社会成员的收入进行必要的再分配调节方式，将高收入者的一部分收入适当转移给另一部分缺少收入的人"：社会保障旨在通过再分配——劫富济贫——促进社会公平。译文没有受原文约束，而是重新表达了这个意思，层次很清楚。

（5）"从而在一定程度上缩小社会成员之间的贫富差距，弥补市场经济的缺陷，缓和社会矛盾，以促进社会公平目标的实现"：中文几个并列分句，译文用 by 短语，译出了意思层次。

例 2.

一九七八年我们党的十一届三中全会才制定了一系列新的正确的路线、方针和政策，根本内容就是建设具有中国特色的社会主义。

It was not until 1978 that the Eleventh CPC Central Committee issued new and correct guidelines, strategies and policies at its third plenary session. These can be summed up as decision to develop Chinese socialism.

这个句子并不长，但如果翻译为从句，如：

It was not until 1978 that the Eleventh CPC Central Committee issued new and correct guidelines, strategies and policies at its third plenary session, which can be summed up as the decision to develop Chinese socialism.

which 的指代不清楚。分为两句，these 很清楚指代 guidelines, strategies and policies。

例 3.

中国科学技术落后，困难比较多，特别是人口太多，现在就有十亿五千万，增加人民的收入很不容易，短期内要摆脱贫困落后状态很不容易。（Deng-III）

China lags behind in science and technology. We have quite a few problems to solve, especially the problem of our huge population, which already stands at 1.05 billion. This makes it very difficult for us to raise the people's income and to eliminate poverty and backwardness in a short time.

原来的一句断为英语三个句子。

例4.

目前，居民储蓄存款增加较多，银行资金比较充裕，利率水平较低，市场价格稳定，国债余额占国内生产总值的比重仍在安全线以内，发行长期建设国债还有一定的空间，不会有大的风险。（国务院总理朱镕基2002年3月5日在第九届全国人民代表大会第五次会议上的政府工作报告）

Savings deposits have increased considerably; banks have adequate capital; interest rates are low; market prices are stable; and the ratio of national debts to GDP is healthy. The market can absorb more long-term infrastructure bonds without incurring much risk.

上例中，原文是一个长句，包含许多分句，英译中几乎把每个分句都译为一个独立的英语短句。

例5.

如果在抓法治建设上喊口号、练虚功、摆花架，只是叶公好龙，并不真抓实干，短时间内可能看不出什么大的危害，一旦问题到了积重难返的地步，后果就是灾难性的。(Xi-II)

In a short term, it may not appear harmful to simply shout out slogans, put on appearances, and feign support instead of taking real action. But the moment problems grow beyond our ability to resolve, the consequences of our inaction will be catastrophic.

原文一句话，译为改为两句。原文隐含的转折，译文明确用 but 表达。

例6.

有些失误，我也有责任，因为我不是下级干部，而是领导干部，从一九五六年起我就当总书记。(Deng-III)

There were some mistakes for which I am also to blame, because I was not a junior cadre but a leading cadre — beginning in 1956, I was General Secretary of the CPC Central Committee.

原文一句话，译文变为两句，用破折号引隔开。原文隐藏的补充说明关系，通过破折号显化。

15.4.1.2 分清层次

汉语的流水句在形式上看是并列的，但意思可能存在包含、因果、递进等关系，翻译时要体现出来。前面几个例子已经说明这个问题，这里再举几例。

例 7.

强化企业内部改革，选择少量中央管理的大型企业和境外上市公司，进行收入分配制度改革试点，建立对企业经营者有效的激励和约束机制。（政府工作报告）

发布译文：

We should deepen the reform in businesses, initiate pilot reform of the income distribution system in selected large corporations managed by the central authorities and in foreign-listed companies, and develop effective incentive and control mechanisms for business managers.

这里把汉语的并列也译为英语的并列，笔者认为可以完善。从上下文的意义来看，"选择少量中央管理的大型企业和境外上市公司，进行收入分配制度改革试点"是"强化企业内部改革"的内容；而"建立对企业经营者有效的激励和约束机制"是"收入分配制度改革"的目的。所以可以改为：

We will deepen internal reform of SOEs. We will initiate pilot reform of the income distribution system in selected large enterprises managed by the central authorities and in companies listed on overseas stock markets, in order to develop incentives and disincentives for business managers.

例 8.

这五年,首先是农村改革带来许多新的变化,农作物大幅度增产,农民收入大幅度增加,乡镇企业异军突起。(Deng-III)

During those five years rural reform brought about many changes: grain output increased substantially, as did the peasants' income, and rural enterprises emerged as a new force.

译文把原文的逗号变为冒号,显示了前后逻辑关系。

例 9.

农村改革取得了明显的成效,农村经济迅速活跃起来,农产品生产快速增长,农民收入显著增加,使中国能够以占世界7%的耕地养活世界22%的人口,为整个改革创造了最重要的物质基础和市场环境,对城市改革产生了很好的示范效应。

原译:

As a result, noticeable progress had been achieved in rural reform, the rural economy had quickly turned vigorous, a rapid growth had been witnessed in the output of farm products and the farmers' incomes had increased greatly. This laid the most important material foundation and created the most favorable environment for the overall reform, *and enabled China to feed 22 percent of the total population of the world with only 7 percent of the arable land.* The rural reform had produced a satisfactory demonstrative impact for the reform in the urban areas.

修改 1:

The success of rural reform was obvious: the rural economy was boosted, agricultural production increased quickly, and the farmers' incomes grew substantially, enabling China to feed 22 percent of the world's population with 7 percent of the world's arable land. Moreover, the rural reform created a material foundation and market environment for the reform of the whole economy and served as a model for reform in the urban areas.

斜线部分维持了中文的并列关系,修改后的译文体现了原文前后的包含关系：农村改革取得的成效包括以下几点……

修改 2：

Success of rural reform was reflected in the booming rural economy, the rapid growth of agricultural production, and a substantial increase in farmers income, an achievement that enabled China to feed 22 percent of the world's population with 7 percent of the world's arable land. Moreover, the rural reform provided the material foundation and market environment to reform the whole economy and served as the model of reform in urban areas.

尽管简明英语要求尽量使用动词句，但并不排除使用名词句，因为名词结构会更加紧凑，修改 2 就使用了更多名词，结构也更为紧凑。

有时并列成分很多，译者无法确信各分句之间的逻辑关系，同时条件也不允许咨询或调查，这时往往沿用原文结构，以规避错误解读的风险：

例 10.

坚持实施扩大国内需求的方针，继续深化改革，扩大开放，加快结构调整，整顿和规范市场经济秩序，提高经济增长质量和效益，促进国民经济持续快速健康发展和社会全面进步。（政府工作报告）

We will continue to expand domestic, deepen reform, open our country, restructure our economy, and rectify the market order to improve the quality of growth and to promote sustainable, rapid and robust economic development and social progress.

本例加点部分难以看出层次，译文同样维持并列关系。注意不能矫枉过正，即在没有偏正关系的分句之间通过翻译建立偏正关系。如：

亚单位疫苗/基因重组蛋白疫苗：安全性好，副作用小，成分明确，稳定性好，但制备工艺复杂，技术难度较大，且往往免疫原性较弱，需要添加佐剂提高免疫原性。

原译：

Subunit vaccines/recombinant protein vaccines: This kind of vaccines are safer. With few side-effects and ingredients that are clearly settled, they are more stable. But the production of them is complex and the technology is hard to control. And adjuvants are usually needed so as to strengthen their immunogenicity.

译文第二句在句首使用了 with 短语，但该短语表示原因。比如：

- *With* exams approaching, it's a good idea to review your class notes.
- *With* its widespread reach and viral potential, it allows your business to connect with prospects in ways that no other marketing medium can.

然而，with few side-effects（副作用小）和 more stable（稳定性好）并无因果关系。经调查，是因为成分明确，所以安全性好（＝副作用小）、稳定性好。因此改为：

Subunit vaccines/recombinant vaccines: *these vaccines contain specific components of a pathogen and are generally safer, more stable, and causes fewer side effects.* However, their preparation and production often involve sophisticated technologies and complicated processes. Subunit vaccines are usually poorly immunogenic and necessitates the use of adjuvants.

15.4.2 复杂句

汉语中也有一些结构复杂的嵌套句子，翻译时应当分解为短句（可以运用核心句分析的方法）。

例 11.

针对中国发展中党治与法治的内在矛盾——中国在 1924 年由国民党提出"以党建国""以党治国"，20 世纪 50—70 年代，共产党把"以党治国"发展到极至，后来共产党主动推进开放和改革，在 1997 年提出"依法治国"和建设"社会主义法治国家"，而在走向开放之中法治的准则和中国在 20 世纪 50—70 年代形成的已成定式的行为和思维模式之间实际存在着一种内在的紧张——本项目将集合地方党和政府领导人、人大领导人，及法院院长、法官和律师，以及第三部门负责人和基层自治组织负责人，以培训的形式，共同探寻在地方推行法治的路径。（一份学术报告）

To resolve the inherent conflict between the rule of the Party and the rule of law in China's development, the project will offer training to leaders of local Party and government organizations, leaders of the legislature, presidents of courts, judges, lawyers, and NGO officers and officials of grassroots self-governing organizations to promote rule of law at the local level.

In 1924, the Nationalist Party (KMT) proposed the concepts of "build the country through the Party" and "governing the country through the Party". From the 1950s to 1970s, the Communist Party of China (CPC) took the latter to the extreme. Later, the CPC initiated the reform and opening-up policy. In 1997, it proposed to "govern the country by law" and build "a socialist country governed by law". But as the country progressively opens up, there is always a tension between the rule of law and the set behaviors and mindsets formed during the 1950s-70s.

这段汉语文字从结构上看，只有一句话，翻译为英语显然要断开。另外，在表达的先后顺序上，译者也作了调整：开门见山提出重点，另起一段交代背景。

总的来说，汉译英断句操作比较简单，因为汉语没有太复杂的结构。英译汉断句，则需要经过仔细分析，需要花费大量时间。对于初学翻译的人来说，需要培养断句的意识。遇到结构复杂的句子，可以通过核心句分析的方式，化繁为简。

15.5　如何化简为繁

句子简短当然便于读者理解，但通篇都是短句也会使读者感到单调乏

味,所以应当在简明的基础上适当追求一些句式的变化,追求一定程度的"雅"。比如,下面一段话全部都是简单句,十分单调:

> The moon is now drifting away from the earth. It moves away at the rate of about one inch a year. This movement is lengthening our days. They increase a thousandth of a second every century. Forty-seven of our present days will someday make up a month. We might eventually lose the moon altogether. Such great planetary movement rightly concerns astronomers, but it need not worry us. It will take 50 million years.

可以通过合并一些句子,做到长短句结合:

> The moon is now drifting away from the earth <u>about one inch a year</u>. <u>At a thousandth of a second every century</u>, this movement is lengthening our days. Forty-seven of our present days will someday make up a month, <u>if we don't eventually lose the moon altogether</u>. Such great planetary movement rightly concerns astronomers, but it need not worry us. It will take 50 million years.

在修改中,下划线部分原来是单句,现在变成了长句中的一个成分。通过主句表达主要意思,从句、短语或单词表达次要意思,句子的主要意思也更加清楚。把单句接单句变为复合句或复杂句的手段有两种——并列和从属结构,下面分别介绍。

15.5.1 并列结构

使用并列连词(for、and、nor、but、or、yet、so)和过渡词或连接副词(however、therefore、for example、in fact)连接起来的句子,叫作并列结构[1]。前者如(见图 15.2):

---

[1] http://www.laspositascollege.edu/raw/lpcraw-coordinationandsubordination.php, accessed September 5, 2021.

> **Coordinators**
>
> Here are some examples of coordinators. You may find it helpful to remember the acronym **FANBOYS**.
>
> - **For** (effect/cause): Jasmine is afraid of dogs, **for** she was bitten by a dog when she was young.
> - **And** (addition): Isaiah lives in Livermore, **and** his parents live nearby in Pleasanton.
> - **Nor** (addition of negatives): Mary doesn't want to go to college, **nor** does she want to find a job.
> - **But** (contrast): Abdul likes to read, **but** he prefers to watch television.
> - **Or** (alternative): Jose thinks he wants to study math, **or** he might be interested in fire fighting.
> - **Yet** (contrast): Justin really likes to run in the morning, **yet** he hates getting up early.
> - **So** (cause/effect): Maria loves dogs, **so** she went to the animal shelter to adopt one.

图 15.2　英语并列结构举例（一）

后者如（见图 15.3）：

> **Transition Words**
>
> You can also use transition words (also known as conjunctive adverbs) to coordinate sentences, although they require different punctuation. If you are joining two sentences with a conjunctive adverb, you need to have a semi-colon before the word and a comma after it.
>
> - however (contrast): Cycling class is a tough workout; **however**, I still attend three times a week.
> - therefore (cause/effect): Erin takes regular pilates classes; **therefore**, she is very strong.
> - for example (general to specific): There are many fun exercises; for example, I take kickboxing and weight lifting.

图 15.3　英语并列结构举例（二）

请大家看英文解释，注意连接副词之前用分号。这两种搭建并列结构的方法在翻译中都很常见。例如：

例 12.

中国不觊觎他国权益，不嫉妒他国发展，但决不放弃我们的正当权益。（Xi-II）

China does not covet other countries' rights and interests or become jealous of their achievements, *nor* do we give up our legitimate rights and interests.

此句以 nor 连接。

例 13.

法律是成文的道德，道德是内心的法律。法律和道德都具有规范社会行为、调节社会关系、维护社会秩序的作用，在国家治理中都有其地位和功能。（Xi-II）

Law is a set of virtues in writing; virtue represents the law in one's inner world. Both function to regulate people's conduct and social relations and maintain social order, *yet* each plays a different role in national governance.

第二句两部分用 yet 连接。

例 14.
党和政府主办的媒体是党和政府的宣传阵地，必须姓党。

Media run by the Party and the government are responsible for Party and government publicity; they must *therefore* be led by the Party.

本句两部分以分号分开。

例 15.
目标远未完成，我们仍须努力。

Yet these goals are far from being achieved; *therefore* we must continue our endeavors.

此句以 therefore 连接。注意：therefore 前面也可以用句号，这样就是另起一句，不再与上句构成并列结构。

15.5.2 从属结构

从属结构是用从属连词连接起来的句子，从句可以表示让步、因果、时间或条件。比如（见图 15.4）[①]：

> **Subordinators/Subordinating Conjunctions**
> To subordinate one sentence to another, use a connecting word called a "subordinator." The following words are examples of subordinators.
>
> ■ although (contrast): Michelle loves coffee although it upsets her stomach.
> ■ because (cause/effect): Marty drinks tea because it is filled with healthy antioxidants.
> ■ when (time): When Kisha gets up in the morning, she drinks a glass of water with lemon.
> ■ if (condition): If Angelo doesn't have his morning coffee, he feels grumpy all day.

图 15.4　英语从属结构举例

---

① 出处同上。

从属结构在翻译中也很常见。即使原文没有用词语表达从属关系，如果存在这种关系，英文也需要明确表达出来。

例 16.

我们改革开放的成功，不是靠本本，而是靠实践，靠实事求是。（Xi-II）

The reform and the open policy have been successful not because we relied on books, but *because* we relied on practice and sought truth from facts.

原文没有"因为"，译文加上了 because。

例 17.

看准了的，就大胆地试，大胆地闯，走不出一条新路，就干不出新的事业。

If we don't have the pioneering spirit, *if* we're afraid to take risks, *if* we have no energy and drive, we cannot break a new path, a good path, or accomplish anything new.

原文没有用"如果"，但译文用了三个 if。

例 18.

我们提的供给侧改革，完整地说是"供给侧结构性改革"，我在中央经济工作会议上就是这样说的。"结构性"3个字十分重要，简称"供给侧改革"也可以，但不能忘了"结构性"3个字。（Xi-II）

What we have raised is "supply-side structural reform". As I mentioned at the 2015 Central Conference on Economic Work, the word "structural" is critical to the full expression, *although* we can call it "supply-side reform" for short.

本句话原文用了"但"，译文改用 although，但使用位置变了。

例 19.

不发展生产力，不提高人民的生活水平，不能说是符合社会主义要求的。

Unless you are developing the productive forces and raising people's living standards, you cannot say that you are building socialism.

原文没有"除非",译文根据意思表达,增加 unless。

常见的从属连词有这些(见图 15.5):

COMMON SUBORDINATORS	
Subordinator	Relationship/Meaning
although, even though, though, whereas, while	contrast
since, because	cause/effect
if, unless	condition
after, as soon as, before, whenever, when, until	time

图 15.5　英语常见从属连词

从中我们可以看到,表示原因的从属连词有 since、because,而并列连词中,也有表示原因的两个词:for、therefore。用从属连词结构紧凑,用并列连词结构松散。如果行文比较拖沓,可以考虑使用从属连词。特别提醒:从属连词不能单独构成句子。如,只能说:We didn't enjoy the day because the weather was so awful. 不能说:We didn't enjoy the day. Because the weather was so awful.

15.6　三种修饰方法

除了上述并列结构、从属结构可以加长句子之外,还可以学习使用以下三种修饰方式,让句子变得更为优雅:重复式修饰语(resumptive modifiers)、总结式修饰语(summative modifiers)和自由修饰语(free modifiers)。

15.6.1　重复式修饰语

重复式修饰就是重复句子中的某个词,然后给该词加上一个修饰语,从而拓展句子长度。请看英语中的例子:

例 20.

A: For several years, the Columbia Broadcasting System created and developed situation comedies that were the best that American TV had to offer, *such as* "The Mary Tyler Moore Show" and "All in the Family" that sparkled with wit and invention.

B: For several years, the Columbia Broadcasting System created and developed situation comedies that were the best American TV had to offer, *comedies* such as "The Mary Tyler Moore Show" and "All in the Family," *comedies* that sparkled with wit and invention.

A 句的 comedies 与修饰语 such as 相距较远，句子显得拖沓，B 句重复两次 comedies，马上提高了句子的档次。

例 21.

Statement by Donald J. Trump, 45th President of the United States of America

Joe Biden gets it wrong every time on foreign policy, and many other issues. Everyone knew he couldn't handle the pressure. Even Obama's Secretary of Defense, Robert Gates, said as much. He ran out of Afghanistan instead of following the plan our Administration left for him — a plan that protected our people and our property, and ensured the Taliban would never dream of taking our Embassy or providing a base for new attacks against America. The withdrawal would be guided by facts on the ground.

本句中重复了 plan。

例 22.

It was American writers who first used a vernacular that was both *true* and *lyrical*, *true* to the rhythms of the working man's speech, *lyrical* in its celebration of the land.

前两句被重复的词是名词，这句被重复的词是形容词。

例 23.

Humans have been defined by some as the only animal that can *laugh at grief, laugh* at the pain and tragedy that define their fate.

这句话被重复的词是动词。在翻译中可以尝试使用重复式修饰：

例 24.

找到医治艾滋病的方法，要靠生物学家和医学家的努力，但解决今天肆虐全球的、作为一种社会病症的艾滋病问题，却不是仅靠生物学家和医学家所能做到的。

To find a cure for AIDS, we need biologists and medical experts; but to cure AIDS as a social problem, *a problem* that has run wild globally, biologists and medical experts alone are not enough.

例 25.

本报告的撰写前提是：我们相信在一个人们能够自主选择，且对自己选择负责任和对别人尊重与同情的社会中，在一个公正的社会中，人类是能够战胜艾滋病的。

When I wrote this report, I assumed that human beings are able to defeat AIDS in *a society* where individuals enjoy freedom of choice, are held accountable for their choice, and show respect and sympathy for others — *a society* where fairness prevails.

15.6.2　总结式修饰语

总结式修饰就是用一个词或短语总结本句中的某个概念，然后在此基础上补充信息，拓展句子长度。请看英语中的应用：

例 26.

A: In the last five years, European population growth *has dropped to almost zero, which* in years to come will have profound social implications.

B: In the last five years, European population growth has dropped to almost zero, *a demographic event* that in years to come will have profound social implications.

A 句中 which 是指 has dropped to almost zero 这一事实，但需要较多思考才能做出判断。B 句将这一事实概括为 a demographic event，在此基础上与从句拓展，意思就更加清楚。

例 27.

A: *Scientists have finally unraveled the mysteries of the human gene,* which may lead to the control of such dread diseases as cancer and birth defects.

B: Scientists have finally unraveled the mysteries of the human gene, *a discovery* that may lead to the control of such dread diseases as cancer and birth defects.

A 句中 which 是指整个主句，但有可能被理解为修饰 gene 或 mysteries；B 句将主句概括为 a discovery，再作补充拓展，意思就十分清楚。

例 28.

In 2018, *Trump enacted a law that requires the U.S. Department of State to punish Chinese officials who bar Americans from traveling freely to Tibet, a move* that China's Foreign Ministry condemned as "grossly interfering in China's domestic affairs."

在本句中，a move 也是总结了整个主句的意思。请看总结式修饰语在翻译中的应用：

例 29.

在一年多的时间内，公司推行了 BEE，即于现有资源下提升表现而达致最佳水平计划，令产量由 5 千吨飙升至 7 千吨，而公司内部也产生了一连串的变化。

For more than a year, the company has implemented the Baseline Enhancement to Entitlement (BEE), *a program* that uses existing resources to achieve the best performance. As a result, output has increased from 5,000 tonnes to 7,000 tonnes, and many changes have also taken place.

在本句中，a program 总结了 BEE 的意思。

例 30.

以往主流社会的意识形态以及一些不恰当的宣传，加大了艾滋病恐慌及人们对艾滋病病人和艾滋病病毒感染者的厌恶，而无助于预防和控制艾滋病。

Mainstream mindsets and misinformation about AIDS have increased public fear of the disease and prejudice against AIDS patients, *a situation which hinders prevention and control.*

在本句中，a situation 总结了整个主句的意思。

15.6.3 自由式修饰语

自由式修饰语是一个用来修饰其他句子成分或整个句子的短语，需要与其他成分用逗号隔开，可以是1）名词短语；2）动词短语；3）形容词短语；4）副词短语；5）介词短语；或6）分句变体。请见以下例子[①]：

1. nominal cluster: noun, e.g. *A cautious soul, Jim opened the door against his best judgment* (a.k.a. an *appositive*);

2. verbal cluster: present participial, past participial, infinitive, e.g. *Jim opened the door to see what was up* (=verbal ["to see"] + modifiers or a noun);

3. adjectival cluster, e.g. *Curious about the kerfuffle outside, Jim opened the door* (=adjective that modifies a noun: here, "Jim");

4. adverbial cluster, e.g. *Gingerly but eagerly, Jim opened the door* (=adverb that modifies the verb — or the sentence as a whole);

5. prepositional phrase, e.g. *With bat in hand, Jim opened the door.* (N.B. prepositional phrases are usually adverbial); and

---

① https://seansturm.wordpress.com/2009/07/07/free-modifiers/, accessed September 5, 2021.

6. altered clause a.subordinate clause; b. free relative clause (which, for which); c. free absolute, e.g. *His bat at the ready, Jim opened the door* (=noun + free modifier); d. free that clause, e.g. *His goal — that the door be open — was achieved;* e. quote-attributing clause.

自由修饰大多数以现在分词开头：

The Scopes monkey trial was a watershed in American religious thinking, *legitimizing the contemporary interpretation of the Bible and making literal fundamentalism a backwater of anti-intellectual theology.*

也可能以过去分词开头：

Leonardo da Vinci was a man of powerful intellect, *driven by an insatiable curiosity and haunted by a vision of artistic expression.*

或者以形容词开头：

In 1939 the United States began to assist the British in their struggle against Germany, *fully aware that it faced another world war.*

自由式修饰语在翻译中很常用。

例 31.

1985年以后，改革在城市推开，允许公有制之外的多种经济形式存在，使城市中的一些人有可能离开原有的单位体制。

After 1985, reform was extended to the cities. Non-public ownership was allowed, *making it possible for some urban residents to leave the work-unit (danwei) system.*

本句后置的现在分词短语就是自由修饰语。

例 32.

"文化大革命"结束后，邓小平同志再度出来工作，依然表示："我出来工作，可以有两种态度，一个是做官，一个是做点工作。"（Xi-II）

Returning to leading positions after the Cultural Revolution, Deng spoke frankly about his attitude towards work, "Now I've come back to work. I could take two different attitudes. One, be a bureaucrat; two, do some solid work."

本句采用前置现在分词短语作为自由修饰语。

例 33.

社会保障基金经过长期的积累，会形成庞大的资产，成为投资融资的一大财源。

Over time, a significant asset base can be accumulated in the social security account, *which will represent a major source of investment capital.*

本句采用 which 从句修饰整个句子。

例 34.

全面建成小康社会，强调的不仅是"小康"，而且更重要的也是更难做到的是"全面"。(Xi-II)

To realize a moderately prosperous society in all respects, we must not only have in our mind "a moderately prosperous society", we must also focus on the issue of "in all respects"—*the latter being more important and more difficult to achieve.*

本句采用"绝对短语"作为自由修饰语。

15.7 平行结构

增强译文优雅性的另一个方式，是使用平行结构（parallel structure）。平行结构就是语法结构相同的一组短语或句子。请看例子（A 不平行，B 平行）：

可以是名词的平行：

A: Mary likes hik**ing**, to swim, and bicycl**ing**.

B: Mary likes hik**ing**, swimming, and bicycl**ing**.

可以是副词的平行：

A: The production manager was asked to write his report quick**ly**, accurate**ly**, and **in a detailed manner.**

B: The production manager was asked to write his report quick**ly**, accurate**ly**, and thorough**ly**.

可以是谓语部分的平行：

A: The teacher said that he was a poor student because he wait**ed** until the last minute to study for the exam, complet**ed** his lab problems in a careless manner, and **his motivation was** low.

B: The teacher said that he was a poor student because he wait**ed** until the last minute to study for the exam, complet**ed** his lab problems in a careless manner, and lack**ed** motivation.

可以是从句的平行：

A: The coach told the players **that they should get** a lot of sleep, **that they should not eat** too much, and **to do** some warm-up exercises before the game.

B: The coach told the players **that they should get** a lot of sleep, **that they should not eat** too much, and **that they should do** some warm-up exercises before the game.①

平行结构在翻译中也经常使用。比如：

例 35.

在行动上紧紧跟随，就是要自觉向党中央看齐，向党的基本理论、基本路线、基本方略看齐，把"四个意识"落实到教育改革发展的方方面面，融入教育教学研究的各个环节，真正解决好培养什么人、怎样培养人、为谁培养人这一根本问题。

Following the Central Committee in action means we must align our-

---

① https://owl.purdue.edu/owl/general_writing/mechanics/parallel_structure.html, accessed September 5, 2021.

selves with the Party Central Committee, adhere to the Party's basic theory, basic line and basic strategy, and mainstream the "Four Consciousness"① in all aspects of education reform, development and research. In this way, we will be able to answer the fundamental questions of *what types of talent to nurture, for whom and how*.

"培养什么人、怎样培养人、为谁培养人"翻译为 what types of talent to nurture, for whom and how 就是平行结构。有的地方翻译为 the purposes of and approaches to higher education，也是平行结构，但内容少了一项——译者（或审校者）可能认为培养什么人和为谁培养人意思相同。但笔者认为，前者强调学生的专业知识，后者强调学生的家国情怀，不完全一样。

例 36.
　　世界语言博物馆通过科学的体系、合理的设计以及丰富的藏品，将历史与现实、知识与技能、本体与运用融为一体。
　　The Museum of the World's Languages integrates *the past and the present, knowledge and skills*, as well as *ontology and application* through a scientific system, rational design, and a rich collection.

原文加点部分的排比，翻译为英语的平行结构。

例 37.
　　中国的权力系统的级别自 20 世纪 50 年代后有过多次变化，目前大致为：一，中央；二，省、自治区、直辖市；三，地级市；四，县级市、县；五，乡、镇、街道办事处。但加上：一，大区，在曾经设立党的地方局的位置，目前还保有军队的机构，新近又设有银行的机构，要求在这一级别上设立审判机构的呼声也正高②；二，较大的市（副省级）；三，在有的地方设于市、县之下的区，以及，从文本上看并非是一个政府级别，但实际上确是一级权力机构（设有执政党的支部）的行政村

---

① Consciously maintaining political integrity, thinking in big-picture terms, following the leadership core, and keeping in alignment with the central authority.
② 此例较早，但仍有意义。目前最高法院已在深圳、沈阳、南京、郑州、重庆、西安设立六个巡回法院，分别管邻近的几个省。

(村民委员会)、居民委员会。

China's administrative hierarchy has changed many times since the 1950s. It now includes: first, the central government; second, subnational governments; third, prefectural cities; fourth, county level cities and counties; and fifth, townships/towns and sub-districts offices. And more: first, large regions, or circuits, each covering several provinces, where *regional Party bureaus once existed, military commands still exist today, banking institutions have been just established, and courts are being debated*; second, large (sub-provincial level) cities; third, districts under counties/ county level cities; and fourth, rural and urban communities, which are theoretically not part of the power hierarchy, but in fact are, because of the presence of ruling party branches.

原文加点部分结构并不统一,译文力求统一,增强节奏感。

例 38.

根据当前两种经济体制转换过程的实际,社会保障制度改革需要一个渐进过程。要坚持低水平、广覆盖、多层次的基本方针,逐步由"全部包揽"向"国家、单位、个人"三方负担转变,由"企业自保"向"社会互济"转变,由"福利包揽"向"基本保障"转变,由"现收现付"向"部分积累"转变,由"政策调整"向"法律规范"转变。应该指出,我国的社会保障法制化程度较低,尚不能给国家解决社会保障面临的严峻而复杂的问题提供充分、有效的法律支持。

During the economic transition period, the reform of the social security system needs a gradual process. The objective should be to establish a multi-tiered system that covers a large population and offers modest levels of benefits. In particular, reforms should achieve the following transformations:

• *from the "state-does-all" model to a mixed-funding model where the state, employers, and individuals all contribute;*

• *from enterprise sponsorship to resource pooling across society;*

- *from "full package of welfare" to "basic protection";*
- *from the pay-as-you-go system to a partially-funded system; and*
- *from the "policy-based adjustment" to "regulation by law".*

It should be noted that China lacks an adequate legal infrastructure for the social security regime. Existing legislation is unable to resolve the difficult and complex problems.

加点部分在汉语中是一系列排比，英语中努力再现这一结构。

需要注意的是，汉语中的排比结构很多，有些是同义反复，翻译中不必重复。例如：万物皆有始，万事皆有源。译文是：Everything has a beginning. 译文没有用不同方式表达相同的意思。

15.8 小结

本章按照简明英语长短句搭配的要求，基于英语写作规则，提出如何把长句变短、短句变长的方法。把长句变短，适用于翻译英语结构复杂的长句，以及汉语的流水句、主题句；把短句变长，适合于汉语简单句过多，译为英文较为零碎的情况。本章提到的三种修饰方法以及平行结构，在翻译实践中似乎重视不够，值得大家尝试。

〔课后练习〕

1. 请阅读 *Style: Toward Clarity and Grace* 或者在网上搜索 repetitive modifier、summative modifier 和 free modifier，进一步学习这三种修饰方式。
2. 请搜索 sentence variety 并阅读相关内容。
3. 请搜索 parallel structure 并阅读相关内容。
4. 请搜索 coordination and subordination 并阅读相关内容。
5. 请按照本章的要求，进一步修改自己的某篇译文。

第十六章　语篇的衔接与连贯

扫码预习

请扫码下载本章涉及的例句。先做练习，再看解答，学习效果更佳。

16.1　语篇的衔接

　　语篇由词、句或段组成，但却不是语句的机械叠加，而是一种有机的、动态的组合。韩礼德和哈桑认为：在一个语篇里，一个句子内的某些词与上下文有一脉相承的关系，或者说，某些词语的具体意义要从上下文有关词语中推断出来。正是这种衔接关系使语篇成为形式和意义的完整统一体。衔接分为两大类：

　　（1）语法衔接，包括照应（reference，指的是人称代词、指示代词等）；替代（substitution，指的是代动词 do，以及 one, the same 这种词，以及答语中的 so, nor 等。比如，"do"可替代动词，"one"可替代可数名词，"so"可替代从句）；省略（ellipsis，指的是名词性词、动词、小句等的省略）；和连接（conjunction，指的是虚词 and, but 及句间连接手段 in that case、of course、anyway、firstly、secondly 等）。

　　（2）词汇衔接，是通过词汇选择手段建立的衔接关系，主要方式有

reiteration（复现）和 collocation（搭配）。复现包含四种情况：1) 用相同的词；2) 用同义或近义词；3) 用上义词；4) 用统称词和代词。而搭配是经常出现在一起的词，如"交通""客运""货运""道路""汽车""堵塞""燃油"。对于译者而言，掌握衔接手段的分类并不重要，重要的是了解英汉衔接手段的主要差异，从而在翻译时进行必要转换，使译文更加符合目的语的习惯。多数情况下，汉译英意味着要把汉语的重复性衔接手段变为英语的省略性衔接手段（见第十一章第二节"调整篇章衔接手段"）；把汉语潜在的逻辑关系和层次关系用英语明示的连接词表示出来；英译汉时，则意味着把省略的东西补充出来。由于汉语连接词趋于增加，所以英译汉时连接词很少省略。

了解衔接还有一个重要作用，即是在理解出现障碍时，能够有意识地通过识别一系列词的衔接关系，确定这些词在该文本中的具体意义，从而透彻理解原文，保证译文意思连贯。

16.1.1 识别原文的衔接关系

对于译者来说，识别衔接关系是理解原文过程中不可缺少的一步。在篇章中，指称同一对象的词语在语篇中先后出现，形成一条共指链。共指链可能以人称代词的形式存在，也可能由指示代词或复现的名词所组成。若不能认清共指链的存在，译文的连贯性就会成为问题。有时共指链很长，成链的词与词之间又相距很远，会给译者造成一些理解上的困难，需特别小心。汉语的共指链重复名词的较多，而英语的共指链往往对同一对象使用多种表达方法，要注意从意义上加以判断：

例 1.

In 1914, in U.S. v. Lexington *Mill* and Elevator Company, *the Supreme Court* issues *its* first ruling on food additives. *It* ruled that in order for bleached flour with nitrite residues to be banned from foods, the government must show a relationship between the chemical additive and the harm it allegedly caused in humans. *The court* also noted that the mere presence of <u>such an ingredient</u> was not sufficient to render *the food* illegal.

1914年，在美国诉莱克星顿**面粉加工**和电梯公司一案中，**最高法院**第一次就食品添加剂问题作出判决。**最高法院**认为，如果要禁止在食品中使用残留<u>亚硝酸盐</u>的**漂白面粉**，政府就必须证明<u>这种化学添加剂</u>和政府所指控的人身伤害之间存在某种关系。**最高法院**还认为，仅靠面粉中存在<u>亚硝酸盐</u>这一事实，不足以认定**该面粉**非法。

英语中的共指链包括：

court 系列（斜体）：the Supreme court—its—it—the court；汉语译为：最高法院—（省略）—最高法院—最高法院。汉语使用了更多的重复。

food additives 系列（下划线）：food additives—nitrite residues—the chemical additive—it—such an ingredient；汉语译为：食品添加剂—亚硝酸盐—这种化学添加剂—（省略）—亚硝酸盐；汉语中使用了更多的重复。

bleached flour 系列（斜体+下划线）：bleached flour—the food。汉语译为：漂白面粉 — 该面粉。原文用上义词 food 与 bleached flour 衔接，而汉语重复使用了"面粉"，表示上下文意思的关联。另外，bleached flour 和 the food 也与 mill 构成衔接链。实际上，如果不是文中关于面粉的叙述，就无法判断 mill 是指面粉厂还是其他加工厂。

例2.

In 1959, the U.S. *cranberry crop* was recalled three weeks before Thanksgiving for FDA tests to check for aminotriazole, a weed killer found to cause cancer in laboratory animals. Cleared *berries* were allowed a label stating that *they* had been tested and had passed FDA inspection, the only such endorsement ever allowed by FDA on *a food product*.

1959年，在感恩节前三个星期美国**越橘**被召回，接受食品与药物管理局检测，以确定是否含有氨三唑（一种在实验室中已证明能引起实验室动物癌症的除草剂）。通过检查的**越橘**可以贴上认证标签。这是 FDA 批准的唯一一次**食品**认证。

英语共指链是 cranberry crop—berries—they—a food product；汉语是：

越橘—越橘—（省略）—食品。如果没有把 berries 还原为"越橘"，而是按照字典意思翻译为"浆果"，共指链就会断裂，意思无法连贯。

例3.

The 1945 Penicillin Amendment requires FDA *testing and certification of safety and effectiveness* of all penicillin products. Later amendments extended *this requirement* to all antibiotics. In 1983 such control was found no longer needed and was abolished.

如果翻译为：

1945年的《盘尼西林修正案》要求食品与药物管理局对所有盘尼西林产品的安全性和有效性进行检测和认证。随后的修正案把这一要求扩大到所有抗生素。1983年，国会认定这样的控制已没有必要，于是取消了这样的控制。

读者需要在"安全性和有效性进行检测和认证""这一要求"和"这样的控制"之间建立等价关系才能理解句子的意思；如果把替代性衔接换为重复或部分重复，意思会十分明确：

1945年的《盘尼西林修正案》要求FDA对所有盘尼西林产品的安全性和有效性进行检测和认证。随后的修正案把检测和认证扩大到所有抗生素。1983年，国会认定检测和认证已没有必要，于是取消了检测和认证。

例4.

下面两段话选自某专家委员会向中国政府所提建议。斜体部分是与transport有关的衔接链。如有必要，在方括号中指出了斜体部分与transport的具体联系。

Transport

As the Council has said on previous occasions, China is no different from any other country in needing an integrated *transport policy* in *which* [the integrated transport policy] the advantages and disadvantages of *different modes* [transport] can be judged against *each other* [other modes of transport]. As the number of *private cars* [a mode of transport] increases and *traffic congestion* [caused by cars] worsens, so does the need for better and more reliable *public transport* [a mode of transport]. Prices for *all kinds of transport*, whether [transport] *of people* or [transport of] *freight*, should reflect *the real social, economic and environmental costs* [of transport]. Throughout environmental standards need to be strictly *applied* [to transport].

If, as seems inevitable, use of *cars* and *road transport* increases, at least in the short term, strict environmental standards need to be applied to *motor vehicles* [a mode of transport], and best available clean technologies need to *be used* [*in transport*]. Throughout *the impact* [of transport] on city and town life should be carefully assessed. Smaller more compact cities, including home, work and recreation, should minimize the need for *transport*. These cities have their own sustainable *transport* arrangements, including the use of *bicycles* [a mode of transport], *which* [the use of bicycles] is being increasingly favored elsewhere in the world.

交通

正如委员会在其他场合曾经指出的，中国与其他国家一样，需要制定一项综合性的交通政策，借以[in which]衡量各种交通方式[different modes]的优缺点。随着家用轿车数量增加，交通堵塞加剧，公众对公共交通的状况和可靠性会提出更高要求。各种交通手段的定价，包括客运价格[of people]与货运价格[freight]，要反映实际的社会、经济和环境成本，要始终坚持严格适用环境标准。

小汽车和公路交通的发展似乎难以避免，至少短期如此。在这种情况下，机动车辆要适用严格的环境标准，并使用最先进的清洁技术。要始终坚持认真评估交通对城市和城市生活的影响[impact (of transport)]。在生活、工作和娱乐场所相对集中的小城市，要尽量减少机动车辆的使用。小城市有其独特的，对环境无害的交通方式，包括自行车。自行车[which]在其他国家越来越受到人们的青睐。

对比原文和译文可以看出，这些衔接项有的直译出来，如交通堵塞（traffic congestion），表明英汉衔接手段有相同之处；有些按汉语习惯把省略的部分补充了出来，如"包括客运价格与货运价格"原文是 whether of people or freight；"各种交通方式"原文是"各种方式"（different modes）。如果不补充出来，而直译为"各种方式"和"各类交通的价格，无论人或货物的"，可能会造成意思不连贯，或需要更大努力才能理解。

原文中除了与 transport 有关的衔接项外，其他词语也存在衔接关系，如 … so does the need for better and more reliable public transport 当中，so does 就是替代性衔接，补充完整是 the need for better and more reliable public transport also increases; smaller more compact cities 与下面的 these cities 构成衔接关系。另外，汉语虽然喜欢重复，但也使用省略性的衔接手段，如"至少短期如此（指小汽车和公路交通会增加）。在这种（指小汽车和公路交通增加的）情况下"。

胡壮麟（1994）在《语篇的衔接与连贯》中提到"零式指称"这个概念，即"语篇中本该出现的指称词被省略了"。它表现为汉语中众多的无主句，要求译者根据英语的指称习惯进行适当的变通，如添加代词：

例5.
　　非洲国家要利用这一有利的和平国际环境来发展自己。[非洲国家]要根据本国的条件制定发展策略与政策，搞好民族团结，通过全体人民的共同努力，使经济得到发展。

　　African countries should take advantage of this favorable peaceful environment to develop. *They* should work out strategies and policies for development in accordance with the actual situation in each country, and *they* should unite to promote economic development.

汉语主语一贯到底，第二句主语缺位（零式指代）。英语则断为三句，分别用 African countries—they—they 作主语。

例6.
　　所以，从一九七八年我们党从十一届三中全会开始，确定了我们的根本政治路线，把四个现代化建设，努力发展生产力，作为压倒一切的中心任务。[我们党]在这个基础上制定了一系列新的方针政策，主要是改革和开放政策。

So in 1978, at the third Plenary session of the Eleventh Central Committee, *we* formulated a new basic political line: to give first priority to modernization and to develop the productive forces. Based on the new political line, *we* drew up new strategies and policies, the essential items being reform and the open policy.

汉语中"我们党"作为主语，将两个句子一统到底，读者丝毫不会感到困惑，而英译文中两次使用"we"点明主语。

16.1.2　转换衔接手段

认清了原文中的衔接关系之后，还必须在译文中建立相应的衔接关系，使译文能具有原文一样的连贯性。译者必须充分认识源语和译语在衔接方式上的异同，按照译语的要求用恰当的衔接手段构建译文语篇。当然，译语的衔接模式与原文完全一致也是可能的，但毕竟属于少数情况；大多数的情形之下，都要进行必要的转换。

例 7.

The EU considers China as a non-market economy (NME) country or "state-trading" country, therefore, different standards are applied to China on *the normal value and the export price side, the main parameters* in deciding whether or not a product is dumped.

欧盟认为，中国是一个非市场经济国家或国有贸易国家，因此，在确定正常价值和出口价格方面，对中国适用不同的标准。正常价值和出口价格是决定产品是否构成倾销的主要指标。

英语通过语法结构表示 the main parameters 与 the normal value and the export price side 是衔接关系，汉语通过重复"正常价值和出口价格"表示。

例 8.

The United States will work for a *just* and *secure* peace; *just*, because it fulfills the aspirations of peoples and nations for freedom and progress; *secure*, because it removes the danger of foreign aggression. (*Joint Communiqué of the People's Republic of China and the United States of America* Issued in Shanghai, February 28, 1972)

美国将致力于建立公正而稳定的和平。这种和平是公正的，因为它满足各国人民和各国争取自由和进步的愿望。这种和平是稳定的，因为它消除外来侵略的危险。(《上海公报》中文本)

在本例中，英语采用重复的衔接方法，汉语也使用重复，但重复部分不同。

例 9.

What should we estimate, why and how often?

我们应当估算什么，为什么进行估算，及多久估算一次？

英语是小句性省略（why 和 how often 后面省略了 should we estimate），汉语是重复。

也可以译为：

估算的内容、原因和方式是什么？

这时，原因和方式后面省略了"估算的"。

例 10.

China's laws are *consistent* with WTO standards but China's anti-dumping practice thus far *is not*.

中国法律与 WTO 标准一致，但中国反倾销的实践目前与 WTO 不一致。

英语省略了形容词 consistent，汉语则重复"一致"。

例 11.

  中国作为一个大国，既不应当害怕结盟，也不应当害怕不结盟。
  As a great power, China should fear neither alignment nor non-alignment.

汉语属于动词性重复，英语改变了句子结构，没有使用重复。

例 12.

  共同富裕的设想是这样提出的：一部分地区有条件先发展起来，一部分地区发展慢点，先发展的地区带动后发展的地区，最终达到共同富裕。如果富的愈来愈富，穷的愈来愈穷，两极分化就会产生，而社会主义制度就应该也能够避免两极分化。解决的方法之一就是先富起来的地区多交点利税，支持贫困地区的发展。(Deng-III)
  Our plan is as follows: where conditions permit, some *areas* may develop faster than *others*; *those* that develop faster can help *those* that lag behind, until *all* become prosperous. If *the rich* keep getting richer and *the poor* poorer, polarization will emerge. The socialist system must and can avoid polarization. One way is for *areas* that become prosperous first to support the poor *ones* by paying more taxes or turning in more profits to the state.

原文中与"地区"有关的衔接链包括六个"地区"，加上两处省略："富的（地区）"和"穷的（地区）"；译文的衔接链却只留下来两个"areas"，"富的"和"穷的"保持不变，其余的转换成了代词（those, all）和替代衔接（ones），还增加了一个（others）。

例 13.

  要抓住机会，现在就是好机会。我就担心丧失机会。不抓[住机会]呀，看到的机会就丢掉了，时间一晃就过去了。(Deng-III)
  We must grab *opportunities*. This is an excellent *time*. The only thing that I worry about is that we may lose *opportunities*. If we don't grab *them*, *they* will slip away, as time flies by.

原文的衔接链如下：机会—机会—机会—（省略）—机会；对应译文中的 opportunities — time — opportunities — them — they。原文的原词复现转换成译文中的替代和代词衔接。

16.1.3 显化隐含的衔接关系

在有些情况下，原文中衔接关系是隐性的，语义却是连贯的；但译文中却需要选择使用一些衔接手段建立显性衔接。这种从无形到有形的转化，在汉译英中尤为多见。

例 14.

去年，中央作了经济体制改革的决定。全世界都在评论［这个决定］，认为这是中国共产党的勇敢的创举。

Last year, the Central Committee adopted *a decision* on reform of the economic structure. The whole world is now commenting on *that decision* and thinks *that is* a bold invention by the Chinese Communist Party.

本句译文补充了汉语中省略的"评论"的宾语（"决定"），以建立衔接关系。

例 15.

城乡改革的基本政策，一定要长期保持稳定。当然，随着实践的发展，该完善的［政策］完善，该修补的［政策］修补，但总的［政策］要坚定不移。即使没有新的主意也可以。就是不要变［政策］，不要使人们感到政策变了。（Deng-III）

The *basic policies* for urban and rural reform must be kept stable for a long time to come. Of course, as the reform progresses, *some of these policies* should be improved or amended as necessary. But we should keep firmly to *our general direction*. It doesn't <u>matter</u> whether we can come up with new *ideas*. What <u>matters</u> is that we should not change our *policies* and people should not feel that we are changing *them*.

加点的词语时围绕"政策"的衔接链，在中文里多处采用语法省略（见方括号），译文则用词语复现、上义词等再现这一逻辑链条。另请注意，原文用"也可以"和"不要"一对反义词形成逻辑链条，译文改为 doesn't matter 和 matter，对比的意味更加强烈。

例 16.

对改革开放，一开始就有不同的意见，这是正常的。不只是经济特区问题〔有不同意见〕，更大的问题是〔对〕农村改革〔有不同意见〕，搞农村家庭联产承包，废除人民公社制度。开始的时候只有三分之一的省干起来，第二年超过了三分之二〔干起来〕，第三年才差不多全部跟上，这是就全国范围讲的。(Deng-III)

In the beginning opinions were *divided* about the <u>reform and the open policy</u>. That was normal. *The difference* was not only over the special economic zones but also over the bigger issues, such as the rural reform that introduced the household contract responsibility system with remuneration linked to output and abolished the system of people's communes. Initially, in the country as a whole, only one third of the provinces <u>launched the reform</u>. By the second year, however, more than two thirds of them <u>had done so</u>, and the third year almost all the rest <u>joined in</u>.

原文的第一和第二句之间靠语法省略构成衔接，而译文中的"divided"和"difference"却构成了近义词复现的衔接关系。另外，原文中的"改革开放""干起来""跟上"形成近义词衔接链，英文变为 reform and the open policy—launched the reform—had done so—joined in，一些衔接的形式发生了变化。

16.2 语篇的连贯

语篇的衔接是指语篇在形式上通过一定的手段，联结成为一个整体；语篇的连贯则是指在意义上，语篇也是一个能够被读者理解的整体。我们在翻译的过程中，应当学会瞻前顾后，确保译文逻辑清楚，前后贯通。以下从调整衔接手段、确保用词一致、局部服从整体、重构逻辑关系等各方面，举例说明如何做到语篇连贯。

16.2.1 调整衔接手段

由于汉英的衔接手段不同，如果把汉语的衔接方式（如重复）直接翻译为英文，会使译文显得松散，缺乏逻辑；同时汉语中的同义反复，翻译为英文也要适当简化。下面是一本书的序言，注意修改前后语篇连贯性的变化。

坚守与革新：美国一流大学校长访谈录

2019年2月，中共中央、国务院印发了《中国教育现代化2035》，中共中央办公厅、国务院办公厅印发了《加快推进教育现代化实施方案（2018—2022年）》。[1] 在提升一流人才培养与创新能力方面，《中国教育现代化2035》指出，要分类建设一批世界一流高等学校，建立完善的高等学校分类发展政策体系，引导高等学校科学定位、特色发展。[2] 在推进高等教育内涵发展方面，《实施方案》指出，要加快"双一流"建设，建设一流本科教育，提升研究生教育水平，完善高等教育质量标准和监测评价体系，提升高等学校科学研究与创新服务能力等。[3]

在这一新征程中，中外一流高校互学互鉴具有重要的意义。[4] 为此，中国驻芝加哥总领事馆与《世界教育信息》杂志共同组稿、合作开展"美国一流大学校长访谈录"，内容涵盖"双一流"建设、一流本科教育、创新创业教育、质量标准和评价以及国际化战略等多个议题，以为我国教育现代化建设提供中美高校对话的平台。[5]

原译：

Persistence and Innovation: Dialogue with U. S. World-Class University Presidents

In February 2019, the CPC Central Committee and the State Council issued *China's Education Modernization 2035*, and the General Offices of the CPC Central Committee and the General Offices of the State Council issued the *Implementation Plan for Accelerating the Modernization of Education (2018–2022)*. In terms of enhancing the cultivation of first-class talents and innovation capability, *China's Education Modernization 2035* pointed out that it is necessary to build a number of world-class higher education institutions <u>by classification</u>, establish a sound policy system for <u>classified development</u> of higher education institutions, and guide <u>the scientific orientation and characteristic development</u> of higher education institutions. <u>In terms of promoting the connotative development of higher education,</u> <u>the implementation plan</u> points out that it is necessary to accelerate the construction of "double first-class", build first-class undergraduate education, improve the level of graduate education, improve the quality standards and monitoring and evaluation system of higher education, and enhance the scientific research and innovative service capacity of higher education institutions.

In this new journey, it is of great significance for first-class universities and colleges at home and abroad to learn from each other. To this end, Consulate-General of the P. R. China in Chicago and the *Journal of World Education* jointly compiled a book entitled "Dialogues with American World-Class University Presidents", covering the First-Class initiative, undergraduate education, innovation and entrepreneurship oriented education, quality standards and evaluation, internationalization strategy, and other topics, so as to provide a platform for dialogue between China and the United States in the modernization of education. (261 words)

改译：

Tradition and Innovation: Dialogues with Presidents of First-Class American Universities

In February 2019, the CPC Central Committee and the State Council issued <u>Modernize China's Education by 2035</u>, and <u>subsequently</u>, the General Offices of the CPC Central Committee and the State Council issued the <u>implementation plan for 2018–2022</u>. <u>The first document</u> highlights the importance of top-notch talent and innovation and sets the targets of building a number of world-class universities. It provides a complete policy framework and guidance for <u>differentiated</u> development of universities. The second document calls for the building of <u>"first-class universities and disciplines" (the First-Class initiative) through measures that improve</u> undergraduate education, post-graduate education, quality control and evaluation, and research and innovation.

<u>To achieve these targets</u>, it is important for Chinese universities to learn from their counterparts. The Chinese Consulate-General in Chicago and the Journal of World Education <u>have thus</u> jointly organized dialogues with presidents of first-class American universities. The book covers the First-Class initiative, undergraduate education, education for innovation and entrepreneurship, quality control and evaluation, and internationalization. In so doing, we hope to provide a communication platform that helps modernize China's higher education. (188 words)

解释：

第 1 句：两个文件之间的关系，一个是长远规划，一个是近期计划，近期计划中包含了长远规划的名字。原译按字面忠实译出，译者必须仔细对比两个文件名才能理解两者之间的关系。改译简化了第二个文件的译法，使两者的关系一目了然。

第 2 句：原译还像原文一样，重复了第一个文件名，译者必须回头查看，才知道原来是第一个文件；译文把重复的衔接手段变为替代，直接说 the first document，省却读者的思考；第 3 句提及第二份文件，译文同样不用全称，而是译为 the second document，与 the first document 形成清楚的对照：一个设定目标，一个负责具体实施。

从形式上看，第 2 句"在提升一流人才培养与创新能力方面"与第 3 句"在推进高等教育内涵发展方面"构成两个文件内容的对比，似乎有照应关系，但从两个文件的关系来看，两者不可能构成对比，因为后者是为了实施前者。因此改译改变第 2 句的结构，把作为话题（topic）的"提升一流人才培养与创新能力"降级为"分类建设……"的并列成分。

改译省略了最先出现的"分类建设"，因为这个句子已经有一个重要信息，即建设一流高校；把"分类建设"放在下面表达，作为下一句的重点，这样两句各有侧重。

原文的"分类建设""分类发展""科学定位""特色发展"是同义关系，都是强调差异化发展；原译全部按字面翻译，让人眼花缭乱，改译合并简化，表达逻辑清晰。

第 3 句省略了"在推进高等教育内涵发展方面"，只翻译内涵发展的具体措施，即"双一流"建设。关于"双一流"建设的具体内容，译文措辞也进行了简化。

第 4 句开头"在这一新征程中"没有直译，而是译为 to achieve these targets，与前文的 targets 形成更清楚的衔接关系。

第 5 句"共同组稿"和"合作开展……"应该是指同一件事，即共同开展访谈活动，访谈本身就是组稿，故翻译简化。另外，原文"开展……访谈录"搭配不当，予以纠正。

总之，改译主要通过把重复性的衔接手段改为指代，并通过编辑、简化原文等方式，大大提高了译文的连贯性，同时将篇幅压缩了近三分之一。

16.2.2　确保用词一致

概念的译法一致，表面上是衔接问题，背后是为了确保意思连贯。通常情况下，如果是一个人翻译一份完整的文件，很容易做到前后用词一致、意思连贯，因为人具备宏观思维能力。但如果多人翻译或机器翻译，则可能把同一个词翻译为多个说法。下面一组例句，来自同一篇文章，其中的"翻供"一词，竟然被机器翻译为 9 种说法：

- 首先，要审查分析其翻供的原因。
- First of all, we must examine and analyze the reasons for the <u>confession</u>.
- 如何对待和审查犯罪嫌疑人翻供
- How to Treat and Review Criminal Suspects' <u>Refusal</u>
- 从司法实践来看，如果侦查人员存在刑讯逼供、指供、诱供等情况，犯罪嫌疑人翻供的概率比较大。

- From the perspective of judicial practice, if investigators extort confessions by torture, refer to confessions, induce confessions and other circumstances, the probability of criminal suspects to withdraw confessions is relatively high.
- 司法人员应当仔细分析犯罪嫌疑人是在什么情况下翻供的,以查明其翻供的具体原因,从而判断翻供是否真实合理。
- Judicial personnel should carefully analyze the circumstances under which the criminal suspect retracted his confession, so as to find out the specific reasons for the retraction and judge whether the retraction is true and reasonable.
- 然而,翻供、翻证往往是发现冤假错案的契机,而且证人翻证后,如果证人与被告人之间没有利害关系,其翻证证言的真实性较大。
- However, the turning over of confession and evidence is often an opportunity to discover unjust, false and misjudged cases. Moreover, if there is no interest between the witness and the defendant after the witness turns over the evidence, the authenticity of the turned-over testimony is greater.
- 另一方面,可以通过口供中提到的线索找到其他证据,可以堵死犯罪嫌疑人的辩解,从而避免翻供。
- On the other hand, other evidence can be found through the clues mentioned in the confession, which can block the criminal suspect's defense, thus avoiding confession reversal.

这些说法都是机器参照不同的文本提取出来的,而这些文本的来源不一定可靠,因此这些译法不一定全部正确。即使全部正确,重要的术语用词相对一致,也是学术论文的一项基本要求。译者必须在机器翻译的基础上,反复查证,找到最通行的译法。通过查证,我们认定 withdraw confessions、retraction、recantation 是正确的说法,其余都不可取。翻译中使用这些译法,才能确保意思连贯。在分工协作或利用机器翻译的情况下,尤其要注意表达方式的一致性和逻辑连贯。

16.2.3 局部服从整体

译者对一个词、一句话的理解和表达，<u>应当符合上下文和宏观背景</u>，不能任意发挥。比如，在一篇关于新加坡城市建设情况的介绍中有这样一段话：

In some ways, however, the city's housing stock was <u>decent</u>. Stamford Raffles, who founded modern Singapore in 1819, set out regulations in his 1823 Town Plan requiring that buildings be built of brick walls and tiled roofs to discourage fires. He also mandated a continuous, covered public veranda, or 'five-foot-way', in front of buildings to shield pedestrians from intense equatorial heat, glare and rain. Internally, the traditional courtyard brought natural light and ventilation into these narrow and deep structures. The result was a <u>reasonably safe and comfortable</u> building. <u>Shophouses were of essentially sound design and construction</u>, and are now valuable heritage properties. However, *in the 1950s, they were deemed slums 'ripe for demolition'.* The root of Singapore's slum problem was overcrowding.

原译：

然而从某些方面讲，新加坡市的住房状况<u>还算不错</u>。于1819年一手开创了现代新加坡的史丹福·莱佛士（Stamford Raffles），在1823年的《市区规划蓝图》（1823 Town Plan）中规定，为防范火灾，建筑物必须以砖筑墙，以瓦铺顶。考虑到赤道热浪炎炎，日照强烈，气候多雨，他还要求在建筑前铺设长长的、有篷遮挡的公共行人道，或称"五脚基"（five-foot-way），为行人遮阳挡雨。室内，因为传统庭院的关系，再狭窄深长的建筑构造，也能有自然光照进来，自然风吹进来。这些因素成就了相对安全、舒适的建筑。<u>尤其是店屋，布局考究，建筑精巧</u>，是当下十分宝贵的文化遗产。<u>然而就在20世纪50年代，店屋还被认为是"应该拆毁"的贫民窟</u>。当时新加坡贫民窟这个问题的症结，是过度拥挤。

这段话中的Shophouses were of essentially sound design and construction翻译为"尤其是店屋，布局考究，建筑精巧"用词华丽，朗朗上口，但意思

上与前文和本段的基调不符。前文描述新加坡 20 世纪 50 年代住房状况很差，本段话锋一转，说新加坡的住房还说得过去（decent，注意这个词的意思是"还凑合"，程度上低于汉语的"体面"）。把说得过去的房屋，描述为"布局考究，建筑精巧"言过其实。原文也不过说"reasonably safe and comfortable"（相对安全、舒适）、"essentially sound"（基本上可以）。因此，在表述上也要有宏观思维，做到前后逻辑一致，不可以想到佳词丽句就忘乎所以。造成这个问题的原因，可能是两段并非一个人所译。

改译：

然而从某些方面讲，市区的住房状况<u>还算不错</u>。于 1819 年一手开创了现代新加坡的史丹福·莱佛士（Stamford Raffles），在 1823 年的《市区规划蓝图》（Town Plan）中规定，为防范火灾，建筑物必须以砖筑墙，以瓦铺顶。考虑到赤道热浪炎炎，日照强烈，气候多雨，他还要求在建筑前建造连续的、有篷遮挡的公共走廊，或称"五脚基"（five-foot-way），为行人遮阳挡雨。在内部，这些狭窄的大进深传统庭院还可以自然通风采光。这些因素成就了相对安全、舒适的建筑。<u>尤其是店屋（上屋下店的商住两用楼），设计和建造基本可靠，</u>是当下十分宝贵的文化遗产。然而，<u>在 20 世纪 50 年代，人们认为这种贫民窟似的店屋'应该拆除'"</u>。新加坡贫民窟问题的症结，是过度拥挤。

改译还把"However, in the 1950s, they were deemed slums 'ripe for demolition'."原译文中"就在……年代……还被认为……"这个强调的说法，改为没有强调的平铺直叙（"在 20 世纪 50 年代……被认为"），因为原文没

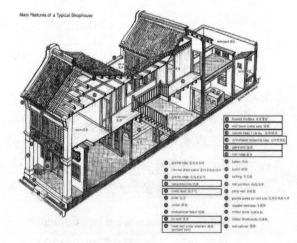

图 16.1　新加坡的店屋（并排多个中的一个）①

有强调。改译还用括号补充了什么是"店屋",是为了照顾读者需要,属于变通的范畴。①

局部服从整体,要求译者具备宏观思维能力,即任何时候都要瞻前顾后,确保自己的理解和表达与宏观背景和其他部分不冲突,确保译文的连贯性。

16.2.4 重构逻辑关系

原文的逻辑不一定清晰,甚至语无伦次,即便如此,译者也要尽最大努力,做最符合情理的推测,并以证据支持自己的判断。比如:

> In relation to a number of questions provided by the participants, panellists noted that States had the obligation to not remove peasants from their lands and to help facilitate food aid. They also had the obligation to protect them and to protect the prices of agricultural products <u>so that peasants could access households and food</u>. They noted that States must have the right to establish agricultural policies to further enable work with sustainable methods and sustainable development.

原译:

> 关于与会者提出的一些问题,专题小组成员指出,各国有义务不把农民赶出他们的土地,并促进粮食援助。各国也有义务保护农民和农产品价格,<u>使农民能够获得家庭和粮食</u>。专题小组指出,各国有权通过制定农业政策,进一步推动可持续农业和可持续发展。

这是联合国一次会议的记录,讨论主题是农民的权利,打算起草一个农民权利宣言。原文难以理解的是下划线部分 peasants could access households and food。peasants could access food 可以理解:农民能够得到吃的。access households 难道是有钱讨个媳妇儿(或打发闺女)?恐怕没有

---

① The Singapore Shophouse Tour—Stories, Experiences & Photos—TravelBuddee.com, accessed September 11, 2021.

根据不能这么说。深切怀疑是 <u>peasants and households</u> could access food，即原文的单词顺序有些错乱。

既然会议记录中有专家的名字，我们不妨用专家的名字和 peasant rights 之类的关键词来搜索。因为专家很可能在别的地方也发表过类似观点。调查发现，同一作者这样写道：

> <u>Household food security</u> refers to a household's ability to acquire food. A working definition is: "A household is food secure when it has access to the food needed for a healthy life for all its members (adequate in terms of quality, quantity, safety and culturally acceptable), and when it is not at undue risk of losing such access."①

同一专家组的另一位专家也发表过关注家庭粮食安全的言论：

> Most studies devoted to the food crisis have only analysed rising food commodity prices. It is taken for granted that higher prices on the world and then local markets normally make more people go hungry. However, the effects of rising food prices on <u>the ability of households, rich or poor, to feed themselves</u> vary from one country to another, from city to countryside. This calls for a deeper analysis, in particular, of two major causes of the growing number of the hungry from 2007 to 2009: the abandonment of policies in favour of smallholder farmers over the past 30 years and the extreme poverty in the cities of developing countries.②

据此，我们可以相当肯定地说原文单词的排列确实出现了混乱。改译：

> 专家回答与会者提出的几个问题时强调，国家有义务不将农民迁离其土地，并有义务促进对农民的粮食援助。国家还有义务保护农民和农产品价格，<u>满足农民及其家庭的食物需求</u>。专家指出，国家有权通过农业政策，进一步推行可持续农作方法，促进可持续发展。

---

① https://www.unscn.org/web/archives_resources/files/Policy_paper_No_10.pdf, accessed September 11, 2021.
② https://poldev.revues.org/145, accessed September 11, 2021.

大家可能有疑问：农民种粮食还没有吃的？首先，本宣言关注的是自给自足的小农（peasants），不包括农场主（farmers）；第二，不要忘记，我们自己的农民也曾经挨饿。后来发布的宣言序言段有这样一句话：

> Concerned that peasants and other people working in rural areas suffer disproportionately from poverty, hunger and malnutrition…

原文逻辑不通的情况很常见，尤其是在汉译英的时候。这是某次翻译竞赛的试题，主题是中非关系：

> 在中国外交的整体布局中，发展中国家是基础，非洲是"基础中的基础"。2013年习近平主席访非时，提出了"真、实、亲、诚"的对非外交新理念。"真"，就是在交往上真诚以待，"真朋友最可贵"。中非传统友谊弥足珍贵，值得倍加珍惜。"实"，就是在合作时真心实意，"中国不仅是合作共赢的倡导者，更是积极实践者。""亲"，就是强调"中国人民和非洲人民有着天然的亲近感。""诚"，就是在解决合作中出现的问题时，讲求实效，"中方坦诚面对中非关系面临的新情况新问题，对出现的问题，我们应该本着相互尊重、合作共赢的精神加以妥善解决"。

我们作为普通读者，并没有感到原文有何不妥。我们只需要理解中国和非洲是一种真诚的、实实在在的合作关系就可以了。但如果作为译者，就会发现很多逻辑问题。比如，把"真"解释为"真诚"，名副其实，英文可以翻译为sincerity；但把"实"解释为"真心实意"，尽管与"真诚"说法不同，但意思相同，翻译为英文也是sincerity或它的同义词，这在逻辑上就行不通了。把"亲"解释为"亲近感"名副其实，但接下来把"诚"解释为"讲求实效"，就名不副实了。"诚"的基本意思是"诚恳"，翻译为英文还是sincerity。一段话中三个有区别的概念都翻译为sincerity或其同义词，这是不可接受的。下面是一位选手的译稿（省略了前两句），"真、实、亲、诚"四个字，采用了官方媒体的译法（Sincerity, Real Results, Affinity/Friendship, Good Faith）[①]，但两个双划线的句子仍无法自圆其说（"实在的结

[①] "亲"也可以用rapport（读作 [ræ'pɔr /ræ'pɔː]）: a relationship of mutual understanding or trust and agreement between people。

果"意思是真诚合作?"诚信"强调实实在在的结果?):

"Sincerity" is to treat each other sincerely in communication. "True friends are the most valuable. China-Africa traditional friendship is precious, which we must cherish all the more dearly." "Real results" is to cooperate with sincerity. "China is not only an advocate for win-win cooperation, but also an active practitioner." "Affinity" stresses that "The Chinese and African people have a natural feeling of kinship toward each other." "Good faith" stresses practical results when resolving problems arising in cooperation. "China will face squarely and sincerely the new developments and new problems confronting our relations. We should properly handle any problem that may arise in the spirit of mutual respect and win-win cooperation."

如果我们外宣中出现这样文理不通的英文,宣传效果可想而知。选手2的翻译效果类似:

"Sincerity" means China insists on treating each other honestly in interactions. "True friends are most valuable. The traditional friendship between China and Africa is precious and worth cherishing." "Practical results" means China values good faith in cooperation. "China not only advocates win-win cooperation, but also actively puts it into practice." "Affinity" means to emphasize that the Chinese people and the African people enjoy natural amity. "Good faith" means China focuses on practical results while addressing problems in cooperation. "China faces squarely and sincerely the new developments and problems confronting China-Africa relations, and believes that the two sides should adhere to the principles of mutual respect and win-win cooperation and settle problems in an appropriate manner."

像这种不能逻辑自洽的原文为数不少,但译者通常无法拒绝翻译。译者能做的,就是在力所能及的范围内,通过变通取舍,尽量让译文逻辑通畅。比如,在本例中,"实"的解释可以选择"实实在在",而不是原文所用的"真心实意";"诚"不采用原文的"讲求实效""诚恳",而采用官方译法的思路,译为"诚信"(good faith)。试译如下:

> When it comes to China's diplomatic strategy, developing countries are the foundation and Africa is the foundation of foundations. In his visit to Africa in 2013, President Xi Jinping put forward a new concept for China's interactions with Africa, namely "sincerity, real results, affinity and good faith". <u>"Sincerity" means China is sincere</u> in our relationship with the African counterparts—<u>sincere friends</u> are our most valuable asset and so our friendship is of paramount value and should be cherished. <u>"Real results" means that China takes a pragmatic approach</u> to cooperation with Africa. "China not only preaches, <u>but also practices win-win cooperation</u>." "Affinity" refers to the natural sense of connection between the Chinese and African peoples. <u>"Good faith" means solving problems</u> that may arise during our cooperation <u>in good faith</u>. "China will face problems squarely, and resolve them in the spirit of mutual respect and win-win cooperation".

请大家注意重构原文逻辑之后,译文通过意思相近的衔接链,做到了前后连贯:"Sincerity" means China is sincere—sincere friends;"Real results" means …a pragmatic approach—practices win-win cooperation;"Good faith" means solving… in good faith。

这些例子说明,尽管译者对原文有忠实的义务,但对读者也有通顺的义务,对委托人更肩负"好用"的责任。如果委托人拿到的译文逻辑不通,就无法发挥任何作用。因此,我们要优先考虑委托人的利益。当然,这里对原文的变通处理,并不损害作者的利益,相反,还无形中为作者增添了光彩。作者如果知道,应该感激译者才对。

16.3 小结

本章讲解了语篇的衔接和连贯。衔接是语言表象,目的是达到意思连贯。译者要通过仔细阅读和宏观思维、批判性思维，发现语篇内部的各种指代和同义关系、对比关系，从而理解原文的逻辑，并通过符合译语习惯的衔接手段，再现原文的逻辑关系。在极端情况下，即使原文没有逻辑关系，译者也要尽量创造逻辑关系。当然，这样做以不损害作者和用户的利益为前提，最好与用户或审校商量后决定如何处理。

〔课后练习〕

1. 请利用任意一篇中文或英文材料，指出其中特定概念的衔接链。
2. 对比一篇文章的中英文版本，总结特定概念衔接方式的变化。
3. 从衔接链的角度重新审查自己翻译过的一篇文章，看是否可以通过改变译文的衔接方式，提高译文的连贯性。
4. 在下一次翻译中，确保能够发现文章所有的衔接链，并在译文中充分再现。
5. 回顾自己翻译过的文件，看是否有逻辑不通的地方，你当时是如何处理的，今后应该怎么办。

第四部分　翻译中的变通

第十七至十九章为本书的第四部分，探讨变通中重点关注的问题。比喻、俗语、口号等文化负载词的翻译，往往不能直译，需要通过各种办法变通处理，所以归入变通部分。还有些情况下需要根据英语的写作习惯或读者的喜爱，对原文结构或内容进行删减、编辑、调整，甚至把原文作为创作素材，这属于更高层次的变通。

是否变通以及如何变通，取决于翻译的委托人是谁、为何翻译、预设读者是谁、译文使用场景、发布媒介等各种信息，也可以用 6W1H 表示：Who is asking you to translate? For whom? When, where, why, and how is the translation to be used, by whom?

第十七章　比喻、口号、简称的翻译

扫码预习

请扫码下载本章涉及的例句。先做练习，再看解答，学习效果更佳。

17.1　比喻的概念

比喻是描写事物或说明道理时，用相似的事物或道理打比方，包括隐喻、明喻、借喻、借代、比拟等。

明喻有本体和喻体，并且以"如""像""若"等联系词连接本体和喻体，如"人生好比是趟旅行""六月的天，就像孩子的脸，说变就变"。隐喻也有本体与喻体，用"是""成为"等联接本体和喻体，也叫暗喻，如"人生是趟旅行""群众是汪洋大海，个人只不过是其中的一滴水"等。借喻既没有比喻词，本体也不出现，而是直接把喻体用在本体应该出现的地方。借喻的基本形式是以乙代甲。如"如果不打落水狗，它一旦跳起来，就要咬你，最低限度也溅你一身的污泥"。此句中"落水狗"比喻挨了打的敌人。借代是用甲事物来代替乙事物，甲乙两事物之间的联系是有某些相关之处。比如：北京认为。"北京"是借代，指中国政府。再比如：枪杆子里面出政权。"枪杆子"是借代，用"枪杆子"来代替"武装斗争"。因为"武装斗争"必须得用枪杆子，二者之间有联系。"龙井"是用地名来代一种茶，"胸无点墨"是用"墨水"来代学问，"停止了呼吸"是用一个不刺眼的现象来代死亡。比拟是按照人的想象和联想直接把人当作物或物当作人来写。比如：鸟儿歌唱，花儿欢笑。"鸟"和"花"本来不会像人那样"歌唱"和"欢笑"，但是人可以想象它们会歌唱、会欢笑。①

英语中也有类似的语言现象：A figure of speech is a word or phrase that possesses a separate meaning from its literal definition. It can be a metaphor or simile, designed to make a comparison. It can be the repetition of alliteration or the exaggeration of hyperbole to provide a dramatic effect.②

metaphor（隐喻）的定义为：a comparison between two things, based on resemblance or similarity, without using "like" or "as"，如 *tying up loose ends, a submarine sandwich, a branch of government* 以及大多数 clichés，如 *Rome wasn't built in a day. When the going gets tough, the tough get going. No guts, no glory. There are plenty more fish in the sea.* simile（明喻）是指：A comparison using "like" or "as"，如 *Her face was pale as the moon;* metonym（借代）是指：The substitution of one term for another with which it is commonly associated or closely related. 如 the *pen* is mightier than the *sword*, the *crown* (referring to a Queen or King); synecdoche（提喻，借代的一种）是指 the substitution of a part for the whole or vice versa (a kind of metonym)。如 give us this day our daily bread.③

我们讨论的重点是翻译方法，不是比喻形式上的分类和区别，所以，凡是具有象征意义的语句，包括各种比喻，都在我们的讨论范围。

比喻没有一定的语言形式，它可能是一个词、一个词组、一个句子或一段文章。比如，He *hatched* a clever scheme. 其中的 hatch 就是一个比喻（隐喻），它把一项计划的产生比作孵化过程；Our nation was *born out* of a desire for freedom. 这里把国家的建立比作"生育"；An eye for an eye. "以眼交换

---

① http://www.pep.com.cn/200403/ca375103.htm, http://www.xxjyw.com/Article_Show.asp?ArticleID=883, http://www.whedu.com.cn/../jiaoyu/ztjz/ztjz27.htm, accessed September 6, 2004.
② https://examples.yourdictionary.com/figure-of-speech-examples.html, accessed September 7, 2021.
③ http://owl.english.purdue.edu/handouts/general/gl_metaphor.html, accessed September 6, 2004.

眼"（以牙还牙，以眼还眼），这里把公正比作天平，做坏事和受惩罚要平衡；The *angry* waves *calmed down* as the dawn came. 这里把海浪比作人，可以发怒，可以平静。再如：There is no comfort in the truth. The truth is just as meaningful as the lie. 汉语中的比喻也是有多种形式："血缘的纽带""城市生活的脉搏""钉子户""铁公鸡""空手套白狼""不入虎穴，焉得虎子""三过家门而不入""狗咬吕洞滨，不识好人心"，唐诗"春怨"："打起黄莺儿，莫教枝上啼。啼时惊妾梦，不得到辽西"，鲁迅的《狂人日记》可以作为篇章级隐喻的代表。①

有些成语也是比喻。成语和比喻的共同点是都具有深刻的隐含意义；不同点有二：（1）成语都是短短数字，比喻则字数不限；（2）成语通常有其典故，而比喻则讲求创新性。既然判断比喻的标准不是语句结构，而是是否含有象征性的意义或具有概念上的不协调性，因此合乎此项标准的成语，也可视为一种比喻，如：过河拆桥、井底之蛙、一毛不拔、虎头蛇尾、半斤八两等。

已经普遍为人所知的比喻，有些学者称之为"死喻"（dead metaphor）。死喻的隐含意思已经成为常规词义，即所谓比喻意义，所以有些学者认为这些比喻已经不能算是比喻。例如"山腰"的"腰"，原来是个比喻，把山比作人；今天已经约定俗成，我们不再觉得是个比喻。"铁拳""蚕食""鲸吞""酝酿""覆没"，都属于这种情况。比喻意义不同于字面意义。我们用祖国的心脏来比喻首都，但首都不是心脏的意义。更有甚者，用来比喻的意思逐渐成了主要的意思，原来的意思反倒被人淡忘了，例如"穷困"原指走投无路，后用来比喻没钱，但这个比喻义现在成了穷困的主要意思，乃至于我们很难用另外什么表达方式来称谓没钱的状况。这是词义转变的一例。"桌腿""桌面""发火""责任"也属此类。②

Mouth 原只用于动物的口，不用于瓶子、河流，现在则应用于这些事物，从而 the mouth of the river〔河口〕就成了一个死喻。荷马把 wounds 叫作 mouth，是一个比喻，汉语里的伤口则不是比喻，这个说法在荷马那里是

---

① http://www.sil.org/LinguaLinks/lexicon/MetaphorsInEnglish/ConventionalMetaphorsInEnglish.htm, accessed September 6, 2004.

② http://www.xianxiang.com/0310101.htm, accessed September 6, 2004.

生动的，而在汉语里是理所当然的，因此是平淡无奇的。"发火"〔burned up〕是个死喻，无非是说他很生气，但这个比喻还活着时，我们就会想象生气时着火冒烟的样子。

用人作为山的喻体，英语有 the foot of the mountain 的说法，却没有 the waist of the mountain 的说法。西方还有 the shoulder of the mountain（山肩）的说法，汉语里则有"山脚""山腰"的说法，却没有"山肩"的说法。"山腰"在汉语里是个常用的比喻（stock metaphor），若在英语里说到 the waist of the mountain，那将是形象说法。由此再进一步，我们将不难看到，采用何种比喻是因文化而不同的。

纽马克（2001b）所谓的 metaphor 采用了广义，即我们所说的"比喻"：

> *By metaphor I mean any figurative expression*: the transferred sense of a physical word; the personification of an abstraction ("*modesty* forbids me"); the application of a word or collocation to what it does not literally denote, i.e., to describe one thing in terms of another. All polysemous words (a "heavy" heart) are potentially metaphorical. Metaphors may be "single" — viz. one-word — or "extended" (a collocation, an idiom, a sentence, a proverb, an allegory, a complete imaginative text).

其中的 transferred sense of a physical word，即词义的转移，如用"诞生"表示任何事物的起源；personification of an abstraction，即抽象行为的拟人化，如"*modesty* forbids me"，其中 forbid 本来只能用人做主语，现在用 modesty，即把 modesty 拟人化；the application of a word or collocation to what it does not literally denote，即用一个单词或语句表示字面意思之外的意思，如用 in cold blood 表示 without feeling or pity; in a purposely cruel way; coolly and deliberately；所谓"All polysemous words are potentially metaphorical"，即所有的多义词都可能带有隐含意思，如 a heavy heart 当中的 heavy，本来表示（物体）沉重，但这里的意思是 sad（悲伤、心情沉重），与汉语的比喻正好吻合。

17.2　比喻的翻译方法

比喻是翻译实践的难题和翻译研究的热门话题。人们经常讨论的两个问题是，比喻是否可译和比喻的翻译方法。Dagut（1976）认为，比喻是否可以翻译不在于比喻的新颖性和独创性，而取决于译入语读者在多大程度上享有比喻所利用的文化经验和关联语义（What determines the translatability of a source language metaphor is not its 'boldness' or 'originality', but rather the extent to which the cultural experience and semantic associations on which it draws are shared by speakers of the particular target language）。这句话的意思是，两种语言的文化越接近，两种语言词语的关联词义越接近，越容易翻译。这似乎是不言自喻的道理。实际情况是，由于文化背景差异，词语的各种意义并不对应，直译无法为读者理解，这时就不得不采取其他翻译策略。

纽马克在《翻译问题探讨》（2001a）中，把比喻划分为五种类型（dead, cliché, stock, recent, original metaphors）（后又增加一种 adapted metaphor，见《翻译教程》（2001b））。前面已经举了一些例子，这里再解释一下 stock metaphor。stock metaphor 也叫 standard metaphor，就是普通比喻、标准比喻。比如，on the eve of 表示在某一事件的前一天或前夕；keep the pot boiling 表示养家糊口；in a fog 表示 mentally confused, not sure what is happening；get in touch with someone 表示 to contact someone by either phone, fax, or email。还有些资料提到 conventional metaphor（常规）的概念，比如，在关于时间的比喻（隐喻）中，有时把时间比作消费品，例如：This method will *save* time. Time is *money*. She's *wasting* her time. How *long* do we have to wait? *Use* your time well. He is making up for *lost* time；有时把时间比作移动的物体，例如：The time will *come* when ... The time has long since *gone* when ... Coming up in the weeks *ahead* ... Next week and the week *following* it ...

纽马克（2001a）提出普通比喻（stock metaphor）的以下 7 种翻译方法。从逻辑上看，该归纳十分详尽，其他类型的比喻也不外乎这几种翻译方法或其组合。所以下文中所举的例子就不一定是普通比喻。需要指出的是，每个比喻的翻译不只一种方法，不同的场合，需要作出不同选择。

1）直译（在译入语中再现相同意象）。条件是该意象在译入语中出现频率、常用程度和文体相当。如：a ray of hope 一线希望，spend money like water 花钱如流水（也可借用"挥金如土"）；be armed to the teeth 武装到牙齿，crocodile tears 鳄鱼的眼泪，God helps those who help themselves 自助者天助也。这几个例子，除了前两对正好相当外，其余在笔者看来，还是有外来痕迹，年轻学子可能已经不知道这些比喻来自外语。既要直译，又要符合"出现频率、常用程度和文体相当"，是很难达到的标准。

2）借用（用标准的译入语意象替代源语意象，但不得和译入语文化相抵触）。如：sunny smile 灿烂的微笑；Among the blind the one-eyed man is king. 山中无老虎，猴子称大王；He who keeps company with the wolf will learn to howl. 近朱者赤，近墨者黑；Old dog will not learn new tricks. 人过三十不学艺；Talk of the devil (and he will appear). 说到曹操，曹操就到；物不平则鸣 Injustice will cry out. 负荆请罪 abject apologies；又如：burn one's boats (bridges)，用来比喻"不留后路，下定决心干到底"，意思同汉语的"破釜沉舟"，但形象稍有差异；kill the goose to get the eggs. 比喻只贪图眼前利益，没有长远打算，与汉语"杀鸡取卵"意思相同，喻体也相近。上述几例中，"说到曹操，曹操就到"就可能产生文化冲突。

3）把隐喻翻译为明喻，保留原来的意象，这样可以避免隐喻造成的突兀。如：龙飞凤舞 *like* dragons flying and phoenixes dancing；狗咬吕洞宾，不识好人心 *Like* the dog that bit Lu Tung-pin — you bite the hand that feeds you.

4）直译＋意译（把比喻翻译为比喻＋意思）。A skeleton in the closet 衣柜里的骷髅，见不得人的事儿；龙飞凤舞 like dragons flying and phoenixes dancing — bold cursive calligraphy；Pandora's box 潘多拉的盒子——灾难、麻烦、祸害的根源；病来如山倒，病去如抽丝 Getting better is always a lengthy business. You know what they say "Sickness comes like an avalanche but goes like reeling silk".

5）意译（把比喻转换为直白的意思）。Every family is said to have at

least *one skeleton in the cupboard.* 据说家家户户至少也有一桩家丑；The teenagers don't invite Bob to their parties because he is *a wet blanket.* 青少年们不邀请鲍勃参加聚会，因为他总是扫别人的兴；Old dog will not learn new tricks. 老人学不了新东西；Achilles' heel 唯一致命弱点；meet one's Waterloo 一败涂地；说得天花乱坠，不由得尤老娘不肯：He *painted such a glowing picture* that naturally old Mrs. Agreed.

6) 删除。如果隐喻多余或没有什么意义，可以删除。例如：他不但不去管约，反助纣为虐讨好：He had not checked his disgraceful behavior but actually abetted him in order to curry favor.

7) 直译＋解释。To carry coals to Newcastle 运煤到纽卡斯尔，多此一举（注："纽卡斯尔"是英国的一个产煤中心地，运煤到此是多余的事）；班门弄斧 show off one's skill with the axe before Lu Ban the master carpenter（也可直接翻译意思：show off one's talent/skill before an expert）；卧薪尝胆 sleep on brush-wood and taste gall—undergo self-imposed hardship (to strengthen one's resolve to wipe out a national humiliation or to accomplish some ambition)。

中国学者也提出过类似的翻译方法。例如，张培基（1980）等提出三种常见的方法，郭著章等（1996）提出五种常见的方法。

图里（Toury, 1995）认为，这些翻译方法是把原文中的比喻作为考察对象提出的，如果观察译文中比喻的使用情况，可以发现另外两种情况：一是把原文直白的意思译为比喻；二是原文不存在语言诱因，却在译文中增加比喻。

尽管以上方法可能适用于所有种类的比喻，但不同种类的比喻使用某种翻译方法的频率可能不同。比如，死喻可能更倾向于直接翻译意思，因为比喻的新鲜意味在原文中已经消失，如果把比喻翻译出来，读者的感受会产生差异；而原创比喻则更倾向于保留原文的意象。同时，笔者也认为，比喻的翻译方法不仅与比喻的类型有关系，还与译入语对外来文化的态度有关，以致产生比喻翻译的双重标准。

17.3　比喻翻译的双重标准

李运兴（2001）总结了译者处理文化成分的五种模式，与纽马克归纳的方法存在对应关系：

1. 文化直入模式（Go-ahead Model）——源语文化表达形式直接进入译文。

2. 文化阻断模式（Block Model）——源语文化表达形式消失，文化意义未进入译语语篇。

3. 文化诠释模式（Annotation Model）——为源语文化表达形式提供文化语境信息。

4. 文化融合模式（Integration Model）——源语文化表达形式与译语表达形式融合，以一种新语言形式进入译语。

5. 文化归化模式（Adaptation Model）——源语表达形式略去，代之以译语表达形式，源语文化意义丧失。

李运兴认为（2001）：从文化交流的角度看，这五个模式可以分为两类：模式1、3、4促成不同文化的交流和沟通，而模式2、5则使源语文化成分被阻隔在译语文化之外。

对文化成分的翻译原则主要取决于原作文化背景、原文作者的权威性、翻译的社会背景、翻译发起者（initiator）和译者的文化观念以及译文读者群的文化接受心态等因素，而这些因素又是密切相关，相辅相成的。

促成选择模式1的因素主要有：1）源语文化在经济和政治上具有强大优势或侵略性；2）源语文化对译语文化有着极强的吸引力，译语读者极想了解；3）译文的预想读者群有较强学术倾向，想了解源语文化真面目；4）翻译发起者要求译者或译者迫于社会形势，将源语文化成分植入译文；5）表现源语文化意义的词语在译语中没有现成的相应词语，译者只能采取音译或直译。

促成选择模式2、5的因素有：1）译语文化属封闭文化，或有强烈优越感，或对源语文化成分表现敏感或反感；2）源语文化意义在语言形式上太独特，以至无法以译文语言形式再现；3）翻译的目的只是愉悦读者或提供大致信息；4）译语社会有严格检查制度，对异域文化实施严格控制。

促成选择模式3、4的因素有：1）当今社会的"全球化"及"民主化"趋势，使不同文化间敌视减少，交流增多，相容性增强；2）译语文化属开放型，在保持自己文化传统的同时，乐于接受外来文化；3）翻译的发起人或译者有强烈的促进文化交流的动机和目的。

Fung（1995）通过比较指出，英语的比喻翻译为汉语时，经常保留原文的意象，而汉语比喻翻译为英语时，经常采用替换的方法。她认为，其中一个原因可能是中国受众可能对西方文化比较熟悉且乐于接受西方文化，而西方读者却并非如此。"一石二鸟"进入了中文，"一箭双雕"没有进入英语，就是一个很好的例子。

其实，Fung仅仅指出了造成翻译策略差异的表面原因，真正的原因是中国文化处于劣势。尽管中华民族有四大发明，有光辉灿烂的历史，为世界文明进步作出了不可磨灭的贡献，但近几百年来，中国确确实实落在了西方列强的后面，所以，我们才不得不向西方寻求救国的真理。不是我们乐于接受西方文化，而是我们不得不接受；不是我们不愿意把祖国璀璨的文化瑰宝直译出去，而是不得不照顾人家的口味。如果我们成了世界一流的强国，全世界的人都向中国取经，那就用不着我们自己把自己的东西翻译出来求人家看，他们会找上门来学习我们的语言、翻译我们的典籍；会像我们现在那样，唯恐翻译得不够准确。其实，这是很自然的现象：中国文明鼎盛时期，周边国家学习中国文化更彻底，把文字都照搬过去了；而在日本明治维新之后，中国反过来向日本学习，我们现在的很多政治经济词汇都是日本人首先从西方文字翻译为中文的。

我们接受西方影响的渠道多种多样。首先是翻译西方典籍、资料，这个过程已经持续了一百多年。"近朱者赤，近墨者黑。"一种新的概念，当它第一次被直译过来的时候，可能需要解释；当它被翻译了一百次的时候，恐怕就不需要解释了。相比之下，从汉语翻译为英语的作品数量极其有限，在西方根本不成气候，在语言上、文化上对西方的影响甚微。当然，随着中国的日趋强大，对中国感兴趣的人越来越多，学习中文的人越来越多，我们的许多说法，也有可能进入西方语言。其次是外语教育。外语教育为西方文化的传播提供了肥沃的土壤，培养了人们对西方文化的亲和力和接受能力。通过外语教育，我们一方面直接学习了西方的一些比喻，另一方面，我们也更容易看懂比喻的直译。还有各种各样的国际交流、派遣留学生、出国考察，这些都是中国了解西方的重要途径。可以说，我们的普通百姓对西方国家的了解水平，远远大于西方百姓对中国的了解，这也说明了为什么中国人对外来的东西更容易接受。

在这样大的历史、文化背景下，在今后相当长的时间内，恐怕在翻译上还要实行双重标准，即英译汉时更多地采取文化直入、文化诠释、文化融合的模式；汉译英时，更多地采取文化阻断和文化归化模式。或者说，在翻译中实行一边倒的翻译策略，即无论汉译英，还是英译汉，一律照顾英文习惯。

当然，这样的标准不是绝对的。即使在这样的大环境下，也不排除局部存在有利于中国文化向西方传播的因素，如在特定翻译情景下，西方读者可能急欲了解中国文化，或译者极力推动中国文化向西方传播。再者，在文学翻译中，因为文学作品本身的特点，使得文化直入、文化诠释和文化融合具有天然的合法性，无论是汉译英，还是英译汉，都是如此；而在非文学翻译中，因为信息的准确传递是第一位的，所以采取文化阻断和文化归化模式也许就足以达到传递信息的目的，没有必要为了传递一个意象而大费周章。但鉴于汉语的巨大包容性以及几千年以来形成的"美文"传统，英译汉时引入英语的意象，甚至酌情增添比喻也许并无文体上的不妥。实际上，在科技名词的翻译中，要尽可能直译，保留原文的意象，因为直译最容易记忆、最容易统一、最容易回译，所以生命力最强。相反，汉译英时就要特别注意照顾英语的需要，以翻译意思为主，不要轻易引入英语中没有的表达方式，尤其是要注意把汉语中特别有文采的地方朴实化。

总之，笔者对比喻翻译的看法是，如果"直译"可以为读者理解，读起来不感到突兀或滑稽可笑，符合特定交际情景，可以直译；否则考虑意译、借用或其他折中方法。具体到汉英非文学翻译，考虑到英语朴实无华的表现手法，一般情况下只需翻译意思。英语作为我们的外语，我们很多时候也许无法判断比喻直译过去是否可以为读者接受，这时翻译意思是最保险的做法。

这样的概括也许还是太绝对，因为非文学翻译的情况也是千差万别，需要根据具体情况作出具体判断。别忘了，翻译中存在 5% 的个人品味，如果你有强烈的促进文化交流的动机和目的，在不违背客观需求的情况下，你可以表现自己的特色。

17.4 特色表达翻译举例

除了比喻,汉语还有很多特色表达方法,如典故、习语、成语。凡是具有特色的表达方式,其翻译方法不外乎中外学者归纳的几种。下面分别举出几个例子,看这些特色说法在特定语境中是如何处理的。

17.4.1 比喻

有一些比喻是汉英通用的,可以直译;但更多情况下,汉语中的比喻直译过去读者可能无法理解,这时,就直接用白话表达汉语的意思。

例1.
   当前,国有经济战线太长,重复建设严重,布局过于分散,企业规模偏小,素质较差,这是造成国有企业经营困难,高投入、低产出,高消耗、低收益的重要原因。

原译:
   At present, *the strength of the state-owned sector is spread too thin*. Moreover, it is haunted by such problems as repeated construction, excessively scattered distribution of industry, small scale of the enterprises and poor product quality. These problems cause many difficulties for the management of state-owned enterprises, such as high input, low output, high consumption of energy and other resources and low efficiency. (Foreign Languages Press)

分析比喻的意义:
"战线长":指行业分布广。证据:"一是行业分布广泛,战线拉得过长"。另外,"布局分散"这一表达方法很抽象,它的意思是指涉足的领域多,和"战线长"意思相同。例如:

   目前,国有经济布局过于分散,涉足的领域众多,没有集中在能够有效发挥其经济功能的领域,这就像让一个举重运动员去跑马拉松一样,其结果是可以想象的。

所以翻译时有必要把比喻和抽象的内容落到实处,把重复的信息合并:

Lack of focus, duplication, small scale, and poor quality are major causes of operational difficulties such as low efficiency and high energy intensity in the state-owned sector.

译文以 lack of focus 概括了"战线长""布局分散"。

例2.

近年来,世界经济低迷给国际航空运输业的发展蒙上了一层阴影,去年发生的"9·11"恐怖事件,更是雪上加霜,使国际航空运输业再次遭受重创。

Global economic slowdown in recent years has *encumbered growth of* the international air transport industry. Last year's September 11th attack only *made it worse.*

两处比喻均没有译出,而是直接翻译意思。

例3.

没有社会的稳定,就没有经济的发展和社会的进步。而社会保障则是维护社会稳定的重要防线。

Without social stability, neither economic growth nor social progress is possible. And social security *is essential for* stability.

同样没有翻译比喻,而是翻译意思。

例4.

第二,是要给实际上处于不利境况或者是社会底层的人以制度化的实际帮助(包括生活救济和其他方面的救助),使法律上的平等对他们而言不再是无实际意义的镜中之花、水中之月。

Second, there must be real institutional support (for living and other needs) for the disadvantaged and the lower social classes, so that equality under the law is no longer mere *rhetoric*.

译文同样没有翻译出比喻。

例 5.

　　我们能漂亮地打赢一场神出鬼没的战役，当然是战略奏效，主帅领导有方，而老百姓也理智地给以充分的配合。对抗沙斯的战役为新加坡赢得了声誉，这个宝贵的资产是属于全国的。

　　Good leadership, effective strategies and active cooperation from the people have helped *conquer the elusive SARS*. The SARS battle has won Singapore international accolades which are national honours.（《早报网》）

译文没有翻译比喻。"神出鬼没"比喻行动变化迅速，让敌人无路可逃。译文改变说法，用 elusive 修饰 SARS，间接表达了"神出鬼没"的意思。

例 6.

　　有人说，新加坡老百姓一向习惯于家长式的管理，反而使得抗沙斯（新加坡用语）的战略更容易行之有效。

　　Some people have argued that the fight against SARS was easier because Singaporeans are *used to a prescriptive style of government*.（《早报网》）

译文没有翻译比喻，而是直接翻译意思。如果翻译为比喻说得过去，当然更好，例如：

　　对 1993 年深圳致丽玩具厂火灾受害打工者的追踪调查在 1999 年和 2000 年已经基本完成，2001 年课题组帮助了该厂客户——意大利某公司提供的补偿款项的发放，包括与香港和内地有关省份发放者的联系，与受害者的联系，到 2001 年 6 月，共有 79 死者家属和 41 伤者分别得到人民币一万多元的补偿。追踪过程已经写出题为"泣血追踪"的报告。

　　Follow-up investigations of the victims of a 1993 fire in Zhili Toy

Factory were basically completed in 1999 and 2000. In 2001, the project team helped distribute compensation paid by the Italian company, including contacting payout centres in Hong Kong and the mainland provinces and contacting the victims. By June 2001, family members of the 79 death victims and 41 injured persons had each received compensation of more than RMB10,000. The tracking process is described in a report entitled *"Trail of Tears."*

译文稍作变化，把"泣血"转变为"泪水"。再如：

> 应当说，中国与俄罗斯和欧洲国家在多极化方面是有共同利益的，中国和欧洲国家也没有什么重大的利益冲突，在建立多极化的进程中可以寻找到更多的共同语言。

Multi-polarity is one area which China, Russia, and Europe share common interests. Without major conflict of interests between them, China and Europe can *find more common ground* in building a multi-polar world.

译文把"共同语言"，换成了译文的比喻"共同立场"。

总的来说，实际翻译活动中，尤其是汉译英时，经常把比喻简化为意思之后再来翻译。一个看似不好解决的问题，就这么简单地解决了。毕竟翻译的最终目的是传达意思，而不是找到对等的语言表达形式。

17.4.2 典故

典故一般没有必要直译过去，除非在特定的情境下，文化交流是文章或谈话的重点，版面或者谈话时间也允许我们对中国文化进行详细解释。

例 7.

> 伊利采用灵活多变的市场营销战略。对不同的地区，伊利采取了不同的营销策略。例如在打入武汉市场时，以"昭君回故里，伊利献真情"为主题，向武汉中小学生赠送 100 万支雪糕，一举占领武汉市场。在打入北京市场时，鉴于北京冷饮品牌众多的情况，采取"农村包围城市"

的战略,由三环路外开始,逐步向内扩展。目前,伊利产品已经广销全国 30 个省市自治区的 500 多个大中城市,并开始打入国际市场。

译文 1:

Flexible marketing strategies. Different strategies are adopted for different regions. For example, in Wuhan, Yili occupied the market by distributing 1 million ice creams for free to the primary and middle school students there through a campaign named *"Care from Yili."* In Beijing, where there were already a lot of brands, it adopted *an encirclement strategy*, starting from the suburbs and gradually expanding into the downtown area. Now Yili products are sold in more than 500 medium and large cities in nearly all parts of China, and it is starting to enter the international market.

该译文把两个典故变为与此处意思相符的白话。

译文 2:

The marketing strategy of Yili is flexible and diversified as it always takes different approaches to deal with different markets. To win over customers of Wuhan, for example, the group donated 1 million servings of ice cream to local primary and middle school students, an offer that really has paid off. In the case of Beijing, Yili, mindful of fierce competition there, decided to start with suburbs outside the Third Ring Road before entering the downtown area. Now Yili sells well in more than 500 cities across the country and, more importantly, it is starting to enter the international market.

该译文完全省略了典故。

译文 3:

Yili adopts different marketing strategies in different target markets. For example, in Wuhan, *under a catchy slogan*, Yili offered 1 million free ice creams to students in primary and secondary schools there. As a result, it took the market overnight. In Beijing, because there are many competitors there, Yili began to sell its products outside the Third Ring Road and gradually moved into the downtown area. At present, Yili's products are available in more than 500 large- and medium-sized cities across the countries. Yili also began to make its presence in the international market.

该译文也采用了简化的手段。

以上三种译文都没有直译文化词。鉴于该译文仅仅是对一个公司情况的简单介绍，译文读者需要获得的是公司信息，不是中国文化信息，所以这样的处理是合适的。虽然没有翻译文化成分，但也达到了翻译目的。

译文 4：

Yili is flexible in adopting different marketing strategies suitable to each specific region. For example, before entering Wuhan, *a southwestern city along the Yangtze River*, we gave out 1 million pieces of ice cream to the local pupils and middle-school students for free, under the theme of "home of beauty, hopes of Yili"[1]. As a result, Yili easily won that market. In Beijing, since there were lots of brands there, we adopted a strategy of "encircling the city from the countryside[2]": selling our products in the outskirts before moving into the city. Currently, Yili products are available in over 500 large- and medium-sized cities on the mainland and even in the international market.

Notes:

1. This refers to Wang Zhaojun, one of the four beauties of ancient China. She was a Wuhan native, but to end the war between her country and a tribe in northern China (where Yili is located), she agreed to be married to the tribal chief to bring peace to her people.

2. A military strategy employed by Mao Zedong to defeat Chiang Kai-shek and the KMT regime, which resulted in victory over the whole of China.

这位学生做得非常认真。如果翻译历史文献，确实需要这样的翻译；如果出于一般的交流目的，则没有这样做的必要。

例8.

  其三、面对经济全球化、金融开放化的国际竞争环境和加入世贸组织的重大战略选择，国家不得不"破釜沉舟"，把国有商业银行推向国际金融市场，促使其在"好银行"的角逐中争得一席之地，以稳固中国金融的阵脚。

  Thirdly, with economic globalization, financial liberalization, and accession to WTO, the government is forced to make *the difficult decision* to push Chinese commercial banks into the global stage to compete and to secure China's place in the international financial market.

没有翻译典故，把"破釜沉舟"翻译为"作出果断的决定"。

例9.

  沙斯战役还没有到可以鸣金收兵的时刻，国人仍须保持警戒之心，以防病毒再次肆虐，这是我们的共识。

  The war against SARS is *far from over*. We must agree to not let our guard down, to prevent another outbreak of the deadly virus.

此处的"鸣金收兵"，也没有按字面翻译。再如：

  大规模减税降费，是要动政府的存量利益，要割自己的肉。所以我说这是一项刀刃向内、壮士断腕的改革。

"刀刃向内、壮士断腕"用在这里表示政府对于实施减税降费相关措施的决心和勇气。如果按照字面意思翻译成 pointing the knife to yourself and severing your own wrist，外国读者可能不理解其背后的含义，官方译文翻译成 "this is a key reform that requires exceptional courage and determination"，省去了一个成语、一个典故，直接解释了背后的意义。

17.4.3 习语和成语

  如果译入语正好有相似或对应的成语，可以使用，否则只能翻译直白的意思。例如：

法律所能提供的制度安排，应是帮助人选择，引导人选择，并非万不得已不实行强制。中国的传统的说法是"己所不欲，勿施於人"，而"己所欲，强施於人"并不应是今天法律的品德。

Institutional arrangements provided by law should serve as guidance on choices, and should not compel unless absolutely necessary. As the saying goes, "do not do unto others what you do not want done unto you," so "do unto others as you would have them do unto you" should not be the spirit of today's law.

"己所不欲，勿施於人"是中国的说法，其内涵并不等于"do unto others what you want to"[①]，因此作者自创了另一个习语"己所欲，强施於人"来表达英文习语的含义。译文严格按照字面翻译翻译，让大家体会两者的区别。

成语（或习语）在汉语中是司空见惯的语言表达方式，对中文读者而言，并无多少新意。如果直译为英语一个很新颖的表达方法，给译文读者的感受是不同的。所以除非要向外国人讲解成语的意思，一般只需要翻译出比喻意义。

例 10.

21 世纪前 10 年，是中国民航承前启后，继往开来的重要时期……

The first decade of the 21st century will be *a period of transition* for China's civil aviation industry …

两个成语合并为一个简单的意思。

例 11.

当时，新中国刚刚成立，百业凋零、百废待兴，国民经济基础相当薄弱。

[①] "己所不欲，勿施于人"常被作为"Do unto others as you would have them do unto you."的同义语，但两者的含义并不完全相同。前者的意思是：自己不想要的，不要强加于人，并不隐含自己认为好的，要强加于人。相反，它可以解释为：自己认为好的，别人如果也认为好，可以来学，我不会强加于你，就像过去日本的学问僧到中国学习一样。而后者的意思，可以理解为我认为好，你不要也得要。这样的做法对方可能乐意，也可能不乐意。可能是办好事，也可能是好心办坏事，还可能以此为借口，强行推广自己的价值观，为世界带来灾难。

At that time, the PRC was just founded and was economically weak. *Industries were devastated by war and needed rebuilding.*

两个成语简化为直白的意思后翻译。

例 12.

何况，难得我国的政治人物一改过去严肃的、近于不苟言笑的态度，而以轻松活泼的方式与老百姓在一起。

It was also rare to see our leaders breaking from their usual serious and *unsmiling demeanour* to mingle with the people in a playful and light-hearted manner.

成语解释后翻译。

例 13.

扶贫干部要真正沉下去，扑下身子到村里干，同群众一起干，不能蜻蜓点水，不能三天打鱼两天晒网，不能神龙见首不见尾。(Xi-II)

Poverty relief officials *must go deep into* the villages and work hard together with the locals. They must not *make token efforts* or *be slack at work*.

原文众多形象的说法几乎消失殆尽。如果翻译出来并不难理解，即使译入语无此说法，也可以译出。如下文的"缘木求鱼"：

爱国有罪，冤狱遍于国中；卖国有赏，汉奸弹冠相庆。以这种错误政策来求集中和统一，真是缘木求鱼，适得其反。(Mao-I)

Patriotism is penalized and innocent people are in jail everywhere; treason is rewarded and traitors are jubilant over their new appointments and honours. To seek centralization and unification by means of this wrong policy is like *climbing a tree to seek fish* and will produce exactly the opposite results.

习语有时甚至没有必要翻译出来，例如：

例 14.

　　社会公平，是人类社会发展中客观产生的一种需要。社会公平体现在经济利益方面主要是社会成员之间没有过份悬殊的贫富差别，即所谓"不患贫、患不均"。

　　Social equity becomes necessary as human societies progress. In terms of wealth distribution, social equity implies keeping a minimum gap between the haves and have-nots.

　　"不患贫、患不均"是对上文意思的概括，不用译出。

　　一些情况下可以概括翻译，如：三从四德 wifely submission and virtues；三纲五常 principles of feudal moral conduct；轻徭薄赋 low tax rates（虽然严格来讲，"徭""赋"并不相同）；循环往复，水涨船高 a spiral；四面楚歌 be besieged；伯乐 talent picker, talent spotter；父母之命，媒妁之言 (parents-and-matchmaker) arranged (marriage)；天时地利人和 all necessary conditions；挂羊头卖狗肉 misbranded, misnamed, sham 等。

　　有不少汉语成语只需要翻译其中的一半即可表达全部的意思："扭亏为盈"，直译为 run from loss making to profit making, turn a loss into a profit，简译为 go into the black (=become profitable) 或 begin to make profit；脱贫致富 shake off poverty (and get rich)；阴盛阳衰 strong women (and feeble men)；男尊女卑 male superiority (and female inferiority)；重男轻女 son preference；男主女从 the domination of men (and the subordination of women)；男主外，女主内 men work outside the home (and women within)。

　　成语和习语在不同的场合可能表示不同的含义，所以不能照搬词典翻译。词典翻译仅仅是参考。

17.5　政策口号的翻译方法

　　在我国的政治、经济生活中，经常把党的施政纲领、方针、政策、措施等以高度浓缩的形式进行概括，形似缩略语，暂且称之为"政策口号"。政策口号言简意赅,节奏感强,为群众喜闻乐见。例如:利改税,是指 reform to replace profit submission with tax payment,英文可以简称 the taxation reform;清产核资,是指 inventory-taking and assets evaluation,英文可以简称 a general assets checkup;孕产保护,是指 prenatal and postnatal care,简称为 maternity protection(maternity 既包括"孕"又包括"产")。政策口号为翻译带来了极大的挑战:首先,政策简称意思具有高度概括性,不容易准确把握;其次,政策简称具有音韵美,在翻译中几乎无法传达。尽管如此,译者也尽量做到准确、通顺、好用。所谓"好用",通常意味着要简洁。以下举例说明几种翻译方法:

17.5.1 保留节奏感

例 15.

立党为公,执政为民

building the Party that serves the public and governs for the people

例 16.

洁身自好、保持童贞、忠于配偶、白头偕老。

Be virtuous, chaste, faithful, and live together until old age.

例 17.

而党政机关在制定政策时最初的考虑是希望通过发展小城镇和乡镇企业,就地消化农村多余劳动力;使农村人离土不离乡。

In the beginning, the Party and government organizations hoped to absorb rural surplus labor locally by developing small towns and rural industries, so that the rural population would "*leave the farm but not the home.*"

例 18.

1983 年,"严打"以毒品犯罪为重点之一,1989 年"除六害"以毒品犯罪为六害之一。

In 1983, one focus of "strike hard" was on drug crime; in 1989, *the "uproot the six evils" campaign* included drug crime as one evil.

例 19.
　　中国能不能在今后严格遵循法治社会中行政机关"依法行政，违法无效"的原则和行政机关必须接受司法的最终裁判的规则，并不再过多地代立法机关起草法律，对中国能否实现法治是至关重要的。
　　Establishing the rule of law in China depends on whether administrative agencies *"govern according to law"*, whether they will accept the judiciary as the final arbitor, and whether they will reduce their involvement in drafting legislation.

"违法无效"，是指行政机关违法行政，其结果无效。这是"依法行政"的应有之义，可以省略。

例 20.
　　谁污染，谁治理
　　PPP (Polluting Party Pays) or "polluter pays"

PPP 更常见的意思是 Purchasing Power Parity（购买力平价），对它进行重新解释很新颖。

17.5.2　稍加变通以保留节奏

例 21.
　　1990 年，公安部《关于严格依法办事，执行政策，深入开展除"六害"斗争的通知》
　　The 1990 Ministry of Public Security Notice on *Implementing Laws and Policies to Eradicate the* "Six Evils"

例 22.
　　12 月，全国人大常委会通过《关于禁毒的决定》，提出"三禁并举，堵源截流，严格执法，标本兼治"的禁毒工作方针。

In December, the NPC Standing Committee passed the Decisions on Prohibition of Narcotic Drugs, proposing a policy of *"triple bans" (ban on smoking, trafficking, and growing) to destroy entire drug chains.*

本句保留了简洁明快的特点，照顾到了意思层次，省略了一些文字（也增加了一些解释），但意思没变。"堵源截流，标本兼治"均已包含在 the whole drug chain 中。"严格执法"加不进去，但可以认为意思不言而喻。"严格执法"在其他地方可能需要翻译出来。

例 23.

中华民族的昨天，可以说是"雄关漫道真如铁"。中华民族的今天，正可谓"人间正道是沧桑"。中华民族的明天，可以说是"长风破浪会有时"。

Citing a few lines, we have "stormed strong passes and come a long way"; we have "turned seas into mulberry fields"; and we will "advance through the wind and waves."

此处引用的诗句仅翻译了其中的关键意思，以保留节奏。如有必要，可以加注说明几句诗的出处，否则，这已经足以传达原文的意思。

17.5.3 只翻译意思，放弃节奏

例 24.

对在西部地区新办交通、电力、水利、邮政、广播电视等企业，企业所得税实行两年免征，三年减半征收。

Businesses in industries such as transportation, power, water conservancy, postal services, and radio and television *will be exempt from income tax in the first 2 years and enjoy a 50% reduction over the following 3 years.*

或者：

For businesses in industries such as transportation, power, water conservancy, postal services, and radio and television, their income tax will *be exempted for the first 2 years and will be reduced by half for the next 3 years.*

例 25.

合理制定"西气东输""西电东送"价格

Reasonable prices should be set for *gas and electricity transmitted from the western region to the east.*

本句也是只翻译了意思。如果必须翻译出来，可以译为 the project to pipe (transfer, convey, conduct, etc.) gas from the west to the east, the (West-to-East) Gas Piping Project; the project to transmit power from the west to the east, "the (West-to-East) Power Transmission Project"等。

例 26.

国家倡导一种整体利益高于一切的伦理主张，要求人们"狠斗私字一闪念"，在行为和思想上自觉与国家（党中央）保持一致。

The state advocated supremacy of collective interests, requiring the people to *"resist every selfish thought"* and to consciously behave and think in line with the state (the Party Central Committee).

例 27.

1994 年，卫生部召开血源用免疫诊断试剂国家检定研讨会时已经认识到"形势严峻"，"到了应提倡全民防止'病从血入'的时候了"。

In 1994, the MOH organized a seminar on national examination of all immunodiagnostic reagents used at blood source. By that time it was clear that "the situation was serious," and *"it was time to prevent transmission of blood-borne diseases."*

原文的联想意义（病从口入）、节奏无法保留。

例 28.

改革是大势所趋、人心所向，停顿和倒退没有出路，必须自强不息,自我革新,逢山开路,遇水架桥。

Reform is the trend of history and the desire of the people. There is no way to stop or reverse. We must keep improving ourselves, innovating and overcoming any obstacles on the way.

译文做了简化处理。

17.5.4 各部分揉合翻译

如果直译太啰嗦,可以把各部分的意思分散在一个句子中来翻译。

例 29.

根据当前两种经济体制转换过程的实际,社会保障制度改革需要一个渐进过程。要坚持低水平、广覆盖、多层次的基本方针……

The objective of reform should be to establish a *multi-tiered regime* with *a wide coverage and modest benefits*.

例 30.

要加强宏观调控,分阶段、按区域、多功能、全方位的发展支线航空。

Various forms of regional air transport will be focused upon and developed in *different phases based on the different local conditions*.

例 31.

在新时代,实现中华民族伟大复兴,更需要以识才的慧眼、爱才的诚意、用才的胆识、容才的雅量、聚才的良方,广开进贤之路……

In the new era, China's rejuvenation is even more reliant on our ability to spot, gather and retain talent. We must have the courage to use them, accept them, and value their contributions.

译文按照逻辑顺序,重新排列了六个并列成分。慧眼、胆识、雅量等词,用于夸赞别人,不能说我自己很有胆识,所以省略。spot:识才;

gather：进贤；retain：聚才；use：用才；accept：容才；value：爱才。

17.6　数字简称的翻译方法

数字简称也是政策口号的一种形式，一般采取直译或直译加解释的方式进行翻译，解释部分可以放在括号内，也可以作为脚注或尾注。第一次用到时，直译加解释；再次提到时，只用缩略形式。例如：

- "二保一"："Two Ensure One" — a woman sacrifices her career to ensure her husband's success or the other way round.
- "两个一百年"奋斗目标：the Two Centennial Goals—the first goal calls for completing the building of a moderately prosperous society, and doubling China's 2010 GDP and per capita income, by the time the CPC celebrates its centenary in 2021, and the second goal calls for building China into a modern socialist country that is prosperous, strong, democratic, culturally advanced, and harmonious, and reaches the level of moderately developed countries, by the time the People's Republic celebrates its centenary in 2049.
- "三个代表"："Three Represents" — Our Party must always represent the development trend of China's advanced productive forces, the orientation of China's advanced culture and the fundamental interests of the overwhelming majority of the Chinese people.
- "三讲"教育：The Three Emphases education — to stress theoretical study, political awareness and good conduct
- "三禁"："Triple Ban" — ban on the production, trafficking and use of drugs
- "三严三实专题教育"：Special Education Program of the Three Guidelines for Ethical Behavior and Three Basic Rules of Conduct — Three Guidelines for Ethical Behavior and Three Basic Rules of Conduct are expectations of leading officials at all levels. They call upon officials to be strict with themselves in self-cultivation, in the exercise of power, and in self-discipline, and act

in good faith when performing official duties, taking initiatives, and interacting with others.

- "三座大山": "Three Big Mountains" — imperialism, feudalism and bureaucratic capitalism
- "双控区": "Double Control" areas — controls of SO_2 and acid rain areas
- "四个全面战略布局": the Four-Pronged Comprehensive Strategy — completing the building of a society which is moderately prosperous in all respects, comprehensively expanding in-depth reform, comprehensively promoting law-based governance, and comprehensively enforcing strict Party self-governance.
- "四个意识": the Four Consciousnesses — maintaining political integrity; thinking in terms of the broader picture; following the leadership core; and keeping in alignment with the CPC Central Committee
- "四个自信": the Four Matters of Confidence — confidence in the socialist path, theory, system and culture
- "四自": "Four-Selves" — woman's self-cultivation in self-esteem, self-confidence, self-reliance and self-improvement
- "五保户": The Five Guarantees System — providing food, clothing, medical care, housing and burial expenses for the childless and infirm elderly and for the weak, sick and disabled who have lost their ability to work
- "五通"（政策沟通、设施联通、贸易畅通、资金融通、民心相通）: The Five-Pronged Approach to Connectivity (FPAC) — policy coordination, infrastructure connection, unimpeded trade, integrated financial service, people-to-people exchange
- "五位一体总体布局": the Five-Sphere Integrated Plan (SPIP) — The Five-sphere Integrated Plan for Chinese Socialism (the development of socialism with Chinese characteristics encompassing economic, political, cultural, social and eco-environmental development
- "一带一路"倡议: the Belt and Road Initiative (BRI) — China's proposal to cooperate with other countries in building a Silk Road Economic Belt

and a 21st-century Maritime Silk Road

- "中央八项规定": the Eight-Point Decision (on Improving Party and Government Conduct) — doing better research and analysis and truly understanding actual conditions when doing grassroots-level studies; streamlining meetings and improving the way meetings are conducted; making documents and briefing papers more concise and improving writing styles; standardizing procedures for working visits abroad; improving security guard work and continuing to observe the principle of doing what improves relations with the people; improving news report; having strict rules on the publication of articles; and promoting frugality and the strict observance of rules on incorruptibility in government

在某时政文献中有这样一段话，译文中的解释作为注释出现：

> 全党要以自我革命的政治勇气，着力解决党自身存在的突出问题，不断增强党自我净化、自我完善、自我革新、自我提高能力，经受"四大考验"、克服"四种危险"，确保党始终成为中国特色社会主义事业的坚强领导核心。

此处的"四大考验""四种危险"表达的内容十分丰富，如果展开翻译可能会使译文过于冗长，所以先简化处理（four tests, four risks），再在文章最后通过注释解释含义。

根据资料，"四大考验"是指长期执政考验、改革开放考验、市场经济考验以及外部环境考验。"四种危险"是指精神懈怠危险、能力不足危险、脱离群众危险以及消极腐败危险。

该书的英文版翻译如下：

> The entire Party needs the courage to conduct self-revolution to solve the Party's prominent problems. We must constantly enhance the Party's capability to carry out self-purification, self-improvement, self-innovation and self-cultivation. We must stand the "four tests*" and overcome the "four risks*". Only by doing so, can we make sure that the Party will always stay

at the core of the firm leadership of socialist society with Chinese characteristics.

注释：

　　*This refers to exercising governance, carrying out reform and opening up, developing the market economy, and responding to external development.

　　*This refers to inertia, incompetence, being divorced from the people, and corruption and other misconduct.

17.7　小结

　　本章总结了中文特色说法的翻译方法。尽管特色元素看起来比较难，但大多数情况下并不需要逐字翻译出来。能找到英文对等说法更好，仅仅把意思翻译出来也可以达到翻译目的。毕竟，翻译的意义在于沟通。如果比喻自身的意义并不大，是否翻译出去，也就显得不太重要。

〔课后练习〕

　　1. 中文进入英文的说法多，还是英文进入中文的说法多？为什么？"一石二鸟""血浓于水""免费的午餐"是中国成语还是外国成语？
　　2. 遇到难以翻译的特色说法时，都有哪些处理办法？是否有必要把字面意思都翻译出来？为什么？
　　3. 带有数字的政策口号，最常用的翻译方法是什么？是否需要解释？
　　4. 书中给出的政策口号例子，是否存在其他译法？有无优劣？
　　5. 请以"准确""通顺""简洁"为标准，分析自己翻译过的特色说法。

第十八章　段落与篇章的布局和重组

扫码预习

请扫码下载本章涉及的例句。先做练习，再看解答，学习效果更佳。

18.1　是否调整原文结构取决于多种因素

李运兴认为，语篇中的文化成分体现在两个不同的语篇层次上：信息单位和语篇结构。信息单位上所体现出的是与文化相关的基本概念或形象，其具体表现形式即文化词语和形象语言；语篇结构上所体现的是语言使用者组句成篇的特定模式（李运兴，2001）。为了达到更好的交流目的，翻译时经常需要对原文进行调整，根据翻译目的、原文性质、译者权限和交际的需要，确定调整幅度大小：可能是单词、短语的调整，也可能是句子、段落的调整，还可能是整个篇章的调整；最大的调整就是对原文进行改写。如有必要，甚至可以把原文信息抽出来，逐项填到译入语"模板"。如新闻报道，中文可能遵循起承转合的模式，翻译（或编译）为英语时，可能需要变为倒金字塔式。翻译政府文件、法律文书或古典作品时，译者可能感到没有调整的权力；而翻译一般性的文章，作者在不违背原意（或征得作者同意）的情况下，可以根据译文需要，对原文结构进行一定幅度的调整。这种调整在汉译英时似乎更为必要，一个重要原因是我们文化处于劣势地位。

我认为，在小范围内（如段落内）进行大的调整是可行的，通篇进行个别调整也是可行的，这些都在译者的权限之内；但把原文完全打乱重来，则需要用户提出要求或与用户协商；对于一般的翻译任务，我个人认为在在篇章结构上不宜做大规模调整；如必须做，则需告知用户原因。

18.2 调整或增加段落主题

英语写作中强调把一个段落为两部分：开头较短的部分提出问题（issue），后面较长的部分讨论问题（discussion）。提出问题可能用一句话，也可能用几句话。请看例子（斜体部分）：

例 1.

<u>*Though most economists believe that business decisions are guided by a simple law of maximum profits, in fact they result from a vector of influences acting from many directions.*</u> When an advertiser selects a particular layout, for example, he depends not only on sales expectations or possible profit but also on what the present fad is. He is concerned with what colleagues and competitors will think, beliefs about the actions of the FTC, concerns about Catholics or the American Legion, whether Chicanos or Italian-Americans will be offended, how the "silent majority" will react. He might even be worried about whether the wife or secretary of the decision maker will approve.

本段用一句话点出本段主题，然后予以论述。

例 2.

Our main concern was to empirically test the theory that forms the background for this work. <u>*To a great extent, we have succeeded in showing our theory is valid.*</u> Chapter Two reports a study which shows that the rate of perceiving variations in length relates directly to the number of connectives in the base structure of the text. In Chapter Three, we report a study that found that subjects perceive as variable units only what the theory claims is a unit. Another series of crucial studies is the comparison and contrast experiments reported in Chapter Three, which show that we do not distinguish complex concepts of different lengths as some current theories do.

本段用两句话点出主题，然后予以论述。

例3.

The United States is at present the world's largest exporter of agricultural products. Its agricultural net balance of payments in recent years has exceeded $10 billion a year. <u>As rising costs of imported petroleum and other goods have increased the U.S. trade deficit, this agricultural surplus has taken on great financial importance in both the domestic and international markets.</u> First, agricultural exports maintain profitable market prices for the American farmer and bolster the national economy by providing over one million jobs. The income from farm exports alone is used to purchase about $9 billion worth of domestic farm machinery and equipment annually. Exports of U.S. agricultural products also reduce price-depressing surpluses. Without exports, the government would be subsidizing American farmers by more than $10 billion a year over the current rate. Finally, agricultural exports provide an entry to foreign markets that can be exploited by other industries.

本段用三句话点出主题，然后予以论述。

每个段落还要有一两句话概括本段的论点（point）或作者要说明的问题，这句话可以放在段落主题部分，也可以放在讨论部分。在上面三段话中，论点分别为斜体且下划线的部分。下面一段话中，论点则出现在段落讨论部分末尾（下划线部分）：

Something has happened to the American male's need to display the signs of stereotypical masculinity that once seemed necessary for survival *on the frontier.*（提出问题）For a long time, American males were confident in their manhood, sure of their sexual roles and images. Indeed, the rugged frontiersmen never even thought about their masculinity; they were simply men surviving in a dangerous world and dressing the part. Then in the nineteenth century, our ideal male became the cowboy, then the world adventurer, then the war hero. They all were confident of themselves and unselfconsciously dressed their part. But in this century, something happened: Hemingway's heroes, for example, seemed to feel that they had to prove that it was still important to be a man among men, and our image of them is one of a kind of Brooks Brothers ruggedness. They seemed less confident that their masculinity had a real function. Now one can detect a new theme: as the male image as conqueror and survivor has lost its value, men have felt free to dress in ways once thought feminine, to wear earrings, even to wear makeup. <u>These signs of a change in the American male's sexual image of himself suggests something deeper than changes in appearance: he is adapting to a world in which the image of traditional masculinity is no longer necessary for survival.</u>（论点）

汉语中多数文件也符合上述规律，所以翻译时不需要调整。例如，下面一段话第一句既是提出问题，又是论点：

> 2. 社会保障制度的建立和发展，与社会发展阶段和经济发展水平相适应。世界各国的社会保障制度，都不是凭空建立起来的，立法所确定的社会保障对象、社会保障项目、社会保障待遇水平，无一不受到本国社会经济发展阶段和经济发展水平的制约与影响。各国的社会保障制度都随着本国经济的发展，呈现出社会保障对象的范围由窄到宽、社会保障项目由少到多、社会保障标准由低到高的共同特点。例如，德国于1883年建立社会保障制度时，其保障对象仅为工商业和手工业工人，直到1957年，农业工人才被纳入社会保障的范围。美国从1935年公布《社会保障法》以后，到1950年通过立法确定了养老保险待遇标准；从1950年到1998年，根据美国的社会经济发展水平，

此标准先后被修改了 32 次，养老保险待遇水平不断提高。

Second, social security systems are established and developed to align with the country's level of socioeconomic development. No country has built its social security institutions in a vacuum. Programs, eligibility, and benefits as provided by legislation are defined and influenced by the social and economic realities of each country. The general pattern is that, as the economy grows, the size of beneficiaries will be expanded, new programs added, and benefits increased. For example, when Germany first set up a social security system in 1883, the system covered only workers in the industrial, commercial, and handicrafts sectors. It was not until 1957 that agricultural workers were included in the system. The United States introduced its Social Security Act in 1935, but it was not until 1950 that old age pension benefits were established by law. Between 1950 and 1998, benefit levels were amended 32 times in accordance with the country's state of socioeconomic development, and benefits continued to increase.

下面这段话提出问题在前，段落的论点放在在讨论部分最后：

例 4.

　　应当指出，近些年来，西方经济发达国家对社会保障制度的调整，是在原有的较高社会福利待遇基础上进行的。由于高福利国家社会福利支出过大，开始出现福利危机被迫进行调整，主要是降低社会福利待遇水平，削减福利支出，减少国家在社会保障方面的负担，增加劳动者在社会保障资金筹集方面的责任。美国前总统里根和英国前首相撒切尔夫人采取的调整措施被认为是搞"缺少人情味的市场经济"，而产生社会公众对执政党的信任危机；法国前总理朱佩因要对社会福利待遇做大手术而承受了全国铁路瘫痪和工人大罢工的震荡。这些事实给我们以醒示：社会保障的水平必须与经济发展水平相适应，不能规定得过高，否则，会给以后的调整带来阻力；调整社会保障待遇标准涉及每个社会成员的切身利益，必须持慎之又慎的态度。

It should be noted that social security reforms in western developed countries have been designed primarily to reduce expenditure, which were at very high levels. These countries were forced into reforms due to an emerging welfare crisis caused by heavy spending. They reform primarily to reduce the burden on the state, and to give employees greater responsibility in funding the system. Social security reforms implemented by President Reagan in the US and Prime Minister Thatcher in the UK were criticized as heartless market economy measures, and in both cases, fueled a public confidence crisis in the ruling parties. When France's prime minister Allan Jupe sought to perform major surgery on that country's existing social welfare system, he triggered nationwide strikes and paralysis in the national railway system. *These lessons point to the fact that the level of social security in a country must match that country's level of development. If the level of social security is too high, later attempts to adjust downward will trigger resistance. Since the interests of every member of society are directly affected by social security reforms, utmost prudence is required.*

本段翻译中基本未作结构调整。但在提出问题部分，还是做了微小的调整。原文点题的字眼（"削减福利支出"）前移放在了第一句，更便于读者获取。

汉译英时，如果汉语篇章布局不符合英语篇章布局习惯，或者没有点明问题或论点，在条件允许时，出于促进沟通的道义责任，可以在译文中作些调整和补充。

其中《打工妹》杂志目前还是《农家女》杂志的增刊，基本的经费靠XX基金会的资助。但是该杂志副主编、"农家女文化发展中心"副秘书长李涛先生认为，办一本严肃的、为打工妹服务的杂志是一件不易的事情，如果两年后她能够自立，全靠她独树一帜的办刊理念和质量，以及多元化的社会资源的支持。其中，读者是支持的重要来源，每一个《打工妹》杂志的读者都是"打工妹之家"的天然会员。这对于办刊的理念和形式,可能是一个突破。

原译:

The Journal was still a supplement to RWKA, and was mainly funded by the XX Foundation. *But Mr. Li Tao, deputy chief editor of the Journal and deputy secretary-general of the Center,* says it was no easy task to run a serious journal that serves migrant women. If it was able to fund itself in two years, that can only be attributed to its unique philosophy, its quality and the support from various sources. Support of readers was of paramount importance. Each reader of the journal was a member of the Club by right. That, according to Mr. Li, might be a breakthrough in the philosophy and mode of operation.

仔细分析发现,加点部分(译文斜体)虽有"但是"一词,但与上一句在意义上似乎不构成转折关系。纵观上下文发现,转折关系是隐含的,即"尽管该杂志目前还是另一杂志的增刊,但他希望该杂志两年后自立"。这句话理应是作者心里要说的话,是段落的论点,但在文字上没有交代清楚,所以可以把这个论点补充出来放在段落主题部分:

改译:

The Journal was still a supplement to RWKA, mainly funded by the XX Foundation. *But Mr. Li Tao, deputy chief editor of the Journal and deputy secretary-general of the Center, said he hoped the journal could become independent in two years.* He said it was no easy task to run a serious journal that served migrant women. If it could become self-sufficient in two years, it is because of its unique philosophy, quality and support from various sources. Support of readers was of paramount importance. Every reader of the journal is a natural member of the Club. That, according to Mr. Li, might be a breakthrough in the philosophy and mode of operation.

篇章的构成与段落一样，也是 issue + discussion。如果汉语篇章缺乏 issue，或者 issue 不完整，在翻译的时候可以补充出来。以下这段文字是文章《中国实行大国外交战略势在必行》的开头一段，但这段文字没有像一般的论文那样将文章的主要观点概括出来。学生在翻译时没有作任何变动，指导老师在修改时，把文章的主要观点概括后，补充在这一段，见译文下划线部分：

原文：
导言
　　科索沃战争以来，国内不少报刊发表了许多关于国际形势与中国外交的文章，形成了声势较大的关于中国外交战略的大讨论。21世纪的中国应当实行什么样的外交战略呢？

Introduction
　　Since the war in Kosovo, a broad and vocal discourse has emerged in China over China's foreign policy strategy, with the publication of numerous newspaper and magazine articles on the international situation and China's diplomacy. The key question in this debate is, what strategy should China adopt in its diplomacy in the 21st century? <u>This paper will propose a great-power strategy that responds to China's foreign policy challenges, contributes to multi-polarization, and is conducive to China's modernization.</u> (Revised by Andrew Dawrant)

18.3　各句主题相对一致

在对相关问题的讨论中，要遵循新信息后置的原则，这就要求创造出一个"主题链"（topic string）（类似于第十四章所说的衔接链），即大致相同的一系列主题，围绕这个主题进行讨论。例如：

修改前：
　　We think it useful to provide some relatively detailed illustration of the varied ways "corporate curricular personalities" organize themselves

in programs. We choose to feature as a central device in our presentation what are called "introductory," "survey," or "foundational" courses. It is important, however, to recognize the diversity of what occurs in programs after the different initial survey courses. But what is also suggested is that if one talks about a program simply in terms of the intellectual strategies or techniques engaged, when these are understood in a general way, it becomes difficult to distinguish many programs from others.

修改后:

<u>Our programs</u> <u>create</u> varied "corporate" curricular personalities, particularly through their "introductory," "survey," or "foundational" <u>courses</u>. After <u>these initial courses,</u> *they* continue to <u>offer</u> diverse <u>curricula</u>. But in <u>these curricula</u> *they* seem to employ similar intellectual strategies. (Antonyan, 2021)

修改后的段落形成了"主题链"(斜体部分),各句围绕这一主题讨论。另外注意,各句主位和述位(下划线部分)也呈现层层推进的态势。一些层层递进的段落,鉴于两句之间首尾相接,各句主语自然无法构成一个"主题链"。例如:

The relationship between steam economy and the overall heat transfer coefficient is shown in <u>Figures 3 and 4</u>. <u>Both graphs</u> show that higher heat transfer coefficients reflect increased <u>steam economy</u>. <u>The steam economy</u>, in turn, reflects <u>the rate and amount of water evaporated</u>. <u>These values</u> are recorded in Table 2.

在本段中,前一句的结尾和后一句的开头层层推进,句子主题当然无法一致。除了这种情况外,汉语段落的主题一般比较集中,翻译时不构成主要问题,只需要对个别地方进行调整。

例 5.

她有幸就读的专门招收流动人口子女的杭州明珠实验学校,是三年前由下城区政府、企业、社会共同创建的。如今,这所学校已有来自二十个省市的在校生 2100 多名,师资和教学设备被联合国教科文组织的教育专家认为是发展中国家基础教育行列中的一流。明珠实验学校的老师说,我们不仅要让民工子女得到正规教育,更要营造一种"文化亲和力的环境",让孩子们感受到"城市温情",尽快融入我们的城市文化。(2003年翻译学院入学考试)

修改前:

Mingzhu Experimental School of Hangzhou, the school she was lucky to attend, was jointly built for migrants' children by the district government, local businesses and the community three years ago. There are *more than 2,100 students* in this school now. *They* come from 20 provinces and municipalities. *UNESCO experts* said its teachers and facilities were first class among primary schools in developing countries. *Teachers of the school* said, "we are not only teaching the children of farmers to read and write, we are also creating a culturally inclusive environment; we want the children to feel the warmth of the city and become part of it as soon as possible."

修改后:

She was lucky. *The school* she attended, Mingzhu Experimental School, was specially built for the children of migrants. *It* was jointly founded three years ago by the district government, local businesses and the community. *On its campus* were more than 2,100 students from 20 provinces and municipalities. The school's *teachers and facilities* were considered by the UNESCO experts as first class among primary schools in developing countries. "*We* are not only teaching the children of farmers to read and write," said the teachers. "*We* are also creating a culturally inclusive environment. *We* want the children to feel the warmth of the city and become part of it as soon as possible."

修改前,各句的主题变换了几次:Mingzhu Experimental School of Hangzhou—more than 2,100 students—they—UNESCO experts—teachers of the school。修改后,除了第一句作为过渡句的主语是 she 之外,其余的都

是学校或与学校有直接关系：the school—it—on its campus—teachers and facilities there—we—we—we，构成一个"主题链"。

18.4　重组逻辑不清的段落

有些段落如果直译为英语，显得结构臃肿、逻辑不清。这种情况下可以对译文进行重组。重组一般发生在修改译文的阶段，就像英文写作中的修改那样。

例 6.
重组前：
　　Under the Clean Water Act, the EPA will promulgate new standards for the treatment of industrial wastewater prior to its discharge into sewers leading to publicly owned treatment plants, with pretreatment standards for types of industrial sources being discretionary, depending on local conditions, instead of imposing nationally uniform standards now required under the Act.

第一步：
　　Under the Clean Water Act, the EPA will promulgate new standards for the treatment of industrial wastewater prior to its discharge into sewers that lead to publicly owned treatment plants. Standards for types of industrial sources will be discretionary. They will depend on local conditions, instead of imposing the nationally uniform standards now required under the act.

第二步：
　　Under the Clean Water Act, the EPA will promulgate new standards for the treatment of industrial wastewater before it is discharged into sewers leading to public treatment plants. Unlike standards under the current act, the new standards will not be uniform across the whole nation; instead, they will be discretionary, depending on the local conditions.

这一过程可以借助核心句分析来完成。翻译过程中，同样需要不断修改，甚至重组。

例 7.

所有这些都意味着，在国际局势日益复杂的情况下，必须始终以邓小平的外交思想为指导，以有利于中国实现现代化这一最大、最重要的国家利益为核心，以创造有利于中国的和平与发展的国际环境为目的，以邓小平的高度现实主义的立场和方法为指导，分析新情况，寻找新的思路，探索新的战略。

第一稿：（合并相似的信息，即原文加点部分）

All these imply that when the international situation becomes increasingly complex, *we must use Deng Xiaoping's diplomatic thinking, i.e., his strong pragmatic position and methods,* to guide us in analyzing new developments, considering new ways of thinking, and exploring new strategies. In this way we will create an international environment that is favorable for peace and development in China, an environment that will help China's modernization, which is China's paramount national interest.

第二稿：（根据上下文删除冗余信息，使译文更为简洁。另外注意重复式修饰的运用）

All these facts imply that in an increasingly complex world, we must *follow the strong pragmatism of Deng Xiaoping* when we analyze new developments, consider new ways of thinking, and explore new strategies. The new strategies should aim at creating an international environment that favors peace and development in China, *an environment* that serves China's paramount national interest—modernization.

例 8.

本文第一部分证明，农民进城受到了巨大的经济利益的推力和拉力的驱动。这里的数据又证明，虽然有巨大的经济利益的驱动，但是，由户籍锁定的生活目标却是一道巨大的心理鸿沟，对于许多农民来说是不可逾越的。所以，虽然推力和拉力都是巨大的，但只是对于近期的活动发生作用，对于长远的"生命周期"（life cycle）或人生目标设计却不发生作用。对于长远生活预期、生活目标发挥最大作用的还是户籍制度。所以，中国的户籍制度仍然是最主要的社会结构，它在总体上，改变了一般自由市场经济下，劳动力流动的通常规律。户籍在计划经济时代形成了严格的"铁律"，这样就在广大人群中建立起一种长久的"生活预期"或"生活目标"，这种"心理定位"的现象一旦出现，几代人都无法改变。所以，本文也在一定程度上解释了威廉·奥格本"文化滞后"的心理原因。

译文1（逐句翻译）：

The first part of this paper shows that farmers' entry into cities is driven by the push and pull of economic interests. *The data also show that, although driven by huge economic benefits, the life goal locked by household registration is a huge psychological gap insurmountable for many farmers.* Therefore, although the pushes and pulls are strong, they only work for the short-term activities, but not for the life goal design. The household registration system plays the biggest role in long-term expectations. Therefore, China's household registration system is still the most important social structure, which, on the whole, has changed the usual law of labor mobility under the free market economy. In the era of planned economy, household registration created an absolute law that determined the "life expectation" or "life goal" among the people. Once this mentality of destination is developed, it cannot be changed for generations. Therefore, this paper also explains, to a certain extent, the psychological reasons for William F. Ogburn's "Cultural Lag."

译文2：

The first part of this paper has explained that farmers are pushed and pulled into cities by economic forces. However, the above figures also show that despite such forces, most farmers do not change their goals because the *hukou* policy has set their expectations. PPF [push and pull factors] can only affect short-term activities. It is the *hukou* policy that has the greatest impact on the farmers' long-term expectations and even life's goals. As an important part of the social structure, the *hukou* policy changes the general rules of labor flow in the free market economy. It set up hard-and-fast rules under the planned economy, which shape people's expectations. Once the goals are set, they remain for many generations. This, to some extent, explains the psychological reason for William F. Ogburn's "Cultural Lag."

原文加点部分，逻辑不清楚（句子结构简化后就成了"生活目标是鸿沟"，没有意义），按照这个结构翻译出来（斜体部分），虽然语法正确，但同样没有意义。但好在这段话的中心思想还算明确，审校干脆删除了这句话，并在原文基础上重写（译文2），以更精炼的语言，用同样的意思表达清楚了。

例9.

有些人可能会认为，中国只有成为一个真正发达的世界大国才能推行大国外交战略。中国成为一个世界大国是一个长期的过程，并非某一天某个指标（如综合国力超过美国，或人均国民产值达到多少）实现才是一个世界大国，在此之后才能实现大国外交。国民生产总值和国防开支指标很重要，是一个大国的根本和基础，但这只是其中的因素之一，并不是唯一的因素。而如果按人均产值作为唯一指标，恐怕中国永远也成不了世界大国。中国现在的综合国力并不很强，不必过高估计中国国力，但也不必过低估计中国。外交战略和外交意识如何，也是决定一国综合国力的重要组成部分，在同等国力的情况下，一个好的外交战略，可以提升本国在世界事务中的作用和地位，而一个不好的外交战略，可能削弱本国在国际社会的地位。

加点部分虽不是相似信息，但在逻辑上更为紧密，所以译文归结为一段；剩下的部分逻辑关系也更为紧密。总的来说，如果原文写得不很好，译文可以对原文进行改进。

Some may argue that a great-power strategy cannot be adopted until China becomes a truly developed world power. That is, in my view, a misconception. Certainly, China's rise as a great power is a long-term process. But it does not mean that China can only adopt a great-power strategy in diplomatic affairs after it has achieved the status of a great power measured by specific indicators, such as its overall strength surpassing that of the United States, or its per capita GNP reaching a certain figure. Indeed, if per capita GNP were the sole indicator, China might never become a great power. Now, China is overall not strong. Its strength should not be overestimated; neither should it be underestimated.

For while gross national product and defense spending are important indicators, they are not the only ones. Foreign policy strategy and vision are equally important parts of a nation's overall strength. Other factors being equal, a good diplomatic strategy can enhance the role and status of a country in world affairs, while a bad one may be crippling.

例 10.

（美国对中国驻南联盟使馆的轰炸，大大恶化了中国人民对美国的情绪。美国当然为此应负主要责任。）但从中国的大国外交战略出发，还是应当超越情感的波动，从中国现代化的外部环境，从中国国内经济发展的大局，从中国国家统一和国家安全这样一些中国最高层次的国家利益出发，更理智和谨慎地处理中美关系。

But in keeping with a great-power foreign policy strategy, China should transcend emotional reactions and become more dispassionate and more judicious in its handling of China-US relations. This is so because such an approach is conducive to achieving China's highest-level national priorities: creating an external environment favorable to its modernization program, promoting economic development, facilitating reunification, and safeguarding national security.

译文把原文加点部分合并，作为提出的问题和论点，置于段落开头。

18.5 简化臃肿的段落

汉语中的重复有些是衔接的需要，有些是表达习惯问题，有些仅仅起到修辞作用（如为了读起来上口），有些纯粹就是原文没有写好（如前文例子）。无论哪种重复，翻译为英语时，都应在保持原文意思不变的情况下，对原文进行简化处理。第十一章"删减冗余信息确保语言简洁"，主要从词语和句子的角度探讨了消除臃肿的方法，这里强调段落一级也需要这样做。

例 11.

　　三是一些法律规定缺乏合乎逻辑的理由支撑，如：何以见得对于一个国家或是一个省份来说，进入其境居住的外国人——如果是个艾滋病病毒感染者的话，进入留居一年就有危险将艾滋病传给别人，而进入留居半年就不具有这种危险呢？同样，何以见得中国人在国外留居一年就有可能染上艾滋病，而留居半年就不可能染上呢？

这一段原文逻辑很清楚，但如果直译为英语，可能显得繁琐。我们可以通过一系列修改改进译文。

第一步，按照汉语结构翻译出各部分（实际就是简单的核心句分析）：

Third, some laws lack coherent reasoning. For example: how can we explain that for a country or a province, when a foreigner enters it to reside—if he or she happens to be an HIV carrier—if he stays for 1 year, he is likely to infect others, and if he stays for 6 months, he is not likely to infect others? How can we explain that when a Chinese stays in a foreign country for over 1 year, he is likely to be infected with AIDS, while if he stays for 6 months, he is not likely to be infected?

第二步，按照英语的特点重组。例如，英语一般不用主题句，所以 for a country or a province, when a foreigner enters it to reside 应当改为 when a foreigner enters a country or a province to reside。又如，英文要求把重要信息后置（本句是比较半年和一年，所以半年和一年应视为重要信息），所

以，就把 if he stays for 1 year, he is likely to infect others, and if he stays for 6 months, he is not likely to infect others? 重组为 he or she is likely to infect others *if he or she stays for 1 year, and is not if he or she stays for 6 months.*

第三步，简化重复的内容：

Third, some laws lack coherence. For example: how can we explain that when a foreigner with HIV/AIDS may infect others if he or she stays in a country or province for 1 year and will not do so for *a 6-month stay*? Similarly, how can we explain that a Chinese national is more likely to be infected with AIDS *if the person stays in a foreign country for more than 1 year as against 6 months?*

例 12.

改革资金缴拨方式，将以多重账户为基础的分散收付制度，改为以国库单一账户体系为基础、资金缴拨以国库集中收付为主要形式的现代国库管理制度。

原译：

Chinese government will reform its capital payment and allocation style, and change the decentralized revenues and expenditures system on the basis of multiple accountings into the modern treasury management system with the treasury unitary accounting system as its basis and treasury concentrated revenues and expenditures as its main style of capital payment and allocation. (54 words)

可以按以下程序进行修改。首先，在核心句基础上进行翻译：

中国政府将改革资金缴拨方式 The Chinese government will reform the way in which funds are collected and allocated.

分散收付制度建立在多重账户基础之上 The decentralized collection and allocation system is based on multiple accounts.

现代国库管理制度以国库单一账户体系为基础 A modern treasury management system is based on a single account.

现代国库管理体制中，资金缴拨主要是国库集中收付 In a modern

treasury management system, collection and allocation of funds are centralized by the treasury. ("缴拨"和"收付"应当是同一概念）

第二，根据逻辑关系组合：

The Chinese government will reform the way in which funds are collected and allocated. The decentralized collection and allocation system based on multiple accounts will be replaced by a modern treasury management system, a system based on a single account. In this modern treasury management system, collection and allocation of funds are centralized by the treasury.

第三，去掉多余信息、读者可推知信息和重复信息：

译文1：

The Chinese government will set up a modern treasury management system to centralize the funds collection and allocation. The current multiple accounts will be replaced by a single account. (30 words)

译文2：

The Chinese government will set up a modern treasury management system by replacing the current multiple accounts with a single account, thus centralizing collection and allocation of funds. (28 words)

译文3：

The Chinese government will centralize funds collection and allocation by replacing the multiple accounts with a single account to modernize the country's treasury management. (27 words)

例13.

　　第三，国际上的人口大规模向城市集中往往与农民失去土地密切相关。中国实行联产承包责任制以后，土地承包给农民，承包以后几十年不变。所以，不存在国际上那种因为失去土地而不得不流入城市的农民。反而，很多农民不愿意承包土地，或者索性将土地转包给他人，或者甚至撂荒不种。中国的个案证明，农民在没有失去土地的情况下，也是要大量流往城市的，土地并不能留住农民。当然，在这方面，中国的农民比起国际上那些失去土地的农民来说，还是有其优势的，土地是流入城市的农民的最后一道保障。

译文1（逐句翻译）：

Third, the large-scale population concentration in cities in other countries is often closely related to farmers' loss of land. After China implemented the contract responsibility system, the land was contracted to farmers and the tenure will remain unchanged for decades. Therefore, there are no situations in which farmers who have to flow into cities because they have lost their land. On the contrary, many farmers are unwilling to work on the contracted land; they subcontract the land to others, or even abandon the land for cities. Cases in China have shown that farmers will flow to cities in large numbers even if they have not lost their land, and land cannot retain farmers. Of course, compared with farmers who have lost their land in other countries, Chinese farmers still have their advantages because land provides the ultimate guarantee for farmers who flow into cities. (144 words)

译文2（改写）：

Third, internationally, migration to cities is often caused by dispossession of land. Farmers who have no land are forced to leave for the city. In China, the HCRS (Household Contract Responsibility System) enables farmers to own land under contract. But land cannot keep the farmers who are reluctant to farm. They re-contract the land to others or just leave it to waste. Actually, compared with farmers of other countries who lose their land, Chinese migrant workers enjoy a better situation. At least, they have land as their last fall back. (90 words)

原译并无不妥，但改译更加简练，必要时可以采用。

例14.

中国西部论坛秉承交流信息、聚合智慧、共谋发展的宗旨，架起了一座让世界了解西部、让西部走向世界的桥梁，构建了一个世界与西部、东部与西部、西部与西部相互沟通、平等交流的平台。中国西部论坛随着西部大开发的启动而诞生，也将随着西部大开发的推进而延续。我相信各位极具创造精神、富有远见卓识的专家学者、企业家和政要们，必将为中国西部大开发提出宝贵的意见和建议，使中国西部论坛闪烁着智慧的光芒。

The purpose of the Forum is to exchange information, pool wisdom, and promote cooperation for common development. *The Forum will build a bridge for the world to know the western region* and for this region to reach out to the world. It will also serve as a platform of communication between western and eastern China and within the region. The Forum has materialized because of the launch of the Western Development Program and more such fora will be held as development advances. As innovative and visionary scholars, businesspeople, and statesmen, your insights on how best to develop this region will be valuable and make this forum shine with wisdom.

"世界与西部……相互沟通、平等交流"与"让世界了解西部、让西部走向世界的桥梁"意思有重复的地方。省略不译，反而使意思层次更清楚。

例 15.

　　第一，中国现有的外交战略是建立在不结盟、不对抗基础之上的，但北约东扩和美日安保条约范围的西扩形成了这样一种局面：一方面是冷战结束，国际形势有所缓和，但另一方面冷战时期形成的北约和美日军事同盟反而有扩大的趋势，这对中国独立自主的不结盟战略形成重大挑战。

The first pillar of China's current strategy is non-alignment and non-confrontation. These principles face serious challenges due to *the eastward expansion of NATO and the westward expansion of the coverage of the US-Japan Security Treaty,* despite the general abatement of tensions following the end of the Cold War.

加点部分的意思重复，翻译时合并。

例 16.

适应经济全球化的发展趋势，对社会保障制度进行必要的调整。经济全球化趋势使各国经济的相互依存、相互影响日益加深，要求各国积极参加国际经济合作，按照平等互利原则处理双边甚至多边的国际经济关系，要求各国的法律作出相应的调整。

Globalization calls for *new social security reforms*. As economies become *increasingly interdependent*, countries need to collaborate more closely both bilaterally and plurilaterally, based on equality and mutual benefit.

Interdependent 隐含了"相互影响"的意思；"参加国际经济合作"与"处理国际经济关系"意思重复，翻译时合并；"要求各国法律作出相应调整"，具体地讲，就是"对社会保障制度进行必要的调整"，而后者作为本段的 point 已经在开头提出，所以翻译时省略。请大家把以上例句的译文翻译回中文，看和原文相比有什么变化。

18.6　大规模调整

篇章之内还可以进行更大程度的调整。下面一篇文章取自 2001 年 7 月 28 日的《早报网》，原文是汉语，英文是作者自己翻译的。通过这个例子我们可以再次看到汉英篇章结构的差异，以及译者（特别是自译者）可能具有的灵活度。

原文：（为方便对比，每段加了编号。加点部分是翻译为英文后保留的内容）

印尼华人姓名与认同问题
廖建裕

1. 苏哈多对印尼华人采取同化政策。他以"土著"为"国族"的模式，视华族文化为外族文化，不能成为所谓"印尼文化"的组成部分。

2. 他因此禁封华族文化的三大支柱（即华团，华校与华文媒体），只准许华人在家庭范围内庆祝传统节日，限制华文的使用，严禁华文读物入口，只批准半印半华的官方《印度尼西亚日报》出版。

3. 但是，冲淡华人身份认同最重要的措施，是印共政变后，在1966年12月所发布的改名换姓法令。

4. 1998年5月暴乱后苏哈多下台，哈比比接任，开始初步改革。1999年10月瓦希德当选总统，推行"亲华人"政策，恢复部分华族文化三大支柱，废除1967年禁止华人公开庆祝节日的法令，准许华文报刊出版及华人团体成立，也允许设立华文培训中心，唯不得复办华校。

5. 有鉴于此，有些观察家认为，这是印尼"华族文化复兴"的大好机会。当瓦希德提出印尼华人可恢复使用华人姓名时，有人以为印尼华人会争先恐后改回使用华人姓名。

6. 事实却不是如此。其原因何在？在回答前，且让我们看看改名换姓法令的来龙去脉。

7. 早在苏卡诺时代，印尼政府已颁布1961年的改名换姓法令，可是手续繁杂且有附带条件。申请人必须获得省长或市长与警长的推荐信。然而，政府并不积极推行此项法令，因此鲜为人知。

8. 但是苏哈多时代的1966年法令手续简单且没有附带条件。申请人只要呈文地方长官，由他们转呈司法部，在三个月内若无人反对，新姓名即可生效。

9. 必须指出的是，改名换姓并不是强制性的，有意改名者得正式呈文申请，也只有印尼籍民方能申请。华侨（外侨）无权改用印尼姓名。

10. 虽然改名并非强制性，但是在条例颁布时，由于政府大力推行，且把改名与国家认同及效忠问题拉在一起，致使大部份华裔印尼籍民，纷纷采用"印尼姓名"。

11. 所谓"印尼姓名"，其实是非华族姓名，洋名及印度名也算是"印尼姓名"。

12. 如果在苏哈多时代，改名带有"半强迫性"，那么为什么他下台后，国家脆弱，民主思潮及族群认同抬头之际，特别是当瓦希德说印尼华人可以重新使用华族姓名时，华人并没有反应？其原因是在于华社本身以及印尼社会的变迁。

13. 首先，我们必须记住印华社会是多元体，其中有讲印尼语的土生华人与讲华语的"新客华人"。然而,32年的苏哈多统治使"新客华人"的后裔"土生华人化",甚至是"印尼化"。

14. 一般上,印尼土生华人与印尼认同已经是公认的事实。在漫长的日子里,印尼"国族"以"土著"为基础,土生华人也逐渐接受,采用"印尼姓名"就是一种认同方式。即使是新客华人在入籍后也采用"印尼姓名",不过,在生活中仍保留原名。

15. 应该指出的是,在"新秩序"时代诞生与长大的印华孩童一般上都只取印尼姓名,有些也取华族姓名但只在家庭使用。没有华族姓名者可能是占多数。

16. 他们如果现在要取华族姓名,就得创造新姓名。许多华裔长期以来都用印尼姓名,若突然改换华族姓名觉得有点不惯,尤有进者,他们已不谙华语。至于老一辈的土生华人,在32年来用惯"印尼姓名",所有的法定文件都用"印尼姓名",如果再改名,手续繁杂,很不方便。此外,印尼土著民族主义方兴未艾,印尼华人仍深感使用"印尼姓名"的压力。然而,有些华人认为,用回华族姓名是原则问题,但是持有此观点者仍属少数。

17. 印尼政局还未明朗,人们不知在后瓦希德时代的印尼华人政策是否会有改变,也难怪印尼华人在应付局势变迁时颇为谨慎。

作者为新加坡国立大学政治系教授。

译文:(各段后括号中的编号是该段在原文中的编号。斜体部分是原文没有的)

Chinese Names and Chinese-Indonesian Identity

By Leo Suryadinata

1. When former Indonesian President Abdurrahman Wahid adopted a so-called "pro-ethnic Chinese policy", many observers considered it to be a golden opportunity for a "renaissance" of Chinese culture in Indonesia. They thought Chinese Indonesians would be ready to change their Indonesian names to ethnic Chinese names again. (4+5)

2. However, there was no response from the ethnic Chinese

community. Before answering the question, a brief historical background on the law will be useful. (6)

3. In fact, the name-changing regulation was first introduced in 1961 during the Sukarno era. The applicant was required to obtain recommendation letters from governors or mayors and local police chiefs. (7)

4. In December 1966, the Suharto government simplified the procedure to *encourage name-changing among the Indonesian citizens of foreign descent.* (8)

5. According to the regulation, Chinese who were Indonesian citizens simply submitted their applications to local authorities to be registered and the applications would be passed to the Justice Department. If no objection was raised by the local community within three months, the new name would be legal. (8)

6. It should be noted that name-changing was not compulsory and only Chinese citizens are allowed to change their names to "Indonesian names". Alien Chinese were/are not allowed. Nevertheless, as the state was actively promoting name-changing, to retain Chinese names was then seen as in disagreement or even disloyalty to the country, *and would face possible repression from the state.* (9+10)

7. The majority of Chinese Indonesians eventually changed their names. Even those alien Chinese who were naturalized also adopted "Indonesian names". They used both Indonesian and Chinese names in daily life but for official purposes, only "Indonesian names" were/are used. (10+14)

8. It should also be mentioned that there is no rigid definition of "Indonesian names". Any name, as long as it is not obviously Chinese, was regarded as "Indonesian". Western and Indian names are accepted as "Indonesian names". (11)

9. After the fall of the Suharto regime, the state became weak and with democratisation and the revival of ethnicity, *theoretically* the Indonesian Chinese should immediately change their names. But this is not the case. (12)

10. The explanation lies in the Chinese Indonesians themselves and the change in Indonesian society. Firstly, the ethnic Chinese in Indonesia are heterogeneous. They consist of peranakan—local-born and Indonesian-speaking Chinese and totoks — foreign-born Chinese-speaking Chinese. (12/13)

11. However, the 32 years of Suharto's rule resulted in the peranakanisation, even Indonesianisation, of the descendants of the totoks. It is an established fact that many peranakan Chinese have identified themselves with the Indonesian nation. (13)

12. In the long period of Suharto's rule, the concept of Indonesian nation had been defined in indigenous terms. These peranakans began to accept "Indonesian names" as part of their official identity. (14)

13. Even the totok Chinese continued to use two names, i.e. adopted Indonesian names as well as original Chinese names. (14)

14. It should be stated that the Chinese-Indonesian children who were born during the New Order are likely to have been given Indonesian names and *have no official Chinese names.* If they want to adopt Chinese names now, it has to be created for them. (15+16)

15. However, the majority might feel uneasy to use Chinese names as many are already known with their Indonesian names. Furthermore, they do not understand Chinese at all. (16)

16. For the older generation Chinese peranakans who have adopted Indonesian names, for 32 years they were known by their Indonesian names. As all their legal documents are in Indonesian names, it will be very inconvenient to change their names back to Chinese. (16)

17. In addition, indigenous Indonesian nationalism is still strong and many Chinese still feel the pressure to continue using Indonesian names. However, some may change or adopt Chinese names as a matter of principle, but these still belong to a minority. (16)

18. In fact, the Indonesian political situation is still very fluid. People do not know whether or not there will be policy changes again in the post-

Gus Dur period. Not surprisingly, the ethnic Chinese have been quite cautious in responding to the change. (17)

(This abridged English version is also written by the author who is a Professor in the Department of Political Science at the National University of Singapore.)

对比原文和译文发现，译文除了省略原文前 4 段背景介绍外，基本没有变化。增加的个别词句也是原文意思中所隐含的。另外，译文和原文在段落上不完全对应。从编号可以看出，部分段落信息进行了重组。

从汉语篇章结构看，前 4 段是背景介绍，第 5 段和第 6 段提出问题，其余部分回答问题。从英语的篇章结构看，采用的是开门见山的叙述方式。第 1 段和第 2 段属于全文的 topic，其余部分属于 discussion。符合英语文章的一般习惯。

那么，译文为什么要省略前 4 段呢？我推测有两个原因。第一，作者在翻译（或用英语写作）时，考虑了英语篇章布局的特点，把汉语结构转换为英语结构；第二，本文的题目是《印尼华人姓名与认同问题》，而前面 4 段是大的背景介绍，与姓名没有直接关系，所以翻译中省略了。如果要插进去，只能插在第 2 段后面，但现在英文本的结构已十分紧凑，在这里插入关系不大的内容似乎没有必要。

18.7　小结

对原文进行加工取舍可能发生在微观层面，也可能发生在句段甚至篇章层面。是否调整，如何调整，取决于主客观情况。如果译者是翻译自己的作品，则有无限制地裁量权；如果翻译他人作品，经与作者协商，也可以在作者授权的范围内进行调整。在没有作者授权的情况下，要看译者本身的地位和文本的权威性、行文质量、客户要求等因素。

〔课后练习〕

1. 是否对篇章结构进行调整以及在多大程度上调整，取决于哪些因素？

2. 调整的方法有哪些？

3. 在你翻译的语篇中，是否做过重大调整？是否征求了用户或作者的同意？

4. 请你把自己翻译的某个段落缩短三分之一，看是否仍然能够把原文意思表达清楚。

第十九章　改写原文的原因

扫码预习

请扫码下载本章涉及的例句。先做练习，再看解答，学习效果更佳。

根据翻译目的或译文用途，可以采取不同的翻译策略，有时需要紧扣原文，有时需要对原文进行微调，有时需要对原文进行改写。在对外宣传中，如新闻报道、企业推介、产品宣传、观光介绍等，由于文化背景、意识形态不同，把我们惯用的语言直接翻译为英语不一定达到宣传效果，在翻译时往往要对原文进行加工改造，甚至重写。第十八章"段落与篇章的布局与重组"即对原文的改写。本章侧重改写的原因分析。

19.1　文化差异

从理论上讲，把文化差异翻译出来（采用"异化"的翻译方法），才能起到文化交流的作用；完全采用"归化"的翻译方法，不利于文化的传播，因为读者永远无法知道对方的文化习俗。我们在英译中时，就通过"异化"引入了大量的新鲜说法，有些甚至颇具文化特色的说法已在汉语中扎根，成为本民族文化的一部分。比如，很多学生不知道"血浓于水""一石二鸟"

等成语来自国外。但反过来,通过翻译进入英语的汉语说法寥寥无几,最多就是几个菜名。

之所以如此,是因为英语是强势文化,汉语是弱势文化。强势文化往往高傲自大,不屑引进外来东西。弱势文化往往虚怀若谷,认为外来东西都是好的,因此会大量引入。虽然这对于有丰富文化资源的中国极为不公,但也只能承认这个现实。将来中国强大之后,不用我们亲自去推销我们的文化,而是他们主动翻译,那时走出去的概念就可能会多起来,就像古代朝鲜半岛、日本、越南引进中国文化那样。

基于当前的现实,如果我们在翻译中过于强调特色,效果可能适得其反。这时,我们要尽量剔除文化色彩过浓的表达方式,用直白或者中性的语言把信息传达出去。下面举例说明过去几十年的对外传播实践。

例 1.

与日本的交流

从隋朝到唐朝这段时期,以派遣遣隋使小野妹子为发端,日本多次派遣遣隋使、遣唐使。

这期间,遣唐使和很多遣唐留学生学习了中国的先进文化后回国,也有的留学生留在了大唐,像侍奉玄宗皇帝的阿部仲麻吕,当时在长安极其活跃。特别是753年玄宗皇帝在含元殿举行正月朝贺仪式时,遣唐大使藤原清河、副使大伴古麻吕与新罗的使节因为座次问题发生争执,这个事件在中日外交史上非常有名。

Exchange with Japan

During the Sui and Tang dynasties, several Japanese missions visited China. These missions were frequently accompanied by students who were eager to study advanced Chinese culture and who later exerted great influence on the society after their return to Japan. The Hanyuan Hall is often mentioned in the archives of the diplomatic history between Japan and the Tang Dynasty.

这个例子选自教科文组织出版的宣传册《大明宫含元殿遗址保护工程》,中、英、日对照。对比英汉内容可以看出,英语省略了很多内容。对比日语发现，日语和汉语在内容上完全一致，没有任何删减。笔者认为这是由于中日两国文化相近，对这段历史都很熟悉，翻译出来不会造成任何交流障碍；相反，由于文化差异，西方读者对这么多细节可能不感兴趣。再者，如果把所有人名、历史名称都翻译出来，对西方读者来说，读出来也有困难，就像我们读西方名字的汉语译文一样。另外，小册子以英日汉三种文字编排，英语最占地方，全译出来不容易排版。当然，如果这段话出现在学术论文中，译文的读者是研究中日外交史的西方学者，恐怕这样的编译就不够了。

中文在介绍产品时，往往使用许多华而不实之辞，而英语崇尚质朴、实事求是，所以翻译时应注意对原文进行简化或改写。

例2.

MA PROMESSE Moisturizing Toner contains natural licorice, astragalus, and ginseng. It is *absolutely* alcohol free. It is a deep cleanser and moisturizes, hydrates and tones the skin. After application, the skin feels fresh, clean and revitalized. Suitable for all skin types.

把英语直译为通顺的汉语是这样的：

诺美思柔嫩爽肤水含有天然甘草、紫云英和人参，绝对不含酒精，是一种深层皮肤清洗液，可以软化、滋润皮肤，恢复皮肤弹性，用后感到皮肤干爽，充满活力。适合各类皮肤使用。

而产品自带的汉语说明：

诺美思柔嫩爽肤水温和配方，不含酒精，能够彻底清除肌肤深层残垢。更重要的是它能软化皮肤表层，为肌肤做好准备，吸收各种滋润成分。内含多种天然植物精华：甘草、紫云英、人参。适合各类肌肤使用。

汉语中的加点部分是英文没有的，应当是商家为照顾中国商品的宣传习惯，补充虚妄夸大的表达方法，如"温和配方""彻底清除""各种滋养成分""天然植物精华"。而英语原文内容除了 absolutely 以外，文字朴实无华，句子结构平铺直叙。再举一例：

（福州仓山区江心公园）演艺广场：1995年，中央电视台与福州市政府在此联合举办"元宵晚会"，江心公园也因此扬名全国。晚会上，时任市委书记的习近平同志在台下观看演出，夫人彭丽媛女士携弟弟妹妹一起上台，在《家庭接力唱》节目中，献唱山东民歌《沂蒙山小调》反响热烈。国内许多著名歌唱家、艺术家也到场表演，如姜昆、陈佩斯、朱时茂、黄宏、毛阿敏等，场面十分热闹。也正是那场元宵晚会，让全国人民通过电视认识了福州，知道了福州有一座美丽的江心公园。

The Performance Square: In 1995, the national television CCTV and Fuzhou Municipal Government jointly organized the "Lantern Festival Gala Evening" on the island. Xi Jinping, then secretary of the CPC Fuzhou Municipal Committee, was among the audience. His wife Peng Liyuan, together with her brother and sister, went on the stage and sang a folk song from her hometown Shandong. Many other celebrities were also present. It was that gala evening that made the people of the whole country know Fuzhou and its beautiful River Island Park.

译文删除了外国人不熟悉的歌曲名、人名，以及重复和不言自喻的内容，还补充了背景（the national television CCTV），简化了信息（a folk song from her hometown Shandong）。

19.2　意识形态差异

对内宣传中经常使用意识形态色彩很浓的语言，如果直译过去，容易引起读者反感，起不到教育作用，达不到应有的宣传效果。因为我们面临的读者，与国内读者所接受的教育完全不同。黄友义（2002）指出：

这本小说（指英国人乔治·奥维尔的《动物农庄》）以嘲讽的口气采用了大量30和40年代苏联使用甚至后来社会主义国家都使用的

词汇，如"党""社会主义生产高潮"等。西方人更习惯的是"某某政府""克林顿政府""经济增长"等。所以，西方人一看到这样的词汇就联想到苏联式的社会主义。二是描述了社会主义计划经济下的高度物质贫乏。国家宣传机器的任务就是编报虚假数字，欺骗公众和当权者的政敌。这使西方人认定，社会主义国家特有词汇下讲的都是假话。

我们可以想象，当没有真正了解中国的外国人看到我们对外宣传品当中与《动物农庄》中相似的写法时，会是一种什么反应。在国际舆论由西方大国操纵的情况下，我们必须时刻想到我们的国外读者基本上都是乔治·奥维尔的门生，都是经过西方宣传机器洗过脑的。他们常常对社会主义国家振奋人心、鼓舞干劲的宣传报道从反面理解。

所以，翻译此类文件要注意"内外有别"。沈苏儒指出：

> 第二，对外译品的中文材料不符合对外传播、对外宣传的要求，或者本来不必要、不适宜作对外用的材料也被译成外文，供外国人阅读、视听。简言之，就是"内外不分"的问题。段文中的"乙型病状"举了四个"病例"，照我看来，它们的共同的、根本的病因，都在"内外不分"。固然，作为一种社会文化现象或具体的翻译问题来考察，中外文化（广义的文化）差异甚大、中国大陆有许多特殊情况不易为外人理解等等是必须考虑研究的因素，但如果从整体上来考察，则中译英对外译品质量问题的解决，不"治本"而只"治标"恐怕难望有"彻底治愈"的一天，这里所说的"治本"就是要解决这个内外不分的问题。十分明显，这四个"病例"都是把对内的材料对外照搬，要想使之成为为外国人所喜闻乐见（至少看得下去）的外文资料，恐怕只有在外文阶段"重写"Rewrite 之一法。这样的"重写"按段文中关于"解释性翻译"的说明应该是许可的，但实际上做起来并不容易。（沈苏儒，1991）

张键更是认为，不要等到输出阶段，在原文审读阶段，就应当进行编辑加工：

> "实践证明，这样大轰大嗡式的对外报道，不但达不到预期的目

的，反而会使受众望而生厌，产生逆效应。有鉴于此，若要达到对外传播效果，英译前必须对汉语新闻稿的语言进行一番'译前处理'。即在抓住原文主旨、领会原文精神的前提下，对原文语言的方方面面进行处理，或重组，或增删，或编辑，或加工"。（张健，2001）

把对内稿件直接翻译为英文，结果可能不如不翻。翟树耀指出："文化大革命"中照搬国内宣传方法曾给我们带来了许多教训。（翟树耀，2001）

在专业的对外宣传中，译者和编辑对原文内容进行增删（主要是删减）已经成为常态。据了解，在中央电视台第9套节目（CCTV9），导播确定将要播出的内容后，如果是外电，撰稿人（writer，就是译者）要负责改写；如果是中文稿件，撰稿人要负责编译。所谓编译，就是翻译时删除外国听众可能不感兴趣的内容（如套话），添加背景资料（解释中国特有说法，如"双一流""八项规定"等）。编译后的稿件交给以英语为母语的编辑（polisher）润色、加工。经润色加工的稿件交给主编审查，主要是在政治上把关，如不要把朝鲜译成North Korea，要说成DPRK；台湾地区领导人要称为Taiwan's leader。经过这些程序，最后播出的内容和原文（原材料）之间可能有很大的不同。这样做虽然表面上不忠实于原文，但实质内容不变，而且可以达到更好的宣传效果。例如，2004年中央1号文件发布后，各大中文媒体一般都这样报道：

中新网　2月8日电　据新华网报道，新华社8日受权全文播发《中共中央国务院关于促进农民增加收入若干政策的意见》。《意见》指出，全党必须从贯彻"三个代表"重要思想，实现好、维护好、发展好广大农民群众根本利益的高度，进一步增强做好农民增收工作的紧迫感和主动性。

《意见》共22条，分九部分，约9 000字。包括：集中力量支持粮食主产区发展粮食产业，促进种粮农民增加收入；继续推进农业结构调整，挖掘农业内部增收潜力；发展农村二、三产业，拓宽农民增收渠道；改善农民进城就业环境，增加外出务工收入；发挥市场机制作用，搞活农产品流通；加强农村基础设施建设，为农民增收创造条件；深化农村改革，为农民增收减负提供体制保障；继续做好扶贫开发工作，解决农村贫困人口和受灾群众的生产生活困难；加强党对促进农民增收工作的领导，确保各项增收政策落到实处。

《意见》指出，在党的十六大精神指引下，2003年各地区各部门按照中央的要求，加大了解决"三农"问题的力度，抵御住了突如其来的非典疫情的严重冲击，克服了多种自然灾害频繁发生的严重影响，实现了农业结构稳步调整，农村经济稳步发展，农村改革稳步推进，农民收入稳步增加，农村社会继续保持稳定。同时，应当清醒地看到，当前农业和农村发展中还存在着许多矛盾和问题，突出的是农民增收困难。

《意见》强调，农民收入长期上不去，不仅影响农民生活水平提高，而且影响粮食生产和农产品供给；不仅制约农村经济发展，而且制约整个国民经济增长；不仅关系农村社会进步，而且关系全面建设小康社会目标的实现；不仅是重大的经济问题，而且是重大的政治问题。

《意见》确定，当前和今后一个时期做好农民增收工作的总体要求是：各级党委和政府要认真贯彻十六大和十六届三中全会精神，牢固树立科学发展观，按照统筹城乡经济社会发展的要求，坚持"多予、少取、放活"的方针，调整农业结构，扩大农民就业，加快科技进步，深化农村改革，增加农业投入，强化对农业支持保护，力争实现农民收入较快增长，尽快扭转城乡居民收入差距不断扩大的趋势。

而对外宣传的窗口——CCTV9并没有把上述新闻直译为英语播发，而是根据《意见》内容，作了如下总结。注意汉语中被划掉的在英语中省略，同时，英语篇章结构也符合英语新闻报道所要求的倒金字塔格式：

> Sensing the urgency of raising farmers' income, the Central Committee of the Communist Party of China and the State Council have issued a document on policies for boosting the growth in the income of farmers.
>
> The document, the key points of which were made public Sunday, prescribes a number of measures to increase farmers' income, stressing raising farmer's income is a significant issue both economically and politically.
>
> The document urges stronger support for grain production in major

grain-producing areas to help raise the income of grain farmers. Resources will be concentrated for the construction of a number of state-class high-quality special grain production bases beginning this year.

In order to reduce the financial burden on farmers, the general level of agricultural tax rates will be cut by one percentage point this year and tax levies on special farm products except tobacco leafs will be annulled.

The document calls for continued efforts to push forward the readjustment of the structure of agriculture to tap its full potential in yielding profits for farmers, and to develop secondary and tertiary industries in the countryside to open up more money-earning opportunities for farmers.

A good environment should be created in cities so that farmers can find jobs for more income, and the role of the market mechanism should be brought into full play to improve the market circulation of agricultural products.

According to the document, construction of infrastructure facilities in the countryside should be strengthened to lay a foundation for farmers to earn more, and the rural reform should be deepened to provide a guarantee for farmers to increase income and reduce financial burden.

The document also calls for continued efforts to carry out the task of poverty reduction and development in the rural areas and help the poverty-stricken people and victims of natural disasters overcome difficulties in production and daily life.

The leadership of the Party should be strengthened to ensure that all the policies to help farmers increase their income are implemented to the letter, the document says.

Despite steady economic development in the rural areas, numerous problems still exist in the countryside, it says. The most salient of these problems is that it is difficult for farmers to increase their income.

The document points out that if farmers' income remains stagnant for long, their living standards will be affected; moreover, grain production and the supply of agricultural products will be impaired.

It will also constrain the growth of the rural economy and the national economy as a whole, and hamper social progress in the countryside and the realization of the goal of building a relatively affluent society in an all-round way.

The income growth of China's 900 million farmers has lagged behind that of urban residents. The disposable per-capita income of urban residents grew by 9.3 percent in 2003, five percentage points higher than that of rural residents, according to the National Bureau of Statistics.

Editor: Hope

Source: Xinhuanet

02-09-2004 09:19, cctv.com

仔细对照可以发现，被删除部分文本都是涉及意识形态的部分或针对国内读者的内容。以上是近 20 年前的新闻报道，最近在美国出版的国情资料同样采取类似的做法。比如：

~~金秋时节，丹桂飘香。~~2017 年 10 月，在北京人民大会堂，万众瞩目的中国共产党第十九次全国代表大会隆重召开。习近平总书记在会上作了题为《~~决胜全面建成小康社会~~ 夺取新时代中国特色社会主义伟大胜利》的报告，2300 多名代表济济一堂，共谋党和国家发展大业，同绘民族复兴壮丽画卷。这次被称为"站在世界地图前"召开的大会，吸引了全球目光，160 多个国家和地区的 450 多个主要政党发来 1000 多份贺电贺信，130 多个国家和地区的 1800 多名境外记者进行了报道，~~世界进入"十九大时间"。~~

~~今朝襄盛会，华夏谱新篇。~~在中国特色社会主义进入新时代的关键时期，党的十九大站在历史和全局的高度，顺应浩浩荡荡的时代潮流，~~承载亿万人民的光荣梦想，擘画了决胜全面建成小康社会、夺取新时代中国特色社会主义伟大胜利的宏伟蓝图，指明了"中华号"航船驶向伟大复兴胜利彼岸的前进方向。~~（中共中央宣传部理论局，2018）

本段选自中共中央宣传部理论局 2018 年编写的《新时代面对面》，"本书以习近平新时代中国特色社会主义思想为指导，紧密联系新时代中国特色社会主义生动实践，紧密联系干部群众思想实际，对这些问题作出了深入浅出的解读阐释，观点权威准确，语言通俗易懂，文风清新简洁，是干部群众、青年学生进行理论学习和开展形势政策教育的重要辅导读物。"很显然，本书面对的是国内读者。但国外读者也希望了解中国十九大的情况。如果逐字翻译中文稿，会把有用的信息淹没在被西方认为无用的信息中，因此，在美国出版的英文版就进行了大胆的删节和改写：

> On October 2017, during *the early autumn* of Beijing, the Communist Party of China (CPC) held its 19th National Congress. The widely anticipated conference was attended by over 2,300 delegates *from different parts of the country*, who convened in the Great Hall of the People where General Secretary Xi Jinping delivered his report on reaching the goal of a moderately prosperous society, and pursuing socialism with Chinese characteristics in a new era. *United in their resolve* to achieve national renewal, the delegates deliberated on important issues for the future development of both the CPC and the nation. The event drew global attention, with more than 1,000 congratulatory messages from over 450 major political parties in 160 countries and regions, and coverage by more than 1,800 reporters from 130 countries.
>
> The 19th CPC National Congress marks a new chapter in Chinese history. Held at a critical time when socialism with Chinese characteristics is entering a new era, it unveiled a roadmap for *realizing the dream of the people*. This *draws on lessons from the past, and has adjusted to the changing times*, and will guide us towards national renewal. (Li Wen, 2018)

译文来自 Li Wen 编写并在美国出版的 *Understanding China in the New Era*。对比原文和译文发现，原文中慷慨激昂、催人奋进、激励人心的政治话语，在译文中消失殆尽。这不是译者偷懒，而是因为勉强译出，效果可能适得其反。这里再摘录一段供大家学习：

全面改革的攻坚期。惟改革者进，惟鼎新者强。党的十八大以来，面对改革进入深水区、攻坚期，面对一个又一个"硬骨头"，改革全面发力、多点突破、纵深推进，夯基垒台、立柱架梁，共推出了1500多项改革举措，重要领域和关键环节取得突破性进展，主要领域改革主体框架基本确立。接下来，关键是要以钉钉子的精神抓落实，确保各项改革举措落地生根。随着改革的深入推进，思想障碍和利益藩篱越来越难以突破，改革的难度越来越大，能不能啃下改革的"硬骨头"，决定着改革成败、事业兴衰。

China's reform is now in a critical stage. We need the courage and resolve to fight many uphill battles. Since the reforms entered a most difficult phase after the 18th CPC National Congress held in 2012, over 1,500 new measures have been implemented, and substantial progress made in crucial areas, laying the groundwork for more in-depth reforms. As these proceed and deepen, there is bound to be greater resistance: inertia and networks of vested interests will present increasingly serious challenges. But we cannot waver. We must forge ahead and overcome them, for our nation's future depends on successful reforms.

把这段回译为中文，看是否能够概括原文的意思：

中国的改革现在正处于关键阶段。我们需要勇气和决心去打"攻坚战"。自2012年党的十八大以来，改革进入最困难阶段，实施了1500多项新措施，关键领域取得实质性进展，为更深入的改革奠定了基础。随着这些进展和深化，必然会有更大的阻力：惰性和既得利益网络将带来越来越严重的挑战。但是我们不能动摇。我们必须勇往直前，克服挑战，因为我们国家的未来取决于成功的改革。

本段中原文传达的信息几乎没有损失，译文只是改用更加朴实的方式。比如："进入深水区""思想障碍和利益藩篱越来越难以突破，改革的难度越来越大"，意味着改革需要勇气，因此译文当中的 courage 不是"空穴来风"；"以钉钉子的精神"就是"决心"（resolve）；"全面发力、多点突破、纵深推进，夯基垒台、立柱架梁"在这句话中都可以找到踪迹：1,500 new measures have been implemented, and substantial progress made in crucial areas, laying the groundwork for more in-depth reforms. 请大家对照双语，在中英文表达之间寻找其他的对应关系。当然，意思对等并不是终极目的，有些不适合的内容该删要果断删除。

黄友义在《把好编辑和翻译两道关 不断提高外宣品的质量》详细列举了各类宣传文稿的问题，比如在谈到"地理位置介绍"时指出：

> 任何一本介绍地方情况的小册子或指南都免不了要介绍这个地方的地理位置和面积。我看到的大多数出版物用外国人的话说，都像是写给地理专家的；不论一个地方大小，知名度如何，都精确地写上"地处东经XX度，北纬XX度"，然后是共辖多少平方公里，再接下来是一一列出本行政单位所属的各个市、县、区等等。我向许多外国读者了解过，除去个别中国问题学者外，大都表示看了这些材料，他们头脑中无法产生具体的地理位置和面积的形象，要么看到这里跳过去，要么看了也没有留下什么印象。（黄友义，2000）

既然这些内容没有多大用处，如果译者碰到这样的内容如何处理？这恐怕不是译者一人能决定的问题。最好有懂得国际传播的专家，提醒撰稿人在编写对外宣传的内容时，就做到有的放矢，而不是把编辑的责任交给翻译。如果没有专门用来翻译的原文，译者在与用户协商之后，可以进行改写；或者依据专业判断，直接改写，然后向用户说明利弊。

19.3　外语能力不足

我们大多数人在国内学习英语，即使学习非常努力，也只能达到工作英语的水平，要做到译文传神、达意而又雅致，几乎是不可能的。但好在实用文本翻译的目的是信息交流，即使不够传神和雅致，只要把实质性信息传递过去，就达到了翻译目的。

汉译英时，感到尤其困难的是对景物的描写和场景的渲染。这类文本需要译者在原文基础上进行创作,虽然最能够体现翻译工作的创造性,但对译者的外语水平提出很高的要求,我们的外语能力这时就显得捉襟见肘。在确定需要忠实翻译的情况下,广泛搜集有关资料,临时学习英语表达方法,是弥补外语能力不足的有效手段。这时,我们实际上把创造转换为仿写,大大降低了难度。据观察,很多旅游景点的介绍采用简化的翻译方法,如下面关于九寨沟的两段中文介绍有不少佳词丽句,而英文介绍要平实得多:

九寨沟 1:

　　位于四川省北部南坪县境内,是一条纵深 40 余公里的山沟谷地,因周围有 9 个藏族村寨而得名,总面积约 620 平方公里,自然景色兼有湖泊、瀑布、雪山、森林之美。沟中地僻人稀,景物特异,富于原始自然风貌,有"童话世界"之誉。河谷地带有大小湖泊 100 多处,其中"五花海",湖底为沉积石,色彩斑斓,在阳光照射下,呈现出缤纷色彩。诺日朗瀑布,高约 30 米,宽约百米。1992 年 12 月九寨沟作为自然遗产被列入《世界遗产名录》。

九寨沟 2:

　　人们说,如果世界上真有仙境,那肯定就是九寨沟。它是一个以高原湖泊众多,瀑布宏伟壮观,植物景观奇妙著称的美丽的名胜;是一个佳景荟萃、神奇莫测的旷世胜地;是一个不见纤尘、自然纯净的"童话世界",那里还生活着大熊猫等多种珍禽异兽。1992 年,被联合国教科文组织纳入《世界自然文化遗产名录》;1997 年,又被纳入世界"人与生物圈"保护网络,是迄今为止世界上唯一同时获得这两项殊荣的景区。

国外有关九寨沟的英文资料:

Jiuzhaigou

　　Situated more than 400 km south of Chengdu, Jiuzhaigou (Gully of Nine Villages) is a gully in Nanping County in Ngawa Tibetan Autonomous Prefecture which derived its name from the 9 Tibetan villages in the gully. Its 80-km-long ravine covers an area of 60,000 hectares and is strewn with lakes, waterfalls, snowy mountains and forests teeming with such precious animals as giant and lesser pandas and golden-haired monkeys. For its fairyland and dreamlike fascinations it is a UNESCO world natural heritage site and part of the UN Man and Biosphere program.

即使是世界自然文化遗产委员会的评价，文字也比较平实：

Jiuzhaigou Valley Scenic and Historic Interest Area
Brief description:

Stretching over 72,000 ha in the northern part of Sichuan Province, the jagged Jiuzhaigou valley reaches a height of more than 4,800m, thus comprising a series of diverse forest ecosystems. Its superb landscapes are particularly interesting for their series of narrow conic karst land forms and spectacular waterfalls. Some 140 bird species also inhabit the valley, as well as a number of endangered plant and animal species, including the giant panda and the Sichuan takin.

评价的译文：

九寨沟位于四川省北部，面积72000多公顷。蜿蜒曲折的九寨沟海拔4800多米，因而形成了一系列多样的森林生态系。它壮丽的景色因一系列狭长的圆锥状喀斯特溶岩地貌和壮观的瀑布而尤其令人感兴趣。沟中现存140多种鸟类，还有一些濒临灭绝的动植物物种，包括大熊猫和四川扭角羚。

再看乐山大佛的中英文介绍：

乐山大佛坐落在乐山市峨眉山东麓的栖鸾峰，依凌云山的山路开山凿成，面对岷江、大渡河和青衣江的汇流处，造型庄严，虽经千年风霜，至今仍安坐于滔滔岷江之畔。又名凌云大佛。

佛像依山临江开凿而成，是世界现存最大的一尊摩崖石像，有"山是一尊佛，佛是一座山"的称誉。大佛为弥勒倚坐像，坐东向西，面相端庄，通高71米，是世界最高的大佛。大佛头长14.7米，头宽10米，肩宽24米，耳长7米，耳内可并立二人，脚背宽8.5米，可坐百余人，素有"佛是一座山，山是一尊佛"之称。雕刻细致，线条流畅，身躯比例匀称，气势恢宏，体现了盛唐文化的宏大气派。

乐山大佛古称"弥勒大像""嘉定大佛"，开凿于唐玄宗开元初年（公元713年）。当时，岷江、大渡河、青衣江三江于此汇合，水流直冲凌云山脚，势不可挡，洪水季节水势更猛，过往船只常触壁粉碎。凌云寺名僧海通见此甚为不安，于是发起修造大佛之念，一使石块坠江减缓水势，二借佛力镇水。海通募集20年，筹得一笔款项，当时有一地方官前来索贿，海通怒斥："目可自剜，佛财难得！"遂"自抉其目，捧盘致之"。海通去世后，剑南川西节度使韦皋，征集工匠，继续开凿，朝廷也诏赐盐麻税款予以资助，历时90年大佛终告完成。佛座南北的两壁上，还有唐代石刻造像90余龛，其中亦不乏佳作。

乐山大佛具有一套设计巧妙，隐而不见的排水系统，对保护大佛起到了重要的作用。在大佛头部共18层螺髻中，第4层、第9层和第18层各有一条横向排水沟，分别用锤灰垒砌修饰而成，远望看不出。衣领和衣纹皱折也有排水沟，正胸有向左侧，与右臂后侧水沟相连。两耳背后靠山崖处，有洞穴左右相通；胸部背侧两端各有一洞，但互未凿通，孔壁湿润，底部积水，洞口不断有水淌出，因而大佛胸部约有2米宽的浸水带。这些水沟和洞穴，组成了科学的排水、隔湿和通风系统，防止了大佛的侵蚀性风化。

大佛胸部有一封闭的藏脏洞。封门石是宋代重建天宁阁的纪事残碑。洞里面装着废铁、破旧铅皮、砖头等。据说唐代大佛竣工后，曾建有木阁覆盖保护，以免日晒雨淋。从大佛棱、腿臂胸和脚背上残存的许多柱础和桩洞，证明确曾有过大佛阁。宋代重建之，称为"天宁阁"，后遭毁。维修者将此残碑移到海师洞里保存，可惜于后来被毁。

大佛头部的右后方是建于唐代的凌云寺，即俗称的大佛寺。寺内有天王殿、大雄殿和藏经楼等三大建筑群。

英文介绍1：

Located on the cliff in the Lingyun Mountain on the eastern bank at the confluence of the Min-jiang, the Dadu River and the Qingyi River, the statue is 71 meters high. Its shoulders are 28 meters broad and its head is 14.7 meters long and 10 meters broad. It is the biggest of such carvings in the world.

The construction started in the Tang Dynasty and lasted 90 years. There is a well- designed drainage system under the statue. It has been well preserved for over 1200 years.

英文介绍2：

A huge Buddha statue stands on the rock slope of Lingyuan Shan mountain at the confluence of Dadu and Minjiang rivers in the southeast district of the city. It is a 71-m-high portrayal of the seated Maitreya, finished in 803 after 90 years of work. Its head is 14.7 m high, 10 m wide and ends at the tip of the cliff. Its eyes are 3.3 m wide, its ears 7 m long. Its feet rest just above the surface of the water. It was the Buddhist monk Taitong who arranged the construction of the Great Buddha. He was to watch over the dangerously powerful currents in this area and to protect the boats. The sculpture can best be seen from the water. One can take a tourist-boat or ferry from the port of Leshan.

世界自然文化遗产委员会关于峨眉山和乐山大佛的评价：

Mt. Emei and Leshan Giant Buddha

Brief description:

The first Buddhist temple in China was built here in Sichuan Province in the 1st century A.D. in the beautiful surroundings of the summit of Mount Emei. The addition of other temples turned the site into one of Buddhism's holiest sites. Over the centuries, the cultural treasures grew in number. The most remarkable is the Giant Buddha of Leshan, carved out of a hillside in the 8th century and looking down on the confluence of three rivers. At 71m high, it is the largest Buddha in the world. Mount Emei is also notable for its exceptionally diverse vegetation, ranging from subtropical to subalpine pine forests. Some of the trees there are more than 1,000 years old.

评价的译文：

  1 世纪，在四川省峨眉山景色秀丽的山巅上，落成了中国第一座佛教寺院。随着四周其他寺庙的建立，该地成为佛教的主要圣地之一。许多世纪以来，文化财富大量积淀。其中最著名的要属乐山大佛，它是 8 世纪时人们在一座山岩上雕凿出来的，仿佛俯瞰着三江交汇之所。佛像身高 71 米，堪称世界之最。峨眉山还以其种类繁多的植被闻名天下，从亚热带植物到亚高山针叶林可谓应有尽有，有些树木树龄已逾千年。

以上例子说明，即使我们没有能力把汉语传神地翻译为英语，也可以把基本意思传达出去，而且这样做反而更加符合英语的习惯。这些例子还说明，对于我们没有把握的文体，可以先通过网络或其他手段，查找相关英语资料，学习英语的写作风格和表达习惯，然后运用到自己的翻译中。

19.4　小结

  由于文化差异、意识形态差异等原因，对外传播决不能亦步亦趋翻译原文，而是要根据读者所处的社会文化背景和意识形态，对原文进行适当的变通取舍，以读者喜闻乐见的形式把原文的基本信息传达出来。尤其是要注意面向国内受众的那一套话语体系，在翻译中尽量不要再现出来，以免国外读者产生反感，从而让宣传效果适得其反。

〔课后练习〕

  1. 请在"知网"下载阅读黄友义《把好编辑和翻译两道关 不断提高外

宣品的质量（二）》一文（《对外大传播》第 1 期增刊），审查自己翻译的材料中，是否存在文中列举的问题，今后遇到此类材料应该如何处理？

2. 请在"知网"下载并阅读沈苏儒《关于中译英对外译品的质量问题》（《中国翻译》1991 年第 1 期），判断自己在翻译中所犯的错误，属于段连城所说的"甲型病状"还是"乙型病状"。

3. 请审查自己翻译过的文章，看有些篇目以改写的方式翻译是否更为合适。

第五部分　译文的修改

　　第二十章为本书的第五部分，举例说明如何通过反复修改和审校，实现翻译中的"信达切"。

第二十章　译文的审校

扫码预习

请扫码下载本章涉及的例句。先做练习，再看解答，学习效果更佳。

20.1　关注事项

　　文章是改出来的，译文也是改出来的。自己翻译的东西，过几天拿出来再看，又发现可以改进的地方；即使已经交稿或发表，也难免发现错误或不当之处，这时再改，为时已晚，造成终生遗憾。因此有人说，翻译是一个遗憾的艺术。审校自己的译文尚且如此，审校别人的译文，发现的问题就更多了。因为对同一篇文章，不同的人可能有不同的理解；即使理解相同，表达习惯也不一样。审校最好是由别人来做，自译自审很难发现问题，因为人的知识是互补的，一个人不懂或没想到的地方，另一个人没准儿正好知道。自译自审最好是隔一段时间再做，减少制作初稿时思维定势的影响。

　　笔者在审校自己的译文时，仍然坚持翻译中的"忠实"（信）、"通顺"（达）、"好用"（切）三个标准。

　　在忠实方面，从完整性、准确性和逻辑性三方面着手。首先对照原文看有无遗漏；如有遗漏，看是有意省略不译，还是疏忽。第二，对照原文看有无意思表达错误。初译时可能只见树木，不见森林；做完后回头再看，可能产生新的理解。第三，通读译文（不看原文），看文章是否有逻辑不通之处。如有，再对照原文，看是原文本身不通，还是理解错误，或者是表达不准确引起的歧义。如果是原文错误，按照第五章（5.2.4"识别原文瑕疵"）相关论述处理。如果是理解错误或者表达有歧义，要想办法改正。还要看是否需要把汉语隐含的逻辑关系（意合）显化为英语外在的逻辑关系（形合）。

在语言通顺方面，主要关注以下问题：

- 基本语言问题，包括用词不当、搭配不当、句子冗长等问题。
- 信息流动问题，必要时调整句子中各信息片段出现的顺序。
- 衔接手段审查，即看译文衔接方法是否需要调整，包括是否需要把汉语中重复出现的名词、动词、短语甚至句子转化为英语中的代词、助动词等简略形式。
- 简洁性审查，即看译文是否有意思重复、不言自喻的地方。重复在汉语中更容易被容忍，但移植到英语可能无法忍受。造成译文意思重复有几个原因：
  - 汉语本身不够简洁；
  - 汉语意思虽然重复，但措辞有变化，不显得重复；翻译为英语后，用词相近或相同，造成明显重复；
  - 汉语本身不重复，但翻译理解或表达偏差，导致译文重复。

要根据文本的权威性和译者的权限，考虑是删除重复部分，还是从形式上修改重复，使重复看起来不太明显。

在好用方面，主要进行文化和政治审查，思考针对不同受众，一些内容是否有必要呈现，是否需要改变呈现方式，是否需要调段落或整篇章结构。

笔者在为别人审校译文时，同样从信达切三方面入手，重点看译文的准确性和表达是否规范，包括：

- 是否有标点符号错误。标点错误十分明显，包括：
  - 在英文中使用中文标点。有的译者没有受过专门训练，在英文行文中不区分中英文标点，特别是使用汉语的逗号和引号，有人甚至还在英文中使用汉语的顿号，这在英文读者来看，是不可容忍的错误，一定要改正；

- 在中文中使用英文标点符号。在中文中混杂使用英文标点，也影响到译文的规范性；

- 空格错误。汉语的标点符号前后都没有空格；英语多数标点符号前面没有空格，后面有一个空格；括号和引号则是外部有空格，内部无空格。

- 大小写错误。标题的实词首字母该大写没有大写；不该大写的介词首字母大写；人名、地名没有大写或大写错误；

- 专有名词拼法错误。中国的人名、地名使用汉语拼音。人名分为两个部分：姓和名，如水稻专家袁隆平拼写为 Yuan Longping，不是 Yuan Long Ping 或 Yuan Long-ping。少数民族人名、地名要使用本民族语言直接转写的罗马化拼法（如有可能），如呼和浩特为 Hohhot，哈尔滨为 Harbin，二连浩特是 Erenhot。中国大陆之外的华人可能有自己的专门拼法，要做到名从主人。音译汉语词语时要符合汉语拼音习惯，如"户口"拼为 *hukou*，不要写为 Hukou，HuKou，或者 Hu Kou。

- 拼写错误。一般计算机可以检查出来。

- 语法错误。包括：

  - 时态；
  - 单复数是否一致；
  - 句子结构、搭配是否站得住脚。

- 是否符合简明英语的各项原则，主要看：

  - 是否用了过多的名词化动词，如该用 suggest，却用了 make a suggestion。
  - 是否有太多从句；
  - 信息流动是否通畅；

- 段落的各个句子的主题部分是否有关联性（是否构成一个 topic string）；
- 被动语态使用是否得当。

20.2　审校他人译文

本节提供一些审校实例，说明审校中关注的信达切问题。

例 1.

语言人造说

文艺复兴以后，西方的许多学者开始反对语言起源神造说，倡导人造说。德国哲学家赫尔德最具有代表性。他认为："当人还是动物的时候，就已经有了语言。"人类语言之所以能够脱离动物语言，是因为人有悟性，这是人类独有的能力。

原译及改译：

Language as a Human Invention

After the Renaissance, many Western scholars began to reject the divine theories ~~on the origin of language~~ and advocated the humanistic ones. A leading exponent, the German philosopher Johann Gottfried Herder, argued that "Even as an animal man has language ~~had already existed when humans were still animals~~." The reason why human language was able to <u>surpass</u> ~~break out of~~ animal forms of communication is that humans have the power of comprehension, an ability unique to its kind.

说明：本段来自北外世界语言博物馆的解说词，原译是经过学生一稿、外教审核过的译文。改译是笔者的修改。改译删除了 on the origin of language，因为一级标题是"人类语言的起源"（The Origin of Human Language），二级标题是"语言神造说"（Language as a divine creation）、"语言人造说"（Language as a Human Invention）。上级标题已经提及的概念，下级标题和正文如果不重复不会引起误解，就不用重复。这是翻译中的宏观思维。

"当人还是动物的时候，就已经有了语言"，原译意思并不错，语言也地道。但此处引用的是德国人的表述，翻译为英语时，应尽量接近德语的表达方法。可以把这句英语输入谷歌搜索框，再加上德国人的名字，就可以找到维基百科中的一篇德语文章，用谷歌翻译译为英语，便可找到相应的德语："Schon als Tier hat der Mensch Sprache."用谷歌或其他翻译为英语，就是 Even as an animal man has language. 这个译法不仅与德语意思对应，字面也对应，是全面对等。

第三处措辞修改，是想使用更确切的词；原译也未尝不可。

例 2.

这种学说近年受到了质疑。2016 年的研究发现，猕猴的声道已很接近人类发音的解剖学结构，但为什么没有发展出语言？科学家认为："人类语言能力的进化靠的主要是神经系统的变化。猕猴确实有了一个会说话的声道，但还缺乏一个会说话的大脑来控制它。"

原译：

This theory has been questioned in recent years. A 2016 study on the anatomy of the macaque vocal tract suggests that *it could already produce an adequate range of speech sounds to support spoken language, then why could macaques not speak?* Scientists argue that "the evolution of human speech capabilities required neural changes rather than modifications of vocal anatomy. Macaques have a speech-ready vocal tract but lack a speech-ready brain to control it."

改译：

This theory has been questioned in recent years. A 2016 study on the anatomy of macaque vocal tracts *asked why macaques had not developed the ability to speak even though they could already produce an adequate range of speech sounds to support spoken language.* The study argues that "the evolution of human speech capabilities required neural changes rather than modifications of vocal anatomy. Macaques have a speech-ready vocal tract but lack a speech-ready brain to control it."

原译因为下划线的两处没有形成衔接链，给人的印象是两拨科学家，其实都是 2016 年这项研究。实际上，原文也看不出来是一批科学家还是不同科学家。笔者查阅了当初研究的相关资料，才发现是同一批科学家。改译两处形成明确的共指关系。斜体部分不修改也完全可以。修改是为了让句子的主次分明。

例 3.

连接欧亚大陆东西方的远古商道、丝绸之路，推进了沿途语言的接触和传播。明代郑和七下西洋，促进了中国语言文化与东南亚各国、阿拉伯世界等的广泛交流。15—16 世纪以来新航路的发现，更是开启了人类历史上波澜壮阔的五大洲语言交流进程。

原译：

The <u>ancient trade routes and the Silk Road</u> connecting <u>the east and the west</u> of Eurasia promoted the interaction and spread of languages along the way. During the Ming Dynasty, Zheng He, a Chinese <u>explorer</u> and diplomat, led seven maritime <u>expeditions to the West</u>, which boosted the extensive exchange of Chinese language and culture with those of the countries in Southeast Asia and the Arab world. The opening of <u>new sea routes</u> from the 15th to the 16th centuries ushered in the magnificent process of language exchanges among the five continents <u>in human history</u>.

改译：

<u>The Silk Road</u> that connected the East and the West of Eurasia promoted the interaction and spread of languages along the way. During the Ming Dynasty <u>(1368–1644)</u>, Zheng He, a Chinese <u>mariner</u> and diplomat, led seven <u>voyages</u> to <u>Western Ocean</u>, which boosted the exchange of language and culture between China and Southeast Asia and the Arab world. <u>The Age of Exploration</u> from the 15th to the 16th centuries ushered in an even more extensive process of language exchange among the five continents.

说明："远古商道、丝绸之路"就是指丝绸之路，译文简化；"明代"补

充了时间;"西洋"并不是指"西方",而是指东南亚、印度洋一带,改为传统译法"Western Ocean";"15—16世纪以来新航路"有个专有名词,叫 The Age of Exploration 或者 The Age of Discovery,用大写,以明确与郑和下西洋区分开来。其他用词的修改,比如 explorer 改为 mariner,是因为我们把郑和称为"航海家",西方可能称其为"探险家"。expeditions 改为 voyages,是因为前者有军事征伐的意思,而郑和是友好使者。in human history 删除,因为不言自喻。

例 4.

选择同意——向个人信息主体明示个人信息处理目的、方式、范围等规则,征求其授权同意。

原译:

Optional consent-make clear to PI Subjects the purpose, method, scope and other rules for PI processing, and seek the PI Subjects' consent.

改译:

Consent. PI Controllers shall explicitly inform PI Subjects of the purpose, method, scope, etc. of PI processing and seek the PI Subjects' consent.

这个例子取自《个人信息安全规范》。从上下文看,"选择同意"的意思很清楚:网站收集个人信息时,让用户选择是否同意。原译者应该不会误解,可能是机器翻译为 optional consent,原译者疏于审校,造成意思错误。因为 optional consent 意思是"网站可以征求同意,也可以不征求"。

另外,原译中用连字符代替破折号也不正确。英文破折号[①]可以用前后无空格的两个连字符输入(--)。改译没有再使用破折号,而是改用完整句子。

例 5.

个人信息控制者通过个人信息或其他信息加工处理后形成的信息,例如,用户画像或特征标签,能够单独或者与其他信息结合识别

[①] 英文中有四个相似的符号:连字符(-)、连接号(–)、破折号(—)、负号(-),请搜索"英文破折号、连接号、连字符、负号的区别,注意事项和输入方法",阅读相关文章(http://blog.sciencenet.cn/blog-437026-733739.html, accessed September 11, 2021)。

特定自然人身份或者反映特定自然人活动情况的，属于个人信息。

原译：

The <u>information</u> resulting from personal information controller's processing of personal information or other information, <u>such as</u> user profiling or feature labels, <u>which</u> can be used alone or in combination with other information to identify a particular natural person or reflect the activity of a particular natural person, is personal information.

原译中的 such as 和 which 都修饰 information，但距离太远，很难理解。改译如下：

<u>Information</u>, <u>such as</u> user profiles and feature labels, <u>that results from</u> PI Controller's processing of PI or other information <u>and can be used</u> alone or in combination with other information to identify a particular natural person or reflect the activity of a particular natural person, is also deemed PI.

例 6.

行政诉讼检察监督改革二题

摘要：依据司法公正原则、尊重和维护审判独立与裁判权威原则、遵循行政诉讼基本原理原则、坚持国家利益和社会公共利益原则，进一步完善行政诉讼抗诉机制；依据现实需要，建立检察机关提起行政诉讼机制。

关键词：行政抗诉机制；存废；检察机关；行政诉讼

作者：

工作单位：

原译：

Two Theses on the Reformation of Procecutorial Supervision of Administrative Litigation

Abstract: Under the following principles: judicial justice、honoring and maintaining the independence of judicial power and the authority of judgment and order、 following the basic theories of administrative litigation、 insisting on the state's interests and social public interests, the system of protest to administrative litigation should be improved; Under the demands of reality, the system of bringing a administrative suit before court by procecutorial organs should be established.

Key words: system of protest to administrative litigation; preserve or abolish; prosecutorial organs; administrative litigation

Author:

Employer: The Law Department of The National Women's University of China

一改：

Two Theses on Reform of Prosecutorial Supervision over Administrative Litigation

Abstract: Based on the principles of fairness, judicial independence and authority, doctrines of administrative litigation, and priority of state and public interests, the author suggests improving the "protest mechanism" (i.e., appeal by the prosecutor) in administrative litigation, and establishing, as appropriate, a mechanism where the prosecutor may initiate a legal action against the government.

Key words: prosecutorial supervision, appeal by the prosecutor, protest mechanism, administrative litigation

Author:

Institution: The Law Department of the National Women's University of China

说明：

1）标点符号。原译文使用的汉语标点更换为英语标点；去掉一处标点前面的空格（见原译文下划线部分）；

2）拼写错误：电脑已经显示 procecutorial 拼写错误；正确拼写是 prosecutorial；

3）语法错误：电脑已经显示 a administrative 是语法错误，改为 an administrative；

4）简化了原译文的一些措辞，如省略了"尊重和维护""遵循""坚持"等，意思并没有损失。

5）进行了必要的解释：把抗诉制度改译为 the protest mechanism，然后加解释"i.e., appeal by the prosecutor"，因为英美法系没有抗诉的说法，解释为检察官的上诉很容易理解。

6）特别改掉了"坚持"的译法 insist on。insist on 的意思是：固执己见，别人不让你干什么，你非要去干。坚持可以翻译为 adhere to，be committed to，很多时候可以不译。

7）根据译文调整了关键词，使关键词简短并真正体现文章的关键内容。

二改：

Reform of Prosecutorial Supervision over Administrative Litigation

Abstract: Based on the principles of justice, judicial independence and judicial authority, the rationale for administrative litigation, and the priority of state and public interest, the author suggests improving the "protest mechanism" (i.e., appeal by the prosecutor) in administrative litigation; and considering China's reality, she suggests that prosecutors be allowed to bring legal actions against the government.

说明：

1）修改了一些词。如 fairness→justice；doctrines→rationale。这两处不改也可以。interests→interest，这是因为查"公共利益"的英语搭配，发现都用单数形式。

2）去掉了题目中的 two theses on，因为 thesis 除了可以表示"问题"外，还可以表示"论文"，从而引起歧义。去掉后意思已经包含在 reform 之中。

3）恢复了原译中体现出来的"依据现实需要"，因为这是第二条建议的前提，与前半句"依据……原则"相对应。

4）对"行政诉讼"作了适当解释（actions against the government）。

三改：

Reform of Prosecutorial Supervision in Administrative Litigation

Abstract: Based on the principles of justice, judicial independence and judicial authority, and considering the purpose of administrative litigation and the priority of state and public interest, the author suggests improving the prosecutors' appeal system in legal actions against the government. In light of the actual needs, she also suggests giving prosecutors the power to initiate an action.

说明：

1）第一句话有五个概念并列，英文最多三个，改译分为两部分，情况有所改善；

2）查 rationale for administrative litigation，网站并没有出现用例，倒是有 the purpose of administrative litigation，意思与原文相同，故采用；

3）"抗诉"进一步简化，不再使用 protest 这个中国特色的表达方法。

4）最后一句进一步理顺。

例 7.

2000 年，纺织品和服装的进口税率是 24.35%，2001 年降为 20.25%，从 2002 年到 2005 年，将逐年下降为 17.15%、15.33%、12.99% 和 11.64%。

原译：

On an average, the import tax rate of textile clothing in 2000 was 24.35%, and that of 2001 decreased to 20.25%, and from 2002 to 2005, the annual average tax rate will decrease to 17.15%、15.33%、12.99%、11.64% respectively.

改译：

The average tariff on textile and clothing was 24.35% in 2000 and dropped to 20.25% in 2001. From 2002 to 2005, it will be further reduced to 17.15%, 15.33%, 12.99% and 11.64% respectively.

说明：

英文中不应有中文标点；单词后面只留一个字母的间距；标点后留一个字母的间距；句子后面用句号；列举最后两个项目之间用 and；选词：import tax rate 就是 tariff。

例 8.

致斯帝格利茨先生：

尊敬的斯帝格利茨先生：

  北京朝阳国际商务节组委会向您致以诚挚的问候，并热情地邀请您于 2003 年 10 月正式访问北京。

  加入世贸组织之后，中国以及北京的经济发展和国际经济合作迎来了前所未有的机遇与挑战，取得了长足发展。北京在今年上半年遭受了"非典型肺炎"突如其来的袭击，面对疫情，北京采取了严密的防治措施，并取得了明显的成效，6 月 24 日，世界卫生组织决定解除对北京的旅行警告，同时将北京从"近期有当地传播"的非典疫区名单中删除。相信在中央政府的正确领导下，在全市人民的共同努力下，"非典型肺炎"过后，中国经济一定会持续、稳定、健康地发展。

  10 月，北京将举办第四届朝阳国际商务节，期间将组织北京 CBD 国际金融发展论坛，探讨中国经济如何加快发展、加快国际化进程，特别要研讨加快北京 CBD 国际金融和服务贸易领域合作问题。本次研讨会将是北京市在今年秋天举办的大型经济类国际研讨会之一。

  因此，第四届北京朝阳国际商务节组委会衷心地邀请您届时能够来访北京并参加研讨会活动，就中国未来经济与世界经济融合的内容发表演讲。

  金秋十月，是收获的季节，也是北京最美的季节。我们相信您的访问也一定会取得圆满成功！

  我们期待着在北京与您会面。

  此致

平安

北京朝阳国际商务节组委会

原译：

To Mr. 斯帝格利茨

Dear Mr. 斯帝格利茨,

  Sincere greetings from the Organizing Committee of Beijing Chaoyang International Business Festival. We warmly invite you to visit Beijing in October 2003.

  China's WTO accession has brought with it unprecedented opportunities and challenges. The economic development and international economic cooperation of China, and Beijing in particular, have enjoyed great progress since then. Beijing suffered from the unexpected Sars disease during the first half of this year. The prevention and control measures proved to be effective and the fight against the epidemic has been successful. On June 24th, the World Health Organization removed its travel advice on Beijing, which is now also off the list of areas having "recent local transmissions of Sars". We believe that with the strong leadership of central government and the joint efforts of the people, China will win the battle against Sars and China's economy will enjoy sustainable, steady and health development.

  In October, Beijing will hold the fourth Beijing Chaoyang International Business Festival as well as the Forum of Beijing CBD International Financial Development. The Forum will discuss various issues such as how to speed up the economic development and internationalization process of China, and particularly how to enhance the cooperation in the fields of international finance, service and trade in Beijing CBD. The Forum will be one of the big international events discussing economic issues in Beijing this autumn.

  The Organizing Committee sincerely invites you to visit Beijing and to be our guest speaker at the Forum. We would like to share your views about the integration of China's economy into the world economy in the future.

  Autumn is the harvest season in Beijing. We believe your visit would be a complete success and expect to meet with you in Beijing.

Cordially

Organizing Committee of Beijing Chaoyang International Business Festival

改译:

June dd, yyyy [请改为实际日期]

Professor Joseph E. Stiglitz

Columbia University

New York, NY, USA

[对方地址请核实，并加上邮政编码]

Dear Professor Stiglitz,

We are pleased to invite you to the Forum on Development of International Finance to be held in Beijing, China from October [ ] to [ ], 2003, on the occasion of the Beijing Chaoyang International Business Festival. China's WTO accession has brought unprecedented opportunities and challenges. Since then, China, including Beijing, has made substantial progress in economic development and international business cooperation.

In October 2003, we will hold the Fourth Beijing International Business Festival at Chaoyang, the city's central business district (CBD). The festival includes a Forum on Development of International Finance, where we will discuss how to speed up China's economic expansion and internationalization, and in particular, how to develop international financial services and enhance cooperation in trade in services at the CBD. The forum is a big international event on economic issues in Beijing this fall.

We sincerely invite you to Beijing and to be our guest speaker at the forum. We hope that you can share with us your views on China's economic integration into the global economy.

Beijing suffered from the unexpected SARS epidemic during the first half of this year. But the prevention and control measures proved to be effective. Out fight against the disease has been successful. On June 24th, the World Health Organization lifted its travel warning on Beijing and also removed the city from its list of places with "recent local transmissions of SARS". We believe that with the strong leadership of the central government and the joint efforts of the people, the Chinese economy will continue to enjoy sustainable, steady and healthy growth after the epidemic.

Fall is the best season of Beijing. We believe that your visit will contribute to our forum's success, and we look forward to meeting you in Beijing.

Sincerely,

［主办机构邀请人签名］

［签字人姓名印刷体］

［职务］

Organizing Committee of Beijing Chaoyang

International Business Festival

［邮政地址］

［电话］

［传真］

［E-mail］

说明：

- 按照英语的邀请函格式（可以在网上查到），应在左上角写上日期、姓名、地址，所以改译把这一部分内容加了上去。原译没有翻译出人名，看来是等组委会的人提供姓名拼法。其实，这种场合受邀请的一定是名人，不妨到网上查一查，很可能查到。大家可以试一试。
- 称大学教授为先生不够礼貌。
- 原译没有加工信息。改译按照英语邀请函常用的格式，开门见山，把会议的内容（从原文后面提取）、时间、地点都交待清楚了。因为原文没有具体时间，译文留出了括号，供组委会作出决定后填补。
- 中文先介绍背景：中国入世和"非典"。原译文没有作调整。改译把与会议内容关系密切的背景统一放在前面交待，把与会议内容关系不大，但与会者关心的"非典"部分分离出来，另起一段，放在后面。这样译文的层次就很清楚。
- 译文需要查证与核实"解除对北京的旅行警告"以及"近期有当地传播"这样的意思世卫组织是如何表达的。在网上很容易查到。
- 结尾部分按照英语的格式,要求组委会填补必要的信息。
- 全文进行了结构调整,力图使译文符合英语同类文体的习惯("好用")。对原文的调整,又没有背离原文的意图,所以也做到了"准确"。

对译文的审校不是一遍、两遍可以解决问题的,如果时间允许,尽量多看,因为每次都会发现问题。举例如下:

原文(为便于对照,加上了段落编号):

1. 《CBD 国际金融服务暨商务写字楼综合项目展》邀请函
2. 金秋十月,是北京最美的时节,也是收获的季节。适逢其时,第四届北京朝阳国际商务节也将于 10 月 7 日—9 日隆重举行。作为北京最重要的商务活动之一,本届商务节在历届商务节的成功基础之上,将规模更大、规格更高、国际化氛围更浓、参展参会嘉宾更多。
3. 几年来,北京朝阳国际商务节实现了让世界了解中国,让世界关注北京的目标,成为各界全面了解北京市及朝阳区投资环境,考察合作项目,以及广泛接触合作伙伴的大型商务活动,并以主题鲜明,活动丰富,成效显著,国际性强等特点形成了自己独特的品牌。
4. 本届商务节将以"优化 CBD 投资环境,深化国际金融服务"为核心理念,隆重推出《北京 CBD 国际金融服务暨商务写字楼综合项目展》,并以此共促商务合作。
5. 本次展会特设主题活动推介日举办期间,市区主要领导亲临讲解推介北京市及朝阳区最新投资政策和重点招商项目,推出北京 CBD 核心区规划,每个参展单位也都将有机会在展会中心推介区展示自身。
6. 作为北京市重要的商务盛会,本次展会还将邀请政界、商界等贵宾莅临。
7. 我们盼望有机会与您相约在太阳升起的地方,共同奏响新世纪商务合作的乐章。

原译：

1. **CBD International Financial Services and Business Office Building Comprehensive Expo Letter of Invitation**

2. Golden autumn in October is the most beautiful season in Beijing, and the harvest, too. Coming just at the right time, the Fourth Beijing Chaoyang International Business Festival (BCIBF) will be solemnly hosted on October 7~9. As one of Beijing's most important business activities, the current Business Festival will, based on the success of all previous festivals, be more imposing and internationalized. It will have more honored guests visit the exhibition.

3. During the past years, BCIBF has been deeply committed to the goal of introducing China, Beijing in particular, to the world. It has become a large business event, which let people comprehensively understand the investment environment of Beijing and Chaoyang District, inspect cooperation projects and make extensive contacts with the partners. With clear theme, effective organization, evident achievements and active international involvement, the BCIBF has successfully established its unique brand.

4. With "optimizing the CBD investment environment and improving the international financial service" as the core concept, the current Business Festival will grandly put out the *CBD International Financial Services and Business Office Buildings Comprehensive Expo.* It will facilitate the business cooperation.

5. On the promotion day of theme activities specifically set by the current exhibition, major municipal and district leaders will come in person to introduce Beijing and Chaoyang District latest investment policies and key merchant projects, and launch Beijing CBD center planning. Every participant unit will have the opportunity to display itself in the exhibition central promotion area.

6. As the important business grand gathering in Beijing, the current exhibition will request the presence of distinguished guests from political and

commercial circles.

7. We are hoping to meet you in Chaoyang District, Beijing and jointly deliver the best start of business cooperation in the new century.

改译1：

1. **Letter of Invitation to the Exhibition on International Financial Services and Office Building Projects to be held at Beijing Central Business District**
2. The Fourth Beijing Chaoyang International Business Festival will be held from October 7th to 9th, 2003, in the golden fall of Beijing. The festival is one of the city's most important business activities and has been successfully held for three times. The coming event will surpass its predecessors in terms of scale, the level of participation and the number of visitors coming from China and abroad.
3. The festival has become a window to China, and to Beijing in particular. Through the events, people come to know the investment environment of Beijing and Chaoyang District, find projects of cooperation, and establish contacts with their partners. The event is characterized by its clear themes, colorful activities, good results, and active international involvement.
4. To optimize the investment environment and provide better international financial services, we will organize an Exhibition on International Financial Services and Comprehensive Office Projects during the festival, in the hope of promoting business cooperation.
5. On the day when major promotional activities are carried out, senior municipal and district officials will be present to introduce latest policies on and key projects for investments, and announce the development plan for the core area of the CBD. All participating organizations will have an opportunity to promote themselves at the central promotion area.
6. Important political and business personages will also be invited.
7. We look forward to meeting you at Chaoyang, which literally means the morning sun, and start our business cooperation from there.

说明：（数字编号为段落号；英文字母编号为修改项目）

1. A) 原译文题目像中文一样用了一连串的名词（noun sandwiches），修饰关系不明确，改为用介词短语作修饰语。需要通过上下文或其他资料确定各部分之间的修饰关系。B) Expo 现在一般用来表示"博览会"，规模很大，所以笔者认为还是 Exhibition 合适一些。C) 对于"国际金融服务"如何"展出"，笔者有疑问，可以进一步询问主办者是什么意思；暂且认为是可能的。

2. A) "金秋十月，是北京最美的时节，也是收获的季节"似乎是所有讲话稿开头的套话。直接翻译为英语，似乎和邀请的主题没有关系。英语要求开门见山。所以，在这里简化处理。B) 中文中像 solemnly 一样的形容词很多，不是真正需要，都可以省略。C) "A festival will be hosted by 一个单位"，这里仅说举办的日期，应该用 be held from … to … D) "将规模更大、规格更高、国际化氛围更浓、参展参会嘉宾更多"没有直译为 The coming event will be of a larger scale, higher standards, more internationalized, and with more participants."规格更高"是指与会代表的级别更高；"国际化氛围更浓"是指更多外国人参加。根据这里理解，作了以上具体化处理。

3. A) 少用生僻的缩写，所以不要说 BCIBF。B) 原译倾向于直译，有一些语法错误，但从交际功能看，是可以达到沟通目的的。C) 改译对原译进行了简化。

4. A) 不用完全遵守原文结构（with … as the core concept）。B) 不用总是重复 CBD，因为一切活动都在 CBD 进行，不言而喻。C) "隆重推出"不用翻译为 grandly put out；不用吹嘘。可以在网上查有没有 grandly put out，或者 grandly organize。D) 组织展览的是人，所以用 we 作主语。

5. "specifically set by the current exhibition" 不言自喻；"in person" 是多余的；"Beijing and Chaoyang District latest investment policies and key merchant projects" 又是名词串，改为介词短语。"招商项目"译为"merchant projects"很奇怪，想必是受到"招商银行"英译的影响；可以译为"projects inviting investments"。"display" 的解释为"If you display something that you want people to see, you put it in a particular place, so that people can see it easily." 所以，用在这里不合适，因为人不可能是展品。

6. "As the important business grand gathering in Beijing" 这个意思在第一段已经表达过，不用重复；不是展会邀请，而是人邀请。

7. 原译 deliver the start 搭配不当；原译省略了原文的比喻，这样做是适当的。改译补充了"朝阳"二字，把它和升起的太阳联系起来。

进一步审校说明：

根据前面一封邀请信的格式，本来打算把第一句改为：We are pleased to invite you to the Fourth International Business Festival to be held from October 7th to 9th, 2003 in Chaoyang District, Beijing, China. 但后来发现与题目不符，造成前后矛盾。如果两者是同一事物的不同名字，这样改倒是没有实质性后果。

如果既要照顾英语邀请函格式，又要做到前后连贯，可以翻译为：We are pleased to invite you to the Exhibition on International Financial Services and Comprehensive Office Projects… 但这时需要知道这一活动的时间，与 Festival 的关系，而上下文没有说清楚。最后只能放弃这方面的努力。

最后一段又稍修改，并把原来第一段省略的部分加在文章最后。作为服务提供者，感觉自己没有权利丢掉太多的东西。即便省略是有道理的，也恐怕审校译文的人看不出你的用意，责怪你漏译。这里修改和补充如下：

8. Fall is the most pleasant season and the season of harvest. We are sure you will enjoy your stay in Beijing and have a bumper harvest from the activities.

20.3 接受他人审校

重要的翻译活动，都需要多人反复审校。每人的视角不同，每次审校都有可能发现或大或小的问题。我们作为译者，要以平常心对待他人的修改，并努力从修改中不断提高。这里是几个笔者修改之后，外专/用户进一步修改的例子。

例 9.

结束语

人类对语言的认识没有完结。人类的自身发展和科技的进步为认识语言、认识自身、认识世界提供了广阔的研究和探索空间。语言能力的强弱关系到社会的发展和国运兴衰。在当今世界，语言与国家的关系已经发生了前所未有的深刻变化，语言问题已经得到世界各国的广泛关注，同时渗透到科技的核心领域和经济的热点地带。世界各国都面临着如语言服务、语言技术、语言红利、语言矛盾、语言竞备等诸多全新且十分重要的语言问题。这些问题已成为事关国家战略大局和发展全局的重大课题，也日益成为影响世界和平、人类文明和社会进步的重要因素。

笔者提交的译文和外专修改：

Conclusion

There is no end to the ~~understanding~~ comprehension of language. Humanity's ~~own~~ development and ~~advances in technology~~ technological advances have provided a vast space for research and exploration in understanding language, ourselves, and the world. The strength of language skills is related to the development of society and the rise and fall of a nation. In today's world, the relationship between language and the state has undergone unprecedented and profound changes. ~~Language issues~~ Language-related issues have received attention from all countries ~~around the world~~ worldwide and have penetrated ~~into~~ the core areas of science and technology and economic hotspots. ~~Countries~~ Nations around the world are facing many new and important issues concerning language services, language technology, language dividends, language tensions, and language competition. These issues have gained strategic importance for national development and ~~are becoming factors~~ affecting world peace, civilization and social progress.

可以看出，其中有些修改让译文更加简练（advances in technology→technological advances, around the world→worldwide, are becoming factors affecting→affect），有些让语言更加正式、专业或精准（understanding→comprehension, Language issues→Language-related issues, Countries—Nations）。

例 10.

第一，混合所有制经济的发展速度大大加快。中国企业联合会前几个月刚刚评出中国企业的 500 强，中国企业 500 强同世界企业 500 强比有相当大的差距，有的差距之大是令我们吃惊的。比如中国企业 500 强的人均资产只等于世界企业 500 强的 1.57%。在中国加入 WTO 的背景下，中国的企业不仅在国内市场与外资企业竞争，而且要走向国际，那就必须扩大自己的规模，提高自己的核心竞争力。出路在哪里？就是要加快发展混合所有制经济。积极发展混合所有制经济，这是十六大提出的要求。以前我们一般叫混合经济，现在叫混合所有制经济。1990 年我国的混合所有制经济只占各类企业总数的 9% 左右，现在已达到 40% 左右。我估计未来的五年左右，混合所有制经济能够达到 60% 左右。如果是这样，我国企业的规模和它的竞争力都会由此得到明显提升。

学生翻译稿：

1. Development of economy of different forms of ownership began to accelerate. Several months ago, China's Association of Enterprises chose Chinese enterprises Top 500. But these enterprises lag far behind the world enterprises Top 500. For example, the per capita asset of China Top 500 is only 1.57% of World Top 50. In the post-WTO era, if the Chinese enterprises want to compete with the foreign enterprises in the domestic market, even in the international market, they have to enlarge their scale and enhance their core competitiveness. But how? One way out is to develop the economy of different forms of ownership, which is also proposed in the 16th Party Congress. In the past, the economy of different forms of owner-

ship is called the mixed economy. In 1990, such economy only accounted for 9% of all enterprises, now it accounted for 40%. And in my view, it will increase to 60% in the next five years. If so, the scale and competitiveness of the Chinese enterprises will be improved dramatically.

笔者的审校稿：

First, development of an economy of mixed ownerships began to accelerate. Several months ago, China's Association of Enterprises selected the top 500 Chinese businesses. But these businesses lag far behind the world's top 500. For example, assets of China's top 500 businesses on a per capita basis are only 1.57% those of the world top 500. In the context of China's WTO accession, if the Chinese businesses want to compete with the foreign businesses in the domestic market, even in the international market, they have to enlarge their scale and enhance their core competitiveness. But how? One way out is to develop an economy of mixed ownership, which was also proposed at the 16th Party Congress. The economy of mixed ownership used to be called the mixed economy. In 1990, such an economy accounted for only 9% of all businesses, now it accounts for 40%. In my view, it will increase to 60% in the next five years. If so, the scale and competitiveness of the Chinese businesses will be improved dramatically.

《中国日报》最终稿：

First, development of the mixed sector of the economy began to accelerate. In 1990, the mixed sector only accounted for 9 percent of all businesses, now it accounts for 40 percent. In my view, it will increase to around 60 percent in the next five years. If this is the case, the scale and competitiveness of Chinese businesses will dramatically improve.

笔者感到不解的不是《中国日报》删除了中间一段（这是编辑的权利），而是为什么把"混合所有制经济"翻译为 the mixed sector。文章说，

"混合所有制经济"就是过去的"混合经济"。毫无疑问,"混合经济"翻译为a mixed economy,这都是耳熟能详的概念,英语是这样定义的: A mixed economy is an economic system in which some companies are owned by the state and some are not. 就是多种所有制共存的经济制度。至于"混合所有制经济",既然与"混合经济"概念相同,翻译为an economy with mixed ownership应该没问题,怎么会错呢?

带着这些疑问,上网查阅有关资料:

中文资料:

"发展混合所有制经济"是一种制度创新

"混合经济"的概念来自西方经济学家萨缪尔森,是指在国家经济成分中多种经济成分并存的状态,我国"公有制为主体、多种所有制经济共同发展"的基本经济制度要求实行的就是"混合经济";而"混合所有制经济"是指在微观主体上实行多种所有制构成的股份制,即:在企业股权构成上既不都是由公有制企业参股形成的股份制,譬如我们过去建立的某些股份制公司,也不是都由私人参股形成的股份制,而是将不同的所有制经济融为一体。"混合所有制经济"借用了"混合经济"的说法,赋予它在企业股权改革方面的新的涵义,是党的十六大报告在理论创新的基础上提出的一种制度创新。

英文资料1:

On the other hand, the private sector was to be based on non-exploiting private ownership. The state was to protect and encourage it and organize its functions so as to enable it to play a positive and active role in the national economy. The mixed sector is based on joint ownership by the state and private sector. It is within this constitutional framework that foreign investment legislation and policy in Sudan were considered in the 1970s and 1980s.

英文资料2:

In fact, the Chinese economy is becoming very diverse. The heart of the system remains statist and centralised. Quantitatively, however, its weight is shrinking, to limit itself to the sectors of "State security, natural monopolies, major suppliers of public goods and services, as well as the mainstay firms of key sectors and of high technology". It is a strategic role that it retains, linked to the maintenance of planning. The main beneficiary of the reduction of the weight of the state is not the private sector but the public decentralised sector, with the aim of "exploring a variety of forms of application of the system of public property"[14]. *A very wide private or mixed sector, in which the state often retains a blocking minority share has also been created.* It covers nearly a million private companies and 30 million one-man operations. China believes in the "establishment of a system of competition based on the survival of the fittest". It gives preference to a shareholding system because it "can be used both under capitalism and socialism (…) The key is to see who holds the shares". Big industrial groups are being formed. The three major sectors (state, public decentralised and private) tend to be of similar size, with the second having the edge over the others.

看来，从严格意义上讲，"混合经济"和"混合所有制经济"并非一回事。原文作者认为相同，是因为在现阶段的中国，无论哪一种提法，其重点都是发展非公有制经济。可以说，两种说法都是"非公有制经济"的代名词。而在英语中，两个概念是完全不同的。所以才有最后发表的译法。

令人惊奇的是，在查找 mixed sector 的过程中，笔者又发现 The World Bank Group 杂志 *Transition Newsletter* 发表的同一作者另一篇文章中的类似内容，译文也是在原来译文的基础上审校的：

> Increasing numbers of state enterprises will sell their assets to private firms and become mixed companies, that is, jointly owned by entrepreneurs and the state. In 1990 mixed companies accounted for only 9 percent of all businesses, but now account for 40 percent; however, on a per capita asset basis China's top 500 businesses account for only 1.6 percent of the

world's top 500 businesses. If Chinese businesses want to compete with foreign businesses in both the domestic and international arenas, they will have to enlarge their scale of operations and enhance their competitiveness. One way that China could achieve this is by developing the mixed sector of the economy. The proportion of jointly-owned enterprises could increase to around 60 percent of all businesses in the next five years, which would dramatically increase both the scale and competitiveness of Chinese businesses.

这个例子的教训是，翻译永远不要想当然。其实，如果批判性地审视译文，本来可以发现问题：既然已认定混合经济是包括各种所有制在内的经济，即经济的全部——100%，那么怎么会有其在经济中所占比例（9%—40%—60%）呢？如果以此为契机，深入研究这两个概念，是会发现问题的。

最后需要指出，外专审改的译文，在意思和表达上也不一定到位，因为外专可能不懂原文，只能在原译的基础上猜测修改，从而造成错误；有些外专也不一定十分用心。

例 11.

语言的历史长河

在历史长河中，不断涌现具有世界或地区共通语性质的语言。由于国民教育、国家治理、科技、贸易、宗教、外交等原因，语言教育对社会进步变得不可或缺，从而引发了世界各种语言的教学活动。<u>在历史长河中，不断涌现具有世界或地区共通语性质的语言。</u>

- 古波斯亚拉姆语
- 古希腊语
- 拉丁语
- 英语
- ……

这是北外语言博物馆的一段说明。原文第一句话和下面一句话没有逻辑关系。原译没有发现这一问题，外专也没有发现这一问题，轮到笔者审校时，发现这个逻辑瑕疵，建议把第一句话移到本段末尾（包括原文和译文），这样正好与下面列举的几个地区性／国际性语言衔接起来：

~~The Evolution of~~ <u>Major</u> Languages <u>in History</u>

~~Throughout history, languages used across regions and across the world appear one after another. These languages~~ Languages play an important role in national education and governance, science and technology, trade, religion and diplomacy. As a result, language education ~~becomes~~ <u>has become</u> indispensable for the society to move forward. To this end, language education is carried out around the world. <u>In history, several languages emerged as universal languages across a region or even the world.</u>

- Aramaic
- Ancient Greek
- Latin
- English

例 12.

语言扶贫

扶贫先扶智，扶智先通语。语言是助力脱贫减贫的基础要素。中国语言扶贫是人类历史上的伟大实践，是人类语言减贫事业的有益探索。

外专审校稿：

Poverty Alleviation Through Language

Poverty elimination requires the support of education. To educate the impoverished population, helping them in understanding and communicating in the national language is the first step. Therefore, language is a fundamental factor in poverty eradication. China's poverty relief through language is great experience in human history and makes contributions to the global poverty reduction through language. (60 words)

改译：

Poverty Alleviation Through Language Education

Educating the poor and helping them communicate in the national language is the first step to eliminate poverty. China's poverty relief through language education is a great endeavour in human history and has contributed to global poverty reduction. (43 words)

原文只有短短两行，译文为五行，作为展览馆的内容，应以图片和实物为主，介绍尽量简短，因为观众没有太多时间看文字。改译几乎减少三分之一篇幅。

例 13.

大约 10 世纪，回鹘人已经学会雕版印刷技术。12—13 世纪，回鹘文已用木活字印刷。敦煌莫高窟曾先后四次发现回鹘文木活字实物，<u>使用年代应在 12—13 世纪上半叶之间</u>。这些回鹘文活字开创了拼音文字活字印刷的先河，为中国活字印刷术进一步向西传播提供了确凿的实物证据。

外专审校稿：

Around the 10th century, the Uighurs had already grasped block printing technology. In the 12th and 13th centuries, Uighur script was printed with wooden movable-type. <u>Dating to the 12th to the first half of the 13th century</u>, the physical wooden movable type of Uighur script have been discovered four times in Dunhuang Mogao Grottoes. This pioneered the movable-type printing of alphabetic script while providing solid physical evidence for the further spread of Chinese movable-type printing to the West.

改译：

Around the 10th century, the Uighurs had already learned block printing technology. In the 12th and 13th centuries, the Uighur script had been printed with wooden movable types. <u>Wooden Uighur movable types dating from the 12th to 13th century</u> have been discovered four times in Dunhuang Mogao Caves. This showed that movable types were being used for alphabetical scripts and offered physical evidence of Chinese movable-type printing spreading westward.

原文画线部分是指活字的使用年代，外专审校稿可能被理解为活字被发现的年代。造成这个错误的原因，可能是原译如此，审校不懂原文没有看出来。改译把时间状语变为活字的定语。

例 14.

汉朝

张骞出使西域，胡人堂邑父，为翻译官员随行。张骞经 13 年流亡，最后回国时，唯堂邑父一人伴随左右，功不可没。

外专审校稿：

Interpreting in the Han Dynasty

Tangyifu, an expatriate Hun, served Zhang Qian as an interpreter and official during his envoy to the <u>West</u>. When he finally returned to China after 13 years of exile, Zhang Qian was only accompanied by Tangyifu, whose contribution has indeed made a difference.

改译：

Interpreting in the Han Dynasty

During Zhang Qian's envoy to <u>Central Asia</u>, Tangyifu, an expatriate Hun, served him as an interpreter. When Zhang finally returned after 13 years of exile, the only other person who survived was Tangyifu. We thus see the value of an interpreter.

说明：西域不是西方，是中亚地区（Central Asia）。

例 15.

大约在 4 世纪末叶，中国造纸法传入朝鲜。7 世纪初，中国纸和造纸术通过朝鲜传入日本。

外专审校稿：

Around the end of the 4th century, Chinese papermaking technology reached <u>North Korea</u>, through which both Chinese paper and the technology were introduced to Japan in the early 7th century.

改译：

Around the end of the 4th century, Chinese papermaking technology reached <u>the Korean Peninsula</u>, from where it further spread to Japan in the early 7th century.

说明：这个朝鲜不是今天的朝鲜民主主义人民共和国，是指朝鲜半岛，这类错误属于荒谬的错误。

20.4　小结

无论是审校自己的译文，还是审校他人，只要本着信达切的原则，以批判性思维发现问题，以调查研究解决问题，就能尽量减少理解、表达方面的错误，并根据翻译的情景对原文进行适当变通。对于他人的审校，一方面要虚心学习，另一方面也不要迷信专家，发现专家审校错误，照样可以反馈或纠正。持之以恒，早晚会成为专业翻译。

〔课后练习〕

1. 你平时翻译完成后修改几遍？
2. 如何平衡速度和质量？
3. 审校时从哪些方面入手？每个方面具体包括哪些事项？请你制作一个清单。
4. 请你按照自己的清单，再次审校自己的一篇译文。

附录一　欧洲委员会英语写作与翻译指南

请扫描二维码获取

附录二　汉英翻译综合训练

请扫描二维码获取

附录三　汉英翻译综合训练参考译文

请扫描二维码获取

参考文献

请扫描二维码获取